Springer Proceedings in Business and Economics

Springer Proceedings in Business and Economics brings the most current research presented at conferences and workshops to a global readership. The series features volumes (in electronic and print formats) of selected contributions from conferences in all areas of economics, business, management, and finance. In addition to an overall evaluation by the publisher of the topical interest, scientific quality, and timeliness of each volume, each contribution is refereed to standards comparable to those of leading journals, resulting in authoritative contributions to the respective fields. Springer's production and distribution infrastructure ensures rapid publication and wide circulation of the latest developments in the most compelling and promising areas of research today.

The editorial development of volumes may be managed using Springer Nature's innovative EquinOCS, a proven online conference proceedings submission, management and review system. This system is designed to ensure an efficient timeline for your publication, making Springer Proceedings in Business and Economics the premier series to publish your workshop or conference volume.

This book series is indexed in SCOPUS.

Nicholas Tsounis • Aspasia Vlachvei
Editors

Applied Economic Research and Trends

2023 International Conference on Applied Economics (ICOAE), Brno, Czech Republic, June 29-July 1, 2023

Volume 1

Editors
Nicholas Tsounis
Department of Economics
University of Western Macedonia
Kastoria, Greece

Aspasia Vlachvei
Department of Economics
University of Western Macedonia
Kastoria, Greece

ISSN 2198-7246 ISSN 2198-7254 (electronic)
Springer Proceedings in Business and Economics
ISBN 978-3-031-49104-7 ISBN 978-3-031-49105-4 (eBook)
https://doi.org/10.1007/978-3-031-49105-4

© The Editor(s) (if applicable) and The Author(s), under exclusive license to Springer Nature Switzerland AG 2024
This work is subject to copyright. All rights are solely and exclusively licensed by the Publisher, whether the whole or part of the material is concerned, specifically the rights of translation, reprinting, reuse of illustrations, recitation, broadcasting, reproduction on microfilms or in any other physical way, and transmission or information storage and retrieval, electronic adaptation, computer software, or by similar or dissimilar methodology now known or hereafter developed.
The use of general descriptive names, registered names, trademarks, service marks, etc. in this publication does not imply, even in the absence of a specific statement, that such names are exempt from the relevant protective laws and regulations and therefore free for general use.
The publisher, the authors, and the editors are safe to assume that the advice and information in this book are believed to be true and accurate at the date of publication. Neither the publisher nor the authors or the editors give a warranty, expressed or implied, with respect to the material contained herein or for any errors or omissions that may have been made. The publisher remains neutral with regard to jurisdictional claims in published maps and institutional affiliations.

This Springer imprint is published by the registered company Springer Nature Switzerland AG
The registered company address is: Gewerbestrasse 11, 6330 Cham, Switzerland

If disposing of this product, please recycle the paper.

Preface

The 2023 conference was co-organised by the Faculty of Business and Economics of the Mendel University in Brno and the Department of Economics of the University of Western Macedonia, Greece, after the kind invitation by Profs. Martina Rašticová and Veronika Solilová who were also co-chairs of the conference.

The aim of the conference was to bring together economists from different fields of Applied Economic Research in order to share methods and ideas.

The topics covered include:

- Applied Macroeconomics
- Applied International Economics
- Applied Microeconomics including Industrial Organisations
- Applied work on International Trade Theory including European Integration
- Applied Financial Economics
- Applied Agricultural Economics
- Applied Labour and Demographic Economics
- Applied Health Economics
- Applied Education Economic

All papers presented in ICOAE 2023 and published in the conference proceedings were peer reviewed by at least two anonymous referees. In total, 105 works were submitted from 22 countries while 73 papers were accepted for publication in the conference proceedings.

The acceptance rate for ICOAE 2023 was 69.5%.

The full-text articles will be published on-line by Springer in the series Springer Proceedings in Business and Economics, and they will be included in the SCOPUS database for indexing.

The organisers of ICOAE 2023 would like to thank:

- The Scientific Committee of the conference for their help and their important support for carrying out the tremendous workload organising and synchronising the peer reviewing process of the submitted papers in a very specific short period of time.

- The anonymous reviewers for accepting to referee the submitted conference papers and submitting their reviews on time for the finalisation of the conference programme.
- Prof. Svatopluk Kapounek, Dean of the Faculty and Professors Martina Rašticová and Veronika Solilová, for accepting to host the conference at the Faculty of Business and Economics of the Mendel University in Brno and providing the required resources.
- Dr. Hana Vránová and Barbora Šiklová, members of the local organising committee, for the time and effort they put for the successful organisation of the conference.
- Mr. Gerassimos Bertsatos for running the reception desk of the conference and Mr. Lazaros Markopoulos and Mr. Stelios Angelis from the Department of Economics and Informatics, of the University of Western Macedonia, respectively, for technical support.

Kastoria, Greece

Nicholas Tsounis
Aspasia Vlachvei

Contents

Volume 1

1　The Nexus Between Geopolitical Risks and Confidence
Measures in G7 Countries 1
Milan Christian de Wet

2　International Trade Flows and Geo-Political
Episodes—Network Perspective 17
Ahaan Shah, Keyaan Shah, and Homa Hosseinmardi

3　A South African Perspective on the Corporate Cash Holding
Conundrum 37
Ilse Botha and Carol Thompson

4　Simulating the Impacts of Productive Development Policies
in Algeria: Computable General Equilibrium Model Analysis 51
Mohammed Touitou

5　Forecasting the Main Energy Crop Prices in the Agricultural
Sector of Thailand Using a Machine Learning Model 63
Jittima Singvejsakul and Chukiat Chaiboonsri

6　Extreme Events and Stock Market Efficiency: The Modified
Shannon Entropy Approach 77
Joanna Olbrys

7　Examining Public Expenditure on Education
and the Relationship Between Expenditure and Corruption
in Greece Through a Nonparametric Statistical Analysis Method .. 91
Kyriaki Efthalitsidou, Nikolaos Sariannidis, Marina Vezou,
and Konstantinos Spinthiropoulos

8　Does Clove Export Cause Economic Growth in Nigeria? 113
Okezie A. Ihugba, Alexander A. Orji, Erasmus E. Duru,
and N. C. Ebomuche

9 The Share of Dependent Work Income in Greece: Main Domestic and External Determinants 143
George Petrakos, Konstantinos Rontos, Chara Vavoura, and Ioannis Vavouras

10 Export-Led and Import-Led Growth Hypotheses: Empirical Evidence from Greece 159
Melina Dritsaki and Chaido Dritsaki

11 An Empirical Analysis of the Trade Impediments in Greece's Global Trade Relationships: A CGE Approach 187
Gerasimos Bertsatos and Nicholas Tsounis

12 Employee Benefits Required by Women of Generation Y in the Food and Agricultural Sectors 205
Jiří Duda

13 How Is Economic News Tone Driven: An Analysis of the Longitudinal Data (1998–2017) of Korean Economic News 219
Wansoo Lee

14 The Role of Trust and Contracts in the Expansion of Technology-Intensive SMEs 235
Ewa Baranowska-Prokop and Jacek Prokop

15 Improving Employee Retention: Evidence from "Best Practices" in the Craft Sector to Tackle the Labor Shortage of Skilled Workers 245
Romina Klara Haller

16 Blockchain Research Trends in Information Systems: A Systematic Review 265
Van Nguyen Nhu Tam and Cao Tien Thanh

17 Analysis of Customer Perception of E-banking Services in India ... 283
Amit Kumar Gupta, Manoj Kumar Srivastava, Imlak Shaikh, and Ashutosh Dash

18 Defense Spending and Economic Growth: An Empirical Investigation in the Case of Greece 299
Antonis Tsitouras, Nicholas Tsounis, and Harry Papapanagos

19 Quality of IFRS Reporting: Developed, Transitional, and Developing Economies 321
Patrik Svoboda and Hana Bohušová

20 Influencer Marketing and Its Impact on Consumer Behavior: Case Study from Slovakia 337
Roman Chinoracky, Tatiana Corejova, and Natalia Stalmasekova

Contents

ix

**21 The Reflection of COVID-19 Pandemic in the State Budget
of the Slovak Republic: Selected Problems** 351
Janka Grofčíková and Katarína Izáková

**22 Role of Information Technology in the Efficiency of HR
Processes in Educational Institutions: A Case Study of Greece** 367
Olympia Papaevangelou, Stavros Kalogiannidis,
Dimitrios Syndoukas, Zacharias Karantonis, and Despoina Savvidou

**23 US Museums: Digitization, Social Media Engagement,
and Revenue Diversification in the Pandemic** 393
Angela Besana, Martha Friel, Enrico Giorgio Domenico Crisafulli,
and Cristina Rossi

**24 Understanding Customer Perception and Brand Equity
in the Hospitality Sector: Integrating Sentiment Analysis
and Topic Modeling** 413
T. D. Dang and M. T. Nguyen

**25 Business Ethics and Green Taxonomy in an Era that
Energy Consumption and Prices Are Defined by a War: An
Empirical Study in Western Macedonian Enterprises** 427
A. Metsiou, G. Broni, E. Papachristou, M. Kiki, and P. Evangelou

**26 Economics and Marketing of Skills. *Pass the Point of No
Return* in Arts and Tourism** 445
Angela Besana, Annamaria Esposito, Chiara Fisichella,
and Maria Cristina Vannini

**27 Risk-Taking Behavior and Effects of Framing in Group
and Individual Decisions: Evidence from Chamas
and Student Subjects in Kenya** 465
Mercy Inyangala Kano, Gülnur Muradoğlu, and John Olukuru

**28 Empirical Study on the Role of Cultivation in the Acceptance
of ICT Technologies in the Agricultural Sector of Kozani** 487
Deligiannis Dimitrios, Saprikis Vaggelis, Avlogiaris Giorgos,
and Antoniadis Ioannis

**29 How Has the COVID-19 Pandemic Affected the Utilization
of the Company's Working Capital?** 499
Janka Grofčíková

**30 Trainer's Characterization of Entrepreneurs to Reduce
Unemployment Gap, Lambayeque** 521
Vidal Taboada Silvia Lourdes, Guillermo Segundo Miñan Olivos,
Jairo Jaime Turriate Chávez, Luis Alberto Vásquez Caballero,
Mercedes Alejandrina Collazos Alarcón,
and Mónica del Pilar Pintado Damián

31 LNG Carriers' Discharge Waiting Time and Energy Inflation...... 531
Stavros Karamperidis, Nektatios A. Michail, and Konstantinos Melas

**32 Big Data Analytics in Management Reporting: A Systematic
Literature Review** 537
Simon Luca Kropf

**33 Using Enterprise Social Media Networks to Foster
Team-Level Collaboration in a Project Organization** 559
Thomas Ruf

**34 Bankruptcy Prediction Using Machine Learning: The Case
of Slovakia** 575
Hussam Musa, Frederik Rech, Zdenka Musova, Chen Yan,
and Ľubomír Pintér

35 Value Creation in Automotive Industry in Slovakia 593
Ľuboš Elexa

**36 Does German Hospital Financing Lead to Distorted
Incentives in the Billing of Intensive Care Ventilation Therapy?** ... 613
Peter Kremeier

Volume 2

**37 Life Cycle Cost Analysis: Applying Monte Carlo Simulation
on Energy Costs in Case Studies for Investments in Natural
Gas Infrastructure** 625
Stefan Wieke

**38 Examination of the Beliefs About the Role of Psychological
Approaches in Economic Growth and National Development** 641
Stavros Kalogiannidis, Christina Patitsa, Dimitrios Syndoukas,
and Fotios Chatzitheodoridis

**39 Heterogenous Consumption Responses and Wealth
Inequality over the Business Cycle** 667
Rachel Forshaw

**40 Consumer Behavior When Buying Clothes in Slovakia in the
Context of Environmentally Responsible Trends** 701
Simona Bartošová, Zdenka Musová, and Zlatica Fulajtárová

41 Impact of Gender Diversity Boards on Financial Health SMEs 729
Mário Papík and Lenka Papíková

**42 Sustainable Banking Practice: The Role of Environmental,
Social, and Governance Factors** 741
Imlak Shaikh, Ashutosh Dash, Amit Kumar Gupta,
and Manoj Kumar Srivastava

Contents

43 Corporate Social Responsibility as a Swap for Reducing Firm Risk: Evidence from Stock Market Reaction to FDI Announcements 757
Mei Liu and Qing-Ping Ma

44 The Impact of Housing Market Policy on House Prices in China ... 793
Mei Liu and Qing-Ping Ma

45 Changes in the Use of Employee Training Methods in Slovakia in the Context of the COVID-19 Pandemic: A Quantitative and Qualitative Perspective 815
Jozef Ďurian, Lukas Smerek, and Ivana Simockova

46 Centralized Governance in Decentralized Autonomous Organizations 831
Ivan Sedliačik and Kamil Ščerba

47 Do Consumers Seek Terroir Elements When Choosing a Wine? Insight from Four Generational Cohorts 839
Spyridon Mamalis, Irene (Eirini) Kamenidou, Aikaterini Karampatea, Elisavet Bouloumpasi, and Adriana Skendi

48 Recreational Uses of the Protected Natural Ecosystem of Grammos in the Region of Western Macedonia 853
Katerina Melfou, Georgia Koutouzidou, Dimitrios Kalfas, Stergios Loudovaris, and Ioannis A. Giantsis

49 National and Regional Disparities: How Recovering? 867
Anna Maria Bagnasco, Viviana Clavenna, and Federica Fortunato

50 The Impact of Insurance Needs Satisfaction on Consumers' Purchase and Repurchase Intention 889
Dimitrios Karnachoritis and Irene Samanta

51 Factors Determining Business Eco-Innovation Activities: A Case of Slovak SMEs 907
Miroslava Vinczeová, Ladislav Klement, and Vladimíra Klementová

52 The Impact of COVID-19 and Lockdowns on Media: The Greek Case 923
Athanasios Papathanasopoulos

53 The Impact of Macroeconomic Indicators on Exchange Rates of the Visegrad Group 939
Kitty Klacsánová, Mária Bohdalová, and Nico Haberer

54 Working Capital Management Policy and Its Financing Across Selected Enterprises According to Size in the Czech Republic 955
Markéta Skupieňová

55 Effects of Monetary Policy and the External Sector on Peru's Economic Cycles 969
Vony Sucaticona-Aguilar and Polan Ferro-Gonzales

56 Importance of Business Digitization: The Case of the Region of Western Macedonia, Greece 987
Ioannis Metsios, Vaggelis Saprikis, and Ioannis Antoniadis

57 Using the Predictive Model IN05 to Assess the Business Environment in Czechia 1009
Tomáš Pražák

58 The WWW Factor: Understanding Generation Z's Website Preferences 1021
Tereza Ikášová

59 Factors Affecting the Effectiveness of Email Marketing 1035
Lola Maria Sempelidou, Giorgos Avlogiaris, and Ioannis Antoniadis

60 E-commerce to Increase Sales in a Peruvian Importer of Hardware Items 1051
Guillermo S. Miñan Olivos, María Y. Del Busto Valdez, Johan H. Espinoza Tumpay, Williams E. Castillo Martínez, and Jairo Jaime Turriate Chávez

61 Big Data in Economics Research 1063
Aristidis Bitzenis and Nikos Koutsoupias

62 Testing Horizontal Support and Resistance Zones on Cryptocurrencies 1073
Prodromos Tsinaslanidis

63 Pre-bankruptcy Consolidation Process and Business Reorganization: A Case Study 1085
Araviadi Ioanna and Katarachia Androniki

64 Tourist Clusters and the Tourist Experience as a Tool for Smart, Sustainable, and Integrated Development of Rural Areas: The Case of Troodos in Cyprus 1095
Electra Pitoska and Panayiotis Papadopoullos

65 Entrepreneurship of Winemaking Enterprises in Mountain Less-Favored Areas: An Empirical Study 1113
Electra Pitoska, Evagelia Theodorli, and Agapi Altini

66 Consumer Attitudes Toward Artificial Intelligence in Fashion 1127
Katerina Vatantzi, Aspasia Vlachvei, and Ioannis Antoniadis

	Contents	xiii

67 What Determines Supply and Demand for Occupational Pension Provision in Germany? Results of a Current Expert Surveys 1143
Robert Piotr Dombek

68 Population Aging: How Much Time Do We Still Have? 1175
Jure Miljevič and Cveto Gregorc

69 The Impact of Capital Adequacy on Banking Risk-Evidence from Emerging Market 1209
Osama Samih Shaban

70 Digital Entrepreneurship Activities Among Gender Groups in Greek Agrifood Firms 1223
Afroditi Kitta, Ourania Notta, and Aspasia Vlachvei

71 The Dynamics of Tourist Flows in Greece 1241
G. Bertsatos, Z. Kalogiratou, Th. Monovasilis, and N. Tsounis

Index 1249

Chapter 1
The Nexus Between Geopolitical Risks and Confidence Measures in G7 Countries

Milan Christian de Wet

Abstract Geopolitical risks (GPRs) and shocks such as military conflicts, terrorist attacks, and tensions of wars are known to cause significant economic downturns. The main aim of this study is to determine the nexus between geopolitical risks and both consumer and business sentiments of the G7 countries. This study is motivated by the importance of consumer and business confidence in financial and economic activities. It achieves its main aim by means of employing a panel quantile regression model and provides several key findings. First, it provides evidence that geopolitical risks do have a statistically significant negative impact on consumer confidence at a median level, with the United States as the base case. Furthermore, consumer confidence in Japan, Italy, and Canada has proved to be significantly more severely impacted by geopolitical risks at a median level. Evidence also shows that geopolitical risks have an asymmetrical impact on consumer confidence across quantiles in all countries. The results show that consumer confidence across all countries is more severely impacted by geopolitical risks during low-confidence regimes, i.e., at the 10th–30th quantiles. The negative impact tends to diminish at higher-confidence regimes, except for Japan, Canada, and Italy. Second, geopolitical risks tend to have an insignificant impact on business confidence in the United States, Japan, and Italy at a median level; however, they have proved to have a significantly negative impact on business confidence in the United Kingdom, France, Germany, and Canada. The asymmetrical relationship between geopolitical risks and the various confidence measures makes policy formulation for geopolitical risks challenging. The results of this study provide information that could be used to improve policy formulation related to geopolitical risks.

Keywords Geopolitical risk · Business and consumer confidence · Panel quantile regression · G7 countries

---

M. C. de Wet (✉)
University of Johannesburg, Johannesburg, South Africa
e-mail: miland@uj.ac.za

© The Author(s), under exclusive license to Springer Nature Switzerland AG 2024
N. Tsounis, A. Vlachvei (eds.), *Applied Economic Research and Trends*, Springer Proceedings in Business and Economics,
https://doi.org/10.1007/978-3-031-49105-4_1

1.1 Introduction

The role of geopolitical risk in determining economic growth and financial stability has attracted considerable research interest recently. Evidence shows that geopolitical risks play an increasingly important role in shaping decision-making and, in turn, having an impact on real economic and investment activities (Dogan et al., 2021). For example, Eckstein and Tsiddon (2004) found that an increased geopolitical risk has a significantly negative impact on economic growth. Furthermore, Caldara and Iacoviello (2022) provide evidence that an increased geopolitical risk causes distortions in capital allocations, where funds tend to flow out of investments considered relatively high risk to those that are low risk. Investment opportunities with a relatively high risk are often linked to potentially high growth, and, thus, investment outflows could halt high-growth projects. In this context, the literature shows that monetary policymakers increasingly consider geopolitical risks as a key determinant of future economic conditions and a potential determinant of the business cycle (Caldara & Iacoviello, 2022).

One channel through which geopolitical risks could transmit to real economic and investment activities is through expectation and uncertainty. Sohag et al. (2022) argue that escalating geopolitical tension typically causes uncertainty, which, in turn, could result in consumers postponing consumption and firms postponing investments. This is linked to the Keynesian investment theory, which argues that confidence in future expectations is the cornerstone of investment decision-making (Brue & Grant, 2007). The uncertainty caused by geopolitical risks could therefore distort investment decision-making and, in turn, could lead to an economic slowdown. The empirical literature provides overwhelming evidence that increased uncertainty causes both consumer and business sentiments to diminish, which, in turn, is often a catalyst for shifts in the business cycle (De Wet & Botha, 2022). Therefore, policymakers often resort to confidence measures as a means to estimate future movements in the business cycle and to identify potential pivot points (Lahiri & Zhao, 2016).

In light of this, identifying the link between geopolitical risks and both business and consumer sentiments could provide key information to policymakers. Given our understanding of the link between sentiments and future economic conditions, the results of this study could point toward a potential transmission mechanism between geopolitical risks and economic conditions. Hence, the main aim of this study is to determine the nexus between geopolitical risks and both consumer and business sentiments of the G7 countries. The G7 countries represent a well-established sample of the largest developed countries globally and offer a good starting point for a study of this nature. The study achieves its objective by means of employing a panel quantile regression model. Quantile analysis is commonly used in the literature to capture asymmetric relationships by analyzing variables at different quantiles (Subramaniam, 2022). This approach is particularly prominent in research related to the dynamics between geopolitical risks and economic and financial variables (see, for example, Bouri et al. (2019), Kannadhasan and Das

(2020), Subramaniam (2022), and De Wet (2023)). This approach will allow one to identify the dynamics between geopolitical risks and the various sentiment measures at different sentiment levels. Subramaniam (2022) argues that a geopolitical risk is erratic by nature and therefore requires a nonlinear estimation approach, such as the panel quantile regression model.

The empirical literature on the impact of geopolitical risks within the economic sphere largely focuses on financial markets, economic growth, and tourism. However, the literature that specifically focuses on the dynamics between geopolitical risks and sentiment measures is scarce, and, to the best of my knowledge, to date, only the study by Pehlivanoğlu et al. (2021) has considered this dimension, by focusing on a number of emerging economies and implementing a linear estimation framework to test the dynamics between geopolitical risks and sentiment measures. However, as suggested by Subramaniam (2022), a linear estimation might not be optimal, given the erratic nature of geopolitical risks. Furthermore, it has been shown in the literature that the impact of geopolitical risks is typically not homogeneous (see, for example, Balcilar et al. (2018), Gkillas et al. (2018), Kannadhasan and Das (2020), and De Wet (2023)). It is, therefore, necessary to conduct several studies, on various economies, to gain a holistic understanding of the dynamics between geopolitical risks and sentiment indicators.

To the best of my knowledge, no previous study has been conducted to determine the nexus between geopolitical risks and economic sentiment measures in developed countries. This study contributes toward filling this gap by considering this dimension in seven of the largest developed countries. It also contributes to the generally scarce body of knowledge on the dynamics between geopolitical risks and sentiments. Furthermore, this study is the first to model the nexus between geopolitical risks and sentiment indicators by means of a nonlinear quantile regression analysis. Several studies show that the impact of geopolitical risks on an economic variable is typically asymmetrical and depends on the state of that variable (see, for example, Sohag et al. (2022), Subramaniam (2022), and Kannadhasan and Das (2020)). This study could thus contribute by providing more detailed information on the phenomena at hand. For example, this analysis will show the impact of geopolitical risks on sentiment when the prevailing sentiment indicator under analysis is low, medium, or high. The remainder of this chapter will proceed as follows: hereafter, a review of the most relevant literature will be provided, followed by a data and methodology discussion. Then, the results will be presented and paired with a discussion. Finally, this chapter will end with a conclusion.

1.2 Literature Review

Geopolitical risks have increasingly captured the attention of policymakers and academic researchers over the last decade. They are not a new phenomenon, but their growing importance as a driving factor of global economic growth over the recent decades has been largely a function of an increase in globally integrated economies and financial markets (Gupta et al., 2019; Sohag et al., 2022). The integrated nature of economies and financial markets means that an escalation in geopolitical risks anywhere in the world will likely have a spillover effect on financial assets across economies and markets. A popular measure used in the literature as a good proxy for global geopolitical risks is the geopolitical risk index constructed by Caldara and Iacoviello (2018) (see, for example, the work by Balcilar et al. (2018), Bouri et al. (2019), Le and Tran (2021), and Sohag et al. (2022)). The work on this index is formally published by Caldara and Iacoviello (2022). This index is based on news reports, and the index value is determined by aggregating words linked to geopolitical risks. This index reflects a comprehensive range of geopolitical risk factors, including military threats, wars, terror attacks, and trade wars (Balcilar et al., 2018).

Several studies consider the impact of geopolitical risks on economic activities, including research by Bloom (2009), Glick and Taylor (2010), Nikkinen and Vähämaa (2010), Caldara and Iacoviello (2018), Cheng and Chiu (2018), Gupta et al. (2019), and Akadiri et al. (2020). Glick and Taylor (2010) provide evidence that geopolitical tension causes a significant reduction in trade. Akadiri et al. (2020) also found that increased geopolitical tension has a negative impact on tourism volumes. Given that international trade and tourism constitute approximately 50% and 10% of the global gross domestic product (GDP) pre-coronavirus disease of 2019 (COVID), respectively, reductions in these activities could have a severe impact on global economic growth (World Bank, 2022). To this end, countries with local economies reliant on tourism and export activities might be disproportionally impacted by increased geopolitical tension. From a G7 perspective, countries most reliant on exports are Germany (47.5%), Italy (32.7%), Canada (30.7%), France (29.9%), and the United Kingdom (27%), with the values in the brackets showing exports as a percentage of GDP based on the latest figures by the World Bank (2022). On the other hand, exports only constitute 15.6% of Japan's GDP and 10.2% of the United States' GDP.

Furthermore, Balcilar et al. (2018) assert that geopolitical risks are a key determinant of investment decision-making. The literature on investment decision-making and geopolitical risks includes research by Demir et al. (2019), Kotcharin and Maneenop (2020), Wang et al. (2020), Elsayed and Helmi (2021), Le and Tran (2021), and Sohag et al. (2022). Findings by these researchers broadly concur that geopolitical risks are a key determinant of investment decision-making from both a fixed capital formation investment perspective and a portfolio investment perspective. In this context, Wang et al. (2020) show that increased geopolitical tension causes uncertainty and investor risk aversion, resulting in a postponement of investment activities. Le and Tran (2021) provide evidence that geopolitical shocks have a significantly negative impact on corporate investments and thereby reduce private fixed capital formation investments.

Furthermore, evidence by Caldara and Iacoviello (2018) shows that geopolitical tension causes capital outflows from economies that are perceived to be riskier and more exposed to global growth. Some countries are therefore more susceptible to an increase in geopolitical tension than are others, depending on the composition of the local economy. The results by Hui (2022) reflect this, showing that currencies of emerging economies typically depreciate during periods of increased geopolitical tension. Furthermore, aggregate stock market returns tend to be negative as a result of divestment (Gkillas et al., 2018; Kannadhasan & Das, 2020). The negative impact of increased geopolitical tensions could transmit through the investment channel, given the central role of investments as a driver of economic growth (Brue & Grant, 2007; Hayat, 2019).

It has also been found that increased geopolitical risks redirect economic activity from investment spending to government spending (Balcilar et al., 2018). It could be argued that this could cause geopolitical risks to have an asymmetric impact on different economies. On the one end, governments with a strong fiscal position could absorb and offset the impact of reduced private investing by increasing public spending and investing. However, governments with a weak fiscal position might have limited access to the capital market during high-risk periods and might therefore not have the means to offset reduced investment activities. In this study, an interesting country to consider is Germany because, on the one hand, it has the highest export-to-GDP ratio of all the G7 countries. On the other hand, Germany has consistently held the strongest fiscal position, which could be used to offset potential negative impacts caused by increased geopolitical risks.

Another channel through which an increase in geopolitical risks could transmit to the economy is through consumption. Bloom (2009), Nikkinen and Vähämaa (2010), and Caldara and Iacoviello (2018) provide evidence that geopolitical risks cause consumers to postpone consumption due to uncertainty. Industries most exposed to consumer uncertainty are those involved in the production and sales of discretionary goods and services (Nikkinen & Vähämaa, 2010; De Wet & Botha, 2019). Countries with high levels of final consumer consumption as a percentage of GDP might therefore be more exposed to increased geopolitical risks. From a G7 perspective, countries that are most exposed to a slowdown in consumption are the United Kingdom with the final consumer consumption at 83.5% of GDP and the United States with the final consumer consumption at 82% of GDP (World Bank, 2022).

A key element in the above discussion is the uncertainty that geopolitical risks create, which relates to consumer and investment sentiments. Consumer and investment sentiments could therefore be a potential transmission channel, whereby an increase in geopolitical risks transmits to economic activity. The empirical literature on the impact of both consumer and business sentiments on economic and financial activities is vast. For example, Lahiri and Zhao (2016) and De Wet and Botha (2022) provide evidence that sentiments play an important role in determining business and financial cycles. However, recent work on the determinants and drivers of consumer and business sentiments has been more limited. One study to this end is the work by Alaoui et al. (2020), which shows that economic growth, property prices, unemployment, and borrowing rates are the typical variables that drive consumer sentiment. Furthermore, Wanga et al. (2006) show that stock market volatility, borrowing rates, and economic growth are significant determinants of business sentiment.

Pehlivanoğlu et al. (2021) analyzed the nexus between geopolitical risks and consumer and business sentiments in several emerging markets. The results show that the nexus is not homogeneous among countries. In some cases, the increased geopolitical risks do have a significant long-run relationship with consumer and business sentiments. However, this is not the case for all countries for example, the nexus between South Africa's and Indonesia's consumer confidence is insignificant. On the other hand, the nexus between South African and Indonesian business confidence is significant. The asymmetrical results provided by Pehlivanoğlu et al. (2021) show that the impact of geopolitical risks on sentiments should not be assumed to be homogeneous, and, therefore, any policy to this end should be tailored for each country. Furthermore, as reviewed, the composition of an economy plays an important role in determining the nexus between geopolitical risks and the local economy. Differentials in economic compositions and fiscal positions could explain the heterogeneity in this nexus. This emphasizes the importance of broadening the body of knowledge to this end. This study will contribute to the scarce body of knowledge by focusing on the G7 countries. This will provide policymakers with more information to tailor their policy response to geopolitical risk events.

Additionally, several researchers provide evidence that the impact of geopolitical risks on economic and financial factors depends on the current state of the economic and financial variables under analysis (see, for example, Kannadhasan and Das (2020), Subramaniam (2022), and Sohag et al. (2022)). For example, Kannadhasan and Das (2020) provide evidence that stocks tend to react more negatively to geopolitical risks when the general stock market trades at upper quantile levels. On the other hand, the impact has proved to be insignificant when the stock market is already at relatively low levels. The impact of geopolitical risks is thus not symmetric and linear, and, therefore, nonlinear quantile regression analysis is commonly employed in the literature to assess geopolitical risks (see, for example, Koenker and Xiao (2006), Bouri et al. (2019), Kannadhasan and Das (2020), and Subramaniam (2022)). This approach allows one to determine the relationship across quantiles and thereby allows for heterogeneity (Subramaniam, 2022). Furthermore, quantile regression analysis makes no normality assumptions and is conducive to model variables with outliers (Kannadhasan & Das, 2020). This is ideal for research on shocks, given the erratic nature thereof. Therefore, this study employs a panel quantile regression model.

1.3 Data Discussion and Methodology

This study considers the impact of geopolitical risks on both consumer and business sentiments of the G7 countries. This study employed monthly data from March 1994 to June 2021. This time frame was determined by data availability and was selected to optimize the number of data points without having any missing data points. Two models were estimated in this study: one with consumer confidence as the dependent variable, hereafter the consumer confidence model, and the other with business confidence as the dependent variable, hereafter the business confidence model. To ensure consistency in measurement across countries, the standardized business and consumer confidence indices constructed by the Organization for Economic and Cooperation and Development (OECD) are employed to measure consumer and business confidence in each country (OECD, 2023a, b).

Similar to Balcilar et al. (2018), Bouri et al. (2019), Le and Tran (2021), and Sohag et al. (2022), the geopolitical risk index constructed by Caldara and Iacoviello (2018) and published by Caldara and Iacoviello (2022) is employed as a proxy for geopolitical risks over time. Thus, the geopolitical risk index by Caldara and Iacoviello (2022) is the main explanatory variable in both models. This index is obtained from Matteoiacoviello (2022). Following the literature, the controlled variables in the consumer confidence model are GDP growth rates, 3-year government bond yields as a proxy for borrowing rates, unemployment rates, and house prices (Alaoui et al., 2020). The controlled variables in the business confidence model are GDP growth rates, 3-year government bond yields, and the US volatility index (VIX) as a proxy for market volatility. All the controlled variables are obtained from the Thompson Reuters DataStream database.

Furthermore, cross-sectional dummies are included to distinguish between the various countries in the model in order to account for any cross-sectional heterogeneities. Additionally, interactive dummies are constructed and included in the model to establish the country-specific impact of geopolitical risks on consumer and business confidence. These interactive dummy variables are constructed by multiplying each cross-sectional dummy with the geopolitical risk index. This will allow the author to identify whether the geopolitical risk has a significantly different impact on business and consumer confidence in a specific country, relative to the base country. It should be noted that the United States will serve as the base country in this study, given that it has the largest economy by GDP in this sample of countries.

A panel quantile regression methodology is utilized in this study to determine the asymmetric impact of geopolitical risks on the consumer and business confidence of the G7 countries. This method allows one to identify and assess any heterogeneity in the relationship across quantiles (Subramaniam, 2022). Additionally, quantile regression analysis makes no normality assumptions and is conducive to model variables with outliers (Kannadhasan & Das, 2020). This is ideal for research on shocks, given the erratic nature of geopolitical risks. The quantile regression framework proposed by Koenker and Xiao (2006) is employed but is adjusted for panel data. The consumer confidence model is specified as follows:

$$
\begin{aligned}
Q_{\mathrm{CCI}it} \left(\tau_k | \alpha_i, \mathrm{GPR}_t\right) \\
= \alpha_i + \gamma_i\left(\tau\right) \mathrm{CCI}_{it-1} I\left(\mathrm{CCI}_{it-1}| > \mathrm{CCI}^q\right) + \beta_{1\tau} \mathrm{GPR}_t + \beta_{2\tau} \mathrm{CV}_{it} \\
+ \beta_{3\tau} D_{it} + \beta_{4\tau} D * \mathrm{GPR}_{it} + \mu_{it}
\end{aligned}
\tag{1.1}
$$

where the transcripts i and t denote country and month, respectively, and CCI denotes the consumer confidence index. The unobserved individual effect is shown by α_i, and τ shows the estimation of a coefficient at the τth quantile. Furthermore, GPR denotes geopolitical risk, and the term "$\beta_{1\tau}$" shows the impact of the geopolitical risk on consumer confidence at the τth quantile. Furthermore, CV_{it} represents a vector of controlled variables, and the term "$\beta_{2\tau}$" shows the impact of each controlled variable on the CCI at the τth quantile. The country-specific dummy variables are represented by D_{it}, and the geopolitical risk interactive dummy variables are represented by $D * GPR_{it}$. The term "$\gamma_i(\tau)$" is used to control the influence of extreme confidence levels using an indicator function variable. If consumer confidence exceeds a threshold value of BY^q at month $t - 1$, then the indicator function ($BY_{xt-1} > BY^q$) takes the value of 1, otherwise 0. The BY^q at the 95th quantile of the uncorrelated distribution is taken. Lastly, μ_{it} represents the model residual.

Using the same notation, the business confidence model, where BCI_{it} represents the business confidence index of each country i at month t, is specified as follows:

$$
\begin{aligned}
Q_{BCI_{it}} \left(\tau_k | \alpha_i, GPR_t \right) \\
= \alpha_i + \gamma_i \left(\tau \right) BCI_{it-1} I \left(BCI_{it-1} | > CCI^q \right) + \beta_{5\tau} GPR_t + \beta_{6\tau} CV_{it} \\
+ \beta_{7\tau} D_{it} + \beta_{8\tau} D * GPR_{it} + \mu_{it}
\end{aligned}
$$

$$(1.2)$$

To test whether the variables in both models are co-integrated and, thus, whether a long-run relationship exists between the variables, the residuals of both models are tested for stationarity by means of the Levin–Lin–Chu panel unit root test. Furthermore, the quantile regression model is only robust if the relationships between the variables in the model are asymmetric across quantiles. In accordance with Koenker and Xiao (2006), the symmetric quantiles test is employed to test for these asymmetries. If heterogeneity is present, then the use of a quantile regression analysis is justified. The Wald test setup to test for the following null hypothesis will be used:

$$ H_0 : \frac{\beta \left(\tau_j \right) + \beta \left(\tau_{K-j-1} \right)}{2} = \beta \left(\frac{1}{2} \right) $$

$$(1.3)$$

For $j = 1, \ldots, \frac{K-1}{2}$.

The assumption here is that the mean value $\tau_{(k+1)/2}$ is equal to 0.5, and the remaining τ are symmetric around 0.5.

Furthermore, Koenker and Bassett (1982) propose that the slopes between the quantiles should be tested for differences as a further test of heterogeneity and robustness. To this end, the Wald slope equality test will be conducted across quantiles to test for heterogeneous slopes. In accordance with Koenker and Bassett (1982), the hypotheses for this test are expressed as:

$$ H_0 : \beta_1 \left(\tau_1 \right) = \beta_1 \left(\tau_2 \right) = \beta_1 \left(\tau_k \right) $$

$$H_1 : \beta_1(\tau_1) \neq \beta_1(\tau_2) \neq \beta_1(\tau_k)$$

where β_1 is the slope coefficient at various quantiles, up to quantile τ_k. In this study, the relationship between geopolitical risks and the two confidence measures are evaluated at quantiles 0.1, 0.2, 0.3, 0.4, 0.5, 0.6, 0.7, 0.8, and 0.9. The results and a discussion thereof are presented in the next section.

1.4 Results and Findings

Table 1.1 depicts the median results estimated by both the consumer and business confidence models. Furthermore, Table 1.1 depicts the co-integration test results and the results for both the symmetric quantiles test and the slope equality test. Based

Table 1.1 Aggregate quantile regression results

	CCI results		BCI results	
	Beta	*P*-value	Beta	*P*-value
House price	0.183	0.000	−0.011	0.000
Growth	0.151	0.001	0.199	0.000
VIX	N/A	N/A	−0.062	0.000
Yields	0.673	0.000	−0.053	0.006
Unemployment rate	−0.490	0.000	N/A	N/A
UK	102.706	0.000	102.740	0.000
JP	102.883	0.000	102.370	0.000
IT	103.271	0.000	103.266	0.000
FRA	101.667	0.000	102.534	0.000
DE	102.106	0.000	102.721	0.000
CA	101.179	0.000	103.121	0.000
US	101.876	0.000	101.436	0.000
GPR (base case)	−0.510	0.017	0.071	0.229
UK*GPR	0.058	0.762	−0.235	0.035
JP*GPR	−0.75	0.000	0.335	0.772
IT*GPR	−0.37	0.013	−0.054	0.146
FRA*GPR	0.43	0.074	−0.164	0.041
DE*GPR	0.40	0.034	−0.273	0.077
CA*GPR	−0.68	0.025	−0.454	0.035
ECM(-1)	−0.022	0.000	−0.051	0.000
P-value of the slope equality test	0.000***		0.026**	
P-value of symmetric quantiles test	0.013**		0.048**	
P-value for the co-integration test	ADF: 0.002 PP: 0.000		ADF: 0.000 PP: 0.000	

ADF Augmented Dickey Fuller, *PP* Phillips Perron, *N/A* not applicable, *UK* United Kingdom, *JP* Japan, *IT* Italy, *FRA* France, *DE* Germany, *CA* Canada, *US* United States, *ECM(−1)* Error Correction Model with one period lag
** denotes 95% significance and *** denotes 99% significance

on the latter, the null hypotheses of the symmetric quantiles and equal slopes across quantiles are rejected at a 95% confidence level for both models. This provides evidence that there are asymmetries across quantiles, justifying the employment of a quantile regression analysis that allows for quantile asymmetries. These asymmetries could be due to the economic variations between the G7 countries. For example, the economies of Germany and Italy are much more reliant on exports and tourism than are those of the United States and Japan (World Bank, 2022). This provides a possible explanation for the asymmetric impact of geopolitical risks on the confidence measures between the G7 countries. Furthermore, the co-integration test results show that the residual series for both models are stationary, and, therefore, co-integration exists in both models.

Consider now the results obtained from the consumer confidence model. At a median level, all the controlled variables are significant at a 99% confidence level. Moreover, the country dummy variables are all statistically significant at a 99% confidence level, providing evidence that there are cross-sectional variations. To determine the impact of geopolitical risks on consumer confidence at a country-specific level, interactive dummy variables are included in the model. In this regard, the nexus between geopolitical risks and US consumer confidence is the base case in the model. The results show that geopolitical risks do have a statistically significant negative impact on consumer confidence in the base case. Thus, a one-index-point increase in the geopolitical risk measure will result in a decline of 0.51 consumer index points. This shows that the sentiment of the US consumer is negatively impacted by geopolitical risks, and this aligns with the findings by Cheng and Chiu (2018), Gupta et al. (2019), and Akadiri et al. (2020), which show that geopolitical risks have a significantly negative impact on economic conditions. The results further show that the impact of geopolitical risks on consumer confidence at a median level in Japan, Italy, and Canada is significantly more negative than the base case. The enhanced negative impact on Italian consumer confidence could be explained by Italy's relatively high reliance on tourism. In the case of Canada, the enhanced negative impact on consumer confidence could be due to its reliance on oil exports. In the case of Japan, Japanese exports are relatively low as a percentage of GDP; however, the United States is Japan's fourth largest trading partner, and this could explain why geopolitical risks have an asymmetrically negative impact on Japanese consumer confidence. This could especially be the case if geopolitical risks directly pertain to the United States. On the other hand, the impact of geopolitical risks on consumer confidence in France and Germany is significantly less severe than the base case at a median level. The results could be due to the United States often being primarily involved in geopolitical tensions. Lastly, the results show that the impact of geopolitical risks on consumer confidence in the UK is insignificantly different from the base case.

Consider now the results obtained from the business confidence model. Once again, all the controlled and country dummy variables are statistically significant at a 99% confidence level. Once again, the nexus between geopolitical risks and US business confidence is the base case in the model against which the interactive dummy variables are measured. The results show that geopolitical risks do have

Table 1.2 Results at the quantile level for CCI

Quantile	GPR	UK*GPR	JP*GPR	IT*GPR	FRA*GPR	DE*GPR	CA*GPR
0.1	−0.784***	−0.88**	−0.84***	−0.22*	−0.21*	−0.30**	−0.22**
0.2	−0.721***	−1.21**	−1.47***	−0.85***	−0.30**	−0.34***	−0.57***
0.3	−0.656***	−0.76*	−0.98***	−0.53**	−0.48***	−0.21*	0.30*
0.4	−0.473**	0.47	−0.75***	−0.32**	0.44***	0.32**	−0.04
0.5	−0.510**	0.058	−0.75***	−0.37**	0.43***	0.40**	−0.68***
0.6	−0.289*	0.29	−0.62***	−0.30**	0.49***	0.41**	−0.98***
0.7	0.013	0.11	−0.56***	−0.25*	0.52***	0.51***	−0.62***
0.8	0.014	0.01	−0.67***	−0.21*	0.000	0.59***	0.32**
0.9	0.026	0.016	−0.15	−0.039	0.000	0.007	0.009

Source: Self-constructed
UK United Kingdom, *JP* Japan, *IT* Italy, *FRA* France, *DE* Germany, *CA* Canada, *US* United States
* and *** denote statistical significance at 95% and 99% confidence levels, respectively, based on
P-values

a statistically insignificant impact on business confidence in the base as well as on business confidence in Japan and Italy. The insignificant impact of geopolitical risks on Japanese and US business confidence could be explained by the relatively low reliance of these two economies on exports and tourism. However, Italy is an interesting case; these results go against expectations. On the other hand, the results show that the impact of geopolitical risks on business confidence is significantly more severe in the United Kingdom, France, Germany, and Canada. This could be explained by the asymmetrically high reliance of these economies on exports (World Bank, 2022). To analyze these dynamics in more detail, the relationship between geopolitical risks and consumer and business confidence is considered at a quantile level, ranging from the 10th to the 90th quantiles. This is carried out on each interactive dummy variable as before, with the United States as the base case. The results at the quantile level for the consumer confidence index are depicted in Table 1.2.

Considering the base case first, the results show that geopolitical risks do have a statistically significant negative impact on consumer confidence at the 10th–60th quantiles. It should also be noted that consumer confidence is most severely impacted when consumer confidence is already low, i.e., at the lowest three quantiles. However, the impact becomes insignificant when consumer confidence is already at relatively high levels, i.e., at the 70th–90th quantiles. Thus, when consumer confidence is low, additional geopolitical risks tend to reduce confidence further. However, when confidence is relatively high, additional geopolitical risks tend to have an insignificant impact on consumer confidence. This aligns with the findings of Sohag et al. (2022), Subramaniam (2022), and Kannadhasan and Das (2020), which provide evidence that the impact of geopolitical risks across quantiles is asymmetrical. Furthermore, the results show that geopolitical risks tend to impact all the other G7 countries significantly more severely when consumer confidence is already low in these countries, i.e., at the 10th–30th quantiles. The results further show that from the fourth quantile onward, the impact of geopolitical risks on consumer confidence in the United Kingdom tends to be similar to that of the United States. The impact of geopolitical risks on consumer confidence in both Japan and Italy tends to be more significantly negative than the base case at all the quantiles, except the 90th quantile. On the other hand, the impact of geopolitical risks on consumer confidence in both Germany and France tends to be significantly less severe from the 40th to the 80th quantiles. Lastly, the impact of geopolitical risks on consumer confidence in Canada relative to the base case is mixed. At the 30th and 80th quantiles, the impact is significantly less severe but significantly more severe at the 50th–70th quantiles. These asymmetrical cross-country results align with those of Pehlivanoğlu et al. (2021).

Table 1.3 depicts the results at the quantile level for business confidence index. The result for the base case shows that an increase in geopolitical risks has a statistically significant positive impact on business confidence at the lowest two quantiles and a statistically significant negative impact at the highest two quantiles. Businesses might expect increased geopolitical risks to result in a looser monetary policy when confidence is already low. However, when confidence is high, geopolitical shocks could cause inflation risks that, in turn, could lead to the expectation of a tighter monetary policy. On the other hand, the impact of geopolitical risks on business confidence has proved to be insignificant at the more moderate quantiles. Interestingly, this differs from the dynamics between geopolitical risks and consumer confidence where an increase in geopolitical risks has a significantly negative impact on consumer confidence when confidence is already low. Given these results, it could be argued that geopolitical risks might transmit through the consumption channel rather than the business channel during low- to moderate-confidence regimes. Therefore, to reduce the economic impact of an increase in geopolitical risks, policymakers should focus on the consumer during low- to moderate-confidence regimes. On the other hand, during relatively high-confidence regimes, policymakers should shift their focus to businesses.

The impact of geopolitical risks on business confidence in the United Kingdom tends to be significantly more negative than the base case at the lower to middle quantiles, i.e., the 10th–50th quantiles, but insignificant at the other quantiles. On the other hand, the impact of geopolitical risks on business confidence in Japan tends to be significantly more positive than the base case at the low quantiles, i.e., the 10th–40th quantiles, but significantly more negative at the higher quantiles, i.e., the 70th–90th quantiles. Furthermore, the results show that the impact of geopolitical risks on Italian business confidence tends to be similar to that of the base case at quantiles 10–60 but significantly more severe at the upper quantiles, i.e., the 70th – 90th quantiles. Similarly, geopolitical risks tend to impact business confidence in France significantly more severely at the middle to upper quantiles but significantly less severely at the lowest two quantiles. This dynamic is also significantly more severe in the case of Germany at the 50th–80th quantiles. Lastly, the impact of geopolitical risks on Canadian business confidence tends to be significantly less severe at the lowest quantile but significantly more severe at the 40th–90th quantiles.

1 The Nexus Between Geopolitical Risks and Confidence Measures in G7 Countries

Table 1.3 Results at the quantile level for the BCI

	GPR	UK*GPR	JP*GPR	IT*GPR	FRA*GPR	DE*GPR	CA*GPR
Quantile							
0.1	0.185*	−0.695***	0.219**	0.032	0.323**	0.000	0.361**
0.2	0.129*	−0.263**	0.262**	−0.103	0.200*	0.021	0.054
0.3	0.065	−0.299**	0.299**	0.000	0.174	0.000	−0.149
0.4	0.076	−0.450**	0.448***	−0.031	0.052	−0.098	−0.349**
0.5	0.071	−0.235**	0.335	−0.054	−0.164**	−0.273*	−0.454**
0.6	0.135	0.101	−0.101	−0.165	−0.327**	−0.409***	−0.250*
0.7	0.193	0.208	−0.308**	−0.329***	−0.421**	−0.294***	−0.475***
0.8	−0.206**	0.193	−0.393**	−0.253***	−0.503***	−0.261***	−0.532***
0.9	−0.434***	0.096	−0.296**	−0.582***	−0.836***	0.000	−0.489**

Source: Self-constructed

UK United Kingdom, *JP* Japan, *IT* Italy, *FRA* France, *DE* Germany, *CA* Canada, *US* United States
* and *** denote statistical significance at the 95% and 99% confidence levels, respectively, based on *P*-values

1.5 Conclusions

The main aim of this study was to determine the nexus between geopolitical risks and both consumer and business confidence of the G7 countries. This study was motivated by the importance of consumer and business confidence in financial and economic activities and the increasingly prominent role that geopolitical risks play in decision-making. The aim of this study was achieved by means of employing a panel quantile regression model and using the geopolitical risk index created by Caldara and Iacoviello (2022) as a proxy for geopolitical risks. This study provides several key findings. First, it provides evidence that geopolitical risks do have a statistically significant negative impact on consumer confidence at a median level, with the United States as the base case. Furthermore, consumer confidence in Japan, Italy, and Canada has proved to be significantly more severely impacted by geopolitical risks at a median level. On the other hand, geopolitical risks have proved to have a significantly lower impact on consumer confidence in France and Germany at a median level. Evidence also shows that geopolitical risks have an asymmetrical impact on consumer confidence across quantiles in all countries. The results show that consumer confidence across all countries is more severely impacted by geopolitical risks during low-confidence regimes, i.e., at the 10th–30th quantiles. The negative impact tends to diminish at higher-confidence regimes, except for Japan, Canada, and Italy.

Second, geopolitical risks tend to have an insignificant impact on business confidence in the United States, Japan, and Italy at a median level but have proved to have a significantly negative impact on business confidence in the United Kingdom, France, Germany, and Canada. Interestingly, the results show that geopolitical risks have a significantly positive impact on business confidence in the United States, Japan, France, and Canada at low-confidence regimes. When confidence in the United States is at extremely high levels, i.e., at the 80th and 90th regimes, geopolitical risks tend to have a significantly negative impact on business confidence. This is also the case for Japan, Italy, France, and Canada. Thus, the results show that the impact of geopolitical risks is asymmetrical in several different ways.

First, the impact of geopolitical risks on consumer confidence tends to differ from that on business confidence across quantiles. For example, in the case of the United States, an increase in geopolitical risks tends to have a significantly negative impact on consumer confidence at low-confidence levels but has an insignificant impact on consumer confidence at high-confidence levels. Inversely, business confidence in the United States tends to respond positively to geopolitical risks at low-confidence levels but negatively at high-confidence levels. Second, the impact of geopolitical risks has proved to be asymmetrical across quantiles for both variables in all the countries. Lastly, there are cross-sectional differences, and, thus, the impact of geopolitical risks tends to differ from country to country.

These results point to the need for a heterogeneous policy, both within an economy and across economies, to manage the impact of increased geopolitical risks. The results show that in a given country, consumer confidence reacts differently to an increase in geopolitical risks than does business confidence at different confidence regimes. For example, geopolitical risks tend to cause business confidence to go up and consumer confidence to go down at low-confidence regimes in the United States. There is also a cross-sectional difference that should be considered. It would be optimal for policymakers of a given economy to identify the underlying confidence regime and use these results to establish whether the business or consumer confidence is more vulnerable to an increase in geopolitical risks. Once this is established, policymakers could employ tools specifically developed to target the most vulnerable confidence measure.

References

Akadiri, S. S., Eluwole, K. K., Akadiri, A. C., & Avci, T. (2020). Does causality between geopolitical risk, tourism and economic growth matter? Evidence from Turkey. *Journal of Hospitality and Tourism Management, 43*, 273–277. https://doi.org/10.1016/j.jhtm.2019.09.002

Balcilar, M., Bonato, M., Demirer, R., & Gupta, R. (2018). Geopolitical risks and stock market dynamics of the BRICS. *Economic Systems, 42*(2), 295–306. https://doi.org/10.1016/j.ecosys.2017.05.008

Bloom, N. (2009). The impact of uncertainty shocks. *Econometrica, 77*(3), 623–685. https://doi.org/10.3982/ecta6248

Bouri, E., Demirer, R., Gupta, R., & Marfatia, H. A. (2019). Geopolitical risks and movements in Islamic bond and equity markets: A note. *Defence and Peace Economics, 30*(3), 367–379. https://doi.org/10.1080/10242694.2018.1424613

Brue, S. L., & Grant, R. R. (2007). *The evolution of economic thought* (7th ed.). Thomson.

Caldara, D., & Iacoviello, M. (2018). Measuring geopolitical risk. *International Finance Discussion Paper, 2018*(1222), 1–66. https://doi.org/10.17016/IFDP.2018.1222

Caldara, D., & Iacoviello, M. (2022). Measuring geopolitical risk. *American Economic Review, 112*(4), 1194–1225. https://doi.org/10.1257/aer.20191823

Cheng, C. H. J., & Chiu, C. W. (Jeremy). (2018). How important are global geopolitical risks to emerging countries? *International Economics, 156*, 305–325. https://doi.org/10.1016/j.inteco.2018.05.002

De Wet, M. C. (2023). Geopolitical risks and yield dynamics in the Australian Sovereign Bond Market. *Journal of Risk Financial Management, 16*(3), 144. https://doi.org/10.3390/jrfm16030144

De Wet, M. C., & Botha, I. (2019). Characterising cycles exhibited by important financial sections in the South African economy. *Journal of Economic and Financial Sciences, 12*(1). https://doi.org/10.4102/jef.v12i1.433

De Wet, M. C., & Botha, I. (2022). Constructing and characterising the aggregate South African financial cycle: A Markov regime-switching approach. *Journal of Business Cycle Research, 18*(1), 37–67. https://doi.org/10.1007/s41549-022-00064-y

Demir, E., Gozgor, G., & Paramati, S. R. (2019). Do geopolitical risks matter for inbound tourism? *Eurasian Business Review, 9*(2), 183–191. https://doi.org/10.1007/s40821-019-00118-9

Dogan, E., Majeed, M. T., & Luni, T. (2021). Analyzing the impacts of geopolitical risk and economic uncertainty on natural resources rents. *Resources Policy, 72*. https://doi.org/10.1016/j.resourpol.2021.102056

Eckstein, Z., & Tsiddon, D. (2004). Macroeconomic consequences of terror: Theory and the case of Israel. *Journal of Monetary Economics, 51*(5), 971–1002. https://doi.org/10.1016/j.jmoneco.2004.05.001

El Alaoui, M., Bouri, E., & Azoury, N. (2020). The determinants of the U.S. consumer sentiment: Linear and nonlinear models. *Journal of International Financial Studies, 8*, 38. https://doi.org/10.3390/ijfs8030038

Elsayed, A. H., & Helmi, M. H. (2021). Volatility transmission and spillover dynamics across financial markets: the role of geopolitical risk. *Annals of Operations Research, 305*(1–2). https://doi.org/10.1007/s10479-021-04081-5

Gkillas, K., Gupta, R., & Wohar, M. E. (2018). Volatility jumps: The role of geopolitical risks. *Finance Research Letters, 27*, 247–258. https://doi.org/10.1016/j.frl.2018.03.014

Glick, R., & Taylor, A. M. (2010). Collateral damage: Trade disruption and the economic impact of war. *The Review of Economics and Statistics, 92*(1), 102–127.

Gupta, R., Gozgor, G., Kaya, H., & Demir, E. (2019). Effects of geopolitical risks on trade flows: Evidence from the gravity model. *Eurasian Economic Review, 9*(4), 515–530. https://doi.org/10.1007/s40822-018-0118-0

Hayat, A. (2019). Foreign direct investments, institutional quality, and economic growth. *Journal of International Trade and Economic Development, 28*(5), 561–579. https://doi.org/10.1080/09638199.2018.1564064

Hui, H. C. (2022). The long-run effects of geopolitical risk on foreign exchange markets: evidence from some ASEAN countries. *International Journal of Emerging Markets, 17*(6), 1543–1564. https://doi.org/10.1108/IJOEM-08-2020-1001

Kannadhasan, M., & Das, D. (2020). Do Asian emerging stock markets react to international economic policy uncertainty and geopolitical risk alike? A quantile regression approach. *Finance Research Letters, 34*. https://doi.org/10.1016/j.frl.2019.08.024

Koenker, R., & Bassett, G. (1982). Robust tests for heteroscedasticity based on regression quantiles. *Econometrica, 50*(1).

Koenker, R., & Xiao, Z. (2006). Quantile autoregression. *Journal of the American Statistical Association, 101*(475), 980–990. https://doi.org/10.1198/016214506000000672

Kotcharin, S., & Maneenop, S. (2020). Geopolitical risk and shipping firms' capital structure decisions in Belt and Road Initiative countries. *International Journal of Logistics Research and Applications, 23*(6), 544–560. https://doi.org/10.1080/13675567.2020.1766003

Lahiri, K., & Zhao, Y. (2016). Determinants of consumer sentiment over business cycles: Evidence from the US surveys of consumers. *Journal of Business Cycle Research, 12*(2), 187–215. https://doi.org/10.1007/s41549-016-0010-5

Le, A. T., & Tran, T. P. (2021). Does geopolitical risk matter for corporate investment? Evidence from emerging countries in Asia. *Journal of Multinational Financial Management, 62*. https://doi.org/10.1016/j.mulfin.2021.100703

Matteoiacoviello. (2022). *Geopolitical Risk index*. https://www.matteoiacoviello.com/gpr.htm

Nikkinen, J., & Vähämaa, S. (2010). Terrorism and stock market sentiment. *The Financial Review, 45*.

OECD. (2023a). *Consumer confidence index (CCI)*. https://data.oecd.org/leadind/consumer-confidence-index-cci.htm

OECD. (2023b). *Business confidence index (BCI)*. https://data.oecd.org/leadind/business-confidence-index-bci.htm#indicator-chart

Pehlivanoğlu, F., Akdağ, S., & Alola, A. A. (2021). The causal nexus of geopolitical risks, consumer and producer confidence indexes: evidence from selected economies. *Quality and Quantity, 55*(4), 1261–1273. https://doi.org/10.1007/s11135-020-01053-y

Sohag, K., Hammoudeh, S., Elsayed, A. H., Mariev, O., & Safonova, Y. (2022). Do geopolitical events transmit opportunity or threat to green markets? Decomposed measures of geopolitical risks. *Energy Economics, 111*. https://doi.org/10.1016/j.eneco.2022.106068

Subramaniam, S. (2022). Geopolitical uncertainty and sovereign bond yields of BRICS economies. *Studies in Economics and Finance, 39*(2), 311–330. https://doi.org/10.1108/SEF-05-2021-0214

Wang, H., Keswani, A., & Taylor, S. J. (2006). The relationships between sentiment, returns and volatility. *International Journal of Forecasting*, 22, 109–123. https://doi.org/10.1016/j.ijforecast.2005.04.019

Wang, Y., Liu, C., & Wang, G. (2020). Geopolitical risk revealed in international investment and world trade. *Risk Management, 22*(2), 133–154. https://doi.org/10.1057/s41283-020-00058-z

World Bank. (2022). *Trade as a percentage of GDP*. https://data.worldbank.org/indicator/NE.TRD.GNFS.ZS

Chapter 2
International Trade Flows and Geo-Political Episodes—Network Perspective

Ahaan Shah, Keyaan Shah, and Homa Hosseinmardi

Abstract Today, globalization and international trade have created a network of countries that are deeply interconnected with each other socially, politically and economically. At the same time, however, this network has experienced significant disruptions over the 5-year period of 2016–2020 in the form of the US-China trade war, Brexit and COVID-19. This chapter presents an analysis of the changes observed in bilateral international trade relations from a social networks perspective over this period and draws connections between the network analysis and these phenomena. The analysis has been done based on the IMF database of over 78,000 trading pairs for the 5 years with USD 88.31 trillion volume; after applying materiality filters resulting in 9119 trading pairs accounting for over 90% volume. The analysis reveals a high degree of concentration: The top 20 pairs account for over 25% of world trade. There is a tight cohesion observed by way of cluster formation amongst countries located within a particular geographical region. It is worth noting that modularity of the clusters has reduced over the period which could be because established trading pairs going beyond their regular partners to other countries in order to fulfil their trade requirements. The centrality measures have remained largely consistent at the network level and for individual countries, clusters or regions. China emerged as the most central trading partner over the years. Further, China's centrality improved during the period; while the United States lost some ground. The United Kingdom's centrality also fell consistently, which could be attributed to Brexit. The findings from this report may be subjected to further granular analysis of different product components of the relevant trade flows or may be used to analyze subsequent events, such as the Russia-Ukraine conflict and other such geo-political disruptive episodes.

A. Shah (✉)
Jayshree Periwal International School, Jaipur, India

K. Shah
Dhirubhai Ambani International School, Mumbai, India

H. Hosseinmardi
Computational Social Science Lab, University of Pennsylvania, Philadelphia, PA, USA

© The Author(s), under exclusive license to Springer Nature Switzerland AG 2024
N. Tsounis, A. Vlachvei (eds.), *Applied Economic Research and Trends*, Springer Proceedings in Business and Economics,
https://doi.org/10.1007/978-3-031-49105-4_2

Keywords International trade · Social network analysis · Bilateral trade flows · Centrality · Community detection · Clusters

2.1 Introduction

International trade has been a key catalyst for economic growth across nations. It helps by improving the efficiency of resource allocation, providing access to markets and facilitating specialization based on the comparative advantage of nations. There are several models for understanding international trade. The Ricardian model and the Heckscher–Ohlin model suggest that the quantum and direction of trade are determined by differences in technology and factor endowments between nations. These models imply that so long as these differences exist between nations, international trade should proliferate between market economies. However, international trade is also subject to constant change from various stimuli, including economic, political, technological and environmental triggers.

After having seen consistent growth in trade volumes from USD 15.58 trn to USD 19.12 trn between 2016 and 2018, international trade witnessed major events in 2019 and 2020, which caused disruptions and de-growth to USD 18.6 trn in 2019 and USD 17.11 in 2020. Chief amongst these are the US-China trade tensions, Britain's exit from the European Union and the novel coronavirus (COVID-19) pandemic. These events demonstrated international trade flows are volatile, imbalanced and fragmented across supply chains and are highly sensitive to geo-political events.

International trade between nations is an example of a social network. The trade relationship between various countries can thus be studied by applying the concepts of social network analysis. Thus, network analysis can provide interesting insights into the effect of these events on international trade flows. This report presents the social network analysis of the international trade flows over a 5-year period from 2016 to 2020.

2.2 Background and Literature Review

A social network consists of a set of entities and the relationships between them. Entities interact with each other, and these interaction patterns provide insight into the entities involved. Relationships enable information to flow across a network, enabling one individual to influence another. Relationships in a network can be classified as either valued or dichotomous. A dichotomous relationship is about existence or non-existence of relationship between two entities, whereas a valued relationship includes a weight indicating the strength of the relationship. The weights allow the relationships to be compared to each other (Wasserman & Faust, 2021).

Fig. 2.1 Node-level measures

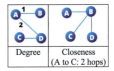

Fig. 2.2 Network-level measures

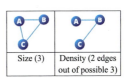

Social network analysis (SNA) provides both a visual and a mathematical analysis of relationships between entities. Visual analysis of network connectivity provides a panoramic perspective of the network, whereas the mathematical approach provides information about the density of a network and the centrality of points in that network. The SNA provides insights such as the level of power, influence, popularity, inter-connectedness and criticality of and within a network.

In a social network, a node represents a social entity, typically a person, an organization or any other relevant unit. There are several concepts related to social networks which help in explaining and understanding the networks better. An edge stands for a specific relationship between its incident nodes. Weight of an edge is the number of times that edge appears between two specific nodes (Telatnik, 2020).

Centrality is used to quantify how important and influential a specific node is to the network as a whole. There are several centrality measures, such as degree, closeness and betweenness. Degree is the number of edges the node has. Closeness measures how well connected a node is to every other node in the network. Betweenness measures the importance of a node's connections in allowing nodes to reach other nodes (Fig. 2.1).

Networks can also be assessed on the network level as against the node level using centrality measures. There are different network measures, such as size and density. Network size is the number of nodes in the network without taking into consideration the number of edges. Density is the number of edges divided by the total possible edges (Fig. 2.2).

Over the past decades, research on networks in economics has grown exponentially. While this can be attributed to the increased data availability and improved computational capabilities for developing complex data models, there are also other reasons for this phenomenon. SNA helps us understand economic behaviors that are driven by patterns of interactions between firms and nations. Further, the different aspects of network analysis such as density, centrality and other attributes help understanding some specific economic behaviors as well. In international trade, trading decisions are made by countries and firms based on several factors, such as conflicts, alliances and competitive advantages. Studying international trade from a network approach helps with better understanding of these factors. This requires continuous assessments of the networks and also developing new models that capture the specific factors that are responsible for evolution of the networks of trade and alliances over time and see the resulting consequences (Jackson, 2014). Social network analysis' measures, such as network density, clustering coefficients and average distance, can help in the assessment of the magnitude and nature of trade relationships. Key aspects of network analysis in the context of international trade flows are outlined in the ensuing part of this section.

2.2.1 Community Detection

A highly relevant area of network analysis is that of community detection or clustering, consisting in the division of nodes into groups, clusters or communities on the basis of features extracted from the network related to the nodes and edges. A cluster can be a set of countries that are closer to each other, compared to the rest of the countries in the network.

2.2.2 Centrality Measures

As mentioned earlier, centrality measures quantify how important or central each node is in a network which helps in assessing the relevance of a country's participation in international trade chains. Links between countries can be further weighted by the value of the trade exchanged between them.

2.3 Methodology

The network analysis has been done based on the dataset drawn from the IMF database for the trade flows between countries of the world. The total value of exports drawn from the DOTS database for each of the trading pairs has been aggregated to analyze the overall trade flows within the network. The total dataset with all the countries in the database created over 78,000 trading pairs for the 5 years. To limit the sample size for a meaningful analysis and network visualization, materiality parameters have been applied. The trade network between countries has been created as a weighted social network using Gephi. Gephi is a visualization and exploration software for all kinds of graphs and networks based on a visualize-and-manipulate paradigm (Bastian & Ors, n.d.). The output generated by Gephi has been validated against code created in Python using tools available on the NetworkX platform—a Python package for the creation, manipulation and study of the structure, dynamics and functions of complex networks.

2.4 Network Analysis

2.4.1 Data collection

The IMF collates and publishes Direction of Trade Statistics (DOTS) about the value of merchandise exports and imports disaggregated according to each country's trading partners. Coverage of the DOTS is augmented by using trade statistics available from other international organizations as well. The reported data are supplemented by estimates whenever relevant data are not available or current. The countries covered in the database represent over 90% of the value of world trade (International Monetary Fund, 2022). The annual value of trade for 2016, 2017, 2018, 2019 and 2020 between each of the trading partners has been drawn from this database. Further, data about the Gross National Income[1] has been drawn from the database of the World Bank collection of development indicators (The World Bank, n.d.).

2.4.2 Creating the Network

The dataset considered for this report has been filtered by making adjustments for materiality[2] from the global database. This dataset has information of over 1800 trading pairs which covers the global trade of USD 82 trillion out of the overall global trade of USD 88 trillion for the 5 years. The overall data and the datasets considered are summarized in Tables 2.1 and 2.2.

The trade network between countries has been created as a weighted social network. Each country of the dataset represents a node in the network and the bilateral trade between any two countries represents the edges of the network. The edges and nodes are weighted based on the trade volume for each pair and GNI of each country, respectively. Further, the region for each country is also added as an

Table 2.1 Dataset considered for creating the network

For the years 2016–2020	Trading pairs	Volume (USD trn)	Countries	GNI (USD bn)
Aggregate	78,885	88.31	212	88,301
Excluded	69,766	6.40	112	1568
Included	9119	81.90	100	86,733
Percentage included	12%	93%	47%	98%

---

[1] GNI has been considered for the years 2019 or 2020 based on the latest available information in the database.

[2] Materiality criteria applied: (i) Top 100 countries by their respective gross national incomes; and (ii) Trading pairs with bilateral volume of over USD 500 in any of the 5 years.

Table 2.2 Yearly aggregates of trade between all countries and between the trading pairs considered

	2016	2017	2018	2019	2020
Trade value—Aggregate (USD bn)	15,584,588	17,332,228	19,123,959	18,601,578	17,111,090
Trade value—Considered (USD bn)	14,458,008	16,086,366	17,749,880	17,228,938	15,763,619
Coverage for analysis	93%	93%	93%	93%	92%
Trading pairs (active)	15,270	15,304	15,512	15,465	15,160
Trading pairs (considered)	1823	1824	1824	1824	1823

Table 2.3 Network summary table across the years

	2016	2017	2018	2019	2020
Edges (total trades)	1824	1823	1824	1823	1823
Network density	0.368	0.368	0.368	0.368	0.368
Degree average (average trading pairs)	36.48	36.46	36.48	36.46	36.46
Degree standard deviation	24.20	24.22	24.20	24.20	24.20
Weighted degree average (USD mn)	2,89,160	3,21,728	3,54,998	3,44,579	3,15,273
Weighted degree standard deviation (USD mn)	5,72,156	6,28,316	6,90,305	6,70,557	6,30,808

attribute for the respective country. A demographic summary of the trade network over the 5 years is shown in Table 2.3.

The above statistics show that the network has an average degree of over 36 across all the years, which is representative of a well-connected trade network. The average weighted degrees range of USD 289 bn to USD 355 bn across the years comes with a very high standard deviation. On an overall basis, the total trading pairs amongst the top 100 countries remained almost constant during the years, which can be seen by the number of edges, the average degree, and graph density of the network. However, the volume of trade varied over the years as is evident from the fall in the average weighted degree. The charts in Fig. 2.3 drawn using Gephi also indicate the high level of inter-connectedness between nations across both years.

2.4.3 Analyzing the Network

2.4.3.1 Top Trading Interactions Between Countries

The ensuing Table 2.4 shows the movement in bilateral trade flows for the top 20 trading partners individually across the years from 2016 to 2020. Collectively, these

2 International Trade Flows and Geo-Political Episodes—Network Perspective 23

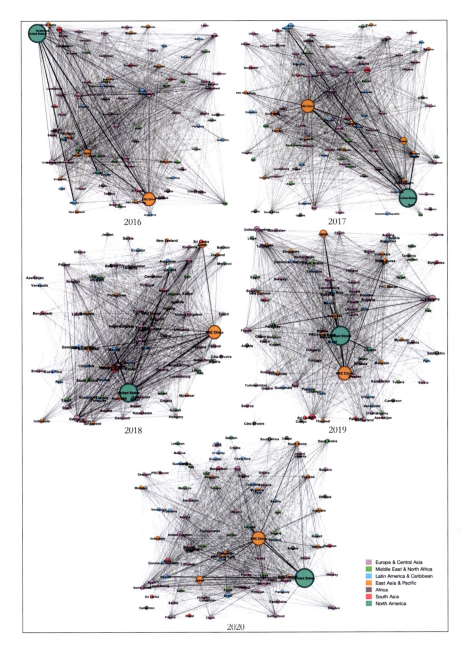

Fig. 2.3 International trade flow network (2016–2020)

Table 2.4 Changes in the international trade flow between the top 20 trading partners

Country 1	Country 2	Trade value (USD mn)										Trendline
		2016 USD mn	2017 USD mn	2018 USD mn	2019 USD mn	2020 USD mn	Delta '16-'20	Delta '16-'18	Delta '18-'20	Delta '18-'19	Delta '19-'20	
PRC China	United States	5,98,475	6,60,530	6,95,763	5,75,479	5,71,572	↓ -4%	↑ 16%	↓ -18%	↓ -17%	↓ -1%	
Canada	United States	5,00,833	5,35,586	5,67,622	5,63,029	4,79,738	↓ -4%	↑ 13%	↓ -15%	↓ -1%	-15%	
Mexico	United States	4,84,440	5,20,273	5,75,305	5,76,195	5,03,222	↑ 4%	↑ 19%	↓ -13%	↑ 0%	↓ -13%	
PRC China	Japan	3,02,085	3,30,127	3,54,016	3,40,756	3,40,009	↑ 13%	↑ 17%	↓ -4%	↓ -4%	0%	
PRC China	PRC Hong Kong	2,68,224	2,70,292	2,89,541	2,73,707	2,58,511	↓ -4%	↑ 8%	↓ -11%	↓ -5%	↓ -6%	
PRC China	South Korea	2,46,159	2,74,572	3,09,445	2,80,744	2,82,357	↑ 15%	↑ 26%	↓ -9%	↓ -9%	↑ 1%	
Netherlands	Germany	2,16,737	2,47,653	2,77,054	2,65,929	2,50,943	↑ 16%	↑ 28%	↓ -9%	↓ -4%	↓ -6%	
Japan	United States	2,01,505	2,10,379	2,26,183	2,24,883	1,91,154	↓ -5%	↑ 12%	↓ -15%	↓ -1%	↓ -15%	
Germany	France	1,87,517	1,93,433	2,04,566	1,93,714	1,69,270	↓ -10%	↑ 9%	↓ -17%	↓ -5%	↓ -13%	
PRC China	Germany	1,63,834	1,78,762	1,95,305	1,91,212	1,99,000	↑ 21%	↑ 19%	↑ 2%	↓ -2%	↑ 4%	
Germany	United States	1,62,406	1,69,795	1,83,282	1,88,093	1,72,970	↑ 7%	↑ 13%	↓ -6%	↑ 3%	↓ -8%	
Germany	United Kingdom	1,30,233	1,35,286	1,39,818	1,30,856	1,15,837	↓ -17%	↑ 7%	↓ -17%	↓ -6%	↓ -11%	
Italy	Germany	1,23,957	1,37,081	1,54,245	1,41,837	1,33,125	↑ 7%	↑ 24%	↓ -14%	↓ -8%	↓ -6%	
PRC China	Australia	1,16,990	1,44,917	1,63,988	1,77,989	1,76,780	↑ 51%	↑ 40%	↑ 8%	↑ 9%	↓ -1%	
Germany	Belgium	1,15,723	1,25,890	1,37,648	1,30,645	1,21,049	↑ 5%	↑ 19%	↓ -12%	↓ -5%	↓ -7%	
United Kingdom	United States	1,13,599	1,13,922	1,26,216	1,32,555	1,08,536	↓ -4%	↑ 11%	↓ -14%	↑ 5%	↓ -18%	
South Korea	United States	1,13,322	1,20,963	1,33,272	1,39,585	1,33,783	↑ 18%	↑ 18%	↑ 0%	↑ 5%	↓ -4%	
Germany	Austria	1,12,887	1,23,823	1,34,938	1,29,516	1,21,946	↑ 8%	↑ 20%	↓ -10%	↓ -4%	↓ -6%	
Poland	Germany	1,11,052	1,27,659	1,44,818	1,42,671	1,47,775	↑ 33%	↑ 30%	↑ 2%	↓ -1%	↑ 4%	
Netherlands	Belgium	1,05,096	1,19,123	1,34,582	1,24,715	1,14,239	↑ 9%	↑ 28%	↓ -15%	↓ -7%	↓ -8%	

2 International Trade Flows and Geo-Political Episodes—Network Perspective   25

pairs contribute in the range of 25% to 28% of the aggregate trade value of the dataset considered.

Top 20 trading pairs saw increase in trade volumes ranging from 8% to 40% between 2016 and 2018. Conversely, almost all these top pairs witnessed reduction in the bilateral trade values between 2018 and 2020 in line with the overall reduction of international trade. Further, for 2019, only five of these pairs had increased trade as compared to 2018. Similarly, in 2020, only three pairs had a minimal increase in the inter-se bilateral trade. These top 20 pairs consistently contributed to the total trade values in the range of 25% to 28%.

Considering this pattern of consistent growth till 2018 and then fall in the years 2019 and 2020, further analysis in the report has been done by combining the first 3 years as a single data set (pre-2019) and subsequently 2019 and 2020 individually.

2.4.3.2 Community Detection and Evaluation

Community detection has been done using the Leiden algorithm[3] in Gephi. The presents the different clusters formed across the periods analyzed (Table 2.5).

Cluster naming has been done based on the country with the highest GNI within the respective community cluster. Changes in the cluster composition have been highlighted by showing these countries in red in the table above.

The above suggests consolidation of trade within tighter clusters over the years. The years 2019 and 2020 witnessed reduction in the number of clusters from 6 to 5 as compared to earlier years. China cluster was a major beneficiary of consolidation in 2019 where all the countries from the Brazil cluster got added. There were minimal other changes within the other clusters. 2020 also saw some minimal changes within each of the clusters. The above table also shows that the geographic proximity results in the formation of clusters. This phenomenon is evident in the Germany cluster, in which 85%–90% members are from Europe or the neighboring North Africa. Similarly, the India cluster has most members across South Asia, the Middle East and Africa, which also form a geographic clique. The US cluster has over 90% members from the Americas. And same is the case with the Russian cluster with members across Europe, Central Asia and the Middle East. The China cluster demonstrates an exception in 2019 and 2020 in addition to the countries from East Asia, Central Asia and Africa, relatively distant Latin American and Caribbean countries contribute significantly in the range of 26%–28%. The clustered networks have been visually presented in Fig. 2.4.

The modularity of the networks across periods is shown in Table 2.6.

---

[3] The Leiden algorithm is an algorithm for detecting communities in large networks. The algorithm separates nodes into disjoint communities so as to maximize a modularity score for each community. Modularity quantifies the quality of an assignment of nodes to communities, that is how densely connected nodes in a community are, compared to how connected they would be in a random network. (Neo4j, n.d.) Parameters applied in Gephi for identifying clusters: Quality Function—Modularity and Resolution: 1.25

Table 2.5 Clusters detected using the Leiden algorithm in Gephi in the trading networks across periods

	Pre-2019 (6 clusters)	2019 (5 clusters)	2020 (5 clusters)
GermanyCluster	33 members (85% European, 12% Middle East & North Africa, 3% Africa) Germany, United Kingdom, France, Italy, Spain, Netherlands, Switzerland, Poland, Sweden, Belgium, Austria, Norway, Denmark, Ireland, Finland, Romania, Portugal, Czech, Greece, Algeria, Hungary, Morocco, Slovak, Bulgaria, Croatia, Côte d'Ivoire, Slovenia, Lithuania, Libya, Serbia, Luxembourg, Tunisia, Latvia)	32 members (88% Europe & Central Asia, 13% Middle East & North Africa) Germany, United Kingdom, France, Italy, Spain, Netherlands, Switzerland, Poland, Sweden, Belgium, Austria, Norway, Denmark, Ireland, Finland, Romania, Portugal, Czech, Greece, Algeria, Hungary, Morocco, Slovak, Bulgaria, Croatia, Slovenia, Lithuania, Libya, Serbia, Luxembourg, Tunisia, Latvia	31 members (90% Europe & Central Asia, 10% Middle East & North Africa) Germany, United Kingdom, France, Italy, Spain, Netherlands, Switzerland, Poland, Sweden, Belgium, Austria, Norway, Denmark, Ireland, Finland, Romania, Portugal, Czech, Greece, Algeria, Hungary, Morocco, Slovak, Bulgaria, Croatia, Slovenia, Lithuania, Serbia, Luxembourg, Tunisia, Latvia
IndiaCluster	23 members (39% Africa, 39% Middle East & North Africa, 22% South Asia) India, Saudi Arabia, UAE, Nigeria, South Africa, Bangladesh, Pakistan, Iran, Egypt, Iraq, Kenya, Ethiopia, Sri Lanka, Oman, Ghana, Tanzania, Lebanon, Congo, Jordan, Cameroon, Bahrain, Uganda, Nepal	24 members (42% Africa, 33% Middle East & North Africa, 21% South Asia, 4% Latin America & Caribbean) India, Saudi Arabia, UAE, Nigeria, South Africa, Bangladesh, Pakistan, Iran, Egypt, Iraq, Kenya, Ethiopia, Sri Lanka, Oman, Ghana, Tanzania, Côte d'Ivoire, Congo, Jordan, Venezuela, Cameroon, Bahrain, Nepal, Uganda	25 members (40% Africa, 36% Middle East & North Africa, 20% South Asia, 4% Latin America & Caribbean) India, Saudi Arabia, UAE, Nigeria, South Africa, Bangladesh, Pakistan, Egypt, Iraq, Kuwait, Kenya, Ethiopia, Sri Lanka, Oman, Ghana, Tanzania, Côte d'Ivoire, Lebanon, Congo, Jordan, Venezuela, Cameroon, Bahrain, Nepal, Uganda
Chinacluster	18 members (78% East Asia & Pacific, 11% Middle East & North Africa, 6% Africa, 6% Europe & Central Asia) China, Japan, South Korea, Australia, Indonesia, Thailand, Philippines, Hong Kong, Malaysia, Singapore, Vietnam, New Zealand, Qatar, Kuwait, Angola, Myanmar, Macao, Turkmenistan	25 members (56% East Asia & Pacific, 28% Latin America & Caribbean, 8% Middle East & North Africa, 4% Africa, 4% Europe & Central Asia) China, Japan, Brazil, South Korea, Australia, Indonesia, Argentina, Thailand, Philippines, Hong Kong, Malaysia, Singapore, Chile, Vietnam, Peru, New Zealand, Qatar, Kuwait, Angola, Myanmar, Uruguay, Macao, Turkmenistan, Bolivia, Paraguay	23 members (61% East Asia & Pacific, 26% Latin America & Caribbean, 4% Middle East & North Africa, 4% Africa, 4% Europe & Central Asia) China, Japan, Brazil, South Korea, Australia, Indonesia, Argentina, Thailand, Philippines, Hong Kong, Malaysia, Singapore, Chile, Vietnam, New Zealand, Qatar, Angola, Myanmar, Uruguay, Macao, Turkmenistan, Bolivia, Paraguay

UScluster	12 members (75% Latin America & Caribbean, 17% North America, 8% Middle East & North Africa) United States, Canada, Mexico, Israel, Colombia, Peru, Ecuador, Dominican Republic, Guatemala, Panama, Costa Rica, Venezuela	11 members (73% Latin America & Caribbean, 18% North America, 9% Middle East & North Africa) United States, Canada, Mexico, Israel, Colombia, Cuba, Ecuador, Dominican Republic, Guatemala, Panama, Costa Rica	12 members (75% Latin America & Caribbean, 17% North America, 8% Middle East & North Africa) United States, Canada, Mexico, Israel, Colombia, Peru, Cuba, Ecuador, Dominican Republic, Guatemala, Panama, Costa Rica
Russia cluster	8 members (88% Europe & Central Asia, 13% Latin America & Caribbean) Russia, Turkey, Kazakhstan, Ukraine, Cuba, Uzbekistan, Belarus, Azerbaijan	8 members (88% Europe & Central Asia, 13% Middle East & North Africa) Russia, Turkey, Kazakhstan, Ukraine, Uzbekistan, Belarus, Lebanon, Azerbaijan	9 members (78% Europe & Central Asia, 22% Middle East & North Africa) Russia, Turkey, Iran, Kazakhstan, Ukraine, Uzbekistan, Belarus, Libya, Azerbaijan
Brazil cluster	6 members (100% Latin America & Caribbean) Brazil, Argentina, Chile, Uruguay, Bolivia, Paraguay		

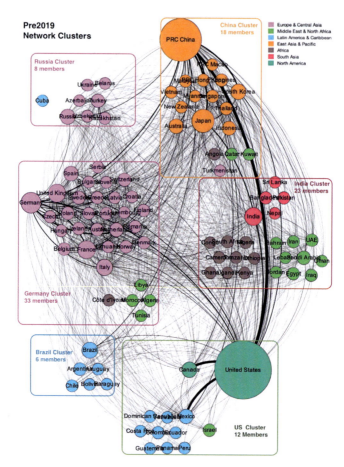

Fig. 2.4 Community clusters suggested by the Leiden algorithm for the periods pre-2019, 2019 and 2020

2 International Trade Flows and Geo-Political Episodes—Network Perspective 29

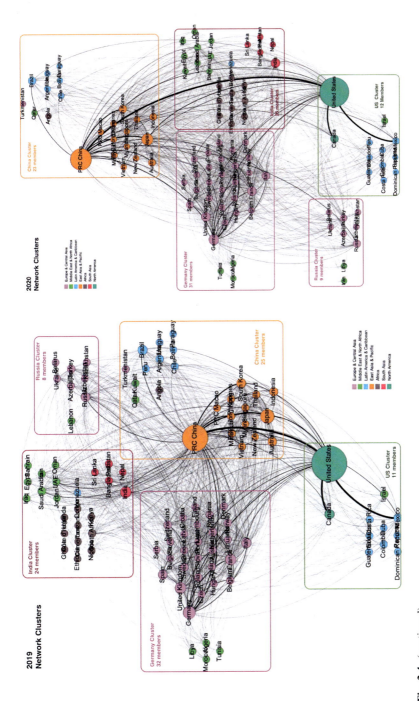

Fig. 2.4 (continued)

Table 2.6 Community orientation of the network based on different parameters

	Pre2019	2019	2020	Trend Line
Modularity (the Modularity is a measure of the structure of a graph, measuring the density of connections within a module or community. Graphs with a high modularity score will have many connections within a community but only few pointing outwards to other communities (Neo4j, n.d.))	0.231	0.249	0.231	
Leiden algorithm—quality	0.188	0.187	0.180	

The year 2019 had witnessed reduced number of clusters and expansion of the resultant clusters. This would mean higher degree of interactions within each of the clusters; hence, the increased measure of modularity is observed in 2019. Reduced modularity in 2020 is indicative of increasing connections outside the communities than within the respective communities. Quality of modularity as per the Leiden algorithm remained almost flat in 2019 and fell in 2020.

2.4.3.3 Node Analysis

Clustering Coefficient

Clustering coefficients,[4] which indicate the interconnectedness of the international trade network, is shown in Table 2.7.

Global clustering coefficient depicts the overall clustering in the network, whereas the local clustering coefficient shows the embeddedness of single nodes (Bisht, 2022). Table 2.7 shows clustering coefficients across clusters and regions and on an overall basis for the entire dataset.

The overall connectedness of the trade network is high at 0.81 and has not undergone significant change significantly between over the period. However, the inter-connectedness for each of the clusters followed a different trend.

The interconnectedness in the Germany cluster has marginally reduced in each of the periods. However, the India cluster and the Russia cluster experienced a dip and then an increase in the interconnectedness. Conversely, the US cluster and the China cluster experienced an increase and then a dip in the interconnectedness. However, geographically, the clustering coefficients moved in very narrow margins relatively within each of the regions.

---

[4] A clustering coefficient is a measure of degree to which nodes in a graph tend to cluster together. If the network is fully connected, the clustering coefficient is 1 and a value close to 0 means that there are hardly any connections in the network.

2 International Trade Flows and Geo-Political Episodes—Network Perspective

Table 2.7 Clustering coefficients for overall network, identified clusters and geographical regions

Clustering coefficients	Pre-2109	2019	2020	Trend line
Overall average	0.81	0.81	0.81	————
Cluster-wise average				
Germany cluster	0.7765	0.7702	0.7649	
India cluster	0.8574	0.8152	0.8642	
United States cluster	0.8148	0.8620	0.8185	
China cluster	0.7893	0.8065	0.8005	
Russia cluster	0.8271	0.8213	0.8313	
Brazil cluster	0.8518	–	–	
Region-wise average				
Africa	0.9043	0.9043	0.9043	
East Asia & Pacific	0.7423	0.7418	0.7418	
Europe & Central Asia	0.7705	0.7704	0.7704	
Latin America & Caribbean	0.8731	0.8731	0.8731	
Middle East & North Africa	0.8599	0.8594	0.8594	
North America	0.5086	0.5085	0.5085	
South Asia	0.8470	0.8463	0.8463	

Centrality

Eigenvector Centrality

Eigenvector centrality[5] scores have been presented in Table 2.8. A high eigenvector score means that a node is connected to many nodes that themselves have high scores.

The eigenvector centrality as seen in the above table suggests that the overall centrality of the trading network has remained almost unchanged. Even among the top 10 countries, there is minimal difference seen for a few countries. However, this measure does not consider the weights of the edges, i.e. the trading volumes are not considered. Hence, the eigenvector centrality consistency suggests that there is no major change in the network without factoring in the quantum of trade.

PageRank Centrality

PageRank centrality,[6] an algorithm that measures the importance of each node within the network, is a variant of the eigenvector centrality algorithm. However, unlike the latter, which is suited for only undirected and unweighted graphs,

---

[5] Eigenvector centrality calculates the centrality of a node based not only on its own connections but also based on the centrality of that node's connections. It measures the transitive influence of nodes (Neo4j, n.d.).

[6] PageRank centrality (also known as the Google algorithm) was first presented by Larry Page and Sergei Brin, founders of Google.

Table 2.8 Eigenvector centrality overall dataset and for top 10 countries

Eigenvector centrality	Pre 2019	2019	2020
Eigenvector centrality—average	0.4992	0.4990	0.4990
Eigenvector centrality—std dev	0.2670	0.2669	0.2669
Eigenvector centrality—top 10			
PRC China	1.0000	1.0000	1.0000
United States	0.9821	0.9821	0.9821
Germany	0.9637	0.9637	0.9637
Italy	0.9600	0.9600	0.9600
Spain	0.9346	0.9346	0.9346
France	0.9343	0.9342	0.9342
United Kingdom	0.9330	0.9329	0.9329
Netherlands	0.9323	0.9322	0.9322
Japan	0.9016	0.9015	0.9015
India	0.9013	0.9013	0.9013

Table 2.9 PageRank centrality for overall dataset and for top 10 countries

	Pre-2019	2019	2020	Trend line
PageRank centrality—average	0.0100	0.0100	0.0100	
PageRank centrality—std dev	0.0166	0.0166	0.0171	
PageRank centrality—top 10				
PRC China	0.1082	0.1108	0.1185	
United States	0.0971	0.0954	0.0948	
Germany	0.0683	0.0664	0.0677	
Japan	0.0358	0.0349	0.0338	
Netherlands	0.0303	0.0308	0.0313	
France	0.0324	0.0320	0.0306	
South Korea	0.0273	0.0265	0.0271	
United Kingdom	0.0284	0.0278	0.0270	
Italy	0.0278	0.0272	0.0270	
Mexico	0.0222	0.0226	0.0216	
India	0.0228	0.0238	0.0216	

PageRank centrality is suited for weighted, directed graphs (Disney, 2020). Table 2.9 shows the page rank centrality for the network and for the top 10 countries.

The average PageRank centrality has remained unchanged at the overall network level. However, the increased standard deviation is indicative of the higher variability observed in 2020 as compared to the earlier periods. Individually, the centrality consistently increased for China and the Netherlands; while it fell for the United States, Japan, the United Kingdom and Italy. Germany and South Korea saw a dip and then a rise, while France, Mexico and India witnessed a dip only in 2020. There is no clear pattern emerging from this analysis other than establishing the volatility in the pattern across different countries (Table 2.10).

Table 2.10 PageRank centrality by regions and community clusters (as suggested in Sect. 2.4.3.2)

	Pre-2019	2019	2020	Trend Line
By regions				
Africa	0.0025	0.0025	0.0025	
East Asia & Pacific	0.0196	0.0198	0.0204	
Europe & Central Asia	0.0112	0.0112	0.0113	
Latin America & Caribbean	0.0045	0.0045	0.0044	
Middle East & North Africa	0.0043	0.0043	0.0040	
North America	0.0594	0.0585	0.0578	
South Asia	0.0067	0.0068	0.0064	
By community clusters				
Germany cluster	0.0113	0.0115	0.0118	
China cluster	0.0159	0.0128	0.0134	
US cluster	0.0138	0.0146	0.0139	
India cluster	0.0044	0.0044	0.0041	
Russia cluster	0.0058	0.0060	0.0055	
Brazil cluster	0.0047	–	–	

In terms of geographical regions, the average centrality of countries in East Asia and Pacific and Europe and Central Asia increased, it reduced for the countries in other regions. Further, East Asia & Pacific region enjoys the highest average centrality, while Africa ranks the lowest. In terms of community clusters, the US Cluster ranks highest while the India Cluster is at the bottom of the table.

2.5 Results

During the 5-year period from 2016 to 2020, international trade patterns show a cyclical trend of consistent growth between 2016 and 2018, followed by a downturn in 2019 and 2020. In terms of bilateral trading pairs, over the 5-year period, i.e. 2020 as compared to 2016, almost equal number of trading pairs registered increase and decrease in trade volumes. However, within this period, in 2018 as compared to 2016, 62% pairs saw an increased volume which is also in line with the 23% increase in the aggregate trade volume for the same period. 2019 witnessed a reversal of the increasing trend with 62% trading pairs showing reduced value as compared to 2018 and the overall trade value also seeing a reduction of 3%. The year 2020 continued to see further reduction with 65% pairs having lower volumes and the aggregate trade value lower by 8% vis-à-vis to 2019. The growth in world trade had been lackluster since 2009 post the global financial crisis of 2008 on account of declining commodity prices and weakened economies the world over. The upward trend in the commodity prices and broad-based economic growth contributed to the growth in international trade seen from 2016 to 2019. However, several factors started playing out in 2019 in the international trade arena, which once again stunted the volumes, chief amongst these were the trade tensions between the United States and China which started playing out in late 2018 and the uncertainty plaguing the United Kingdom – European Union trade arrangements in view of the impending exit. The United States, China, the United Kingdom and members of the European Union have consistently been amongst the top trading pairs globally and these events led to dampened global trade volumes. Individually speaking, the US-China trade fell by 17% in 2019 and UK-Germany (the largest country in the EU) trade fell by 6%. In addition to the reduction in bilateral volumes, a cascading global impact can be seen in broad-based decline because of the formal and informal trade alliances which also got caught in the wake of these issues. The year 2020 caused a much deeper and broad-based impact on account of the spread of the novel coronavirus (COVID-19) at an unprecedented scale globally. The disease' rapid emergence from local outbreak to global pandemic severely disrupted the world economy. The world GDP contracted by an unprecedented 5% and the total international trade fell by 8% year-on-year. The widespread impact is evident from the fact that 65% trading pairs saw reduced trading volumes.

Another interesting phenomenon observed in the international network is in terms of its clusterization and modularity. The reduced number of clusters and expansion of the resultant clusters in 2019 meant higher degree of interactions within each of the clusters. This can be attributed to consolidation of trade on account of the US-China trade issue within their respective trading allies which is evident from the 2019 increase in the respective average clustering coefficients for both US and China clusters. These changes also led to the consolidation of the China cluster with all countries of the Brazil cluster rolling into the former. Brexit-related uncertainties did not result in significant change in the clustering of the Germany cluster or for the European region. Interestingly, in 2020, the network modularity reduced, which is indicative of increasing connections outside the communities than within the respective communities. This could be indicative of established trading pairs going beyond their regular partners to other countries in order to fulfill their trade requirements in view of the COVID19-related containment measures and restrictions on manufacturing and movement of goods. The India cluster, with a higher clustering coefficient in 2020, showed an increased connectedness, whereas the US cluster lost its connectedness during this period. This cluster, which is constituted by countries from Africa, Middle East Asia and South Asia, showed resilience in the inter-se trade; whereas, the US cluster with members from the Americas witnessed a weaker clustering in 2020 indicating that the members were looking outwards due to the trade limitations.

Centrality measures of the international trade network suggest reasonable consistency at the network level and for most of the individual countries, clusters or regions. China has emerged as a significant trading partner globally. This is evident in the high centrality scores across both eigenvector and PageRank models for all the years under consideration. China is followed by the United States and Germany in the centrality ranking. Incidentally, China's PageRank centrality increased in both 2019 and 2020 whereas that of the US fell in both these years. Seemingly, China's position in international trade has improved during the period of US-China trade tensions and COVID-19; while the United States seems to have lost some ground. UK's centrality also fell consistently in 2019 and 2020 which could be attributed to Brexit.

2.6 Conclusions

While international bilateral trade is highly spread across many numbers of countries, there is a high degree of concentration among major trading partners: the top twenty partners account for slightly more than a quarter of world trade. There is a tight cohesion that could be observed by way of community cluster formation amongst countries which are located within a particular region. These clusters remained almost consistent across the period with the exception of a few countries changing trading loyalties between clusters. However, it is worth noting that the modularity or the cliquishness of the clusters reduced over the period which could be indicative of the start of change in trading patterns due to logistical or market reasons. The critical international events till 2020 have led to China increasing or at least maintaining its leadership position in international trade, while the United States seems to have lost some ground or just being able to maintain its strong position. The United Kingdom has slipped a few notches on account of Brexit. The study of geo-political issues for impact on international trade is a continuing exercise. The events subsequent to 2020, such as the Russia-Ukraine conflict, runaway inflation, monetary tightening and COVID-19 re-emergence are likely to further impact the trade patterns.

2.7 Declarations

2.7.1 Study Limitations

This research is based on the reported bilateral trade of physical goods between countries and does not include services. Further, after the outbreak of COVID-19 in February 2020, trade data for the early part of the year were not reported by some countries. As a result, some ad-hoc statistics were used to estimate trade for certain months by the IMF.

Acknowledgements We would like to thank Mr. Arun Kumar (University of Cambridge) for his input during the entire course of this project.

References

Bisht, J. (2022). *Clustering coefficient in graph theory*. [Online] Available at: https://www.geeksforgeeks.org/clustering-coefficient-graph-theory/

Disney, A. (2020). *PageRank centrality & EigenCentrality*. [Online] Available at: https://cambridge-intelligence.com/eigencentrality-pagerank/

International Monetary Fund. (2022). *Direction of Trade Statistics (DOTS)*. [Online] Available at: https://data.imf.org/?sk=9D6028D4-F14A-464C-A2F2-59B2CD424B85

Jackson, M. O. (2014, November). The past and future of network analysis in economics. In *The Oxford handbook of the economics of networks get access arrow*. s.l.:Oxford University Press.

Telatnik, M. (2020). *How to get started with social network analysis*. [Online] Available at: https://towardsdatascience.com/how-to-get-started-with-social-network-analysis-6d527685d374

Wasserman, S., & Faust, K. (2021). *About social network analysis*. [Online] Available at: https://www.ibm.com/docs/pl/spss-modeler/18.0.0?topic=analysis-about-social-network

Chapter 3
A South African Perspective on the Corporate Cash Holding Conundrum

Ilse Botha and Carol Thompson

Abstract In recent years, much media attention has been given to cash holding increases of non-financial companies all over the globe. The objective of this chapter is to investigate the cash holding behavior of South African financial and non-financial firms listed on the Johannesburg Stock Exchange (JSE). Internal and external cash holding determinants of South African financial and non-financial firms listed on the Johannesburg Stock Exchange (JSE) are identified. For the purpose of this study, financial, market, and economic data were analyzed for the period 2005–2019. Panel regression analysis was employed, and it was found that the fixed effects (FE) model suited the data best. The contribution of this study is the inclusion of financial firms to identify internal and external determinants of cash holdings in a South African contexts. Findings show that the determinants between financial and non-financial firms are similar, although the coefficient sizes of the determinants differed between financial and non-financial firms.

Keywords Cash holdings · Internal and external determinants · Panel regression analysis

3.1 Introduction

In recent years, much media attention has been given to cash holdings increases of non-financial companies all over the globe. For example, non-financial companies in the USA reflected $1.82 trillion of cash balances at the end of 2014 and $4 trillion at end of 2019 as reported by Monga (2015) and Stevens (2019). These large cash balances are largely held by technology, pharmaceutical, and industrial companies within the USA. Cash holdings levels in the USA for the period 2014 were at their highest level when compared to the findings of Deloitte UK (2014) and Stevens

---

I. Botha (✉) · C. Thompson
Department of Accountancy, University of Johannesburg, Johannesburg, South Africa
e-mail: ilseb@uj.ac.za

© The Author(s), under exclusive license to Springer Nature Switzerland AG 2024
N. Tsounis, A. Vlachvei (eds.), *Applied Economic Research and Trends*, Springer Proceedings in Business and Economics,
https://doi.org/10.1007/978-3-031-49105-4_3

(2019) for non-financial companies. In this chapter, US companies reflected cash holdings of $1.73 trillion for the third quarter of 2011, indicative of an increasing trend between the periods 2011–2014 and 2014 to 2019. Additionally, UK cash balances in 2019 are estimated to be about £747 billion (Liberto, 2019). The South African Reserve Bank reported that non-financial companies in South Africa had cash holdings of R522 billion at the end of April 2012 and R540 billion at the end of December 2012 respectively (Gunnion, 2012; Johnson, 2013). In 2017, the University of Johannesburg's Centre for Competition, Regulation and Economic Development (CCRED) reported that cash holdings have reached an all-time high of R1.4 trillion (van Rensburg, 2017). Therefore, it would seem that South African firms have started to reflect the same growing trend in cash holdings levels as experienced globally (Clark, 2013; Gunnion, 2012; van Rensburg, 2017).

3.2 Literature Review

Say's law states that all income is used and therefore the possibility of hoarding cash is not possible (Jonsson, 1995). Keynes (1936) postulated the motives of cash holdings and found that cash is held for transactional motives to address the day-to-day needs, as well as external obligations of a business. Further, the precautionary motive exists to be able to service debt obligations in times when the economic conditions are not favorable to access external funds. Lastly, the speculative motive, referred to as the wealth creation motive, is where firms will look at market conditions and will invest funds in favorable conditions opposed to hoarding cash (Keynes, 1936). As a result, the work of Say was found to be flawed. This led to the development of cash management models by Baumol (1952), Tobin (1956), Beranek (1963), Miller and Orr (1966), and Stone (1972), and the research by Keynes (1936) was used to create the capital structure theories namely the Trade-Off Theory by Modigliani and Miller (1958, 1963), Pecking Order Theory by Myers & Maljuf (1984), and the Agency Cost Theory by Jensen (1986). These motives for holding cash and capital structure theories prompted research into the determinants of cash holdings. The seminal paper by Opler et al. (1999) postulated internal (current assets, dividend pay-outs, cash alternatives and substitutes, leverage, firm size, cash flows, and networking capital) and external determinants (economic instability) of cash holdings.

Opler et al. (1999) found that non-financial US firms that perform well seem to accumulate more cash than usual and this study found no evidence that an increase in cash holdings has an effect on the capital expenditure, mergers and acquisitions, and pay-outs in the form of dividends and share repurchases. Accordingly, many research studies were conducted using the work of Opler et al. (1999) to understand cash holdings behavior and identify determinants of cash holdings. Also, all the studies are mainly reflective of non-financial firm level analyses. The research work of Ferreira and Vilela (2004) was done in a developed market setting to evaluate the effects of investment opportunity, cash flow, leverage, and firm size on cash holdings for non-financial firms for the countries Germany, France, the Netherlands, Italy, Spain, Finland, Belgium, Austria, Ireland, Luxembourg, Greece, and Portugal. Moreover, Ferreira and Vilela (2004) found that investment opportunity, cash flow leverage, dividend pay-outs, and firm size concur with the findings of Opler et al. (1999). Then, Ferreira and Vilela (2004) found alignment with the Free Cash Flow Theory of Jensen (1986), which suggests that managers hoard cash for empire building having more assets under their control to influence investment decisions. Another developed market analysis by Naoki (2012), who wrote a paper discussing cash holdings and performance for Japanese non-financial companies found that the more uncertain cash flows become, the more likely the motive of holding cash becomes, thus this view supports the precautionary motive for holding cash, according to Keynes (1936). Since the 1990s, owing to large investment opportunities, the positive relationship of assets to cash holdings has lowered significantly. The Pecking Order Theory by Myers & Maljuf (1984) and the findings by Opler et al. (1999) apply where cash is used to take advantage of investment opportunities making use of internal funds before external funding is considered. Therefore, the higher a firm is leveraged, the higher its cash holdings, and when external funding is not readily available, the firm is likely to hold more cash. Riskier cash flows encourage higher cash holdings levels, implying no optimal cash holdings level. A study conducted by Martínez-Sola et al. (2013) looked at the optimal cash holdings level and the effect on firm value. They evaluated a sample of industrial US firms for the period 2001–2007. Their findings support the Trade-Off Theory of Modigliani and Miller (1958, 1963), i.e. an optimal level of cash, meaning deviations from this optimal cash holding level require the rebalancing of debt and equity. He and Wintoki (2016) conducted an analysis on US industrial firms for the period 1980 to 2012 and found that the average increases observed in the cash to asset ratio are a direct result of research and development investment activities. He and Wintoki's (2016) explanation for the rapid increase in cash holdings for research and development intensive firms as opposed to research and development non-intensive firms is that it is due to the changes in competition, the way financial markets have evolved, and the level of technology available to make things better, faster, and more cost-effective. The findings concur with that of Opler et al. (1999). A study by Abushammala and Sulaiman (2014) on emerging markets for 65 non-financial firms listed on the Amman Stock Exchange observed a positive relationship between GDP and cash holdings due to optimistic managers believing that economic conditions will improve. This finding contradicted the finding of Opler et al. (1999), where a negative relationship is expected. In another emerging market study, Wang et al. (2014) found that high inflationary conditions result in weakened purchase power parity and therefore firms will be inclined to hold more cash for non-financial firms listed on the Shanghai and Shenzhen Stock Exchanges. However, although Wang et al. (2014) found, on a macro-economic level, a positive relationship of cash holdings to inflation, this relationship also changes when inflation reaches a certain level, relative to cash holdings and purchasing power parity dynamics. Mesfin (2016) investigated the cash holdings behavior of manufacturing firms in Ethiopia from 2009 to 2014. The overall results of Mesfin (2016) are in line with the work of

Opler et al. (1999), Bates et al. (2009), Daher (2010), Kim et al. (2011), Gill and Shah (2012), and Daher (2010). Inflation, however, rendered both a positive and negative relationships to cash holdings, concurring with the findings of Wang et al. (2014).

A study by Nyamgero (2014) investigated the levels of cash holdings for non-financial South African listed firms for the period 1990–2014. This study found that cash flows have a positive significant relationship to cash holdings and dividend pay-outs have an insignificant relationship. Furthermore, Nyamgero (2014) found no evidence that South African firms are hoarding cash but found that the findings of Opler et al. (1999) apply. In another South African study, Karwowski (2015) investigated the corporate cash holdings of non-financial mining firms listed on the Johannesburg Stock Exchange (JSE). Karwowski (2015) states that South African firms hold a significant amount of cash on their balance sheets, just as is being reported in the USA. Karwowski (2015) therefore concludes that the finding of the study is due to motives for holding cash and is based on the fundamental building blocks as postulated by Keynes (1936). Additionally, Tambo and Theobald (2017) investigated non-financial companies listed on the Johannesburg Stock Exchange (JSE) and found that these firms do not reflect significant cash holdings level increases; therefore, there is no evidence that non-financial South African firms reflect abnormal (excess) cash holdings. However, the underlying reasons for holding cash relate closely to research conducted by Keynes (1936) and Opler et al. (1999). Similarly, Chireka and Fakoya (2017) investigated non-financial firms listed on the Johannesburg Stock Exchange (JSE) for the period 2000–2015, and the findings were in line with the Pecking Order Theory by Myers & Maljuf (1984) and Opler et al. (1999). They found an insignificant relationship between dividend pay-outs, leverage, and cash holdings, which was different from the findings of Opler et al. (1999), Ferreira and Vilela (2004), Daher (2010), Gill and Shah (2012), and Naoki (2012). Another study on South African non-financial firms found that leverage had no great impact on cash holdings levels (Maleka, 2017). Moreover, Kasongo (2019) evaluated the cash holdings behavior of 80 non-financial South African firms indicating no abnormal (excess) cash holdings and the overall findings concur with those of Opler et al. (1999), Ferreira and Vilela (2004), Daher (2010), and Gill and Shah (2012) except for the firm size, dividends payments, and inflation rate findings. Dividends payments reflect the same relationship observed by Chireka and Fakoya (2017).

In summary, all work discussed in the section above used the study of Opler et al. (1999) as foundational literature in order to conduct cash holdings analyses. Mixed results were recorded for emerging and developed markets. Most international studies are based on non-financial firm level analyses and similarly the case for studies in South Africa. These studies in a South African context indicated conflicting views in terms of determinants as well as whether firms in South Africa hold abnormal (excess) cash. Therefore, there is a need to identify internal and external determinants of cash holdings for both financial and non-financial firms in a South African setting.

3.3 Methodology

The purpose of this chapter is to uncover the cash holdings conundrum of why South African firms listed on the Johannesburg Stock Exchange (JSE) hold cash. It is important to investigate and identify the internal and external determinants of cash holdings for both financial and non-financial firms. A quantitative approach was followed employing panel regression analysis.

3.3.1 Sample, Data, and Variables

Secondary financial, market, and economic data were used for all firms listed on the Johannesburg Stock Exchange (JSE). The time period of this analysis is from 2005 to 2019. The sample data is reflective of 255 firms, 28 sectors, of which 153 are non-financial firms and 102 are financial firms listed on the Johannesburg Stock Exchange (JSE). Furthermore, the sample dataset is grouped as follows: all firms, financial firms, and non-financial firms. Financial and market data were derived from IRESS and the economic data from the South African Reserve Bank (SARB) and Statistics South Africa (Stats SA) for the period 2005–2019.

The first dataset is a combination of financial and market data. Firms listed on the Johannesburg Stock Exchange (JSE) for a minimum of 5 years and maximum of 15 years are included in the research study.

The underlying reason for this period is that firms listed on the Johannesburg Stock Exchange (JSE) have varying listed dates, and furthermore data less than five years old will not provide good trended data to provide significant insights into South African cash holdings behavior. Firms with a suspended status are excluded from the analysis. Consequently, these firms no longer have active statuses as per the rules and regulations of the Johannesburg Stock Exchange (JSE) and are, therefore, excluded from the sample data for the purpose of this research.

The second dataset is representative of economic data and it is sourced from the South African Reserve Bank (SARB) and Statistics South Africa (Stats SA). The data period corresponds with that of the first data set in order to analyze the data and to gain an understanding of the South African cash holdings environment. The sample panel dataset therefore spans from 2005 to 2019 (15 years) for 255 firms and 28 sectors.

The choice of variables (Table 3.1) to identify cash holdings determinants of the South African environment was based on the studies by of Opler et al. (1999), Dittmar et al. (2003), Ferreira and Vilela (2004), Ozkian and Ozkian (2004), Bates et al. (2009), Daher (2010), Kim et al. (2011), and Nyamgero (2014). The financial data (FD) variables are as follows: CA, INV, LEV, NWC, CAPEX, and SIZE. Market data in the equation below is represented by DIV and SHAREB, which did not previously receive much attention in the South African determinants of cash holdings context (Lee & Suh (2011) and Martínez-Sola et al. (2013)). The economic

Table 3.1 Research variables

Data Type	Variables	Variable code	Definition
Financial statement data (FD)	Cash holdings	CASH	Total cash and cash equivalents to total assets expessed as a ratio.
	Current assets	CA	Current assets minus cash and cash equivalents to total assets expressed as a ratio.
	Leverage	LEV	Total debt to total assets expressed as a ratio.
	Investment opportunity	INV	Book value of total assets minus book value of equity plus market value of equity to total assets expressed as a ratio.
	Capital expenditure	CAPEX	Captal expenditure to total assets expressed as a ratio.
	Networking capital	NWC	Current assets, excluding cash and cash equivalents minus current liabilities to total assets expessed as a ratio.
Market data (MD)	Share buy backs	SHAREB	Share buy back $=1$ and no share buy back $= 0$. Dummy variables.
	Dividend pay-outs	DIV	Dividend paid $=1$ and no dtvidends paid $= 0$. Dummy variables.
Economic data (ED)	Gross domestic product	GDP	Yearly historical gross domestic data for South Africa.
	Interest rates	INTR	Yearly historical interest rate data for South Africa.
	Inflation rates	INFR	Yearly historical inflation rate data for South Africa.
Control variable	Firm size	SIZE	Natural logarithm of total assets.

Complied by author

data in the equation is reflective of INFR, INTR, and GDP, and is in relation to the research studies conducted by Keynes (1936), Opler et al. (1999), Modigliani and Miller (1958, 1963), and Wang et al. (2014).

3.3.2 Panel Regression Analysis

Panel data analysis is best suited for this analysis since it accounts for the time and space dimension, combining time series and cross-sectional data (Brooks, 2014).

The dependent variable is cash holdings and the independent variables are the identified variables as indicated in Table 3.1. The specification of the model is below.

$$
\begin{aligned}
\text{Cash}_{it} = {} & \alpha + \beta CA_{it} + \beta LEV_{it} + \beta INV_{it} + \beta CAPEX_{it} + \beta NWC_{it} + \beta SIZE_{it} \\
& + \beta SHARED_{it} + \beta DIV_{it} + \beta INFR_{it} + \beta INTR_{it} + \beta GDP_{it} + \beta UER_{it} + U_{it}
\end{aligned}
\tag{3.1}
$$

where:

CASH = the dependent variable of each firm $(_i)$ for the time $(_t)$

$\beta = 1 \times k$ vector of observations on the explanatory variables (X_{it}) of each firm $(_i)$ for the time $(_t)$ (CA, LEV, INV, CAPEX, NWC, SIZE, SHAREB, DIV, INFR, INTR, and GDP)

Second-order diagnostics are conducted to determine whether the fixed effects or random effects model is the best fit for the data. The redundancy test and the Hausman (1978) test are presented in order to determine which model is the most appropriate model for each dataset.

The redundancy test results are presented in Table 3.2. The p-values of the F and Chi-square test statistics for all firms, financial firms, and non-financial firms cash holdings are less than 0.05. Hence, the null hypothesis of redundant fixed effects can be rejected. This indicates that the cross-sections and period effects are heterogeneous and the fixed effects model is better than the pooled model which assumes homogenous cross-sections and time effects.

The results for the Hausman (1978) test for all categories (all firms, financial firms, and non-financial firms) are presented in Table 3.3. The p-values in Table 3.3 are smaller than 0.05 which indicates a rejection of the null hypothesis and, therefore, the fixed effects (FE) model with cross-sections and time effects is therefore suitable to use for all the specified models. This means that there is heterogeneity between cross-sections and across time in this panel.

3.4 Panel Regression Results: All, Financial, and Non-financial Firms

The panel regression analysis results for all, financial, and non-financial firms are presented in Table 3.4. The adjusted R-squared shows how much the variation in CASH is explained by the independent variables in these models respectively (80% of the variation can be explained by all models).

Table 3.2 Redundancy test results

	Effects test	Cross-section F	Cross-section chi-square	Period F	Period chi-square	Cross-section/period F
All firms	Statistic	3.58	912.05	26.66	127.66	4.79
	d.f.	(254 231)	254	(14 231)	14	(268 231)
	P-value	0.00	0.00	0.00	0.00	0.00
Financial firms	Statistic	2.67	272.60	18.34	73.45	4.01
	d.f.	(101 293)	101	(14 239)	14	(115 293)
	P-value	0.00	0.00	0.00	0.00	0.00
Non-financial firms	Statistic	4.60	704.27	31.19	160.95	5.16
	d.f.	(152 191)	152	(14 191)	14	(166 191)
	P-value	0.00	0.00	0.00	0.00	0.00

Source: Eviews results

Table 3.3 Hausman test

	Chi-sq. statistic	Chi-sq. d.f.	P-value
All firms	67.75	12	0.0000
Financial firms	56.07	12	0.0000
Non-financial firms	81.42	12	0.0000

Source: Eviews Results
Cross-section and period effects applied.

Based on the results in Table 3.4 of the Fixed Effects model for the aggregated categories all firms, financial firms, and non-financial firms, the following is observed: firstly, positive significant relationships between CA, INV, NWC, DIV, INTR, INFR, and CASH; secondly, LEV, CAPEX, and GDP show a negative relationship to CASH, and thirdly no significant relationships between SIZE and CASH are observed for all firms and non-financial firms, where financial firms is the only category that recorded a significant relationship between SIZE and CASH. Furthermore, SHAREB showed no significant relationship to CASH for all categories. The internal (financial and market data) determinants of cash holdings results are discussed first and are CA, LEV, INV, NWC, DIV, CAPEX, and SIZE; and secondly, the external (economic data) determinants of cash holdings, which are INTR, INFR, and GDP, are discussed thereafter.

A comparison of these results with past research reveals that the positive and significant relationship of CA and NWC to CASH are in line with the findings of Opler et al. (1999), Dittmar et al. (2003), Ferreira and Vilela (2004), Bates et al. (2009), and Daher (2010) where cash is held to attend to daily operational needs and meet debt obligations. The relationship of LEV to CASH is expected to be significant and negative according to Opler et al. (1999), Ferreira and Vilela (2004), Al-Najjar (2015), Mesfin (2016), and Das & Goel (2019). The same negative

Table 3.4 Fixed effects model results of all, financial, and non-financial firms

Variable	All firms		Financial firms		Non-financial firms	
	Coefficient		Coefficient		Coefficient	
C	75.558		55.204		111.912	
CA	0.658	***	0.256	**	0.342	***
LEV	−0.345	***	−0.376	***	−0.760	***
INV	0.099	***	0.079	***	0.287	***
CAPEX	−0.375	***	−0.357	***	−0.294	***
NWC	0.099	***	0.079	***	0.296	***
SIZE	−2.988		−3.499	**	−2.746	
SHAREB	−0.612		−1.979		−1.232	
DIV	2.421	**	1.050	**	2.615	**
GDP	−0.281	*	−0.263	*	−1.280	*
INTR	0.431	*	1.898	*	1.342	*
INFR	0.301	*	1.468	*	1.291	*
R-squared	0.854		0.861		0.842	
Adjusted R-squared	0.805		0.819		0.799	
F-statistic	29.123		30.252		28.513	
Prob(F-statistic)	0.000		0.000		0.000	
Durbin-Watson stat	2.788		2.807		2.604	

Significance at 1% ***, 5% **, and 10%* level
Cross-section and period effects applied

significant relationship is observed for all categories, whereby firms that are not highly leveraged will hold more cash to service debt and attend to operational obligations. Additionally, a positive and significant relationship of INV and DIV to CASH is found for all aggregated categories and is found to be in line with the findings of Opler et al. (1999), Ferreira and Vilela (2004), Kim et al. (2011), Gu et al. (2016), Labhane and Mahakud (2016), Seifert and Gonenc (2016), and Weidemann (2016). Cash is used for investments and to pay out dividends. Moreover, a significant negative relationship between CAPEX and CASH is expected to exist according to the findings of Opler et al. (1999), Dittmar et al. (2003), Ferreira and Vilela (2004), Daher (2010), Huang-Meier et al. (2016), He and Wintoki (2016), Lyandres and Palazzo (2016), Cai et al. (2016), and Kim et al. (2011), where cash is used for research and development activities. The relationship between SIZE and CASH is found by this study to be negative and significant only for the financial firms category, but an insignificant relationship is reported for the rest of the categories. The negative relationship observed corresponds with the findings of Opler et al. (1999), Ferreira and Vilela (2004), and Daher (2010), where larger firms are expected to hold less cash, owing to being more established and having easy access to capital markets, and smaller firms will hold more cash due to transactional and precautionary motives (Keynes, 1936).

The external determinants of cash holdings observed the following: GDP showed a negative significant relationship with CASH for all aggregated categories, which implies that as economic performance decreases, CASH will increase, as found by Opler et al. (1999) and Anand et al. (2018). Moreover, past literature indicates that a positive relationship between INFR and CASH is expected to exist, according to emerging market research studies by Wang et al. (2014) and Mesfin (2016), which implies that as inflation increases, purchasing power reduces, making products and services more costly and, therefore, firms will hold more cash. All categories indicate a positive significant relationship between INTR and CASH and this concurs with the findings of Wang et al. (2014) and Mesfin (2016). Additionally, these findings are as expected, as interest and inflation rates start to increase firms that tend to hold more cash, owing to external funding becoming more expensive (Lee & Song, 2007; Mesfin, 2016; Wang et al., 2014).

In summary, the key findings to note are that CA, LEV, INV, CAPEX, NWC, DIV, GDP, INFR, and INTR are identified as determinants of cash holdings for all aggregated categories (all firms, financial firms, and non-financial firms). For financial firms, the relationship between SIZE and CASH was also significant. Furthermore, the coefficient sizes for CA, LEV, INV, NWC, DIV, GDP, INFR, INTR, and GDP are found to be smaller for financial firms as opposed to non-financial firms, indicating a less pronounced effect on cash holdings. The fact that size had a significant impact on cash holdings for financial firms might explain the lower impact of the other determinants of cash holdings for financial firms, meaning that bigger firms are not as reliant on cash holding in times of economic turmoil.

3.5 Conclusion

Data was analyzed for period 2005–2019 for all firms listed on the JSE, which includes 255 firms of which 153 are non-financial firms and 102 are financial firms. Previous research on the determinants of cash holdings focused on the cash holdings behavior of non-financial firms mainly, and as a result, financial firms analysis have not been receiving equal attention. As a result, the contribution of this research is that the internal and external determinants of cash holdings were identified for both non-financial and financial firms listed on the Johannesburg Stock Exchange (JSE).

The internal (financial and market data) and external (economic data) determinants of cash holdings were found to be the same on an aggregated and disaggregated level. The internal determinants are CA, LEV, INV, CAPEX, NWC, DIV, and SIZE and external determinants are GDP, INTR, and INFR. Also the theory and past research agreed with the positive and negative significant relationships identified by this study. These findings indicated that cash holdings levels changed in order to meet daily operational needs of a firm, to meet debt obligations, to pay out dividends, for investment and research, and for development opportunities. Furthermore, these determinants show that increased cash holdings are for transaction, precautionary, and speculative reasons as postulated by Keynes (1936), which lead to the findings concurring with the Trade-Off and Pecking Order Theories as well. Furthermore, the coefficient sizes for CA, LEV, INV, NWC, DIV,

GDP, INFR, INTR, and GDP are found to be smaller for financial firms as opposed to Non-Financial Firms. As a result, the higher coefficients size shows that the internal and external determinants of cash holdings have a greater impact on the cash holding levels of non-financial firms.

What is prevalent is the significant relationships between INTR, INFR, and GDP and cash holdings for both aggregated and disaggregated levels owing to recent poor economic conditions pointing toward the precautionary motive of Keynes (1936). Financial firms holdings reflected a negative significant relationship between SIZE and CASH. Accordingly, the negative significant relationship observed shows that smaller financial firms will hold more cash and as a result corresponds with the findings of the Trade-Off and Pecking order theory. Smaller firms hold more cash due to the transaction and precautionary motives of Keynes (1936) to address daily operational needs and to service debt obligations (incapable to draw from the financial system as opposed to their larger counterparts) when market conditions are unfavorable and external funding becomes too costly. Additionally, there is a lack of research regarding the relationship of DIV to CASH in a South African context, and a positive significant relationship between DIV and CASH was found.

Future research studies should focus more on financial firm analyses to identify internal and external determinants of cash holdings. In addition, research studies should explore the implications of the Agency Cost Theory by Jensen (1986) to understand the qualitative aspects of cash holdings behavior in a South African context to address the lack of research regarding the dividend pay-out and cash holdings relationship. The cash holdings topic is complex and therefore all research done thus far aids in gaining a better understanding of this topic.

References

Abushammala, S. M. N., & Sulaiman, J. (2014). Impact of macroeconomic performance on corporate cash holdings: Some evidences from Jordan. *Asian Economic and Financial Review, 4*(10), 1363–1377.

Al-Najjar, B. (2015). The effect of governance mechanisms on small and medium-sized enterprise cash holdings: Evidence from the United Kingdom. *Journal of Small Business Management, 53*(2), 303–320.

Anand, L., Thenmozhi, M., Varaiya, N., & Bhadhuri, S. (2018). Impact of macroeconomic factors on cash holdings? A dynamic panel model. *Journal of Emerging Market Finance, 17*(1), 1–27.

Bates, T., Kahle, K. M., & Stulz, R. M. (2009). Why do U.S. firms hold so much more cash than they used to? *The Journal of Finance, 64*(5), 1985–2021.

Baumol, W. J. (1952). The transactions demand for cash: An inventory theoretic approach. *The Journal of Economics, 66*(4), 545–556.

Beranek, W. (1963). *Analysis for financial decisions, Homewood, Ill*. Richard D, Irwin.

Brooks, C. (2014). Introductory Econometrics for Finance, 3rd edition, The ICMA Centre, Henley Business School, University of Reading, Cambridge University Press.

Cai, W., Zeng, C.Z., Lee, E., & Ozkan, N. (2016). Do business groups affect corporate cash holdings? Evidence from a transition economy. *China Journal of Accounting Research, 9*, 1–24.

Centre for Competition, Regulation and Economic Development (CCRED). (2017). *Companies hoarding R1.4 trillion in cash*. University of Johannesburg. Available at:

https://www.competition.org.za/seminars/2017/8/4/companies-hoarding-r14-trillion-in-cash. Accessed: 15 Nov 2017

Chireka, T., & Fakoya, M. B. (2017). The determinants of corporate cash holdings levels: Evidence from selected south African retail firms. *Investment Management and Financial Innovations, 14*(2), 79–93.

Clark, J. (2013). *Are SA companies sitting on piles of cash?* MoneyWeb, 23 April. Available at: http://www.moneyweb.co.za/archive/are-sa-companies-sitting-on-piles-of-cash/. Accessed: 20 Sept 2014

Daher, M. (2010). *The determinants of cash holdings in UK public and private firms.* Unpublished Masters Dissertation: Lancaster University Management School.

Das, S., & Goel, U. (2019). Determinants of Excess and Deficit Cash Holdings of Firms: Evidence from Emerging Market. *Global Business Review, 1–14.*

Deloitte. (2014). *The cash paradox: How record cash reserves are influencing corporate behaviour.* Available at: https://www2.deloitte.com/content/dam/Deloitte/uk/Documents/corporate-finance/deloitte-uk-cash-paradox-jan-14.pdf. Accessed 1 Mar 2015

Dittmar, A., Mahrt-Smith, J., & Servaes, H. (2003). International corporate governance and corporate cash holdings. *Journal of Financial and Quantitative Analysis, 28,* 111–133.

Ferreira, M. A., & Vilela, A. S. (2004). Why do firms hold cash? Evidence from EMU countries. *European Financial Management, 10*(2), 295–319.

Gill, A., & Shah, C. (2012). Determinants of corporate cash holdings: Evidence from Canada. *International Journal of Economics and Finance, 4*(1), 70–79.

Gu, X., Wang, P., & Hu, H. (2016). Analysis of the impact of corporate cash holdings on product market performance based on DID evaluation model. *Iberian Journal of Information Systems and Technology, E10,* 225–240.

Gunnion, S. (2012). *S. Africa companies hoard cash on ANC policy concerns, Bloomberg,* 22 June. Available at: https://www.bloomberg.com/news/articles/2012-06-21/s-africa-companies-hoard-cash-on-anc-policy-concerns. Accessed: 29 July 2015

Hausman, J. (1978). Specification tests in econometrics. *Econometrica, 46*(6), 1251–1272.

He, Z., & Wintoki, M. B. (2016). The cost of innovation: R&D and high cash holdings in U.S. firms. *Journal of Corporate Finance, 41,* 280–303.

Huang-Meier, W., Lambertides, N., & Steeley, J. M. (2016). Motives for corporate cash holdings: The CEO optimism effect. *Review of Quantitative Finance and Accounting, 47,* 699–732.

IRESS. (2014). Available at: http://research.mcgregorbfa.com/Login.aspx?ReturnUrl=%2fDefault.aspx. Accessed: 20 Jan 2017.

Jensen, M. (1986). Agency costs of free cash flow, corporate finance and takeovers. *American Economic Review, 76,* 323–329.

Johnson, G. (2013). *Companies with large cash balances can earn better yields by investing in unit trusts,* FANEWS, 18 February. Available at: https://www.fanews.co.za/article/investments/8/unit-trusts/1008/companies-with-large-cash-balances-can-earn-better-yields-by-investing-in-unit-trusts/13158. Accessed: 1 Mar 2016

Jonsson, P. O. (1995). On the economics of say and Keynes's interpretation of Say's law. *Eastern Economic Journal, 21*(2), 147–155.

Karwowski, A. (2015). The finance-mining nexus in South Africa: How mining companies use the south African equity market to speculate. *Journal of Southern African Studies, 41*(1), 9–28.

Kasongo, A. (2019). Determinants of cash holding in South Africa: Evidence from non-financial firms. *African Review of Economics and Finance, 11*(2), 316–337.

Keynes, J. M. (1936). The general theory of employment. In *Interest and money.* Harcourt Brace.

Kim, J., Kim, H., & Woods, D. (2011). Determinants of corporate cash – An empirical examination of the restaurant industry. *International Journal of Hospitality Management, 30*(3), 568–574.

Labhane, N. B., & Mahakud, J. (2016). Factors affecting the likelihood of paying dividends: Evidence from Indian companies. *Journal of Management Research, 16*(2), 59–76.

Lee, Y., & Song, K. (2007). Why have East Asian firms increased cash holdings so much after the Asian financial crisis? 20th Australian Finance & Banking Conference 2007. *Journal of Financial and Quantitative Analysis (JFQA), Forthcoming, 1–48.*

Lee, S.B., & Suh, J. (2011). Cash holdings and share repurchases: International evidence. *Journal of Corporate Finance, 17*(5), 1306–1329.

Liberto, D. (2019). Cash hoarders, Investors' Chronicle, 5 September. Available at: https://www.investorschronicle.co.uk/shares/2019/09/05/cash-hoarders/. Accessed: 12 July 2020.

Lyandres, E., & Palazzo, B. (2016). Cash holdings, competition, and innovation. *Journal of Financial and Quantitative Analysis, 51*(6), 1823–1861.

Maleka, M.M. (2017). *Cash holding levels and performance of JSE-listed firms*. Wits Business School, Available at: http://hdl.handle.net/10539/26104. Accessed: 15 Feb 2019.

Martínez-Sola, C., García-Teruel, P. J., & Martínez-Solano, P. (2013). Corporate cash holding and firm value. *Applied Economics, 45*(2), 161–170.

Mesfin, A. E. (2016). The factors affecting cash holding decisions of manufacturing share companies in Ethiopia. *International Journal of Advanced Research in Management and Social Sciences, 5*(3), 48–67.

Miller, M. H., & Orr, D. (1966). A model of the demand for money by firms. *Quarterly Journal of Economics, 80*, 413–435.

Modigliani, F., & Miller, M. (1958). The cost of capital, corporation finance and the theory of investment. *American Economic Review, 48*, 261–297.

Modigliani, F., & Miller, M. (1963). Corporate income taxes and the cost of capital: A correction. *American Economic Review, 53*(3), 433–443.

Monga, V. (2015). *Record cash hoard concentrated among few companies*, The Wall Street Journal, 11 June. Available at: http://blogs.wsj.com/cfo/2015/06/11/record-cash-hoard-concentrated-among-few-companies/. Accessed: 29 July 2015

Myers, S. C., & Majluf, N. (1984). Corporate financing and investment decisions when firms have information that investors do not have. *Journal of Financial Economics, 13*, 187–221.

Naoki, S. (2012). *Firms' cash holdings and performance: Evidence from Japanese corporate finance. Development Bank of Japan*, RIETI Discussion Paper Series 12-E-031.

Nyamgero, F. (2014). *Are South African firms holding more cash than before?* University of Pretoria, Master of Business Administration, Gordon Institute of Business Science.

Opler, T., Pinkowitz, L., Stulz, R., & Williamson, R. (1999). The determinants and implications of corporate cash holdings. *Journal of Financial Economics, 52*, 3–46.

Ozkian, A., & Ozkian, N. (2004). Corporate cash holdings: An investigation of UK companies. *Journal of Banking & Finance, 28*(9), 2103–2134.

Seifert, B., & Gonenc, H. (2016). Creditor rights, country governance, and corporate cash holdings. *Journal of International Financial Management & Accounting, 27*(1), 65–90.

South African Reserve Bank (SARB). (2020). *Selected historical rates*. Available at: https://www.resbank.co.za/en/home/what-we-do/statistics/key-statistics/selected-historical-rates. Accessed: 01 Jan 2020.

Statistics South Africa. (2020). *Gross domestic product second quarter 2020 Statistical Release P0441*. Available at: http://www.statssa.gov.za/publications/P0441/P04412ndQuarter2020.pdf. Accessed: 1 Oct 2020

Stevens, P. (2019). Here are the 10 companies with the most cash on hand, *CNBC*, 7 November. Available at: https://www.cnbc.com/2019/11/07/microsoft-apple-and-alphabet-are-sitting-on-more-than-100-billion-in-cash.html. Accessed 15 Sept. 2020

Stone, B. (1972). The use of forecasts and smoothing in control-limit models for cash management. *Financial Management, 1*(1), 72–84.

Tambo, O., & Theobald, S. (2017). *The myth of corporate cash hoarding: A study of the cash holdings of south African companies*. Intellidex Researching Capital Markets & Financial Services, Research Report.

Tobin, J. (1956). The interest elasticity of the transaction demand for cash. *The Review of Economic Statistics, 38*, 241–247.

van Rensburg, D. (2017). *Why firms are hoarding R1.4trn*, City Press, 6 August. Available at: https://www.news24.com/fin24/Economy/why-firms-are-hoarding-r14trn-20170806-2/. Accessed: 17 May 2020

Wang, Y., Jib, Y., Chen, X., & Songa, C. (2014). Inflation, operating cycle, and cash holdings. *China Journal of Accounting Research, 7*(4), 263–276.

Weidemann, F. (2016). *Regional differences in the determinants of cash holdings.* Available at: https://ssrn.com/abstract=2764828. Accessed: 12 July 2016

Chapter 4
Simulating the Impacts of Productive Development Policies in Algeria: Computable General Equilibrium Model Analysis

Mohammed Touitou

Abstract In this chapter, we have tried to develop and design a computable general equilibrium model (CGEM) for the Algerian economy with the aim of simulating the impacts of productive development policies in the face of alternative scenarios. The model serves as a powerful analysis tool to evaluate the impacts of economic policies (change in taxes, subsidies, etc.) and autonomous shocks (changes in international prices, changes in technology via increases in productivity and/or quality, etc.).

Keywords CGE model · SAM · Productive development policies

JEL Classifications C68, E16

4.1 Introduction

When economists are interested in studying an economic phenomenon, they resort to what they call "economic models," which have a consistent relationship with economic theory and allow the quantitative and qualitative evaluation of different policy scenarios or economic shocks. A model helps understand an economic problem through a series of assumptions about the agents and their relationships with their economic environment and with each other, for which they "simplify reality" in order to reveal the mechanisms of the problem that they want to study. This "simplification of reality" leaves out numerous details but explicitly places the behaviors that are important for the economic phenomenon to be analyzed, without the results found failing to explain things that happen in the "real world."

M. Touitou (✉)
Faculty of Economics and Business, University of Algiers 3, Dély Ibrahim, Algeria

© The Author(s), under exclusive license to Springer Nature Switzerland AG 2024
N. Tsounis, A. Vlachvei (eds.), *Applied Economic Research and Trends*, Springer Proceedings in Business and Economics,
https://doi.org/10.1007/978-3-031-49105-4_4

An economist builds an economic model as a tool that can be manipulated and thus learns more about what is behind the economic phenomenon to be studied.

Computable general equilibrium models (CGEMs) as the acronym can be applied to measure sector- and economy-wide effects of (shifts in) regulation and the economic situation in general. The theoretical foundation of a CGEM rests on Walras's general equilibrium theory, which describes a cyclical economic process as follows: production generates income, income triggers demand, demand further induces production, and the quantities and prices of goods marketed vary until demand and supply are balanced in the economic system (i.e., equilibrium is reached). The model originated in the 1960s and has been widely applied in the areas of global trade (Fan et al., 2000; Koesler, 2015), environmental protection (Yahoo et al., 2017; Wei, 2009), economic policy reform (Li et al., 2000), tax reform (Shi et al., 2015), transport (Robson et al., 2018), and thus low-carbon and sustainable development (Bednar et al., 2021; Engström et al., 2020).

One of the main benefits that justify the use of a CGEM for analysis and policy recommendations is that these models are built on solid microeconomic foundations that specify the rules of behavior for all agents (consumers, producers, the government, and the external sector). Another reason is that they take into account the interrelationships between all the variables, which makes it possible to capture both their direct and indirect effects. In addition, they ensure internal consistency among all the variables, taking into account macroeconomic balances and sectorial balances of supply and demand. They even provide numerical solutions and not merely the direction of change in the variables. In this sense, packages of measures can be simulated since it is possible to carry out and evaluate several changes simultaneously and to accurately see their effects on key economic variables such as gross domestic product (GDP), tax collection, sectorial added value, household well-being, and informality labor, among others.

4.2   CGEM Structure

A CGEM is a numerical representation of the aggregate equilibrium conditions and each one of the markets of an economy in which producers and consumers intervene with behaviors established through production and utility functions of consumers that depend on relative prices. A CGEM follows the theoretical structure of Walrasian general equilibrium models. In this line, it is assumed that there is a general equilibrium by which a competitive and optimal equilibrium is reached in the Pareto sense (following Wilfredo Pareto, who provided the foundations of welfare economics). According to this logic, there is a set of prices that simultaneously achieve the balance between supply and demand in all markets. To do this, it is assumed that excess demand is: 1) continuous and therefore cannot have inexplicable jumps, 2) depends on relative prices and not absolute ones, and 3) complies with Walras"s first law so that markets are linked through agents" budget constraints, considering that the equilibrium in all markets is relevant, since it is in

4 Simulating the Impacts of Productive Development Policies in Algeria... 53

this way that the income effect, the mobility of factors, and the substitutability of goods for consumers are all captured. On the contrary, partial equilibrium models and sectorial studies leave these effects aside in such a way that the analysis is impoverished by not considering the indirect effects.

4.3 Construction of a CGEM and a Social Accounting Matrix (SAM)

For the construction of a CGEM, it is necessary to have an important volume of information, in addition to its respective consistency. In this, the social accounting matrix (SAM) plays a crucial role. This matrix allows the circular flow of the economy to be represented in a double-entry table, with the income of each one of the accounts in the rows and the expenses in the columns, thus complying with the basic budget restriction (income equals expenses).

A SAM is generally made up of five types of accounts: production, goods, factors, institutions (households and the government), and the external sector. In a SAM, the rows are equal to the columns. In the rows, the income of the sectors is read, whereas, in the columns, the expenses of these sectors are read. The activity, goods, and factors accounts require the specification of the market (supply, demand, and equilibrium conditions), the household and government accounts require behavior rules and budget restrictions, and the investment and rest of the world accounts provide the macroeconomic requirements for the internal balance (savings equal to investment) and external (exports plus capital inflows must equal imports). See Table 4.1 of the annex for a basic model of a sectorial aggregate SAM. Regarding the work of consistency of the information, this can be arduous. It is even possible to have past information and not the analysis period. The RAS and the entropy method (Ver Bacharach (1970) and Stone (1978)) are usually used to ensure that missing or out-of-date transaction data are estimated in such a way that there is a minimum deviation from the real data and that they are consistent with the data available from the national accounts.

The RAS Method

RAS (bi-proportionate adjustment model) is a widely used methodology to balance or update SAMs. It is used when new information on the matrix row and column sums becomes available and we want to update an existing matrix. The problem is to generate a new nXn matrix A^1 from an existing matrix A^0 of the same dimension while respecting new given row and column totals, by applying row and column multipliers, r and s, respectively. The $(2n - 1)$ unknown multipliers are determined by the $(2n - 1)$ independent row and column restrictions using an iterative adjustment procedure.

Define T as a matrix of SAM transactions, where t_{ij} is a cell value that satisfies the condition: $T_j = \sum_i t_{ij}$. A SAM coefficient matrix, A, is constructed from T by dividing the cells in each column of T by the column sums: $a_{ij} = t_{ij} \mathop{/} t_{.j}$.

Table 4.1 Sectorial aggregation social accounting matrix (SAM) for Algeria for the year 2014 (DZD thousand)

	A	C	L	C	H	E	G	S-I	Ytax	Tva	Tariff	ROW	Total
Activities		13,759,741											13,759,741
Commodities	4,403,061				3,922,963		1,862,704	4,545,845				3,427,170	18,161,745
Labor	8,273,639												8,273,640
Capital													
Household			5,286,439		7052	29,228	1,102,359					25,387	6,450,466
Enterprises				2,986,615		5277	542,227					14,000	3,548,120
Government	1,083,040				797,552		701,887		1,984,716	542,063	169,055	598,871	5,877,188
Saving: Investment					1,514,413	1,601,408	1,430,023						4,545,845
Income tax					205,540	1,779,176							1,984,716
Sales tax		542,063											542,063
Tariff		169,055											169,055
ROW		3,690,885	585		2943	133,029	237,986						4,065,430
Total	13,759,741	18,161,745	8,273,640		6,450,466	3,548,120	5,877,188	4,545,845	1,984,716	542,063	169,055	4,065,430	

Source: Author

4 Simulating the Impacts of Productive Development Policies in Algeria... 55

A classic approach to solve this problem is to generate a new matrix A^1, from the old matrix A^0 by means of "biproportional" row and column operations:

$$a_{ij}^1 = r_i\, a_{ij}^0 s_j$$

In matrix notation (revealing the origin of the method's name!),

$$A^1 = \tilde{R}\, A^0\, \tilde{S}$$

where the ($\tilde{\ }$) indicate a diagonal matrix of elements r_i and s_j^2. RAS method is an iterative algorithm of biproportional adjustment.

In what followed, subscriptions 0, 1, 2... refer to iteration steps and ($\hat{\ }$) is used for new column or row values.

This process is continued until the iterations converge. We can summarize these steps by:

Step 1:

$$a_i^1 = \frac{\hat{x}_{i.}}{\sum_j x_{ij}^0} \Rightarrow x_{ij}^1 = a_i^1 x_{ij}^0 \Rightarrow b_j^1 = \frac{\hat{x}_{.j}}{\sum_i x_{ij}^1} \Rightarrow x_{ij}^2 = b_j^1 x_{ij}^1$$

Step 2:

$$a_i^2 = \frac{\hat{x}_{i.}}{\sum_j x_{ij}^2} \Rightarrow x_{ij}^3 = a_i^2 x_{ij}^2 \Rightarrow b_j^2 = \frac{\hat{x}_{.j}}{\sum_i x_{ij}^3} \Rightarrow x_{ij}^4 = b_j^2 x_{ij}^3$$

Step t:

$$a_i^t = \frac{\hat{x}_{i.}}{\sum_j x_{ij}^{2t-2}} \Rightarrow x_{ij}^{2t-1} = a_i^t x_{ij}^{2t-2} \Rightarrow b_j^t = \frac{\hat{x}_{.j}}{\sum_i x_{ij}^{2t-1}} \Rightarrow x_{ij}^{2t} = b_j^t x_{ij}^{2t-1}$$

This process is continued until the iterations converge. We can summarize these steps as follows:

$$x_{ij}^{2t-1} = \left(\prod_{h=1}^{t-1} b_j^h\right)\left(\prod_{k=1}^{t} a_i^k\right) x_{ij}^0; \text{ for odd rank values, } x_{ij}^1, x_{ij}^3, x_{ij}^5, \ldots$$

$$x_{ij}^{2t} = \left(\prod_{h=1}^{t} b_j^h\right)\left(\prod_{k=1}^{t} a_i^k\right) x_{ij}^0; \text{ for even rank values, } x_{ij}^2, x_{ij}^4, x_{ij}^6, \ldots$$

$$\text{With } A_i^t = \left(\prod_{k=1}^{t} a_i^k\right) \text{ and } B_j^t = \left(\prod_{h=1}^{t} b_j^h\right)$$

$$\Rightarrow x_{ij}^{2t-1} = A_i^t B_j^{t-1} x_{ij}^0 \text{ ; for odd rank values, } x_{ij}^1, x_{ij}^3, x_{ij}^5, \ldots$$

$$\Rightarrow x_{ij}^{2t} = A_i^t B_j^t x_{ij}^0 \text{ ; for even rank values, } x_{ij}^2, x_{ij}^4, x_{ij}^6, \ldots$$

When there is a solution, the RAS method has an advantage of being simple to apply. But, this simplicity has many disadvantages: (1) a lack of economic foundations, (2) inability to accommodate other sources of data than those on row and column totals, for example we cannot fix new cell values that we suppose are accurately measured. Because of these disadvantages, many researchers prefer to use the cross-entropy method, which seems more flexible than RAS method.

The Keynesian Theory states that the equilibrium situation is usually expressed in terms of Aggregate Demand (AD) and Aggregate Supply (AS). However, the equilibrium can also be determined when saving (S) is equal to the investment (I).

Simply put, equilibrium is attained when:

$$AD = AS$$

Now, we know that

$$AD = C + I,$$

and $AS = C + S$.

Therefore,

$$C + S = C + I$$

i.e., $S = I$

Ytax: Income tax

Row: Rest of the World

Tva: Value-Added Tax

4.4 Calibration

Once the information is organized in a single table, additional information is needed on substitution and transformation elasticity that serve as the parameters of the chosen behavior functions. This stage is called calibration. More precisely, calibration can be understood as the process by which parameter values are inferred from economic data for a given period, and, once those values are specified in an applied model, the base period data are endogenously replicated as a solution to it (Mansur & Whalley, 1984). In this way, a partial equilibrium is obtained that will later serve as a reference point, that is, it will be the benchmark for the simulations. In other words, the new equilibrium obtained from the simulations is compared with the initial equilibrium or benchmark.

4.5 CGEM Equations

The system of equations underlying a CGEM considers four types of agents (consumers, producers, the rest of the world, and the government) that possess certain behavioral functions.[1] In the first place, consumers or domestic families maximize their utility that depends on consumption subject to their budgetary restrictions that are given by the fact that the total expenses of the families in the purchase of domestic and imported goods cannot exceed the income obtained by their labor activity (payment to work), receipt of dividends and interest (payment to capital), and government transfers. In a simplified way, the following equation is considered.

$$\sum_i p_{c,i} c_i + p_{m,i} m_i = wL + rK + vTR$$

where c: household goods consumption, p_c: domestic goods price, m: consumption of the imported goods, p_m: price of imported goods, w: salary, L: manpower endowment, r: return on capital, k: capital endowment, v: transfer price, and TR: government transfers. Second, domestic producers or firms maximize their net benefits from spending on intermediate inputs. These are equal to the income from production minus the costs incurred by the use of labor and capital factors. Each firm produces a single good i for which a good j has been used as an input according to a fixed coefficient a_i, obtained from the input–output table. In a simplified way, the following equation is considered.

---

[1] The behavioral functions used are mostly Leontief and Cobb–Douglas.

$$\pi_i = \left[(1 + t_i)\, p_{c,i} - \sum_{j \neq i} p_{c,i} a_{i,j} \right] Y_i\, (L_i, K_i) - w L_i - r K_i$$

where t = taxes and Y = production. This specification implies a sales tax. However, the model considers the entire wide range of existing liens. Third, the rest of the world (foreign families) maximizes its consumption that depends on the consumption of our goods (tradable) and goods that are produced abroad subject to the fact that these expenses cannot exceed the income that it has for remunerations and benefits of domestic capital and the rest of the world. Finally, the government is a special agent that receives tax revenue and redistributes or purchases assets. The taxes considered in the model are all relevant, including taxes on foreign trade, value added, factors at the firm level, and income at the family level. The treatment of the General Sales Tax (IGV) is detailed to represent the exemptions and special regimes by destination (for exports or investment goods). Finally, the equilibrium conditions are considered to obtain a maximum by which the marginal utilities are equal to the relative prices, the marginal product value is equal to the factor prices, and the conditions of supply are equal to the demand in the markets for factors used domestically and of the foreign factor, market of goods, market of transfers, and market of bonds. Under unemployment, wages must be determined by adding a condition to the previous ones: the basic scenario contemplates setting them so that real wages remain constant (this addition allows households to choose between work and leisure). Under capital mobility, a fraction of capital is mobile between sectors and for that fraction; the rate of profit is similar.

4.6 Simulations and Results

The simulations explore both the cases of changes in productivity, quality, and efficiency, which can be autonomous, as well as international price shocks and policy measures, such as tax changes and subsidies. The simulations carried out and their respective results are the following:

Research and Development (R&D) Tax Incentives A 10% increase in research and development spending by companies, which arises due to a tax incentive and an increase in productivity as a result of these expenses, is simulated. This increase in spending is interpreted as an increase in intermediate purchases in the professional services sector, since it is the sector that is the most closely related to research and development activities. In turn, the tax incentive is considered in the sense that 49% of the increase in said expense can be deducted from the income tax. Finally, the 3% increase in productivity that would be triggered in conjunction with the previous simulations is evaluated. The results indicate that there is an increase of 3.67% in GDP and a considerable improvement in the trade balance as well as a decrease in unemployment of more than 2% points. The welfare of the government increases, although the collection in terms of GDP decreases with respect to the base, with the latter given by a decrease in the simulated income tax rate as an economic incentive for R&D expenses.

Formalization of Workers The effects of formalizing dependent informal workers are simulated by applying the same tax rate as that applied to formal dependent workers. There is a decrease in GDP and trade balance. Unemployment increases to more than 8 points. The fiscal result increases as does the collection in terms of GDP, also given the increase in the tax. If this effect is evaluated together with a 57% increase in the labor productivity of nonformal workers, then the GDP increases by 3.5% and improves the welfare of the government and the collection in terms of GDP. Unemployment continues to be above the benchmark rate as higher labor productivity means less work is in demand. The primary activity is where the greatest increases in production are seen due to the greater participation of informal workers. By lifting the assumption of inelastic labor supply (including leisure as an alternative to the decision of dependent workers), similar results are observed. However, when carried out together with an increase in productivity, it is observed that the effects are exacerbated, thus increasing the GDP to 6.9%.

Increase in Productivity in the Manufacturing Sector An increase of 5% in productivity and of 10% in the manufacturing sector is simulated. In the first case, the GDP increases by 2.1% and improves the trade balance and the well-being of the government; likewise, the level of activity of the manufacturing sector increases by 7%, which takes resources away from the rest of the economic activities. The tertiary sector increases its level of activity; however, the primary sector decreases by more than two 3%. The meaning of the results is similar to a 10% increase in productivity, although the magnitudes are greater. In this case, the increase in GDP becomes 3%.

Increase in the Quality of Manufacturing Products It is simulated as if the rest of the world provided a subsidy to manufacturing exports. The interpretation revolves around the fact that the quality of manufacturing products increases so that the rest of the world pays more for the same quantity given the increase in quality, which would be similar to a subsidy paid to our exports by foreign importers. Under this scenario, an increase of 0.39% in GDP is observed, but, under the scenario of constant nominal wages, GDP achieves an increase of 2.4%.

Reduction in Mineral Export Prices A 10% reduction in international mineral export prices is simulated. This generates a decrease of 0.41% in GDP. The trade balance falls to 6.2%. The welfare of the government falls because the collection falls, given the fall in exports. The well-being of households increases due to the reduction in prices.

Increased Efficiency in the Use of Infrastructure Through Industrial Parks An increase of 10% in the use of infrastructure (electricity, gas, water, transportation, and rentals) is simulated by the manufacturing sector, in addition to an increase of 3% in spending in investment by the government. The results found show an increase of 2.5% in GDP, a decrease in the unemployment rate, and a slight increase in the well-being of households. It should be taken into account that activity levels not only increase in the manufacturing sector but also in the services sector.

Increase in the Supply of Technical Assistance and Training Through Technological Innovation Centers (TICs) This is simulated through a 10% subsidy from the government for intermediate consumption in the professional services sector for all economic sectors. This can be interpreted as an increase in the supply of technical assistance through the TICs, given that these institutions carry out technological transfer activities and promote innovation in companies, leading to greater efficiency in production. As a result, an increase of 1.3% in GDP is observed, and it should be noted that the level of activity increases for the primary, secondary, and tertiary sectors.

Reduction of Micro, Small, and Medium Enterprise (MSME) Financial Costs[2] The model is calibrated with a 15% differential of capital costs in relation to large companies. The results observed are of low magnitude; however, it is worth mentioning that the level of activity of the MSME manufacturing industries increases by 2.1%.

4.7 Conclusions

Computable general equilibrium models play an important role in applied economic research. These models accommodate the micro-consistent systematic analysis of complex economic problems where analytical solutions are either not available or do not provide adequate information. However, the computational approach to economic policy analysis also has severe shortcomings of its own. In general, scientific publications include a complete listing of neither the algebraic model underlying the numerical simulation nor the data used to calibrate model parameters.

The model used information from the social accounting matrix (SAM) updated in 2014 and prepared through various sources of information, including the 2014 input–output matrix etc., which consistently reflects the circular flow of the economy. It has a sectorial breakdown of 19 productive activities, 4 types of work (based on the combinations that arise from dependent–independent, skilled–unskilled, formal–informal work), 2 types of capital (mobile and fixed), and 10 types of households, with rural and urban households each separated into 5 quintiles according to income.

The model evaluated the effects of the provision of tax incentives in terms of a 49% income tax deduction for research and development spending, and the results

---

[2] In order to analyze specific programs on MSMEs, an additional version of the SAM was carried out. The simulations on MSMEs were carried out with the model that explicitly disaggregates the manufacturing industry according to company size.

indicate that there is an increase of 3.67% in GDP. Regarding the manufacturing sector, an increase in the quality of its products is simulated where the GDP increases by 2.1% as well as progressive increases in its productivity followed by an increase of 0.39% in GDP. In addition, the effect of the formalization of workers is evaluated through the application of the tax rate of formal workers to informal workers. Likewise, the general equilibrium effects are analyzed in the face of an increase in the efficiency in the use of road infrastructure through the implementation of industrial parks. Then, the effects of an increase in the supply of technical assistance and training through technological innovation centers (TICs) are evaluated. Regarding policies for MSMEs, the effects of a reduction on financial costs and tax incentives for job training are evaluated; the results indicated that the level of activity of the MSME manufacturing industries increases by 2.1%.

References

Bacharach, M. (1970). *Biproportional matrices & input-output change.* Cambridge University Press.

Bednar, J., Obersteiner, M., Baklanov, A., Thomson, M., Wagner, F., Geden, O., Allen, M., & Hall, J. W. (2021). Operationalizing the net-negative carbon economy. *Nature, 596,* 377–383.

Engström, G., Gars, J., Krishnamurthy, C., Spiro, D., Calel, R., Lindahl, T., & Narayanan, B. (2020). Carbon pricing and planetary boundaries. *Nature Communications, 11,* 4688.

Fan, M. T., & Zheng, Y. X. (2000). General equilibrium analysis of the impact of trade liberalization on China's economy. *Journal World Economics, 4,* 16–26. (In Chinese) [Google Scholar]

Koesler, S. T. (2015). Computable general equilibrium modelling in the context of trade and environmental policy. *Chembiochem, 7,* 158–164. [Google Scholar]

Li, S. T., Hou, Z. Y., & Zhai, F. (2000). Medium and long term: China's economy still has the potential for rapid growth. China. *Industrial Economist, 6,* 15–19. (In Chinese) [Google Scholar]

Mansur, A., & Whalley, J. (1984). Numerical specification of applied general equilibrium models: Estimation, calibration, and data. In *Applied General Equilibrium Analysis* (pp. 69–127). Cambridge University Press.

Robson, E. N., Wijayaratna, K. P., & Dixit, V. V. (2018). A review of computable general equilibrium models for transport and their applications in appraisal. *Transportation Research Part A Policy and Practice, 116,* 31–53. https://doi.org/10.1016/j.tra.2018.06.003

Shi, J. R., Ling, T., Le-An, Y. U., & Bao, Q. (2015). Impacts of coal resource tax reform on China's economy based on a CGE model. *Systems Engineering - Theory & Practice, 35,* 1698–1707. [Google Scholar]

Stone, R. (1978). *'Forward' to G. Pyatt, A. Roe, et al, Social accounting for development planning.* Cambridge University Press.

Wei, W. (2009). An analysis of China's energy and environmental policies based on CGE model. *Statistics Research, 26,* 3–12. (In Chinese) [Google Scholar]

Yahoo, M., & Othman, J. (2017). Employing a CGE model in analysing the environmental and economy-wide impacts of CO2 emission abatement policies in Malaysia. *Science of the Total Environment, 584,* 234–243. [Google Scholar] [CrossRef]

Chapter 5
Forecasting the Main Energy Crop Prices in the Agricultural Sector of Thailand Using a Machine Learning Model

Jittima Singvejsakul and Chukiat Chaiboonsri

Abstract This study uses a machine learning algorithm to forecast the price of Thailand's primary energy crops. The information is annually compiled from 2000 to 2022 and covers the prices of the five primary energy crops used in the agricultural industry. Empirically, two regimes—the booming market and the recessionary market—are offered by the unsupervised learning k-means method, which is used to cluster the cycle regimes of agricultural prices. Seven years indicate the beginning of a rising market, and 15 years mark the beginning of a recessionary one. Furthermore, the cycle regimes of energy crop prices in the upcoming 5 years are investigated utilizing supervised learning techniques such as linear discriminant analysis (LDA), k-nearest neighbors (kNN), and support vector machines (SVMs). The findings showed that LDA was selected based on the greatest coefficient validation, representing crop price regimes in Thailand's agricultural industry that will continue to experience recessionary periods over the following 5 years. Therefore, the knowledge presented in this chapter might help farmers control their production, especially in the domain of energy crops. To promote the production and use of energy crops, it is essential to maintain stable and competitive prices. Policymakers can support the energy crop industry by providing incentives to farmers, investing in research and development, and promoting the adoption of biofuels in the transportation sector. By doing so, Thailand can enhance its energy security, promote sustainable agriculture, and support economic growth in a recessionary market.

Keywords Energy crop · Machine learning model · Forecasting · Agricultural sector · Crop price

---

J. Singvejsakul (✉)
Department of Agricultural Economy and Development, Faculty of Agriculture, Chiang Mai University, Chiang Mai, Thailand

C. Chaiboonsri
MQERC, Faculty of Economic, Chiang Mai University, Chiang Mai, Thailand

© The Author(s), under exclusive license to Springer Nature Switzerland AG 2024
N. Tsounis, A. Vlachvei (eds.), *Applied Economic Research and Trends*, Springer Proceedings in Business and Economics,
https://doi.org/10.1007/978-3-031-49105-4_5

5.1 Introduction

Agriculture has always been a significant sector of the Thai economy, providing employment to millions of people and contributing to the country's food security. In recent years, however, the sector has also become increasingly important in the context of renewable energy production. The Thai government has set ambitious targets for renewable energy development, including the use of biomass as a source of energy. One of the key components of this strategy is the cultivation of energy crops, specifically those that can be used for biofuel production. The prices of these crops, such as cassava, sugarcane, soybeans, corn, and oil palm, have become an important indicator of the profitability of the renewable energy sector in Thailand. In addition, they are also important for farmers who decide what crops to grow and for investors who consider financing energy projects (Chirapanda et al., 2009). To accurately predict the prices of these crops, it is essential to analyze large amounts of data and identify patterns and trends. Traditional statistical methods may not be able to capture the complex relationships between different variables and may be prone to errors. Machine learning methods, on the other hand, can handle large datasets and identify complex patterns and relationships. Therefore, using machine learning methods to study the main energy crop prices in the agricultural sector of Thailand is crucial for various stakeholders, including policymakers, farmers, and investors. Using these methods, we can develop more accurate models to predict future prices and identify the factors that influence them. This can help farmers make better decisions about which crops to grow and when to sell them and help investors make more informed decisions about financing renewable energy projects. Furthermore, these insights can inform policy decisions about how to best support the development of the renewable energy sector in Thailand (Bayona-Oré & Cerna, 2021). One of the most important statistics for these crops is the average price per ton. The price of these crops has a direct impact on the income of farmers and the profitability of the agricultural sector. For example, a drop in the price of sugarcane can result in lower incomes for sugarcane farmers, which can lead to decreased spending in other areas of the economy. The average price of sugarcane in Thailand was around 778 baht/ton in 2020, whereas cassava was around 2393 baht/ton and oil palm was around 3497 baht/ton. These prices are subjected to fluctuations due to a variety of factors, such as weather patterns, global demand, and government policies. Another critical statistic is the production volume of these crops. Thailand is one of the world's largest producers of sugarcane, cassava, and oil palm. In 2020, the country produced around 70 million tons of sugarcane, 30 million tons of cassava, and 18 million tons of oil palm. These crops are used in various industries, including food and beverage, biofuels, and pharmaceuticals, thus making their production volumes important indicators of the country's overall economic health. The prices of these crops are also influenced by external factors, such as global demand for biofuels and government policies related to the agricultural sector. For example, in 2021, the Thai government implemented a policy to increase the use of biofuels in the transportation sector, which could potentially increase the demand for

5 Forecasting the Main Energy Crop Prices... 65

sugarcane and oil palm (The Office of Agricultural Economics, 2021). One approach to analyzing crop prices is using machine learning algorithms, particularly k-means clustering. K-means is a popular unsupervised learning algorithm that can group data into clusters based on their similarity. This algorithm has been extensively used in various fields, including crop price analysis. In this study, we aim to apply k-means clustering to analyze crop prices in Thailand. We will explore how this approach can be used to identify patterns and trends in crop prices and help farmers make better decisions about their crops.

Specifically, we will focus on the energy crop prices, which are crucial for the renewable energy industry in Thailand. By analyzing the energy crop prices, we can provide insights into the overall energy market in Thailand and help stakeholders make informed decisions. Therefore, we will use a combination of these machine learning methods to analyze the main energy crop prices in the agricultural sector of Thailand. We will explore the factors that influence these prices and use machine learning models to predict future prices based on historical data and provide valuable insights into the dynamics of the renewable energy sector and its potential for sustainable development in Thailand. Furthermore, machine learning model forecasting is then used to predict the price cyclical movement of data from 2000 to 2022. Therefore, to examine the energy crop price cyclical stage and validate the data for better forecasting, machine learning models using both supervised and unsupervised approaches are applied.

5.2 A Literature Review

Agriculture is a critical sector of the Thai economy, significantly contributing to the country's gross domestic product (GDP) and employment. The prices of crops in Thailand are influenced by a range of factors, including climate, market demand, and government policies. With the rise of big data and machine learning techniques, there has been growing interest in applying these methods to analyze and predict crop prices. In this literature review, we will discuss some of the recent studies that have used machine learning algorithms for crop price analysis in Thailand. Historically, several studies considered the machine learning approach to predict crop prices. Raksakulthai and Thepa (2019) developed a model for predicting the prices of rice, rubber, and palm oil in Thailand using machine learning algorithms such as artificial neural networks (ANNs), support vector regression (SVR), and random forest regression (RFR). The authors found that the RFR model outperformed the other models in terms of accuracy, indicating its potential for price forecasting. Kongsawatt and Boonjing (2020) compared the performance of four machine learning algorithms, including ANNs, SVR, RFR, and gradient boosting regression (GBR), for predicting the prices of five agricultural commodities in Thailand: rice, rubber, palm oil, maize, and cassava. The authors found that the GBR model outperformed the other models in terms of accuracy, demonstrating its potential for crop price prediction in Thailand. Hong et al. (2021) developed a model for predicting the prices of six agricultural commodities in Thailand: rice, rubber, palm oil, maize, cassava, and sugar cane. The authors used a machine learning technique called extreme gradient boosting (XGBoost) to forecast commodity prices based on historical data. The results showed that the XGBoost model outperformed traditional statistical models, indicating its potential for crop price prediction in Thailand. Suwannaporn et al. (2021) developed a machine learning model to predict the prices of four major crops in Thailand: rice, rubber, palm oil, and cassava. The authors used the XGBoost algorithm to forecast commodity prices based on historical data and climate factors. The results showed that the model could accurately predict crop prices, thus providing farmers with useful information for decision-making. By utilizing machine learning methods, Chaiboonsri and Wannapan (2020) investigated the nowcasting and forecasting for the macroeconomic cycle in Thailand. Their study included unsupervised and supervised machine learning techniques such as Bayesian structural time series (BSTS), k-means clustering, linear discriminant analysis (LDA), and k-nearest neighbors (kNN).

The empirical results demonstrated that the conclusions drawn from the two approaches were distinct; supervised machine learning discovered that Thailand's expansion period served as a predictive indicator, whereas unsupervised machine learning, or kNN, discovered that Thailand's contraction period served as a sign for the country's cycles over the following 3 years. Predicting the price of assets is one of the most challenging tasks for financial analysts. The ability to accurately forecast future prices is essential for investors, traders, and financial institutions. Over the years, traditional statistical models have been used for this purpose. However, with the advent of machine learning algorithms, researchers have begun to explore their potential for predicting asset prices. Several studies have been conducted to predict asset prices using machine learning models. In 2016, Liu et al. used a support vector regression (SVR) model to predict the closing price of stocks. They compared the performance of the SVR model with those of traditional statistical models such as the autoregressive integrated moving average (ARIMA) and found that the SVR model outperformed the traditional models in terms of accuracy. In 2017, Wang et al. proposed a deep learning model for predicting stock prices. Their model combined convolutional neural networks (CNNs) and long short-term memory (LSTM) networks to capture both spatial and temporal features of stock data. The authors reported that their model outperformed traditional machine learning models such as random forests and gradient boosting machines. In a recent study, Chiu et al. used a recurrent neural network (RNN) to predict cryptocurrency prices. They collected data from several cryptocurrency exchanges and used the RNN to predict the price of Bitcoin, Ethereum, and Litecoin. The authors reported that their model achieved a prediction accuracy of up to 83%. Therefore, machine learning models have shown great potential in predicting asset prices. Researchers have used a variety of machine learning algorithms, including SVR, CNN–LSTM, RNN, and random forest models. These models have demonstrated superior performance compared to traditional statistical models. In the future, it will be interesting to see

5 Forecasting the Main Energy Crop Prices...

how these models evolve and how they can be applied to other asset classes. The studies reviewed above demonstrate the potential of machine learning algorithms for analyzing crop prices in Thailand. Machine learning models can analyze large amounts of data and identify patterns that traditional statistical models may miss, thus making them useful tools for predicting crop prices. The studies also show that different machine learning algorithms may perform better for different crops, indicating the need for further research to identify the optimal algorithm for each crop. Machine learning models can also help farmers make more informed decisions by providing them with accurate price forecasts. This can help farmers plan their planting and harvesting schedules, choose the most profitable crops to grow, and negotiate better prices with buyers. However, there are some challenges associated with implementing machine learning models in the agricultural sector, including data collection and management, access to technology, and the need for specialized knowledge and skills.

5.3 Data Review

Table 5.1 shows the price of the main energy crops used in agriculture as the observed data for the learning model. The data range covers the years 2000–2020, and log return was applied to the data. Table 5.2 also includes descriptive data about yearly price indices in the agricultural sector.

Table 5.1 Energy crop prices in the agricultural sector

Agricultural stocks	Code	Source
Cassava	CASS	CEIE
Corn	COR	CEIE
Sugar cane	CANE	CEIE
Soybean	SOY	CEIE
Palm	PALM	CEIE

CEIC Global Economic Data, Indicators, Charts and Forecasts

Table 5.2 Data description of crop price indexes in the agricultural sector

	CASS	CORN	CANE	SOY	PALM
Mean	1.7331	0.7606	3.4111	2.5779	2.1310
Median	1.7628	0.9289	3.3892	2.6516	2.1298
Maximum	2.1147	2.0155	3.8262	2.7791	2.3547
Standard deviation	1.2020	−0.6198	3.0439	2.3203	1.9830
Skewness	0.2942	0.6664	0.2568	0.1466	0.1029
Kurtosis	−0.3859	−0.4353	−0.0876	−0.4676	0.5444
Jarque–Bera	1.6610	0.9744	1.8908	2.6184	1.2942
Probability	0.4358	0.6144	0.3885	0.2700	0.5236

5.4 Research Methodology

For an analysis of the major energy crop prices in the agricultural sector, a machine learning model is used in this study. First, the price index regimes are clustered using the k-means algorithm, which is used for unsupervised machine learning. Then, to predict the price cycle regimes in the agricultural sector, supervised machine learning techniques, including linear discriminant analysis (LDA), k-nearest neighbors (kNN), and support vector machines (SVMs), are used.

5.4.1 The k-Means Clustering Algorithm of Unsupervised Machine Learning

The k-means algorithm is an unsupervised learning method used for clustering and data mining. It is specified to be a function of the available data type and the purpose of selective analysis (Oyelade et al., 2010). It aims to partition a given dataset into k-clusters such that the data points within each cluster are as similar as possible, whereas the clusters themselves are as dissimilar as possible. The k-means algorithm is simple to implement and is computationally efficient, making it a popular method for clustering large datasets. In this chapter, we will describe the k-means algorithm.

The k-means algorithm works as follows:

1. Initialization: Choose k initial centroids randomly from the dataset.
2. Assignment: Assign each data point to the nearest centroid based on its Euclidean distance.
3. Update: Calculate the mean of all data points assigned to each centroid, and update the centroid to this mean.
4. Repeat: Repeat steps 2 and 3 until convergence, i.e., when the centroids no longer change.

The process of the algorithm begins with selecting a set of k data points randomly to serve as the initial centroids. Each data point is then assigned to the centroid that is nearest to it based on its Euclidean distance. After all data points are assigned to a centroid, the centroid is updated to the average of all data points that are assigned to it. This iterative process continues until the centroids no longer change, which is a sign that the algorithm has converged. Therefore, the k-means algorithm is a powerful clustering method that can be used for a wide range of applications. Its simplicity and efficiency make it a popular method for clustering large datasets. However, its sensitivity to the initial centroid selection and its assumptions about the clusters' shapes and variances limit its effectiveness in certain scenarios. Nonetheless, the k-means algorithm remains a valuable tool for data mining and clustering.

5.4.2 Supervised Machine Learning Approaches

5.4.2.1 Linear Discriminant Analysis (LDA)

LDA is a linear classification method that finds the best linear combination of features that separate the classes. The objective of LDA is to project the data onto a lower-dimensional space while maximizing the distance between the means of different classes and minimizing the within-class scatter. The output of LDA is a set of discriminant functions that can be used to classify new data. Linear discriminant analysis is a powerful classification and dimensionality reduction algorithm that can be used to extract meaningful information from high-dimensional data (Bishop, 1995; Ioffe, 2006). By maximizing the distance between the means of different classes and minimizing the within-class scatter, LDA can effectively separate the classes and improve the performance of a classification model. The formula can be written as follows:

Let μ be the mean of the samples and μ_i N_i be the mean and number of the observation data in the ith class, respectively. Then, Σ_i is the scatter matrix of the observation data, and S_W can be written as follows:

$$S_W = \sum_{i=1}^{n} \Sigma_i, \tag{5.1}$$

where the solution of the between-class scatter matrix, S_B, can be expressed as

$$S_B = \sum_{i=1}^{n} N_i \left(\mu_i - \mu\right) \left(\mu_i - \mu\right)^{\mathrm{T}} \tag{5.2}$$

with the condition that $S_W^{-1} S_B$, eigenvalues, and eigenvectors are solved.

5.4.2.2 The k-Nearest Neighbor (kNN) Algorithm

The kNN algorithm is a widely used machine learning algorithm that is used for classification and regression problems. The kNN is a non-form artificial approach for both linear regression problems and classification (Chakraborty & Joseph, 2017). The basic idea behind kNN is that the class of an unseen data point can be predicted based on the classes of its k-nearest neighbors. In this chapter, we will describe the kNN algorithm and its implementation in detail. The key steps in implementing kNN involve loading the data, splitting them into training and testing sets, calculating distances, finding the k-nearest neighbors, assigning classes, and predicting the class of each test data point. By following these steps, the kNN algorithm can be easily implemented for a wide range of applications. The observation data are allocated in order to cluster the data that were used as the other feature space. Second, the algorithms calculate the searching distance x_i, which is the distance between a single sample and every other point in the feature space. At this point, the closest neighbors $\{x_j\}_i^k$ control the value of k, and the Euclidean distance is typically used to represent the measure distance. The next stage will then presumptively determine that the result of y_i is class membership, such as $y_i \in \{C_1, C_2, \ldots, C_c\}$ $\forall i = 1, 2, \ldots, n$, where c is the number of class levels derived from the majority vote of its kNN. The distance-weighted average of the kNN regression can be represented as follows:

$$y_i = {}^1\big/k \sum_{j=1; x_i \in \{x_j\}_i^k}^k x_j \tag{5.3}$$

where y_i represents the average value of its single nearest neighbor.

5.4.2.3 Support Vector Machines (SVMs)

For classification and regression analysis, powerful supervised learning techniques called support vector machines (SVMs) are employed. When working with complicated, high-dimensional datasets, in which the number of features is significantly more than that of samples, SVMs are especially successful. Finding a hyperplane in the feature space that maximally separates the various classes of data is the core tenet of SVMs. The hyperplane is selected to maximize the margin, which measures the separation between the hyperplane and the nearest data points for each class. Support vectors, which are utilized to define the hyperplane, are the data points that are most closely related to the hyperplane. The SVM algorithm can be formulated as an optimization problem, in which the objective is to find the hyperplane that maximizes the margin. This optimization problem can be solved using quadratic programming techniques. However, in practice, the problem may not be separable by a linear hyperplane. In such cases, the SVM algorithm uses a technique called the kernel trick to transform the input data into a higher-dimensional feature space where a linear hyperplane can be used for separation. The choice of kernel function is crucial for the performance of the SVM algorithm. Common kernel functions include linear, polynomial, radial basis function (RBF), and sigmoid functions. The RBF kernel is one of the most widely used kernels and is known to perform well on a wide range of problems. One of the advantages of SVMs is that they are less prone to overfitting compared to other machine learning algorithms. This is because the objective function of the SVM algorithm includes a regularization term that penalizes large coefficients, thereby reducing the complexity of the model. In addition, SVMs have a good generalization ability, which means that they can perform well on unseen data. Typically, problems are treated as interval ranges of data, a binary 0–1 range, which is logistic regression, when it comes to categorization (logit model). As a result, the position of the hyperplane in the feature space is assigned to the binary 0–1 range, which is also the probability of class memberships. The first step is the linear separation of the

5 Forecasting the Main Energy Crop Prices... 71

separate group of the data feature in the space. The location in the input space that will support the biggest margin in the vectors is then found. The SVM algorithm's key characteristics include the following (Chakraborty & Joseph, 2017):

$$\varepsilon = \varepsilon_{emp} + \varepsilon_{g'},\qquad(5.4)$$

where ε_{emp} is the training error, and $\varepsilon_{g'}$ is the generalization error.

5.5 Empirical Results

5.5.1 The Clustering Results of the k-Means Algorithm

The k-means technique is used in this part to analyze the energy crop price index regimes from 2000 to 2022. The agricultural sector's energy crop price indexes are introduced as a crucial variable in determining the energy crop price index regimes. Therefore, as shown in Table 5.3, we examine the energy crop price index regimes by grouping them into two categories: booming markets and recessionary markets. The findings show that there are 7 periods for a booming market and 15 periods for a recessionary market, which are 22 years from 2000 to 2022. The data of crop price indexes from 22 years are clustered by the k-means algorithm to find the group of price indexes, which can be divided into two groups. A booming market means that the price crop indexes are in an uptrend, whereas a recessionary period means that the price crop indexes are a downtrend. Therefore, the results are analyzed from the k-means algorithm to provide the information of the price index situation from 2000 to 2022. Furthermore, the energy crop price indexes are clustered into two regimes, which are booming and recessionary markets, using the k-means algorithm as shown in Fig. 5.1.

5.5.2 Forecasting of Stock Market Regimes by the Machine Learning Approach

In this section, three learning machine algorithms—linear discriminant analysis (LDA), k-nearest neighbors (kNN), and support vector machines (SVMs)—are used to study the energy crop price index regimes during the next 5 years. In order to

Table 5.3 The frequencies of booming and recessionary markets for energy crop prices

Description	Frequencies (years)
Booming market	7
Recessionary market	15

Source: Computing

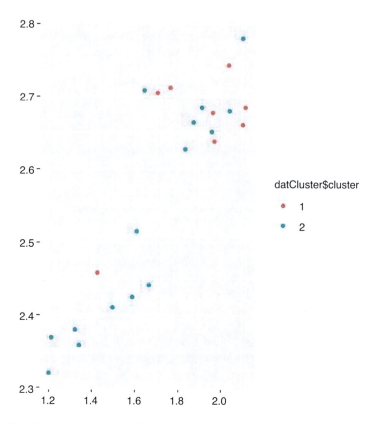

Fig. 5.1 The energy crop price index regime clustering by the k-means algorithm

Table 5.4 The results of three machine learning approaches by Kappa's coefficients

Algorithm	Cross-validation method	Accuracy	Kappa's coefficients
LDA[a]	Cohen's kappa	0.8528571	0.7241792
kNN	Cohen's kappa	0.6000000	0.3333333
SVM	Cohen's kappa	0.6833333	0

Source: The authors
[a]Indicates the chosen algorithm

choose the best machine learning algorithms for prediction and also validate them, Kappa's coefficient is utilized. As shown in Fig. 5.2, the findings showed that the linear form learning algorithm, or LDA, was selected as the most effective validation method. Moreover, Table 5.4 provides specifics on the accuracy and coefficients.

However, Fig. 5.3 shows that the energy crop price index regime category is based on raw data. The findings using LDA to forecast the cycle regimes of the energy crop price indices are shown in Table 5.5, and they are represented as the linear learning category of cycling regimes. The objective of LDA is to project the

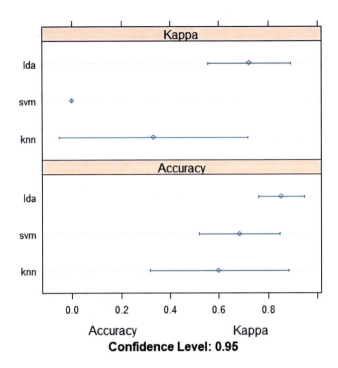

Fig. 5.2 Kappa's coefficient validation. (*Source*: Computing)

Table 5.5 Posterior prediction by LDA

Year/stages	Booming market	Recessionary market
2023	0	1
2024	0	1
2025	0	1
2026	0	1
2027	0	1

Source: Computing

data onto a lower-dimensional space while maximizing the distance between the means of different classes and minimizing the within-class scatter. The output of LDA is a set of discriminant functions that can be used to classify new data. Linear discriminant analysis is a powerful classification and dimensionality reduction algorithm that can be used to extract meaningful information from high-dimensional data.

The linear learning method is used to categorize the data from the crop price indexes and the dataset into booming and recessionary markets. It is interesting to note that the data for grouping are intercepted for one another so that the algorithm can group the most frequent occurrences. The data of crop price indexes from 2000 to 2022 are employed to analyze the prediction of group data, which contain booming and recession periods. As a result, according to the LDA's estimate, the

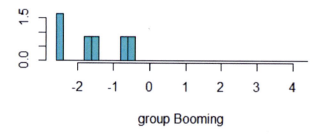

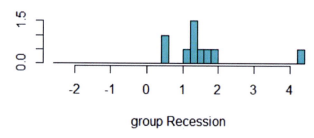

Fig. 5.3 The energy crop price index regime category based on raw data. (*Source*: The authors)

agricultural sector in Thailand will continue to experience periods of recession over the next 5 years, as shown in Table 5.5.

5.6 Conclusions

The range of time series data recorded for the energy crop price indices from Thailand's agricultural industry spans the years 2000–2022. The recession brought on by the coronavirus disease of 2019 (COVID-19) epidemic that started in 2020 is currently affecting the global economy. Machine learning techniques are a tool that can be applied to a variety of data types, such as big data, which has a greater motivation to be employed in problem-solving in the real world. Intriguingly, the strength of the findings in this study demonstrate the highly predictable patterns of variations in the energy crop price indexes in Thailand's agricultural sector using forecasting, clustering, and forecasting of machine learning methodologies. The k-means approach, which is an unsupervised learning technique, can be used to tackle the complexity of the data and categorize the cycle regimes of crop prices in order to perform computational clustering of the energy crop price index regimes. As a result, machine learning techniques can predictably determine the price of energy crops in Thailand's agricultural industry under prospective regimes. The vast amount of high-dimensional data can be estimated using supervised learning, which outperforms the conventional approach. The flexible machine learning model to counter the parametric estimations is the linear discrimination analysis. The outcomes demonstrate that the energy crop price index regimes are a recessionary market for the following 5 years, according to the LDA learning algorithm. In summary, the performance of machine learning can replicate the key features of econometric techniques, including classification, clustering analysis, and predictors with or without parameters. According to the hypothesis, agricultural sector energy crop price indices do not require the use of pro-cyclical policies. The amount of crop prices in a downturn, however, is crucial information for farmers to manage their produce, especially in the agricultural sector during the downturn. Energy crop prices have a significant impact on the energy sector. Thailand is heavily dependent on imported energy sources, which can be expensive in a recessionary market. By producing biofuels from energy crops, Thailand can reduce its dependence on foreign energy sources and enhance its energy security. However, the viability of biofuels as an alternative energy source depends on the price of energy crops. When energy crop prices are high, biofuels may not be competitive with traditional energy sources such as oil and gas. Therefore, energy crop prices play a crucial role in Thailand's economy in a recessionary market. The profitability of energy crops affects the income of farmers, the viability of biofuels as an alternative energy source, and the adoption of biofuels in the transportation sector. To promote the production and use of energy crops, it is essential to maintain stable and competitive prices. Policymakers can support the energy crop industry by providing incentives to farmers, investing in research and development, and promoting the adoption of biofuels in the transportation sector. By doing so, Thailand can enhance its energy security, promote sustainable agriculture, and support economic growth in a recessionary market.

References

Bayona-Oré, S., & Cerna, R. (2021). Machine learning for price prediction for agricultural products. *WSEAS Transactions on Business and Economics, 18*, 969–977. https://doi.org/10.37394/23207.2021.18.92

Bishop, C. (1995). *Neural networks for pattern recognition*. Oxford University Press.

Chaiboonsri, C., & Wannapan, S. (2020). Nowcasting and forecasting for Thailand's macroeconomic cycles using machine learning algorithms. In *International symposium on integrated uncertainty in knowledge modelling and decision making* (pp. 270–282). Springer.

Chakraborty, C., & Joseph, A. (2017). *Machine learning at central banks* (Staff Working Paper No. 647). Bank of England.

Chirapanda, S., Techasriprasert, S., Pratummin, S., Jain, S., & Wongtarua, P. (2009). *Status and potential for the development of biofuels and rural renewable energy: Thailand*. Asian Development Bank.

Hong, W., Chaithanoo, R., & Jirasakuldech, B. (2021). Forecasting agricultural commodity prices in Thailand using extreme gradient boosting. *Sustainability, 13*(2), 739.

Ioffe, S. (2006). Probabilistic linear discriminant analysis. In A. Leonardis, H. Bischof, & A. Pinz (Eds.), *Computer vision – ECCV 2006. ECCV 2006* (Lecture Notes in Computer Science) (Vol. 3954). Springer.

Kongsawatt, S., & Boonjing, V. (2020). Comparison of machine learning algorithms for predicting agricultural commodity prices in Thailand. *Agricultural Economics Review, 21*(2), 37–50.

Liu, S., Shi, Z., & Zhang, Y. (2016). Stock price prediction using support vector regression on daily and up sampled data. In *2016 IEEE, international conference on industrial technology (ICIT)* (pp. 1837–1841). IEEE.

OAE. (2021). *Agricultural prices*. Retrieved from https://www.oae.go.th/view/1/Price/Price7

Oyelade, O. J., Oladipupo, O. O., & Obagbuwa, I. C. (2010). Application of k-means clustering algorithm for prediction of students' academic performance. *International Journal of Computer Science and Information Security, 7*(1), 292–295.

Raksakulthai, V., & Thepa, S. (2019). Prediction of agricultural commodity prices using machine learning algorithms: A case study of Thailand. *Kasetsart Journal of Social Sciences, 40*(2), 225–233.

Suwannaporn, P., Jomnonkwao, S., & Srisuk, S. (2021). Crop price prediction model for Thai major crops using machine learning. *Journal of Agricultural Science, 13*(2), 81–91.

Wang, Z., Zhang, J., Feng, X., & Chen, K. (2017). Stock price prediction based on deep learning. *Procedia Computer Science, 122*, 213–218.

Chapter 6
Extreme Events and Stock Market Efficiency: The Modified Shannon Entropy Approach

Joanna Olbrys

Abstract The aim of this chapter is to investigate whether extreme events influence stock markets' informational efficiency measured by entropy. As an example, the 2-year period from February 24, 2021 to February 24, 2023 is explored. It comprises 1 year before the war in Ukraine and 1 year including the period of the war. The selected European equity markets are analyzed. As the data sample is not long, the modified Shannon entropy based on symbolic encoding with thresholds is utilized. This approach is especially useful in assessing stock market efficiency during extreme events as it allows us to capture extreme changes in market returns. The symbol-sequence histograms are obtained. The empirical results of this dynamic approach indicate that the influence of the war in Ukraine on daily returns of stock market indices was not very significant, but overall market efficiency measured by entropy decreased during this turbulence period.

Keywords Extreme event · Stock market · Informational efficiency · Symbolic time series analysis (STSA) · Shannon entropy

6.1 Introduction

The concept of informational market efficiency is important in finance, and it is inextricably connected with the Efficient Market Hypothesis (EMH) proposed by Fama (1970). In the literature, the following three potential forms of market efficiency are specified: (1) weak-form efficiency (the information set includes only the history of prices or returns), (2) semi-strong-form efficiency (the information set includes all public available information), and (3) strong-form efficiency (the information set includes all information known to any market participant) (see, e.g., Campbell et al., 1997). However, Dimson and Mussavian (1998) emphasize that

---

J. Olbrys (✉)
Bialystok University of Technology, Bialystok, Poland
e-mail: j.olbrys@pb.edu.pl

© The Author(s), under exclusive license to Springer Nature Switzerland AG 2024
N. Tsounis, A. Vlachvei (eds.), *Applied Economic Research and Trends*, Springer Proceedings in Business and Economics,
https://doi.org/10.1007/978-3-031-49105-4_6

the EMH remains an elusive concept, and therefore testing for market efficiency is rather complicated. Among others, Lim and Brooks (2011) point out that empirical findings of market efficiency are not homogenous. Although the literature concerning informational efficiency is vast, for a comprehensive survey of the origins, history, and theoretical background of the EMH, see, for instance, the references Campbell et al. (1997) and Dimson and Mussavian (1998). For a detailed survey of the empirical literature concerning the topic of market efficiency, see, e.g., the paper Lim and Brooks (2011).

Some researchers stress that the idea of market efficiency is connected with the concept of entropy. For instance, Gulko (1999) proposes the so-called entropic market hypothesis, and he advocates that the entropy maximization may be a basic property of efficient pricing and competitive markets.

The definition of information entropy was introduced by Shannon in his seminal paper concerning mathematical theory of information and communication (Shannon, 1948). Entropy is a universal measure of a system complexity and regularity. Many applications of entropy in economics, finance, and management have been proposed in the literature. For the literature review on this topic, see, e.g., Jakimowicz (2020), Olbrys and Ostrowski (2021), Olbrys (2022), Zhou (2013), and the references therein.

The main goal of this research is to investigate whether extreme events influence stock markets' informational efficiency measured by entropy. As an example, the 2-year period from February 24, 2021 to February 24, 2023 is explored. The data comprises 1 year before the Russian invasion of Ukraine and 1 year including the period of the invasion. The sample period is not long as the number of sub-sample observations for particular stock markets varies between 222 and 259. Therefore, the methods that are usually used to detect stock market efficiency within long-time periods (such as the Hurst exponent Hurst, 1951) are not appropriate in this case. For this reason, the modified Shannon entropy based on symbolic encoding with thresholds is utilized.

The research hypothesis states that market efficiency measured by entropy of stock market index returns decreases during extreme event periods. The selected 15 European equity markets are analyzed. The symbol-sequence histograms are obtained. The empirical results of this dynamic approach indicate that the influence of the war in Ukraine on daily returns of stock market indices was not very significant, but overall entropy decreased during this turbulence period. The findings are unambiguous and confirm no reason to reject the research hypothesis.

To the best of the author's knowledge, the empirical findings reported in this chapter are novel and have not been presented in the previous literature.

The remainder of this chapter is organized as follows. Section 6.2 specifies the methodological background. Section 6.3 presents data description, illustrates the findings with histograms, and discusses the informational efficiency results on the selected European stock markets. The last section covers the main findings and indicates directions for further research.

6.2 Methodology

This section presents the methodological background of the modified Shannon entropy based on symbolic encoding with thresholds. This approach is especially useful in assessing regularity in discrete financial time series during extreme event periods as it allows us to capture extreme changes in market returns (Buhlmann, 1998).

6.2.1 Symbolic Time Series Analysis (STSA)

As mentioned in the Introduction section, the sample period is not long. Therefore, the methods that allow for assessing market efficiency within long-time periods (such as the Hurst exponent Hurst, 1951) are not appropriate in this case. Hence, in this study, the modified Shannon information entropy based on symbolic time series analysis (STSA) is utilized. The problem of the STSA is that there is no formal definition of the time series partitions. Therefore, there are several symbolic encoding procedures presented in the literature, see, e.g., Ahn et al. (2019), Buhlmann (1998), Daw et al. (2003), Finney et al. (1998), Kim and Lee (2021), Olbrys and Majewska (2023), Risso (2008), Risso (2009), Sensoy et al. (2014), and Mazzarisi and Marmi (2022).

The symbolic representation of time series is used in many applications. The main idea is that the values of given discrete time series data are transformed into a finite set of symbols. This operation is just a translation into a finite language (Brida & Punzo, 2003). Among others, Schittenkopf et al. (2002) achieve the result that discretization of financial time series can effectively filter the data and reduce the noise. Ahn et al. (2019) emphasize that the symbolic encoding allows us to capture time-varying patterns in stock returns by transforming the real data into a limited number of symbols which reflect the dynamic rise–fall pattern of several consecutive returns.

In this study, financial time series of stock market indices are investigated. Returns of indices are calculated as daily logarithmic rates of return:

$$r_t = ln P_t - ln P_{t-1}, \tag{6.1}$$

where P_t is the closing value of the particular market index on day t.

Letellier (2008) points out that symbolic time series analysis is a useful technique for characterizing any kind of dynamical behavior with symbols. In this chapter, we adapt Letellier's definition of a sequence of symbols for returns of stock market indices, in the case of two thresholds:

Definition 1 A sequence $\{s_t\}$ of symbols is defined according to

$$s_t = \begin{cases} 0 \; if & r_t \le \theta_1 \\ 1 \; if & \theta_1 < r_t \le \theta_2 \\ 2 \; if & r_t > \theta_2, \end{cases} \tag{6.2}$$

where θ_1 and θ_2 are the thresholds of return time series $\{r_t\}$.

According to the literature, various thresholds θ_1 and θ_2 are used in empirical research, for instance:

1. θ_1 is the 5% sample quantile, and θ_2 is the 95% sample quantile (Sensoy et al., 2014).
2. θ_1 is the 2.5% sample quantile, and θ_2 is the 97.5% sample quantile (Buhlmann, 1998).
3. θ_1 and θ_2 are the tertiles (Mazzarisi & Marmi, 2022).

The finite set $A = \{0, 1, 2\}$ of possible $n = 3$ symbols is called an alphabet, while each subset of a sequence of symbols is called a word (Brida & Punzo, 2003; Daw et al., 2003; Lempel & Ziv, 1976). Therefore, a sequence of consecutive returns is symbolized as a sequence of 0s, 1s, and 2s.

6.2.2 Symbolic Sequence Histograms

Based on the symbolic-dynamics literature, after symbolization, the next step in the identification of temporal patterns in time series is the construction of symbol sequences (words). If each possible sequence is represented in terms of a unique identifier, each result creates a new time series referred to as a code series (Daw et al., 2003). The choice of the specific decimal numbers in the alphabet can be arbitrary (Ahn et al., 2019).

Let $n > 1$ be the number of possible symbols and $k \ge 1$ be the length of a code sequence. Hence, there are n^k paths with k symbols that occur in the given symbolic data sequence (Brida & Punzo, 2003). For instance, in the case of $n = 3$ and $k = 3$, the number of possible patterns is equal to $n^k = 3^3 = 27$ permutations (words). These words can be represented by natural numbers $\{1, 2, 3, \ldots, 27\}$.

The structure of patterns in observed data is revealed by the relative frequency of each possible k-length symbol sequence. The observed dynamics can be described by a k-histogram of relative frequencies. The empirical distribution presented in such histogram allows comparison of coded words. In general, direct visualization of the frequencies with histograms provides a convenient way for observing possible patterns in time series (Brida & Punzo, 2003; Daw et al., 2003; Oh et al., 2015).

6.2.3 The Modified Shannon Entropy Based on Symbolic Encoding

In the light of the existing literature, entropy is a widely used indicator that summarizes the information content of a probability distribution. Specifically, the Shannon information entropy (Shannon, 1948) estimates the expected value of information contained in a discrete distribution. The Shannon entropy of k-th order is an information-theoretic measure for symbol-sequence frequencies.

Definition 2 The Shannon entropy of k-th order, $H(k)$, is defined according to

$$H(k) = -\sum_i p_i \cdot log_2(p_i),\qquad(6.3)$$

where p_i is the probability of finding the i-th sequence of length k.

The probability p_i is approximated by the number of times the i-th sequence is found in the original symbolic string divided by the number of all nonzero sequences of length k (Brida & Punzo, 2003). It means that p_i is calculated based on the histogram of symbol-sequence frequencies (Daw et al., 2003).

Daw et al. (2003) emphasize that for increasingly longer sequence from a finite-length time series, entropy given by Definition 2 tends to be underestimated. Hence, following Brida and Punzo (2003), we utilize the definition of the modified Shannon entropy $H_s(k)$ based on symbolic encoding. The $H_s(k)$ is a normalized form of the Shannon entropy $H(k)$.

Definition 3 The modified (normalized) Shannon entropy $0 \leq H_s(k) \leq 1$ based on symbolic representation of time series is defined according to

$$H_s(k) = \frac{-1}{log_2 N} \cdot \sum_i p_i \cdot log_2(p_i),\qquad(6.4)$$

where N is the total number of observed sequences of length k with nonzero frequency, i is the index of a sequence, and p_i is the probability of finding the i-th sequence of length k. It is assumed that $0 \cdot log_2 0 = 0$.

6.3 Data Description and Empirical Findings

This section describes the data set and discusses the empirical findings concerning the assessment of informational efficiency of the 15 European stock markets within the 1-year pre-war in Ukraine period (from February 24, 2021 to February 23, 2022) and the 1-year war in Ukraine period (from February 24, 2022 to February 24, 2023).

6.3.1 Data Description

The data set includes daily observations of the main stock market indices for the 15 European countries. These countries are France, United Kingdom, Germany, Finland, Norway, Turkey, and the so-called Bucharest 9—NATO Eastern flank states (i.e., Poland, Hungary, Czechia, Romania, Bulgaria, Lithuania, Estonia, Latvia, and Slovakia). Table 6.1 presents brief information about the analyzed indices, in order of decreasing value of market capitalization in December 31, 2020, as well as the summarized statistics for daily logarithmic rates of return within two sub-periods.

Table 6.1 The information about the 15 analyzed stock market indices and the basic statistics for daily logarithmic rates of return within the pre-war in Ukraine (from February 24, 2021 to February 23, 2022) and the war in Ukraine (from February 24, 2022 to February 24, 2023) periods

Country	Index	Market cap. EUR Billion Dec 2020	The pre-war period			The war period		
			N	Mean (in%)	Std. Dev. (in%)	N	Mean (in%)	Std. Dev. (in%)
France	CAC40	2480.404	258	0.061	2.357	259	0.022	4.734
United Kingdom	FTSE100	2411.490	253	0.031	1.714	251	0.020	2.502
Germany	DAX	1870.687	255	0.018	2.413	259	0.020	4.865
Finland	OMXH25	289.000	251	0.011	2.481	251	−0.003	4.779
Norway	OSEAX	273.141	252	0.067	2.202	255	0.027	4.128
Turkey	XU100	194.491	249	0.123	7.375	250	0.368	13.957
Poland	WIG	145.379	251	0.035	2.665	253	0.020	5.789
Hungary	BUX	22.908	252	0.040	2.813	254	0.019	7.961
Czechia	PX	21.797	251	0.115	1.207	254	0.001	3.701
Romania	BET	20.895	251	0.103	1.547	252	−0.027	3.403
Bulgaria	SOFIX	14.505	245	0.081	1.323	248	0.008	1.998
Lithuania	OMXV	12.114	249	0.033	0.889	251	0.059	0.971
Estonia	OMXT	3.014	252	0.104	3.284	254	0.000	1.934
Latvia	OMXR	2.971	248	0.028	1.470	254	0.025	4.359
Slovakia	SAX	2.648	249	0.042	1.234	222	−0.077	1.868

Source: https://stooq.pl (accessed on February 28, 2023); http://www.nasdaqomxnordic.com (accessed on February 28, 2023)

Notes: The stock market indices are presented in order of decreasing value of the market capitalization in EUR billion at the end of 2020, and N denotes the number of sample observations. The summarized statistics are based on two sub-sample observations

6.3.2 Empirical Experiments: Histograms

In this chapter, the symbolic encoding method with two thresholds given by Definition 1 is utilized, and the θ_1 threshold is the 5% sample quantile, while the θ_2 threshold is the 95% sample quantile (method 1).

The following codes of possible sequences (words) for $n = 3$ and $k = 3$ (i.e., $n^k = 3^3 = 27$ natural numbers) are assigned: $(0, 0, 0) \rightarrow 1$, $(0, 0, 1) \rightarrow 2$, $(0, 1, 0) \rightarrow 3$, $(1, 0, 0) \rightarrow 4$, $(1, 1, 0) \rightarrow 5$, $(1, 0, 1) \rightarrow 6$, $(0, 1, 1) \rightarrow 7$, $\underline{(1, 1, 1) \rightarrow 8}$, $(2, 2, 2) \rightarrow 9$, $(0, 0, 2) \rightarrow 10$, $(0, 2, 0) \rightarrow 11$, $(2, 0, 0) \rightarrow 12$, $(2, 2, 0) \rightarrow 13$, $(2, 0, 2) \rightarrow 14$, $(0, 2, 2) \rightarrow 15$, $(2, 2, 1) \rightarrow 16$, $(2, 1, 2) \rightarrow 17$, $(1, 2, 2) \rightarrow 18$, $(1, 1, 2) \rightarrow 19$, $(1, 2, 1) \rightarrow 20$, $(2, 1, 1) \rightarrow 21$, $(0, 1, 2) \rightarrow 22$, $(0, 2, 1) \rightarrow 23$, $(1, 0, 2) \rightarrow 24$, $(1, 2, 0) \rightarrow 25$, $(2, 0, 1) \rightarrow 26$, $(2, 1, 0) \rightarrow 27$.

Figures 6.1 and 6.2 present examples of symbol-sequence histograms for one developed (France) and one emerging (Poland) stock markets during the pre-war in Ukraine and war periods. In the case of the remaining stock market indices reported in Table 6.1, the histograms are very similar. The main evidence is that underlined sequence No. 8, i.e., $(1, 1, 1)$, was the most frequently observed. This sequence means that stock index returns are not extremely high or low but lie between the thresholds.

Table 6.2 reports the number of all sequences of length $k = 3$ and the number of the sequence $(1, 1, 1)$ for all investigated indices, within two analyzed sub-periods. The empirical findings are unambiguous for all investigated stock markets. They reveal that the influence of the war in Ukraine on daily rates of return was not very significant as the number of sequence No. 8 was very similar within both sub-periods, for each stock market. It means that the proposed STSA method based on two 5 and 95% thresholds collates the returns properly.

6.3.3 Informational Efficiency of the European Stock Markets

This subsection discusses empirical findings concerning the assessment of informational efficiency of the selected European stock markets with the use of the modified Shannon entropy based on symbolic encoding with thresholds. The main goal is to examine the research hypothesis which states that entropy of stock market index returns usually decreases during extreme event periods. According to the literature, when regularity in time series increases, entropy and market efficiency decrease.

Table 6.3 includes the modified Shannon entropy results within the pre-war in Ukraine and the war periods for the 15 analyzed stock market indices. The last column reports changes in entropy before and during the extreme event period. The down arrows visualize entropy decrease, while the (rare) up arrows show entropy

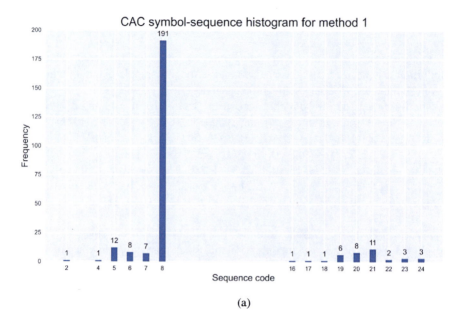

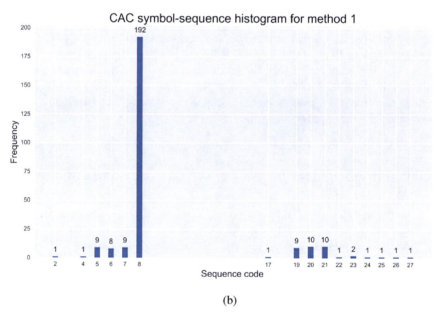

Fig. 6.1 Symbol-sequence histograms for CAC40 (France). (**a**) CAC40 (the pre-war in Ukraine period). (**b**) CAC40 (the war in Ukraine period)

6 Extreme Events and Stock Market Efficiency: The Modified Shannon... 85

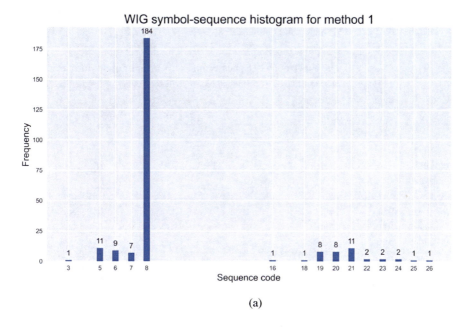

(a)

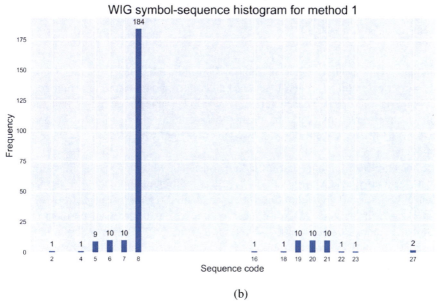

(b)

Fig. 6.2 Symbol-sequence histograms for WIG (Poland). (**a**) WIG (the pre-war in Ukraine period). (**b**) WIG (the war in Ukraine period)

Table 6.2 The number of sequences of length $k = 3$ within the pre-war in Ukraine and war periods for the 15 analyzed stock market indices

Country	Index	The pre-war period		The war period	
		The number of all sequences of length $k = 3$	The number of sequence No. 8 (1, 1, 1)	The number of all sequences of length $k = 3$	The number of sequence No.8 (1, 1, 1)
France	CAC40	256	191	257	192
UK	FTSE100	251	184	249	181
Germany	DAX	253	186	257	193
Finland	OMXH25	249	183	249	185
Norway	OSEAX	250	183	253	186
Turkey	XU100	247	184	248	191
Poland	WIG	249	184	251	184
Hungary	BUX	250	187	252	197
Czechia	PX	249	175	252	198
Romania	BET	249	186	250	189
Bulgaria	SOFIX	243	175	246	191
Lithuania	OMXV	247	181	249	194
Estonia	OMXT	250	194	252	191
Latvia	OMXR	246	178	252	199
Slovakia	SAX	247	183	220	165

Note: Notations as in Table 6.1

increase. The results reported in Table 6.3 require some interpretations. Generally, the empirical findings are homogenous and confirm no reason to reject the research hypothesis. Entropy decreased during the war in Ukraine period for the vast majority of the investigated markets, except for three countries, i.e., the UK, Poland, and Estonia. However, the entropy values were only slightly higher for these three equity markets.

The empirical findings of entropy are consistent with the existing literature. For instance, Olbrys and Majewska (2022) utilize a different approach, i.e., the Sample Entropy (SampEn) algorithm to estimate sequential regularity and entropy of daily time series of 36 stock market indices within two extreme event periods: (1) the Global Financial Crisis in 2007–2009 and (2) the COVID-19 pandemic outbreak in 2020–2021. Their results support the hypothesis that regularity in financial time series usually increases, while entropy and informational efficiency of stock markets usually decrease during various turbulence periods due to the existence of patterns in returns. Moreover, Wang and Wang (2021) document that the informational efficiency of the S&P 500 index substantially decreased during the COVID-19 extreme event. Ozkan (2021) investigates six developed equity markets during the COVID-19 pandemic outbreak and obtains that all markets deviate from market efficiency within this extreme event period.

6 Extreme Events and Stock Market Efficiency: The Modified Shannon... 87

Table 6.3 The modified Shannon entropy results within the pre-war in Ukraine and the war periods for the 15 analyzed stock market indices

| Country | Index | The pre-war period | | | The war period | | | The change of |
		θ_1	θ_2	Entropy	θ_1	θ_2	Entropy	entropy
France	CAC40	−0.016	0.015	0.425	−0.020	0.020	0.412	−0.013 ↓
UK	FTSE100	−0.012	0.013	0.435	−0.018	0.015	0.466	0.031 ↑
Germany	DAX	−0.018	0.014	0.461	−0.022	0.021	0.417	−0.044 ↓
Finland	OMXH25	−0.016	0.014	0.433	−0.022	0.020	0.426	−0.007 ↓
Norway	OSEAX	−0.016	0.015	0.451	−0.022	0.021	0.434	−0.017 ↓
Turkey	XU100	−0.021	0.024	0.407	−0.035	0.035	0.398	−0.009 ↓
Poland	WIG	−0.019	0.017	0.431	−0.023	0.025	0.439	0.008 ↑
Hungary	BUX	−0.017	0.018	0.416	−0.024	0.028	0.370	−0.046 ↓
Czechia	PX	−0.010	0.013	0.532	−0.022	0.019	0.361	−0.171 ↓
Romania	BET	−0.014	0.013	0.417	−0.019	0.015	0.405	−0.012 ↓
Bulgaria	SOFIX	−0.011	0.013	0.464	−0.012	0.013	0.376	−0.088 ↓
Lithuania	OMXV	−0.010	0.010	0.431	−0.006	0.008	0.369	−0.062 ↓
Estonia	OMXT	−0.021	0.019	0.383	−0.013	0.010	0.406	0.023 ↑
Latvia	OMXR	−0.011	0.013	0.456	−0.021	0.019	0.361	−0.095 ↓
Slovakia	SAX	−0.011	0.011	0.438	−0.017	0.013	0.410	−0.028 ↓

Notes: Notations as in Table 6.1. θ_1 and θ_2 denote the 5 and 95% sample quantiles, respectively

6.4 Conclusion

The purpose of this study was to assess whether the war in Ukraine extreme event has substantially influenced stock markets' informational efficiency measured by the modified Shannon entropy. The 15 European stock markets have been investigated. These markets have been selected in the context of the Russian invasion of Ukraine. In general, the results have confirmed no reason to reject the research hypothesis that entropy and informational efficiency of stock markets decreased during the 1-year period of the war in Ukraine compared to the pre-war period. Moreover, the empirical experiments illustrated by symbol-sequence histograms have revealed that the dynamic patterns captured by code sequences in time series of stock index returns have been similar during the pre-war and the war periods for all analyzed markets. The non-extreme returns lying between 5 and 95% thresholds have dominated.

As the topic of stock market informational efficiency during extreme event periods is crucial in finance, a possible direction for further investigation could be an extensive comparative research of various symbolic encoding methods with entropy-based applications to financial time series analyses.

Acknowledgments This study was supported by the grant WZ/WI-IIT/2/22 from Bialystok University of Technology and founded by the Ministry of Education and Science. Moreover, I am grateful to student Natalia Komar for expert programming and visualization assistance.

References

Ahn, K., Lee, D., Sohn, S., & Yang, B. (2019). Stock market uncertainty and economic fundamentals: An entropy-based approach. *Quantitative Finance, Taylor & Francis Journals, 19*(7), 1151–1163.

Brida, J. G., & Punzo, L. F. (2003). Symbolic time series analysis and dynamic regimes. *Structural Change and Economic Dynamics, 14*, 159–183.

Buhlmann, P. (1998). Extreme events from the return-volume process: A discretization approach for complexity reduction. *Applied Financial Economics, 8*, 267–278.

Campbell, J. Y., Lo, A. W., & MacKinlay, A. C. (1997). *The econometrics of financial markets.* Princeton University Press.

Daw, C., Finney, C., & Tracy, E. (2003). A review of symbolic analysis of experimental data. *Review of Scientific Instruments, 74*(2), 915–930.

Dimson, E., & Mussavian, M. (1998). A brief history of market efficiency. *European Financial Management, 4*(1), 1–14.

Fama, E. F. (1970). Efficient capital markets: A review of theory and empirical work. *The Journal of Finance, 25*(2), 383–417.

Finney, C. E. A., Green, Jr., J. B., & Daw, C. S. (1998). Symbolic time-series analysis of engine combustion measurement. *SAE Transactions, 107*(3), 880–897.

Gulko, L. (1999). The entropic market hypothesis. *International Journal of Theoretical and Applied Finance, 2*(3), 293–329.

Hurst, H. (1951). Long term storage capacity of reservoirs. *Transactions of the American Society of Civil Engineers, 116*, 770–799.

Jakimowicz, A. (2020). The role of entropy in the development of economics. *Entropy, 22*, 452.

Kim, K., & Lee, M. (2021). The impact of the COVID-19 pandemic on the unpredictable dynamics of the cryptocurrency market. *Entropy, 23*, 1234.

Lempel, A., & Ziv, J. (1976). On the complexity of finite sequences. *IEEE Transactions on Information Theory, 22*(1), 75–81.

Letellier, C. (2008). Symbolic sequence analysis using approximated partition. *Chaos, Solitons & Fractals, 36*, 32–41

Lim, K.-P., & Brooks, R. (2011). The evolution of stock market efficiency over time: A survey of the empirical literature. *Journal of Economic Surveys, 25*(1), 69–108.

Oh, G., Kim, H., Ahn, S.-W., & Kwak, W. (2015). Analyzing the financial crisis using the entropy density function. *Physica A, 419*, 464–469.

Olbrys, J. (2022). Entropy-based applications in economics, finance, and management. *Entropy, 24*(10), 1468.

Olbrys, J., & Majewska, E. (2022). Regularity in stock market indices within turbulence periods: The sample entropy approach. *Entropy, 24*, 921.

Olbrys, J., & Majewska, E. (2023). Ranking stock markets informational (in)efficiency during the COVID-19 pandemic. In N. Tsounis, & A. Vlachvei (Eds.), *Advances in Empirical Economic Research. Springer Proceedings in Business and Economics.* Springer Nature Switzerland AG.

Olbrys, J., & Ostrowski, K. (2021). An entropy-based approach to measurement of stock market depth. *Entropy, 23*, 568.

Ozkan, O. (2021). Impact of COVID-19 on stock market efficiency: Evidence from developed countries. *Research in International Business and Finance, 58*, 101445.

Risso, W. A. (2008). The informational efficiency and the financial crashes. *Research in International Business and Finance, 22*, 396–408.

Risso, W. A. (2009). The informational efficiency: the emerging versus the developed markets. *Applied Economics Letters, 16*, 485–487.

Schittenkopf, C., Tino, P., & Dorffner, G. (2002). The benefit of information reduction for trading strategies. *Applied Economics, 34*, 917–930.

Sensoy, A., Sobaci, C., Sensoy, S., & Alali, F. (2014). Effective transfer entropy approach to information flow between exchange rates and stock markets. *Chaos, Solitons & Fractals, 68*, 180–185.

Shannon, C. E. (1948). A mathematical theory of communication. *The Bell System Technical Journal, 27*(3), 379–423.

Shternshis, A., Mazzarisi, P., & Marmi, S. (2022). Measuring market efficiency: The Shannon entropy of high-frequency financial time series. *Chaos, Solitons & Fractals, 162*, 112403.

Wang, J., & Wang, X. (2021). COVID-19 and financial market efficiency: Evidence from an entropy-based analysis. *Finance Research Letters, 42*, 101888.

Zhou, R., Cai, R., & Tong, G. (2013). Applications of entropy in finance: A review. *Entropy, 15*(11), 4909–4931.

Chapter 7
Examining Public Expenditure on Education and the Relationship Between Expenditure and Corruption in Greece Through a Nonparametric Statistical Analysis Method

Kyriaki Efthalitsidou, Nikolaos Sariannidis, Marina Vezou, and Konstantinos Spinthiropoulos

Abstract This research aims to explore public expenditure on education and the relationship between expenditure and corruption in Greece through the use of a nonparametric statistical analysis method. Statistical data were retrieved using a nonparametric statistical analysis technique, namely, Spearman's method. In this research, the theoretical framework is first presented, and then Spearman's method of analysis is used in order to draw conclusions about the correlation of the quantities between them.

The chronological series of the data included the years 2001–2019 as they were available for processing at the time. An analysis of public expenditure data in primary, secondary, and higher education in relation to both total expenditure and total expenditure due to corruption in Greece was performed.

Finally, conclusions were drawn regarding the correlation of the dimensions examined in the research and the need for investments in education for future economic development.

Keywords Non-parametrical analysis · Public expenditure · Education · Corruption · Greece

---

K. Efthalitsidou (✉) · N. Sariannidis · M. Vezou · K. Spinthiropoulos
Department of Accounting and Finance and Management Science and Technology, School of Economics, University of Western Macedonia, Kozani, Greece

© The Author(s), under exclusive license to Springer Nature Switzerland AG 2024
N. Tsounis, A. Vlachvei (eds.), *Applied Economic Research and Trends*, Springer Proceedings in Business and Economics,
https://doi.org/10.1007/978-3-031-49105-4_7

7.1 A Nonparametric Statistical Analysis of Public Expenditures at Various Levels of Education (A Comparative Analysis)

7.1.1 Introduction

Empirical investigation of statistical data enabled us to answer the first research question, "what is the appropriate test to examine the validity of a hypothesis regarding the value of a parameter of one or more samples or populations?"

In order to answer the above question, we should separate the tests performed into parametric and nonparametric tests, that is, the methodology to be followed should be determined. Tests that meet some necessary requirements regarding a population and its distribution can be characterized as parametric. Normally, a population should follow a normal distribution or the variances between the samples under consideration should be equal.

On the other hand, when dealing with nonparametric tests, the normality of the population is not relevant because these tests do not focus on population parameters but instead mainly focus on the form of the distributions (Stegos, 2006). The use of these checks began long before the use of computers in statistics, in contrast to parametric ones, which, due to complex calculations, require the use of computers and are therefore considered more reliable. However, both types of criteria have advantages and disadvantages. Thus, while nonparametric tests are much easier in theory, in practice, large samples are needed for reliable results and their calculations.

It can therefore be concluded that both types of controls provide information and illuminate different aspects depending on the research conducted and the analysis that needs to be performed to obtain accurate results; for this reason, their use should not be competitive but should rather aim at complementing each other.

There are several descriptors, which are now available for use and for conducting nonparametric estimations. These are kernel-based estimators, which are included in models used by Darolles et al. (2006) and Hall and Horowitz (2005). Moreover, series or sieve estimators, which have been developed by Blundell et al. (2007) and Newey and Powell (2003), are also available.

Following the methodology, the nonparametric tests are presented, and one of them will be used to reach our conclusions about investments in education. These tests, as mentioned above, do not assume the existence of normality in the population and are the most suitable for analysis of categorical data, something that often occurs in the social sciences.

Finally, when used for two or more samples, an independence test is conducted, whereas, when used for one sample, a fit test is performed.

The second method that is often used, which is suitable for independent samples for a variable, to test whether one sample has greater values than the other, is the Mann–Whitney test. This specific test requires the samples to be random and independent and the observations to be on a hierarchical scale. The size of the samples does not matter, i.e., a different procedure is followed if the samples have a size smaller or larger than 10 (Xekalaki, 2001).

If there are two samples that are not independent and a test is required to examine whether there is a difference between them, then the Wilcoxon test or the Wilcoxon signed rank test is used. It is a nonparametric test corresponding to the Mann–Whitney test. This test is applied to dependent samples, and we should note that because there are differences between samples, the measurement scale cannot be simply hierarchical; rather, it should be proportional (Bakir & Reynolds, 1979).

When there are three or more populations and a test is needed to check whether the populations are the same, the Krustal–Walls test is used. Populations are not required to follow a normal distribution nor have the same variance. The only requirement is that their sample sizes be greater than or equal to 5 (Bhattacharya & Frierson, 1981).

The post hoc test, the next nonparametric test, is a simple test, for cases in which the direction, rather than the magnitude, of the participants' preference in a survey is of interest or for cases in which the interest can be simply compared with a value rather than the magnitude of the difference. No test to assess normality of the population distribution is required. The test is for the median, which is assumed to be the value entering the null hypothesis, and we distinguish cases by sample size or whether they are pairs of values.

Finally, Spearman's rank correlation coefficient test, denoted by rho, or r, is also employed. The coefficient is used to examine the correlation between variables for pairs of dependent sample values. It should be highlighted that the variables may be measured according to numerical scales (Sariannidis & Konteos, 2012).

7.1.2   A Literature Review

There has always been a significant body of research available to investigate the issue of financing education both in the past and in the present, thus stimulating those interested and conveying information that is useful to both the society and economy. Pesmazoglou (1987), at the beginning of his book, makes extensive reference to the distribution of public expenditures in education and also deals with the ways in which education is affected by them; this is stressed as an extremely important issue to determine the composition of specialties and educational orientations as well as the distribution of expenses according to the orientation per era in Greece (ibid).

Pesmazoglou (1987) concludes that education, the mechanisms that frame it, the structure of the expenses made for it, and, in general, financial contributions are factors that have shaped the performance of educational systems.

An important part of this book also refers to the structure of a workforce and how it is shaped and how it affects production in the primary, secondary, and tertiary sectors (ibid). The author's references to the asymptotic or two-way path that develops between the educational and developmental processes are thorough.

Of interest is Pesmazoglou's observation regarding agriculture, the factors that went wrong in agricultural education, and the development of not only agricultural but also other economic activities. Decisive economic upgrading and financing of education combined with educational reforms may succeed in overcoming stagnation and in stopping the vicious circle mentioned above. The main conclusion of Pesmazoglou's study is that education is not linked to economic development in Greece and that, until the end of the period studied, it was mainly used for the purpose of socialization and social integration of the members of society.

Giannakopoulos and Demoussis (2015) make an extensive reference to the financing of education and the positive or negative results that arise in their book *The Economics of Education*. In particular, the interpretation of the production of educational work and the way in which it is achieved, the distribution of the level of education among individuals, and the economic effects on them and on the society as a whole are all exemplified. Their work explicitly supports that education is an investment in knowledge and that this ongoing investment, as Smith (1958) has also pointed out, contributes to the production of human capital and, by extension, to productivity.

In 2014, the European Commission through the Eurydice Report (School Education Gateway, n.d.) contributed to the investigation and analysis of serious issues pertaining to education funding: the ways in which the financing of education is done by public local and nongovernmental bodies and the parties involved in the public financing of education. The survey refers to primary and secondary education in 27 of the 28 members of the European Union as well as in Iceland, Liechtenstein, Norway, and Turkey. It emphasizes the important role played by the political and social environments of each country, with each member state having its own characteristics and priorities, which also played an important role in financing. It was pointed out that many countries use local public funding to pay educational staff.

A special reference of Greece is made to emphasize that in it as well as in some other European countries such as the Czech Republic, France, Austria, and Turkey, the costs of education are not only borne by the central government but also by the local authorities and a part of the costs are borne by the private consumer as well.

Something that is observed in the Greek context and ought to be highlighted is that according to the country's budget and, after approval by the parliament, the money is distributed to the ministries and to the entities that use them.

Significant findings have also emerged from the annual surveys conducted by Center for Educational Policy Development General Confederation of Greek Workers (KANEP GSEE) (2009) (2020a, b), where an attempt was made to show how important the role of educational expenses is in the social and economic development of each country, to eliminate inequalities, to highlight the importance of local funding bodies, and to help modernize and upgrade education.

The financing of education is observed to be directed at specific sectors, such as higher education, in contrast to the other sectors that were sidelined, and this resulted in compulsory education not being part of any strategic planning on the basis of which its funding arises, something that is also found as an assumption for all subsystems of education such as special education, intercultural education, etc.

The common goal of the state and society, as emphasized in the reports, is a school that provides quality education, has no educational inequalities, is democratic, and offers a suitable environment to everyone. This can be achieved by educational reforms and by the creation of an effective educational system under the necessary and properly guided total funding.

Papakonstantinou (2000), through a work text, is of the opinion that it is the family budget that determines the comprehensive education of children; this opinion is a result of his research according to which expenses for education are proportional to family income. However, an equally important role is played by the social environment in which children develop and the conditions that prevail in this environment. What Papakonstantinou (2000) concludes, and is particularly sad, is that the underfunding that still exists may consequently cultivate inequality at school and thus transfer the burden of competition onto the family budget.

Ansell (2010) presents a unified theory of education policy. This theory is based on two basic axes. The first is that education is essentially redistributive. On the one hand, universal education is the sharpest asset of progressive distribution. Not only does it transfer resources from the rich to pay for the education of the poor but it also potentially undermines the position of the rich—and their children—in the income distribution. That is, education promotes a system that rewards achievement over heredity. In addition, the increased supply of education to the masses weakens the view that the more financially affluent are the ones who hold the privilege of education. Consequently, it appears to be in the interest of the financially affluent groups to prevent the existence and expansion of educational expenditure. The second axis is that one cannot examine education policy without linking it to broader trends in the labor market, which help complete the global economy.

Globalization allows citizens to "export their skills" (Ansell, 2010), meaning that the domestic supply of education can increase. Similarly, the demand for an educated workforce also determines the parameters of education policy. New technologies combined with specialized work such as computers and new media generally help increase the number of trainees. To the extent that globalization facilitates this type of technology transfer, it increases the state's incentive to invest in education. Thus, public education policy is greatly influenced by the nature of the global form of education and the backgrounds of the educated citizens around the world.

This book develops the writer's theory of education spending by tracing three stories that roughly trace the historical expansion of the government's role in education. It begins by examining the initial expansion of mass education, relating it to the government's first involvement in education policy. Universal primary education was achieved in the mid-nineteenth century in the United States of America but remains unfulfilled in many states in Africa and Asia. Nevertheless, the second half of the twentieth century marked a period of massive expansion of public expenditure on education. Public spending on education as a percentage of national income rose worldwide from an average of 2.5% in 1960 to 4.6% in 1999.

Between 1960 and 1995, not only did the world average of public education spending double but so did standard deviation. Divergence meant that some states fell behind, whereas others moved ahead and increased their spending on education over a long period of time (Pritchett, 2001). Furthermore, the trend in education spending has not always been upward. Many countries have experienced an impressive volatility in their countries' education spending.

According to the second story, electoral cycles shape how general redistribution takes place. Thus, redistributive politics continually plays a role in the funding of public education, both academic and vocational, but the extent is largely limited by politicians' interactions with voters and political institutions.

The third story takes us to the pinnacle of modern education policy: higher education. Fifty years ago, the higher education policy was extremely narrow in scope. Less than 5% of citizens in even the most advanced industrial nations attended university.

Political parties choose to structure higher educational systems according to the particular preferences of their constituencies but are constrained by the nature of the preexisting system. Thus, the politics of higher education is quite different in mass educational systems as opposed to those that remain selective and elitist.

Particularly informative is the doctoral thesis of Chalkiotis (2003), who emphasizes that the way education is financed plays an extremely important role in the functioning of the educational system.

Another reference is also made by Choleza (2005) in his doctoral thesis in which the multidimensional role of education and the social, cultural, pedagogical, but mainly economic, effects it has on society and the economy are emphasized.

Georgopoulos (2009), in his PhD thesis, also mentions to what extent there is adequate funding in public secondary education, which can help assess, in terms of both quantity and quality, the logistical infrastructure, human resources, and also funding for operational costs.

There has not yet been any substantial research linking the resources given to secondary education in relation to public expenditure and costs to the central government. Although financing of education is an extremely important public expenditure, the state has not made any reforms in favor of it, and, on the contrary, it has simply adjusted the expenses to the changing conditions of education.

The last doctoral thesis dealing with this topic was by Benos (2010), who also emphasizes the importance of human capital in shaping economic growth. The formation of human capital in the present is what will affect the formation of human capital in the future and will bring about economic growth accordingly.

It follows that human capital can reverse the limitation of diminishing returns to scale in a broad definition of capital (including natural and human capital) and lead to long-term per capita growth without exogenous technological progress.

Physaki (2016), in her work, makes a special reference to Greece, once again emphasizing the utmost importance of the creation of human capital, and to the compulsory free education provided in almost all European countries and the United States. Following Benos (2010), Psacharopoulos (2003), and Tsamadias (2021), Physaki (2016) also believes that investing in people and in their education and training will be an investment for countries in the future as doing so will bring about economic growth. To achieve this goal, public spending on education should be increased, which, according to Physaki's (2016) research, was extremely low until 2007; despite being a public cost, it should be prioritized, as the positive impact that it has on the society and the economy will unquestionably compensate for the cost.

In the text of Montenegro and Patrinos (2014), through a thorough analysis of the data concerning the education of young people and together with those of investments in education, it was found that after 1950 and for 60 years, they are directly and positively connected. This means that the more there is a will on the part of young and creative people for education, the greater is the mobilization of the state to invest in it. The value of human capital is recognized again, and it is considered an extremely important factor when examining the economic issues of a country and its participation in development, competitiveness, equality, democracy, institutions, and political freedom. Another fact is that people are particularly interested in higher education, which should be enough to prompt governments to invest more money in higher education and in education in general.

Theodoriadis (2018), in his postgraduate thesis, states that the economic crisis of 2007 affected many sectors, much more so the education sector in Greece, which, to a large extent, depends on state funding; when this fell short, it logically followed that there were insufficient funds for education. What he points out is that an extremely important tool for the social and economic improvement of the Greek state would initially be the investment in primary education, which would naturally result in greater investments in secondary and tertiary education.

In 2017, Papanikos examined how Greece's extreme recession is affecting public investment in education. This work examines Greek education spending before and after the Great Recession of 2008–2016. Greece suffered a shock due to the great recession because it was not prepared for such a thing. However, the Greek economy in the worst years of the twenty-first century surpassed the best years of the entire twentieth century. Education expenditure may have decreased but not as a percentage of gross domestic product (GDP). The educational policy of Greece should not be implemented with a view of short-term results but rather of future perspectives so that it is effective and competitive.

Betsas et al. (2016) analyzed the cost–benefit ratio of investment in education, the correspondence of qualifications with the needs of the economy and society, and the models in the selection of student potential. Despite arguments by many that the relationship between education, human capital, and economic growth is characterized by diminishing of returns, the authors believe that it is actually the opposite. Human capital is the driving force behind economic growth. The research is presented and aims to investigate the relationship between public and private expenses in Greece from 1960 to 2010, to compare them with those of European states, and to examine what would be the most correct and fair way of distributing educational resources.

The above research finds that financing of education is not the only condition for development, but it is one of them.

In Greek education, it is extremely important to strengthen public spending, but, at the same time, private spending and the way in which it may or may not contribute to the creation of a qualified, reliable, and efficient educational system is also an important obstacle to be taken into consideration.

The work of Benos (2010) studies the general equilibrium effects of two types of education policies in an overlapping generation model. It examines private and public spending on education and human capital.

It argues that it is the government that determines the amount of money and that the creation of human capital and economic development both depend on it.

Finally, Psacharopoulos (2003) in his article, "The Social Cost of an Outdated Law: Article 16 of the Greek Constitution" emphasizes that despite Article 16 of the Constitution, which stipulates that higher education be provided free of charge and that private universities be prohibited, Greece holds the world record for students studying abroad. With this article as a trigger, Psacharopoulos (2003) not only analyzed the pros and cons of financing tertiary education but also the return of students studying abroad in the context of Greek economy and society.

What is also clear according to Psacharopoulos (2003) is that Article 16 is nonfunctional and essentially ineffective because it cannot be enforced. This conclusion follows from the fact that higher education is essentially not free and that private universities exist and many graduate from them.

7.2 Public Expenditure at Different Educational Levels

Greek education is a highly interesting field, as, in Greece, services at all educational levels are provided free of charge. Formal education is an integral part of Greek families, and, as such, the public educational system plays a particularly important role.

There are many authors who have dealt with public expenditure and its distribution in education. The first authors who worked in Greece were Tsakloglou and Antoninis (1999) and Antoninis and Tsakloglou (2001). These authors concluded that most of the expenditure mainly concerns primary and secondary education. Moreover, public education was the subject of research for Callan et al. (2008) who mainly refer to higher education when making a comparative analysis.

In the case of Greece, the necessary financial resources come from not only the general state budget but also from private individuals. Here, it is pointed out that the allocation of most government expenditures in favor of the educational sector is made directly by the central government to the active school units, without the involvement of intermediary authorities. These costs include all current costs but do not include the maintenance costs of the school facilities, which were undertaken by the municipal authorities, or the construction costs of the school buildings, which were undertaken by the prefectures. The above financial financing process constitutes the centralized model (Katsikas, 2005).

7 Examining Public Expenditure on Education and the Relationship Between... 99

It is clarified that state funding is not always sufficient, neither for the simple upgrading and modernization of the existing infrastructure and facilities of the school units nor for carrying out all the necessary and required repairs and maintenance works. Here, we are referring to the amounts that barely cover the operational costs of the educational sector. Even these expenditure cases are covered at a low rate of return. Thus, in a case where there is purely direct funding, from the state budget, there is no other alternative than the necessary and unavoidable funding cuts, especially if you take into account the fact of the upward trend in the number of admitted people. According to Tsamadia (2021), at this point, after the Second World War, an increase in demand levels was observed, especially in the case of higher education. This increase had a direct effect on the inflation of the financial costs of the system. This has led to the problematic issue of funding higher education, something that has arisen, on the one hand, in the case of Europe and, on the other hand, in the case of North America. However, both America and the rest of the European states managed to deal with this problematic point by establishing new procedures for the flow of available resources, which led to the revision of the previously existing and prevailing education financing policy and philosophy (Tsamadias, 2021).

7.2.1 Nonparametric Spearman's Statistical Analysis

The non-parametric test which will be used serves the analysis and the investigation of the data we have.

To check the statistical significance of the correlation coefficient, Table 7.1 presented below was used, according to Sariannidis and Konteos (2012):

The formulated hypotheses are as follows:

H_0: There is no correlation and, alternatively
H_1: There is correlation and the value of the statistic we found is compared with the critical value rho.

The null hypothesis is rejected if lrhol $> =$ rho_c, whereas it is accepted when the opposite happens (Fig. 7.1; Table 7.2).

Primary vs. Total Expenditure (Tables 7.3 and 7.4)
The rho index $= 1\text{-}6\Sigma$ d $2/ n$ $(n$ 2-1) $= 1\text{-} \{6*426/19*(361\text{-}1)\} = 1\text{-}(2556/6840)$ $=1\text{-}0.37 = 0.63$.
We formulate the hypotheses:

H_0: There is no correlation between the variables
H_1: There is a correlation between the variables

In the above table, with a level of significance at 1%, we see that the critical value for the 19 pairs of values is 0.63 > 0.584. So, we reject the null hypothesis and conclude that spending in primary education is positively correlated with the

Table 7.1 Critical values of Spearman's coefficient (rho)

One-sided	0.05	0.025	0.01	0.005
Bilateral	0.1	0.05	0.02	0.01
N				
8	0.643	0.738	0.833 _	0.881
9	0.600	0.700	0.783	0.833 _
10	0.564	0.648	0.745	0.794
11	0.536	0.618	0.709	0.755
12	0.503	0.587	0.671	0.727
13	0.484	0.560	0.648	0.703
14	0.464	0.538	0.622	0.675
15	0.446	0.521	0.604	0.654
16	0.429	0.503	0.582	0.635
17	0.414	0.485	0.566	0.615
18	0.401	0.472	0.550	0.600
19	0.391	0.460	0.535	0.584
20	0.380	0.447	0.520	0.570
21	0.370	0.435	0.508	0.556
22	0.361	0.425	0.496	0.544
23	0.353	0.415	0.486	0.532
24	0.344	0.406	0.476	0.521
25	0.337	0.398	0.466	0.511

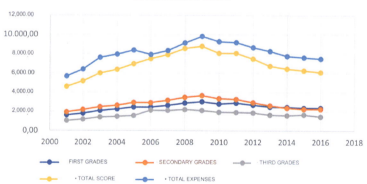

Fig. 7.1 Public expenditure on education (own editing)

total spending as the more the money of total spending increases, the more money is given for the spending in primary education (Fig. 7.2).

Secondary vs. Total Expenditure (Tables 7.5 and 7.6)

The rho index = 1-6Σ d 2/ n (n 2-1) = 1- {6*110/19*(361-1)} = 1-(660/6840) = 1- 0.096 = 0.90.

We formulate the hypotheses:

7 Examining Public Expenditure on Education and the Relationship Between...

Table 7.2 Detailed expenditure table of 2001–2019

Year	First grades	Secondary grades	Third grades	Total score	Total expenses
2001	1617.00	1936.00	1043.00	4596.00	5643.00
2002	1804.00	2178.00	1179.00	5161.00	6395.00
2003	2098.00	2487.00	1410.00	5995.00	7612.00
2004	2264.00	2631.00	1484.00	6379.00	7954.00
2005	2457.00	2942.00	1574.00	6973.00	8389.00
2006	2452.00	2922.00	2134.00	7508.00	7947.00
2007	2640.00	3158.00	2120.00	7918.00	8357.00
2008	2895.00	3488.00	2198.00	8581.00	9130.00
2009	3027.00	3653.00	2120.00	8800.00	9810.00
2010	2789.00	3348.00	1935.00	8072.00	9280.00
2011	2878.00	3280.00	1912.00	8070.00	9182.00
2012	2675.00	2940.00	1869.00	7484.00	8657.00
2013	2485.00	2610.00	1634.00	6729.00	8274.00
2014	2467.00	2366.00	1602.00	6435.00	7758.00
2015	2359.00	2244.00	1657.00	6260.00	7617.00
2016	2376.00	2259.00	1450.00	6085.00	7490.00
2017	2569.7	2425.4	1141.6	6136.7	6682.9
2018	2710.8	2497.3	1236.5	6444.6	7098
2019	2874.9	2369.8	1315.1	6559.8	7289.5

Table 7.3 Primary vs. total expenditure

Year	First grades	Total expenses
2001	1617.00	5643.00
2002	1804.00	6395.00
2003	2098.00	7612.00
2004	2264.00	7954.00
2005	2457.00	8389.00
2006	2452.00	7947.00
2007	2640.00	8357.00
2008	2895.00	9130.00
2009	3027.00	9810.00
2010	2789.00	9280.00
2011	2878.00	9182.00
2012	2675.00	8657.00
2013	2485.00	8274.00
2014	2467.00	7758.00
2015	2359.00	7617.00
2016	2376.00	7490.00
2017	2569.70	6682.90
2018	2710.80	7098.00
2019	2874.90	7289.50

Table 7.4 Calculation of rho primary vs. total expenditure

Xi	Yi	Order of magnitude e Xi	Order of magnitude Yi	Xi − Yi =d	d (2)
1617.00	5643.00	1	1	0	0
1804.00	6395.00	2	2	0	0
2098.00	7612.00	3	7	−4	16
2264.00	7954.00	4	11	−7	49
2359.00	7617.00	5	8	−3	9
2376.00	7490.00	6	6	0	0
2452.00	7947.00	7	10	−3	9
2457.00	8389.00	8	14	−6	36
2467.00	7758.00	9	9	0	0
2485.00	8274.00	10	12	−2	4
2569.70	6682.90	11	3	8	64
2640.00	8357.00	12	13	−1	1
2675.00	8657.00	13	15	−2	4
2710.80	7098.00	14	4	10	100
2789.00	9280.00	15	18	−3	9
2874.90	7289.50	16	5	11	121
2878.00	9182.00	17	17	0	0
2895.00	9130.00	18	16	2	4
3027.00	9810.00	19	19	0	0
					426

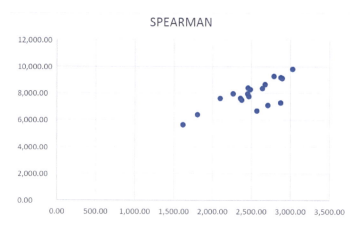

Fig. 7.2 Spearman's index printing in reference to primary education expenditure (own editing)

H_0: There is no correlation between the variables
H_1: There is a correlation between the variables.

In the above table, with a level of significance of 1%, we see that the critical value for the 19 value pairs is 0.90 > 0.584. So, we reject the null hypothesis and conclude that the expenditures in secondary education are positively correlated with

7 Examining Public Expenditure on Education and the Relationship Between... 103

Table 7.5 Secondary vs. total expenditure

Year	Secondary grades	Total expenses
2001	1936.00	5643.00
2002	2178.00	6395.00
2003	2487.00	7612.00
2004	2631.00	7954.00
2005	2942.00	8389.00
2006	2922.00	7947.00
2007	3158.00	8357.00
2008	3488.00	9130.00
2009	3653.00	9810.00
2010	3348.00	9280.00
2011	3280.00	9182.00
2012	2940.00	8657.00
2013	2610.00	8274.00
2014	2366.00	7758.00
2015	2244.00	7617.00
2016	2259.00	7490.00
2017	2425.40	6682.90
2018	2497.30	7098.00
2019	2369.80	7289.50

Table 7.6 Calculation of rho quadratic vs. total expenditure

Xi	Yi	Order of magnitude Xi	Order of magnitude Yi	Xi - Yi $=d$	$d(2)$
1936.00	5643.00	1	1	0	0
2178.00	6395.00	2	2	0	0
2244.00	7617.00	3	8	−5	25
2259.00	7490.00	4	6	−2	4
2366.00	7758.00	5	9	−4	16
2369.8	7289.50	6	5	1	1
2425.4	6682.90	7	3	4	16
2487.00	7612.00	8	7	1	1
2497.3	7098.00	9	4	5	25
2610.00	8274.00	10	12	−2	4
2631.00	7954.00	11	11	0	0
2922.00	7947.00	12	10	2	4
2940.00	8657.00	13	15	−2	4
2942.00	8389.00	14	14	0	0
3158.00	8357.00	15	13	2	4
3280.00	9182.00	16	17	−1	1
3348.00	9280.00	17	18	−1	1
3488.00	9130.00	18	16	2	4
3653.00	9810.00	19	19	0	0
					110.00

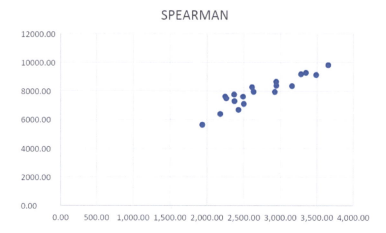

Fig. 7.3 Spearman's index trap of expenditure on secondary education (own editing)

Table 7.7 Tertiary vs. total expenditure

Year	Third grades	Total expenses
2001	1043.00	5643.00
2002	1179.00	6395.00
2003	1410.00	7612.00
2004	1484.00	7954.00
2005	1574.00	8389.00
2006	2134.00	7947.00
2007	2120.00	8357.00
2008	2198.00	9130.00
2009	2120.00	9810.00
2010	1935.00	9280.00
2011	1912.00	9182.00
2012	1869.00	8657.00
2013	1634.00	8274.00
2014	1602.00	7758.00
2015	1657.00	7617.00
2016	1450.00	7490.00
2017	1141.60	6682.90
2018	1236.50	7098.00
2019	1315.10	7289.50

the total expenditures, as the more the latter increases, the more money is given to the former as well (Fig. 7.3).

Tertiary vs. Total Expenditure (Tables 7.7 and 7.8)
The rho index = 1-6Σ d 2/ n (n 2-1) = 1- {6*1214/19*(361-1)} = 1- (7284/6840) = 1−1.06 = −0.06.

Table 7.8 Calculation of rho tertiary vs. total expenditure

Xi	Yi	Order of magnitude Xi	Order of magnitude Yi	Xi – Yi =d	d(2)
1043.00	5643.00	1	1	0	0
1141.6	6682.90	2	17	−15	225
1179.00	6395.00	3	2	1	1
1236.5	7098.00	4	18	−14	196
1315.1	7289.50	5	19	−14	196
1410.00	7612.00	6	3	3	9
1450.00	7490.00	7	16	−9	81
1484.00	7954.00	8	4	4	16
1574.00	8389.00	9	5	4	16
1602.00	7758.00	10	14	−4	16
1634.00	8274.00	11	13	−2	4
1657.00	7617.00	12	15	−3	9
1869.00	8657.00	13	12	1	1
1912.00	9182.00	14	11	3	9
1935.00	9280.00	15	10	5	25
2120.00	8357.00	16	7	9	81
2120.00	9810.00	17	9	8	64
2134.00	7947.00	18	6	12	144
2198.00	9130.00	19	8	11	121
					1214

We formulate the hypotheses:

H_0: There is no correlation between the variables.
H_1: There is a correlation between the variables

In the above table, with a level of significance at 1%, it is evident that the critical value for the 19 value pairs is $-0.06 < 0.635$. So, we reject the null hypothesis and conclude that tertiary expenditures are negatively correlated with total expenditures, as the higher the total expenditures are, the less money is given to the former (Fig. 7.4).

The quantitative research aimed to model the data related to economic growth and spending on education. Initially, it was found that there is indeed a relationship between economic growth and educational expenses, but it is not particularly noticeable in the long term. Therefore, education is not a factor of economic growth in the long run. The specific findings of this research are extremely important, as they are registered in a similar assessment of the relationship between spending on education and the country's development perspective that were reported in previous periods. In particular, the study of education funding for the period 1998–2018 is a further confirmation of the previously established position for the post-war period by Pesmazoglou (1987) and the first years of the post-colonial period by Psaharopoulos (1984) and Kazamias (1985) that education seems to

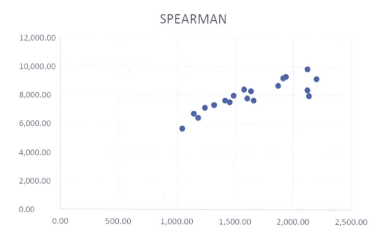

Fig. 7.4 Spearman's index printing in reference to tertiary education expenditure (own editing)

have contributed to a small extent to the economic development of Greece. This finding, which calls into question the theory of human capital for the Greek case, seems to be verified in this research. The interpretation of this phenomenon is a significant challenge. Pesmazoglou (1987) argues that the developmental function of education did not receive the required attention during the post-war years, when school practice prioritized functions such as socialization and social control of students. Psaharopoulos and Kazamias (1985) attributed the lack of relationship between educational investment and economic development to the low quality of the Greek educational system. In this research, insufficient funding is also highlighted on the one side, and the absence of strategic planning, on the other side, with its irrational distribution at the various levels of the educational system.

What we conclude is that total education expenditure is positively correlated with primary and secondary education expenditure and negatively with tertiary education expenditure, i.e., the more money spent on education increases, the more money is distributed to the first two levels, whereas the less money is spent on tertiary education. Observing the time series, we find that over the years, the amount of money may decrease, but after 2010 and the Greek crisis, the fluctuations are smaller, especially in secondary and higher education. This also mainly results from the massification of secondary education followed by tertiary education.

7.3 Public Investment in Education vs. Corruption

Corruption vs. Public Investment (Tables 7.9 and 7.10)

The rho index $= 1-6\Sigma \, d \, 2/ \, n \, (n \, 2-1) = 1-6*2843/22*(484-1) = 1-(17{,}058/10626) = 1-1.6 = -0.6$.

Table 7.9 Corruption and public investment in education

Year	Country	Corruption rate	Public investment in education as a percentage of GDP
1998	Greece	4.9	3.6
1999	Greece	4.9	3.7
2000	Greece	4.9	3.9
2001	Greece	4.2	3.7
2002	Greece	4.2	3.9
2003	Greece	4.3	4.3
2004	Greece	4.3	4.1
2005	Greece	4.3	4.2
2006	Greece	4.4	3.6
2007	Greece	4.6	3.6
2008	Greece	4.7	3.8
2009	Greece	3.8	4.1
2010	Greece	3.5	4.1
2011	Greece	3.4	4.4
2012	Greece	3.6	4.4
2013	Greece	4	4.5
2014	Greece	4.3	4.3
2015	Greece	4.6	4.1
2016	Greece	4.4	3.9
2017	Greece	4.8	3.8
2018	Greece	4.5	3.9
2019	Greece	4.8	3.6

Source: https://www.transparency.org/en/cpi/2021/index/grc

We formulate the hypotheses:

H_0: There is no correlation between the variables
H_1: There is a correlation between the variables

In the above table, at 1% level of significance, we see that the critical value for the 22 value pairs is - 0.6 < 0.544. Thus, the null hypothesis is rejected, and it is concluded that the corruption that exists as a phenomenon in our country is negatively related to public investment in education, since the index of the control we conducted has indicted that it is much smaller than the critical value, and, therefore, as the phenomena of corruption increase, the state invests less money in education (http://www.transparency.org/research/cpi/overview) (Fig. 7.5).

Table 7.10 Calculation of rho of corruption and public investment in education (edited by me)

Xi	Yi	Order of magnitude xi	Order of magnitude yi	xi-yi = d	d (2)
4	4.5	1	22	−21	441
3.4	4.4	2	20	−18	324
3.5	4.1	3	13	−10	100
3.6	4.4	4	21	−17	289
3.8	4.1	5	14	−9	81
4.2	3.7	6	5	1	1
4.2	3.9	7	9	−2	4
4.3	4.3	8	18	−10	100
4.3	4.1	9	15	−6	36
4.3	4.2	10	17	−7	49
4.3	4.3	11	19	−8	64
4.4	3.6	12	1	11	121
4.4	3.9	13	10	3	9
4.5	3.9	14	11	3	9
4.6	3.6	15	2	13	169
4.6	4.1	16	13	3	9
4.7	3.8	17	7	10	100
4.8	3.8	18	8	10	100
4.8	3.6	19	3	16	256
4.9	3.6	20	4	16	256
4.9	3.7	21	6	15	225
4.9	3.9	22	12	10	100
					2843

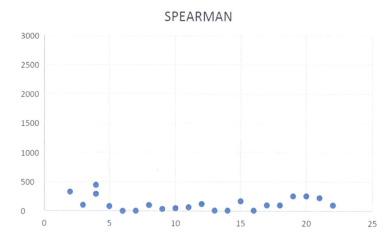

Fig. 7.5 Spearman's index printout of corruption and public investment in education (own edit)

7.4 Conclusions

Upgrading the financing of education has been proven to be particularly important, as an increase in public expenditure in favor of education brings about an increase in the efficiency of public educational institutions at all educational levels. For this reason, particular importance must be given to the government decisions taken on issues of financing the educational sector. Making rational decisions on this issue brings about not only individual benefits to each citizen of the society but also benefits of the social nature. In conclusion, it is pointed out that the total expenditure on education shows a positive correlation, which means that the more the money spent on education are, the more money are distributed by expenditure category.

As far as corruption is concerned, according to the research results, it was shown that it is negatively associated with funding. This occurs, as expected, as the more corruption phenomena increase, the less money there is in reserve to spend on education and other social expenditures.

7.5 Online Resources

1. www.Eurostat.Gr
2. https://www.statistics.gr/el/statistics?p__id=documents_WAR_publications portlet_INSTANCE_qDQ8fBKKo4lN&p_p_lifecycle=2&p_p_state=normal& p_p_mode=view&p_p_cacheability=cacheLevelPage&p_p_col_id=column-2&p_p_col_count=4&p_p_col_pos=1&_documents_WAR_publicationsportlet _INSTANCE_qDQ8fBKKo4lN_javax.faces. resource=document&_documents_ WAR_publicationsportlet_INSTANCE_qDQ8fBKKo4lN_ln=downloadResources &_documents_WAR_publicationsportlet_INSTANCE_qDQ8fBKKo4lN_ doc-umentID=452881&_documents_WAR_publicationsportlet_INSTANCE_qDQ8f BKKo4lN_locale=el
3. http://www.transparency.org/research/cpi/overview
4. https://ec.Europe.eu/eurostat/databrowser/view/educ_uoe_fine06/default/table? lang=en
5. https://www.schooleducationgateway.eu/el/pub/resources/publications/financing _schools_in_europe_m.htm(15/2/2021)

References

Greek

Antoninis, M., & Tsakloglou, P. (2001). Who benefits from public education in greece? Evidence and policy implications. *Education Economics, 9*(2), 197–222. https://doi.org/10.1080/09645290110057001

Betsas, I., Mavroskoufis, D., & Tzimourtou, A. (2016). The Financing of Education in Greece (1960–2010). In *Proceedings of the ninth Panhellenic Conference "Greek Pedagogy and Educational Research"* (pp. 321–334). Interaction.

Chalkiotis, D. (2003). *The financing of universities in Greece and the effects on their efficiency, Doctoral thesis*. National and Kapodistrian University of Athens.

Cholezas, I. (2005). *Private returns to education in Greece and the European Union*. Doctoral thesis. Economical University of Athens.

European Commission. (2014). *Funding schools in Europe: Mechanisms, methods and criteria for public funding. EACEA/Eurydice report*. Publications Office of the European Union. https://www.schooleducationgateway.eu/el/pub/resources/publications/financing_schools_in_. europe_m.htm(15/2/2021)

Georgopoulos, I. (2009). *Financial resources – Expenditure and development of secondary education in the region of Epirus*. Doctoral thesis. Ioanina.

Giannakopoulos, N., Demoussis M. (2015). The Economics of Education, Athens, Publications: Association of Greek Academic Libraries. Available at: http://www.kallipos.gr/ ISBN: 978-960-603-336-0 (5/4/2021).

KANEP/GSEE. (2020a). 2017–2018 Annual Report on Education of the Center for Development of Educational Policy of GSEE in collaboration with the "Observatory of Disability Issues" of the National Confederation of Persons with Disabilities on the subject: "Basic figures of Special Education and Education: Discrimination and Inequalities in Education and at Work". Athena. https://www.kanep-gsee.gr/ekdoseis/-/etisia-ekthesi-2017-2018-gia-tin-ekpaidefsi-tou-kentrou-anaptyksis-ekpaideftikis-politikis-tis-gsee-se-synergasia-me-to-paratiritirio-thematon-anapirias-tis-ethnikis-synomospondias-atom/.

KANEP/GSEE. (2020b). *Annual report on formal education 2009*, Athens. https://www.kanep-gsee.gr/ekdoseis/-/etisia-ekthesi-gia-tin-typiki-ekpaidefsi-2009/

Katsikas, X. (2005). *European higher education area and capitalist restructuring: The mutation of the university*. Gutenberg Publications.

Papakonstantinou, G. (2000). *The cost of education: From the withdrawal of the state to the competitive penetration of the family*. National Center for Social Research.

Papakonstantinou P. (2000). *The second political changeover in Greece in the 20th Century*. Kathimerini

Pesmazoglou, S. (1987). *Education and Development in Greece 1948–1985. The asymptote of a relationship, Athens*. Themelio Publications.

Physaki, P. (2016). The financing of secondary education in Eurozone countries at the beginning of the twenty-first century: cross-country comparisons—The position of Greece. *Education, Lifelong Learning, Research and Technological Development, Innovation and Economy, 1*, 357–370. https://doi.org/10.12681/elrie.800

Psacharopoulos, G. (2003). The Social Cost of an Outdated Law: Article 16 of the Greek Constitution. *European Journal of Law and Economics, 16*, 123–137.

Sariannidis, N., & Konteos, G. (2012). *Statistics, non-parametric tests* (pp. 630–667). Kozani.

Stegos, D. (2006). *Nonparametric statistics*. University Notes for the Department of Statistics and Actuarial Science, University of Piraeus.

Theodoriadis, K. (2018). *Financial analysis of resources in primary education*. (Unpublished master's thesis). Piraeus University.

Tsakloglou, P., & Antoninis, M. (1999). On the distributional impact of public education: evidence from Greece. *Economics of Education Review, 18*(4), 439–452.

Tsamadias, K. (2021). *The Financing of Higher Education in Greece Needs a New Approach*. http://galaxy.hua.gr/~ctsamad/files/research_insp/insp_xrim.pdf (27/2/2021).

Xekalaki, E. (2001). *Non-parametric statistics*. OPA.

Foreign

Abel-Smith, B. (1958). Whose welfare state? In N. Mackenzie (Ed.), *Conviction*. McGibbon & Kee.

Ansell, B. W. (2010). *From the ballot to the blackboard: The redistributive political economy of education*. Cambridge University Press.

Bakir, S. T., & Reynolds, M. R. (1979). A nonparametric procedure for process control based on within-group ranking. *Technometrics, 21*(2), 175–183.

Bhattacharya, P., & Frierson, D. (1981). A nonparametric control chart for detecting small disorders. *The Annals of Statistics, 9*(3), 544–554. Retrieved April 14, 2021, from http://www.jstor.org/stable/2240818

Benos, N. (2010). Education policy, growth and welfare. *Education Economics, 18*(1), 33–47.

Blundell, R., Chen, X., & Kristensen, D. (2007). Semi-nonparametric IV estimation of shape-invariant engel curves. *Econometrica, 75*, 1613–1669.

Callan, T., Smeeding, T., & Tsakloglou, P. (2008). Short-run distributional effects of public education transfers to students in seven European countries. *Education Economics, 16*(3), 275–288. https://doi.org/10.1080/09645290802338144

Darolles, S., Florens, J.-P., & Renault, E. (2006). *Nonparametric instrumental regression*. Working Paper, University of Toulouse.

Hall, P., & Horowitz, J. L. (2005). Nonparametric methods for inference in the presence of instrumental variables. *The Annals of Statistics, 33*, 2904–2929.

Montenegro, C. E., & Patrinos, H. A. (2014). *Comparable estimates of returns to schooling around the world*. The World Bank.

Newey, W. K., & Powell, J. L. (2003). Instrumental variables estimation of nonparametric models. *Econometrica, 71*, 1565–1578.

Papanikos, Gr. (2017). *The Great Recession and its effect on Greek education spending*. https://www.researchgate.net/publication/321747742_The_Great_Recession_and_its_Effect_o n_Greek_Education_Spending (20/5/2021).

Pritchett, L. (2001). Where has all the education gone? *The World Bank Economic Review, 15*(3), 367–391. http://www.jstor.org/stable/3990107

Psacharopoulos, G. (1984). The contribution of education to economic growth: international comparisons. In J. W. Kendrick (Ed.), *International comparisons of productivity and causes of the slowdown* (pp. 335–355). Ballinger Publishing.

Psacharopoulos, G., & Kazamias, A. M. (1985). *Education and growth in Greece: SocioEconomic research of the third level education*. Nationa l Centr e of Social Research.

Chapter 8
Does Clove Export Cause Economic Growth in Nigeria?

Okezie A. Ihugba, Alexander A. Orji, Erasmus E. Duru, and N. C. Ebomuche

Abstract Using annual data from 1970 to 2019, this study investigated the causal relationships between clove export and economic growth in Nigeria, using econometric techniques to empirically evaluate the hypotheses generated. In this regard, utilizing a systems simultaneous equation, a co-integration analysis was introduced to capture long- and short-run relationships among variables. Ex ante forecasting employing impulse response and variance decomposition simulations, as well as ex post forecasting to evaluate the period under study, were also used in this study. This study looked at causality relationships between series using the vector error correction model (VECM) and the Granger causality technique, which is used in F-/Wald test simulation to investigate short-run causation. Non-oil export trade has a positive and significant relationship with economic growth in its first and second lags, according to empirical findings, but oil exports have a positive and substantial effect on economic growth in its first, second, and third lags. Both oil and non-oil exports influence economic growth, according to the VECM–Granger causality results. A closer examination of the impulse response function reveals that non-oil exports will contribute to economic growth in both the short and long run. Meanwhile, the data point to oil export as an export that can stifle economic growth. Furthermore, data show that non-oil exports have always played a significant role in contributing to economic growth. This study advises that the money supply be expanded since it is beneficial to investors, based on the findings. When it rises, it lowers interest rates and stimulates more investment, resulting in economic growth.

Keywords C10 · O4 · F1 · O55

O. A. Ihugba (✉) · N. C. Ebomuche
Department of Economics, Alvan Ikoku Federal College of Education, Owerri, Imo State, Nigeria

A. A. Orji
Department of Economics, Nnamdi Azikiwe University, Awka, Anambra State, Nigeria

E. E. Duru
Department of Financial Management Technology, Federal University of Technology, Owerri, Imo State, Nigeria

© The Author(s), under exclusive license to Springer Nature Switzerland AG 2024
N. Tsounis, A. Vlachvei (eds.), *Applied Economic Research and Trends*, Springer Proceedings in Business and Economics,
https://doi.org/10.1007/978-3-031-49105-4_8

8.1 Introduction

Export trade, according to both classical and neoclassical economists, expands the market for both developing and developed countries' output. It has the potential to boost national output and serve as a growth engine (Mohsen & Javad, 2016). Expansion of a country's export trade may energize a stagnating economy and propel it forward on the path to prosperity and growth. Increased foreign demand may result in large-scale production and lower unit costs as a result of economies of scale. Export growth will generate funding for domestic investments, support the creation of new jobs, strengthen knowledge transfer, and boost overall economic growth (Dritsaki & Stiakakis, 2014). For any country to thrive sustainably, trade gains must be complemented by autonomous productivity increases, savings, and investment as well as favorable economic policies for private enterprise, capital incursions, and resource efficiency (Ali & Koko, 2018). Nigeria, like all emerging countries, is working hard to attain and maintain long-term economic growth. It is endowed with immense natural resources that can help it become a major player in the world market and so achieve economic growth through commerce; however, crude oil accounts for the majority of the country's exports (Nageri et al., 2013).

The export-led growth hypothesis (ELGH) believes that one of the most important measures of growth is export growth. It promotes the idea that a country's overall progress can be achieved not only by expanding the number of personnel and the amount of investment in the economy but also by growing exports (Saaed & Hussain, 2015). Causality also runs from growth to exports, indicating that it is unidirectional from economic growth to exports but not the other way around. There is also the possibility of a two-way causality link among exports and growth, and vice versa (Mehta, 2015).

Over the study period, the Nigerian economy has witnessed more positive than negative economic growth, and this pattern of positive economic growth has been accompanied by an even faster growth in total trade. The Central Bank of Nigeria (CBN)'s data (2005 and 2018) reveal a causal relationship between economic growth and trade. Higher rates of gross domestic product (GDP) growth are likewise associated with higher rates of trade growth as a percentage of output, according to the data. Figure 8.1 depicts the basic relationship between average annual changes in real GDP per capita and trade growth (average annual change in export value).

Export trade statistics, according to the CBN (2005 and 2018), reveal that in 1970, the total export was valued at ₦885.4 million and it increased to 19280 trillion in 2018. Years that recorded a positive economic growth were associated with a higher rate in the volume of export trade, except in 1986 (when a structural adjustment program (SAP) was introduced as a measure to diversify the Nigerian economy and revamp the non-oil exports), 1997, 1998, 2001 (upon signing the United States African Growth and Opportunity Act (AGOA) in the previous year), 2002, 2009, 2012, 2014, and 2015. Years that recorded a negative economic growth were associated with a higher rate in the volume of export trade, except in 1970

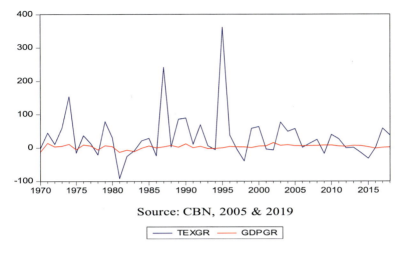

Fig. 8.1 Total export growth rate and GDP growth rate (1970–2019)

(GDP had a negative growth of 12.4, whereas export was −1.4) and 1983 (GDP had a negative growth of 10.9, whereas export was −8.5) (see Fig. 8.1).

Compared to other oil-exporting nations, Nigeria's export performance has been backward. Unlike some other fuel producers, the country has not managed to diversify its economy so that oil continues to account for almost all merchandise exports. In 1970, the total export earnings stood at ₦885.4 million with oil export accounting for about 57.6%, whereas the share of non-oil export fell to 42.4%. Since then, the share of non-oil exports has not been impressive. It has been declining, from 26.3% in 1971 to 7.4% in 2019 (see Fig. 8.2). This dominance of fuel exports has made Nigeria highly dependent on developments in the world oil market and has prevented it from taking advantage of dynamic opportunities in other sectors. Past attempts to foster nonfuel merchandise exports through export subsidies and other incentive measures have had extremely limited success, as many of the programs have been undermined by corruption.

Previous studies have been conducted on the short- and long-run relationships between exports and economic growth without disaggregating exports into oil and non-oil exports, and those that did were inconclusive, for example, previous studies did not properly check the problem of non-stationarity related to time series data. Those that did, did not test the ex ante forecast. Some of these studies include those by Ambreen and Abdul (2018), Ali and Koko (2018), Iyoha and Okim (2017), Sayef and Mohamed (2017), and Ugwuegbe and Uruakpa (2013), among others. Therefore, modern statistical time series procedures like the unit root test will be properly used to know the nature of the series, i.e., whether they are stationary or not, in order to select the appropriate study model. More so, this study serves as an update to the previous studies, more especially those by Ali and Koko (2018), Iyoha and Okim (2017), and Ugwuegbe and Uruakpa (2013). Some of the studies suffered from theoretical and methodological problems, in which the authors did not

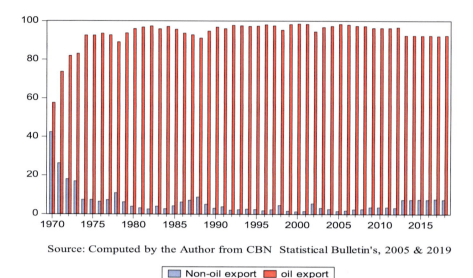

Fig. 8.2 Percentage of non-oil and oil to total export (1970–2019)

relate their study to any theory. Furthermore, many of the studies used ordinary least squares (OLS), correlation analysis, and co-integrated vector autoregression (VAR). These statistical techniques were unable to draw useful conclusions. Thus, their study may be prone to spurious results. Furthermore, none of the reviewed study used the F-/Wald test simulation to investigate the causality relationship between the variables in Nigeria. Similarly, some the literature studies reviewed here used annual or quarterly data, which were meant to be extended further, and some used cross-country data. Most recent among the works include Ambreen and Abdul (2018), Ali and Koko (2018), and Iyoha and Okim (2017), among others. Many of these studies have a wider time gap. Therefore, there is a need to extend the period to cover more recent years for which data are available to ensure compressive and up-to-date analysis.

Finally, the objective of this study was to quantify the significance of clove (disaggregate) exports in Nigeria's economic enactment and also to find out whether non-oil exports that contributed 6.2% to the economy during the period of study (1970–2019) caused economic growth in Nigeria using a vector error correction model (VECM). A VECM was used instead of a co-integration model because co-integration only captures the long-run relationship, whereas VECM also captures the short-run dynamics of the variables.

To achieve this objective, this chapter is structured as follows. In Sect. 8.2, we present a literature review and also review Nigeria's trade policy. Next, we discuss the data source and model specification in Sect. 8.3. Section 8.4 presents the empirical results as well as the analysis and discussion of findings. Finally, Sect. 8.5 is dedicated to our conclusion and policy implications.

8.2 Literature Review

8.2.1 Theoretical Framework

8.2.1.1 Comparative Advantage

David Ricardo proposed the idea of comparative advantage in 1817 because he was dissatisfied with the looseness of Smith's theory (Carbaugh, 2004). According to the comparative advantage principle, a country should focus on producing and exporting goods in which it has a comparative or a relative cost advantage over other countries while importing goods in which it has a comparative disadvantage. It is argued that as a result of this advantage, everyone will benefit more. According to Ricardo's theory, there is still a basis for mutually beneficial trade even if a nation has an absolute cost disadvantage in the production of both goods. The less efficient nation should focus on producing and exporting goods in which it is relatively less inefficient (and so has the smallest absolute disadvantage), whereas the more efficient nation should focus on producing and exporting goods in which it is relatively more efficient (where its absolute advantage is the greatest). The idea also assumed that both countries' technological levels were fixed. Different countries may use different technologies, but, for each commodity, all firms inside each country use the same production method. It is also assumed that the trade and flow of money between countries are both balanced. Trade does not affect the distribution of income inside a country. This hypothesis surpassed Smith's absolute advantage theory because it is possible for a country to have no absolute advantage in anything, but one country cannot have a comparative degree of advantage in everything while the other country has a comparative degree of advantage in nothing. This is because comparative advantage is based on relative costs (Carbaugh, 2004). As a result, the comparative advantage theory proposed by David Ricardo serves as the theoretical framework for this study.

8.2.2 Review of Empirical Studies

Different studies and research works were conducted by academics and policymakers to assess both exports and economic growth. A variety of studies have shown different results about the relationship between these two variables. Our review of the literature is limited to studies that focus on the impact of export on economic growth (Table 8.1).

Table 8.1 Studies related to the relationship between exports and economic growth

Authors	Countries	Period	Econometric techniques	Keys findings
Qazi Muhammad, A.A. (2012)	China	1978–2009	ARDL	GDP<=>EXP
Velnampy, T. and Achchuthan, S. (2013)	Sri Lanka	1970–2010	Correlation regression analysis	EXP=>GDP
Ugwuegbe, S.U. and Uruakpa, P.C. (2013)	Nigeria	1986–2011	OLS	GDP<=>EXP
Seipati, M. and Itumeleng, P. (2014)	South Africa	1990 Q1–2013 Q2	Co-integrated vector autoregression	EXP=>GDP
Afaf, A.J. and Majeed, A.H. (2015)	Tunisia	1977–2012	Granger causality and Johansen co-integration	EXP≠GDP
Sayef Bakari, M.M. (2017)	Panama	1980–2015	VAR and the Granger causality tests	EXP=>GDP
Iyoha, M. and Okim, A. (2017)	ECOWAS Countries	1990–2013	Pooled OLS, fixed effects model, random effects model, and dynamic panel regression model	EXP=>GDP
Fatemah, A. and Qayyum, A. (2018)	Pakistan	1971–2016	Co-integration analysis and dynamic error correction mechanism	EXP=>GDP
Elias, I.A., Agu, R.E., and Eze, L.O. (2018)	Nigeria	1980–2012	Multiple regression analysis technique	EXP=>GDP
Ali, A. and Koko, M.A. (2018)	Nigeria	1970–2016	Multivariate vector error correction approach, co-integration analysis, and Granger causality test	EXP<=>GDP
Adesoye, A. B., Adelowokan, O.A., and Alimi, Y.O. (2018).	Nigeria	1975–2003	Vector error correction model (VECM)	EXP<=>GDP
Yuna, Z. (2019)	Pakistan	1980–2011	Johansen co-integration and OLS	EXP=>GDP

Source: Authors' compilation, 2021
ARDL autoregressive distributed lag

8.2.3 An Overview of the Trade Policy in Nigeria

This section will look at Nigeria's trade policies in two major periods: before the structural adjustment program (SAP) was implemented and after it was implemented. These regimes' trade policies all had the same objective of enhancing economic growth and development through achieving specific goals like export promotion and ensuring balance of payments viability. These policies were also intended to support other policy initiatives such as job creation, self-sufficiency policies, and industrialization policies, among others. The following were the trade policies in place during the study period:

8.2.3.1 The Pre-SAP Trade Policy of 1970–1985

The import substitution industrialization strategy, which had been implemented before the Nigerian civil war, was carried on after the war ended in 1970. Due to the necessities of postwar reconstruction, trade policy was less restrictive between 1970 and 1976. Only nonessential consumer goods were prohibited, whereas raw material tariff rates were reduced and quantitative restrictions on spare parts, agricultural equipment, and other goods were eased. Similarly, the reconstruction tax on imports was reduced from 7.5% to 5% and then repealed entirely, as were exchange restrictions and profit repatriation (Analogbei, 2000). Import licensing was adopted as a trade barrier to promote import substitution industrialization policy and to supplement import tariffs in import control as well as to protect indigenous sectors that were set up to manufacture import substitutes.

Export tariffs were imposed soon after independence and lasted until the early 1970s. Agricultural exports such as palm oil, cotton, rubber, groundnuts, cocoa, and palm kernel were subjected to taxes ranging from 5% to 60%. Due to the oil boom and the need to encourage agricultural exports as part of the export diversification policy, these taxes were removed in 1973. This period of liberalization, however, came to an end in 1977, when a wide range of imported finished items requiring permits were subjected to extremely high tariffs or were outrightly banned. In 1979, this new stringent trade policy resulted in the ban of 82 commodities and restriction of 25 others.

The tariff structure for capital goods and raw materials was purposefully discriminatory. Luxury products were either placed on an import restriction list or were subjected to extremely high import levies. Nigeria's imports and exports were concentrated in the western hemisphere, even though this was not an intentional policy but was rather done owing to historical inheritance.

The Second National Development Plan (1970–74) was created to incorporate and improve on the 1962–68 plans' priority areas. It also attempted to achieve economic growth through restoring the country's productive potential and ensuring equal distribution. Nigeria will be able to create its goods and services, finance its growth, rely on its labor, and seek the best conditions for its exports by the end of the plan period, according to the plan. The abrupt and unexpected increase in crude oil prices in 1973, according to the CBN (1979), resulted in a surplus of revenues in 1974. As a result, in 1974, the limits on import payments were lifted.

The Third National Development Plan benefited from the surge in crude oil export earnings (1975–80). This was designed to be exceedingly ambitious, based on increased earnings from the oil sector of the economy. As a result, trade policies were loosened. The economy had begun to experience reductions in foreign exchange earnings by the time the Fourth National Development Plan (1981–85) was introduced, which were climaxed by the oil shock of the early 1980s. Although oil prices plummeted, import demand remained strong. In 1974, the level of external reserves could finance roughly 24 months of imports; by the end of 1978, it could only sustain 1.8 months, and, by the early 1980s, it could only fund less than 1 month. This reflected the reality that import demand had become price-inelastic, with the effect of balance of payments deficits. Then, with the imposition of stricter trade restrictions, a concerted attempt was made to curb the import pattern. Administrative delays were exacerbated by the increasing number of controls implemented by a large number of people. The authorities' incapacity to successfully ensure downward adjustment to import demand against the backdrop of falling export profits resulted in a significant payments imbalance that necessitated immediate and drastic corrective action (Analogbei, 2000).

8.2.3.2 Trade Policies During and After the SAP

The challenges in the economy caused by poor controls made it expedient for the government to take drastic actions to salvage the situation. Thus, in July 1986, a structural adjustment program (SAP) was introduced to tackle the problem of imbalances in the economy and thereby pave the way for growth and development. According to Analogbei (2000), a number of strategies specific to international trade were enunciated to achieve the broad objectives of the SAP. The primary focus was on liberalization of trade and the pricing system. The main elements of the program included:

(i) Restructure and diversify the productive base of the economy in order to lessen the dependence on the oil sector and on imports.
(ii) Achieve fiscal and balance of payments viability over time.
(iii) Lay the basis for sustainable, noninflationary growth.
(iv) Lessen the dominance of unproductive investments in the public sector, improve the sector's efficiency, and intensify the growth potential of the private sector.

A number of strategies were enunciated to achieve the broad objectives of the SAP, and they included:

• The Second-Tier Foreign Exchange Market (SFEM): This was introduced in order to determine the exchange rate of the naira by the market forces of demand

and supply. The price determination mechanism provided the means for the ultimate allocation of foreign exchange as against the use of administrative discretion.

- Abolition of Import and Export Licensing: The application of import and export licensing became important in the new dispensation and was consequently abolished. The policy that required exporters to surrender their export proceeds to the Central Bank of Nigeria was abolished. Moreover, exporters were allowed to retain 100% of their export earnings in their domiciliary accounts from which they could freely draw to meet all their foreign exchange transactions. More so, under the new scheme, exporters/producers could import raw materials and intermediate products free from import duty and other indirect taxes and charges.
- The Export Incentive and Miscellaneous Provisions Decree of 1986: This was promulgated to encourage exports. Through this, the CBN could provide refinancing and rediscounting facilities to other banks to encourage them to provide export financing to their customers.
- The Nigerian Export Credit Guarantee and Insurance Corporation came on stream in 1988 and was subsequently renamed the Nigerian Export-Import Bank (NEXIM), to provide credit and risk-bearing facilities to banks, so as to encourage them to support exports. In the area of imports, the devalued exchange rate of the naira at the different types of the Foreign Exchange Market, such as SFEM, the Autonomous Foreign Exchange Market (AFEM), or the Inter-Bank Foreign Exchange Market (IFEM), was meant to make imports dearer and thus discourage excessive importation and thereby reduce the pressure on the balance of payments. Import licensing was abolished, and reliance was placed on the use of customs tariff for the control of imports. The list of items on the imports prohibition list was also drastically reduced.
- The Customs, Excise, and Tariff Consolidation Decree of 1988: The Customs, Excise, Tariff (Consolidation) Decree, enacted in 1988, was based on a new customs goods classification, namely, the Harmonized System (HS) of Customs Goods Classification Code. This provided for a 7-year (1988–1994) tariff regime, with the aim of achieving transparency and predictability of tariff rates. Imports under the regime thus attracted ad valorem rates applied on the most favored nation (MFN) basis.

8.2.3.3 Trade Policy in the NEEDS Era

Recent economic policy reforms (since National Economic Development Strategy (NEEDS)) have aimed to lessen the trade policy regime's unpredictability, provide a timeline for the adoption of the Economic Community of West African States (ECOWAS) common external tariff (CET), and adhere to multilateral trading system responsibilities (Adenikinju 2005). Nigeria has several export incentives, but it continues to rely on import restrictions to protect its manufacturing and agricultural sectors. The justification is because the manufacturing base is relatively weak, import-dependent, and technologically constrained. A wide range of manufactured consumer goods that were frequently dumped in Nigeria's relatively big market is included on the import prohibition list. To protect the local industry and encourage job creation, a few agricultural products (such as fresh fruits, pork, and frozen chicken) that are produced in considerable numbers locally are also included in the list. Staple foods/crops that are crucial for food security, commodities that could serve as raw materials for local industries, and live organisms that are becoming uncommon are all on the export prohibition list. Maize, hides and skins, scrap metals, and wildlife animals categorized as endangered species are examples of such commodities (Chete et al., 2016).

There are also elaborate export incentives, such as the Manufacture-in-Bond Scheme, which allows exporting manufacturers to import intermediate products duty-free, the Duty Drawback Scheme, which provides refunds for duties/surcharges on raw materials, the Export Development Fund Scheme, which provides financial assistance to exporting companies to cover part of their initial expenses, and the Telecommunications Development Fund Scheme, which provides financial assistance to exporting companies to cover part of their initial expenses. The government has also established the Oil and Gas Export Free Zone (1996) and the Export Processing Zones (EPZs), which provide businesses with special tax treatment and other benefits. Furthermore, international investors can repatriate their profits and dividends tax-free. The Nigerian Investment Promotion Commission (NIPC) Act guarantees that no business will be nationalized or expropriated by the government (Chete et al., 2016).

8.3 Methodology

8.3.1 Data Source

The study employed the use of secondary data that were mainly sourced from the Central Bank of Nigeria (CBN) Statistical Bulletin of 2005, 2012, and 2018 and the World Bank. The scope of the study covered the period between 1970 and 2019. All data were converted into a log–log equation for time series processing. Thus, the coefficient was interpreted as elasticity. The variables and their sources are presented in Table 8.2.

8.3.2 Model Specification

The model of this study has been adopted from Iyoha and Okim (2017) with some modifications to realize the objective of this study. The basic exogenous growth model suggested by Solow (1956) explains the growth rate of output or income as depending on the rate of growth of technical change, labor or population, and capital

Table 8.2 Variables, measurement, and sources of data

S. No.	Variables	Measurement	Sources of data
1.	Economic growth (GDP per capita (GDPPC))	GDP per capita (constant 2010 US$): it is a proxy for the level of economic growth	https://data.worldbank.org/indicator
2.	Gross fixed capital formation (PCAP)	It measures additions of capital goods, such as equipment, tools, transportation assets, and electricity (in billions),and is a proxy for infrastructure	https://data.worldbank.org/indicator
3.	Human capital (HCAP)	Average years of secondary schooling, representing the numbers of years in school	https://data.worldbank.org/indicator
4.	Total oil export (OEXP)	Total value of oil export (in billions)	CBN Statistical Bulletins of 2006, 2010, and 2018
5.	Total non-oil export (NOEXP)	Total value of non-oil export (in billions)	CBN Statistical Bulletins of 2006, 2012, and 2018
6.	Government policy (GOVP)	Money supply (in billions) and total quantity of money in circulation at a point in time	CBN Statistical Bulletins of 2006 and 2018
7.	Exchange rate (EXR)	Official exchange rate (local currency unit per US$, period average). It has long been considered to be a key factor in driving macroeconomic performance and business cycles. A depreciation in the exchange rate should make Nigerian exports more competitive and should increase demand	CBN Statistical Bulletins of 2005 and 2018
8.	Inflation rate	Annual percentages of average consumer prices based on year-on-year changes	https://data.worldbank.org/indicator
9.	Population growth rate (POPGR)	Number of individuals by which population increases. It is measured in terms of annual percentages	https://data.worldbank.org/indicator

Source: Researcher's compilation, 2020

stock. Consider the standard neoclassical production function:

$$Y = f(A, K, L) \tag{8.1}$$

where A is the level of technology, K is the capital stock, L is the quantity of labor, and Y is output. Assume that the production function is twice differentiable and is subjected to constant returns to scale and that technical change is Hicks-neutral.

Differentiation of Eq. (8.1) with respect to time, division by Y, and rearrangement of terms yields:

$$Y'/Y = A'/A + (F_K K/Y) \cdot (K'/K) + (F_L L/Y) \cdot (L'/L) \tag{8.2}$$

where Y'/Y is the continuous time rate of growth of output, K'/K is the rate of growth of capital stock, and L'/L is the rate of growth of labor force; F_K and F_L are the (social) marginal products of capital and labor, respectively; and A'/A is the Hicks-neutral rate of change of the technological progress.

Thus, the basic Solow (exogenous) growth model gives the growth rate of output or income as depending on the rate of growth of technical change, labor or population, and capital stock. In empirical applications, this basic Solow model is modified to obtain the augmented Solow growth model, in which the rate of growth of income depends not only on technical change, labor, and capital but also on policy variables like exchange rate and inflation (Iyoha & Okim, 2017). The central bank tries to maintain price stability through controlling the level of money supply, and, according to standard macroeconomic theory, an increase in the supply of money should lower the interest rates in the economy, leading to more consumption and lending/borrowing. Based on this statement, this chapter will expand policy variables to include money supply as a proxy for government policy, non-oil exports, and oil exports. Disaggregating the total stock of capital into two components, namely, physical capital and human capital, the augmented Solow theory of economic growth yields the following specification for the determinants of economic growth in Nigeria:

$$GDPPC = f(\text{OEXP, NOEXP, GOVP, PCAP, HCAP, POPGR, EXCR, INF}) \tag{8.3}$$

$f_1 > 0, f_2 > 0, f_3 > 0, f_4 > 0, f_5 > 0, f_6 < 0, f_7 < 0, f_8 < 0.$

This means that all the identified variables have a positive relationship with economic growth, whereas the population growth rate, the exchange rate, and inflation are expected to exert a negative influence on economic growth.

where

GDPPC = real GDP per capita
OEXP = total oil exports
NOEXP = total non-oil exports
GOVP = money supply as a proxy for government policy

PCAP = real gross fixed capital formation
HCAP = human capital, proxied by the number of years spent in secondary school
POPGR = population growth rate
EXCR = exchange rate
INF = inflation rate

Equation 8.3 can be written in the econometric model and in their respective natural log form as thus:

$$LGDPPC_t = \beta_0 + \beta_1 LOEXP_t + \beta_2 LNOEXP_t + \beta_3 LGOVP_t + \beta_4 LPCAP_t$$
$$+ \beta_5 LHCAP_t + \beta_6 POPGR_t + \beta_7 LEXCR_t + \beta_8 INF_t + \varepsilon_t$$

$$(8.4)$$

In the production function, LGDPPC is the natural log of real GDP per capita, LOEXP is the natural log of total oil exports, LNOEXP is the natural log of total non-oil exports, LGOVP is the natural log money supply as a proxy for government policy, LPCAP is the natural log of real gross fixed capital formation, LHCAP is the natural log of human capital, proxied by the number of years spent in secondary school, LEXCR is the natural log of exchange rate, L is the natural logarithm, β_0 is the intercept or autonomous parameter estimate, $\beta_1. . ...\beta_8$ is the parameter estimate associated with the determinants of economic growth in Nigeria, and ε_t is the stochastic error term.

The entire estimation procedure consists of six steps: performing the unit root test, lag selection, performing the co-integration test, performing fort, which is the error correction model estimation, performing Granger causality analysis, and the using VAR stability model. This chapter is based on the following hypotheses for testing the causality and co-integration between GDPPC, LNOEXP, and LNOEXP: (i) whether there exists a short-run relationship between GDPPC, LNOEXP, and LNOEXP in Nigeria, (ii) whether there exists a long-run relationship between GDPPC, LNOEXP, and LNOEXP in Nigeria, and (iii) whether there is causality between GDPPC growth and LNOEXP and LNOEXP.

8.4 Data Presentation and Analysis

The analysis will be divided into two, namely, descriptive statistics and empirical analysis.

8.4.1 Descriptive Statistics

Table 8.3 provides a summary of the descriptive statistics, namely, sample means, maximum values, minimum values, medians, standard deviations, skewness, kurto-

Table 8.3 Summary statistics of the variables (1970–2019)

	LEXCR	LGDPPC	LHCAP	INF	LGOVP	LNOEXP	LOEXP	LPCAP	LPOPGR
Mean	1.14	1.40	0.80	1.15	2.55	4.07	5.39	0.83	0.41
Median	1.34	1.42	0.78	1.11	2.46	4.00	5.59	0.94	0.41
Maximum	2.55	1.48	0.85	1.86	4.41	6.15	7.25	1.17	0.49
Minimum	-0.26	1.33	0.78	0.54	0.97	2.31	2.71	0.37	0.15
Std. Dev.	1.04	0.05	0.03	0.30	1.21	1.30	1.44	0.29	0.05
Skewness	-0.19	0.12	0.77	0.63	0.25	0.14	-0.20	-0.40	-3.68
Kurtosis	1.38	1.58	1.60	3.06	1.50	1.53	1.55	1.46	23.09
Jarque–Bera	5.75	4.30	9.07	3.30	5.18	4.64	4.73	6.27	953.4
Probability	0.06	0.12	0.01	0.19	0.08	0.10	0.09	0.04	0.00
Sum	56.81	70.22	39.98	57.55	127.56	203.72	269.67	41.29	20.74
Sum Sq. Dev.	53.36	0.12	0.05	4.27	71.81	83.15	101.91	4.10	0.11
Observations	50	50	50	50	50	50	50	50	50

Source: Authors' computation using Eviews 10, 2020
Std. Dev. standard deviation, *Sum Sq. Dev.* sum of the squared deviations

8 Does Clove Export Cause Economic Growth in Nigeria?

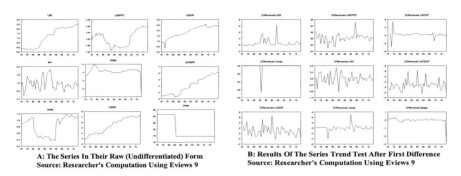

Fig. 8.3 Trend Analysis

sis, and the Jarque–Bera tests with their *P*-values. It is clear that all the statistics show characteristics that are common with most time series, for instance, for normality in the form of a platykurtic distribution, there are a number of noticeable differences between the variables. First, oil export has the largest unconditional average of 5.39%, whereas human capital has the least unconditional average of 0.80%. The standard deviation shows the level of volatility in the variables. It displays the rate at which each variable deviates from the mean value. From the above table, oil export is the most volatile at 1.44%, whereas real human capital is the least volatile at 0.031%. The skewness measures the asymmetric nature of the data.

8.4.2 Series Trend Analysis

Time series data often exhibit increasing or decreasing trends, with fluctuations. As such, a trend analysis is necessary before unit root testing, to establish whether the series has a unit root or not. The results of the graphical display in Fig. 8.3a indicate that the series exhibit a random walk with drift and trend, except inflation rate. Fig. 8.3b shows that the series reflect a trend with a pattern of large fluctuations, meaning that the series are nonstationary.

8.4.3 The Stationarity Test

8.4.3.1 Unit Root Tests

Unit root tests will be conducted based on the Enders (2014) approach. The second augmented Dickey–Fuller test (ADF) test at level involved a trend and an intercept, whereas in the third, none were included. Later data were tested at first difference. Following Dickey and Fuller (1979) and Davidson and Mackinnon's (1993) method, the series are estimated. The results of the ADF tests at level, constant and trend, none, and first difference are summarized in Table 8.4 below.

As indicated by the asterisk (*), the inflation variable (LINF) is stationary when tested at level with a constant and a constant and trend. However, as indicated by the asterisk for population growth rate (LPOPGR), the series are nonstationary in all cases, including at first difference. We therefore conclude that the series for LPOPGR are nonstationary because data are stationary when the ADF test statistics are less than the test critical values at 5 % (ADF test statistics < test critical value at 5%). The corresponding probability value for stationary data is less than $0.05(P$ - value $< 0.05)$. The corresponding probability value for stationary data is less than $0.05(P$ - value $< 0.05)$. Following the ADF test, all series, except INF, are nonstationary at level but stationary at first difference. However, ADF tests are often affected by the choice of the lag length (p) and lose power while estimating a large sample. As such, the ADF test results are validated by the Phillips–Perron (PP) test.

8.4.3.2 The Phillips–Perron Unit Root Test

The advantage of the PP test over the ADF test is that the PP test corrects any heteroscedasticity and serial correlation in the errors terms(u_t). In addition, it does not require lag selection and is based on a serially correlated regression error term. Similar to the ADF test, the null for PP is also based on the null that the series are nonstationary. The results of the PP test are indicated in Table 8.4 below. These results indicate that the series are nonstationary at level but stationary at first difference, except inflation and population growth rate. Figure 8.3b shows the variables in their differenced form. This result justifies the use of the VAR model for estimation.

8.4.4 Determination of Lags

Table 8.5 reports lag-order selection statistics. The criteria of Schwarz criteria (SC), final prediction error (FPE), Hannan–Quinn information criterion (HQIC), likelihood ratio (LR), and Akaike information criterion (AIC) show a lag order of four. AIC has the lowest value. So, the study will proceed with further tests with lags (4).

8.4.5 The Co-integration Test

Having verified that all variables are integrated to order one $I(1)$, the next step is to perform the co-integration test. Due to the fact that there are multivariate time series,

Table 8.4 Unit root test results

Variables	ADF test statistics				PP test statistics			
	Constant	Constant and trend	None	First difference	Constant	Constant and trend	None	First Difference
LGDPPC	−0.34	−0.85	0.89	−6.27*	−0.67	−1.04	0.72	−6.35*
LOEXP	−1.72	−1.49	2.81	−7.12*	−1.82	−1.40	2.88	−7.12*
LNOEXP	−0.05	−2.74	2.53	−7.12*	−0.07	−2.75	2.92	−7.17*
LGOVP	0.32	−2.29	1.70	−5.16*	0.51	−2.49	3.96	−5.25*
LHCAP	−1.45	−1.59	−1.06	−6.93*	−1.45	−1.62	−1.06	−6.93*
LPCAP	−1.16	−1.50	−0.13	−6.00*	−1.27	−1.50	−0.18	−5.96*
LPOPGR	−0.47	−0.50	−0.79	−0.95	−0.97	−0.60	−0.79	−0.51
INF	−3.43*	−4.02*	−2.11	−7.17*	−3.27*	−3.26	−1.96*	−14.59*
LEXCR	−0.17	−1.64	2.20	−5.64*	−0.27	−1.89	1.51	−5.64*

Notes (ADF): Test critical values at 5% (at level: constant = −2.92, constant and trend = −3.50, none = −1.94, whereas at first difference = −2.92); *P*-value = probability value, * signifies stationarity

Notes (PP): Test critical values at 5% (at level: constant = −2.92, constant and trend = −3.50, none = −1.94, whereas at first difference = −2.92); *P*-value = probability value, * signifies stationarity

Table 8.5 VAR lag-order selection criteria

Lag	LogL	LR	FPE	AIC	SC	HQ
0	229.5395	NA	1.48e-13	−9.675633	−9.397361	−9.571390
1	533.4440	502.1030	2.33e-18	−20.75843	−18.53226*	−19.92450
2	583.7067	67.74534	2.56e-18	−20.81333	−16.63926	−19.24970
3	638.2727	56.93847	3.07e-18	−21.05533	−14.93336	−18.76201
4	734.3553	71.01755*	1.04e-18*	−23.10240*	−15.03253	−20.07938*

Source: Researcher's calculations from Eviews 9, 2020
Indicates lag-order selected by the criterion

the multivariate co-integration technique proposed by Johansen (1995) is applied to determine whether there is a stable long-run relationship.

Table 8.6 indicates the presence of a long-run economic relationship among all the variables as both trace and max-eigen statistics indicated six co-integrating equations among the variables. For this reason, it can be concluded that there was a long-term relationship among the variables and that the VECM could be estimated to detect the long- and short-term dynamics of these variables.

8.4.6 Vector Error Correction Model (VECM) Estimation

Table 8.7 accounts for a −1.17 error correction. The fact that this term has a negative impact explains how disequilibrium eventually dissipates from the short to the long run. As a result, the short-run output values will eventually converge to the long-run trend, with an annual adjustment of 117%. However, the results show that in the first and second lags, the coefficient of non-oil export has a substantial positive relationship with economic growth, which is consistent with the a priori expectation. According to the findings, a 1% increase in LNOEXP raises LGDPPC by 0.03% in the first lag and by 0.05% in the second. LOEXP's first, second, and third lags all demonstrate a substantial positive connection with economic growth, which matches our a priori prediction. According to the findings, a 1% rise in LOEXP raises LGDPPC by 0.05% in the first lag, by 0.02% in the second lag, and 0.04% in the third lag. A 1% increase in the exchange rate will increase economic growth by 0.07% in the first lag of LEXCR, which is not in line with our a priori expectation, but a 1% increase in the exchange rate will reduce economic growth by 0.07% in the fourth lag, which is in line with our a priori expectation. Human capital's first, second, and third lags all have a strong positive correlation with economic growth. From the first to the fourth LCAP difference, there is a substantial negative link to economic growth throughout the study year. Furthermore, as shown by the coefficient of determination value of 0.931159, R^2 measures the combined statistical influence of explanatory variables in explaining the dependent variable, with the variables controlled in the model accounting for 93% of the variation in GDP between 1970 and 2019, whereas the remaining 7% is explained by other variables not controlled in the model.

Table 8.6 Co-integration test results

Hypothesized No. of CE(s)	Trace Statistics	0.05 Critical value	Probability**	Hypothesized No. of CE(s)	Max- eigen Statistics	0.05 Critical value	Probability**
None *	463.1366	125.6154	0.0001	None *	173.8238	46.23142	0.0000
At most 1 *	289.3128	95.75366	0.0000	At most 1 *	97.31783	40.07757	0.0000
At most 2 *	191.9949	69.81889	0.0000	At most 2 *	79.19594	33.87687	0.0000
At most 3 *	112.7990	47.85613	0.0000	At most 3 *	61.11434	27.58434	0.0000
At most 4 *	51.68466	29.79707	0.0000	At most 4 *	25.74687	21.13162	0.0104
At most 5 *	25.93779	15.49471	0.0010	At most 5 *	21.78475	14.26460	0.0027
At most 6 *	4.153045	3.841466	0.0416	At most 6 *	4.153045	3.841466	0.0416

Source: Researcher's calculations from Eviews 9, 2020

Denotes rejection of the null hypothesis at the 0.05 level

Table 8.7 Error correction results

	Coefficient	Std. Error	*t*-Statistics	Probability
ECT	−1.167282	0.193675	−6.027020	0.0000
D(LGDPPC(-1))	0.094916	0.148833	0.637738	0.5333
D(LGDPPC(-2))	0.115120	0.118825	0.968820	0.3480
D(LGDPPC(-3))	0.263397	0.119659	2.201235	0.0438
D(LGDPPC(-4))	−0.015152	0.108090	−0.140180	0.8904
D(LEXCR(-1))	0.066152	0.016213	4.080177	0.0010
D(LEXCR(-2))	0.057870	0.016717	3.461805	0.0035
D(LEXCR(-3))	−0.005459	0.016857	−0.323846	0.7505
D(LEXCR(-4))	−0.065884	0.017376	−3.791804	0.0018
D(LHCAP(-1))	1.014596	0.145273	6.984077	0.0000
D(LHCAP(-2))	1.477479	0.262598	5.626389	0.0000
D(LHCAP(-3))	0.919987	0.231569	3.972836	0.0012
D(LHCAP(-4))	0.013569	0.173994	0.077987	0.9389
D(LNOEXP(-1))	0.025294	0.009970	2.537112	0.0228
D(LNOEXP(-2))	0.048955	0.009896	4.946787	0.0002
D(LNOEXP(-3))	0.016963	0.012333	1.375445	0.1892
D(LNOEXP(-4))	0.010709	0.008986	1.191752	0.2519
D(LOEXP(-1))	0.054012	0.011943	4.522505	0.0004
D(LOEXP(-2))	0.024559	0.011927	2.059169	0.0573
D(LOEXP(-3))	0.040635	0.010461	3.884570	0.0015
D(LOEXP(-4))	0.007995	0.009060	0.882430	0.3915
D(LPCAP(-1))	−0.135108	0.026363	−5.124815	0.0001
D(LPCAP(-2))	−0.106488	0.021373	−4.982443	0.0002
D(LPCAP(-3))	−0.063298	0.020754	−3.049993	0.0081
D(LPCAP(-4))	−0.058154	0.018938	−3.070747	0.0078
D(LGOVP(-1))	0.037205	0.018865	1.972103	0.0673
D(LGOVP(-2))	−0.009057	0.016853	−0.537415	0.5989
D(LGOVP(-3))	−0.037423	0.016711	−2.239403	0.0407
D(LGOVP(-4))	−0.037751	0.019431	−1.942863	0.0710
C	−0.012604	0.002752	−4.580686	0.0004

Source: Researcher's calculations from Eviews 9, 2020
Std. Error standard error
R^2, 93%; adjusted R^2, 80%

8.4.7 Simultaneous Equation Short-Run Simulation and Analysis

The results of the short-run test are presented below in Table 8.8.

According to our findings, there exists a short-run relationship between the explanatory variables and the independent variables, as indicated by the chi-squared joint statistics probability values. The *P*-value of the chi-squared test for nominal exchange rate (EXCR), human capital proxied by the number of years spent in

8   Does Clove Export Cause Economic Growth in Nigeria?   133

Table 8.8 Wald tests and short-run test

Dependent variable: DLGDPPC			
Variables	Chi-squared test	Probability	Relationship
D(LEXCR)	27.4	0.00	Short-run causality
D(LHCAP)	63.5	0.00	Short-run causality
D(LNOEXP)	27.6	0.00	Short-run causality
D(LOEXP)	26.8	0.00	Short-run causality
D(LPCAP)	40.4	0.00	Short-run causality
D(LGOVP)	12.9	0.01	Short-run causality
ALL	156.7	0.00	Short-run causality

Source: Researcher's calculations from Eviews 9, 2020

secondary school (LHCAP), total non-oil exports (LNOEXP), oil export (LOEXP), real gross fixed capital formation (LPCAP), and money supply as a proxy for government policy (GOVP) is less than 0.05, the null hypotheses ($H0$): $\beta 5=0$ will be rejected, and, therefore, all the variables cause LGDPPC in the short run. The next step is to conduct ex ante forecasting involving impulse response and variance decomposition tests.

8.4.8   Impulse Response Function

The impulse response function plays a pivotal role in assessing how and to what extent shocks on independent variables influence economic growth. Table 8.9 displays the dynamic effects of one standard deviation shock from the independent variables in Nigeria over a 5-year period on LGDPPC (Tables 8.9 and 8.10).

Nigeria's economic growth prediction shows a good trend with fluctuations due to shocks and innovations. Economic growth's shock, nominal exchange rate (EXCR), human capital proxied by the number of years spent in secondary school (LHCAP), total non-oil exports (LNOEXP), real gross fixed capital formation (LPCAP), and money supply as a proxy for government policy (GOVP) will all contribute to the country's economic growth. A one standard deviation positive own shock, for example, will cause a change from 0.005 in the short run to 0.014 in the long run. Second, forecasts show that the nominal exchange rate (EXCR) harms economic growth in the short run but improves in the long run. According to the simulation, a one standard deviation positive shock to the nominal exchange rate (EXCR) will reduce economic growth by −0.001 in the short run. In the long run, the shocks will increase by 0.004, therefore weakening the naira and hurting economic growth in the short run. This demonstrates that at the outset of a depreciation, aggregate demand will not be met by adequate increases in domestic output and imports of goods and services. Third, human capital innovations, as measured by the number of years spent in secondary school (LHCAP), induce economic growth to improve for 5 years but with diminishing benefits. According to

Table 8.9 Impulse response analysis

Response of LGDPPC							
Period	LGDPPC	LEXCR	LHCAP	LNOEXP	LOEXP	LPCAP	LGOVP
1	0.005878	0	0	0	0	0	0
2	0.007894	−0.00095	0.005351	0.005208	−0.00029	−0.00035	0.002854
3	0.009076	0.001967	0.005792	0.003995	−0.00706	0.003557	0.001707
4	0.012226	0.001857	0.002779	0.003793	−0.00784	0.003443	0.001043
5	0.014466	0.004391	0.001314	0.007456	−0.00746	0.00214	0.001998

Source: Researcher's calculations from Eviews 9, 2020

Table 8.10 Variance decomposition

Period	LGDPPC	LEXCR	LHCAP	LNOEXP	LOEXP	LPCAP	LGOVP
Short-run	79.9	0.3	8.8	8.4	0.0	0.0	2.5
Medium-term	63.8	1.2	10.7	9.9	9.9	2.1	2.3
Long-run	55.1	5.4	8.3	13.5	14.1	2.1	1.6

Source: Researcher's calculations from Eviews 9, 2020

simulations, a one positive standard deviation shock to LHCAP will raise economic growth by 0.005 in the short run and decline to 0.001 in the long run. This suggests that while the number of years spent in secondary school is crucial for the nation's economic growth, it does not lead to faster growth in the long run. This result can be attributable to the percentage of secondary school graduates who work after graduation. Fourth, forecasts show that total non-oil exports (LNOEXP) will be a source of concern for the country and will rise. LNOEXP increases by 0.005 in the short run and by 0.007 in the long run as a result of a one standard deviation negative own shock. This suggests that growing non-oil exports will have a significant long-term impact on Nigeria's economic growth. We can see that growing non-oil export volume has a positive impact on the economy of the country. Sixth, both in the short and long run, innovations to the money supply as a proxy for government policy (GOVP) account for positive fluctuations in economic growth. According to the findings, one positive standard deviation shock to GOVP accounts for a 0.003 increase in Nigeria's economic growth. In the long run, a positive one standard deviation innovation similar to GOVP causes economic growth to increase by 1.002.

However, oil export innovations (LOEXP) suggest that Nigeria's economic growth would slow down in the coming years. This is because a one positive standard deviation shock to LOEXP will lead economic growth to fall by 0.003 in the short run. In the long run, a one positive standard deviation shock to LOEXP reduces economic growth by 0.007. This is not a positive trend for the country. This could be ascribed to corruption and the government's inability to get the refineries to run at full capacity over the years. Fifth, the impact of real gross fixed capital creation (LPCAP) is mixed, implying both negative and positive effects. In the short run, a one standard deviation positive shock to LPCAP reduces economic growth by −0.0003 but boosts it by 0.0021 in the long run.

8.4.9 Variance Decomposition

Variance decomposition is adopted to forecast the error variance effects for each endogenous variable within a system. In a simple linear equation, for any change in x at time (t), there is a corresponding change in y as a dependent variable (Wickremasinghe, 2011). In this study, based on the Monte Carlo procedure and ordering by Cholesky, the forecast is comprised of short run (2 years), medium term (5 years), and long run (10 years). The results of variance decomposition forecast for endogenous variables are economic growth, nominal exchange rate, human capital, total non-oil exports, oil export, real gross fixed capital formation, and government policy.

In the short run, impulses, innovations, or shocks to economic growth account for 79.9% of fluctuations in economic growth's own shock. However, fluctuations in the economic growth's own shock continuously decline to 55.1% in the long run. Meanwhile, shocks to the exchange rate account for 0.3% of fluctuations of economic growth in the short run. The fluctuations of economic growth due to exchange rate increase to 5.4% in the long run. In the short run, shocks to human capital account for 8.8%, non-oil export for 8.4%, oil export for 0.0%, physical capital for 0.0%, and government policy for 2.5%. In the long run, shocks to human capital decrease to 8.3%, non-oil export increases to 13.5%, oil export accounts for 14.1%, physical capital accounts for 2.1%, and government policy decreases to 1.6%. Shocks to economic growth will account for the highest fluctuations in Nigeria's economic growth, followed by non-oil export.

8.4.10 VAR Model Checking

Employing VAR, the model was estimated via the VECM procedure using four lags, where the endogenous variables were transformed to first difference via the error correction term. The error correction term, which indicates the long-run equilibrium, has been reported in Table 8.7, whereas the short-run relationship is reported in Table 8.8. Before discussing the findings, the VECM will be validated for serial correlation and stability.

8.4.10.1 Autocorrelation Residual Lagrange Multiplier (LM) Test

The LM test is commonly used to test for serial correlation in autoregressive model one $[AR(1)]$. The LM test statistics compute lag order p based on an auxiliary regression of the residuals of the estimated regression under the hypothesis that there is no serial correlation from lag one. The results of the LM test are indicated below.

Table 8.11 Breusch–Godfrey serial correlation LM test

F-statistic	0.190555	Probability F(4,11)	0.9383
Obs*R-squared	2.916114	Probability chi-squared (4)	0.5720

Source: Researcher's calculations from Eviews 9, 2020

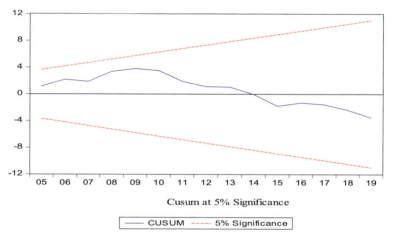

Fig. 8.4 Cusum at 5% significance

The results of Table 8.11 show that the null hypothesis of no serial autocorrelation will be accepted for Godfrey LM test for four lags since their *P*-values are greater than the significance value of 0.05 and the four lags reject the null hypothesis that there is serial autocorrelation. Hence, we can conclude that there is no serial autocorrelation since the majority of the lags accept the null hypothesis.

8.4.10.2 Test for Stability

The actual and fitted tables, as well as the CUSUM (cumulative sum) test and recursive coefficients stability test, are used to determine stability. Figures 8.4, 8.5, and 8.6 depict the outcomes. All of the experiments showed that the systems equation is correct and offers enough results for economic analysis. To check for structural change instability, recursive residual estimations were used. The CUSUM and CUSUM of the test statistics of the squares plots, as well as the recursive coefficients, are all proven to be within the 5% critical bounds of parameter stability, indicating that there is no instability. This indicates that we accept the null hypothesis and infer that our parameters are stable and, as a result, do not have any misspecification.

8 Does Clove Export Cause Economic Growth in Nigeria?   137

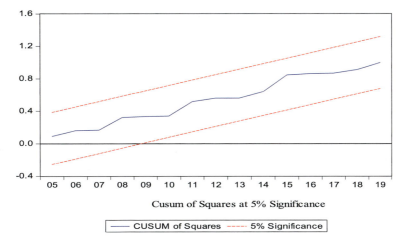

Fig. 8.5 Cusum of squares at 5% significance

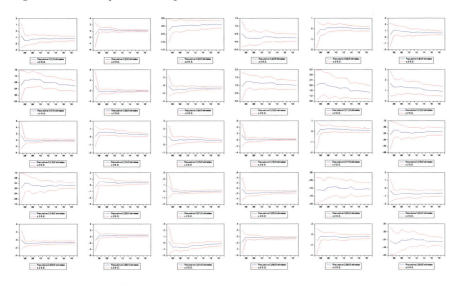

Fig. 8.6 Recursive coefficients test

8.4.11 Discussion of Findings

As a result of the foregoing, a positive relationship between LGDPPC and LNOEXP is observed, which indicates that when LNOEXP grows by any amount, LGDPPC increases by the same amount, as interpreted above, as does LOEXP. This is true because, in theory, exports raise per capita income, which ideally translates into the economic growth of an economy when all other factors remain constant. The findings support Ricardo's comparative advantage hypothesis, which holds that a country should specialize in producing and exporting commodities in which it has a comparative or a relative cost advantage over others. The fact that the labor force is positively related to economic growth in the study indicates that the country has a surplus of labor, which translates to low-cost labor. Nigeria's main non-oil exports are agricultural products and services, both of which are plenty. Similarly, the exchange rate, which is theoretically negative concerning LGDPPC growth, was found to be positively related to LGDPPC in Nigeria throughout the time under review. This is not surprising because, since the SAP period, when the Nigerian government depreciated its currency, Nigeria has continuously recorded or experienced growth. The increase in RGDP between 2017 and 2018 is a clear validation of this result. In 2017, the RGDP growth rate was at 1%, with a 305.8 naira to a dollar exchange rate in the same year, and a 306.8 naira to a dollar exchange rate in 2018. Nigeria's RGDP, on the other hand, grew at a pace of 1.9%. This indicates that rising currency rates in Nigeria have never prevented the country from growing its gross domestic product. Similarly, money supply, which serves as a proxy for government policy, was found to be negatively related to LGDPPC, even though this was not expected. In most cases, increasing the supply of money decreases interest rates, resulting in greater investment and more money in the hands of consumers, thus promoting expenditure. However, interest rates in Nigeria have stayed high. In the last 21 years, the prime lending rate of Nigerian commercial banks, which is the rate at which commercial banks lend to their valued customers, has averaged 17%. The findings suggest that the amount of money available in the economy is insufficient to lower the interest rates in Nigeria. When interest rates are high, according to John Maynard Keynes' theory of interest, it discourages investments and diminishes aggregate demand by translating into higher prices of consumable items, which is detrimental to an economy's growth. LPCAP (infrastructure) was also discovered to be negatively associated with LGDPPC, which is contrary to theory. The state of Nigeria's infrastructure, on the other hand, is consistent with the findings. The state of its roads, power supply, train, and other infrastructure, as well as the amount of money earmarked for capital investment, has never exceeded 50% in the last 40 years. This has had a significant detrimental impact on the country's costs of production.

8.5 Conclusions

Finally, the aim of estimating the economic growth equation was to look at the short- and long-run effects of clove trade (oil and non-oil) and other explanatory factors included in the systems equation on Nigeria's economic growth using annual data from the period 1970 to 2019. This was accomplished by first determining whether co-integrating vectors exist. This was also done to see whether the co-integrating series have any sort of long-term relationship. The use of trace test statistics and max-eigen test statistic vectors co-integrates, according to the findings. The long-run relationship between the series was interpreted using normalized co-integrating coefficients. According to the data, there is a long-term association between the series.

Second, the researchers looked into whether there is a short-run relationship between the series. A co-integration analysis was used in the first part to explain the long- and short-run relationships between the series. According to the findings, the series are co-integrated to the same order (1), implying that the variables studied have a long-run relationship. A VECM systems model was constructed to validate the long-run relationship explained by the normalized coefficients of the co-integration simulation. In addition, a VECM systems model for a short-run relationship among variables was developed. A VECM simultaneous systems model with six endogenous variables was created to fulfil these goals. The long-run relationship is indicated by an error correction term section after modeling the aforementioned VECM systems model, whereas the short-run relationship is indicated by the second part. However, the VECM systems model was evaluated for stability, serial correlation, and heteroscedasticity before the results were interpreted. The VECM systems model was found to be valid for policy analysis, according to the findings. The error correction term coefficient results show a long-run relationship between the dependent variables' economic growth and the independent variables' nominal exchange rate, human capital, total non-oil exports, oil exports, real gross fixed capital formation, and government policy. The fact that the explanatory variables are 6.03 in absolute terms implies the existence of a long-run relationship.

An F-/Wald test simulation was used to establish a short-run link among the endogenous variables. All endogenous factors have a short-run association, according to the findings. The major goal of this research is to see whether clove commerce contributes to economic growth. The findings show that in Nigeria, non-oil exports and oil exports both induce Granger-cause economic development with no feedback. According to impulse response analysis, oil export will slow Nigeria's economic growth, whereas non-oil export will accelerate it. Meanwhile, variance decomposition shows that oil export has no effect on economic growth in the short run but does in the medium and long run, but non-oil export has an effect in all periods.

8.5.1 Policy Implications

1. To encourage economic growth in Nigeria, the government should provide necessary financial and technical assistance to the productive sector to enable it to create enough for exports.
2. Government spending on infrastructure and initiatives that assist export trade, such as free trade zones, should be increased (EPZs).
3. The government should design and manage export protection measures with defined objectives and firm pledges.

4. Finally, it is suggested that the money supply be raised because it is beneficial to investors. When it rises, it lowers interest rates and stimulates more investment, resulting in increased economic growth.

References

Adenikinju, A. F. (2005). African imperatives in the new world order: Country case study of the manufacturing sector in Nigeria. In O. E. Ogunkola & A. Bankole (Eds.), *Nigeria's imperatives in the new world trade order* (pp. 101–158). African Economic Research Consortium/Trade Policy Research and Training Programme.

Adesoye, A. B., Adelowokan, O. A. &, Alimi, Y.O. (2018). Time series analysis of non-oil export demand and economic performance in Nigeria. *Iranian Economic Review* Vol. 22, No. 1, pp. 295–314.

Afaf, A. J., & Majeed, A. H. (2015). Impact of exports and imports on economic growth: Evidence from Tunisia. *Journal of Emerging Trends in Economics and Management Sciences, 6*(1), 13–21.

Ali, A., & Koko, M. A. (2018, August). Effect of non-oil sector trade on economic growth in Nigeria: Evidence from agriculture and mining sector. *International Journal of Humanities, Art and Social Studies (IJHAS), 3*(3).

Ambreen, F. & Abdul, Q. (2018). Modeling the Impact of exports on the economic growth of Pakistan. *Munich personal RePEc Archive (MPRA)* Paper No. 83929, posted 16 Jan.

Analogbei, F. C. O. (2000). Trade reforms and productivity in Nigeria. In *Proceeding of the ninth conference of the zonal research unit of the CBN titled productivity and capacity building in Nigeria* (p. 159). Lagos Press.

Carbaugh, R. (2004). *International economics* (10th ed.). Thomson.

Chete, L.N, Adeoti, J. O, Adeyinka, F. M & Ogundele, F. O. (2016). Industrial policy in Nigeria: Opportunities and challenges in a resource-rich country @ https://www.oxfordscholarship.com/view/10.1093/acprof:oso/9780198776987.001.0001/acprof 9780198776987-chapter-6 25/03/2020

Davidson, R. & MacKinnon. J. G. (1993). *Estimation and inference in econometrics.* New York: Oxford University Pres.

Dickey, D. A., & Fuller, W. A. (1979). Distribution of the estimators for autoregressive time series with a unit. *Journal of the American Statistical Association, 77*, 427–431.

Dritsaki, C., & Stiakakis, E. (2014). Foreign direct investments, exports, and economic growth in Croatia: A time series analysis. *Procedia Economics and Finance, 14*, 181–190.

Elias, I. A., Agu, R. E., & Eze, L. O. (2018). Impact of international trade on the economic growth of Nigeria. *European Journal of Business and Management., 10*(18).

Enders, W. (2014). *Applied econometric time series: Wiley series in probability and mathematical statistics* (4th ed.).

Fatemah, A., & Qayyum, A. (2018). Modeling the impact of exports on the economic growth of Pakistan. *Munich personal RePEc Archive (MPRA). Paper No. 83929, posted 16 Jan.*

Iyoha, M., & Okim, A. (2017, June). The impact of trade on economic growth in ECOWAS Countries: Evidence from panel data. *CBN Journal of Applied Statistics, 8*(1).

Johansen, S. (1995). *Likelihood-based inference in cointegrated vector autoregressive models.* Oxford University Press.

Mehta, S. N. (2015, July). The dynamics of relationship between exports, imports and economic growth in India. *International Journal of Research in Humanities & Soc. Sciences, 3*(7).

Mohsen, M. & Javad, B. (2016). The contribution of industry and agriculture exports to economic growth: The case of developing countries, Tehran, Iran world scientific news (46), pp. 100–111. www.worldscientificnews.com

8 Does Clove Export Cause Economic Growth in Nigeria?

Nageri, K. I., Ajayi, O., Olodo, H. B., & Abina, B. M. (2013). An empirical study of growth through trade: Nigeria evidence. *Arabian Journal of Business and Management Review, 3*(5), 31–42.

Qazi Muhammad Adnan Hye. (2012). Exports, imports and economic growth in China: An ARDL analysis. *Journal of Chinese Economic and Foreign Trade Studies, 5*(1), 42–55.

Saaed, A. J., & Hussain, M. A. (2015, July). The causality relationship between exports, imports and economic growth in Jordan: 1977–2012. *EPRA International Journal of Economic and Business Review, 3*(7).

Sayef, B., & Mohamed, M. (2017). The relationship among exports, imports and economic growth in Turkey. *Munich Personal RePEc Archive*. Paper No. 76044, posted 07 Jan. 10:34 UTC.

Sayef Bakari, M. M. (2017). Impact of exports and imports on economic growth: New evidence from Panama. *Journal of Smart Economic Growth, 2*(1).

Seipati, M., & Itumeleng, P. (2014). The impact of international trade on economic growth in South Africa: An econometrics analysis. *Mediterranean Journal of Social Sciences, 5*(14).

Solow, R. M. (1956, February). A contribution to the theory of economic growth. *The Quarterly Journal of Economics, 70*(1), 65–94.

Ugwuegbe, S. U., & Uruakpa, P. C. (2013, November). The impact of export trading on economic growth in Nigeria. *International Journal of Economics, Business and Finance, 1*(10).

Velnampy, T., & Achchuthan, S. (2013). Export, import and economic growth: Evidence from Sri Lanka. *Journal of Economics and Sustainable Development., 4*(9).

Wickremasinghe, G. (2011). The Sri Lankan stock market and the macroeconomy: An empirical investigation. *Studies in Economics and Finance, 28*(3), 179–195.

Yuna, Z. (2019). Impact of foreign trade, FDI, exchange rate and inflation on economic growth. *Global Journal of Economics and Business Administration., 3*(17).

Chapter 9
The Share of Dependent Work Income in Greece: Main Domestic and External Determinants

George Petrakos, Konstantinos Rontos, Chara Vavoura, and Ioannis Vavouras

Abstract The stability of functional income distribution, that is, the distinction between labor and capital income, was considered for many decades as a "stylized fact of growth." More recently, however, the prevailing hypothesis has been that this share is declining over time, at least in developed economies. Greece, contrary to the prevailing hypothesis of a downward trend of labor share in total income, has been associated with an upward trend of this share during the last decades. We look into the evolution of labor income share in total income in Greece in the period 1995–2021, for which reliable data are available, and our objective, in this chapter, is to highlight its main domestic and external determinants. We find that certain factors determine this upward trend, namely, the real gross domestic product (GDP) growth rate, the risk of poverty rate, the real labor productivity, the rate of trade to GDP, and the effect of economic crises that materialized during the years 2011–2016 of the great Greek economic slump and the years 2020–2021 of the coronavirus disease of 2019 (COVID-19) crisis.

G. Petrakos
Department of Public Administration, Panteion University of Social and Political Sciences, Athens, Greece

Research Institute for Tourism, Athens, Greece
e-mail: petrakos@panteion.gr

K. Rontos
Department of Sociology, University of the Aegean, Mytilene, Greece
e-mail: K.Rontos@soc.aegean.gr

C. Vavoura
Department of Economics, University of Athens, Athens, Greece
e-mail: cvavoura@econ.uoa.gr

I. Vavouras (✉)
Panteion University of Social and Political Sciences, Athens, Greece
e-mail: vavouras@panteion.gr

© The Author(s), under exclusive license to Springer Nature Switzerland AG 2024
N. Tsounis, A. Vlachvei (eds.), *Applied Economic Research and Trends*, Springer Proceedings in Business and Economics,
https://doi.org/10.1007/978-3-031-49105-4_9

Keywords Income shares · Factor shares · Real labor productivity · Risk of poverty · Compensation of employees

JEL Classifications D33, E25, F16, J30

9.1 Introduction

According to the income approach of gross domestic product (GDP), the total income of an economy sums up the compensation of employees, the gross operating surplus and mixed income, and taxes less subsidies on production and imports. Compensation of employees is the total remuneration in cash or in kind payable by employers to employees in return for their provided work. It is distinguished into two main components, namely, wages and salaries and employers' social contributions. For the purposes of our analysis, we consider the compensation of employees as the broad concept of the labor income share, whereas wages and salaries are viewed as the narrow concept of the labor income share.

When examining the evolution of wages and salaries as a percentage of GDP in Greece during the period 1995–2021, for which data are available by Eurostat

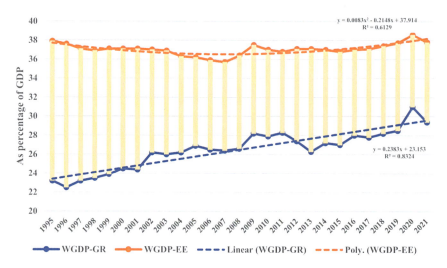

Fig. 9.1 The evolution of wages and salaries in Greece and in the European Union of 27 during the period 1995–2021 *Source*: Eurostat database, GDP, and main components (NAMA_10_GDP_custom_5720898) *Notes*: (1) WGDP-GR = wages and salaries as a percentage of GDP in Greece. WGDP-EE = wages and salaries as a percentage of GDP in the European Union of 27 countries. The vertical distance measures the discrepancy between WGDP-EE and WGDP-GR, that is, WGDP-EE − WGDP-GR

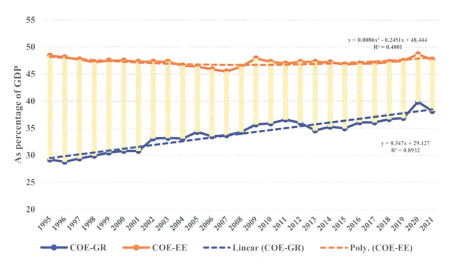

Fig. 9.2 The evolution of compensation of employees in Greece and in the European Union of 27 during the period 1995–2021 *Source*: Eurostat database, GDP, and main components (NAMA_10_GDP_custom_5814374)*Notes*: (1) COE-GR = compensation of employees as a percentage of GDP in Greece. COE-EE = compensation of employees as a percentage of GDP in the European Union of 27 countries. The vertical distance measures the discrepancy between COE-EE and COE-GR, that is, COE-EE – COE-GR

for all European Union (EU) member states,[1] we observe a clear upward trend (see Fig. 9.1). The same conclusion is reached in the case of Greece if we consider the evolution of the compensation of employees, as presented in Fig. 9.2. In other words, regardless of which concept of the labor income share we use, narrow or broad, in the case of Greece, we observe an upward trend between 1995 and 2021. On the contrary, we observe that in the case of the European Union of 27 countries (EU-27), wages and salaries as well as compensation of employees followed a downward trend till the years of the outbreak of the global financial crisis of 2007–2008 that subsequently turned into a global economic crisis, and then an upward trend. However, neither the downward trend nor the upward one was of any significant extent. Therefore, the general conclusion for the EU-27 is that the long-run share of labor in total income during the period 1995–2021 remained relatively constant.

Before proceeding with our analysis, we must point out the major problems associated with the division of total income between labor and capital, the so-called functional distribution of income. The difficulties are greater in countries with high rates of self-employment or work in family businesses, such as Greece. The essence of the problem lies in the distinction between labor and nonlabor income, since in reality there are many different types of labor and economic agents that may derive

---

[1] Eurostat database, GDP, and main components (output, expenditure, and income) (NAMA_10_GDP).

their earnings from several different sources (Krueger, 1999). Since earnings from self-employment and family business represent both returns to work and returns to capital, returns to work from self-employment and family business should in principle be incorporated into labor income.[2] To avoid the limitations of the labor income share highlighted above, we define the compensation of employees as the broad concept of dependent work income and wages and salaries as the narrow concept of dependent work income.

The objective of this chapter is to investigate the main domestic and external determinants of the labor share in total income in its broad and narrow concepts, as defined above, in the case of Greece. We find that during the period under consideration, namely, during the years 1995–2021, certain factors seem to decisively determine the share of dependent work income,[3] namely, the real GDP growth rate, the risk of poverty rate, the real labor productivity, the country's openness to international trade as measured by the rate of trade to GDP, and the years of economic crisis in Greece, that is, the years 2011–2016 of the great Greek economic slump and the years 2020–2021 of the COVID-19 crisis. The first three factors could be considered as mainly domestic, whereas the next two as mainly external determinants of dependent work income share. Interestingly, we find that the rate of unemployment, the degree of income inequality as measured by the Gini coefficient, and the past values of the dependent variables examined do not seem to affect, in a statistically significant way, the share of dependent work income within the context of our empirical analysis.

9.2 Literature Review

By definition, the labor share of income measures the proportion of total income that accrues to labor. The labor share is conventionally calculated by dividing the total compensation of employees by national income. Compensation of employees is considered a better measure of the labor share of income than the simple notion of "wages and salaries" (in cash and in kind), since it also includes employers' social contributions (employers' actual social contributions and imputed social contributions). However, as already been stated, even this measure of the income share suffers from serious limitations and weaknesses, which have already been outlined.[4]

---

[2] This particular problem has been pointed out several decades ago. See among others Johnson (1954), Kravis (1959), and Kuznets (1959).

[3] The issue of factor income shares in general and labor income share in particular and its determinants in the case of Greece has been the subject of empirical analysis, using, however, different notions of income and explanatory contexts. See mainly Koutsampelas and Tsakloglou (2013) and Agiomirgianakis et al. (2022).

[4] In more recent considerations on the issue, see Krueger (1999), Gollin (2002), Glyn (2009), and Guerriero (2019).

The issue of labor share in total income and, more generally, functional income distribution is one of the first issues that occupied both theoretical and empirical economic research emerging from Ricardo's theory of distribution (Ricardo, 1817). Since then, many different approaches on the subject of factor shares have been supported, and each major school of economic thought has developed its own theory on the distribution of income.[5] For many decades, the stability of functional income distribution was considered a "stylized fact of growth" (Kaldor, 1961; Gottschalk & Smeeding, 1997; Goldfarb & Leonard, 2005; ILO & OECD, 2015). More recently, however, the prevailing hypothesis is that the labor share has been declining since the 1980s, not only in developed or advanced economies[6] but also in emerging economies (Dao et al., 2019). Moreover, it seems that labor income share is reduced with capital account openness, since trade openness increases the bargaining power of capital vis-à-vis labor (Jayadev, 2007).

However, some researchers argue that the decline of income share could be attributed to measurement problems[7] and if labor income share is adjusted for self-employment income, indirect taxes, and capital depreciation, factor shares in total income are rather constant over time.[8] Finally, we must note that most empirical research on the labor income share issue provides only a partial analysis,[9] focusing mainly on industrialized or developed economies, covering mainly a relatively short time period,[10] and depending heavily on the methodology used.[11]

Several factors have been proposed as possible determinants of changes in the labor income share. Financialization, which is defined as the tendency of economic agents to pursue profits through financial channels or financial transactions, has been recognized as one of the main forces behind the decline of the labor income share experienced by most economically developed economies. This has been confirmed by many empirical studies (Pariboni and Tridico, 2019). Globalization and openness to trade that increase trade flows and specialization between countries is another important factor that might have significant effects on the labor share in income, mainly by altering the balance of power between capital and labor. These effects are found to be mainly negative for labor income (Rodrik, 1998; Guscina, 2006; Dao et al., 2019; Stockhammer, 2017). Technological progress is also regarded as another dominant factor that caused the decline of labor income share (Dao et al., 2019). It is argued that the skill-biased technological change caused the reduction of wage share due to substitution of capital for low-skilled labor.[12]

---

[5] See mainly Atkinson (2009) and Glyn (2009).

[6] See among others Blanchard (1997), Guscina (2006), Hogrefe and Kappler (2013), Elsby et al. (2013), Karabarbounis and Neiman (2014), Piketty and Zucman (2014), ILO and OECD (2015), and Pariboni and Tridico (2019).

[7] See among others Cho et al. (2017) and Grossman and Oberfield (2022).

[8] See among others Guerriero (2019) and Gawrycka and Szymczak (2019).

[9] See Elsby et al. (2013), Piketty and Zucman (2014), and Guerriero (2019).

[10] See IMF (2017).

[11] See Izyumov and Vahaly (2015), Bridgman (2017), and Mućk et al. (2018).

[12] See Hutchinson and Persyn (2012), Karabarbounis and Neiman (2014), and Kheng et al. (2023).

Another source of imbalance between labor and capital income shares could be the structural change in employment, which is the reduction of industrial employment to total employment, since the remuneration of labor tends to be higher in manufacturing than in most service industries (Pariboni & Tridico, 2019). Labor market institutions, such as changes of market regulations, of the extent of public ownership and of the bargaining power of workers and trade unions, might also affect factor income shares.[13]

Moreover, focus has also been placed on technological progress. Technological changes are often proposed as the main factor affecting the labor income share.[14] If technological progress is labor-augmenting, then the increase in the effectiveness of labor inputs raises real wages and, as a result, increases the share of labor income. On the contrary, if technological progress is capital-augmenting, then it increases the returns to capital and, as a result, raises the share of capital income (Guscina, 2006).

Changes in labor productivity might also affect labor income shares. It is argued that when wages increase more rapidly than labor productivity, the labor share in income increases, whereas when wages increase slower than labor productivity, the labor share in income is reduced (ILO & OECD, 2015).

Economic crisis might also exert positive effects on the labor income share since wages and salaries tend to be less volatile than profits during economic downturns (ILO & OECD, 2015). This countercyclical behavior of labor income shares in developed economies has also been documented by the International Monetary Fund (IMF) (2012). However, another aspect of the issue has been proposed: there is no clear tendency for the labor income share to rise during the slump (Kalecki, 1938).

9.3 Data, Methodology, and Results

As already stated, the objectives of this chapter are to identify in the case of Greece the main domestic and external determinants of the labor share in total income in its broad and narrow concepts, as they have been defined above, during the period 1995–2021. We limit our analysis to this period because it is only during this period that reliable data regarding the variables employed in our models following the EU statistical base (Eurostat) are available. Prior to 1995, there are no official data regarding the variables of our analysis. Our second objective is to test whether the compensation of employees as a percentage of GDP is affected by the same variables. In our analysis, we use the dependent variables expressed as percentages of GDP and not as absolute values in order to avoid any multicollinearity problems.

To achieve these objectives, we have constructed and tested regression models using the following variables:

---

[13] See Guerriero and Sen (2012), ILO and OECD (2015), and Guschanski and Onaran (2022).

[14] See, for example, Arpaia et al. (2009) and Hutchinson and Persyn (2012).

A. Dependent variables:

1. *Wages and salaries as a percentage of GDP (WGDP)*, which is the share of wages and salaries in GDP, as estimated by the Hellenic Statistical Authority (ELSTAT) and the Eurostat methodology. We have defined wages and salaries as the narrow concept of work income.
2. *Compensation of employees as a percentage of GDP (COE)*, as estimated by the Hellenic Statistical Authority (ELSTAT) and the Eurostat methodology. We have defined compensation of employees as the broad concept of dependent work income.

B. According to the above literature review and the stated objectives of our chapter, we specify the following explanatory (independent) variables that are used in the empirical models listed below:

1. *The real GDP growth rate (GDPGR)* (gross domestic product at market prices, chain-linked volumes (2010), and percentage change in the previous period), as estimated by the Hellenic Statistical Authority (ELSTAT) and the Eurostat methodology.
2. *The real labor productivity per person (RLPP)* (Index, $2010 = 100$), as estimated by the Hellenic Statistical Authority (ELSTAT) and the Eurostat methodology.
3. *Trade as a percentage of GDP (TRGDP)*, which is the sum of exports and imports of goods and services as a share of gross domestic product, as measured by the World Bank (World Development Indicators). The ratio of trade to GDP is the most frequently used proxy variable to express a country's openness to international trade.
4. *The at risk of poverty rate (ROPR)* (cutoff point: 60% of median equalized income after social transfers) as a percentage of total population, as estimated by the Eurostat methodology.
5. *The real GDP per head in euros (GDPH)* (gross domestic product at market prices, chain-linked volumes (2010), euros per capita), as estimated by the Hellenic Statistical Authority (ELSTAT) and the Eurostat methodology.
6. *The total annual unemployment rate (UNR)*, which is unemployed persons as a percentage of the labor force, as estimated by the Hellenic Statistical Authority (ELSTAT) and the Eurostat methodology.
7. *The Gini coefficient of equivalized disposable income (GINI)*, as defined and measured by Eurostat (EU Statistics on Income and Living Conditions (EU-SILC) surveys) and the Hellenic Statistical Authority (ELSTAT).
8. *Wages and salaries as a percentage of GDP in the previous year (WGDP-1)*, which is the share of wages and salaries in GDP in the previous year, as estimated by the Hellenic Statistical Authority (ELSTAT) and the Eurostat methodology.
9. *Compensation of employees as a percentage of GDP in the previous year (COE-1)*, as estimated by the Hellenic Statistical Authority (ELSTAT) and the Eurostat methodology.

10. *Period of the great Greek economic slump and COVID-19 (GESCOV)*, a binary variable taking the value of 1 in the years 2011–2016 of the great Greek economic slump as well as in the years 2020–2021 of COVID-19 and the value of 0 otherwise. We introduce this binary variable into our analysis in order to investigate whether and to what extent this period influenced the share of wages and salaries in GDP.[15]

9.3.1 Regression Model Fitting

In order to investigate the main determinants of the share of labor income in GDP in the case of Greece, we used WGDP and COE as dependent variables in our analysis. We must note that by definition, the compensation of employees (COE) is equal to wages and salaries (WGDP) plus employers' social contributions. The purpose of examining WGDP and COE as dependent variables is twofold: (a) to determine whether wages and salaries and compensation of employees are affected by the same set of independent variables and, (b) since the two dependent variables constitute different measures of labor shares in GDP, namely, broad and narrow, to investigate to what extent they are influenced by the same factors.

Let y_{ni} denote, for $n = 1$ and 2, respectively, the WGDP and the COE yearly indices, consequently considered as the response variable on the ith time segment ($i = 1,2,\ldots,27$). Let $x_{ji}, j = 1, 2, \ldots, 9$, denote the values of X_j corresponding to the nine quantitative variables defined above. In addition, let z_i denote the observed values of the dichotomous variable.

We start off by assuming that the mean of the response variable can be modeled as a linear combination of both the quantitative and dichotomous variables in the following way:

$$E\left(y_{ni}\right) = \beta_0 + \sum_{j=1}^{9} \beta_j x_{ji} + \gamma z_i$$

Using the stepwise backward elimination process, we end up with two different models of the general form in equation 1. Model 1 has variable WGDP as the dependent variable, whereas in model 2, the variable COE is considered as the dependent variable.

---

[15] We have shown that the period of the great Greek economic slump and COVID-19 significantly affected the level of total real GDP and the rate of unemployment. See Petrakos et al. (2021) and Vavouras and Vavoura (2022).

Table 9.1 Regression coefficients of model 1

Term	Coefficients	SE coefficients	T-value	P-value	VIF
Constant	28.51	4.51	6.32	0.000	
GDPGR	−0.1480	0.0404	−3.66	0.002	1.51
ROPR	−0.642	0.178	−3.60	0.002	2.34
RLPP	0.0698	0.0185	3.77	0.001	1.22
TRGDP	0.0744	0.0185	4.02	0.001	2.65
GESCOV	1.726	0.622	2.77	0.012	3.62

SE standard error

9.3.2 Statistical Analysis

In model 1, the dependent variable is WGDP, whereas the explanatory (independent) variables are GDPGR, ROPR, RLPP, TRGDP, and GESCOV. All independent variables were found to be significant at the 0.01 level. The overall performance of the model was extremely high, explaining more than 89% of WGDP's variability, whereas the basic results concerning the overall model fitting are summarized in the analysis of variance (ANOVA) table in Appendix A. The basic assumptions regarding model residuals were graphically tested (Appendix B), revealing no significant violation of them. In addition, Variance Inflection Factor (VIF) <5 in Table 9.1 concludes that there is no multicollinearity effect among the predictors of model 1.

When GESCOV = 1, a value of 1.726 is added to the constant of the model. The variables GDPGR and ROPR have negative signs, implying that increases of GDPGR and ROPR are associated with reductions of WGDP. On the contrary, the variables RLPP, TRGDP, and GESCOV have positive signs, implying that increases of RLPP, TRGDP, and GESCOV are associated with increases of WGDP. In other words, increases in real labor productivity per person, increases of the country's openness to international trade, as measured by the ratio of trade to GDP, as well as the period of economic crisis, which is the period of the great Greek economic slump and COVID-19, are associated with increases of the share of wages and salaries to GDP. On the contrary, increases of the growth rate of real GDP and the at risk of poverty rate are associated with reductions of the share of wages and salaries to GDP.

In model 2, the dependent variable is COE, whereas the explanatory (independent) variables are the same as in model 1, namely, GDPGR, ROPR, RLPP, TRGDP, and GESCOV. Moreover, in model 2, all independent variables were found to be significant at the 0.05 level. The overall performance of the model was extremely high, explaining more than 90% of COE's variability, whereas the basic results concerning the overall model fitting are summarized in the ANOVA table in Appendix A. The basic assumptions regarding model residuals were graphically tested (Appendix B) and revealed no significant violation of them.

Table 9.2 Regression coefficients of model 2

Term	Coefficients	SE coefficients	T-value	P-value	VIF
Constant	31.30	6.04	5.18	0.000	
GDPGR	−0.2257	0.0541	−4.17	0.000	1.51
ROPR	−0.618	0.239	−2.59	0.018	2.34
RLPP	0.0830	0.0248	3.35	0.003	122
TRGDP	0.1259	0.0248	5.08	0.000	2.65
GESCOV	1.989	0.834	2.39	0.027	3.62

SE standard error

When GESCOV $= 1$, a value of 1.989 is added to the constant of the model. The variables GDPGR and ROPR have again negative signs, implying that increases of GDPGR and ROPR are associated with reductions of COE. On the contrary, the variables RLPP, TRGDP, and GESCOV have positive signs, implying that increases of RLPP, TRGDP, and GESCOV are associated with increases of COE. In other words, increases in real labor productivity per person, increases of the country's openness to international trade as measured by the ratio of trade to GDP, andthe period of economic crisis, which is the period of the great Greek economic slump and COVID-19, are associated with increases of the compensation of employees as a percentage of GDP. On the contrary, increases of the growth rate of real GDP and the at risk of poverty rate are associated with reductions of the share of compensation of employees to GDP. It is worth noting that, although both models 1 and 2 share the same significant regressors, which also appear in both with the same sign, in model 2, the coefficients of most variables, namely, GDPGR, RLPP, TRGDP, and GESCOV, have higher values than those in model 1. This result suggests that the impact of those regressors is higher in model 2. Only the coefficient of variable ROPR is associated with a smaller value (Table 9.2).

Finally, we must note that in the above ordinary least squares (OLS) models, homoscedasticity has been graphically tested (res vs. fitted) in the usual model assumption checking. As can be seen from Appendix B, no evidence of heteroscedasticity was found in our models.

9.3.3 Discussion of the Results

The basic objective of this chapter is to investigate the main domestic and external determinants of labor share in total income in its broad and narrow concepts in the case of Greece during the period 1995–2021. Our empirical research has revealed that common factors affect the share of labor income in total income regardless of whether the narrow or the broad concept of dependent work income is used. These factors are the real GDP growth rate, the real labor productivity per person, trade as a percentage of GDP, the at risk of poverty rate, and the effect of economic crises.

These common features could be considered as an indication of the stability of the empirical models used.

More specifically, regarding the at risk of poverty rate (ROPR), we find that increased risk of poverty rates is associated with reduced labor income shares. This result is expected since high labor shares are generally regarded as a force toward income equality tending to suppress relative poverty (e.g., Erauskin (2020)).

Moving on to the effect of economic growth (GDPGR), we find that increases in the growth rate of real GDP are associated with reductions in the labor income share. This result is commonly linked to the effect of processes like technical progress and automation that shift income away from labor and toward capital. It can be reconciled with the hypothesis of declining income share in developed economies, if we consider real income as the sole determinant of income share in GDP.

Regarding the effect of trade (TRGDP), we find that, contrary to the majority of empirical papers on developed economies, in the case of Greece, trade appears to drive labor income up. This result is probably related to the fact that Greece mainly exports labor-intensive primary sector goods and services (like tourism and travel) but could also be driven from the dramatic decrease in imports during the great Greek economic slump years, which, according to Eurostat estimates, amounted to €20.04 billion. Unfortunately, data availability prevents us from breaking down the effect of trade so as to differentiate between the effect of exports, imports, and foreign direct investment inflow and outflow whose coefficients could differ in terms of both sign and magnitude (e.g., Doan and Wan (2017)). Differentiating between time periods (before, during, and after the great Greek economic slump) could also yield interesting results.

Moving on to the impact of economic crises (GESCOV), it appears to have been beneficial for the labor incomes share. This result is backed by the literature (ILO & OECD, 2015) and can be attributed to the lower relative volatility of labor, as opposed to capital earnings.

Finally, we find that increases in real labor productivity (RLPP) are associated with increases in the labor income share. This result implies that, in Greece, wages have increased more rapidly (or decreased less sharply) than labor productivity (ILO & OECD, 2015).

We must note that in the contexts of our two models specified above, we examined the possible contributions of other numerical explanatory variables, namely, the real GDP per head, the total unemployment rate, the Gini coefficient of equalized disposable income, and the two lagged dependent variables, namely, wages and salaries as a percentage of GDP in the previous year and compensation of employees as a percentage of GDP in the previous year. However, none of these variables proved to be statistically significant. Moreover, we examined the possible effects of some other explanatory variables not listed above, mainly some fiscal variables, namely, the actual budget balance as a percentage of GDP and the total general government expenditure as a percentage of GDP as well as the employers' social contributions as percentages of GDP and a dummy variable for the years of general elections. In this case, none of these variables proved to be statistically significant in the context of our analysis.

At this point, it is interesting to note that an important part of the existing empirical and theoretical research refers to the relationship between labor income shares and income distribution. A declining labor income share is expected to be associated with increasing income inequality. However, this relationship depends not only on the specific distribution of labor and capital incomes but also on some other factors that play a critical role, such as the impact of the system of social transfers and taxes (Petrakos et al., 2022). As a result, the relationship between labor income shares and income inequality is not as straightforward as it seems (Erauskin, 2020). Although we have shown that increases of the labor income share in GDP reduce income inequality in Greece (Petrakos et al. 2022), the opposite direction of causality does not seem to hold. That is, the variations of the Gini coefficient of equalized disposable income in Greece do not seem to significantly affect the share of the labor income in GDP.

9.4 Summary and Conclusions

In this chapter, we looked into the key driving factors of the labor share in total income in its broad (compensation of employees) and narrow (wages and salaries) concepts in the case of Greece during the period 1995–2021. We examined the possible effects of several explanatory variables listed above.

Our empirical analysis has demonstrated that common factors affect the share of labor income in total income regardless of whether the narrow or the broad concept of dependent work income is used. These factors are the real GDP growth rate, the real labor productivity per person, trade as a percentage of GDP, the at risk of poverty rate, and the period of economic crises in Greece. An interesting outcome of our analysis is that the period of the great Greek economic slump and COVID-19, namely, the years 2011–2016 and 2020–2021, respectively, was associated with increases of the share of wages and salaries as well as compensation of employees to GDP. Obviously, we are led to this conclusion because of the specific mix of policy measures adopted during this period to deal with the consequences of the crisis, which seemingly were more supportive of wage labor than of self-employment and capital.

According to our analysis, the most important factors that could support a long-run strategy of increasing labor income share in GDP are the rise in real labor productivity and the increase in the openness of the Greek economy to international trade or the strengthening of the degree of globalization of the economy. Therefore, these objectives constitute the primary pillars of the country's strategies of economic growth and income distribution.

A.1 Appendices

A.1.1 Appendix A: ANOVA Tables

Analysis of variance table for model 1

Source	DF	Adj SS	Adj MS	F-value	P-value
Regression	5	99.807	19.9615	33.74	0.000
GDPGR	1	7.942	7.9418	13.42	0.002
ROPR	1	7.669	7.6693	12.96	0.002
RLPP	1	8.400	8.4001	14.20	0.001
TRGDP	1	9.570	9.5704	16.18	0.001
GESCOV	1	4.552	4.5524	7.69	0.012
Error	20	11.833	0.5916		
Total	25	111.640			

DF = Degrees of Freedom
SS = Sum of Squares
MS = Mean Sum (of Squares)

Analysis of variance table for model 2

Source	DF	Adj SS	Adj MS	F-value	P-value
Regression	5	198.772	39.754	37.42	0.000
GDPGR	1	18.477	18.477	17.39	0.000
ROPR	1	7.110	7.110	6.69	0.018
RLPP	1	11.903	11.903	11.20	0.003
TRGDP	1	27.440	27.440	25.83	0.000
GESCOV	1	6.051	6.051	5.70	0.027
Error	20	21.249	1.062		
Total	25	220.020			

A.1.2 Appendix B: Residual Plots

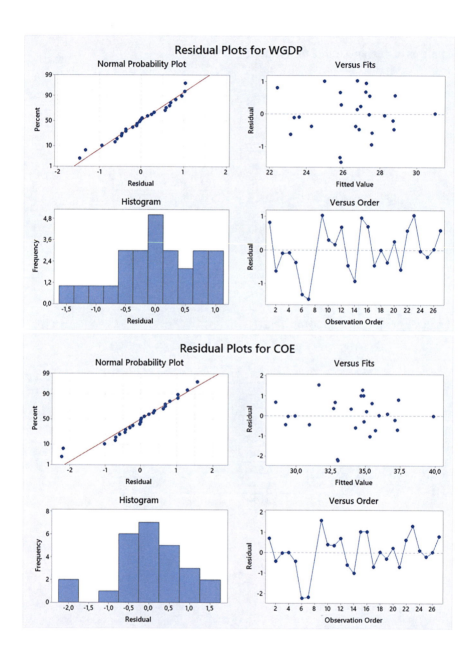

References

Agiomirgianakis, G. M., Sfakianakis, G., Manolas, G., & Grydaki, M. (2022). Chapter 2: Labour share developments in Greece: Important drivers and possible turning points. In *Essays in economic theory and policy. In honour of Professor Stella Karagianni* (pp. 15–26).

Arpaia, A., Pérez, E., & Pichelmann K. (2009). Understanding labour income share dynamics in Europe. *European Economy Economic Papers*, No. 379, European Commission, Brussels, May.

Atkinson, A. B. (2009). Factor shares: The principal problem of political economy? *Oxford Review of Economic Policy, 25*(1), 3–16.

Blanchard, O. (1997). The medium run. *Brookings Papers on Economic Activity*, Brookings Institution, No. 2, 1–52.

Bridgman, B. (2017). Is labor's loss capital's gain? Gross versus net labour shares. *Macroeconomic Dynamics, 22*(8), 1–18.

Cho, T., Hwang, S., & Schreyer, P. (2017). Has labour share declined?: It depends. In *OECD Statistics Working Papers, No 2017/01*. OECD Publishing.

Dao, M. C., Das, M., & Koczan, Z. (2019). Why is labour receiving a smaller share of global income? *Economic Policy, 34*(100), 725–759.

Doan, H., & Wan, G. (2017). *Globalization and the labor share in national income*. No. 639. Asian Development Bank Institute.

Elsby, M.W.L., Hobijn, B., & Şahin, A. (2013). The Decline of the U.S. Labor Share. *Brookings Papers on Economic Activity*, Brookings Institution, Fall 2013, 1–52.

Erauskin, I. (2020). The labor share and income inequality: Some empirical evidence from the period 1990-2015. *Applied Economics Analysis, 28*(84), 173–195.

Gawrycka, M., & Szymczak, A. (2019). Reasons behind changes in the share of labour in national income in the Polish economy: Selected aspects. *Journal of Economics and Management, 36*(2), 5–18.

Glyn, A. (2009). Functional distribution and inequality. In W. Salverda, B. Nolan, & T. M. Smeeding (Eds.), *The Oxford Handbook of Economic Inequality* (pp. 101–126). Oxford University Press.

Goldfarb, R.S., & Leonard, T.C. (2005). Inequality of what and among whom?: Rival conceptions of distribution in the 20th Century. *Research in the History of Economic Thought and Methodology*. In A Research Annual, 23, part 1, 75–118.

Gollin, D. (2002). Getting income shares right. *The Journal of Political Economy, 110*(2), 458–474.

Gottschalk, P., & Smeeding, T. M. (1997). Cross-national comparisons of earnings and income inequality. *Journal of Economic Literature, 35*(2), 633–687.

Grossman, G. M., & Oberfield, E. (2022). The elusive explanation for the declining labor share. *Annual Review of Economics, 14*. https://doi.org/10.1146/annurev-economics-080921-103046

Guschanski, A., & Onaran, Ö. (2022). The decline in wage share: Falling bargaining power of labour or technological progress? Industry-level evidence from the OECD. *Socio-Economic Review, 20*(3), 1091–1124.

Guscina, A. (2006). *Effects of globalization on labor's share in national income*. International Monetary Fund, IMF Working Paper, No. WP/06/294, December.

Guerriero, M., & Sen, K. (2012). *What determines the share of labour in national income? A cross-country analysis*. IZA, Discussion Paper No. 6643, June.

Guerriero, M. (2019). *The labor share of income around the world: evidence from a panel dataset*. In G. Fields & S. Paul (Eds.), *Labor income share in Asia* (ADB Institute Series on Development Economics) (pp. 39–79). Springer.

Hogrefe, J., & Kappler, M. (2013). The labour share income: Heterogeneous causes for parallel movements? *Journal of Economic Inequality, 11*, 303–319.

Hutchinson, J., & Persyn, D. (2012). Globalisation, concentration and footloose firms: In search of the main cause of the declining labour share. *Review of World Economics, 148*(1), 17–43.

International Labour Organization and Organization for Economic Co-operation and Development (ILO and OECD) (2015). *The Labour Share in G20 Economies*. Report prepared for the G20 Employment Working Group, Antalya, Turkey, 26–27 February 2015.

International Monetary Fund (IMF). (2017). Understanding the downward trend in labour income shares, Chapter 3, *World Economic Outlook: Gaining Momentum?* Washington, April.

International Monetary Fund (IMF). (2012). *World economic outlook: Growth resuming, dangers remain.* Washington, April.

Izyumov, A., & Vahaly, J. (2015). Income shares revisited. *Review of Income and Wealth, 61*(1), 179–188.

Jayadev, A. (2007). Capital account openness and the labour share of income. *Cambridge Journal of Economics, 33*(3), 423–443.

Johnson, D. G. (1954). The functional distribution of income in the United States, 1850–1952. *The Review of Economics and Statistics, 36*(2), 175–182.

Kaldor, N. (1961). Chapter 10: Capital Accumulation and Economic Growth. In F. A. Lutz & D. C. Hague (Eds.), *The Theory of Capital* (pp. 177–222). St. Martin's Press.

Kalecki, M. (1938). The determinants of distribution of the national income. *Econometrica, 6*(2), 97–112.

Karabarbounis, L., & Neiman, B. (2014). The global decline of the labor share. *The Quarterly Journal of Economics, 129*(1), 61–103.

Kheng, V., Mckinley, J., & Pan, L. (2023). The decline of labour share in OECD and non-OECD since the 1980s. *Applied Economics*. https://doi.org/10.1080/00036846.2023.2177604

Koutsampelas, C., & Tsakloglou, P. (2013). The distribution of full income in Greece. *International Journal of Social Economics, 40*(4), 311–330.

Kravis, I. B. (1959). Relative income shares in fact and theory. *The American Economic Review, 49*(5), 917–949.

Krueger, A. B. (1999). Measuring labor's share. *The American Economic Review, 89*(2), 45–51.

Kuznets, S. (1959). Quantitative aspects of the economic growth of nations: IV. Distribution of national income by factor shares. *Economic Development and Cultural Change*, 7(3), Part 2, 1-100.

Mućk, J., McAdam, P., & Growiec, J. (2018). Will the "true" labor share stand up? An applied survey on labor share measures. *Journal of Economic Surveys, 32*(4), 961–984.

Pariboni, R., & Tridico, P. (2019). Labour share decline, financialisation and structural change. *Cambridge Journal of Economics, 43*(4), 1073–1102.

Petrakos, G., Rontos, K., Salvati, L., Vavoura, C., & Vavouras, I. (2021). Political budget cycles and the effects of the excessive deficit procedure: The case of Greece. *Regional Statistics, 11*(2), 1–20.

Petrakos, G., Rontos, K., Vavoura, C., & Vavouras, I. (2022). Quantifying the effects of recent economic and fiscal crises on income inequality in Greece. In *Advances in Empirical Economic Research, Springer Proceedings in Business and Economics*, International Conference in Applied Economics (ICOAE) 2022, Chapter 28, forthcoming.

Piketty, T., & Zucman, G. (2014). Capital is back: Wealth-income ratios in rich countries 1700-2010. *The Quarterly Journal of Economics, 129*(3), 1255–1310.

Ricardo, D. (1817). *On the principles of political economy and taxation.* John Murray.

Rodrik, D. (1998). Has globalization gone too far? *Challenge, 41*(2), 81–94.

Stockhammer, E. (2017). Determinants of the wage share: A panel analysis of advanced and developing economies. *British Journal of Industrial Relations, 55*(1), 3–33.

Vavouras, I., & Vavoura, C. (2022). Income inequality and poverty in Greece during the recent economic, fiscal, and Covid-19 crises. *Social Cohesion and Development,* March, 17(1), 5-21.

Chapter 10
Export-Led and Import-Led Growth Hypotheses: Empirical Evidence from Greece

Melina Dritsaki and Chaido Dritsaki

Abstract This chapter examines the impact of exports and imports on economic growth in Greece alongside empirical analysis of the export-led growth hypothesis (ELGH), the import-led growth hypothesis (ILGH), the growth-led export hypothesis (GLEH), and the growth-led import hypothesis (GLIH), both in the short and long run. To analyze these hypotheses, we used Johansen's approach to examine whether there is a long-run equilibrium relationship between the variables, the vector error correction model (VECM) to discover how variables behave in the long and short run, and the Granger causality test for the direction of the behavior of variables. The results of this study show that there is a long-run relationship between the variables. The results of the controls show evidence to favor the case for export-led growth in the long run and import-led growth in the short run but not in the long run.

Keywords Export · Economic growth · Imports · Foreign direct investment · Government expenditure · Co-integration · Granger causality · Variance decomposition (VDC · Impulse response function (IRF) · Greece

JEL Classifications C32, E62, F43, J38

M. Dritsaki (✉)
Department of Economics, University of Western Macedonia, Kastoria, Greece
e-mail: mdritsaki@uowm.gr

C. Dritsaki
Department of Accounting and Finance, University of Western Macedonia, Kila Kozanis, Kozani, Greece
e-mail: cdritsaki@uowm.gr

© The Author(s), under exclusive license to Springer Nature Switzerland AG 2024
N. Tsounis, A. Vlachvei (eds.), *Applied Economic Research and Trends*, Springer Proceedings in Business and Economics,
https://doi.org/10.1007/978-3-031-49105-4_10

10.1 Introduction

It is widely accepted among economists that economic development is an extremely complex process, which depends on many variables such as capital accumulation (physical and human), trade, investments, price fluctuations, government spending, political conditions, income distribution, and even geographical characteristics.

The export-led growth hypothesis (ELGH) argues that the expansion of exports is one of the main determinants of growth. Overall development of countries occurs not only by increasing the amounts of labor and capital within the economy but also by expanding exports. According to this view, exports can act as an "engine of growth."

The relationship between exports and growth is often attributed to the potential positive externalities of the domestic economy resulting from its participation in world markets. However, these mechanisms are frequently invoked without any theoretical support or any empirical proof.

A considerable amount of research on the ELGH has been carried out over the past 30 years. A key aspect concerning early studies relates to both the methodology and the econometric technique used. In fact, during the 1990s, a new series of empirical studies were conducted with different methodologies, time periods, and countries. The theoretical benchmark can be considered generally weak and is based on bivariate and ad hoc production functions, whereas the empirical results obtained from traditional econometrics have been criticized as spurious. Therefore, these studies could have been misleading, in that they supported the expansion of exports in an indiscriminate way.

The ELGH has been proposed by many researchers using different econometric techniques. In general, the recent empirical literature has shown that causality relations vary depending on the period of the study, the use of econometric methods, the treatment of variables (nominal or real), the presence of other relevant variables, or the inclusion of variables in the estimated equation. For example, the role of foreign trade in economic growth has been a critical debate among economists for decades. Classical economists see the relationship between foreign trade and economic growth optimistically. Smith (1977) perceived international trade as a key element in creating an opportunity for a country through specialization, division of labor, and surplus production efficiencies.

The impact of exports and imports on economic growth has been a critical topic of debate and research among academics and policymakers for decades. Most studies demonstrate the theoretical relationship between trade and economic growth, disagreeing with the magnitude of effects and causal direction (Edwards, 1998). Most of the previous studies exclusively focused on the role of exports in economic growth and used bivariate causal models that ignored the contributions of imports (Rahmaddi & Ichihashi, 2011). Imports play a critical role in economic growth in the long run, since significant export growth is usually associated with rapid growth in imports (Rodrik, 1999). Empirical results on the relationship between exports and economic growth can be spurious, resulting in misleading conclusions if the model excludes imports (Esfahani, 1991). In addition, the role of exports in economic growth analysis that excludes imports may suffer from omitted variable biases, leading to an overstatement of the dynamic relationship between exports and economic growth.

Government spending can be a useful economic policy tool for governments. Fiscal policy can be defined as the use of government spending and/or taxation as a mechanism to influence an economy. There are two types of fiscal policies: expansionary fiscal policy and contractionary fiscal policy. Expansionary fiscal policy is increasing government spending or reducing taxation, whereas contractionary fiscal policy is reducing government spending or increasing taxes. Expansionary fiscal policy can be used by governments to stimulate the economy during a recession. For example, an increase in government spending directly increases the demand for goods and services, which can contribute to an increase in output and employment. On the other hand, contractionary fiscal policy can be used by governments to ease the economy during an economic boom. Reducing government spending can help control inflation.

10.1.1 Research Questions and Hypotheses

The research questions and hypothesis testing to be examined regarding the correlation between export and import growth for Greece are the following:

RQ1: Do exports cause economic growth in Greece? Export-led growth (ELG)
H01: Exports do not cause economic growth in Greece.
Ha1: Exports cause economic growth in Greece.
RQ2: Does economic growth cause exports in Greece? Growth-led exports (GLEs)
H01: Economic growth does not cause exports in Greece.
Ha1: Economic growth causes exports in Greece
RQ3: Do imports cause economic growth in Greece? Import-led growth (ILG)
H01: Imports do not cause economic growth in Greece.
Ha1: Imports cause economic growth in Greece
RQ4: Does economic growth cause imports in Greece? Growth-led imports (GLIs)
H01: Economic growth does not cause imports in Greece.
Ha1: Economic growth causes imports in Greece

This chapter contributes to the existing literature in the following ways: First, it focuses on a European Union (EU) country that, after the memorandums, the global financial crisis, and the pandemic, is experiencing a rapid growth, the highest of the EU countries. Second, employing the traditional neoclassical growth model, this chapter estimates the impact of both exports and imports on economic growth. Third, this chapter uses, in addition to exports and imports, foreign direct investment (FDI) as a control variable, as an increase in foreign direct investment can be linked to the improvement of technology and is expected to have a positive impact on economic growth. Furthermore, government spending, including all government consumption, investments, and transfer payments, which are expected to have a positive impact on economic growth, are all included in the model. Fourth, as empirical results using causality are sensitive to unit roots and lags (Xu, 1998), we used the Dickey–Fuller and Phillips–Peron tests. Fifth, this study examines the short- and long-run dynamic relations among the relevant variables within an error correction framework. Finally, impulse response function (IRF) and variance decomposition examine the configuration of the endogenous variables of the vector error correction model (VECM) from a structural change of a standard deviation of the innovation term in the equation itself or other equations of the system.

This chapter contributes to the existing research by providing a new analysis of exports, imports, and economic growth in the Greek economy. The remainder of this chapter is organized as follows: Section 10.2 presents a literature review in relation to the topic under investigation. Section 10.3 presents the data and Sect. 10.4 the methodology and results. Section 10.5 presents a discussion. Finally, Sect. 10.6 presents the conclusions and limitations of this study.

10.2 Literature Review

Economic growth is one of the most important indicators of a country's well-being. Economists interpret the fluctuations of economic growth from the relationship between trade (exports and imports) and economic growth. Exports are one of the most significant sources of foreign income because they create employment opportunities and therefore income. Imports also play an important role in boosting economic growth when managed properly. They can also generate overall economic growth as they provide local businesses with access to foreign technologies and knowledge. In addition, imports have a positive effect on productivity growth through innovation and research (Hashem & Masih, 2014).

The allegation that justifies the role of international trade in economic growth is nothing new. The classical economic theories of Adam Smith and David Ricardo argue that international trade is the key factor in economic growth. Nevertheless, Smith and Ricardo's theories did not exactly specify what factors would give a country a trade advantage.

In order to overcome the shortcomings in these theories, the economic theories of the twentieth century were developed to explain international trade in more detail. More specifically, Heckscher (1919) focused on his work on how a country could gain comparative advantage by producing products that utilize their abundant factor of production. Moreover, economic theory states that trade between countries is not a win–loss situation, but each country is improving (Mankiw, 2016).

However, in the last decade, there has been a surprising and impressive resumption of activity in the literature on economic growth triggered by endogenous growth theory, leading to an extensive inventory of models that emphasize the importance of trade in achieving sustainable economic growth. These models have focused on different variables, such as degree of openness, real exchange rate, tariffs, terms of trade, and export performance, to verify the hypothesis (see Edwards 1998).

Empirical work on the causal relationship between exports, imports, and economic growth has attracted many researchers' attention in recent decades (see Awokuse, 2007; Hagemejer & Muck, 2019; Arteaga et al., 2020). The causal relationship between exports, imports, and economic growth shows that the dynamic relationship between these three variables produces mixed results. Differences in the results can be explained by the sampling period used, the methodologies applied, and the different countries under examination.

Ghartey's analysis (1993) studied the causal relationship between exports and economic growth for the case of Taiwan, the United States, and Japan using the vector autoregression (VAR) approach. The results of his work showed that an increase in exports is causing economic growth in Taiwan and economic growth is causing exports to the United States to increase. Furthermore, this study highlighted that a bidirectional causal relationship exists between exports and economic growth in Japan.

Islam (1998) used a multivariate vector error correction model (VECM) to examine the causal relationship between exports and economic growth in 15 Asian countries between 1967 and 1991. The results of his work showed that a long-run equilibrium relationship exists between exports and gross domestic product (GDP) in five countries: Bangladesh, India, Nepal, Sri Lanka, and Fiji.

Ronit and Divya (2014) analyzed the relationship between exports and GDP growth in the case of India using annual data for the period between 1969 and 2012. To achieve this goal, they used a VAR model, the Granger causality test, and an impulse response function (IRF). The results of their work rejected the assumption that growth is driven by exports.

Bakari and Mabrouki (2017) investigated the relationship between exports, imports, and economic growth in Panama. The data were tested using Johansen co-integration, VAR model analysis, and the Granger causality test. The results of their work showed that there is no co-integrated relationship between exports, imports, and growth. The Granger causality test showed a strong bidirectional causality between imports and economic growth as well as between exports and economic growth.

Najaf and Ye (2018) examined the impact of foreign direct investment (FDI) on economic growth in Sri Lanka, Pakistan, the Philippines, and Thailand using panel data for the period 1990–2014. In their work, they applied the Johansen co-integration test and vector error correction model analysis as evaluation techniques. Their results showed that there is a positive, significant, and long-run link between FDI and economic growth. Their results also revealed that there is a long-run Granger causality from foreign direct investment, gross capital formation, government consumption, trade openness, and labor toward gross domestic product.

Zahra and Hassouneh (2019) explored the relationship between exports, imports, and economic growth for the Palestinian economy in the period 2000–2018, using quarterly data. To analyze their work, they used Johansen's approach as well as the vector error correction technique. Their findings confirmed the presence of a long-run equilibrium relationship between exports, imports, and production growth. Their results also supported the existence of bidirectional long-run causality between exports, imports, and production growth. In terms of short-run causality, their findings suggested that exports are driven by imports and that imports trigger economic growth.

Kumar et al. (2020), to confirm the export-led growth hypothesis (ELGH), selected four South Asian countries, Bangladesh, India, Pakistan, and Sri Lanka, and used the panel unit root, panel autoregressive distributed lag (ARDL), and an error correction model (ECM) for the time span of 1991–2017. Their findings demonstrated a significant and positive impact of exports and foreign direct investment on growth, whereas a negative but significant impact of imports on GDP growth in South Asian countries.

Schmidt (2020) analyzed the causal effects of exports on economic growth in the case of Brazil. Annual data for the years 1990–2018 were used. The variables included were GDP, exports, gross capital formation, FDI, and labor force. This study placed export-driven development theory in the context of correcting vector errors and Granger causality. Contrary to the findings of previous researchers, this study showed that neither export-led growth nor growth-led export could be determined for the case of Brazil.

Wani and Mir (2021) aimed to explore the relationship between globalization, which includes foreign direct investment (FDI), exports, imports, foreign remittances, and economic growth in India. To achieve this goal, they used the autoregressive distributed lag bounds testing approach. The results of their work showed that imports and FDI positively affect economic growth in India. On the other hand, exports and remittances from abroad also have a negative relationship with economic growth. This suggests that exports and foreign remittances take longer to extend the positive impact on India's economic performance.

Onose and Nuri (2021) examined whether the export-led growth assumption holds in the case of five emerging economies, including Brazil, India, Nigeria, China, and South Africa (BINCS), for the period 1980–2019. In their work, they used the panel mean group autoregressive distributed lag (ARDL) process to identify the causal relationship between exports and gross domestic product (GDP) per capita. The findings of their work showed that the export-led growth hypothesis has a positive effect on economic growth only in the short run, whereas other variables, including foreign direct investment (FDI), gross capital, and labor, increase economic growth in the long run.

Humnath et al. (2022) examined equilibrium relationships and dynamic causality between economic growth, exports, and imports in Nepal using time series data between 1965 and 2020. To analyze their data, they used Johansen's approach to examine the long-run equilibrium between variables as well as the VECM through which short- and long-run causal relationships are tested. The findings of their work showed that the assumption of import- and export-driven growth holds not only in the short run but also in the long run.

10.3 Data

To test both ELGH and ILGH, we used annual time series data at constant 2015 prices from the Greek economy for the period 1970–2021. All data were obtained from the World Bank's World Development Indicators (WDI). The dependent variable representing economic growth, driven by exports and imports, used data on gross domestic product at constant 2015 prices in million dollars. The main independent variables used were exports of goods and services, imports of goods and services, foreign direct investment, and government spending. Independent variables were measured in constant 2015 prices in million dollars. All variables were converted to the natural logarithmic (L) form.

All researchers, working with export-driven growth theory, have included variables representing the output of an economy (such as GDP or gross national product (GNP)) and exports as their main variables for analysis in their econometric model. Very often, the growth rates of variable data are used, taking the natural logarithm.

Some studies, however, differ in which additional variables to include in their empirical model, whereas most scholars have included only one output variable and one export variable (Ghartey, 1993; Gokmenoglu et al., 2015; Hatemi & Irandoust, 2000; Maneschiöld, 2008; Mangir, 2012). Other researchers, such as Ram (1985), Yaghmaian and Ghorashi (1995), and Malhotra and Kumari (2016), included variables representing imports, capital, government spending, and labor or population.

Many studies on developing countries (Hagemejer & Muck, 2019; Krasniqi & Topxhiu, 2017; Shan & Tian, 1998) have used in their model a variable for investment, as a substitute for the change in technology. This is because investment, particularly foreign direct investment, can be regarded as a means to improve technology for developing countries (Lensink & Morrissey, 2006).

The variables included in our model, in order to examine whether or not there is an effect of export and import growth on economic growth (GDP), are as follows:

Gross Domestic Product (GDP)
Gross domestic product is the dependent variable in this study, describing economic growth. It includes the market value of all final goods and services in Greece produced during the period 1970–2021.

Exports (EXPP)
Exports are one of the independent variables of this study. It is the variable with the highest priority, alongside GDP, as it revolves around the research question. Here, it is defined as exports of goods and services at constant 2015 prices and in US dollars. It is expected to have a positive impact on economic growth (GDP) according to economists such as David Ricardo, but studies have shown different results.

Imports (IMP)
Imports are also an independent variable. The import-driven growth hypothesis suggests that imports are one of the key sources of economic growth. Moreover,

the import-driven growth hypothesis suggests that imports can be a channel for long-run economic growth. Imports stimulate economic growth through access to intermediate factors such as foreign technology to domestic enterprises as well as the transfer of growth-enhancing research and development (R&D) knowledge from developed countries (Coe & Helpman, 1995).

Foreign Direct Investment (FDI)

Foreign direct investment is also an independent variable defined as the net inflows of foreign direct investment at constant 2015 prices and in US dollars into Greece. It serves as a control variable and is expected to have a positive impact on economic growth, as FDI growth can be linked to improved technology (Lensink & Morrisey, 2006). The latter can only be assumed for the case of developing countries. However, it also heavily depends on government decisions and policies.

Government Expenditure (GOV)

Government spending includes all government consumption, investments, and transfer payments (government payments to individuals). The acquisition by governments of goods and services for current use, for the direct satisfaction of the individual or collective needs of the community, is classified as government final consumption expenditure. Government acquisition of goods and services that intends to generate future benefits, such as investment in infrastructure or research expenditure, is classified as government investment. These two types of government expenditures, on final consumption and on gross capital formation, together constitute one of the main components of gross domestic product. Therefore, we expect government spending to have a positive impact on economic growth.

Figure 10.1 shows the variables of the model in their logarithmic form throughout the period under investigation.

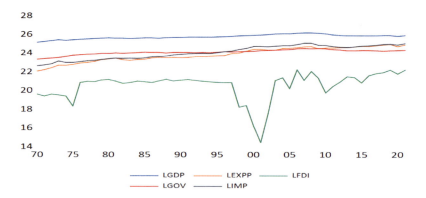

Fig. 10.1 Gross domestic product, exports, imports, foreign direct investment, and government expenditure (constant 2015 US$)

10.4 Methodology and Results

Before testing for a causal relationship between time series, the first step is to check for the stationarity of variables used as regressors in the model to be estimated. and also to test for co-integration using the model below

$$LGDP_t = \beta_0 + \beta_1 LEXPP_t + \beta_2 LIMP_t + \beta_3 LFDI_t + \beta_4 LGOV_t + e_t \qquad (10.1)$$

10.4.1 The Unit Root Test

To examine data stationarity, we used the augmented Dickey and Fuller (1979) and Phillips and Perron (1988) tests. For the case of both stationarity tests, the null hypothesis states that data are not stationary.

Table 10.1 presents the results of both ADF and Phillip–Perron stationarity tests at levels and first differences. The findings suggest that all variables under examination are nonstationary at their levels but become stationary at their first differences. In other words, the time series used for the purpose of this analysis

Table 10.1 Unit root test results

	Levels		First differences	
	C	C, T	C	C, T
Augmented Dickey–Fuller				
LGDP	−2.089 (1)	−1.664(1)	−4.662(0)*	−4.844(0)*
LEXPP	−2.597(0)	−3.102(0)	−6.219(0)*	−6.449(0)*
LIMP	−1.581(1)	−1.800(1)	−5.634(0)*	−5.745(0)*
LFDI	−2.645(0)***	−2.740(0)	−6.872(0)*	−6.801(1)*
LGOV	−2.207(1)	−3.102(2)	−4.137(0)*	−4.694(0)*
Phillips–Perron				
LGDP	−2.578[4]	−1.681[4]	−4.655[3]*	−4.895[3]*
LEXPP	−2.585[1]	−3.102[0]	−6.208[1]*	−6.413[2]*
LIMP	−1.768[1]	−1.611[2]	−5.634[0]*	−5.753[1]*
LFDI	−2.645[0]***	−2.740[0]	−6.914[4]*	−6.833[4]*
LGOV	−2.594[3]	−2.268[3]	−4.102[2]*	−4.749[2]*

Notes:
1. *, **, and *** show significance at the 1%, 5%, and 10% levels, respectively
2. The numbers within parentheses followed by ADF statistics represent the lag length of the dependent variable used to obtain white noise residuals
3. The lag lengths for the ADF equation were selected using the modified Akaike information criterion (MAIC)
4. The MacKinnon (1996) critical value for rejection of hypothesis of unit root was applied
5. The numbers within square brackets followed by the PP statistics represent the selected bandwidth based on the method by Newey and West (1994) using the Bartlett kernel
6. C constant; T trend

Table 10.2 Optimal lag length selection

Lag	LogL	LR	FPE	AIC	SC	HQIC
1	265.7135	NA	3.04e-11[a]	−10.0297[a]	−9.05514[a]	−9.66143[a]
2	285.9426	32.02946	3.83e-11	−9.830944	−7.881776	−9.094350
3	309.5546	32.46643	4.37e-11	−9.773108	−6.849356	−8.668218
4	328.1079	21.64553	6.72e-11	−9.504496	−5.606161	−8.031309

[a]Indicates lag order selected by the criterion; LR, sequential modified likelihood ratio (LR) test statistic (each test at 5% level); *FPE* final prediction error, *AIC* Akaike information criterion, *SC* Schwarz criterion, *HQIC* Hannan–Quinn information criterion, *NA* not applicable

are first-order integrated or I(1). Hence, the results imply the possibility of co-integrating relationships in our variables.

10.4.2 Optimal Lag Length Selection

Having tested for stationarity, we can determine the optimal hysteresis length to select the number of lags that should be included in both the Johansen co-integration test and the error correction vector model (vector error correction model (VECM)). The optimum lag length is presented in Table 10.2 from selected criteria.

The results in Table 10.2 provide an optimal hysteresis length of 1, based on all criteria. Therefore, this optimal hysteresis length applies to the entire model.

10.4.3 The Johansen Co-integration Test

After determining both the order of integration of the series and the optimal hysteresis length based on the final prediction error (FPE), Akaike information criteria (AIC), Schwarz criterion (SC), and Hannan–Quinn information criterion (HQIC), we investigated the existence of the long-term equilibrium relationship with the Johansen co-integration test (Johansen & Juselius, 1990) at the levels of variables to test the co-integration of model variables (1).

Table 10.3 shows the results of the Johansen co-integration test, using a lag length of one.

The null hypothesis of non-co-integration is rejected by both tests (trace and maximum eigenvalue) for the cointegration equation. Both tests show that there is a co-integration equation at a significance level of 5%.

10 Export-Led and Import-Led Growth Hypotheses: Empirical Evidence from Greece 169

Table 10.3 The results of the Johansen co-integration test

Series: LGDP LEXPP LFDI LGOV LIMP Lags interval (at first differences): 1 to 1 Unrestricted co-integration rank test (trace)

Hypothesized number of CE(s)	Eigenvalue	Trace statistic	0.05 Critical value	Probability**
None*	0.639416	116.4560	88.80380	0.0001
At most 1*	0.414709	65.45457	63.87610	0.0366
At most 2	0.301408	38.67230	42.91525	0.1247
At most 3	0.258682	20.73791	25.87211	0.1908
At most 4	0.109019	5.771606	12.51798	0.4898

Unrestricted co-integration rank test (maximum eigenvalue)

Hypothesized Number of CE(s)	Eigenvalue	Maximum eigenStatistic	0.05 Critical value	Probability**
None*	0.639416	51.00146	38.33101	0.0011
At most 1	0.414709	26.78227	32.11832	0.1951
At most 2	0.301408	17.93440	25.82321	0.3822
At most 3	0.258682	14.96630	19.38704	0.1954
At most 4	0.109019	5.771606	12.51798	0.4898

The trace test indicates two co-integrating equation(s) at the 0.05 level. Max-eigenvalue test indicates one co-integrating equation at the 0.05 level. *Denotes rejection of the hypothesis at the 0.05 level. ** MacKinnon et al. (1999) values

Table 10.4 Long-run co-integration function of VECM

Cointegrating variables	Cointegrating coefficients
LGDP(-1)	1.0000
LEXPP(-1)	−0.147574 (0.04696) [−3.14270]
LFDI(-1)	−0.025612 (0.00377) [−6.78850]
LGOV(-1)	−0.046781 (0.06370) [−0.73441]
LIMP(-1)	−0.588151 (0.03835) [−15.3379]
@trend	0.022821 (0.00197) [11.5999]
C	−7.037797

Standard errors are in () and t-statistics in []

10.4.4 Vector Error Correction Model

Since the Johansen co-integration test shows a co-integration equation between variables, it is possible to continue with the vector error correction model (VECM) estimation to discover how variables behave in the long and short run (Dritsaki & Dritsaki, 2012). As co-integration implies the existence of a long-run relationship of variables, the number of lags for the VECM are selected based on the optimum hysteresis length defined in Table 10.2.

Table 10.4 shows the long-run co-integration function of VECM. Long-run equilibrium is based on level data.

The co-integration function (long-term relationship) can be defined as follows:

$$LGDP_t = 7.03 - 0.02t + 0.147LEXPP_{t-1} + 0.025LFDI_{t-1} + 0.046LGOV_{t-1}$$

$$+0.588LIMP_{t-1} + e_t$$

$$(10.2)$$

In the long-term VECM, we observed that all coefficients are positive and statistically significant at the level of 1% (except for LGOV(-1)), according to the theory to which the variables of the model refer. In the long-run VECM, we observed that all coefficients are significant at the level of 1% (except the LGOV(-1) factor). The coefficient of the variable LEXPP = 0.147 indicates that a 1% change in exports causes growth to increase by 1.47% over the long run, ceteris paribus (keeping the other variables constant). Looking at the investment ratio LFDI = 0.025, it is implied that a 1% change in investment causes growth to increase by 0.25% in the long run. Moreover, the government expenditure ratio is LGOV = 0.046, which indicates that a 1% change in government spending causes growth to increase by 0.46% in the long run. Finally, the import rate is LIMP = 0.588, which means that a 1% change in imports causes growth to increase by 5.88% in the long run. The findings show that imports have the largest increase in Greece's growth in the long run. Therefore, we can say that in Greece, imports stimulate economic growth in the long term through access to intermediate factors such as foreign technology to domestic enterprises as well as the transfer of R&D knowledge that enhances growth. These findings are consistent with the works of Zahra and Hassouneh (2019) and Wani and Mir (2021) who have shown that imports drive growth.

10.4.5 Short-Run VECM

Table 10.5 shows the short-run VECM that is based on first-differenced data.

Looking at this table, we can interpret the results as follows. The coefficient for the error correction term (ECT) = −0.139 predicts the speed of adjustment, in terms of one lag, from the short to the long run. This value should be negative if a convergence of the short to the long run can be expected. It is interpreted as follows: the deviation of the previous period from the long-run equilibrium is corrected in the current period with an adjustment speed of approximately 14% (a factor for ECT). Moreover, the short-run relationship between exports and growth is described by the coefficient D(LEXPP) (−0.074) as a percentage change in exports that is associated with a decrease in growth of 0.074% on average, ceteris paribus. The coefficient of the variable D(LFDI) (0.0004) is described as a percentage change in investment that is associated with a 0.0004% increase in growth on average, ceteris paribus. The coefficient for D(LGOV) (0.316) is interpreted as a percentage change in government spending that is associated with a 0.316% increase in growth on average, ceteris paribus. For variable D(LIMP), the coefficient (−0.115) is understood as a percentage change in imports that is associated with a 0.115% decrease in growth on average, ceteris paribus.

Table 10.5 Short-run VECM

Error correction	D(LGDP)	D(LEXPP)	D(LFDI)	D(LGOV)	D(LIMP)
Co-int Eq	−0.139 (0.162) [−0.855]	1.215 (0.396) [3.066]	11.102 (4.255) [2.609]	−0.222 (0.149) [−1.501]	0.514 (0.354) [1.452]
D(LGDP)(-1)	0.472 (0.217) [2.176]	−0.121 (0.529) [−0.229]	2.708 (5.679) [0.476]	0.458 (0.198) [2.315]	0.640 (0.472) [1.355]
D(LEXPP)(-1)	−0.074 (0.077) [−0.963]	−0.113 (0.188) [−0.604]	−4.839 (2.023) [−2.391]	0.032 (0.079) [0.458]	−0.107 (0.168) [−0.640]
D(LFDI)(-1)	0.0004 (0.005) [0.077]	0.008 (0.013) [0.660}	0.025 (0.143) [0.179]	0.0004 (0.004) [0.095]	0.003 (0.011) [0.320]
D(LGOV)(-1)	0.316 (0.150) [2.105]	0.658 (0.365) [1.798]	3.801 (3.938) [0.967]	0.293 (0.137) [2.145]	0.234 (0.327) [0.718]
D(LIMP)(-1)	−0.115 (0.127) [−0.904]	0.586 (0.311) [1.881]	4.026 (3.344) [1.203]	−0.137 (0.116) [−1.175]	0.175 (0.278) [0.629]
C	0.010 (0.007) [1.419]	0.022 (0.017) [1.239]	0.021 (0.191) [0.112]	0.011 (0.0006) [1.730]	0.031 (0.015) [1.968]

(continued)

Table 10.5 (continued)

Error correction	D(LGDP)	D(LEXPP)	D(LFDI)	D(LGOV)	D(LIMP)
R^2	0.297	0.244	0.243	0.378	0.180
Adjusted R^2	0.199	0.139	0.138	0.291	0.066
Sum of squared residuals	0.063	0.380	43.801	0.053	0.303
SE equation	0.038	0.094	1.009	0.035	0.084
F-statistic	3.034	2.319	2.311	4.359	1.577
Log likelihood	95.59	51.038	−67.638	100.16	56.657
AIC	−3.543	−1.761	2.98	−3.726	−1.986
SC	−3.276	−1.493	3.253	−3.459	−1.718
Mean-dependent	0.013	0.054	0.056	0.018	0.046
SD-dependent	0.043	0.101	1.087	0.041	0.086
Determinant resid covariance (degrees of freedom (dof) adj.) 1.64E-11					
Determinant resid covariance 7.73E-12					
Log likelihood 284.9040					
Akaike information criterion −9.756158					
Schwarz information criterion −8.188299					

SE standard error, *SD* standard deviation
Standard errors are in () and *t*-statistics in []

10 Export-Led and Import-Led Growth Hypotheses: Empirical Evidence from Greece

Table 10.6 The Breusch–Godfrey autocorrelation test

Null hypothesis: no serial correlation		
Lags	LM statistics	Probability
1	22.49845	0.6068
2	19.52625	0.7712

Probabilities are from chi-squared with 25 degree of freedom (d.f)
LM Lagrange multiplier

These statements refer to the short-run period of the VECM. A quick summary of the short-run effects of the selected variables on the growth variable is as follows: In the short run, exports have a negative effect on growth, investment has a positive effect on growth, government spending has a positive effect on growth, and imports have a negative effect on growth. However, these conclusions are insignificant as the absolute *t*-values of each variable do not exceed the 95% confidence interval for the critical level of 2473.

10.4.6 Validity Tests

To ensure the validity of the vector error correction model, we performed several diagnostic tests, such as the Breusch and Godfrey (1981) autocorrelation test (Table 10.6), the Jarque and Bera regularity test (1981) (Table 10.7), and the White (1980) heteroscedasticity test (Table 10.8).

According to the Breusch–Godfrey autocorrelation test, the VECM showed no serial correlation at a significance level of 5% for 1 and 2 hysteresis, as the null hypothesis of non-serial correlation could not be rejected due to *p*-values greater than the significance level.

Furthermore, the Jarque–Bera normality test did not reject the assumption of normality at a significance level of 5% (*p*-value $= 0.05$), so the residuals are normally distributed in the model.

Finally, White's heteroscedasticity tests the model for non-heteroscedasticity, which could not be rejected at a significance level of 5% (*p*-value $= 0.07$). Therefore, we concluded that the model is stable.

10.4.7 The Granger Causality/Wald Test

After performing the validity of the model, we determined the causal relationships of the variables. Table 10.9 shows the Granger causality/Wald test to measure the possible short-run effects between variables.

The results of the above table show that there is a one-way causal short-term relationship between government spending and growth, exports and investment,

Table 10.7 The Jarque–Bera normality test

VEC residual normality tests				
Orthogonalization: Cholesky (Lutkepohl)				
Null hypothesis: residuals are multivariate normal				
Component	Skewness	Chi-squared	d.f.	Probability
1	−0.9211	7.0704	1	0.0078
2	0.0049	0.0002	1	0.9885
3	−0.0455	0.0173	1	0.8953
4	0.0833	0.0579	1	0.8098
5	−0.5408	2.4380	1	0.1184
Joint			5	0.0879
Component	Kurtosis	Chi-squared	d.f.	
1	4.6347	5.5677	1	0.0183
2	2.4810	0.5610	1	0.4538
3	2.9956	3.99E-05	1	0.9950
4	3.0319	0.0021	1	0.9633
5	3.0860	0.0154	1	0.9011
Joint			5	0.2922
Component	Jarque–Bera	d.f.	Probability	
1	12.638	2	0.0018	
2	0.5612	2	0.7553	
3	0.0173	2	0.9914	
4	0.0600	2	0.9704	
5	2.4534	2	0.2933	
Joint	15.730	10	0.1076	

d.f. degrees of freedom

Table 10.8 The white heteroscedasticity test

VEC residual heteroscedasticity tests: No cross terms (only levels and squares)		
Joint test		
Chi-squared	d.f.	Probability
208.0521	180	0.0746

d.f. degrees of freedom

exports and government spending, and growth and imports. These results answer the fourth question of the hypotheses posed in the Introduction section of this chapter.

10.4.8 The Pairwise Granger Causality Test

To further emphasize the causal relationship between variables of growth, exports, imports, investment, and government spending, the pairwise Granger causality test was performed. Table 10.10 shows the results of the same. The results of the table

10 Export-Led and Import-Led Growth Hypotheses: Empirical Evidence from Greece

Table 10.9 Granger causality/Wald test dependent variable: D(LGDP)

VEC Granger causality/block exogeneity Wald tests			
Dependent variable: D(LGDP)			
Excluded	Chi-squared	d.f.	Probability
D(LEXPP)	0.9282	1	0.3353
D(LFDI)	0.0060	1	0.9379
D(LGOV)	4.4345	1	0.0352
D(LIMP)	0.8178	1	0.3658
All		4	0.0481
Dependent variable: D(LFDI)			
Excluded	Chi-squared	d.f.	Probability
D(LEXPP)	4.9354	1	0.0263
D(LGDP)	0.4893	1	0.4842
D(LGOV)	0.0248	1	0.8747
D(LIMP)	5.08E-05	1	0.9943
All	7.3607	4	0.1180
Dependent variable: D(LGOV)			
Excluded	Chi-squared	d.f.	Probability
D(LEXPP)	4.0969	1	0.0430
D(LFDI)	0.5503	1	0.4582
D(LGDP)	0.0898	1	0.7644
D(LIMP)	1.1379	1	0.2861
All	5.3229	4	0.2557
Dependent variable: D(LIMP)			
Excluded	Chi-squared	d.f.	Probability
D(LEXPP)	0.0013	1	0.9709
D(LFDI)	0.0010	1	0.9743
D(LGDP)	3.8304	1	0.0503
D(LGOV)	0.3589	1	0.5491
All	5.4354	4	0.2455a

d.f. degrees of freedom

show that there is a unidirectional causal relationship between exports and growth at a level of 10% directed from exports to growth. These results answer the first question of the hypotheses raised in the Introduction section of this chapter. There is a bidirectional causal relationship between government spending and growth at the 1% level. In addition, there is a unidirectional causal relationship between imports and growth at a level of 5% directed from growth to imports. These results answer the fourth question of the hypotheses raised in the Introduction section of this chapter. There is a unidirectional causal relationship between exports and investment at a level of 10% directed from exports to investment.

Causality effects (short and long-term) show that growth is driven by long-term growth (the export-led growth hypothesis (ELGH)) and imports are driven by growth in the short term (the growth-led import hypothesis (GLIH)).

Table 10.10 The results of the pairwise Granger causality test (lags: 1)

Null hypothesis	Obs	F-statistic	Probability
D(LEXPP) does not Granger Cause D(LGDP)	50	2.9828	0.0907
D(LGDP) does not Granger Cause D(LEXPP)		2.0659	0.1572
D(LFDI) does not Granger Cause D(LGDP)	50	0.0847	0.7722
D(LGDP) does not Granger Cause D(LFDI)		0.0203	0.8872
D(LGOV) does not Granger Cause D(LGDP)	50	6.2923	0.0156
D(LGDP) does not Granger Cause D(LGOV)		7.8805	0.0073
D(LIMP) does not Granger Cause D(LGDP)	50	1.9414	0.1701
D(LGDP) does not Granger Cause D(LIMP)		5.2212	0.0269
D(LFDI) does not Granger Cause D(LEXPP)	50	0.0068	0.9345
D(LEXPP) does not Granger Cause D(LFDI)		3.4323	0.0702
D(LGOV) does not Granger Cause D(LEXPP)	50	2.7195	0.1058
D(LEXPP) does not Granger Cause D(LGOV)		2.3391	0.1329
D(LIMP) does not Granger Cause D(LEXPP)	50	0.5484	0.4626
D(LEXPP) does not Granger Cause D(LIMP)		9.7E-05	0.9922
D(LGOV) does not Granger Cause D(LFDI)	50	0.5535	0.4606
D(LFDI) does not Granger Cause D(LGOV)		0.8095	0.3729
D(LIMP) does not Granger Cause D(LFDI)	50	0.7851	0.3801
D(LFDI) does not Granger Cause D(LIMP)		0.2438	0.6237
D(LIMP) does not Granger Cause D(LGOV)	50	2.4145	0.1269
D(LGOV) does not Granger Cause D(LIMP)		1.5610	0.2177

10.4.9 *Impulse Response Function and Variance Decomposition*

VECM tests can only indicate the Granger causality of the dependent variable within the sample period and provide little evidence on the dynamic properties of the system. The VDC, by dividing the variance of a particular variable's prediction error into the ratios attributed to innovations (or vibrations) in each variable in the system, including its own, can provide an indication of these relativities and can be called extra-sample causality test (Kling & Bessler, 1985). The VDC, by partitioning the variance of the forecast error of a certain variable into the proportions attributable to innovations (or shocks) in each variable in the system, including its own, can provide an indication of these relativities and may be termed as out-of-sample causality test (Kling & Bessler, 1985). The variable that is the optimum prediction from its own lagged values will have all the variances of the prediction errors explained by its own shocks (Sims et al., 1982). In addition, impulse response functions (IRFs) examine the structure of the VECM's endogenous variables from a structural change of the standard deviation of the novel term of the same equation or other equations of the system. A change in one variable in the system affects not only the variable itself, but this change is also transferred to the other variables of the VECM through the dynamic lags of the model (see Dritsakis et al., 2021, p. 247).

10 Export-Led and Import-Led Growth Hypotheses: Empirical Evidence from Greece 177

The VDCs shown in the table below are used to ascertain how important the innovations are for predicting the decomposition error of variance. The error of decomposition of variance indicates the percentage of information of each variable that contributes to the other variables of autoregression. In other words, it determines the percentage of error of the variance of predictions for each variable that can be affected by exogenous changes of other variables (see Dritsakis et al., 2021, p. 249).

From the results of the above table, we can observe that growth explains only its own variances in the first year. It explains about the 2.5% fluctuations of export shocks in the second year, the 0.18% fluctuations of import shocks, the 0.05% fluctuations of foreign direct investment shocks, and the 2.37% fluctuations of government expenditure shocks in the same year. The export shock variable explains 30.32% of growth variances in the first year but does not explain fluctuations in the uncertainty for imports, direct investment, and government spending in the same year. Moreover, the export variable explains more than 30% of the fluctuations for the remaining years. Finally, the import variable explains 47.69% of growth variances in the first year and 12.4% of export variances. The variations in deviations for foreign direct investment and government spending are 0.78% and 0.07%, respectively.

Figure. 10.2 in Appendix A shows how the variance decomposition for all variables of the VECM evolve in the course of 10 years according to Choleski's method.

Figure 10.3 in Appendix B shows all the results of the impulse response function with the values obtained by the endogenous variables of the VECM in the 10 years since the innovative shocks of standard deviations in the innovative terms.

From the above chart, we can observe that growth has the longest positive course after a shock of the standard deviation in the innovative terms of exports, whereas imports show a shock of the standard deviation in the innovative terms of growth. Therefore, it can be concluded that GDP has the largest impact on export change as shown in Table 10.11 as well as in Figs. 10.2 and 10.3 and that imports have the biggest impact on growth.

10.5 Discussion

This chapter widely applies econometric methodologies such as the ADF and Phillip–Perron unit root tests, the Johansen co-integration test, and the VECM to test the ELGH, using data from Greece from 1970 to 2021. The results of the unit root test suggest that time series data on GDP, exports, imports, foreign direct investment, and government spending are nonstationary at their levels but become stationary at their first differences. The results of the Johansen test show a co-integration relationship between variables.

Later on, the VEC, which is specified for both the long and the short run, determined a significant positive long-run relationship of exports, imports, and foreign investment with GDP, whereas exports, imports, and foreign investment

Table 10.11 VECM forecast error VDCs

Period	SE	LGDP	LEXPP	LFDI	LGOV	LIMP
Variance decomposition of LGDP						
1	0.038	100.00	0.000	0.000	0.000	0.000
2	0.064	94.882	2.513	0.048	2.375	0.180
3	0.087	91.904	4.714	0.053	3.000	0.326
4	0.108	91.311	5.246	0.053	2.746	0.642
5	0.128	91.511	5.009	0.057	2.374	1.047
6	0.146	91.886	4.558	0.063	2.033	1.457
7	0.164	92.251	4.087	0.069	1.746	1.845
8	0.181	92.556	3.657	0.074	1.511	2.199
9	0.198	92.797	3.284	0.080	1.320	2.517
10	0.213	92.984	2.965	0.085	1.164	2.799
Variance decomposition of LEXPP						
1	0.103	30.326	69.673	0.000	0.000	0.000
2	0.152	37.581	61.668	0.095	0.646	0.007
3	0.190	43.082	55.838	0.124	0.948	0.005
4	0.224	47.099	51.740	0.138	0.985	0.035
5	0.256	49.984	48.831	0.149	0.925	0.109
6	0.287	52.108	46.686	0.157	0.837	0.210
7	0.317	53.721	45.042	0.164	0.748	0.323
8	0.346	54.977	43.744	0.170	0.667	0.439
9	0.373	55.979	42.695	0.175	0.596	0.552
10	0.400	56.792	41.830	0.180	0.536	0.659
Variance decomposition of LFDI						
1	1.071	0.189	2.1660	97.64	0.000	0.000
2	1.574	0.087	13.940	85.67	0.165	0.131
3	1.951	0.116	15.940	82.94	0.485	0.515
4	2.260	0.240	16.262	81.85	0.756	0.887
5	2.529	0.447	16.088	81.23	0.997	1.232
6	2.772	0.709	15.766	80.76	1.208	1.554
7	2.996	1.000	15.407	80.34	1.391	1.853
8	3.205	1.302	15.051	79.96	1.552	2.127
9	3.402	1.604	14.711	79.60	1.695	2.379
10	3.588	1.898	14.393	79.27	1.823	2.610
Variance decomposition of LGOV						
1	0.029	5.257	1.911	10.53	82.29	0.000
2	0.043	20.92	3.799	9.256	65.87	0.138
3	0.057	40.70	2.40	7.917	46.49	2.435
4	0.074	54.25	1.502	6.712	32.33	5.196
5	0.091	62.57	1.208	5.770	23.04	7.421
6	0.110	67.63	1.271	5.057	16.92	9.113
7	0.128	70.73	1.487	4.523	12.87	10.37
8	0.147	72.69	1.751	4.120	10.11	11.32
9	0.165	73.96	2.016	3.810	8.159	12.05
10	0.183	74.81	2.263	3.567	6.742	12.61

(continued)

Table 10.11 (continued)

Period	SE	LGDP	LEXPP	LFDI	LGOV	LIMP
Variance decomposition of LIMP						
1	0.085	47.69	12.40	0.781	0.079	39.03
2	0.134	61.26	7.767	0.774	0.340	29.84
3	0.171	66.33	5.032	0.792	1.165	26.67
4	0.204	69.42	3.615	0.776	1.520	24.65
5	0.233	71.91	2.814	0.762	1.610	22.89
6	0.259	73.94	2.320	0.753	1.607	21.37
7	0.284	75.62	1.998	0.749	1.564	20.06
8	0.308	77.02	1.778	0.746	1.506	18.94
9	0.330	78.21	1.624	0.744	1.444	17.97
10	0.352	79.22	1.514	0.743	1.384	17.13

Cholesky ordering: LGDP LEXPP LFDI LGOV LIMP
Cholesky one SE (d.f. adjusted)
SE standard error

were found to have a negative and nonsignificant long-run relationship with government spending. The long-run positive effect on foreign direct investment in GDP is in line with expectations that increased foreign direct investment is expected to improve technology and infrastructure in Greece, which, in turn, will increase productivity and stimulate economic growth. This positive relationship confirms the results of previous studies that foreign direct investment has a positive impact on economic growth. Moreover, the results of the VECM have shown a small negative and nonsignificant short-run relationship of exports and imports to GDP, in contrast to the positive short-run relationship of direct investment as well as the significant short-run relationship of government spending to GDP.

Moving on to the discussion of the short-term VECM, the negative factor for the error correction term as defined in the model implies convergence of the short-run model, which is as one would expect as the model moves toward long-run equilibrium. However, the *p*-value showed non-significance. Exports have a negative impact on GDP, whereas GDP has had a negative impact on exports also in the short run. The negative impact of exports on GDP could be explained by the low export share of GDP compared to other variables. The fact that GDP has a negative impact on exports could be due to several crises and structural changes that have not been accounted for in this research study.

Foreign direct investment and government spending have a positive effect on GDP. Compared to the long-run model, in the short run, government spending has a positive effect on GDP supported by economic theory, as increasing assets (or capital goods) increases productivity and this stimulates economic growth. The positive relationship that foreign direct investment has with GDP in the short run can be explained by similar factors as it is in the long run, by technology and infrastructure improvements. However, the interpretations for short-run VECM were based on nonsignificant coefficients, so these interpretations apply only in theory.

Later on, validity tests were run to ensure VECM reliability. No serial correlation and or any heteroscedasticity has been proved, and the model is seen to be normally distributed.

Discussion on Granger/Wald causality proceeds with the results being quite surprising; the variable of government spending seems to have a causal relationship with GDP in the short run. The results also show a one-way causal short-term relationship between exports and investment, exports and government spending, and growth and imports. However, these go hand in hand with the outcomes of the short-run VECM, which has resulted in nonsignificant coefficients for all other variables (except government spending) considering GDP as a dependent variable.

The pairwise Granger causality test was performed as a support to the Granger causality/Wald test and showed the following results: there is a causal relationship between exports and GDP, which is in line with what most studies on export-driven growth theory have found. Moreover, there is a causal relationship between GDP and imports (in this case, imports are driven by growth) and causal relationship between exports and foreign direct investment (in this case, investment is driven by exports). Finally, there is a bidirectional causal relationship between GDP and government spending.

The impulse response function and variance decomposition examined the configuration of the endogenous variables of the VECM from a structural change of a standard deviation of the innovation term in the same equation or other equations of the system. The results revealed that over the next 10 years, GDP will have the greatest impact on export change, and imports will have the greatest impact on growth.

This discussion has shown that the short-run VECM results deviate from those of the long-run VECM even though there is long-run convergence at an adjustment speed of 13.9% for the short-run VECM.

The current work answers the research questions posed in the Introduction section in the following way:

- Exports cause economic growth in Greece.
- Imports cause economic growth in Greece.
- Economic growth causes imports in Greece.
- Economic growth causes exports in Greece.

Since a causal relationship between exports and GDP was determined by the Granger causality test, the theory of export-driven growth applies to the case of Greece in 1970–2021. The same test also identified a causal relationship between GDP and imports, where imports are driven by economic growth. In conclusion, we can say that the theory of export-driven growth applies to the case of Greece and to the specific period under investigation.

10.6 Conclusions and Limitations

As shown in the literature review section, mixed results of export-driven development theory have been observed. Using data from the World Bank's database for the years 1970–2021 for Greece, the time paths of variable GDP, exports, imports, foreign direct investment, and government expenditures were first analyzed. These time paths showed a steady increase for all variables (except foreign direct investment). The purpose of this research was to find out whether exports and imports cause economic growth in Greece or whether economic growth causes an increase in exports and imports in Greece. The findings of this chapter are that exports cause economic growth and that economic growth causes imports to increase in Greece. Therefore, both hypotheses, hypothesis 1 "export growth causes economic growth in Greece" and hypothesis 2 "economic growth causes an increase in imports into Greece," should be accepted.

From the literature review, we find that the empirical evidence on the relationship between exports and growth is not strong, and although the results of our study suggest that exports have a positive effect on economic growth and could be considered an "engine of growth" as ELGH argues, their impact is quantitatively relatively small, especially in the short term.

This work is just a small contribution to development research with exports and imports. The main limitation of this study is represented by a limited number of variables. It is reasonable to recognize that a large number of factors, such as accumulation capital, entrepreneurship, innovation, learning by doing, and human capital, determine economic growth. However, in this particular case, growth was mainly driven by traditional factors of production and it was investigated whether exports and imports acted as an engine of growth in Greece.

One research proposal would be to focus on a wider number of variables, as many previous researchers have done. Moreover, future studies on the export- and import-driven growth theory for Greece could try to take structural changes into account over a given period of time by adjusting their models.

Appendices

Appendix A

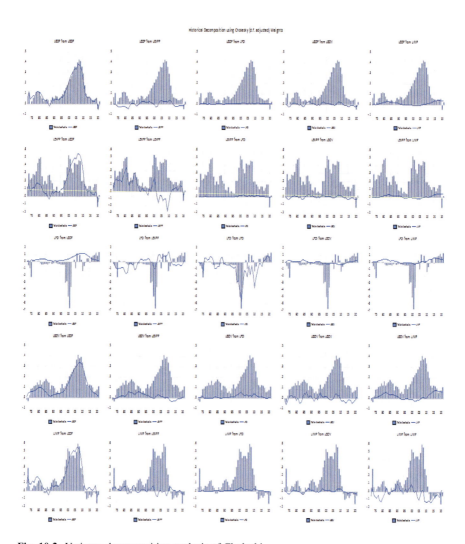

Fig. 10.2 Variance decomposition analysis of Choleski

Appendix B

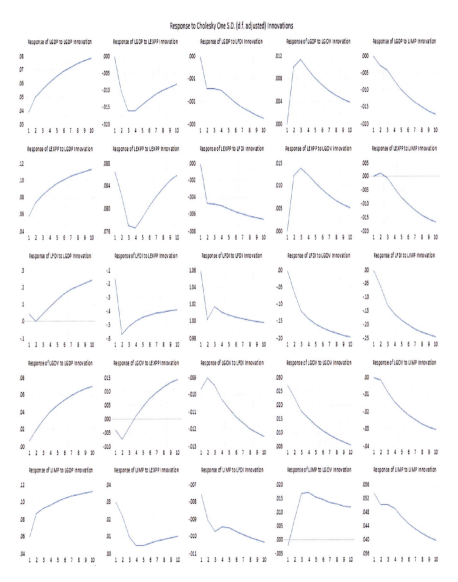

Fig. 10.3 VECM orthogonal impulse responses

References

Arteaga, J. C., Cardozo, M. L., & Diniz, M. J. T. (2020). Exports to China and economic growth in Latin America, unequal effects within the region. *International Economics, 164*, 1–17.

Awokuse, T. O. (2007). Causality between exports, imports, and economic growth: Evidence from transition economies. *Economics Letters, 94*(3), 389–395.

Bakari, S., & Mabrouki, M. (2017). Impact of exports and imports on economic growth: New evidence from Panama. *Journal of Smart Economic Growth, 2*(1), 67–79.

Breusch, T. S., & Godfrey, L. G. (1981). A review of recent work on testing for autocorrelation in dynamic simultaneous models. In D. Currie, R. Nobay, & D. Peel (Eds.), *Macroeconomic analysis: Essays in macroeconomics and econometrics* (pp. 63–105).

Coe, D. T., & Helpman, E. (1995). International R&D spillovers. *European Economic Review, 39*, 859–887.

Dickey, D. A., & Fuller, W. A. (1979). Distribution of the estimators for autoregressive time series with a unit root. *Journal of the American Statistical Association, 74*, 427–431.

Dritsaki, C., & Dritsaki, M. (2012). Inflation, unemployment and the NAIRU in Greece. In *Procedia economics and finance* (pp. 118–127). Elsevier.

Dritsakis, N., Dritsaki, C., & Dritsaki, M. (2021). *Special topics in econometrics*. Klidarithmos Publications.

Edwards, S. (1998). Openness, productivity and growth: What do we really know? *The Economic Journal, 108*, 383–398.

Esfahani, H. S. (1991). Exports, imports, and economic growth in semi-industrialized countries. *Journal of Development Economics, 35*, 93–116.

Ghartey, E. (1993). Causal relationship between exports and economic growth: Some empirical evidence in Taiwan, Japan and the US. *Applied Economics, 25*(9), 1145–1152.

Gokmenoglu, K., Sehnaz, Z., & Taspinar, N. (2015). The export-led growth: A case study of Costa Rica. *Procedia Economics and Finance, 25*(C), 471–477.

Hagemejer, J., & Muck, J. (2019). Export-led growth and its determinants: Evidence from Central and Eastern European countries. *The World Economy, 42*, 1994–2025.

Hashem, K., & Masih, M. (2014). *What causes economic growth in Malaysia: Exports or imports?* (MPRA Paper 62366). University Library of Munich.

Hatemi, J. A., & Irandoust, M. (2000). Time-series evidence for Balassa's export-led growth hypothesis. *The Journal of International Trade & Economic Development, 9*(3), 355–365.

Heckscher, E. (1919). The effects of foreign trade on the distribution of income. *Ekonomisk Tidskrift, 21*, 497–512.

Humnath, P., Devkota, M. L., & Banjade, D. (2022). Exports and imports-led growth: Evidence from a small developing economy. *Journal of Risk and Financial Management, 15*, 1–14.

Islam, M. N. (1998). Export expansion and economic growth: Testing for cointegration and causality. *Applied Economics, 30*(3), 415–425.

Jarque, C. M., & Bera, A. K. (1981). Efficient tests for normality, homoscedasticity and serial independence of regression residuals: Monte Carlo Evidence. *Economics Letters, 7*, 313–318.

Johansen, S., & Juselius, K. (1990). Maximum likelihood estimation and inference on cointegration with application to the demand for money. *Oxford Bulletin of Economics and Statistics, 52*(2), 169–210.

Kling, J. L., & Bessler, D. A. (1985). A comparison of multivariate forecasting procedures for economic time series. *International Journal of Forecasting, 1*(1), 5–24.

Krasniqi, F. X., & Topxhiu, R. M. (2017). Export and economic growth in the West Balkan countries. *Romanian Economic Journal, XX*(65), 88–104.

Kumar, M., Nargis, & Begam, A. (2020). Export-led growth hypothesis: Empirical evidence from selected South Asian countries. *Asian Journal of Economic Modelling, 8*(1), 1–15.

Lensink, R., & Morrissey, O. (2006). Foreign direct investment: Flows, volatility, and the impact on growth. *Review of International Economics, 14*(3), 478–493.

MacKinnon, J. G. (1996). Numerical distribution functions for unit root and cointegration tests. *Journal of Applied Econometrics, 11*(6), 601–618.

MacKinnon, J. G., Haug, A. A., & Michelis, L. (1999). Numerical distribution functions of likelihood ratio tests for cointegration. *Journal of Applied Econometrics, 14*, 563–577.

Malhotra, N., & Kumari, D. (2016). Revisiting export-led growth hypothesis: An empirical study on South Asia. *Applied Econometrics and International Development, 16*(2), 157–168.

Maneschiöld, P. (2008). A note on the export-led growth hypothesis: A time series approach. *Cuadernos de economía, 45*(132), 293–302.

Mangir, F. (2012). Export and economic growth in Turkey: Cointegration and causality analysis. *Economics, Management and Financial Markets, 7*(1), 67–80.

Mankiw, N. G. (2016). *Principles of microeconomics*. Cengage Learning.

Najaf, A., & Ye, M. (2018). An application of vector error correction model approach in explaining the impact of foreign direct investment on economic growth of Asian developing countries. *International Journal of Economics and Financial Issues, 8*(4), 133–139.

Newey, W. K., & West, K. D. (1994). Automatic lag selection in covariance matrix estimation. *The Review of Economic Studies, 61*(4), 631–653.

Onose, O. L., & Nuri, A. O. (2021). *Does the export-led growth hypothesis hold for services exports in emerging economies?* (MPRA Paper No. 108350). University Library of Munich.

Phillips, P. C. B., & Perron, P. (1988). Testing for a unit root in time series regression. *Biometrika, 75*, 335–346.

Rahmaddi, R., & Ichihashi, M. (2011). Exports and economic growth in Indonesia: A causality approach based on multi-variate error correction model. *Journal of International Development and Cooperation, 17*, 53–73.

Ram, R. (1985). Exports and economic growth: Some additional evidence. *Economic Development and Cultural Change, 33*(2), 415–425.

Rodrik, D. (1999). *The new global economy and developing countries: Making openness work* (Council, policy essay no. 24). Overseas Development/The Johns Hopkins University Press.

Ronit, M., & Divya, P. (2014). The relationship between the growth of exports and growth of gross domestic product of India. *International Journal of Business and Economics Research, 3*(3), 135–139.

Schmidt, F. (2020). *Export-led growth? The case of Brazil*, Bachelor thesis, Jonkoping University.

Shan, J., & Tian, G. (1998). Causality between exports and economic growth: The empirical evidence from Shanghai. *Australian Economic Papers, 37*(2), 195–202.

Sims, C. A., Goldfeld, S. M., & Sachs, I. D. (1982). Policy analysis with econometric models. *Brooking Papers on Economic Activity, 1*, 107–164.

Smith, A. (1977). In E. Cannan & G. J. Stigler (Eds.), *An inquiry into the nature and causes of the wealth of nations*. University of Chicago Press.

Wani, S. H., & Mir, M. A. (2021). Globalisation and economic growth in India: An ARDL approach. *The Indian Economic Journal, 69*(1), 51–65.

White, H. (1980). A heteroskedasticity-consistent covariance matrix estimator and a direct test for heteroskedasticity. *Econometrica, 48*(4), 817–838.

Xu, Z. (1998). Export and income growth in Japan and Taiwan. *Review of International Economics, 6*, 220–233.

Yaghmaian, B., & Ghorashi, R. (1995). Export performance and economic development: An empirical analysis. *The American Economist, 39*(2), 37–45.

Zahra, F., & Hassouneh, I. (2019). The causal relationship between exports, imports and economic growth in Palestine. *Journal of Reviews on Global Economics, 8*, 258–268.

Chapter 11
An Empirical Analysis of the Trade Impediments in Greece's Global Trade Relationships: A CGE Approach

Gerasimos Bertsatos and Nicholas Tsounis

Abstract In this work, a multi-sector computable general equilibrium (CGE) model for the trading relationship between Greece and the rest of the world (RoW) countries is developed. It is examined how an import tariff and various quotas will affect the Greek economy. To measure the magnitude of these trade barriers and how Greece's output changes as a result of lower RoW imports, the 2015 Input–Output (I-O) for the Greek economy has been used. As a scenario, quotas of 67% on energy imports and 35% on the remaining imports from RoW are implemented, combined with a 30% ad valorem import tariff. The results shed light on the fact that the output level and the domestic use level are considerably decreased since Greece is an energy-dependent country and is heavily reliant on RoW imports. When the effect of the quotas is combined with that of the import tariff, where prices increase and quantities decrease, the pollution/energy haven effect emerges, in which firms may reallocate to countries with less rigorous energy regulations and continue to produce as before.

Keywords CGE model · Greece · RoW relationship · Input · Output table · CES function

JEL Classification C51, C63, C67, C68, F11, F14

11.1 Introduction

Economic cooperation between Greece and the rest of the world (RoW) had always been a significant characteristic of their trade relationship, which is primarily driven by its exports and imports of goods and services. As a member of the European Union (EU), Greece trades extensively with its EU partners as well as with countries

---

G. Bertsatos (✉) · N. Tsounis
University of Western Macedonia, Athens, Greece
e-mail: decon00001@uowm.gr

© The Author(s), under exclusive license to Springer Nature Switzerland AG 2024
N. Tsounis, A. Vlachvei (eds.), *Applied Economic Research and Trends*, Springer Proceedings in Business and Economics,
https://doi.org/10.1007/978-3-031-49105-4_11

187

outside the EU. In terms of exports, Greece's largest trading partners are the EU countries, which account for about 60% of its exports. The most important export sectors are food and beverages, petroleum products, pharmaceuticals, and aluminum. Outside of the EU, Greece also exports to countries such as Turkey, the United States, and China. In terms of imports, Greece relies heavily on its EU partners, which account for about 40% of its imports. The most important import sectors are petroleum products, machinery, and vehicles, which are mostly related to energy. Outside of the EU, Greece imports from countries such as Russia, China, and the United States. Tourism is also a significant contributor to Greece's economy, with millions of tourists visiting the country each year. This has led to a significant trade surplus in services, which helps offset Greece's trade deficit in goods.

Computable general equilibrium (CGE) models are a class of economic models that simulate the behavior of an economy in response to various policy and economic shocks. CGE models are widely used for policy analysis, as they can capture the complex interactions between different sectors of an economy and provide insights into the effects of policy changes. A CGE static model includes a starting scenario, typically referred to as the benchmark scenario, which depicts reality before the implementation of the policy. By changing one or more parameters, both scenarios may be compared to see how the policy affects other measures and how it interacts with them (Johansen, 1960; Scarf & Hansen, 1973; Deardorff & Stern, 1985; Hertel, 1997; Dixon & Jorgenson, 2012). A CGE model of international trade includes ties with other nations, where each nation has its own set of consumers, producers, and government. The growth of a foreign sector involves the understanding of one critical issue, i.e., the interchangeability of imports and domestic products, since, in international trade, products are distinguishable by their country of origin.

In this chapter, a CGE model was developed to simulate the effects of trade control measures on energy trade and trade in general for Greece and RoW countries. This chapter will provide an answer to the question of the effect of these trade barriers on the Greek economy, specifically the impact of enforcing a two-third quota on RoW energy imports and a one-third quota on the rest of the imports, along with a 30% ad valorem import tariff. The novelty of this work stems from the scarcity of the modern literature on CGE models for the Greek economy, particularly those relating to energy use limitation and the pollution haven hypothesis. Furthermore, the research addresses the question of how the Greek economy will react to reduced imports from the rest of the world.

The rest of the text is organized as follows: Sect. 11.2 describes the CGE model and data; Sect. 11.3 describes the estimation method for substitution elasticities, presents the estimation results and those of the CGE model, along with a discussion and a sensitivity analysis; and Sect. 11.4 concludes the study.

11.2 Model Description for Greece

11.2.1 Conceptual Framework

The trade relationship between Greece and the rest of the world countries has been modeled in this study. Trade barriers are proposed as a counterfactual scenario to examine the Greek industry's reaction to lower imports from the RoW. These measures will determine whether energy-intensive firms relocate to countries with laxer energy restrictions or continue to produce and pollute in Greece. If the former is true, then the Heckscher–Ohlin–Samuelson (H-O-S) model's factor endowment theory is correct; if the latter is true, then the pollution/energy haven theory emerges, and Greece should end up using less energy.

An outline of the CGE model is presented in Fig. 11.1, including the flows of goods and services in the economy. The sector's i output (Y_i) and imports (M_i) are divided between uses (USS_i) and exports (EX_i). "Uses" is further split into two categories: intermediate inputs (II_i) and final consumption (FC_i), which is further divided into domestic and imported final consumption and intermediate inputs. Utility depends on the final consumption of outputs from all sectors.

In this trade relationship, 35 production sectors are taken into account divided into 4 major groups: agriculture, energy, manufacturing, and services. In each sector, production is based on constant returns to scale and perfect competition. All goods in the economy are traded, and, thus, consumer's utility is derived from the consumption of all available goods. In the model, a tariff on consumption and a quota on RoW imports are introduced as a counterfactual scenario to quantify the extent of the endogenous variables' response to reduced imports.

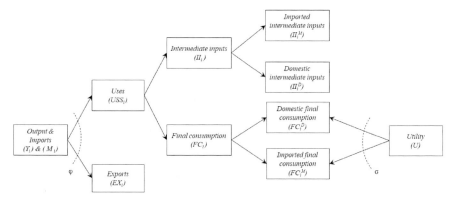

Fig. 11.1 Outline of the model. (Source: Construction by the authors)

11.2.2 Data Description

This section provides an introduction to the general form of the Input–Output (I-O) table as well as an analysis of Greek economy-specific characteristics, particularly those related to RoW energy imports. The 2015 I-O table for the Greek economy was employed for the purposes of the analysis.

The I-O table depicts the flows between several economic sectors in order to provide a static image for a given year. Each row of the intermediate inputs contains transactions from the output of a sector. These transactions are divided into two categories: intermediate usage and final consumption.

The I-O table used in this work was obtained from the Organization for Economic Cooperation and Development (OECD)s statistical office (2015). Eurostat database (2022) was used to obtain imported intermediate inputs for RoW countries. Besides, the I-O table is aggregated into 35 sectors, with production inputs for all sectors distinguished between domestic and RoW imports, yielding two 35 × 35 I-O tables. The final consumption for each source is also included in the two tables.[1]

To examine how Greece's production activities respond to changes in RoW imports, intermediate inputs are divided into domestic and imported from RoW. The OECD (2015) bilateral trade database (BTDIxE) was utilized to build this aggregated I-O table. This dataset contains bilateral trade values broken down by industry and end use.

11.2.3 Model Equations and Description

11.2.3.1 Behavior of the Producer

For each sector, a single output-producing firm selects input quantities of non-energy intermediate inputs (II_i), energy inputs (E_i), and primary factors (K_i) and (L_i). Each commodity is generated using a constant elasticity of substitution (CES) production function, with each sector having constant elasticity of substitution on its own but deviating from the others; this occurs since the substitution parameters are independently estimated for each sector.

In the model, a two-level nesting structure describes Greece's production output; nesting structures are widely used in CES functions and CGE models (Kemfert, 1998; Koesler & Schymura, 2012; Lagomarsino, 2020; Prywes, 1986). Figure 11.2 depicts a nested structure. In the lower fragment of the nest, energy is aggregated with capital and labor; in this part, we assume that the inputs are substitutes with constant elasticity of substitution for each other. Going up the nest, energy,

---

[1] Final consumption in the typical I-O table is divided into three categories: household and government consumption and investment. In this work, it is assumed that utility is derived only from household consumption, and, thus, investment and government consumption are not included.

capital, and labor are once again aggregated with non-energy intermediate inputs from all sources but with different substitution elasticities than before. In each nest, we assume that inputs are substitutes but not perfect substitutes (imperfect substitutability is assumed due to region/country aggregation).

$$Y_i = A_i \left\{ \delta_i \sum_{j=1}^{35} \sum_{k=1}^{2} \mu_{jk} II_{jk}^{\rho} + (1-\delta_i) \left[\sum_{k=1}^{2} a_k E^{\varepsilon}_{1k} + \sum_{k=1}^{2} \beta_k E^{\varepsilon}_{2k} + \pi_i K_i^{\varepsilon} \right. \right.$$

$$\left. \left. + \left(1 - \sum_{k=1}^{2} a_k - \sum_{k=1}^{2} \beta_k - \pi_i \right) L_i^{\varepsilon} \right]^{\frac{\rho}{\varepsilon}} \right\}^{\frac{1}{\rho}} \quad (11.1)$$

where ρ and ε are the substitution parameters, $\frac{1}{1+\rho}$ is the substitution elasticity between the intermediate and the remainder of the inputs, $\frac{1}{1+\varepsilon}$ is the substitution elasticity between energy, capital, and labor, i is sector i, $i = 1, \ldots, 35$, and μ_{kj} is the share parameter of the sector j input into sector i ($i, j = 1, \ldots, 35$) from source k (domestic and imported from RoW).

In Fig. 11.2, the joint effort of intermediate inputs, energy, capital, and labor to produce sector i's final output is depicted. In the model, two sorts of energy and intermediate inputs are present: domestic (E_i^D) and imported energy (E_i^M) and domestic (II_i^D) and imported (II_i^M) non-energy intermediate inputs. Here, ρ is the substitution parameter between non-energy intermediate inputs and all other inputs, ε is the substitution parameter between energy and capital–labor inputs, σ_{II_i} is

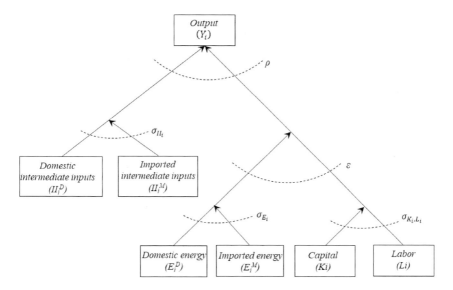

Fig. 11.2 A nested structure of the production. (Source: Construction by the authors).

the substitution elasticity between domestic and imported non-energy intermediate inputs, and σ_{E_i} is the substitution elasticity between domestic and imported energy inputs. Finally, σ_{K_i,L_i} is the substitution elasticity between the primary factors of production.

11.2.3.2 Behavior of the Consumer

Assume that the representative household maximizes utility within the constraints of its budget. The income of the household is made up of its labor and capital endowment, both of which are supplied to firms for production. Household utility is defined as the consumption of all goods available in the economy in quantity terms. A CES-type function is assumed for its utility. The following optimization problem explains the behavior of the household:

$$\max \ U = \left(\sum_{i=1}^{35} \gamma_i^{\frac{1}{\sigma}} FC_i^{\frac{\sigma-1}{\sigma}} \right)^{\frac{\sigma}{\sigma-1}} \tag{11.2}$$

$$s.t. \sum_i P_{FC_i} FC_i = \sum_v P_{FE_v} FE_v \tag{11.3}$$

Equation (11.2) represents the utility function to be maximized, whereas household preferences are characterized by a CES utility function of final consumption, with FC_i representing the final consumption of good i, γ_i being its share parameter, and σ being the elasticity of substitution. The household's utility is a CES consumption composite of agriculture, energy, and non-energy manufacturing goods and services both domestic and imported from RoW. The income constraint, Eq. (11.3), specifies that the total expenditure on the left-hand side must equal the total income on the right-hand side, where P_{FE_v} is the price of factor v, FE_v is the factor endowment of factor v, and P_{FC_i} is the price of the consumed product i.

The Lagrange method was used to resolve this optimization problem:

$$L = \left(\sum_{i=1}^{35} \gamma_i^{\frac{1}{\sigma}} FC_i^{\frac{\sigma-1}{\sigma}} \right)^{\frac{\sigma}{\sigma-1}} - \lambda \left(\sum_i P_{FC_i} FC_i - \sum_v P_{FE_v} FE_v \right) \tag{11.4}$$

The demand function (11.5) is generated for each commodity i by taking the first-order criteria of (11.4) and some calculations, as shown below:

$$FC_i = \frac{\sum_v P_{FE_v} FE_v}{P_j - P_j^{\sigma} \sum_{i=1}^{35} \left(P_i^{1-\sigma} - 1 \right) \gamma_i} \tag{11.5}$$

The derived demand function of good i is influenced not only by its own price (P_i) but also by the price of another good (P_j) as well as by income ($P_v FF_v$).

Furthermore, for the purpose of the analysis, the substitution elasticity value is assumed to be equal to 0.3, a value proposed by Welsch and Ehrenheim (2004), Schumacher and Sands (2007), Allan (2007), and Lutz et al. (2021).

11.2.3.3 Transformation

In the final phase, firms transform their output into uses and exports with constant elasticity of transformation (*CET*) technology as described by Eq. (11.6) below:

$$Y_i = \Theta_i \left(\vartheta_i USS_i^{\varphi} + (1 - \vartheta_i) EX_i^{\varphi} \right)^{\frac{1}{\varphi}} \tag{11.6}$$

where φ is the substitution transformation parameter and $\frac{1}{1+\varphi}$ is the elasticity of transformation among domestic and exported commodities. Nonetheless, exports are regarded to be entirely transformable with uses, which indicates that even if Greece stopped producing one unit of exports, it could still supply one unit of domestic use, meaning that substitution elasticity is one. Thus, Eq. (11.6) collapses to:

$$Y_i = USS_i + EX_i \tag{11.7}$$

11.2.4 Calibration

The I-O table is used to specify the model. In order to describe the model and perform simulations, we must provide parameters such as i in the utility function or A_i and δ in the production function, ϑ in the transformation function, and so on. These parameters are shown in Table 11.1. The model designed for this work contains many parameters that need to be specified. As a result, estimating the model parameters econometrically as a system of simultaneous equations is challenging since the number of unknown parameters exceeds the number of equations. Thus, simple functional forms with a few parameters are favored, with the number of unknown parameters equaling the number of equations in the model and the unknown parameters inversely solved at the benchmark equilibrium.

The parameters of the functions are determined by the reference quantity from the I-O table. Separability is essential since benchmark data from the I-O table are presented as price multiplied by quantity. By setting all prices to one, values may be read as quantity figures.

Table 11.1 Calibration parameters

Parameter	Explanation
γ_i	Utility function share parameter
A_i	Production function scale parameter
δ_i	Production function share parameter
a_k, β_k	Energy share parameter (source)
$\mu_{j,k}$	Intermediate inputs share parameters (source, sector)
Π_i	Capital share parameter
Θ_i	Transformation function scale parameter
ϑ_i	Transformation function share parameter

Source: Construction by the authors

11.2.5 General Equilibrium

A general equilibrium model takes into account each economic agent's competitive behavior. Consumers earn money in the factor market by amassing factor rewards from the factors they own, and they maximize their utility by buying the final products. Producers, on the other hand, use raw materials and sell their finished commodities on the market. Consumers or other manufacturers supply raw resources for manufacturing.

In all markets, equilibrium is not always ensured only by conditions derived from demand and supply behavior, in which agents assume that prices are given and that their demand and supply are met regardless of how they behave at given prices. As a result, for all markets to attain general equilibrium, market-clearing conditions are essential.

Two market-clearing conditions (11.8) and (11.9), as well as a zero-profit condition, are assumed to establish the general equilibrium:

$$Y_i = \sum_{i=1}^{35} \sum_{k=1}^{2} II_{i,k} + \sum_{i=1}^{35} \sum_{k=1}^{2} FC_{i,k} \tag{11.8}$$

$$\sum_i F_{v,i} = FE_v \tag{11.9}$$

The first is the market-clearing condition for goods, which assures that all demanded and supplied goods are equal. The market-clearing condition for factors follows, in which the total of the provided factors ($F_{v,i}$) equals the market factor demand. In other words, market-clearing conditions compel that the aggregate supply of each good and factor in equilibrium be equal to the total intermediate and final demand.

$$\Pi_i = P_{Y_i} Y_i - \left(P_{L_i} L_i + P_{K_i} K_i \right), \Pi_i = 0 \tag{11.10}$$

$$P_{Y_i} Y_i = P_{L_i} L_i + P_{K_i} K_i \qquad (11.11)$$

The zero-profit condition (11.11) assures that the cost of production equals the value of output; this condition is used in conjunction with the accompanying activity levels. In order to satisfy the zero-profit condition, no producer must gain an excess profit in equilibrium. The sum of the outputs per unit activity must not be more than the sum of the inputs. The model is solved as a nonlinear problem under these conditions.

11.3 Results and Discussion

11.3.1 CGE Model Results

The research' goal is to evaluate and isolate the impact of lower RoW imports on Greek output using counterfactual scenarios. We analyze Greece's dependency on RoW imports, notably energy imports, by imposing a quota of 67% on RoW energy imports and 35% on the remainder of RoW imports as well as a 30% ad valorem import tariff. Tables 11.2, 11.3 and 11.4 show the outcomes for the quota and tariff scenarios.

Because imports are endogenous in the model, they respond to parameter changes. Placing a 67% tariff on energy imports and a 35% quota on all other imports decreases output and uses in the Greek economy. The production and domestic usage of each sector are lowered correspondingly. The introduction of quotas has the greatest impact on the energy, industrial, and service sectors. Greece's own energy generation is mostly reliant on solar power (7.55%) and fossil fuel combustion (71.01%). Greece's energy imports, however, surpass its exports, rendering the country energy-reliant. Imposing a quota on its energy supply drastically reduces energy usage, forcing it to rely on its own energy production. As a result, output and, consequently, domestic consumption in the energy sector are severely reduced. Services and manufacturing also play a significant role in Greece's comparative advantage, with output and consumption reductions surpassing 20% and 30%, respectively. Decreased RoW imports, on the other hand, have a far lesser impact on labor-intensive sectors like agriculture than on capital and/or capital-intensive sectors like manufacturing.

According to the calibration specification, the implementation of quotas resulted in a decrease in all sectors. Reduced RoW imports have an influence on both consumption (through tariffs) and output (via quotas), as imported energy is the

Table 11.2 Changes in the output for Greece

Sectors	Benchmark	Quota effect	Change percentage (%)
Agriculture			
Agriculture, forestry, and fishing	46394,80	41446,33	−10,666
Mining and quarrying of non-energy-producing products	3539,40	3250,939	−8,150
Energy			
Mining and extraction of energy-producing products	3264,57	3070,034	−5,959
Coke and refined petroleum products	49806,70	40880,84	−17,921
Electricity, gas, water supply, sewerage, waste, and remediation services	126215,90	90831,27	−28,035
Manufacturing			
Food products, beverages, and tobacco	137713,40	117957	−14,346
Textiles, wearing apparel, leather, and related products	15604,70	12268,73	−21,378
Wood and products of wood and cork	20143,70	16539,79	−17,891
Paper products and printing chemicals and pharmaceutical products	40876,30	30819,91	−24,602
Chemicals and pharmaceutical products	118207,60	93921,85	−20,545
Rubber and plastic products	52755,90	39760,01	−24,634
Other nonmetallic mineral products	29829,10	23520,54	−21,149
Basic metals	83121,90	72674,31	−12,569
Fabricated metal products	77734,10	56829,85	−26,892
Computer, electronic, and optical products	46516,60	37788,69	−18,763
Electrical equipment	63755,70	50812,02	−20,302
Machinery and equipment, NEC	158896,50	124843,4	−21,431
Motor vehicles, trailers, and semi-trailers	248510,80	183234,5	−26,267
Other transport equipment	30852,70	25100,52	−18,644

Other manufacturing; repair and installation of machinery and equipment	55118,80	40296,25	−26,892
Construction	152475,80	106893,2	−29,895
Publishing, audiovisual, and broadcasting activities	40278,00	28328,725	−29,667
Services			
Mining support service activities	60524,13	60450,9	−0,121
Wholesale and retail trade; repair of motor vehicles	219266,20	148954,1	−32,067
Transportation and storage	232156,87	161650,8	−30,370
Accommodation and food services	47733,60	33277,48	−30,285
Telecommunications	47441,29	33108,8	−30,211
IT and other information services	60111,27	41684,76	−30,654
Financial and insurance activities	178716,70	122571,1	−31,416
Real estate activities	134570,58	91494,54	−32,010
Other business sector services	252403,69	173166,6	−31,393
Public administration and defense; compulsory social security	105912,12	72568,87	−31,482
Education	49348,76	33697,3	−31,716
Human health and social work	102087,54	70230,1	−31,206
Arts, entertainment, recreation, and other service activities	57517,25	39633,987	−31,092

Source: Estimated by the authors

NEC not elsewhere classified, *IT* information technology

Table 11.3 Greece's domestic use changes

Sectors	Benchmark	Quota effect	Change percentage (%)
Agriculture			
Agriculture, forestry, and fishing	44.295	39350,07	−11,164
Mining and quarrying of non-energy-producing products	3.299	3011,116	−8730
Energy			
Mining and extraction of energy-producing products	3.261	3066,549	−5965
Coke and refined petroleum products	43.545	36869,83	−15,330
Electricity, gas, water supply, sewerage, waste, and remediation services	126.195	90811,4	−28,139
Manufacturing			
Food products, beverages, and tobacco	135.042	115300,4	−14,619
Textiles, wearing apparel, leather, and related products	14.955	11627,43	−22,249
Wood and products of wood and cork	20.090	16486,97	−17,936
Paper products and printing chemicals and pharmaceutical products	40.703	30649,06	−24,700
Chemicals and pharmaceutical products	116.433	92168,62	−20,840
Rubber and plastic products	52.170	39184,16	−24,891
Other nonmetallic mineral products	29.344	23042,16	−21,477
Basic metals	80.774	70337,47	−12,921
Fabricated metal products	77.122	56230,54	−27,089
Computer, electronic, and optical products	46.263	37537,24	−18,861
Electrical equipment	63.364	50425,36	−20,420
Machinery and equipment, NEC	158.251	124206,2	−21,513
Motor vehicles, trailers, and semi-trailers	248.463	183186,6	−26,272
Other transport equipment	30.660	24909,46	−18,755

Other manufacturing; repair and installation of machinery and equipment	54.719	39904,67	−27,073
Construction	152.482	106896,2	−29,796
Publishing, audiovisual, and broadcasting activities	40.183	28236,4	−29,731
Services			
Mining support service activities	60.515	60442,14	−0,119
Wholesale and retail trade; repair of motor vehicles	215.056	144838,2	−32,651
Transportation and storage	220.233	150070,8	−31,858
Accommodation and food services	47.720	33264,24	−30,293
Telecommunications	47.133	32809,57	−30,390
IT and other information services	59.729	41313,51	−30,832
Financial and insurance activities	177.983	121854,5	−31,536
Real estate activities	134.551	91475,81	−32,714
Other business sector services	251.435	172227,6	−31,502
Public administration and defense; compulsory social security	105.894	72551,19	−31,487
Education	49.289	33639,09	−31,751
Human health and social work	102.086	70229,14	−31,206
Arts, entertainment, recreation, and other service activities	57.485	39602,464	−31,108

Source: Estimated by the authors

NEC not elsewhere classified, IT information technology

Table 11.4 Household consumption and price changes

Sector	Benchmark	Price percentage (%) change	Quantity percentage (%) change	Tariff effect on household consumption
Agriculture				
Agriculture, forestry, and fishing	3801,9	0,618	−30,002	2661,253
Mining and quarrying of non-energy-producing products	7,8	1,035	−15,132	6,6197
Energy				
Mining and extraction of energy-producing products	4,7	0,298	−12,485	4,113
Coke and refined petroleum products	2746,1	0,375	−22,208	2136,246
Electricity, gas, water supply, sewerage, waste, and remediation services	3001,4	1,626	−34,552	1964,356
Manufacturing				
Food products, beverages, and tobacco	10569,9	1,054	−31,640	7225,584
Textiles, wearing apparel, leather, and related products	643,0	1,308	−11,113	571,543
Wood and products of wood and cork	16,6	0,836	−17,732	13,656
Paper products and printing chemicals and pharmaceutical products	311,3	1,078	−16,014	261,448
Chemicals and pharmaceutical products	565,1	1,752	−17,306	467,306
Rubber and plastic products	105,4	0,353	−19,589	84,753
Other nonmetallic mineral products	172,6	0,801	−10,872	153,835
Basic metals	96,4	0,57	−15,156	81,790
Fabricated metal products	372,5	0,580	−14,439	318,715
Computer, electronic, and optical products	140,8	1,530	−13,722	121,479
Electrical equipment	281,9	0,848	−13,006	245,237
Machinery and equipment, NEC	46,1	1,580	−12,289	40,435
Motor vehicles, trailers, and semi-trailers	126,2	1,918	−11,572	111,596

Other transport equipment	106,1	0,344	−10,856	94,582
Other manufacturing; repair and installation of machinery and equipment	411,7	1,308	−10,139	369,958
Construction	166,1	2,164	−37,422	103,942
Publishing, audiovisual, and broadcasting activities	443,8	1,153	−36,706	280,901
Services				
Mining support service activities	102,5	0,161	−7,989	94,311
Wholesale and retail trade; repair of motor vehicles	13712,8	1,787	−29,272	9698,759
Transportation and storage	5260,7	2,063	−6,556	4915,832
Accommodation and food services	14471,7	1,681	−5,839	13626,714
Telecommunications	3951,5	0,471	−5,122	3749,095
IT and other information services	5,9	1,271	−4,406	5,640
Financial and insurance activities	2399,7	1,896	−3,689	2311,178
Real estate activities	22012,7	2,582	−28,972	15635,132
Other business sector services	1967,9	2,100	−7,256	1825,118
Public administration and defense; compulsory social security	518,3	2,525	−9,539	468,860
Education	1453,7	1,930	−11,822	1281,840
Human health and social work	9626,7	2,057	−5,106	9135,203
Arts, entertainment, recreation, and other service activities	4095,6	1,925	−13,611	3538,143

Source: Estimated by the authors

Note: In the benchmark equilibrium, prices are fixed to unity *NEC* not elsewhere classified, *IT* information technology backbone of the Greek economy. By fitting the elasticity of substitution values[2] in the model, we get the following results:

Tables 11.2 and 11.3 show the results of the introduction of quotas on RoW imports in terms of output and domestic usage. Greece's overall energy consumption falls in tandem with the continuous decline in RoW imports. In terms of output, the "Electricity, gas, water supply, sewerage, waste, and remediation services" sector has had the most substantial decrease (-28.035%). The drop in this sector was the most pronounced since electricity and gas are the most often used power sources in Greece's manufacturing activity, which are mostly provided by RoW imports. Construction and publishing, audiovisual, and broadcasting industries have had the biggest decreases in the manufacturing sector, with $-29,895\%$ and $-29,667\%$ declines, respectively. As Greece's construction index and publishing activities have grown in recent years, both sectors have become the most energy- and import-demanding and consequently, suffer the most. The services industry is Greece's source of comparative advantage, since it uses both domestic and foreign inputs from the rest of the world. "Wholesale and retail trade; repair of motor vehicles" ($-32,067\%$) and "Real estate activities" ($-32,010\%$) have witnessed the most dramatic decreases in the service sector. Since they rely the most on RoW, these industries have seen large decreases. On the one hand, "Wholesale and retail trade; motor vehicle repair" and "Real estate activities" are highly energy-intensive sectors. The "Real estate activities" sector in Greece has experienced a surge in recent years, largely due to tourism arrivals; thus, the RoW import restriction has the greatest impact on it. Yet, due to the modest amount of RoW agricultural imports and Greece's lack of specialization in agricultural output, the decline in agricultural sectors is less substantial compared to the other sectors.

Domestic uses fall as a result of lower output since the amount available in the economy for both exports and domestic consumption falls. The greatest significant reduction ($-28,139\%$) in Greece's energy sectors may be seen in the "Electricity, gas, water supply, sewerage, waste, and remediation services" area, which incorporates power consumption. The largest reduction ($-29,796\%$) in the manufacturing sector is also seen in the "Real estate activities" sector. As previously stated, the significant reduction ($-32,651\%$) in the service sector is seen in the "Wholesale and retail trade; maintenance of motor vehicles." Finally, the agricultural sector saw the least decrease ($-11,164\%$), followed by the "Agriculture, forestry, and fisheries sector.

Table 11.4 shows the effects of a 30% ad valorem import tariff on RoW imports. Import tariffs raise the price of the consumed goods in the economy. According to Table 11.4, prices in all sectors have risen, resulting in a decrease in consumption owing to the law of demand. The most substantial price increase in the energy sector is visible in the "Electricity, Gas, Water Supply, Sewerage, Waste, and Remediation Services" sector, which constitutes the most dominant power source for Greek

---

[2] The elasticity substitution parameter estimation and the elasticities of substitution can be found in the Appendix.

households' energy consumption. The price of electricity and gas rises by 1,626%, resulting in a drop of −34,552% in the available supply. The "Construction" sector has had the most significant price increase in the manufacturing sector (2,164%), corresponding to a significant drop in quantity (−37,422%). After that, the "Real Estate Activities" sector has the most substantial price rise (2,582%) as well as the most dramatic decrease in quantity (−28,972%). Lastly, the price increase in agriculture is rather low, reflecting the small decrease in quantity related to the remaining sectors.

These trade barriers allow the energy haven hypothesis to be incorporated into the Heckscher–Ohlin–Samuelson (H-O-S) theory by demonstrating preferences for lower energy consumption and causing energy usage to deviate from the original H-O-S forecast, in which energy consumption would increase in the face of trade liberalization. Greece has always held a competitive advantage in service activities, particularly those connected to tourism, and will continue to increase energy consumption as imports from RoW increase in order to preserve this advantage. Nevertheless, trade restrictions cause Greece to consume less energy for both household and industrial activities since energy-intensive enterprises' substitution and energy usage across sectors are no longer prevalent. As energy consumption falls, so does the output of Greece's manufacturing activity. As a result, industrial prices will grow since the economy must rely on its own electricity generation and distribution capacity. Therefore, profits will plummet, causing a snowball effect. This circumstance permits the energy haven theory to emerge because enterprises may choose to reallocate to countries with laxer energy rules while continuing to produce as before.

11.4 Conclusions

Computable general equilibrium models are a common technique for investigating policy implications via counterfactual experiments and their influence on diverse economic agents. They provide a consistent framework for studying the relationships between various sectors and the rest of the economy.

Using Greece's I-O table for 2015 as the basis year, this study built a multi-sector CGE model with special characteristics for the Greek–RoW trade relationship. This model examines the Greek economy's response to decreased energy and other imports by including trade obstacles (such as tariffs and quotas) on RoW imports through counterfactual scenarios. To examine how Greece's energy usage responds to a reduction in RoW imports, the intermediate inputs in the I-O have been separated into domestic and imported from the rest of the world countries. Greece is an energy-dependent country; therefore, any constraints on its energy supply have a significant impact on its consumption and production activities, simulating a 67% quota on energy imports and a 35% quota on the remainder of RoW imports, as well as a 30% ad valorem import tariff, resulting in a fall in production and domestic uses from the quota, as well as an increase in costs from the import tariff, resulting in a decrease in consumed quantities. The most substantial decreases are observed in the energy sector of "Electricity, gas, water supply, sewerage, waste, and remediation services," the manufacturing sector of "Construction," and the service sector of "Real estate activities." These sectors are anticipated to consume the most energy; hence, the reduction was the greatest.

The introduction of trade barriers causes the pollution/energy haven effect to arise. Companies pressed by rising energy prices and lower output as well as the fact that Greece must rely on its own energy capacity, which is relatively limited and unable to cover its demands, may opt to reallocate to nations with laxer energy regulations and continue to produce as before.

References

Allan, G. (2007). The impact of increased efficiency in the industrial use of energy: A computable general equilibrium analysis for the United Kingdom. *Energy Economics, 29*(4), 779–798.

Deardorff, A. V., Stern, R. M., Robert, M., & (Robert Mitchell) Stern. (1985). *The Michigan model of world production and trade: Theory and applications*. MIT Press. Print.

Dixon, P. B., & Jorgenson, D. W. (2012). *Handbook of computable general equilibrium modeling*. Newnes.

Eurostat. (2022). *International trade in goods – Annual data*. Eurostat Publications. https://ec.europa.eu/eurostat/web/international-trade-in-goods/data/database

Hertel, T. W. (1997). *Global trade analysis: Modeling and applications*. Cambridge University Press.

Johansen, L. (1960). *A multi-sector study of economic growth*. North-Holland Publishing Company.

Kemfert, C. (1998). Estimated substitution elasticities of a nested CES production function approach for Germany. *Energy Economics, 20*(3), 249–264.

Koesler, S., & Schymura, M. (2012). *Substitution elasticities in a CES production framework-an empirical analysis on the basis of non-linear least squares estimations* (ZEW-Centre for European Economic Research Discussion Paper (12–007)). Zentrum für Europäische Wirtschaftsforschung (ZEW).

Lagomarsino, E. (2020). Estimating elasticities of substitution with nested CES production functions: Where do we stand? *Energy Economics, 88*, 104752.

Lutz, C., Becker, L., & Kemmler, A. (2021). Socioeconomic effects of ambitious climate mitigation policies in Germany. *Sustainability, 13*(11), 6247.

Prywes, M. (1986). A nested CES approach to capital-energy substitution. *Energy Economics, 8*(1), 22–28.

Scarf, H. E., & Hansen, T. (1973). *The computation of economic equilibria*. Yale University Press.

Schumacher, K., & Sands, R. D. (2007). Where are the industrial technologies in energy–economy models? An innovative CGE approach for steel production in Germany. *Energy Economics, 29*(4), 799–825.

Welsch, H., & Ehrenheim, V. (2004). Environmental fiscal reform in Germany: A computable general equilibrium analysis. *Environmental Economics and Policy Studies, 6*, 197–219.

Chapter 12
Employee Benefits Required by Women of Generation Y in the Food and Agricultural Sectors

Jiří Duda

Abstract The relationship of women of generation Y with employee benefits is often unresolved. There are several commercial surveys on employee benefits, and, in this context, this contribution is complementary to the views of prospective employees. The purpose of this chapter is to define what employee benefits are required by women of generation Y from their future employer. It is long-term research. The data of this study were collected from a sample of 2916 women, students of the Mendel University in Brno. As the main method of data acquisition, a questionnaire survey among students was conducted. The hypotheses were tested by ordinary least squares regression analyses (contingency table and chi-squared test). For the results that showed statistical dependence, there was determined association dependence. The results highlight the demands of university-educated women. The results also show that women have similar demands for employee benefits as men do. Women more than men demand these four employee benefits: coverage of language courses, children's nurseries and kindergartens, contribution to recreation, and contribution to cultural events. The results confirm the trend of interest in benefits related to the work–life balance (sick days, home office). The cafeteria system is appropriated to provide employee benefits.

Keywords Czech Republic · Employee benefits · Generation Y · Millennials · Women

12.1 Introduction

Motivating employees is one of the key aspects of managerial work and one of the tools that can affect the results and competitiveness of a company. Labor is the most important resource available to an enterprise, and, in a market environment, it is

---

J. Duda (✉)
Faculty of Business and Economics, Mendel University in Brno, Brno, The Czech Republic
e-mail: jiri.duda@mendelu.cz

© The Author(s), under exclusive license to Springer Nature Switzerland AG 2024
N. Tsounis, A. Vlachvei (eds.), *Applied Economic Research and Trends*, Springer Proceedings in Business and Economics,
https://doi.org/10.1007/978-3-031-49105-4_12

usually the most expensive resource, especially skilled labor. Providing employee benefits is one of the motivating factors. Specific material remuneration, which includes employee benefits, often has a more significant subjective value. Employers are aware that their success and competitiveness crucially depend on the workforce and their abilities, work behavior, satisfaction, and their relationship with the employer. When an employee perceives the company's interest in their person, they realize that they are valuable to the company, as a result of which their self-confidence grows and their sense of belonging is strengthened. In addition to traditional remuneration, employee benefits are becoming one of the main factors in employee care. An organization has a relatively wide range of options for rewarding its employees for their work. Rewards can be in a monetary or nonmonetary form; they can be linked to the nature of the work performed and its importance, they can take the form of public recognition of merit and good work, etc. (Armstrong, 2007; Urbancová & Šnýdrová, 2017). Students, who graduate from university and often gain their first work experience during their studies, have certain ideas about employee benefits. If employers want to motivate these future employees, then they should know their preferences. The aim of this chapter is to identify the employee benefits that an employer conducting business in the food and agricultural sectors should provide to women of generation Y, especially to those holding a university degree.

12.2 Literature Review

Determining the beginning of generation Y is not easy. Many authors define generation Y as a generation of people born in the years 1985–1994 (Constantine, 2010; Zhao & Xu, 2019), but many authors assign this birth interval to a later time as well (e.g., Clark (2007), Strauss and Howe (2010), and Beekman (2011)). A later birth interval, 1982–2009, has also been reported by Alexander and Sysko (2012).

The common name for this generation is millennials (children of the millennium) (Jayson, 2012; Balda & Mora, 2011; Van der Bergh & Behrer, 2011; Norum, 2009; McCrindle, 2014; Howe & Strauss, 2000).

At present, generation Y is entering the labor market. By 2025, generation Y should be a significant part of the workforce (Costanza et al., 2012). Currently, more than half of the world's population is under 30 (Van der Bergh & Behrer, 2011). Employers are beginning to adapt to the demands and opinions of generation Y.

The preferences of one generation may be different from those of another. Generation Y is more optimistic, confident, and often wants to try new challenges. They expect a better future (Cogin, 2012; Zhao & Xu, 2019).

Stojanová et al. (2015) and Eisner (2005) point to the more frequent usage of modern technologies (mobile phones, computers) by this generation and their demand to use these technologies in the work process as well. They consider new technologies to be an integral part of both personal and work life. At the same time, they assume that the employer will evaluate the results of their work regardless of where, how, and when they perform it. Bannon et al. (2011) state that generation Y workers can be considered more flexible than the previous generation X workers.

This generation is considered highly technologically advanced, and they discuss and share information over the Internet (Bolton et al., 2013). They are active on social networks and use the available modern technologies (Woodman & Wyn, 2015).

For generation Y, work–life balance is crucial. The millennials seek out future employers who will have an understanding of their need to find a balance between their work goals and personal life goals. Companies should concentrate on the formation of incentive programs, an attractive work environment, and a comprehensive system of human resource management. Many authors (Hershatter & Epstein, 2010; Smola & Sutton, 2002; Tulgan, 2009) recommend that employers create an interesting and diverse work environment, including a clearly defined motivation system. Generation Y has specific requirements of the labor market, including in the field of education. Generation Y workers expect hands-on collaboration.

Employee preferences are different, and, therefore, their motivation differs as well. Women are more motivated by the needs of their family; they try to find a work–family balance (Almobaireek & Manolova, 2013; Mcintosh et al., 2012). On the contrary, men are driven by economic welfare and professional success at work, and, so, they prefer independence (Adams et al., 2010; Buttner, 1993). The conducted studies also revealed that women and men have different motivations to work. Research has shown that interpersonal relationships are important to women at work, and they prefer to balance their private and work activities. They attach more importance to these factors than do men (Godlewska-Werner et al., 2020; Lubrańska, 2014). According to Chusmir and Parker (1991), women are the ones who prefer flexible working hours and choose less time-consuming occupations. If we analyze the importance of salary and job satisfaction, we find that these factors are equally important motives for both women and men (Carli & Eagly, 2016; Godlewska-Werner et al., 2020; Linz, 2004). It could be stated that, in addition to a quality work environment, the most important job aspect for women is recognition for work done, and, on the contrary, for men, participating in the processing of new work challenges and work problems is an important motivator (Wiley, 1997).

The workers of generation Y require more flexible working hours and refuse to work overtime (Campione, 2016). They are likely to stop working if they were financially solvent (Becton et al., 2014). The main causes of generation Y fluctuation include lack of meaningful tasks, work–life imbalance, lack of incentives, or poor leadership style (Nolan, 2015).

In an organization, the employment of employees and the length of employment are both important for providing employee benefits. Armstrong (2007) and Chandra (2012) define employee benefits as a reward that an employee receives because he/she is the employee of the company. Employee performance for providing employee benefits is usually not assessed.

Employee benefits may constitute the extremely expensive parts of remuneration. Armstrong (2007) and Hewitt Associates (2002) report that they can account for up to a third of labor costs. It is important to plan and manage the process of providing employee benefits. The importance of employee benefits increases when they reflect the needs of the employee or his/her family. The employee feels supported by the employer and realizes that the employer cares about them. All this increases the loyalty of the employee, and, thus, the employee becomes more responsible in the performance of his/her tasks and identifies with the goals of the company (Dulebohn et al., 2009). Employee benefits also have a major impact on employee loyalty and are a substantial part of the employee motivation program (DeCenzo & Robbins, 1999). Holding a similar view, Backes-Gellner and Tuor (2010) and Chandra (2012) have identified other important business characteristics such as a good working atmosphere and career advancement opportunities, which are also an important part of recruiting. This view is supported by the research of the readers of the Employee Benefits magazine (2013), which explored the reasons for providing employer benefits. Most employers adopted efficiency as a tool to attract and retain employees. The main reasons behind this were the efforts put into rewarding employees, promoting their well-being and health, and striving to provide a work–life balance. Wages only are not the motivating factor for talented employees to work for a particular employer (Rowland, 2011; Schlechter et al., 2015). In addition, Zhaohong et al. (2011) and Dencker et al. (2007) see the advantages of quality systems for providing employee benefits to retain their existing employees, thus making the employer more attractive to new employees and reducing possible social conflicts in the work process. The tax advantage of the benefits provided compared to the salary provided contributes to the attractiveness of the provision of employee benefits (Duda, 2014; Hammermann & Mohnen, 2014).

The demands of the young generation (generation Y) are changing, and creating a workable and competitive payroll system is a challenging task for employers (Prasad, 2015).

In the Czech Republic, research on employee benefits is not very extensive. There are surveys published in the past by various consulting companies (e.g., Aon HR Solutions, Grafton recruitment, LMC). One of the major surveys was a several-year comparison made by NN in cooperation with the Confederation of Industry of the Czech Republic (NN, 2015).

The provision of employee benefits is not mandatory in the Czech Republic, but research by the Ministry of Labor and Social Affairs (2016) points out that 99% of research respondents (companies) offer employee benefits. On average, these companies offer 12 employee benefits. Some of the most offered employee benefits provided by the company include allowance for company catering, mobile phone for private use, medical examinations, drinking regime, and professional development of the employee.

Moreover, in the Czech Republic, the provision of some employee benefits is supported by tax reliefs (e.g., meal vouchers, pension insurance, life insurance, and sports and cultural benefits (Macháček (2019)).

12.3 Materials and Methods

The respondents were students of master-level courses of business management and human resources management at the Faculty of AgriSciences and the Faculty of Business and Economics, Mendel University, in Brno, Czech Republic. The period of research covered the years 2002–2022, and a total of 4376 students participated in the survey (of which there were 2916 women). The number of students in the respective years of research ranged from 175 to 321 (women: 93–246). This corresponds to approximately 75–95% of all students in the final year of their study program. Participation in the research was voluntary and with the consent of the students. The completion of the questionnaire was anonymous. Only gender was filled in from personal data.

In the research, a list of 40 employee benefits that can be expected from an employer was presented, and students were expected to evaluate the particular benefits by the level of their interest in their provision. The author compiled this list after a careful survey of the employee benefits offered by many companies of various specializations. The suitability of individual benefits was confirmed by later commercial research of the consulting companies (e.g., NN, 2015 and others), which used the same benefits. Students evaluated their preference of the particular benefits on a Likert-type scale of 1 (definitely yes) to 4 (definitely not). This chapter only focuses on those benefits that were demanded the most and were evaluated by students as "definitely yes."

First, those employee benefits that women would most appreciate in the offer of benefits provided by employers were identified. Tables 12.1 and 12.2 were created based on the frequency of the top ten and top five most desired benefits for each year of the survey. The order of popularity of employee benefits for the whole research period (2002–2022) and for the last 5 years (2017–2022) is provided here. In Table 12.1, the frequency between the 5 most desirable benefits (under the column "Frequency in 5") and the 10 most desirable benefits (under the column "Frequency in 10") can be seen.

Based on the frequencies, the ranking of employee benefits for women was determined. In the case of equal frequency in "Top 10" benefits (column "Rank 10"), the ranking is determined by the frequency of appearance of the particular benefits in the "Top 5" (column "Rank 5") benefits. In the case of equal frequency in "Top 5" benefits, the ranking is determined by the average value over a period of 20 (respectively 5) years (Φ).

In each year of the research, for each employee benefit, monitoring was carried out to assess whether the gender of the respondent has an effect on the popularity of the employee benefit. Employee benefits, for which the influence of the respondent's gender on the popularity of the benefit in 7 and more years was found, are listed in Table 12.3.

When processing the answers, selected contingency tables were compiled, both with empirical frequencies (n_{ij}) and expected frequencies (n'_{ij}) in order to conduct a statistical analysis of the dependence. The chi-squared (χ^2) test criterion was

Table 12.1 Ranking of the frequency of the most desirable benefits in the top 10 most wanted benefits for women during the research years 2002–2022

Employees benefit	Frequency in 5	Frequency in 10	Rank 5	Rank 10	Φ (%)
Contribution to corporate catering	20	20	1	1	73.37
On-site parking	20	20	2	2	66.69
Use of a company car for business reasons	20	20	3	3	63.76
Extra week holiday	9	20	6	4	45.78
Additional salary (mid-year bonus)	6	20	7	5	43.39
Contribution to pension insurance	5	20	8	6	42.49
Employee discount on company product and services	0	20	10	7	38.48
Language courses	11	18	4	8	49.64
Contribution on pension leave	1	17	9	9	37.24
Sick day	9	10	5	10	61.43

Φ, the average share of answers "definitely yes" in the period 2002–2022

used to analyze this, and, in case of verification of the dependence, the intensity of dependence was calculated using Pearson's contingency coefficient (P) (Budíková et al., 2010).

$$\chi 2 = \sum_{i=1}^{r} \sum_{j=1}^{s} \frac{\left(n_{ij} - n'_{ij}\right)}{n'_{ij}} \tag{12.1}$$

$$P = \sqrt{\frac{\chi 2}{\chi 2 + n}} \tag{12.2}$$

When observing the possible gender influence on the benefit preferences, coefficients of contingency were calculated based on the data in the contingency tables and the level of gender dependence was determined.

For the results that showed statistical dependence, there was determined association dependence. Association dependence explores the relationship between two qualitative alternative variables. The association coefficient V measures the intensity of the association in values ranging from -1 to $+1$. In the case of this research, a positive number means a benefit preferred by men and not by women; a negative number means a benefit not preferred by men but by women.

$$V = \frac{n \cdot n_{11} - n_{1*} \cdot n_{*1}}{\sqrt{n_{1*} \cdot n_{*1} \cdot n_{0*} \cdot n_{*0}}} \tag{12.3}$$

where n represents the total response rate, n_{11} is the frequency of positive responses among men, n_{1*} is the overall response rate of men, n_{*1} is the overall rate of positive responses, n_{0*} is the overall response rate of women, and n_{*0} is the frequency of negative responses of women.

12.4 Results and Discussion

In Table 12.1, we can see those employee benefits that women most demanded throughout the survey period. The most popular employee benefits include use of a company car for business reasons, on-site parking, and contribution to corporate catering. The average share of answers "definitely yes" in the period 2002–2022 (the value of "Φ") is between 61% and 74% of the surveyed students. The most important employee benefit for women according to the survey is contribution to corporate catering (meal vouchers).

Providing a contribution to corporate catering is a popular employee benefit among employers. According to Urbancová and Šnýdrová (2017), this benefit is among the most used benefits by employers. This opinion is also supported by other research by commercial research companies (e.g., Kučera (2011) and NN (2015)). A survey by Trexima (2019) states that more than 72% of companies provide this benefit. Contribution to corporate catering is among the tax-advantaged employee benefits for employers (Macháček, 2019). To employees, quality food is provided at a lower price.

The use of a car for business reasons, especially parking at the workplace, is also a significant benefit requested by women. Parking in the vicinity of their place of work is one of the problems that current employees have to deal with, and allowing parking on the company's premises or in its parking lots is a welcome benefit. The importance of this benefit is confirmed by research conducted by the Society for Human Resource Management (2013), which indicates that 87% of employers offer car parking in company parking lots. Moreover, Armstrong (2007) in the research "Survey of Reward Management" confirms the privileged position of this benefit because this benefit is provided by 74% of respondents and thus became the third most important benefit provided.

Research has shown that an extra week holiday is among the significant benefits that women demand. The importance of this benefit is confirmed by the fact that it was among the 10 most requested employee benefits in individual years of research. The importance of this benefit is confirmed by Přikryl (2012) in the study "Salary & Benefits Guide 2011–2012" by Robert Half and Kučera (2011). Surveys by the Ministry of Labor and Social Affairs (2016) and "Survey of Reward Management" by Armstrong (2007) also rank it among the most frequently provided benefits. These surveys consistently consider this benefit to be the second-most provided employee benefit. In the survey by Profesia, which processed the development of employee benefits in the years 2007–2012, this benefit is also regularly ranked second or third and is required by almost 25% of respondents (Kolerová, 2014).

Table 12.2 Ranking of the frequency of the most desirable benefits in the top 10 most wanted benefits for women during the research years 2017–2022

Employees benefit	Frequency in 5	Frequency in 10	Rank 5	Rank 10	Φ_{5w} (%)
Contribution to corporate catering	5	5	1	1	73.25
Sick day	5	5	2	2	69.04
On-site parking	5	5	3	3	68.06
Use of a company car for business reasons	5	5	4	4	59.63
Extra week holiday	3	5	5	5	52.78
Contribution to pension insurance	2	5	6	6	47.72
Additional salary (mid-year bonus)	0	5	7	7	43.81
Flextime	0	5	8	8	40.90
Employee discount on company products and services	0	5	9	9	39.76
Language courses	0	3	10	10	40.95

Φ_{5w}, the average share of answers "definitely yes" in the period 2017–2022

Research shows that women have begun to demand a similar type of benefit, so-called sick days (several days off with full pay), over the course of the last 12 years. This employee benefit was among the top five benefits over the past 5 years (see Table 12.2). If the employer introduces paid sick days, it will reduce contagion in the workplace, improve productivity, and reduce employee turnover (Milli et al., 2016). This opinion is also shared by Drago and Kevin Miller (2010), who state that if the employer offers a sick days benefit, then it is less likely that employees will work when sick and thereby pass on their infection to their coworkers. Losses in work productivity can be prevented using this benefit. Stewart et al. (2003) defined the time value of lost work productivity due to illness as 1.32 h per week.

Based on the evaluation of research data, we can observe a decrease in student interest in "language courses" (see Table 12.2), which in the last 5 years were not among the five most requested employee benefits.

On the other hand, another benefit, i.e., contribution to pension insurance, became a more popular benefit during the monitored years and more emphasis is placed on its provision. Research by the commercial company NN (2015) also confirms the growing popularity of contribution to pension insurance. According to the survey, 77% of the approached companies offer contribution to pension insurance. Galanaki (2020) also confirms the importance of pension insurance in his research.

The results of the presented research confirm that the gender of the respondent does not play an important role in the most popular employee benefits mentioned by female respondents of generation Y.

The most frequent correlation of the requested benefits with the gender of the respondents can be found only in the benefit "coverage of language courses" (14 years, with the association coefficient "V" reaching the values between -0.089 and -0.240). Other employee benefits for which the dependence of the respondent's gender on benefit preference was more often (over 7 years of measurement) manifested are children's nurseries and kindergartens, contribution to cultural events, and contribution to recreation (see Table 12.3). These benefits are among the less requested among the respondents.

In the case of the "children's nurseries and kindergartens" benefit, the dependence of the respondent's answers on the respondent's gender was found. In 11 of the 20 years of the survey, the preference of women was proven for this benefit. The level of significance was also extremely high ($P \leq 0.001$), and dependence reached high values (essentially the highest that were found in the whole research, with the "V" values between -0.183 and -0.337).

Currently, also due to the increased number of Ukrainian refugees, women, and children, there is a shortage of kindergartens in the Czech Republic. For this reason, women who want to continue working for their employer demand the establishment of kindergartens at their place of work as well. For women, this benefit means an important part of reconciling private and working life. The establishment of company nurseries is also advantageous for employers, as qualified women may return to the workforce earlier. This also results in lower costs for the employer for recruiting and selecting new employees. The employer can also gain higher employee loyalty (Urbancová & Šnýdrová, 2017).

12.5 Conclusions

The aim of the presented research was to find employment benefits that future employers would offer to women with a university degree. The research took place in the years 2002–2022, and for women, there were presented the 40 most offered employee benefits by employers in the Czech Republic. According to the research results, we can state that women of generation Y want the following benefits the most: on-site parking, meal tickets, additional salary, use of a company car for business reasons, contribution to pension insurance, extra week of holiday, coverage of language courses, contribution to pension leave, and employee discount on company products and services.

As part of the research, monitoring was carried out to assess whether there was a correlation between the answers and the gender of the respondent. In the case of the most requested employee benefits, which include additional week of holiday, use of a company car for business reasons, and contribution to corporate catering, the nonexistence of this correlation was demonstrated by the respondents' answers.

In the research, it was also proven that women statistically more significantly than men require the provision of only four employee benefits. These benefits include contribution to recreation, children's nurseries and kindergartens, contribution to cultural events, and coverage of language courses.

Table 12.3 Gender influences on benefit preference: chi-squared (χ^2) test and the association coefficient (V)

Year/benefit	Coverage of language courses	Children's nurseries and kindergartens	Contribution to recreation	Contribution to cultural events
2002/2003	4.510	24.879*** $V = -0.330$	14.065** $V = -0.200$	2.017
2003/2004	4.104	13.454** $V = -0.183$	13.131** $V = -0.260$	4.538
2004/2005	4.580	6.086	8.090* $V = -0.190$	3.092
2005/2006	8.099* $V = -0.151$	4.954	3.386	14.040** $V = -0.240$
2006/2007	14.102** $V = -0.163$	2.934	9.043* $V = -0.161$	8.515* $V = -0.181$
2007/2008	10.903** $V = -0.129$	19.254*** $V = -0.216$	7.378	7.567
2008/2009	19.398*** $V = -0.207$	16.447*** $V = -0.229$	10.238* $V = -0.129$	7.128
2009/2010	7.901* $V = -0.153$	32.832*** $V = -0.322$	3.312	2.670
2010/2011	12.973** $V = -0.164$	15.472** $V = -0.220$	9.222* $V = -0.158$	24.012*** $V = -0.238$
2011/2012	22.504*** $V = -0.229$	24.451*** $V = -0.230$	5.114	7.806
2012/2013	13.955** $V = -0.125$	7.130	2.765	7.453
2013/2014	6.698	37.5147*** $V = -0.337$	12.086** $V = -0.104$	8.210* $V = -0.124$
2014/2015	15.678** $V = -0.214$	24.325*** $V = -0.264$	0.637	2.769
2015/2016	3.816	6.377	7.672	11.511** $V = -0.189$
2016/2017	14.184** $V = -0.089$	24.833*** $V = -0.323$	4.341	2.822
2017/2018	8.521* $V = -0.118$	6.574	3.888	9.523* $V = -0.245$
2018/2019	14.615** $V = -0.124$	7.661	4.652	3.751
2019/2020	17.329*** $V = -0.240$	6.447	2.530	8.565* $V = -0.171$
2020/2021	8.836* $V = -0.167$	15.835** $V = -0.268$	1.637	5.384
2021/2022	6.283	4.629	7.019	4.598

Gender differences significant at ***$P \leq 0.001$, **$P \leq 0.01$, and *$P \leq 0.05$

Employee benefits such as flexible working hours, home office, and sick days (several days off in case of health indisposition) play a significant role in balancing work and private life.

A modern trend in providing employee benefits is the cafeteria system. This system meets the requirements of individual demand for employee benefits. Using this method of providing benefits, employers can solve any specific requirements of employees with regard to the gender and age of employees.

References

Adams, S. M., Gupta, A., & Leeth, J. D. (2010). Maximising compensation: Organisational level and industry gender composition effects. *Gender in Management: An International Journal, 25*(5), 366–385. https://doi.org/10.1108/17542411011056868

Alexander, C., & Sysko, J. (2012). A study of the cognitive determinants of generation Y's entitlement mentality. *Academy of Educational Leadership Journal, 16*(2), 63–68.

Almobaireek, W. N., & Manolova, T. S. (2013). Entrepreneurial motivations among female university youth in Saudi Arabia. *Journal of Business Economics and Management, 14*(Suppl 1), 56–75. https://doi.org/10.3846/16111699.2012.711364

Armstrong, M. (2007). *A handbook of employee reward management and practice*. Kogan Page Limited.

Backes-Gellner, U., & Tuor, S. N. (2010). Avoiding labor shortages by employer signaling: On the importance of good work climate and labor relations. *Industrial and Labor Relations Review, 63*(2), 271–286. https://doi.org/10.2139/ssrn.1346915

Balda, J. B., & Mora, F. (2011). Adapting leadership theory and practice for the networked. *Millennial generation. Journal of Leadership Studies, 5*(3), 13–24. https://doi.org/10.1002/jls.20229

Bannon, S., Ford, K., & Meltzer, L. (2011). Understanding millennials in the workplace. *CPA Journal, 81*(11), 61–65.

Becton, J. B., Walker, H. J., & Jones-Farmer, A. (2014). Generational differences in workplace behaviour. *Journal of Applied Social Psychology, 44*, 175–189. https://doi.org/10.1111/jasp.12208

Beekman, T. (2011). Fill in the generation gap. *Strategic Finance, 93*(3), 15–17.

Bolton, R. N., Parasuraman, A., Hoefnagels, A., et al. (2013). Understanding generation Y and their use of social media: A review and research agenda. *Journal of Service Management, 24*(3), 245–267. https://doi.org/10.1108/09564231311326987

Budíková, M., Králová, M., & Maroš, B. (2010). *Guide to basic statistical methods* [in Czech: Průvodce základními statistickými metodami]. Grada Publishing.

Buttner, E. H. (1993). Female entrepreneurs: How far have they come? *Business Horizons, 36*(2), 59–65. https://doi.org/10.1016/S0007-6813(05)80039-4

Campione, W. (2016). Volunteer work experience: Can it help millennials to find meaning and interest in their work and to negotiate their role within the workplace? *Journal of Leadership, 13*(3), 11–27.

Carli, L. L., & Eagly, A. H. (2016). Women face a labyrinth: An examination of metaphors for women leaders. *Gender in Management, 31*(8), 514–527. https://doi.org/10.1108/GM-02-2015-0007

Chandra, V. (2012). Work–life balance: Eastern and Western perspectives. *The International Journal of Human Resource Management, 23*(5), 1040–1056. https://doi.org/10.1080/09585192.2012.651339

Chusmir, L. H., & Parker, B. (1991). Gender and situational differences in managers' values: A look at work and home live. *Journal of Business Research, 23*(4), 325–335. https://doi.org/10.1016/0148-2963(91)90018-S

Clark, A. D. (2007). The new reality: Using benefits to attract and retain talent. *Employment Relations Today, 34*(3), 47–53. https://doi.org/10.1002/ert.20164

Cogin, J. (2012). Are generational differences in work values fact or fiction? Multi-country evidence and implications. *International Journal of Human Resource Management, 23*(11), 2268–2294. https://doi.org/10.1080/09585192.2011.610967

Constantine, G. (2010). *Tapping into generation Y: Nine ways community financial institutions can use technology to capture young customers.* First Data Corporation [online]. Available at: https://www.firstdata.com/downloads/thought-leadership/geny_wp.pdf. Accessed 13 Aug 2021.

Costanza, D. P., Badger, J. M., Fraser, R. L., Severt, J. B., & Gade, P. A. (2012). Generational differences in work-related attitudes: A meta-analysis. *Journal of Business Psychology, 27,* 375–394. https://doi.org/10.1007/s10869-012-9259-4

DeCenzo, D. A., & Robbins, S. P. (1999). *Human resource management.* Wiley.

Dencker, J. C., Joshi, A., & Martocchio, J. J. (2007). Employee benefits as context for intergenerational conflict. *The International Journal of Human Resource Management, 17*(2), 208–220. https://doi.org/10.1016/j.hrmr.2007.04.002

Drago, R., & Kevin Miller, K. (2010). *Sick at work: Infected employees in the workplace during the H1N1 pandemic.* Institute for Women's Policy Research.

Duda, J. (2014). The requirements of university students in the employee benefits by a prospective employer. *Procedia Economics and Finance, 12,* 130–137. https://doi.org/10.1016/S2212-5671(14)00328-1

Dulebohn, J. H., Molloy, J. C., Pichler, S. M., & Murray, B. (2009). Employee benefits: Literature review and emerging issues. *Human Resource Management Review, 19*(1), 86–103. https://doi.org/10.1016/j.hrmr.2008.10.001

Eisner, S. P. (2005). Managing generation Y. *SAM Advanced Management Journal: Society for the Advancement of Management, 70*(4), 4–15. https://doi.org/10.1109/EMR.2011.5876168

Employee Benefits magazine. (2013). *Benefits research* [online]. Available at: http://www.employeebenefits.co.uk/Journals/2013/05/02/n/g/f/BBResearch2013.pdf. Accessed 13 May 2021.

Galanaki, E. (2020). A hidden deterioration in equal pay achievements? The case of employee benefits during the Greek recession. *Gender in Management, 35*(5), 423–444. https://doi.org/10.1108/GM-09-2019-0150

Godlewska-Werner, D., Peplińska, A., Zawadzka, A. M., & Połomski, P. (2020). Work motives in the context of generational differences, gender differences, and preferred values. *Polish Psychological Bulletin, 51*(2), 116–125. https://doi.org/10.24425/ppb.2020.133769

Hammermann, A., & Mohnen, A. (2014). Who benefits from benefits? Empirical research on tangible incentives. *Review of Managerial Science, 8*(3), 327–350. https://doi.org/10.1007/s11846-013-0107-3

Hershatter, A., & Epstein, M. (2010). Millennials and the world of work: An organization and management perspective. *Journal of Business and Psychology, 25*(2), 211–223. https://doi.org/10.1007/s10869-010-9160-y

Hewitt Associates. (2002). *Archival records and benefit communications.* Lincolnshire.

Jayson, S. (2012). *The millennial generation is highly motivated and overwhelmed with work.* Greenhaven Press.

Kolerová, K. (2014). Trend of employee benefits in the Czech Republic. In *Proceedings of the international scientific conference Hradec economic days 2014, Hradec Králové* (Vol. 2, pp. 28–34).

Kučera, P. (2011). *The most common benefit in the Czech Republic is five weeks of holiday* [in Czech: Pět týdnů dovolené, to je nejčastější benefit v Česku] [online]. Available at: https://zpravy.aktualne.cz/finance/pet-tydnu-dovolene-to-je-nejcastejsi-benefit-v-cesku/r~i:article:725935/. Accessed 21 Oct 2019.

12 Employee Benefits Required by Women of Generation Y in the Food and...

Linz, S. J. (2004). Motivating Russian workers: Analysis of age and gender differences. *Journal of Socio-Economics, 33*(3), 261–289.

Lubrańska, A. (2014). Work – Family and family – Work conflict in terms of gender and intergenerational differences [Konflikt praca – rodzina i rodzina – praca w aspekcie różnic międzypłciowych i międzypokoleniowych.]. *Medycyna Pracy, 65*(4), 521–533. https://doi.org/10.13075/mp.5893.00040

Macháček, I. (2019). *Employee benefits and taxes* [in Czech: Zaměstnanecké výhody a daně]. Wolters Kluwer.

McCrindle, M. (2014). *The ABC of XYZ: Understanding the global generations*. UNSW Press.

McIntosh, B., McQuaid, R., Munro, A., & Dabir-Alai, P. (2012). Motherhood and its impact on career progression. *Gender in Management: An International Journal, 27*(5), 346–364. https://doi.org/10.1108/17542411211252651

Milli, J., Jenny Xia, J., & Min, J. (2016). *Paid sick days benefit employers, workers, and the economy*. Institute for Women's Policy Research [online]. Available at: https://iwpr.org/wp-content/uploads/wpallimport/files/iwpr-export/publications/B361.pdf. Accessed 9 May 2020.

Ministry of Labour and Social Affairs Czech Republic. (2016). *Working conditions information system*. Annual Report for 2016.

NN – Insurance and Pension Company. (2015). *Companies are doing well, offering more benefits to employees than last year* [in Czech: Firmám se daří – nabízejí zaměstnancům vice benefit než loni] [online]. Available at: https://www.nn.cz/spolecnost-nn/tiskove-centrum/tiskove-zpravy/firmam-se-dari-nabizeji-zamestnancum-vice-benefitu-nez-loni.html. Accessed 18 May 2020.

Nolan, L. (2015). The roar of millennials: Retaining top talent in the workplace. *Journal of Leadership, Accountability, 12*(5), 69–75.

Norum, P. S. (2009). Examination of generational differences in household apparel expenditures. *Family and Consumer Sciences Research Journal, 32*(1), 52–75. https://doi.org/10.1177/1077727X03255901

Prasad, C. V. (2015). Emerging trends in HRM. *International Journal of Economic Research, 12*(2), 511–517.

Přikryl, J. (2012). *Benefits: Specialists and managers appreciate the extra weeks holiday* [in Czech: Benefity-specialisté a manažeři si nejvíce cení delší dovolené] [online]. Available at: http://kariera.ihned.cz/c1-55918420-benefity-specialiste-a-manazeri-si-nejvice-ceni-delsi-dovolene. Accessed 3 Aug 2020.

Rowland, M. (2011). How to cement a diversity policy: The key role of talent development. *Human Resource Management International Digest, 19*(5), 36–38. https://doi.org/10.1108/09670731111153357

Schlechter, A., Thompson, N. C., & Bussin, M. (2015). Attractiveness of non financial rewards for prospective knowledge workers an experimental investigation. *Employee Relations, 37*(3), 274–295. https://doi.org/10.1108/ER-06-2014-0077

Smola, K. W., & Sutton, C. D. (2002). Generational differences: Revisiting generational work values for the new millennium. *Journal of Organisational Behaviour, 23*(4), 363–382. https://doi.org/10.1002/job.147

Society for Human Resource Management – SHRM. (2013). *Employee benefits: An overview of employee benefits offerings in the U.S.* Research report SHRM.

Stewart, W. F., Judith, A., Ricci, E. C., & Morganstein, D. (2003). Lost productive work time costs from health conditions in the United States: Results from the American productivity audit. *American College of Occupational and Environmental Medicine, 45*(12), 1234–1246. https://doi.org/10.1097/01.jom.0000099999.27348.78

Stojanová, H., Tomšík, P., & Tesařová, E. (2015). The approach to the work mobility in generation Y – Enthusiasm for change. *Human Resources Management and Ergonomics, 9*(1), 83–96.

Strauss, W., & Howe, N. (2010). *Generational archetypes* [online]. Available at: http://www.lifecourse.com/about/method/generational-archetypes.html. Accessed 18 June 2021.

Trexima. (2019). *In 2019, companies offered their employees 5 benefits* [in Czech:V roce 2019 nabízely firmy svým zaměstnancům průměrně 5 benefitů] [online]. Available at: https://www.trexima.cz/aktualita/v-roce-2019-nabizely-firmy-svym-zamestnancum-prumerne-5-benefitu. Accessed 13 Aug 2021.

Tulgan, B. (2009). *Not everyone gets a trophy: How to manage generation Y*. Jossey-Bass.

Urbancová, H., & Šnýdrová, M. (2017). Remuneration and employee benefits in organizations in The Czech Republic. *Acta Universitatis Agriculturae et Silviculturae Mendelianae Brunensis, 65*(1), 357–368. https://doi.org/10.11118/actaun201765010357

Van der Bergh, J., & Behrer, M. (2011). *How cool brands stay hot*. Kogan Page.

Wiley, C. (1997). What motivates employees according to over 40 years of motivation surveys. *International Journal of Manpower, 18*(3), 263–280. https://doi.org/10.1108/01437729710169373

Woodman, D., & Wyn, J. (2015). *Youth and generation: Rethinking change and inequality in the lives of young people*. SAGE Publications.

Zhao, Y., & Xu, Q. (2019). Understanding the achieving styles of Chinese millennials and implications on HRM policy. *International Journal of Manpower, 41*(3), 303–317. https://doi.org/10.1108/IJM-08-2018-0271

Zhaohong, L., Kelly, J., & Trenberth, L. (2011). Antecedents and consequences of the introduction of flexible benefit plans in China. *The International Journal of Human Resource Management, 22*(5), 1128–1145. https://doi.org/10.1080/09585192.2011.556787

Chapter 13
How Is Economic News Tone Driven: An Analysis of the Longitudinal Data (1998–2017) of Korean Economic News

Wansoo Lee

Abstract This study examined what drives the tone of media coverage. In particular, this study measured who and what causes the tone of news change and how it is done through a 20-year longitudinal data analysis of Korean economic news. The analysis results are as follows. First, the tone of Korean economic news showed a similar pattern with no significant difference between the headlines and leads. Second, the tone of economic news during the same period showed a different pattern according to the ideology of the media. Third, the current economic situation had a greater impact on the tone of economic news than did any potential economic situation of the future. Fourth, economic index change had a greater effect on tone change in economic news than did levels of economic conditions. The effect of changes in the economic index affecting the tone of economic news was greater than the simple lagged levels. Fifth, the positive outlook index for the future economy had no effect on the tone change of economic news, but the negative outlook index had a distinct effect on the same. Sixth, the economic news coverage of the Korean Broadcasting System (KBS), a public broadcaster, had the most statistically significant positive effect on the overall economic news tone change, whereas the commercial broadcaster Seoul Broadcasting System (SBS) had a statistically significant negative effect. This study multidimensionally confirmed the causes and consequences that affect the change of the tone of Korean national economy news and discussed the norms of Korean economic journalism.

Keywords Economic news · News tone · Level and change · Negativity bias · Media ideology

---

The research for this paper was conducted with a grant from the Ministry of Education of the Republic of Korea and the National Research Foundation of Korea in 2021 (NRF-2021S1A2A01070066).

W. Lee (✉)
Faculty of College of Media Contents, Dongseo University, Busan, Republic of Korea

© The Author(s), under exclusive license to Springer Nature Switzerland AG 2024
N. Tsounis, A. Vlachvei (eds.), *Applied Economic Research and Trends*, Springer Proceedings in Business and Economics,
https://doi.org/10.1007/978-3-031-49105-4_13

13.1 Introduction

Who and what causes the tone of news change and how is it done? Media coverage tone is an important variable in news research. Researchers have paid considerable attention right from the issue of norms of reporting by the media to the effects of these arguments on people's perceptions, evaluations, and behaviors in the context of social reality. The same is true for economic news, which has a large impact on people's daily lives. The economic news tone affects not only the economic realities of an individual, a business, and government economic entities but also economic behavior and the policy decision-making process.

People rely heavily on information provided by the media when evaluating the economic realities and governments of their communities. Among them, the attitude of valance shown by the media has a decisive influence on the evaluation of the economic reality and the government (McCarthy & Dolfsma, 2014). The "bad news" distributed by the media gives people a negative perception of the economy, which, in turn, influences investors' decisions, corporate strategies, stock markets, employment decisions, education investments, and voting behavior (Abo-Zaid, 2014).

For this reason, many researchers have explored how economic news is negatively or positively biased (Soroka, 2014; Soroka & Mcadams, 2015), how negative economic news affects people's perceptions of economic reality (Soroka & Mcadams, 2015), and whether economic news conventions affect government ratings and electoral voting (Erikson & Wlezien, 2012; Lewis-Beck & Stegmaier, 2007).

However, only limited empirical studies on what factors influence tone change in the process of reporting economic news, under what conditions the tone change is caused, and the extent of the tone effect (Heinz & Swinnen, 2015; Fogarty, 2005) are available. Most of the existing studies have mainly focused on the effect of economic news tone as an independent variable and the effects of people's perceptions and evaluations of economic reality as well as political decisions, such as presidential, political, and government evaluations, by tone as a dependent variable. However, little is known about the extent to which the economic news tone we encounter daily change and are affected (more specifically negative biased) under what factors and conditions, reaching the magnitude (Soroka, 2014).

In other words, previous studies have not adequately explained what internal/external factors and conditions change the economic news tone as a dependent variable. Economic news tone does not consistently move in the same direction and with the same size under all conditions. In fact, it is common for economic news tone to change in different directions and sizes depending on various political and economic factors and conditions (Lischka, 2016). The existing argument that economic news tone is biased in some way and that it affects people's perception of economic reality or decision-making is only a post-evaluation of the news effect. However, it does not explicitly explain the conditional factors that affect them.

Therefore, this study attempted to test the following research problems: (1) What is the difference between a newspaper and a broadcasting in terms of the economic news tone? (2) How can tone be changed according to the economic index? (3) Does tone change according to the levels, simple indicators, or changes in the indicators? (4) Does media ideology makes a difference to the economic news reporting tone? (5) Does it differ according to the political ideology of the government?

13.2 A Literature Review

Many previous studies have pointed out that economic news tone is more likely to be negatively biased than positive, regardless of political and economic conditions or circumstances (Lischka, 2016; Soroka, 2014). Interpreted the negative bias of economic news, as economic journalists are more sensitive to changes in a negative economic situation. In addition, Soroka (2006) argued that news consumers tend to prefer negative economic information, which is why reporters adopt negative reporting practices regardless of their interests. Garz (2014), on the other hand, looked at the cognition limitations that the reporters face in their information processing to assess why they have a negative bias. Tversky and Kahneman (1991) argued that reporters also respond differently to favorable and unfavorable changes in economic variables because of their tendency to loss aversion. This asymmetric cognitive tendency of reporters influences their reporting of economic news.

Wlezien et al. (2017) stated that "a lot of research on the relationship between economic news and public attitudes to the economy have been conducted, but the nature of the economic news is not properly identified" (p. 1). In another study, Soroka et al. (2017) pointed out that media coverage of economic issues focuses more on future economic conditions than on past ones. Moreover, these researchers have suggested that changes rather than simple levels of economic conditions are more sensitive. This indicates how necessary it is to study the causes and consequences that affect the change of media tone. More specifically, Blood and Phillips (1995), Wu et al. (2004), and Dalen et al. (2015) suggested the importance of reviewing media's economic reports regarding both the economic situation and government characteristics.

These studies suggested a review on examining the effect of economic news tone on other economic factors (e.g., people's assessment of the political and economic environment) and on the necessity of looking at the relationship between external economic factors and how they intervene and influence the change in economic news tone. For example, previous studies that suggested that media tone is influenced by specific factors or conditions are summarized as follows. First, the media tend to report more negatively when economic issues are salient (Ju, 2014), to change tone when the index changes rather than the economic situation itself (e.g., levels) (Dalen et al., 2015; Soroka et al., 2017), to pay more attention to the future economic outlook than the current economic conditions (Soroka et al.,

2017; Wlezien et al., 2017), and to follow the changes in future economic situations (Wlezien et al., 2017). In addition, some research studies have also shown that the so-called "asymmetric effects" (Ju, 2008; Soroka, 2006) indicate that when the economy deteriorates, it turns into a more negative tone, but, on the contrary, it does not change more positively when the economy improves.

On the other hand, there have been discussions regarding whether the tone change in economic conditions, such as the economic expansion or contraction period, and the economic news tone differ according to the government (Blood & Phillips, 1995). Earlier, Harrington (1989) found that US television tended to report more negatively when economic indicators such as unemployment rate, inflation, and growth rate deteriorated and that the media were overly negative for bad economic conditions. Heinz and Swinnen (2015) have also found in a recent study that newspaper coverage was 10 times higher when the job market was getting worse than when it was better. In contrast, Lischka (2016) argued that there is a difference in economic reporting between public and commercial broadcasting, which is related to the broadcasting company's revenue model.

In addition, there is a study on the relationship between media's political interests and changes in economic news tone. According to previous studies, the political attitudes of journalists are closely related to article content, headline selection, or framing decisions (Larcinese et al., 2011; Patterson & Donsbagh, 1996). Larcinese et al. (2011) argued that some newspapers, which have a partisan bias, report favorably on their preferred president or government when reporting economic news. These researchers point out that pro-Democratic government newspapers in America tend to report higher unemployment rates when their president is a Republican than a Democrat. In other words, the partisanship of the media affects the direction of media tone. Lott Jr. and Hassett (2014) reported that American newspapers treated economic problems more positively during the administration of a Democratic government than a Republican one. Besley and Prat (2006) argued that the political bias of journalists occurs more often when media companies are expected to benefit from their cooperation with the government, when there is ease of access to public officials to gather information, and when their intervention in administrative decisions of the government is possible. In a research in South Korea, there are studies that conservative media treated economic problems negatively during Roh Moo-hyun's liberal government due to their political interests regardless of the actual economic situation.

However, previous research studies were sporadically measured using short-term data, so they have not systematically presented the factors and conditions of the economic news tone. In particular, since the existing studies are mainly focused on the data of Western society, it is not certain whether they appear in the Korean society where the political and economic environments and conditions are different. As Wlezien et al. (2017) mentioned earlier, previous studies on the changes in the economic news tone have been mostly conducted in Western countries (Soroka, 2014) such as the United States, Canada, and the United Kingdom.

Advanced Western countries comprise a society that is more practical and substantial in value, with the market economy working relatively reasonably, and, so, the economic prospects as well as the political and economic values and attitudes of reporters may differ from those of other regional reporters (Wlezien et al., 2017). In this respect, I would like to point out how Korean reporters, who have interpreted the social problems of a bureaucratic ideology, have been covering the economic news for a long time in the government-led economic system. As a result, without knowing the mechanism by which the media report economic news in what factors, conditions, and circumstances, it is difficult to make political evaluation or prospects of the economic reality.

13.3   Research Questions and Hypotheses

RQ 1 and RH 1: Media coverage and tone change
RQ 1: Is there any discrepancy between the headline and the lead in the economic news tone?
RQ 2: How do economic news headlines and lead tones work by events?
RH 1: The economic news tone will differ depending on the characteristics of the media.

RH 2: Media tone change on future economic outlook vs. current economic situation
RH 2-1: Future economic outlook changes will have a greater impact on the tone change of media coverage than will future economic outlook levels.
RH 2-2: Future economic situation will have a greater impact on the tone change of media coverage than will the current economic situation.

RH 3: The bias tone of media coverage on the future economy
RH 3-1: The media will report a more negative tone on the outlook of future economic changes.
RH 3-2: Media reporting will also change negatively, if the future economic situation is expected to deteriorate rather than improve.
RH 3-3: Public broadcasting will report the outlook of the future economy less negatively than will (conservative) newspapers.
RH 3-4: Commercial broadcasting will report the outlook of the future economy more negatively than will (conservative) newspapers.

RH 4: The partisan bias tone of media coverage on the future economy according to the ideology of the government
RH 4-1: Public broadcasting will report the outlook of the future economy less negatively regardless of the ideology of the government.
RH 4-2: Commercial broadcasting will report the outlook of the future economy more negatively regardless of the ideology of the government.

RH 4-3: Conservative newspapers will report more negatively on the future economic outlook when it is a liberal government in charge and less negatively in the case of a conservative government.

13.4 Methods

1. Analysis Data and Analysis Frame

In order to resolve the abovementioned research questions, the economic news index and economic real indicators of individual media were used as independent variables. As a dependent variable, monthly economic news tone data were used. The analysis covered the main daily newspapers in Korea, one each of the major conservative and less conservative newspapers, and the broadcasting included both public and commercial broadcasting.

The news data included all economic news about the national economy reported on the front page in the case of newspapers. The broadcasting included national economic news reported in the evening news. The front page of the newspapers and the evening prime time news of the broadcasting were analyzed in terms of dealing with the most important issues of the day. On the other hand, we excluded news on indirect economic issues related to corporate news and economic scandals that were not directly related to the national economy.

The actual economic indicators use the Composite Coincident Index (CCI) and the Composite Leading Index (CLI), which represent the national economic reality, as well as official statistical data regularly announced by the National Statistical Office and the Bank of Korea. Variables of the actual economic indicators also use the coincident index and the leading index of the economy, which the government announces each month. The coincident index removes seasonal trends and extracts purely cyclical fluctuations that reflect seasonal volatility. The cyclical fluctuation value of the coincident index is the current economic condition and that of the leading index is the economic index that forecasts the future economic situation. In 2010, these indices had a base value of 100. If the economic index is below 100, then this means that the economic situation (or economic outlook) will deteriorate, and, if it is above 100, then this means that the economic situation (or economic outlook) will improve. The coincident index and the leading index are reconstituted with a level index showing the indicator itself (e.g., level) and a change index showing the change of the indicator.

The government ideological variables to be used as arbitration variables are divided into liberal government (Kim Dae-jung and Roh Moo-hyun terms of office), and conservative government (Lee Myung-bak and Park Geun-hye terms of office). Each of these categories is further divided into individual government or political ideology.

2. Data Collection Procedures and Analysis Variables

A coding operation of media data was performed according to a codebook prepared in advance. The media variable data is the conservative newspaper *Chosun Ilbo*, and *Dong-A Ilbo*, public broadcasting KBS, and commercial broadcasting *SBS*. Data were collected from the archives of the newspapers and the broadcaster's online homepage with the keywords "economy" and "national economy." In South Korea, *Chosun Ilbo* and *Dong-A Ilbo*, which have the most circulation among newspapers, and the KBS as a public broadcaster, and the SBS as a commercial broadcaster were included for data analysis. Economic news was collected from the front page of newspapers and from the evening general news of broadcasting.

The total economic news data was taken from the *Chosun Ilbo* 1285, *Donga Ilbo* 1224, *KBS* 2616, and *SBS* 3101. Data analysis was conducted on an extensive scale in 20 years (240 months in total) from February 1998, when the Kim Dae-Jung government was sworn in, to February 2017, when Park Geun-hye stepped down due to political impeachment. This period included two progressive governments (Kim Dae-jung and Roh Moo-hyun) and two conservative governments (Lee Myung-bak and Park Geun-hye).

The analysis used data from the Korea economic news for 20 years (1998–2017). The analysis unit was set on a monthly basis. The dependent variable, economic news tone change index, refers to the monthly average tone value. The tone was measured on a five-point interval scale from very negative (-2) to very positive (+2). The average news tone was minus 0.59.

This study was divided into two parts. First, we analyzed the overall landscape of the Korea economic news tone and then tried to systematically analyze what factors and conditions change the economic news tone. There were two reasons for showing the terrain of the economic news tone. First of all, the research on this was not conducted in Korea, and this study suggested that it is possible to follow-up on finding the factors and conditions that may change the economic news tone.

After analyzing the overall tendency of the economic news tone, the independent variables such as the economic reality index, the political and economic ideology of the media, the government structure, and the economic situation were carried over to the second stage. The purpose of this study was to determine the causes and consequences affecting the change of economic news tone.

13.5 Findings

1. *Tone of Media Coverage: Headlines* vs. *Leads by Events*

Let me start with some basic diagnostics by events. Here is a figure comparing the tone of coverage in headlines to the tone of coverage (1998.02–2017.02) using the "lead" paragraph. The results are highly similar. All the media's economic news had a distinctly positive tone when the financial crisis was completely overcome around early 2001. However, one interesting finding was that economic news took a rather positive tone during the course of the financial crisis (the International Monetary

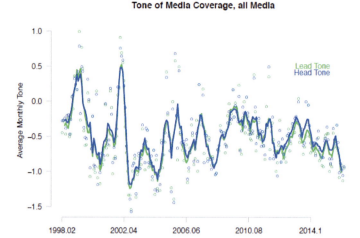

Fig. 13.1 Tone trend of media coverage by events

Fund (IMF) crisis). In addition, the tone of economic news changed negatively during Roh Moo-hyun's administration in 2003, which caused political conflicts with the media, and during Park Geun-hye's administration in early 2017, which faced political impeachment (Fig. 13.1).

2. *Tone of Media Coverage: Chosun Ilbo, Dong-A Ilbo, the KBS, and the SBS*

There are relatively small differences between the sources most of the time. There are a few periods that show differences. In early 2001, at the time of overcoming the financial crisis, all the media showed a generally positive tone. However, during the Roh Moo-hyun period in 2003, which was a progressive government in political conflicts with the conservative media, the tone of economic news in conservative newspapers such as the *Chosun Ilbo* and the *Dong-A Ilbo* was extremely negative, whereas economic news in broadcasting showed a relatively positive tone. The KBS was more positive than were other sources in mid-2006 and less positive than were other sources in early 2008. It is also noteworthy that the *Chosun Ilbo*, a conservative newspaper, showed a more positive tone than did other media around 2010, during the Lee Myung-bak period, the conservative government (Fig. 13.2).

3. *What Drives Media Coverage Tone? The CCI* vs. *The CLI and Lag* vs. *Change*

What drives media coverage? The table below shows some basic error correction models regressing changes in media tone as a function of either the CCI (Composite Coincident Index) or the CLI (Composite Leading Index). These results show no real difference between the two. Media tone does respond to these economic indicators but does so roughly to the same degree. Past US work suggests that

13 How Is Economic News Tone Driven: An Analysis of the Longitudinal...

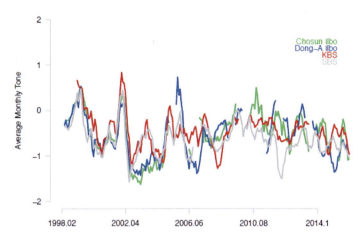

Fig. 13.2 Tone trend of individual media coverage by media

Table 13.1 Tone change as a function of the CCI vs. the CLI and lag vs. change

	Dependent variable: lead.tone.ch	
lead.tone.lag	−0.823***	−0.811***
	(0.011)	(0.011)
cci.cycle.ch	0.480***	
	(0.181)	
cci.cycle.lag	−0.058***	
	(0.005)	
cli.cycle.ch		0.375**
		(0.146)
cli.cycle.lag		−0.022***
		(0.004)
Constant	5.388***	1.757***
	(0.536)	(0.410)
Observations	8215	8215
R2	0.412	0.406
Adjusted R2	0.412	0.405
Residual Std. Error (df = 8211)	1.019	1.024
F Statistic (df = 3; 8211)	1918.483***	1868.227***

Note: $*p < 0.1$; $**p < 0.05$; $***p < 0.01$

leading indicators matter more in media coverage than do the current indicators. However, in terms of coefficient values alone, the current economic indicators have a somewhat greater influence on the tone of economic news than do the leading economic indicators in South Korea. Changes in the economic index had a greater effect on the tone change in economic news than levels (Table 13.1).

Table 13.2 Negativity bias of economic news coverage tone through the CLI

	Dependent variable: lead.tone.ch
lead.tone.lag	−0.811***
	(0.011)
cli.cycle.lag	−0.022***
	(0.004)
cli.cycle.ch.pos	0.294
	(0.196)
cli.cycle.ch.neg	0.478**
	(0.222)
Constant	1.750***
	(0.410)
Observations	8215
R2	0.406
Adjusted R2	0.405
Residual Std. Error	1.024 (df = 8210)
F Statistic	1401.161*** (df = 4; 8210)

Note: $*p < 0.1$; $**p < 0.05$; $***p < 0.01$

4. *A Negativity Bias of Economic News Coverage Tone*

Is there a negativity bias in response to the economy? The following table tests this possibility, by allowing upward changes in the CLI to have a different impact than downward changes. The results are similar to what has been shown in other countries—negative changes matter more than positive ones (Table 13.2).

5. *Differences Across Sources*

There are some differences across sources. On average, the KBS was more positive than were the newspapers and the SBS was more negative. That is, the public broadcaster KBS had the most positive and the SBS had the most negative influence on the tone of economic news, whereas the conservative newspaper *Dong-A Ilbo* had a negative effect, but it did not affect the tone change (Table 13.3).

6. *Differences Depending on Who Is in Power?*

Are there differences depending on who is in power? Here is the same model estimated for the four different leaders in power during this period (Table 13.4):

There are some interesting differences here. The KBS was more positive than were newspapers during the administration of the Dae-jung and Moo-hyun governments. They became less positive than newspapers during Myung-bak's administration. The SBS followed a roughly similar trend—more positive than newspapers during Moo-hyun and less positive during Myung-bak and Guen-hye. The two TV stations differed from each other during Dae-jung and Guen-hye.

The public broadcaster KBS treated economic news in a generally positive tone under the progressive government, whereas the commercial broadcaster SBS treated economic news relatively less positively under the conservative government.

Table 13.3 Tone differences by media sources

	Dependent variable: lead.tone.ch
lead.tone.lag	−0.813***
	(0.011)
cli.cycle.ch	0.368**
	(0.146)
cli.cycle.lag	−0.026***
	(0.004)
sourceDong-A Ilbo	−0.021
	(0.041)
sourceKBS	0.069**
	(0.035)
sourceSBS	−0.077**
	(0.034)
Constant	2.169***
	(0.418)
Observations	8215
R2	0.408
Adjusted R2	0.407
Residual Std. Error	1.022 (df = 8208)
F Statistic	941.699*** (df = 6; 8208)

Note: $*p < 0.1$; $**p < 0.05$; $***p < 0.01$

13.6 Discussion

This study examined the factors affecting the tone change of Korean economic news. In particular, we measured who and what caused the tone change and how it was done so through a 20-year longitudinal data analysis of Korean economic news. The analysis results are as follows. First, the tone of Korean economic news showed a similar pattern with no significant difference between the headlines and leads. However, the tone of economic news differed according to political and economic events. Contrary to expectations, despite the national financial crisis, the tone was positive, and when the crisis was overcome, the tone changed to a more positive tone. However, the tone of economic news changed negatively during Roh Moo-hyun's administration in 2003, which caused political conflicts with the conservative media, and during Park Geun-hye's administration in early 2017, which faced political impeachment.

Second, the tone of economic news during the same period showed a different pattern according to the ideology of the media. The public broadcaster KBS treated economic news more positively than did other media. In contrast, the commercial broadcasting SBS treated it in a generally negative tone compared to other media. In particular, the SBS treated national economy with an extremely negative tone in 2012, during Lee Myung-bak's administration, which emphasized economic issues.

Table 13.4 Tone differences by Korean presidents

	Dependent variable: lead.tone.ch			
	Dae.jung (1)	Moo.hyun (2)	Myung.bak (3)	Guen.hye (4)
lead.tone.lag	−0.781***	−0.798***	−0.894***	−0.875***
	(0.019)	(0.024)	(0.021)	(0.024)
cli.cycle.ch	0.252	0.649	1.072***	−1.610*
	(0.187)	(0.512)	(0.341)	(0.903)
cli.cycle.lag	−0.019***	−0.032	0.039**	−0.124**
	(0.005)	(0.028)	(0.015)	(0.061)
sourceDong-A Ilbo	−0.008	0.129	−0.011	−0.144*
	(0.071)	(0.095)	(0.079)	(0.086)
sourceKBS	0.159**	0.303***	−0.134**	0.042
	(0.069)	(0.078)	(0.063)	(0.074)
sourceSBS	−0.052	0.225***	−0.264***	−0.155**
	(0.061)	(0.078)	(0.063)	(0.072)
Constant	1.521***	2.440	−4.124***	11.948*
	(0.535)	(2.795)	(1.513)	(6.158)
Observations	2592	1728	2172	1723
R2	0.392	0.400	0.452	0.446
Adjusted R2	0.391	0.398	0.451	0.444
Residual Std. Error	1.125 (df = 2585)	1.044 (df = 1721)	0.911 (df = 2165)	0.932 (df = 1716)
F Statistic	277.984*** (df = 6; 2585)	191.487*** (df = 6; 1721)	297.707*** (df = 6; 2165)	230.623*** (df = 6; 1716)

Note: $*p < 0.1$; $**p < 0.05$; $***p < 0.01$

Third, actual economic indicators influenced the tone of economic news. The CCI, which indicates the current economic situation, and the CLI, which indicates the future economic situation, influenced the tone of economic news at almost the same degree. This result differed from previous research results (Soroka, 2014) that showed that the future economic situation has a greater effect on the tone of economic news than does the current economic situation. Rather, in terms of the regression coefficient alone, the current economic situation had a greater impact on the tone of economic news than did the future economic situation.

Fourth, economic index change had a greater effect on tone change in economic news than levels. The effect of changes in the economic index affecting the tone of economic news was greater than the simple lagged levels.

Fifth, the positive outlook index for the future economy had no effect on the tone change of economic news, but the negative outlook index had a distinct effect on the tone change. Here, the positive change in the economic outlook is statistically insignificant, but the negative change is clearly significant.

Sixth, the economic news coverage of the KBS, a public broadcaster, had the most statistically significant positive effect on the overall economic news tone change, whereas the commercial broadcaster SBS had a statistically significant negative effect. However, newspapers did not influence the change in the tone of economic news.

13.7 Conclusions

The results of this study provide several theoretical implications. The economic news reporting tone of the Korean media appeared positive in the midst of a national crisis. The Korean media tended to report the state of the national economy positively in situations of severe national economic crises such as the financial crisis (IMF crisis). The so-called "rally effect" that the media contributes to national unity and order in times of a national crisis was confirmed in the process of reporting on the national economy by the Korean media.

The tone of the national economy report was biased due to the partisan nature of the media. In particular, the tone of economic news reports by conservative media with different political ideologies was extremely negative. Under Roh Moo-hyun's administration, during which the actual national economic indicators were not bad, the economic news tone was negative.

The Chosun Ilbo, a conservative newspaper, reported the national economy in an extremely negative tone under the progressive Roh Moo-hyun administration but reported in a positive tone under the conservative Lee Myung-bak government, showing a bias toward "press–government parallelism." The KBS, whose personnel and finances are controlled by the government, showed positive reporting unlike other media during Roh Moo-hyun's administration, showing bias in reporting as well.

Economic news tone was influenced by the current national economic situation (Composite Coincident Index) and was more influenced by the change than the lag of the economic situation indicator. The tone of the national economy news appeared to be more influenced by the current economic situation, showing a different result from the preceding study (Soroka, 2014) that it was influenced by the future national economic situation (Composite Leading Index). In addition, when the economic situation indicator was announced as lagged levels, it did not affect the tone, but, when it was presented as change, it did affect the tone.

The economic news tone showed a correlation with the negative bias of the actual economic situation. In other words, the Korean national economy news did not affect the tone when the national economic situation changed positively, but it did affect the tone when the national economic situation changed negatively, thus confirming the negativity bias. In the case of the CCI, asymmetric reactions were shown in which change had a greater influence on tone than levels. The CLI also showed a similar pattern and an asymmetrical negative bias that only negative changes affect the tone of the news and not positive changes.

It was confirmed that the effect on the tone of national economic news was different depending on the media. The KBS, a public broadcaster, had the most positive effect on the tone of the national economic news, whereas the SBS, a commercial broadcaster, had the most negative effect on the tone. On the other hand, the newspaper media had a limited impact on the change in tone of national economy news.

The tone of the power source's national economic news differed depending on the relationship between the government and the media. The KBS, a public service news outlet, tended to pursue a positive reporting tone rather than critically reporting the national economy. This shows that the KBS plays a role as a guide that consistently drives public opinion on the Korean national economy in a positive direction. However, it can be interpreted that the SBS, a private news outlet, tends to adjust the tone of reporting differently according to market conditions and principles rather than political positions. In the case of newspapers, it was not possible to confirm the effect of different governments on the tone of national economy news, but, only under Park Geun-hye's administration, the *Dong-A Ilbo* reported more negatively than did the *Chosun Ilbo*, showing a difference.

Public opinion on the national economy affects a wide range of economic agents such as individuals, corporations, and countries. The media's reporting tone plays an extremely important role, and, therefore, the biased tone distorts the national economic reality. In the process of reporting national economic news, the Korean media excessively reflects partisan ideology, and the bias in tone is noticeable. We cannot overlook the fact that the media's bias tone in this partisan can make the national economic reality worse and distort public opinion on the economy. Above all, the press–government parallelism, in which the media reports in a positive tone on a government consistent with their political ideology and a negative tone on a government that contradicts it, shows the obstacles of economic news reporting.

References

Abo-Zaid, S. (2014). Revisions to US labor market data and the public's perception of the economy. *Economics Letters, 122*(2), 119–124.

Besley, T., & Prat, A. (2006). Handcuffs for the grabbing hand? Media capture and government accountability. *American Economic Review, 96*(3), 720–736.

Blood, D. J., & Phillips, P. C. (1995). Recession headline news, consumer sentiment, the state of the economy and presidential popularity: A time series analysis 1989–1993. *International Journal of Public Opinion Research, 7*(1), 2–22.

Dalen, A. V., de Vreese, C., & Albæk, E. (2015). Economic news through the magnifying glass. *Journalism Studies, 18*, 1–20.

Erikson, R. S., & Wlezien, C. (2012). The objective and subjective economy and the presidential vote. *PS: Political Science & Politics, 45*(4), 620–624.

Fogarty, B. J. (2005). Determining economic news coverage. *International Journal of Public Opinion Research, 17*(2), 149–172.

Garz, M. (2014). Good news and bad news: evidence of media bias in unemployment reports. *Public Choice, 161*(3–4), 499–515.

Harrington, D. E. (1989). Economic news on television: The determinants of coverage. *Public Opinion Quarterly, 53*(1), 17–40.

Heinz, M., & Swinnen, J. (2015). Media slant in economic news: A factor 20. *Economics Letters, 132*, 18–20.

Ju, Y. (2008). The asymmetry in economic news coverage and its impact on public perception in South Korea. *International Journal of Public Opinion Research, 20*(2), 237–249.

Ju, Y. (2014). Issue obtrusiveness and negative bias: exploring the moderating factors for asymmetric news coverage of the economy. *Asian Journal of Communication, 24*(5), 441–455.

Larcinese, V., Puglisi, R., & Snyder, J. M., Jr. (2011). Partisan bias in economic news: Evidence on the agenda-setting behavior of US newspapers. *Journal of Public Economics, 95*(9–10), 1178–1189.

Lewis-Beck, M. S., & Stegmaier, M. (2007). Economic models of voting.

Lischka, J. A. (2016). *Economic news, sentiment, and behavior: How economic and business news affects the economy*. Springer.

Lott, J. R., & Hassett, K. A. (2014). Is newspaper coverage of economic events politically biased? *Public Choice, 160*(1–2), 65–108.

McCarthy, K. J., & Dolfsma, W. (2014). Neutral media? Evidence of media bias and its economic impact. *Review of Social Economy, 72*(1), 42–54.

Patterson, T. E., & Donsbagh, W. (1996). News decisions: Journalists as partisan actors. *Political Communication, 13*(4), 455–468.

Soroka, S. N. (2006). Good news and bad news: Asymmetric responses to economic information. *Journal of Politics, 68*(2), 372–385.

Soroka, S. (2014). *Negativity in democratic politics*. Cambridge University.

Soroka, S., & McAdams, S. (2015). News, politics, and negativity. *Political Communication, 32*(1), 1–22.

Soroka, S., Daku, M., Hiaeshutter-Rice, D., Guggenheim, L., & Pasek, J. (2017). Negativity and positivity biases in economic news coverage: Traditional versus social media. *Communication Research, 1*(21), 1–21.

Tversky, A., & Kahneman, D. (1991). Loss aversion in riskless choice: A reference-dependent model. *Quarterly Journal of Economics, 106*(4), 1039–1061.

Wlezien, C., Soroka, S., & Stecula, D. (2017). A cross-national analysis of the causes and consequences of economic news. *Social Science Quarterly, 98*(3), 1010–1025.

Wu, H. D., McCracken, M. W., & Saito, S. (2004). Economic communication in the 'Lost Decade' news coverage and the Japanese recession. *Gazette (Leiden, Netherlands), 66*(2), 133–149.

Chapter 14
The Role of Trust and Contracts in the Expansion of Technology-Intensive SMEs

Ewa Baranowska-Prokop and Jacek Prokop

Abstract The main objective of this chapter is to provide an insight into the collaboration between technology-intensive small- and medium-sized enterprises (SMEs) and a large multinational firm. In this context, the role of trust and contracts has been assessed. It is argued that technology-intensive SMEs have to rely on trust with large multinational companies. However, it is crucial to have some mechanism that enables small firms to attract a large company to be committed to a stable relationship with a smaller partner. Such a mechanism is demonstrated by a simple model of profit sharing which may allow to develop a trustworthy collaboration between asymmetric partners.

Keywords Trust · Contracting · Technology-intensive SMEs

JEL Classification L14, L25

14.1 Introduction

A contract is complete when all relevant decisions (regarding, for example, trade, transfer, etc.) depend on verifiable variables, including announcements by the parties concerning their valuation, costs, etc. However, contracts are usually incomplete, and, therefore, transaction costs arise (see, e.g., Coase (1937) and Williamson (1975)). The costs of transacting are exacerbated by a turbulent environment faced by small- and medium-sized enterprises (SMEs) who plan to expand internationally.

E. Baranowska-Prokop
Department of International Marketing, SGH Warsaw School of Economics, Warsaw, Poland
e-mail: ebarano@sgh.waw.pl

J. Prokop (✉)
Department of Business Economics, SGH Warsaw School of Economics, Warsaw, Poland
e-mail: jacek.prokop@sgh.waw.pl

© The Author(s), under exclusive license to Springer Nature Switzerland AG 2024
N. Tsounis, A. Vlachvei (eds.), *Applied Economic Research and Trends*, Springer Proceedings in Business and Economics,
https://doi.org/10.1007/978-3-031-49105-4_14

Contracting by itself cannot replace the need for trust. Trust could be seen as a complementary mechanism that helps reduce transaction costs in the world of incomplete contracts (Blomqvist, 2002).

There is an asymmetry between technology-intensive SMEs and their partners; therefore, trust is of significant value in the context of incomplete contracting. In many cases, trust might be viewed as a sine qua non condition for not only collaboration but also contracting. A technology-based SME may be interested in collaboration with a large multinational firm with effective distribution channels in order to reach global (international) markets.

The SME grants the right to use its core technology if the larger firm, in return, offers access to their distribution channels in foreign countries and complementary resources. This situation creates significant risks for the technology-based SME. Without careful contracting, the SME could lose its most important source of competitive advantage. In the most extreme case, its strong business partner might take over the SME's technology, leaving the small firm with nothing (Oviatt & McDougall, 1994).

The main objective of this chapter is to provide an insight into the collaboration between technology-intensive SMEs and a large multinational firm. In this context, the role of trust and contracts has been assessed.

This chapter is organized as follows. In Sect. 14.2, the issue of imperfect contracting between firms is identified. Section 14.3 describes the role of trust in the relationships between contracting parties. In Sect. 14.4, the model of collaboration between asymmetric firms is offered. The last section contains the conclusions and directions of further research.

14.2 Imperfect Contracting

A highly dynamic technological environment is a major cause of imperfect contracting. Coase (1937) and Williamson (1975) have identified four types of incompleteness resulting from transaction costs. Two of them occur at the moment of contracting, and the remaining two occur during contract implementation.

Ex ante, some contingencies may not be foreseeable. Even if they could be predicted, there might be too many contingences to include in the contract. Monitoring the implementation of the contract involves costs and time. Contract enforcement may call for significant legal expenses (comp. Tirole, 1997).

All-inclusive contracts could be too rigid to allow for the cooperation to function (see e.g., Hart (1989) and Pisano (1990)). Actual contracts are often ambiguous and leave out many unexplained areas. The situation becomes even more complex in the international environment. The laws governing business practices vary across countries, and it may take too much time to identify all specificities and differences.

Companies internationalizing at a slow pace have more time to gather experience and information about laws and customs abroad. However, SMEs that would like to expand internationally at a rapid pace and scope face additional challenges. Moreover, their resources and size are limited.

In the world of incomplete contracts, the critical point is who has the right to be the decision-maker when a situation unforeseen by the formal contract arises (Hart, 2017). Stipulating the appropriate action in the agreement between the parties creates an intermediate form of transacting between two extreme situations. On the one hand, we have unconstrained bargaining (the simplest decision process), and, on the other hand, we have the theoretical benchmark of a complete contract. Intermediate forms can save transaction costs relative to complete contracts but without the perverse effects of unconstrained bargaining.

In this case, two possibilities arise. In the first one, both concerned parties rely on intermediation by a third party; that is, external arbitration. The second possibility is to give one of the concerned parties the right to be the decision-maker when an unspecified contingency occurs; that is called authority.

Arbitration by outside experts tends to be expensive, especially when they may have no immediate knowledge of the specificity of the given situation. Therefore, assigning authority to one of the parties may be viewed as a more efficient solution. However, authority does not exclude ex post negotiations. Grossman and Hart (1987) and Hart and Moore (1988) stress that authority changes the status quo point in the bargaining process by granting more power to the party that was given authority. There could be situations in which the preferred decision of the party with authority is extremely costly to the other party. In such cases, a mutually beneficial solution may be a good alternative to exercising the authority rights.

Despite our great abilities to determine optimal contracts, the research literature shows serious doubts about the possibility of their efficient implementation in practice. Macauloy (1963) pointed out that business relations between firms are much more informal than predicted by the theory. When firms engage in long-run cooperation, their reputation supports the efficient behavior. A firm that decides to deviate from its typical characteristics at some point faces the risk of losing future profitable ventures with its partner (see, e.g., Williamson (1975), chapter 6; Kreps (1990); and Tirole (1997), chapters 2 and 6)). Reputation contributes to building trust and enables a firm to save on the costs of preparing complete contracts. However, informality makes the firms vulnerable to the hazard of opportunism and typical holdup problems in business relationships when ex ante investments need to be undertaken.

14.3 The Role of Trust

Informal norms and customs augment formal contracts. These are labeled as "relational contracts" or "social contracts" (Macneil, 1980, Wathne & Heide, 2000). Knights et al. (2001, p. 314) state that "a long tradition of management thought conceptualizes trust and control as opposing alternatives" in which high trust allows for limited formal control, and vice versa. We define trust as the "willingness of a party to be vulnerable to the actions of another party based on the expectation that the other will perform an important action to the trustor, irrespective of the ability to monitor or control that other party" (Mayer et al., 1995: 712).

There are numerous situations in which a contract may not be enough or it may not be the most efficient way to conduct business. For instance, technology-intensive SMEs engaged in international collaboration need to share important information and know-how with their partners. Selling expertise leads to a disclosure of confidential information to potential partners in order to attract them. Unfortunately, this kind of knowledge cannot be fully protected by formal contracts, patents, or copyrights.

Limited trust provides large firms and SMEs with a fragile base to build mutual trust (Bachmann, 2001). The existing theories of trust show that trust is hard to build when the power relationship is asymmetrical (Fawcett et al., 2004; Sawers et al., 2008; Schoorman et al., 2007). Moreover, SMEs are more likely to view and experience trust in different ways, which can further intensify the asymmetry in trust (Graebner, 2009; Gulati & Sytch, 2008; Kramer & Tyler, 1996).

Mutual trust facilitates more efficient transfer of tacit knowledge and creates good bases for successful market operations (Blomqvist, 2002). It is particularly valuable to the international expansion of technology-intensive SMEs in forming partnerships. Lack of observability could be compensated by trust in order to mitigate the principle agent problem. Trust can substitute for costly monitoring in this case.

It can be argued that failure of trust significantly reduces the gains from business cooperation (Putnam, 1992). In particular, it is relatively a more important governance mechanism for SMEs that try to expand internationally relatively fast (Blomqvist et al., 2008). Researchers indicate that asymmetry in size and resources in contracting parties is an intrinsic feature of interfirm exchange that must be taken into account when explaining business relations (McEvily et al., 2003; Zaheer & Kamal, 2011). Moreover, asymmetry in trust can lead to misinformation, misrepresentation, and misinterpretation (Weber et al., 2005). Several authors have recognized that trust asymmetry could be overcome by active investment in trust (Child & Möllering, 2003; Sheppard & Sherman, 1998; Tsui-Auch & Möllering, 2010; Williams, 2007).

Trust is a complex phenomenon, and it is not easy to obtain. It is a multidisciplinary concept comprising sociopsychological, economic, and potentially other aspects. It may be based on cultural values, personality, and/or education. In international collaborations, the nature of trust and its levels vary across different national environments. Thus, the business relationship of partners based in different countries is expected to demonstrate strong asymmetries in the approach to trust. In the power asymmetry context of SMEs–large firms, there is a little guidance in the existing literature on how trust asymmetry is emerging and can be overcome among SMEs and large firms, what aspects are important, and how trust building evolves over time (Wang et al., 2015).

Technology-intensive SMEs must rely on trust with large multinational companies. However, it is crucial to have some mechanism that enables small firms to attract a large company to be committed to a stable relationship with a smaller partner. Such a mechanism could be provided by a relationship based on profit sharing demonstrated by a simple model in the next section.

14.4 A Simple Model of Profit Sharing

We consider a one-period model in which a technology-based SME would like to boost its international expansion by entering into an agreement with a large global company. The agreement stipulates that the SME share its profit with the global company (denoted by GC) for access to production facilities and international distribution channels.

We assume that the SME produces a single good at the cost given by the function $C_{SME}(\bullet)$. Given its own distribution channels, it can produce and sell in the relatively small (local) market described by the following inverse demand function $P_L(\bullet)$:

$$p_L = P_L(q_L), \tag{14.1}$$

where q_L denotes quantity demanded at price p_L.

By entering into the agreement with GC, it would have access to a much larger (global) market given by the inverse demand function $P_G(\bullet)$:

$$p_G = P_G(q_G), \tag{14.2}$$

where q_G denotes quantity demanded at price p_G.

The objective of the SME is to maximize its profit. By deciding to sell in the local market, the SME managers will choose the production level q_L to maximize:

$$\pi_{SME}^L(q_L) = p_L q_L - C_{SME}(q_L), \tag{14.3}$$

where π_{SME}^L is the profit achieved by the SME in the local market.

From the maximization of the profit function given by (14.3), we obtain the optimal decision of the SME regarding the production level; we denote it as q_L^*.

By deciding to access the global market through the marketing channels of GC, the SME managers will choose the production level q_G to maximize:

$$\pi_{SME}^G(q_G) = p_G q_G - C_{SME}(q_G). \tag{14.4}$$

We assume that by deciding to collaborate with GC, the SME will agree to pay the share of $(1 - s)$ of the total profit, resulting from the global market access enabled by GC, i.e.,

$$(1 - s) \pi_{\text{SME}}^{G} (q_G), \qquad (14.5)$$

where s $(0 < s < 1)$ denotes the share of the profit retained by the SME.

A higher s means that the benefit to the SME from its collaboration with GC will be greater.

The SME will be interested in such a collaboration as long as its profit resulting from the global market access will be greater than the profit achieved from selling in the local market alone, i.e.,

$$s\pi_{\text{SME}}^{G} (q_G) > \pi_{\text{SME}}^{L} (q_L), \qquad (14.6)$$

or

$$s > \frac{\pi_{\text{SME}}^{L} (q_L)}{\pi_{\text{SME}}^{G} (q_G)}. \qquad (14.7)$$

As long as the share of profit retained by the SME is larger than the ratio of profits from the local market and from the global market, the SME will have incentives to enter into the agreement with the GC.

An Illustrative Numerical Example

We provide a numerical example to illustrate the application of the general model. Let us assume that the inverse demand functions for the SME are specified as follows:

$$p_L = 1000 - q_L,$$

while operating in the local market only, and

$$p_G = 5000 - q_G,$$

while in agreement with GC.

The production costs of SME are given by the following function:

$$C_{\text{SME}}(q) = q^2 + 5000.$$

The profits of SME are calculated, respectively, as follows:

$$\pi_{\text{SME}}^{L} (q_L) = p_L q_L - C_{\text{SME}} (q_L) = (1000 - q_L) q_L - q_L^2 - 5000,$$

$$\pi_{\text{SME}}^{G} (q_G) = p_G q_G - C_{\text{SME}} (q_G) = (5000 - q_G) q_G - q_G^2 - 5000.$$

The above profits are maximized at $q_L = 250$ and $q_G = 1250$, respectively, and the actual amounts of maximal profits are $\pi^L_{SME}(250) = 120\,000$ and $\pi^G_{SME}(1250) = 3\,120\,000$, respectively.

$$ s > \frac{120\,000}{3\,120\,000} \approx 0.0385. $$

Clearly, the share of the profit at 0.0385 (3,85%) is the bottom line for any discussion of collaboration. The SME may expect a significantly higher share of the profit than this minimal ratio. The actual split of profits between firms will be the subject of negotiations. The bargaining power of the SME will very much depend on outside options, e.g., another global company that is ready to collaborate with the technology-based SME.

Once the profit-sharing collaboration starts, it will contribute to building trust for the longer-term relationship between firms.

14.5 Conclusions

In this chapter, we provided an insight into the collaboration between technology-intensive SMEs and a large multinational firm. The main focus was on the interrelationship between trust and contracts in such cooperation.

We argued that trust plays a crucial role for the technology-intensive SMEs engaging in business with large multinational companies. However, there must be some mechanism that enables small firms to attract a large company to be committed to a stable relationship with a smaller partner. We offered a simple model of profit sharing which may allow to establish a trustworthy cooperation between asymmetric business partners.

Clearly, it is necessary to further analyze the role of trust in contracting by applying formal modeling. For example, we may consider the probability of GC expropriating the know-how of the SME as a factor in evaluating the profitability of the collaboration for the vulnerable firm.

References

Bachmann, R. (2001). Trust, power and control in trans-organizational relations. *Organization Studies, 22*(2), 337–365.

Blomqvist, K. (2002). *Partnering in the dynamic environment: The role of trust in asymmetric technology partnership formation*, Ph.D. Dissertation, Lappeenranta University of Technology, Finland.

Blomqvist, K., Hurmelinna-Laukkanen, P., Nummela, N., & Saarenketo, S. (2008). The role of trust and contracts in the internationalization of technology-intensive born Globals. *The Journal of Engineering and Technology Management (JET-M), 25*(1–2), 123–135.

Child, J., & Möllering, G. (2003). Contextual confidence and active trust development in the Chinese business environment. *Organization Science, 14*(1), 69–80.

Coase, R. (1937). The nature of the firm. *Economica, 4*(4), 386–405.

Fawcett, S. E., Magnan, G. M., & Williams, A. J. (2004). Supply chain trust is within your grasp. *Supply Chain Management Review, 8*(2), 20–26.

Graebner, M. E. (2009). Caveat venditor: Trust asymmetries in acquisition of entrepreneurial firms. *The Academy of Management Journal, 52*(3), 435–472.

Grossman, S. J., & Hart, O. (1987). Vertical integration and the distribution of property rights. In A. Razin & E. Sadka (Eds.), *Economic policy in theory and practice* (pp. 504–548). Palgrave Macmillan.

Gulati, R., & Sytch, M. (2008). The dynamics of trust [review of handbook of trust research]. *The Academy of Management Review, 33*, 276–278.

Hart, O. (1989). An economist perspective on the theory of the firm. *Columbia Law Review, 89*(7), 1757–1774.

Hart, O. (2017). Incomplete contracts and control. *American Economic Review, 107*(7), 1731–1752.

Hart, O., & Moore, J. (1988). Incomplete Contracts and Renegotiation. *Econometrica, 56*(4), 755–785.

Knights, D., Noble, F., Vurdubakis, T., & Willmott, H. (2001). Chasing shadows: Control, virtuality and the production of trust. *Organization Studies, 22*(2), 311–336.

Kramer, R. M., & Tyler, T. R. (Eds.). (1996). *Trust in organizations: Frontiers of theory and research*. Sage.

Kreps, D. (1990). Corporate culture and economic theory. In *Perspectives on positive political economy* (pp. 90–142). Cambridge University Press.

Macauloy, S. (1963). Non contractual relations in business. *American Sociological Review, 45*(28), 55–70.

Macneil, I. R. (1980). *The new social contract: An inquiry into modern contractual relations* (pp. 134–137). Yale University Press.

Mayer, R. C., Davis, J. H., & Schoorman, F. D. (1995). An integrative model of organizational trust. *The Academy of Management Review, 20*, 709–734.

McEvily, B., Perrone, V., & Zaheer, A. (2003). Trust as an organizing principle. *Organization Science, 14*(1), 91–103.

Oviatt, B. M., & McDougall, P. P. (1994). Toward a theory of international new ventures. *Journal of International Business Studies, 25*(1), 45–64.

Pisano, G. (1990). The R&D boundaries of the firm: An empirical analysis. *Administrative Science Quarterly, 35*(1), 153–176.

Putnam, R. (1992). *Making democracy work: Civic traditions in modern Italy*. Princeton University Press.

Sawers, J. L., Pretorius, M. W., & Oerlemans, L. A. G. (2008). Safeguarding SMEs dynamic capabilities in technology innovative SME-large company partnerships in South Africa. *Technovation, 28*(4), 171–182.

Schoorman, F. D., Mayer, R. C., & Davis, J. H. (2007). An integrative model of organizational trust: Past, present, and future. *The Academy of Management Review, 32*(2), 344–354.

Sheppard, B. H., & Sherman, D. M. (1998). The grammars of trust: A model and general implications. *The Academy of Management Review, 23*(3), 422–437.

Tirole, J. (1997). *The theory of industrial organization*. The MIT Press.

Tsui-Auch, L. S., & Möllering, G. (2010). Wary managers: Unfavorable environments, perceived vulnerability, and the development of trust in foreign enterprises in China. *Journal of International Business Studies, 41*(6), 1016–1035.

Wang, H., Peverelli, P. J., & Bossink, B. A. G. (2015). The development of asymmetric Trust in Cooperation between Large Firms and SMEs: Insights from China. *Group Decision and Negotiation, 24*, 925–947.

Wathne, K., & Heide, J. B. (2000). Opportunism in Interfirm relationships: Forms, outcomes, and solutions. *Journal of Marketing, 64*(4), 36–51.

Weber, J. M., Malhotra, D., & Murnighan, J. K. (2005). Normal acts of irrational trust: Motivated attributions and the trust development process. In B. M. Staw & R. N. Kramer (Eds.), *Research in organizational behavior* (pp. 75–101). JAI Press.

Williams, M. (2007). Building genuine trust through interpersonal emotion management: A threat regulation model of trust and collaboration across boundaries. *The Academy of Management Review, 32*(2), 595–621.

Williamson, O. E. (1975). *Markets and hierarchies: Analysis and antitrust implications, a study in the economics of internal organization*. Free Press.

Zaheer, A., & Kamal, D. F. (2011). Creating trust in piranha-infested waters: The confluence of buyer, supplier and host country contexts. *Journal of International Business Studies, 42*, 48–55.

Chapter 15
Improving Employee Retention: Evidence from "Best Practices" in the Craft Sector to Tackle the Labor Shortage of Skilled Workers

Romina Klara Haller

Abstract The labor markets have undergone several significant transformations in recent years. Though companies used to be able to choose from many applicants, today, the issue of the "labor shortage of skilled workers," especially in the craft sector, is very present. Young skilled workers are highly sought after, and new retention measures are needed to retain them instead of only recruiting new talents. The chapter addresses the research question, *What are the leading factors for employees to stay in a firm and to what extent are these transferable to the craft sector?* A systematic literature review identified factors that keep people in the company. In the second step, qualitative expert interviews were conducted with managers or owners of craft enterprises, which were suggested as "Best Practices" by the self-regulated German Chambers of Crafts. Based on the literature review results, the interviewees confirmed three important stay factors for young people after their apprenticeship in the craft sector: autonomy, team spirit, and further education. Furthermore, extrinsic factors like money play a subordinate or given role. The results are also transferable to small- and medium-sized companies and give insight into the needs and motivation of Gen Z. They serve as an essential basis to derive countermeasures against the shortage of skilled workers and the increasing brain drain.

Keywords Employee retention · Shortage of skilled workers · Human resource management · Craft sector

---

R. K. Haller (✉)
Faculty of Business and Economics, Mendel University, Brno, Czech Republic
e-mail: xhaller@mendelu.cz

© The Author(s), under exclusive license to Springer Nature Switzerland AG 2024
N. Tsounis, A. Vlachvei (eds.), *Applied Economic Research and Trends*, Springer Proceedings in Business and Economics,
https://doi.org/10.1007/978-3-031-49105-4_15

15.1 Introduction

The demand for skilled workers has increased significantly, and employees are almost free to choose where they want to work (Allen et al., 2010). Due to the many jobs on offer, the labor market has become extremely dense. Therefore, terminating long-term employee contracts usually leaves a significant gap in experience and expertise, which is challenging to close again (Frank et al., 2004). Especially in the craft sector, a shortage of skilled workers can be identified in many countries and forecasts for the future show that demographic change and an increasing tendency toward academization will not improve the situation long term. Qualified skilled workers often migrate to industrial companies and leave the craft sector (Schirner et al., 2021).

On the one hand, companies will have to be even more attractive in the future to recruit skilled workers. On the other hand, the focus must shift to trained young workers and how to retain them in the company. Long-term employee retention is decisive in securing skilled labor in the future (Das & Baruah, 2013), meaning that new retention measures are needed (Haverkamp & Proeger, 2020). Historically, apprenticeship has been established as an integral part, to build up qualified professionals. The craft sector is the most important to train young people in Germany in the so-called "Dual System," a 3-year apprenticeship with a double learning site: the craft enterprise and the vocational school (Deißinger, 1998). After the apprenticeship, there are various options for the person: to stay in the company, to do a master craftsman apprenticeship, to continue with a school or academic career, or to change the industry. Since training involves high costs and commitment by the company, the aim is to be able to keep young skilled workers in the company.

15.2 Research Design and Literature Review

A two-stage research is applied to find out the leading factors for employees to stay in a firm and to what extent these are transferable to the craft sector. First, a detailed literature review followed by qualitative research through expert interviews was conducted. These interviews were carried out with managers and executives in the craft sector (construction and finishing trade) named by the regional chambers of craft as a benchmark for the underlying research focus. The aim is to analyze and categorize secondary data and then complement it with primary data.

This is a common ground in the literature that employees are the most important asset of a firm and successful retention measures are therefore crucial to secure them (Esser, 2022; Singh, 2019; Winterton, 2004). As a consequence, turnover results in different problems. *Firstly*, recruiting and turnover are both very costly processes. The most important positions are replacement costs, training costs, and costs of managers and others (Hennemann et al., 2018). These costs include recruiting, selecting, as well as training new employees and personal experiences combined with the workplace. According to Allen et al. (2010), the costs often exceed the position's annual salary. *Second*, turnover affects the organizational performance of the company. When highly qualified employees leave the company, this significantly impacts the work of the remaining employees (Shaw et al., 2005). *Third*, turnover threats will increase in the future regarding demographic change, globalization, and a shortage of skilled workers. That means companies must be aware of these scenarios and derive measures accordingly, to gain a relative advantage in times of crisis and staff shortages (Schirner et al., 2021).

It has long been assumed that the reasons why employees quit are identical to the factors why people stay. However, numerous studies have contradicted this assumption (e.g. Holtom & Interrieden, 2022; Reitz & Anderson, 2011). The present study, therefore, addressed the question of what makes people stay in a company rather than the reasons for turnover.

15.2.1 *Procedure and Methods*

This research intends to create a profound base of relevant factors that make people stay in firms as a basis for further qualitative research. The underlying research question is *"What are the leading factors for employees to stay in a firm and to what extent are these transferable to the craft sector?"* For this purpose, the following databases and library catalogs were used for the literature search: SCOPUS, JSTOR, ProQuest, Google Scholar, Google Search, Web of Science, Springer Link.

The following English search terms and their corresponding German terms were used as part of a targeted literature review. The Boolean operators AND/UND | NOT/NICHT | OR/ODER were used to connect the search terms.

retention
employee retention
employee retention AND craft sector
employee retention factors
retention factors AND craft sector
employee retention AND craft sector
employee retention management
employees AND craft sector
stay factors AND employees

The literature review identified a total of 2338 potential sources, of which 340 proved to be relevant to the stated research question. All sources were sorted and structured according to scientific requirements and quality. The year of publication was also considered in the selection. Consequently, the literature since 2002 was consulted for this study except for essential definitions and foundations from the earlier scientific literature.

The literature was coded with MAXQDA software, following an inductive, data-driven approach (Kuckartz & Rädiker, 2019). For this purpose, 10 principal

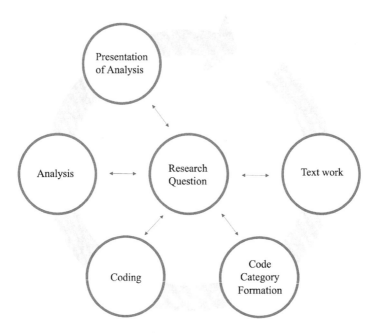

Fig. 15.1 Qualitative content analysis of Kuckartz (2016)

codes and 29 subcategories were developed inductively and deductively. Then, the literature was analyzed and systematized according to structured content analysis (Kuckartz & Rädiker, 2019). The relevant passages were encoded in 2328 codings and subsequently analyzed concerning the research question. Figure 15.1 shows an overview of the structured content analysis approach.

15.2.2 Results from Literature Analysis

The following graphic gives an overview of the codes developed through the structured content analysis and the belonging subcategories. Ten main codes and additional 29 subcodes were made to analyze the topic (Fig. 15.2).

Overriding Stay Factors The two primary motives why people stay are *job embeddedness* and the directly connected with it, *job satisfaction*. Employees having many connections to a company are more embedded and have numerous reasons to stay in a company (Mitchell et al., 2001). Job embeddedness focuses on three stances: (1) fit in an organization, (2) link within an organization, and (3) sacrifice of social benefits and material things like wages etc. (Allen & Shanock, 2013). Whether an employee fits in a company defines the degree to which workers consider themselves compatible with their work, values, and colleagues (Mitchell

Fig. 15.2 Literature code overview

et al., 2001). Some studies have looked at the relationship between job satisfaction and turnover and have found a clear negative relationship. Consequently, dissatisfied employees are likelier to quit their jobs and leave the company, e.g., Kyndt et al., 2009; Tett & Meyer, 1993; Trevor, 2001. In most cases, not a single factor is responsible, but a combination of factors is decisive for a termination. Existing research primarily concentrates on the industry, healthcare, and IT sectors (Hytter, 2007; Walker, 2001).

Autonomy One can follow the definition that autonomy "can be characterized by the ability to choose how to do one's work; having influence over one's work; and flexibility in workload decisions" (George, 2015, p. 106). Autonomy is an influential factor in job retention and reduces the intention to leave (Andrews & Wan, 2009). It is important for employees to have the possibility of free decisions, independent thoughts, and control over the pace and workload. An organization needs to empower its employees by giving them the competence to make decisions, thus ensuring that they feel a sense of belonging to the organization and stay with it (Ghosh et al., 2013). The flexibility of the work schedule represents, especially for women, an essential retention factor (Hausknecht et al., 2009). Horwitz et al. (2003) identified flexible work arrangements as a retention factor. Flexible working reduces absence and promotes employee loyalty (Eldridge & Nisar, 2011). Through the option of workplace flexibility, employees can better coordinate their private and work–life to increase their work–life balance and become happier (Singh, 2019). Happy employees can bring new innovations and creative ideas that are of major significance for self-determination (Idris, 2014).

Lavoie-Tremblay et al. (2006) describe autonomy on the job as a determinant factor and Spence Laschinger et al. (2009) a predictor of job satisfaction. Autonomy as a job characteristic is significant, especially for young professionals. Research indicates that Generation X (1965–1981) prefers autonomy; however, Generation Y focuses more on corporate social responsibility (Singh, 2019). Autonomy is also a core characteristic of high potentials who attach great importance to flexibility (Dries & Pepermans, 2008). Thus, autonomy can be seen as the ability to decide how to do one's work, influence one's work, and have flexibility in making decisions about one's workload (George, 2015).

Compensation and Benefit Compensation is one of the main HR tasks, and there is a positive relationship between compensation and appropriate compensation in the literature (Hong et al., 2012). In some cases, the benefit is limited to monetary compensation, but this should not be the standard because purely financial incentives do not sufficiently retain employees in the long-termed field (Allen & Shanock, 2013). Deferred bonuses can help people stay a short time in a firm but more from a monetary point of view. However, if the aim is to keep an employee short term in the company, a bonus can be a suitable measure (Cappelli, 2000). Poor wages and limited career opportunities lead to employee dissatisfaction and resignation, especially when there is a regional downgrade of extra payments (Abujaber & Katsioloudes, 2015). Since many employees see earnings as their value to the organization, earnings can make workers feel that they have a vested interest in the organization's collective success, heighten their sense of self-worth, and strengthen their commitment and loyalty. In other words, compensation affects a person psychologically, economically, and sociologically (Abbasi & Hollman, 2000). Furthermore, the authors agree that purely monetary incentives do not retain employees in the long term. Many reasons, other than money, make people stay in their organizations. Many companies are dissatisfied with employees' attachment to an organization and their sense of fit in the job and the community (Mitchell et al., 2022). The essential aspects of compensation in terms of employee retention seem to be the perception that compensation decisions are transparent and that salaries are fair based on performance and effort (George, 2015). Employee compensation significantly influences the relationship between types of employee participation and retention (Khalid & Nawab, 2018).

Development Opportunities Training and development opportunities have two sides. On the one hand, many researchers agree that training can counteract fluctuation. Through growth opportunities, employees are well-positioned and stay with the company. If employees do not see opportunities to develop their skills within the company, they may be more likely to move to a competitor or a company where they can thrive (Azeez, 2017).

On the other hand, training can also improve employees' marketability, as they are better trained and more attractive to other companies. Accordingly, they are more likely to be poached or leave the company because of better opportunities in the labor market. However, those who receive more training are slightly less likely to quit than those who receive little or no training. There is also growing evidence that employees are increasingly considering future growth opportunities when making decisions about changing jobs, which means training and development play an important role in this (Allen et al., 2003). In general, developmental opportunities can positively increase an employee's commitment to stay in an organization (Cardy & Lengnick-Hall, 2011). Deery and Jago (2015) support this statement and prove that on-the-job training increases employees' commitment and retention. Failure to invest in training and development can therefore contribute to higher labor turnover (Winterton, 2004).

Management Aspects There are two central recurring management parameters for successful retention: the suitable style of leadership and the perceived management support by employees (Paillé, 2013; Spence Laschinger et al., 2009). Countless research exists about the appropriate style of leadership that is seen as the most critical management topic. Several studies noted that the way people are managed and led has a direct influence on the retention of employees. Participative leadership style significantly affects employee retention (Kroon & Freese, 2013), respectively increases higher employee participation the employee retention (delegative, consultative, worker director, and worker union) (Khalid & Nawab, 2018). This is confirmed by the fact that employee involvement in decision-making motivates employees to stay in an organization (Lavoie-Tremblay et al., 2006). Taking part in decision-making processes makes employees feel being part of the organization, increasing loyalty and, with it, retaining (Noah, 2008).

Organizational Commitment

The concept of organizational commitment, when used as a predictor of employee retention, has become the focus of managers in general and HR departments in many companies. Organizational commitment (OC) is defined as "the relative strength of an individual's identification with and involvement in a particular organization" (Mowday et al., 1979, p. 226).

The OC of people is essential as it affects their commitment to the company and contributes to their loyalty to the company (Meyer & Allen, 1997). Private premises of loyalty, trust, commitment, identification, and attachment with the company directly influence employee retention (Hytter, 2007). In addition, there is a positive relationship between motivation and retention. When a firm can motivate its employees more individually, it will directly increase the productivity and efficiency of its operation (Hong et al., 2012).

Person-Organization-Fit The concept of fit is based on whether the employee meets the criteria for a specific position and organization (Cloutier et al., 2015). Based on the idea that organizational productivity and individual performance will improve as a result of congruity between the value of an individuum and the company's values, beliefs, and goals (Chatman, 1989). Due to Chew and Chan (2004), OC and intention to stay were significantly related to person-organization-fit. The better the P-O-fit, the higher the probability for employees to remain in the firm. Employees who perceive a fit with the company are more likely to survive than those less suited (Chew & Com, 2004). Appreciative learning and working climate contribute positively to employee retention because it makes people feel acknowledged for their strengths and creates possibilities to develop people's qualities (Cooperrider et al., 2003).

Work–Life Balance Work–life balance is defined as being able to find enough time for activities other than work (George, 2015). The balance between work and other life domains means that some professional workers will give up some degree of success if this allows more time for different areas of life. Work–life balance has moved firmly into the requirement profile of employees in recent years.

Some professionals who have achieved significant career success may then decide to emphasize other areas of their life in the following years. Jobs that fulfil personal or family responsibilities enhance retention (Loan-Clarke et al., 2010). Horwitz et al. (2003) describe the working place as a "fun place" to retain employees successfully. A conducive environment can be critical in building a workplace where sufficient resources and fun are also allowed. In organizations where there was a high level of inefficiency, high staff turnover was observed (Alexander et al., 1994). Workers are more likely to stay if the work environment is promising and the reverse is also true (Zuber, 2001).

Reward and Recognition Employees are more willing to invest in their work when they feel that the organization supports their psychological need to feel safe and supported (Maslow, 1958).

For the best workers to stay, companies must provide incentives to keep them and implement personnel services (Abbasi & Hollman, 2000). What the motivation must look like is not primarily monetarily oriented but firmly based on the value generated by the employee. Employee satisfaction and job retention can be achieved through recognition (Buckingham & Coffman, 1999). There is also a greater need for employees to work collaboratively, emphasizing various team-based structures. Firms will need more outstanding commitment and staff engagement to remain competitive in the future and to retain employees successfully (Burke & Ng, 2006). It is important to strengthen employee engagement. This can help retain talent because employees are satisfied and enjoy their work. These employees care about their work and about the company, which they are happy to support with their contribution (Vance, 2006).

Craft The craft sector is an almost untouched field. Binder and Blankenberg (2021) published a unique paper based on data from the craft sector in Germany that investigates the connection between identity and well-being in the Skilled Crafts and Trades. Existing research did not emphasize this category of employees, the sector of the economy or its businesses except a few studies like Kossivi et al. (2016). Analyzing the research clearly shows the general research gap in the craft sector. Merely the fact that the craft sector is problematic in recruiting and retention is mentioned but without clear recommendations or implications for the future. The work "The Craftsmen" by Sennett (2008) sheds light on this craft field but more from a theoretical perspective. However, the calls for research (e.g., Khalid & Nawab, 2018) focus more on the craft sector, and its employees, especially young employees, are straightforward and necessary. The research will therefore lead to a contribution from a practical and theoretical point of view.

Employee retention is very complex and depends on several factors. The aim is to verify that identified factors can be used as a guideline to regularly reflect on and adjust the management strategy. Furthermore, the main codes serve as a basis for the qualitative in the second step and the subsequent quantitative research. The aim is to check to what extent the factors are also applicable in the craft sector, which are the particularly important ones and whether there are other additional factors.

15.3 Expert Interview Study

15.3.1 Descriptive Analysis and Implementation

The craft sector is the number one apprenticeship provider in Germany. The *Dual System* (*Duales System*) combines practical work and learning in the company with reflective theoretical training in the vocational school and is unique and historically grown in German-speaking countries. This is especially true for the dual system, which, at least in some countries, simultaneously functions as historical derivatives of apprenticeships. Examples are Germany, Switzerland, Austria, Denmark, or the Netherlands. Even in Anglo-Saxon countries such as Australia or the United Kingdom, apprenticeship training has been reinvented, usually with the addition of "modern" or "new," in the last two decades. This has occurred in the wake of reforms aimed at creating other pathways into employment alongside non-formal on-the-job training, traditional school-based VET programs and higher education courses designed to provide labor-market-relevant skills (Deissinger, 1996).

In the federal state of Baden-Württemberg in Germany, are eight Chambers of Crafts. All of them were contacted by mail and asked which company or companies should be mentioned as *"Best-Practice"* in their chamber area. The following criteria must be met:

- The craft company must be in the chamber area.
- The craft company must train apprentices regularly.
- The craft company must belong to the construction and finishing trades.
- The company must successfully train apprentices and retain them in the company (takeover rate of more than 50%).

Due to the necessity for further research in the craft sector, all chambers acted very supportively and showed their commitment. The Chambers are located in Freiburg, Heilbronn-Franken, Stuttgart, Karlsruhe, Constance, Mannheim, Reutlingen, Stuttgart, and Ulm. Because Karlsruhe did not show a direct e-mail address, they were not contacted accordingly. Every other Chamber of Crafts ($n = 7$) recommended at least one to six "Best-practice" companies. That means there is a 100% return rate by the Chambers of Crafts. The companies that the Chambers of Crafts recommended were invited via e-mail to conduct an expert interview. Of 20 suggested companies that all were contacted, 10 out of 6 chambers responded via mail, resulting in a response rate of 50%. Some of them had no time in the survey period, and others did not respond at all. All firms had maximum flexibility to appoint the interviews. They could propose one or more dates themselves; the interviews were conducted by telephone or via teams if desired, and all received the guiding questions in advance by e-mail. Afterward, the transcript was sent to them for review and approval. This offer was accepted, and only two interviewees made minimal corrections or adjustments.

Definition of an Expert The interviewees have to be in a management position in the craft sector and directly connected to the apprentices and the training process. For data safety reasons and based on the request of some of the experts, all expert opinions, statements, and company names have been anonymized in this study. The table below gives an overview of the anonymized companies, the function and age of the interviewee, the crafts, the number of trainees, and the number of apprentices (Table 15.1).

Of the 10 interviews, 7 interviewees were male, two were female, and one was mixed with two interviewees because the owner of the firm and his wife lead the firm together. The request for an interview was followed by e-mail or telephone. At the request of the interviewees, all interviews were conducted by telephone or digitally via the Teams platform and recorded by audio, which offered the experts maximum flexibility and allowed them to choose a suitable and convenient date. All interviews were held in German, and the interview questions were sent to the interviewees in advance to show the direction of the interview. At the beginning of the interviews, there was a detailed explanation of the dissertation thesis topic, the supervision situation, and the research questions, as well as an explanation of the consent form for collecting personal data and recording via laptop. The explanation of the general information was not transcribed and lasted about 10 min.

In the consent form, the interviewees confirm the recording of the interview and the subsequent transcription of the interview content, which can be seen as an appendix in the thesis. Furthermore, the interviewees were informed that they could stop or pause the interview at any time and that they did not have to answer selected questions if they did not want to. Depending on the level of detail provided by the respondents, all interviews lasted at least 35 min, sometimes up to an hour. The following question types were asked in the interview (Hussy et al., 2010):

- General and introductory questions: framing concerning the company, the position of the interviewee, number of apprentices.
- Structured questions (fully planned)
- Ad hoc questions to keep flexibility (unplanned)

When conducting the interview, communication rules of active listening were prioritized by giving the interviewee the maximum amount of speaking time, allowing the interviewee to clarify their expertise and point of view better. Furthermore, truth is subjective and should not be commented on or evaluated by the interviewer (Helfferich, 2009).

15.3.2 Quality Criteria

The data in expert interviews is always context-dependent, and each interview would be different if it were conducted several times. Therefore, quality criteria of standardized procedures do not apply to qualitative interviews. The goal of

Table 15.1 Qualitative data collection of expert interviews from December 2022–February 2023, $n = 10$

	Gender	Interviewee (age)	Craft profession	Company size and number of apprentices
1	Male	General Manager (63)	Electronics technician for energy and building technology	150 employees, 23 apprentices
2	Male	General Manager (62)	Bricklayers and draftsmen	45–60 employees, 11 apprentices
3	Male	General Manager and Partner (48)	Carpenter and monument protection	166 employees, 26 apprentices
4	Male	Managing Director (58)	Plasterer	85 employees, 9 apprentices
5	Male	Managing Partner (35)	Building services engineering and building envelope	285 employees, 40 employees
6	Male	General Manager (37)	Carpentry	30 employees, 5 apprentices
7	Female	Human Resource Manager and Successor (27)	Plumbing, heating, and air conditioning	50 employees, 10 apprentices
8	Male	Managing Director (33)	Road construction and construction machinery	130 employees, 8 apprentices
9	Male and female	Managing Director (53) and owner with his wife (Human Resource Manager and Accounting)	Electricity and building installation	25 employees, 6 apprentices
10	Female	Marketing Manager and Successor (24)	Floor and Tile layer	40 employees, 9 apprentices

qualitative research should not be to guarantee objectivity in the classical context but to conduct subjectivity in an appropriate manner. The lack of objectivity is ultimately the starting point of qualitative research (Helfferich, 2009). The reliability test was carried out according to the concept of inter-coding agreement (intra-coder reliability), in which a coder coded the interviews at 1-week intervals. Since the classification of the categories is very clear based on the statements, almost no discrepancies could be determined due to the time interval. A second coder did the coding separately, and the concordance is approved. The reliability of the coding is consequently considered to be given (Döring & Bortz, 2016).

When conducting the interviews, care was taken to ensure that the share of speech lay with the interviewed expert and that the interviewer commented as little as possible. In addition, the guiding questionnaire enabled a clearly structured concept to be adhered to. The validity, whether the implementation measures exactly what it is supposed to be measured, can also be seen as given. All interview partners received the dissertation thesis's exact topic and research questions.

15.3.3 Coding and Results

For the evaluation, a deductive categorization of four areas was already made when designing the guiding questionnaire: Category A, B, C, and D. Area B was divided into two categories: First, general challenges in the craft sector and second, the discussion and confirmation of the literature findings. The categories were by no means worked through statically one after the other during the interview but are considered as a theoretical framework for the interviewer. Depending on the answering technique, the questions could be asked in a different order as desired so as not to disrupt the dynamics of the conversation. Nevertheless, the attempt was made to cover all questions meaningfully in a situationally appropriate order. The following table gives an overview of the categories and the respective subcategories that resulted from the interviews. Quotations are given as examples to obtain the identical wording of the experts and gain insights into the direct argumentation structure.

The following table gives an overview of the respective main categories and subcategories and will be explained in detail (Tables 15.2 and 15.3).

The biggest challenge craft firms are struggling with is securing skilled workers in the future. All interviewees confirmed that this is the biggest challenge for the craft sector in general. Fifty percentage of the interviewees also confirmed that apprenticeship is part of the historical nature of the craft. Learn from each other and give experience as a craftsman to the young people. One possible reason for their struggle seems to be the bad image. The academic education seems to be better regarded in society due to the idea that academic education implies a better professional career. This is also associated with a political problem. The image's relevance was stated by 50% of the experts when they got asked about their current biggest challenge when they got asked about their biggest current challenge. When

15 Improving Employee Retention: Evidence from "Best Practices" in the. . .

Table 15.2 Category scheme of interview study

Category A	Current situation and challenges
Motivation	(a) Securing skilled workers (b) Tradition
Challenges	(a) Individual needs (b) Image (c) Succession (d) Quality and costs of apprentices (e) Poaching
Category B	**B1 retention in craft sector**
	(a) Pre-boarding (b) Seniority (c) Flexibility (d) Working environment (e) Teambuilding (f) Quality in apprenticeship (g) Money (h) Stay-interviews/surveys
	B2 literature
	(a) Autonomy (b) Team (c) Further education (d) Money (e) Work–life balance (f) Recognition/appreciation (g) Employer branding. (h) Person-organization-fit (i) Organizational commitment/job embeddedness/satisfaction
Category C	**Successful retention**
	(a) High quality apprenticeship (b) Humanity (c) Sense (d) Immigration (e) Size of company (f) Onboarding
Category D	**Wishes**
	(a) Better image and information (b) School support (c) Others

asked about their biggest wish for the future, even 100% referred to the craft's image.

Apprenticeship is very costly and intense. Therefore, high quality is key to a successful apprenticeship and subsequent long-term employment. Apprenticeship is very individual concerning personal needs and requirements. A further challenge in the crafts sector is the currently rising need for succession solutions for many craft firms. Due to the shortage of skilled workers and the manager's approaching retirement age, many managers decided already and others will follow them to

Table 15.3 Most relevant questions and answers of interview study

Category A	Current situation and challenges	Consent and support
What is your motivation to train apprentices?	1. Securing skilled workers 2. Tradition	100% 50%
Where do you currently see the most significant challenge in the craft sector?	1. Image 2. Individual needs 3. Succession 4. Quality and costs of apprentices 5. Poaching	50% 30% 30% 30% 20%
Category B	**B1 retention in craft sector**	
How do you concretely retain employees and especially young trainees in your company?	1. Quality in apprenticeship 2. Teambuilding 3. Working environment 4. Pre-boarding 5. Stay-interviews/surveys seniority 6. Flexibility 7. Money	70% 60% 60% 50% 10% 10% .
	B2 literature	
Which employee retention factors do you consider most important? Which of the factors are your TOP 3 and why?	1. Autonomy 2. Team 3. Further education	90% 80% 70%
Category C	**Successful retention**	
What does successful retention of apprentices in the craft sector look like for you in concrete terms?	1. High-quality apprenticeship 2. Humanity 3. Sense/appreciation 4. Immigration 5. Size of company	70% 50% 30% 30% 30%
Category D	**Wishes**	
What is your wish for the craft sector and young people?	1. Better image and information 2. School support 3. Others	100% 40% 40%

close their companies in the upcoming years. The war for talents through poaching continues to rise the tension in the market. The main key to successful retention is a high-quality apprenticeship. Even if there is the prejudice that high-quality apprenticeships will lead to a higher possibility that young people will not stay but continue with further education. A second very important factor is team spirit and the working environment. Sixty percentage mentioned team spirit as essential for retention and the working environment. Flexibility during work, especially with the working hours, is also associated with a good work atmosphere.

Retention already starts with pre-boarding and, therefore, way earlier than the official start of the apprenticeship. As examples can education fairs, internships, traineeships, and cooperation with schools already contribute to successful employee retention (50%). Communication and reflection are very important factors, too. Through stay-interviews and regular surveys, possible topics and issues of the young people and all other staff members can get identified, solved, adapted, or implemented improvements. There has been a significant change in young people's conscientiousness and commitment; therefore, regular exchange is crucial for successful employee retention. Apart from this, the money factor plays a very varying importance. For some companies, wages are only considered as a complete side issue, while for the other it is perceived as a big threat (loose employees to higher paying industries) or as a big opportunity, since many craftsmen get paid wages above the collectively agreed wage. The interviewees were asked about the retention factors from the literature analysis and confirmed that all are important for the craft sector, too. The three most important ones are autonomy, the team, and further education. Especially for the younger employees from Generation Z, autonomy is a very important value. The factor teamwork can even get stronger emphasized (e.g., on the construction side) in the direction of a "working family" that must be suited together.

The third most important factor, further education is training in technical competences and operations and further education that concerns the personal level. Master qualifications or studies with a fixed development plan are also a suitable way to retain young people in a long term. Larger companies score better in terms of development opportunities and promotion prospects. Smaller companies can often work directly with the boss or company owner.

As a central recommendation for other craft enterprises, the highly qualitative training could be mentioned above all. Trainees, for example, want to be seen as human beings, not as unskilled and cheap labor. In the past, the apprentice was a subordinate to the master craftsman, but today it is more becoming a meeting at eye level, which the young people prefer. The topic of humanity and human interaction is indispensable and necessary for this mind set. This point is also contributing to the factor of teamwork. Only those who act fairly, humanely, and collegially can retain employees in the future. The meaning of work is especially relevant for young trainees. Handicraft work brings a sense of purpose through the activity per se and can therefore be made even more conscious using personnel measures. The issue of immigration of skilled workers is also an important point for the future that must not be disregarded alongside all retention methods. Due to the significant, ongoing demographic change, some of the interviewed companies have already moved their recruitment efforts toward immigrant groups. When asked about what they would like to see for the craft sector and young people, the interviewees called not only for an improvement of their industries image, as described before, but also for the support of schools. Schools need to do more educational work in the field of vocational education and in the classroom, which gives students a better insight into the variety and opportunities of craft professions.

As stated before, employee retention begins long before the employee starts working. Through internships, trade fairs, and other binding measures with and in the company, young people can be inspired by the company. Onboarding also plays an important role so that employees arrive and feel comfortable right from the start. One wish that could support the integration of refugees into the labor market is the definition of an additional, new job description for construction workers with lower entry barriers. A simplified job profile would allow a much faster integration of immigrants without the need to learn all the technical and academic content in detail as in the common training. State support and promotion of more training in the craft sector and bonuses for companies that train them successfully would be further ideas to counteract the trend toward a skilled labor shortage in the future. Higher wages for the craft sector and standardization of hourly rates. At least 100 euros per hour must be paid for the craft sector to achieve pay equity with other industries. Another wish is to introduce compulsory basic craft training as a basis for further skill assessments and, therefore, to evaluate an academic path.

All the companies surveyed have a very high general level of commitment and creativity, which should be more intensively explored and utilized by the political, educational, and media sectors. This would enable us to benefit from each other even more and develop constructive solutions.

15.4 Conclusions

The main motivation to train young employees is the securing of skilled workers. Craft firms want to build up the specialists of the future through high-quality apprenticeships. Companies that do not provide training risk losing access to qualified employees in the future. One of the main problems is the social perception that the craft, and especially the apprenticeship, are not sufficiently recognized and valued compared to an academic career. This issue may already need attention during early school levels and is not perceived as sufficiently supported by political authorities. Companies must be aware that autonomy, team, and further education are crucial elements to retain young employees in the future. Autonomy can be granted to the young apprentices in an early phase through self-determined activities on the construction site or by handing over small areas of responsibility. The role of the trainer as coach and life counselor should be considered equally important. Team activities to improve collaborative and supportive behavior should also be strengthened outside of working hours, and team members must be carefully selected accordingly. There are many ways to retain skilled workers in the future successfully. To do so, companies as a whole organization must stay curious and open toward everlasting, changing circumstances and become creative problem solvers. Furthermore, individual training plans must be worked out and aligned with the apprentices, discussed, and reviewed in regular meetings and updated if necessary.

References

Abbasi, S. M., & Hollman, K. W. (2000). Turnover: The real bottom line. *Public Personnel Management, 29*, 333–342. https://doi.org/10.1177/009102600002900303

Abujaber, A., & Katsioloudes, M. (2015). Impact of HR retention strategies in healthcare: The case of Qatar. *Avicenna, 2015*. https://doi.org/10.5339/avi.2015.6

Alexander, J. A., Bloom, J. R., & Nuchols, B. A. (1994). Nursing turnover and hospital efficiency: An organization-level analysis. *Industrial Relations: A Journal of Economy and Society, 33*, 505–520.

Allen, D. G., & Shanock, L. R. (2013). Perceived organizational support and embeddedness as key mechanisms connecting socialization tactics to commitment and turnover among new employees: Socialization and turnover. *Journal of Organizational Behaviour, 34*, 350–369. https://doi.org/10.1002/job.1805

Allen, D. G., Shore, L. M., & Griffeth, R. W. (2003). The role of perceived organizational support and supportive human resource practices in the turnover process. *Journal of Management, 29*, 99–118.

Allen, D. G., Bryant, P. C., & Vardaman, J. M. (2010). Retaining talent: Replacing misconceptions with evidence-based strategies. *Academy of Management Perspectives, 24*, S.48–S.64.

Andrews, D. R., & Wan, T. T. H. (2009). The importance of mental health to the experience of job strain: An evidence-guided approach to improve retention. *Journal of Nursing Management, 17*, 340–351. https://doi.org/10.1111/j.1365-2934.2008.00852.x

Azeez, S. (2017). Human resource management practices and employee retention: A review of literature. *Journal of Environmental Management and Tourism, 18*, 1–10. https://doi.org/10.9734/JEMT/2017/32997

Binder, M., & Blankenberg, A. K. (2021). *Identity and well-being in the skilled crafts and trades* (p. 62). Levy Economics Institute of Bard College.

Buckingham, M., & Coffman, C. (1999). *First, break all the rules: What the world's greatest managers do differently*. Simon and Schuster.

Burke, R. J., & Ng, E. (2006). The changing nature of work and organizations: Implications for human resource management. *Human Resource Management Review, 16*, 86–94. https://doi.org/10.1016/j.hrmr.2006.03.006

Cappelli, P. (2000). A market-driven approach to retaining talent. *Harvard Business Review, 78*(1), 103–111.

Cardy, R. L., & Lengnick-Hall, M. L. (2011). Will they stay or will they go? Exploring a customer-oriented approach to employee retention. *Journal of Business and Psychology, 26*, 213–217. https://doi.org/10.1007/s10869-011-9223-8

Chatman, J. A. (1989). Matching people and organizations: Selection and socialization in public accounting firms. In *Academy of management proceedings* (pp. 199–203). Academy of Management Briarcliff Manor.

Chew, J., & Chan, C. C. A. (2004). Human resource practices, organizational commitment and intention to stay. *International Journal of Manpower, 29*(6), 503–522.

Chew, J., & Com, B. (2004). *The influence of human resource management practices on the retention of core employees of Australian Organisations: An empirical study* (p. 296). Murdoch University.

Cloutier, O., Felusiak, L., & Hill, C. (2015). The importance of developing strategies for employee retention. *Journal of Leadership, Accountability and Ethics, 12*(2), 119–129.

Cooperrider, D. L., Whitney, D. K., & Stavros, J. M. (2003). *Appreciative inquiry handbook: The first in a series of AI workbooks for leaders of change*. Berrett-Koehler Publishers.

Das, B. L., & Baruah, M. (2013). Employee retention: A review of literature. *IOSR Journal of Business and Management (IOSR-JBM), 14*, 08–16. https://doi.org/10.9790/487X-1420816

Deery, M., & Jago, L. (2015). Revisiting talent management, work-life balance and retention strategies. *International Journal of Contemporary Hospitality Management, 27*, 453–472.

Deißinger, T. (1998). *Beruflichkeit als "organisierendes Prinzip" der deutschen Berufsausbildung*.

Deissinger, T. (1996). Germany's Vocational Training Act: its function as an instrument of quality control within a tradition-based vocational training system. *Oxford Review of Education, 22*(3), 317–336.

Döring, N., & Bortz, J. (2016). *Forschungsmethoden und Evaluation in den Sozial- und Humanwissenschaften.* Springer-Lehrbuch/Springer Berlin Heidelberg. https://doi.org/10.1007/978-3-642-41089-5

Dries, N., & Pepermans, R. (2008). "Real" high-potential careers: An empirical study into the perspectives of organisations and high potentials. *Personnel Review.* https://doi.org/10.1108/00483480810839987

Eldridge, D., & Nisar, T. (2011). Employee and organizational impacts of flexitime work arrangements. *Relations Industrielles/Industrial Relations, 66,* 213–234.

Esser, H. (2022). *Alarmstufe Rot auf dem Fachkräftemarkt Bildungs- und Erwerbsmigration stärken.*

Frank, F. D., Finnegan, R. P., & Taylor, C. R. (2004). The race for talent: Retaining and engaging workers in the 21st century. *Human Resource Planning, 27,* 15.

George, C. (2015). Retaining professional workers: What makes them stay? *Employee Relations, 37,* 102–121. https://doi.org/10.1108/ER-10-2013-0151

Ghosh, P., Satyawadi, R., Prasad Joshi, J., & Shadman, M. (2013). Who stays with you? Factors predicting employees' intention to stay. *International Journal of Organizational Analysis, 21,* 288–312. https://doi.org/10.1108/IJOA-Sep-2011-0511

Hausknecht, J. P., Rodda, J., & Howard, M. J. (2009). Targeted employee retention: Performance-based and job-related differences in reported reasons for staying. *Human Resource Management, 48,* 269–288. https://doi.org/10.1002/hrm.20279

Haverkamp, K., & Proeger, T. (2020). Ausbilder der Nation, Integrator und Impulsgeber: Die Rolle des Handwerks im deutschen Bildungssystem. Göttinger Beiträge zur Handwerksforschung.

Hennemann, S., Witthüft, M., Bethge, M., Spanier, K., Beutel, M. E., & Zwerenz, R. (2018). Acceptance and barriers to access of occupational e-mental health: cross-sectional findings from a health-risk population of employees. *International Archives of Occupational and Environmental Health, 91,* 305–316.

Helfferich, C. (2009). *Die Qualität qualitativer Daten. Manual für die Durchführung qualitativer Interviews.* 3., überarb. Aufl. Lehrbuch.

Holtom, B. C., & Interrieden, E. J. (2022). Integrating the unfolding model and job embeddedness model to better understand voluntary turnover. *Journal of Managerial Issues, 18*(4), 435–452.

Hong, E. N. C., Hao, L. Z., Kumar, R., Ramendran, C., & Kadiresan, V. (2012). An effectiveness of human resource management practices on employee retention in institute of higher learning: A regression analysis. *International Journal of Business Research and Management, 3*(2), 60–79.

Horwitz, F. M., Heng, C. T., & Quazi, H. A. (2003). Finders, keepers? Attracting, motivating and retaining knowledge workers. *Human Resource Management Journal, 13,* 23–44. https://doi.org/10.1111/j.1748-8583.2003.tb00103.x

Hussy, W., Schreier, M., & Echterhoff, G. (2010). *Forschungsmethoden in Psychologie und Sozialwissenschaften.* Springer-Lehrbuch/Springer.

Hytter, A. (2007). Retention strategies in France and Sweden. *Irish Journal of Management, 28,* 59–79.

Idris, A. (2014). Flexible working as an employee retention strategy in developing countries: Malaysian Bank managers speak. *Journal of Management Research, 14,* 71–86.

Khalid, K., & Nawab, S. (2018). Employee participation and employee retention in view of compensation. *SAGE Open, 8,* 215824401881006. https://doi.org/10.1177/2158244018810067

Kossivi, B., Xu, M., & Kalgora, B. (2016). Study on determining factors of employee retention. *Open Journal of Social Sciences, 04,* 261–268. https://doi.org/10.4236/jss.2016.45029

Kroon, B., & Freese, C. (2013). Can HR practices retain flexworkers with their agency? *International Journal of Manpower, 34,* 899–917. https://doi.org/10.1108/IJM-07-2013-0169

Kuckartz, U. (2016). *Qualitative content analysis.* [in GER: Qualitative Inhaltsanalyse] [online]. 3., überarbeiteteAuflage. Beltz Juventa. GrundlagentexteMethoden. ISBN 978-3-7799-3344-1.

Kuckartz, U., & Rädiker, S. (2019). *Analyzing qualitative data with MAXQDA: Text, audio, and video.* Springer International Publishing. https://doi.org/10.1007/978-3-030-15671-8

Kyndt, E., Dochy, F., Michielsen, M., & Moeyaert, B. (2009). Employee retention: Organisational and personal perspectives. *Vocations and Learning, 2*, 195–215. https://doi.org/10.1007/s12186-009-9024-7

Lavoie-Tremblay, M., O'Brien-Paallas, L., Viens, C., Brabant, L. H., & Gelinas, C. (2006). Towards an integrated approach for the management of ageing nurses. *Journal of Nursing Management, 14*, 207–212.

Loan-Clarke, J., Arnold, J., Coombs, C., Hartley, R., & Bosley, S. (2010). Retention, turnover and return – A longitudinal study of allied health professionals in Britain: Retention, turnover and return. *Human Resource Management Journal, 20*, 391–406. https://doi.org/10.1111/j.1748-8583.2010.00140.x

Maslow, A. H. (1958). A dynamic theory of human motivation. In C. L. Stacey & M. DeMartino (Eds.), *Understanding human motivation* (pp. 26–47). Howard Allen Publishers.

Meyer, J. P., & Allen, N. J. (1997). *Commitment in the workplace: Theory, research, and application*. SAGE Publications.

Mitchell, T. R., Holtom, B. C., Lee, T. W., Sablynski, C. J., & Erez, M. (2001). Why people stay: Using job embeddedness to predict voluntary turnover. *Academy of Management Journal, 44*, 1102–1121.

Mitchell, T. R., Holtom, B. C., Lee, T. W., & Sablynski, C. J. (2022). Why people stay: Using job embeddedness to predict voluntary turnover. *Academy of Management Journal, 44*(6), 1102–1121.

Mowday, R. T., Steers, R. M., & Porter, L. W. (1979). The measurement of organizational commitment. *Journal of Vocational Behavior, 14*(2), 224–247. https://doi.org/10.1016/0001-8791(79)90072-1

Noah, Y. (2008). A study of worker participation in management decision making within selected establishments in Lagos, Nigeria. *Journal of Social Sciences, 17*, 31–39.

Paillé, P. (2013). Organizational citizenship behaviour and employee retention: How important are turnover cognitions? *The International Journal of Human Resource Management, 24*, 768–790. https://doi.org/10.1080/09585192.2012.697477

Reitz, O., & Anderson, M. A. (2011). An overview of job embeddedness. *Journal of Professional Nursing, 27*, 320–327. https://doi.org/10.1016/j.profnurs.2011.04.004

Schirner, S., Malin, L., Hickmann, H., & Werner, D. (2021). *Fachkräfteengpässe in Unternehmen – Fachkräftemangel und Nachwuchsqualifizierung im Handwerk* (Research report no. 1/2021). KOFA-Studie.

Sennett, R. (2008). *The craftsman*. Yale University Press.

Shaw, J. D., Duffy, M. K., Johnson, J. L., & Lockhart, D. E. (2005). Turnover, social capital losses, and performance. *Academy of Management Journal, 48*, 594–606. https://doi.org/10.5465/amj.2005.17843940

Singh, D. (2019). A literature review on employee retention with focus on recent trends. *International Journal of Scientific Research in Science, Engineering and Technology*, 425–431. https://doi.org/10.32628/IJSRST195463

Spence Laschinger, H. K., Leiter, M., Day, A., & Gilin, D. (2009). Workplace empowerment, incivility, and burnout: Impact on staff nurse recruitment and retention outcomes. *Journal of Nursing Management, 17*, 302–311. https://doi.org/10.1111/j.1365-2834.2009.00999.x

Tett, R. P., & Meyer, J. P. (1993). Job satisfaction, organizational commitment, turnover intention, and turnover: Path analyses based on meta-analytic findings. *Personnel Psychology, 46*, 259–293.

Trevor, C. O. (2001). Interactions among actual ease-of-movement determinants and job satisfaction in the prediction of voluntary turnover. *Academy of Management Journal, 44*, 621–638.

Vance, R. J. (2006). Employee engagement and commitment. *SHRM Foundation, 1*, 1–53.

Walker, J. W. (2001). Zero defections? *Human Resource Planning, 24*, 6–8.

Winterton, J. (2004). A conceptual model of labour turnover and retention. *Human Resource Development International, 7*, 371–390. https://doi.org/10.1080/1367886042000201967

Zuber, A. (2001). A career in food service cons: High turnover. *Nations Restaurant News, 35*, 147–148.

Chapter 16
Blockchain Research Trends in Information Systems: A Systematic Review

Van Nguyen Nhu Tam and Cao Tien Thanh

Abstract Blockchain technology has emerged as a disruptive innovation that has the potential to transform various industries, including information systems. With the increasing adoption of blockchain, researchers have explored various aspects of this technology, including its security, scalability, interoperability, and governance. This chapter presents a systematic review of the blockchain research trends in information systems. The study analyzes the research published between 2018 and 2023 in top-tier information systems journals, conferences, and workshops. The findings of this chapter reveal that blockchain research in information systems has primarily focused on three themes: blockchain architecture and infrastructure, blockchain applications, and blockchain governance. The chapter concludes with recommendations for future research in this area.

Keywords Blockchain · Information system · Research trend · Technology

16.1 Introduction

The blockchain is a decentralized, write-only database that contains transactions and is highly resistant to tampering, even in the absence of a central operator. It is widely believed that the blockchain has the potential to significantly alter our economies and societies by reducing transaction costs and the reliance on trusted intermediaries, as suggested by various studies.

Investments made by public and private organizations in blockchain technology are fueled by its potential to revolutionize societies and markets. Cryptocurrencies enabled by blockchain, such as Bitcoin, have attracted significant attention from investors and generated mixed responses from regulators. Meanwhile, more com-

---

V. N. N. Tam (✉) · C. T. Thanh
Department of Information Technology, University of Foreign Languages and Information Technology, Ho Chi Minh City, Vietnam
e-mail: tamvnn@huflit.edu.vn; thanhct@huflit.edu.vn

© The Author(s), under exclusive license to Springer Nature Switzerland AG 2024
N. Tsounis, A. Vlachvei (eds.), *Applied Economic Research and Trends*, Springer Proceedings in Business and Economics,
https://doi.org/10.1007/978-3-031-49105-4_16

plex applications are being developed, relying on blockchain-based smart contracts that ensure the execution of algorithms stored on the blockchain. Ethereum co-founder Vitalik Buterin introduced this concept in 2014. A partnership between Maersk and IBM was recently announced, with the goal of significantly enhancing the efficiency and security of global product transportation (Nærland et al., 2018). The consensus among influential players is that blockchain technology could have a significant impact on various facets of our society, ranging from environmental sustainability (Chapron, 2017) to healthcare (Gammon et al., 2018) and social networks (Ciriello et al., 2018). Despite organizations investing in exploring the potential of blockchain, research within the field of information systems (IS) investigating blockchain technology is limited. Some initial research has provided valuable insights into the development of applications that utilize blockchain-based smart contracts (Egelund-Müller et al., 2017). Additionally, other studies have explored the practical use of cryptocurrencies, such as Li and Wang's (2017) empirical study on the factors that determine the exchange rates of Bitcoin. So, the field of information systems (IS) has not yet contributed enough to form a theory-driven or empirically derived understanding of blockchain and its implications (Beck et al., 2017). This special issue aims to address this gap in scholarly conversation by presenting cutting-edge IS research, as well as setting an agenda for future research studying the opportunities and challenges of blockchain. The issue emphasizes inclusivity by considering three major paradigms in IS research, including behavioral, design, and economics, both in the three papers included and the research directions provided in this editorial. The following is an overview of the three papers included in the special issue, along with our own suggestions for future blockchain research in the IS community. The article *Self-Organising in Blockchain Infrastructures: Generativity Through Shifting Objectives and Forking'* by Andersen and Ingram Bogusz explores the concept of self-organizing infrastructures. Through a longitudinal case study of forking within the Bitcoin blockchain infrastructure, the authors illustrate how diverging objectives of different implementer groups can result in forks that create incompatible subversions of the infrastructure. These forks are interpreted as manifestations of self-organizing within the growing community. The article provides a valuable contribution to theory by describing various patterns of self-organizing within the Bitcoin blockchain.

Chanson et al. utilize a design science research methodology to create a blockchain-based solution for safeguarding sensor data in Internet of Things (IoT) systems for used cars. The paper aims to address the issue of insecure communications and data storage in IoT devices by iteratively designing a system. The resulting design principles are evaluated by experts and reported as an initial design theory for protecting IoT sensor data generation and processing. The paper presents a unique combination of innovative design, design theorizing, and practical implications, which is uncommon in design science research papers. Their work is detailed in the second paper entitled *Privacy-Preserving Data Certification in the Internet of Things: Leveraging Blockchain Technology to Protect Sensor Data.*

The paper titled *Business on Chain: A Comparative Case Study of Five Blockchain-Inspired Business Models,* by Hua et al., explores how blockchain technology is utilized by companies to generate and acquire value in new and innovative ways. Employing a comparative, exploratory, multiple case study approach, the authors analyzed the experiences of five firms in mainland China that implemented blockchain initiatives. Through this analysis, the authors developed a typology of five blockchain-inspired business models, namely platformer, disintermediator, mediator, transformer, and co-innovator, each with unique market differentiation logics. They also offer valuable insights into the value creation and capturing mechanisms of each model and highlight potential challenges that could impact their long-term viability.

In this chapter, we present our concerns regarding the state of blockchain research in the IS field and introduce a framework that moves the IS discipline's focus beyond the application of blockchain. Specifically, we argue for greater attention to be directed toward understanding the blockchain protocol level and its interactions with blockchain applications. In Sect. 16.3, we describe the systematic review process used to identify the relevant studies. The inclusion and exclusion criteria will be discussed, along with the search strategy used to retrieve the articles. The data extraction and analysis methods will also be explained. In Sect. 16.4, we discuss critical issues related to the blockchain protocol level and its interactions with blockchain applications, both of which we believe are crucial for future IS research on blockchain. The next section will present the findings of the systematic review. The key research trends in blockchain and information systems will be discussed, along with the research methodologies used and the main findings of the studies. Finally, we conclude in Sect. 16.6.

16.2 Related Work

Currently, there are concerns about the state of blockchain research in the IS (Information Systems) field. Many studies tend to focus solely on the applications of blockchain technology, neglecting the fundamental protocol level and its interactions with blockchain applications. This approach can result in limited insights into the potential of blockchain technology and may hinder its wider adoption. To address this issue, a framework has been proposed that directs the attention of the IS discipline beyond blockchain applications toward understanding the blockchain protocol level and its interactions with applications. By doing so, researchers can gain a deeper understanding of the technology and its capabilities, leading to more impactful and meaningful research. Here are some newer concerns regarding blockchain research in the IS field:

– Interoperability: As blockchain technology evolves, there is a growing need for interoperability among different blockchain networks. However, current research in the IS field has not adequately addressed this issue.

- Governance: Blockchain technology often requires decentralized governance mechanisms, but there is a lack of understanding of how such mechanisms can be effectively designed and implemented.
- Scalability: As blockchain technology gains wider adoption, its scalability has become a critical concern. There is a need for research on how to improve the scalability of blockchain systems while maintaining their security and decentralization.
- Energy consumption: The energy consumption of blockchain networks, especially those that use proof-of-work consensus algorithms, is a significant concern. There is a need for research on how to reduce the energy consumption of blockchain systems while maintaining their security.
- Regulation: The regulatory landscape around blockchain technology is constantly evolving, and there is a need for research on how to design blockchain systems that comply with existing regulations while also promoting innovation.

These concerns highlight the need for continued research on blockchain technology in the IS field, focusing on emerging challenges and opportunities to ensure that the technology is effectively utilized and implemented. Lingxiu Dong et al. in (Dong et al. (2022)) investigate how the use of blockchain technology impacts the operational and financial decisions made by different agents in the supply chain and the resulting profit levels. The study aims to provide insights into the potential benefits and challenges of blockchain adoption in a complex supply chain setting and to inform decision-making processes for supply chain managers and practitioners considering the implementation of blockchain technology. The use of blockchain technology in supply chain management has the potential to improve efficiency, transparency, and trust among supply chain participants, ultimately leading to a more resilient and sustainable supply chain ecosystem, as depicted in Fig. 16.1.

The author in (Ali et al., 2022) makes a valuable contribution by creating a forum for sharing manufacturing data related to quality across the entire system. This ensures that all members and processes of the system receive verified information that enhances trust, transparency, and the ability to trace and track products. As a result, manufacturers can improve their product and system quality to meet the expectations of customers and stakeholders. Kumari and Devi in (2022) investigate the impact of FinTech and blockchain technologies on digital banking and financial services. The study reveals that these technologies have a significant impact on the current digitalization trends. The research is primarily concerned with the modernization processes in banking and financial services, with a particular emphasis on the community.

In addition, the authors in Verma and Sheel (2022) describe a general review on blockchain for government organizations. The main goal of this study is to encourage policymakers and governments to allocate resources toward implementing blockchain technology to improve public services and government organizations. The study emphasizes the practical implications of using blockchain in public departments, as it can enhance transparency and efficiency in public life. Addi-

Fig. 16.1 Blockchain-based supply chain

tionally, the social implications of blockchain are highlighted, as it can improve the transparency, traceability, and accountability of public records. This study is innovative as it is one of the first to chronologically emphasize the importance of blockchain in government-controlled public departments.

The following section will outline the methodology on blockchain research trends in information systems.

16.3 Methodology

16.3.1 Components

In general, the most recent studies on blockchain research trends in information systems could include the following components:

- Research Question: Clearly state the research question that the systematic review aims to answer. For example, the research question could be "What are the emerging research themes and areas in blockchain research in information systems?"

- Search Strategy: Describe the search strategy used to identify relevant studies. This may include the databases searched, the search terms used, and the inclusion and exclusion criteria for studies. It is important to ensure that the search strategy is comprehensive and reproducible.
- Study Selection: Describe the process for selecting studies. This may include screening titles and abstracts and full-text screening. It is important to ensure that the study selection process is transparent and reproducible.
- Data Extraction: Describe the process for extracting data from selected studies. This may include extracting information on study characteristics, research themes, and emerging areas. It is important to ensure that the data extraction process is consistent and accurate.
- Quality Assessment: Describe the process for assessing the quality of selected studies. This may include evaluating the rigor of the research design, the validity of the findings, and the relevance of the study to the research question.
- Data Synthesis: Describe the process for synthesizing the data extracted from selected studies. This may involve using qualitative or quantitative methods to identify research themes, emerging areas, and gaps in the literature.
- Results: Present the findings of the systematic review. This may include a summary of the number of studies included, the research themes identified, and the emerging areas in blockchain research in information systems.
- Limitations: Describe any limitations of the systematic review, such as the possibility of publication bias or the exclusion of relevant studies due to language barriers.
- Conclusion: Summarize the main findings of the systematic review, and provide implications for future research in blockchain research in information systems.

The process involves several steps, including identifying research questions, conducting a literature review, data collection and analysis, presenting results and findings, and providing conclusions and recommendations. Overall, the Methodology section should provide a clear and comprehensive description of the systematic review process, from study selection to data synthesis. This will ensure that the study is transparent, reproducible, and rigorous as shown in Fig. 16.2. When conducting blockchain research, it is important to consider the technical, organizational, and social aspects of blockchain technology. The research methodology should be tailored to the specific research problem, and the data collection and analysis techniques should be appropriate to the nature of the data. As shown in Fig. 16.3, blockchain research is expected to address the issues of trust, sharing, and privacy as part of human society (Zhao et al., 2016).

Fig. 16.2 Blockchain research method processing

16 Blockchain Research Trends in Information Systems: A Systematic Review

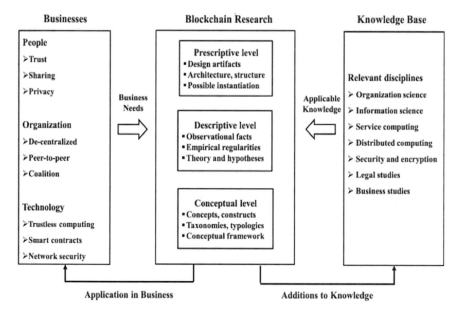

Fig. 16.3 Blockchain research landscape (Zhao et al., 2016)

In addition, Table 16.1 describes a few examples of research trends in information systems. We will synthesize a few case study methods and make objective assessments, thereby proposing effective and appropriate solutions to the current context.

16.3.2 Overview of Consensus Algorithms

Anonymity is a desired feature of blockchain, but it creates a trust issue regarding the honesty of anonymous users who add transactions to the ledger. To address this problem, each transaction must be validated as legal, and then the transactions are added to a block. Consensus algorithms are used to reach agreement on adding a block to the blockchain. These algorithms leverage the common interest of the majority of users in keeping the blockchain honest. The consensus algorithm is crucial in building trust in the blockchain system and ensuring proper storage of transactions on the blocks. Therefore, it can be said that consensus algorithms are the core of all blockchain transactions. Several consensus mechanisms have been specifically designed for blockchains, such as Proof of Work (PoW) (Squarepants, 2022), Proof of Stake (PoS) (Vasin, 2014), Directed Acyclic Graph (DAG) (Digitale et al., 2022), Proof of Elapsed Time (PoET), Delegated Proof of Stake (DPoS) (Larimer, 2017), Practical Byzantine Fault Tolerance (PBFT) (Xu et al., 2021), Proof of Authority (PoA) (Gourisetti et al., 2020), Tendermint (Kwon,

Table 16.1 Blockchain research trends in information systems

Name [Year]	Description	Ref
Financial Innovation and Technology After COVID-19: A Few Directions for Policy Makers and Regulators in the View of Old and New Disruptors [2021]	The authors suggest identifying specific areas for intervention and developing strategies to address them, such as strengthening regulatory frameworks and increasing collaboration among regulatory agencies. They emphasize the importance of balancing regulatory oversight with innovation and the need to engage with stakeholders to create effective policies	Pompella and Costantino (2021)
Ethical Marketing in the Blockchain-Based Sharing Economy: Theoretical Integration and Guiding Insights [2021]	The article ends by suggesting various areas for future research that highlight three different methods of stakeholder theory—the descriptive, instrumental, and normative approaches. The main goal of these directions is to provide guidance to marketing experts on how blockchain technology can facilitate an institutionalized view of ethical marketing activities and practices that promote collaborative marketing, innovation in value chains, and sustainable business models in the sharing economy, as well as in the metaverse	Tan and Salo (2021)
Blockchain Technology in Healthcare: Challenges and Opportunities [2022]	The purpose of this study was to examine how blockchain technology can help address the most pressing and complex issues facing the healthcare industry. A literature review was conducted to identify the roles played by blockchain technology in healthcare and to outline the challenges and opportunities associated with its implementation. The study also provides an overview of the various health-related blockchain products available and highlights key players in this field who are offering solutions across different applications	Attaran (2022)
Blockchain-Enabled Humanitarian Supply Chain Management: Sustainability and Responsibility [2023]	The objective of this paper is to develop a comprehensive theoretical model that can be used to facilitate the adoption of blockchain technology in supply chain management. This will be achieved by identifying the factors that drive blockchain adoption and analyzing how these factors are interdependent and affect the adoption process	Hanna (2023)

2014), Scalable Byzantine Consensus Protocol (SCP) (Damle et al., 2021), Proof of Bandwidth (PoB), Proof of Importance (PoI), Proof of Burn, and Proof of Capacity (PoC) (Jiang & Wu, 2020).

– Proof of Work (PoW) is the original consensus algorithm used by Bitcoin and many other cryptocurrencies. It requires nodes to solve a computational puzzle

16 Blockchain Research Trends in Information Systems: A Systematic Review 273

to add a new block to the chain, which is resource-intensive and can lead to high energy consumption.

- Proof of Stake (PoS) is an alternative to PoW that relies on nodes holding a certain amount of cryptocurrency as "stake" to validate transactions and add new blocks to the chain. This reduces energy consumption but can lead to centralization of power among those with the most stake.
- Delegated Proof of Stake (DPoS) is similar to PoS, but instead of all nodes having an equal chance of being chosen to validate transactions and add blocks, a small group of nodes (referred to as "delegates" or "witnesses") are elected by stakeholders to perform this function.
- Proof of Authority (PoA) is a consensus algorithm that relies on a fixed set of validators who are trusted to add new blocks to the chain based on their identity or reputation. This results in faster transaction processing but can lead to centralization.

These are just a few examples of consensus algorithms used in blockchain technology. Other algorithms, such as Proof of Elapsed Time (PoET) and Byzantine Fault Tolerance (BFT), have also been developed and implemented in various blockchain systems. Each mechanism is uniquely designed to cater to the requirements of specific blockchains. Some of them are shown in Table 16.2.

Table 16.2 Comparison of consensus algorithms

	PoW	PoS	PoET
Energy efficiency	Very low	High	High
Finality and scalability in a network	High	Medium	Medium
Setup	Open blockchain/ private blockchain	Public permissionless/ private blockchain	Open blockchain/ private blockchain
Motivators	The miner who successfully validates the block receives new coins and transaction fees as a reward	The block validator who successfully adds a new block to the blockchain is rewarded with both the transaction fees included in the block and newly minted coins. If the validator tries to add an invalid block to the chain, it will forfeit its stake	The possibility of damaging their reputation and losing their earnings serves as a motivation for delegates to act in an honest manner and ensure the security of the network
Majority or 51% attack	More than 25% of all nodes being malicious can lead to an attack	Decreased likelihood of a 51% attack	Reduced 51% attack probability

The next section will describe some several critical issues related to the blockchain protocol level and its interactions with applications.

16.4 Critical Issues on Blockchain Protocol Level

There are several critical issues related to the blockchain protocol level and its interactions with blockchain applications. One of the key issues is scalability, as blockchain networks struggle with the increasing volume of transactions, resulting in slower transaction processing times and higher transaction fees. Another issue is security, as blockchain networks are susceptible to 51% attacks and other security breaches. Interoperability is also a concern, as different blockchain protocols may not be compatible with one another, hindering the development of decentralized applications that operate across multiple blockchain networks. Additionally, governance and consensus mechanisms within blockchain networks can present challenges, such as conflicts over proposed changes to the protocol and the potential for centralization of decision-making power. These critical issues must be addressed to ensure the continued growth and success of blockchain technology. The key challenges for blockchain adoption are depicted in Fig. 16.4.

16.4.1 Security Issues

As the blockchain ecosystem continues to evolve and new use-cases emerge, organizations across various industries will encounter a complex and potentially chal-

Fig. 16.4 Key challenges for blockchain adoption

lenging set of obstacles and dependencies. Among the issues plaguing blockchain technology are security concerns. Therefore, what are the security vulnerabilities of blockchain?

– 51% attacks: The architecture of blockchain technology varies, resulting in different designs with varying levels of security. Decentralized blockchains, for instance, are more susceptible to 51% attacks compared to centralized ones. This has been a concern for cryptocurrency enthusiasts who prefer to store their assets on decentralized chains. To understand how 51% attacks work, it exploits a loophole in decentralized systems that enables users to take over a chain by controlling over 51% of the processing power. This often occurs on networks that use the proof-of-work (PoW) standard. Permissionless blockchain systems with low hash rates are particularly vulnerable to these types of attacks. A successful 51% attack can reverse transactions, nullify new transactions, and modify new blocks. In many instances, malicious actors behind the attacks aim to create double-spending situations. This anomaly enables hackers to steal funds from a network without hacking embedded crypto wallets. Bitcoin Cash ABC (BCHA), Bitcoin Cash (BCH), and Ethereum Classic are some of the blockchain networks that have experienced 51% attacks in recent years. However, some blockchain ecosystems have implemented robust 51% attack mitigation techniques. For instance, proof-of-work (PoW) systems have deployed blind signatures, while proof-of-stake (PoS) systems use fund locking to prevent majority control and maintain network security.

– Flash loan attacks: Blockchain networks often face flash loan attacks, especially within DeFi ecosystems that provide non-collateralized loans and have relaxed Know Your Customer (KYC) requirements. This type of attack is carried out by exploiting arbitrage loopholes to manipulate token value and withdraw profits to other networks, thereby laundering the funds. Smart contract-based DeFi systems are particularly susceptible to these attacks. It is one of the most significant flash loan attacks occurred in May 2021, when PancakeBunny lost around $200 million in cryptocurrency assets. Other notable attacks include those on Alpha Finance and Spartan Protocol, which resulted in losses of tens of millions of dollars. To prevent such attacks, some blockchain networks are implementing stricter KYC requirements and conducting more comprehensive audits of smart contracts.

– Coding loopholes: In addition to hack attacks, blockchain networks are also vulnerable to coding errors. Centralized blockchains are particularly susceptible because hackers only need to exploit specific points of failure. In some cases, attackers target entities holding the private keys or other important blockchain keys. Once hackers gain access to these keys, they can transfer assets from the wallets that are associated with the blockchain network. This poses a significant risk to the security of blockchain systems and can result in significant financial losses for individuals or organizations that use these networks. Therefore, it is important for blockchain developers and users to take proactive measures to secure their systems against these types of attacks.

– Centralization of information: Blockchain systems face security issues due to the centralization of information, particularly in networks that rely on external sources. Oracle systems, for example, are utilized by some blockchain ecosystems to determine pricing, leading to substantial losses in some cases. The Compound DeFi protocol, for instance, suffered a cumulative loss of $103 million in November 2020 due to a DAI price discrepancy caused by incorrect market price data from Coinbase Pro. As a result, short sellers with highly leveraged positions incurred significant losses. Another significant issue that centralized blockchain systems encounter is susceptibility to rug pulls. This type of manipulative scheme involves promoting projects to attract investors, after which the founders abscond with the funds. These incidents are relatively common in the cryptocurrency world and are likely to persist due to a lack of regulatory oversight. They have led to ethical concerns associated with blockchain technology such as tax evasion and money laundering.

The security risks most frequently associated with blockchain are outlined in Table 16.3

Table 16.3 Blockchain security risk categories

Risk	Description
Network attacks	Due to its limited capacity, a blockchain can only handle a certain number of transactions per second. This leaves it vulnerable to denial-of-service (DoS) attacks, where an attacker can flood the network with more transactions than it can handle, causing the system to become unavailable. Along with DoS attacks, other attacks like BGP attacks, routing attacks, eclipse attacks, stealthier attacks, DNS attacks, and remote side-channel attacks can also fall under this category
Code vulnerabilities	One source of code vulnerabilities is smart contracts that are open to anyone to create, as well as the underlying platform code. Because of the distributed nature of the network, these vulnerabilities can have far-reaching consequences, and once the code is deployed, it cannot be changed. This creates the potential for malicious actors to intentionally create harmful smart contracts
Human negligence	The owners of the logs may stop monitoring them
Data protection	The blockchain, rather than the data owners, is responsible for ensuring the integrity and availability of data protection
Intentional misuse	The attackers could potentially gain control of a larger number of nodes to carry out attacks similar to the 51% attack
Endpoint security	Endpoints, which can be of different types, provide more opportunities for vulnerabilities to be exploited. Alternatively, endpoints can be of the same type, which means that a flaw in one system may exist in all systems

16.4.2 Low Scalability and Interoperability Challenges

Blockchain technology faces significant challenges in terms of scalability and interoperability. Scalability refers to the ability of a system to handle an increasing amount of work in a graceful and efficient manner. Interoperability, on the other hand, refers to the ability of different systems to communicate and exchange data seamlessly. At present, most blockchain systems have limited scalability. This is because most systems are designed to handle a finite number of transactions per second, which is not sufficient for large-scale applications. As the number of users on the network increases, the system may become congested, leading to slow transaction times and high fees. This is a significant barrier to the widespread adoption of blockchain technology. Interoperability is also a major challenge for blockchain systems. Most blockchain networks operate in isolation, which makes it difficult for them to interact with other systems. This limits the potential of blockchain technology to solve complex problems that require data sharing across multiple systems. To address these challenges, there are ongoing efforts to develop new blockchain solutions that are more scalable and interoperable. Some approaches include sharding, sidechains, and cross-chain communication protocols. Sharding involves breaking down a blockchain network into smaller parts to increase scalability. Sidechains allow for the creation of separate blockchains that can communicate with the main chain. Cross-chain communication protocols enable different blockchain networks to communicate and exchange data seamlessly. These approaches show promise in addressing the scalability and interoperability challenges in blockchain technology. However, more research and development are needed to create truly scalable and interoperable blockchain systems that can support large-scale applications in a secure and efficient manner.

To overcome the scalability issue of blockchain technology and make the most of its benefits, data can be shared through a dedicated off-chain channel while recording the link or evidence of the data sharing on the blockchain for auditing purposes. However, implementing off-chain data sharing solutions requires companies to create and maintain inter-company channels, which can be burdensome. Furthermore, the integrity of the shared data cannot be guaranteed as one company may manipulate the original data to meet the requirements of another company. To alleviate the burden of participating companies, data can be shared on a cloud platform. In our filed patent document, we have proposed a blockchain-based access control and data sharing framework for supply chains, which can be referred to in this regard (Lee et al., 2020).

16.4.3 Low Workforce Availability

The rise of non-fungible tokens (NFTs) and decentralized finance (DeFi) projects in the blockchain industry has created a labor market crisis. The demand for blockchain professionals has soared by 300% as both established companies and startups compete for the best talent. This has led to a labor shortage, with major companies such as Google, Amazon, Goldman Sachs, the Bank of New York Mellon Corporation, and DBS Group hiring blockchain specialists in large numbers. Coinbase, a blockchain-centric company, reportedly hires more than 500 people every quarter. LinkedIn lists over 6,000 blockchain and cryptocurrency jobs, with Indeed and ZipRecruiter each listing over 15,000 blockchain jobs. The competition for top talent has resulted in substantial salary hikes of at least 20% compared to other asset classes. Some blockchain companies are consistently paying over a million dollars per year to workers in certain job categories, with software engineers reportedly receiving pay packages of over $900,000 per year. The talent shortage is a major issue for the industry, hindering the development of blockchain projects due to the limited availability of qualified professionals. The mainstream adoption of blockchain technology has led to a rising need for blockchain staff, with companies such as Walmart using blockchain to manage invoices and payments to freight carriers. The labor shortage is expected to continue despite the bearish crypto season because of the need to scale blockchain projects that will take advantage of future price uptrends.

This section provides a concise overview of the challenges and concerns surrounding the implementation of blockchain applications, with a specific focus on the latest studies conducted from 2018 to the present. Furthermore, we highlight the most noteworthy studies and subsequently classify them based on their methodologies and techniques utilized.

16.5 Evaluation on Current Research Trends

One example of the evaluation of blockchain on information systems is its use in supply chain management. Blockchain can be used to track products throughout the supply chain, from the manufacturer to the end consumer. By using a decentralized and transparent ledger, stakeholders in the supply chain can access and verify information about the products, such as their origin, quality, and shipping history. This can help to reduce fraud, counterfeiting, and errors in the supply chain, as well as improve transparency and traceability. An analysis of data on the use of blockchain in supply chain management can provide insights into its effectiveness. For instance, a study conducted by the World Economic Forum and Deloitte found that blockchain-based supply chain systems can reduce the time required for cross-border transactions by up to 40%, administrative costs by up to 50%, and the need for manual interventions and reconciliations by up to 80%. The study also found that blockchain can improve transparency and reduce fraud, as it enables stakeholders to track products in real time and identify any irregularities or discrepancies. Another example of the evaluation of blockchain on information systems is its use in healthcare. Blockchain can be used to store and share medical records securely and transparently while also ensuring patient privacy and data protection. By using

16 Blockchain Research Trends in Information Systems: A Systematic Review 279

Table 16.4 Blockchain-based supply chain system in terms of various parameters

Parameter	Current supply chain system	Blockchain-based supply chain system
Security	Centralized control with risk of single point of failure	Decentralized control with secure cryptographic protocols
Transparency	Limited transparency and traceability	Complete transparency and traceability
Efficiency	Slow and inefficient due to manual processes	Real-time tracking and streamlined processes
Fraud prevention	Lack of transparency and vulnerability to fraud	Reduced fraud and increased accountability
Data privacy	Limited data privacy and control	Enhanced data privacy and control
Interoperability	Limited interoperability between different systems	Improved interoperability with standardized protocols

a decentralized and immutable ledger, healthcare providers can access and update medical records in real time while also ensuring that patients have control over their own data.

An analysis of data on the use of blockchain in healthcare can provide insights into its effectiveness. For instance, a study conducted by the MIT Technology Review found that blockchain-based healthcare systems can improve the accuracy and completeness of medical records, reduce the risk of medical errors and fraud, and enhance patient privacy and data protection. The study also found that blockchain can enable patients to share their medical records with different healthcare providers securely and efficiently, which can improve the quality and continuity of care.

In conclusion, blockchain has shown great potential for improving various aspects of information systems, such as supply chain management and healthcare. The analysis of data on the use of blockchain in these areas provides evidence of its effectiveness in improving transparency, traceability, security, and privacy. However, further research is needed to explore the scalability, interoperability, and sustainability of blockchain-based systems, as well as their potential social and ethical implications. Another example of a comparison table from a paper titled *Blockchain-Based Safety Management System for the Grain Supply Chain* by Zhang et al. (2020). The table compares the current supply chain system with the proposed blockchain-based supply chain system in terms of various parameters such as security, transparency, and efficiency as shown in Table 16.4.

The comparison table provides a clear and concise overview of the benefits of the proposed blockchain-based supply chain system compared to the current system. It highlights the advantages of blockchain in terms of security, transparency, efficiency, fraud prevention, data privacy, and interoperability. Gohil M et al. in (2021) illustrate blockchain technology along with its state-of-the-art applications in healthcare. In this chapter, the author describes the comparison table to compares the current healthcare system with the proposed blockchain-based healthcare system in terms of various parameters such as security, privacy, and interoperability; all things

Table 16.5 Blockchain and its applications in healthcare

Parameter	Current healthcare system	Blockchain-based healthcare system
Security	Centralized control with risk of data breaches	Decentralized control with secure cryptographic protocols
Privacy	Limited privacy and control over personal health data	Enhanced privacy and control over personal health data
Interoperability	Limited interoperability between different healthcare providers and systems	Improved interoperability with standardized protocols
Trust	Trust in healthcare providers is based on reputation and certification	Trust in healthcare providers is based on immutable and transparent blockchain records
Efficiency	Slow and inefficient due to manual processes and redundant data	Streamlined processes and reduced redundant data
Accessibility	Limited accessibility to personal health data	Improved accessibility to personal health data with patient-controlled access
Innovation	Limited innovation due to strict regulations and limited sharing of data	Encouragement of innovation through secure and transparent sharing of data

Table 16.6 Blockchain security issues and challenges (Li & Wang, 2017)

Security feature	Centralized system	Blockchain
Integrity	Centralized authority controls and verifies data	Decentralized nodes reach consensus to validate transactions
Confidentiality	Data are stored on a centralized server, which is vulnerable to hacking	Data are encrypted and distributed among nodes
Availability	Single point of failure makes the system vulnerable to denial-of-service attacks	Decentralized nodes ensure high availability
Auditability	Limited ability to track and audit transactions	Blockchain transactions are recorded in an immutable ledger
Resilience	Vulnerable to cyber-attacks and natural disasters	Blockchain is resistant to tampering and attacks

are depicted in Table 16.5. The comparison table provides a clear overview of the potential benefits of a blockchain-based healthcare system compared to the current system. It highlights the advantages of blockchain in terms of security, privacy, interoperability, trust, efficiency, accessibility, and innovation.

In addition, Li and Wang (2017) highlight the benefits of decentralization, encryption, distributed storage, immutability, and resistance to tampering and attacks. The comparison is depicted in Table 16.6.

16.6 Conclusions

The chapter identifies three primary themes in blockchain research in information systems: blockchain architecture and infrastructure, blockchain applications, and blockchain governance. The first theme focuses on the technical aspects of blockchain, including scalability, security, and interoperability. The second theme explores the various applications of blockchain in information systems, such as supply chain management, healthcare, and financial services. The third theme focuses on the governance of blockchain networks, including the role of regulators, the development of standards, and the management of blockchain networks. The chapter also finds that the majority of the blockchain research in information systems uses a qualitative research methodology, with case studies being the most common research design. The research work contributes to the understanding of the technical, organizational, and social implications of blockchain in information systems.

Blockchain technology has the potential to transform information systems by enabling secure, decentralized, and transparent data management. However, to fully realize its potential, researchers need to address the scalability, interoperability, security, and governance challenges of blockchain networks. The future research directions outlined in this chapter offer a roadmap for researchers to explore innovative solutions that can enable the widespread adoption of blockchain technology in information systems.

References

Ali, S., Shin, W. S., & Song, H. (2022). Blockchain-enabled open quality system for smart manufacturing: Applications and challenges. *Sustainability (Switzerland), 14*, 11677.

Attaran, M. (2022). Blockchain technology in healthcare: Challenges and opportunities. *International Journal of Healthcare Management, 15*, 70–83.

Beck, R., Avital, M., Rossi, M., & Thatcher, J. B. (2017). Blockchain technology in business and information systems research. *Business & Information Systems Engineering, 59*, 381–384.

Chapron, G. (2017). The environment needs cryptogovernance. *Nature, 545*, 403–405.

Ciriello, R. F., Beck, R., & Thatcher, J. B. (2018). The paradoxical effects of blockchain technology on social networking practices. In *Thirty Ninth International Conference on Information Systems, San Francisco 2018*.

Damle, S., Faltings, B., & Gujar, S. (2021). Blockchain-based practical multi-agent secure comparison and its application in auctions. In *In WI-IAT'21: IEEE/WIC/ACM International Conference on Web Intelligence*.

Digitale, J. C., Martin, J. N., & Glymour, M. M. (2022). Tutorial on directed acyclic graphs. *Journal of Clinical Epidemiology, 142*, 264–267.

Dong, L., Qiu, Y., & Xu, F. (2022). Blockchain-enabled deep-tier supply chain finance. *Manufacturing & Service Operations Management, 25*, 2021–2037.

Egelund-Müller, B., Elsman, M., Henglein, F., & Ross, O. (2017). Automated execution of financial contracts on blockchains. *Business and Information Systems Engineering, 59*, 457–467.

Gammon, R. R., Alvarez, H., & Benitez, N. (2018). Rare blood donor needed. *Transfusion, 58,* 1890–1893.

Gohil, M. R., Maduskar, S. S., Gajria, V., & Mangrulkar, R. (2021). Blockchain and its applications in healthcare. *International Journal of Intelligent Networks, 2,* 130–139.

Gourisetti, S. N. G., Mylrea, M., & Patangia, H. (2020). Evaluation and demonstration of blockchain applicability framework. *IEEE Transactions on Engineering Management, 67,* 1142–1156.

Hanna, B., Xu, G., Wang, X., & Hossain, J. (2023). Blockchain-enabled humanitarian supply chain management: sustainability and responsibility. In *Blockchain in a volatile-uncertain-complex-ambiguous world.*

Jiang, S., & Wu, J. (2020). A game-theoretic approach to storage offloading in PoC-based mobile blockchain mining. In Twenty-First International Symposium on Theory, Algorithmic Foundations, and Protocol Design for Mobile Networks and Mobile Computing, pp. 171-180. https://doi.org/10.1145/3397166.3409136

Kumari, A., & Chitra Devi, N. (2022). The impact of fintech and blockchain technologies on banking and financial services. *Technology Innovation Management Review, 12,* 1–11.

Kwon, J. (2014). *Tendermint: Consensus without mining.*

Larimer, D. (2017). *DPOS consensus algorithm - the missing white paper.* https://steemit.com/dpos/@dantheman/dpos-consensus-algorithm-this-missing-white-paper, (2018).

Lee, H. A., Kung, H. H., Udayasankaran, J. G., Boonchai, K., Marcelo, A. B., Chao, L. R., & Hsu, C. Y. (2020). An architecture and management platform for blockchain-based personal health record exchange: Development and usability study. *Journal of Medical Internet Research, 22,* e16748.

Li, X., & Wang, C.A. (2017). The technology and economic determinants of cryptocurrency exchange rates: The case of bitcoin. *Decision Support Systems, 95,* 49–60.

Nærland, K., Beck, R., Müller-Bloch, C., & Palmund, S. (2018). Blockchain to rule the waves - nascent design principles for reducing risk and uncertainty in decentralized environments. In *Proceedings/International Conference on Information Systems (ICIS).*

Pompella, M., & Costantino, L. (2021). Financial innovation and technology after covid-19: a few directions for policy makers and regulators in the view of old and new disruptors. *Ekonomika, 100,* 40–62.

Squarepants, S. (2022). Bitcoin: A peer-to-peer electronic cash system. *SSRN Electronic Journal.*

Tan, T. M., & Salo, J. (2021). Ethical marketing in the blockchain-based sharing economy: Theoretical integration and guiding insights. *Journal of Business Ethics, 183,* 1113–1140.

Vasin, P. (2014). *Blackcoin's proof-of-stake protocol v2 Pavel.* Self-published.

Verma, S., & Sheel, A. (2022). Blockchain for government organizations: past, present and future. *Journal of Global Operations and Strategic Sourcing, 15,* 406–430.

Xu, X., Zhu, D., Yang, X., Wang, S., Qi, L., & Dou, W. (2021). Concurrent practical byzantine fault tolerance for integration of blockchain and supply chain. *ACM Transactions on Internet Technology, 21,* 1–17.

Zhang, X. et al. (2020). Blockchain-Based Safety Management System for the Grain Supply Chain. in IEEE Access, *8,* pp. 36398–36410. https://doi.org/10.1109/ACCESS.2020.2975415

Zhao, J. L., Fan, S., & Yan, J. (2016). Overview of business innovations and research opportunities in blockchain and introduction to the special issue. *Financial Innovation, 2,* 1–7.

Chapter 17
Analysis of Customer Perception of E-banking Services in India

Amit Kumar Gupta, Manoj Kumar Srivastava, Imlak Shaikh, and Ashutosh Dash

Abstract One of the most significant changes in the industry is the introduction of electronic banking. Electronic banking plays a critical role nowadays, as individuals are seeking for alternatives to visiting the bank to perform their transactions, in order to increase financial inclusion by leveraging on the rising adoption of the internet. In India, the usage of the internet and cell phones has grown dramatically during the previous decade. Increased internet usage, cell phone penetration, and government initiatives like the Digital India campaign have all functioned as catalysts, resulting in exponential rise in digital usage. Increased internet use, cell phone penetration, and government initiatives like the Digital India campaign have all functioned as catalysts, resulting in an exponential increase in the use of digital payments. However, there are still barriers to electronic banking acceptability (mental, traditional, and technological). We plan to examine consumers' perceptions of electronic banking and aim to uncover obstacles that may prevent widespread adoption of the technology.

Keywords E-banking services · Intention to use · Perceived usefulness · TAM

17.1 Introduction

Internet banking became widely available in the early 1990s. The Indian banking sector embarked on a digital transformation journey after the LPG (Liberalization, Privatization, and Globalization) era and the Information Technology (IT) era, which is dynamically altering the face of banking as banks move away from traditional banking toward e-banking, which provides many benefits to customers. The surge in innovation and the burning demand for real-time data with convenience has resulted in the increasingly major influence of information systems (IS) in the

---

A. K. Gupta · M. K. Srivastava · I. Shaikh (✉) · A. Dash
Management Development Institute Gurgaon, Gurugram, Haryana, India
e-mail: amitkgupta@mdi.ac.in; mks@mdi.ac.in; imlak.shaikh@mdi.ac.in; ashutosh@mdi.ac.in

© The Author(s), under exclusive license to Springer Nature Switzerland AG 2024
N. Tsounis, A. Vlachvei (eds.), *Applied Economic Research and Trends*, Springer
Proceedings in Business and Economics,
https://doi.org/10.1007/978-3-031-49105-4_17

corporate setting. Organizations may employ evolutionary technologies to enhance their profitability by adjusting to these new future methods of interacting with their consumers now that there is a link between IS and organizational success. In today's competitive world, e-banking plays a critical role, with an increasing number of clients opting for alternatives to traditional banking to perform financial transactions since they have the choice of banks. In India, the usage of the internet and cell phones has increased dramatically over the previous decade. Furthermore, the current scenario has increased the familiarity of both bankers and customers with technology use. These reasons, in combination with government programs like Digital India and the current epidemic, have functioned as catalysts, propelling exponential development in digital payments and e-banking usage.

By allowing consumers to conduct their day-to-day financial operations from the comfort of their own homes, internet banking is bringing the globe into a new era of banking. Regarding "information flow timeliness and accuracy," online banking services offer a significant advantage over traditional banks, which decreases information delay in a high-pressure decision-making environment. TAM (technology acceptance model) is widely used and considered a robust model used for the adoption of technology, mostly in information management research (Kesharwani & Bisht, 2012; Raj et al., 2020; Venkatesh et al., 2003). Using TAM as a theoretical basis, this study hypothesized and analyzed an integrated model to explain several elements impacting individual uptake and usage of online banking services. Environmental sustainability and demographic factors have been included to the model as moderating aspects, in addition to the traditional TAM dimensions.

The banking sector has changed dramatically over the last two decades and is now one of India's fastest-growing industries. Banking has undergone a transformation as a result of the use of e-banking services as a delivery channel for its services (Laukkanen, 2007). The extensive use of online banking services received considerable customer acceptability, resulting in a shift in the economic model of banking services in India and throughout the world. It led to a phenomenal growth of banking services in recent years (Aboobucker & Bao, 2018).

It has been noticed that as Internet banking becomes more widely used and accepted, its utility and acceptance will grow. Banking services have produced a variety of e-banking options. Customers have also benefited from 24×7 service availability, convenience of use, quality services with less hassles than traditional banking services, and reduced reliance on banking people, among other things.

Virtual banking, online banking, or internet banking are various names used for electronic banking, primarily known as e-banking. The emergence of new information and communication technologies (ICTs) has created an ease of access to e-banking for consumers.

However, there are still a few impediments to the adoption of e-banking services in India (image, value, risk, and tradition). This category includes not just online banking but also mobile banking. As a result, we want to investigate the variables impacting the uptake of e-banking services in India (both enablers and impediments). Despite technological advancements, acceptance of new technologies has remained sluggish and e-banking adoption is still in its early stages. A study of the TAM is required to understand the consumer attitude underlying this sluggish adoption. The TAM model is useful for analyzing customer behavior when it comes to adopting a new technology.

Various factors have been taken into consideration while attempting to understand customer perception toward Internet banking. But, from the existing literature, it has been identified that security concerns and environmental sustainability have not been analyzed yet. If a bank does not provide e-banking services that are not environmentally friendly, will it hinder the acceptance of services related to e-banking by the consumer? We understand the presence of eco-consciousness amongst the public nowadays, but to what extent their preferences in banking services depend upon environmental sustainability is yet to be analyzed. We have yet to learn about the effects media has on banking consumers in this age of pervasive social media influence. How much power does a trustworthy social media recommendation hold? What are the effects of TAM variables, PEOU, and PU on the IU? Does the addition of ESG into TAM increase its predictive power? Are recommendations via social media strong enough to make a consumer switch to e-banking services? Some of the general gaps that we identified while performing literature reviews are: Environmental factors, demography and geography, TAM model, etc. This study combines an existing theoretical model with an essential concept called environmental sustainability, which will be evaluated on the intention to use e-banking services (IU) for the first time. As a result of this research, banks may be able to better understand the important elements that impact users and enhance their service delivery model and policies to encourage customers to utilize e-banking services. Furthermore, switching from physical to online banking channels is in both the banks' and customers' interests in order to save money and increase productivity.

The main objective of the study is to understand how social influence, trust, security concerns, and environmental sustainability affect or influence the intention of consumers to accept e-banking. Broadly, study objectives are:

- Identification of antecedents for the adoption and usage of e-banking services.
- Estimation of impact of trust, social impact, PEOU, security, and PU on the intention to use e-banking services.
- To find out how environmental and sustainability concerns influence the use of e-banking services.

17.2 Literature Review

Several research studies have been undertaken to better understand how consumers feel about online banking. Davis (1989) introduced the TAM model, according to which users' adoption of computer systems is based on their behavioral intention to use, which is based on attitude, which is made up of two beliefs: perceived ease of use (PEOU) and perceived usefulness (PU). Davis (1989) has also defined both of these concepts. TAM has been tested in a variety of empirical studies, and it has been found to be more successful than other theories in explaining technology adoption intentions and attitudes. Cost and convenience of use have been linked to a negative association with cost in various research studies (Selvanathan et al., 2016). It was revealed that client loyalty to e-banking is influenced by dependability, privacy, and security. One thing to keep in mind is that customer perceptions of e-banking are culturally specific. Dimensions of e-banking service quality (EBSQ) serve as indicators of client satisfaction levels (Sathiyavany & Shanmugathas, 2018). The adoption of online banking services is influenced by client satisfaction levels. To better understand client perceptions of e-banking adoption, studies have been conducted using a TAM extension (Fonchamnyo, 2012). The findings of the extended model research showed that perceived reliability and quality of internet connectivity had no significant influence on consumer attitudes. Cybersecurity risks have just recently been researched (Jibril et al., 2020), but more study is needed to understand the influence of cybersecurity threats on e-Banking adoption and retention. Mobile banking services are one of the most important channels for enabling e-banking (Alsamydai, 2014). There have been specific research focusing just on mobile banking services. Studies on how the technology acceptance affects e-banking adoption have been conducted (Sinha & Mukherjee, 2016), and in addition to the TAM, the DOI model has been employed in the research. The use of e-banking opens the door to client value co-creation (Carranza et al., 2021), the model in this study had one flaw: it was only dependent on functional qualities of technology adoption, such as PEOU and PU.

The increased use of e-banking services has prompted experts to focus their efforts on understanding and predicting what motivates customers to utilize these services. George & Kumar (2013) investigated the influence of TAM factors such as Perceived Risk (PR), Perceived Ease of Use (PEOU), and Perceived Usefulness (PU) on customer satisfaction connected to Internet banking using the TAM. Arif et al. (2020) investigated the challenges to online banking adoption in Karachi, Pakistan. First, factor analysis and structural equation modeling (SEM) were used to identify important obstacles, and then the neural network model was used to rank the relative importance of these major barriers. Vatnani & Verma (2014) proposed an integrated framework for examining and testing the aspects that impact customer acceptability of online banking services in India, based on the TAM and the technological readiness (TR) model. Sharma & Sharma (2019) proposed a novel research model that expanded the DeLone & McLean information systems (D&M IS) success model to better assess customers' actual use of mobile banking. The study employed a two-staged analytical method that included structural equation modeling and neural network analysis. They have talked about both the theoretical and practical implications of their findings. Yu (2012) investigated the variables that influence people's choice to use mobile banking using the Unified Theory of Acceptance and Use of Technology (UTAUT). Mortimer et al. (2015) investigated the factors that influence a consumer's decision to use mobile banking. Customers' intentions to utilize mobile banking in Thailand and Australia were compared for the first time in this survey. Additional factors not included in the original SST IU model were suggested and verified as part of the study. Ngubelanga and Duffett (2021) investigated the antecedents of customer satisfaction due to the adoption of mobile commerce apps (MCA) by Millennial consumers in South Africa using the extended Technology Acceptance Model. Safeena et al. (2012) investigated the Indian consumer's perspective on mobile banking uptake. By analyzing the key causes of a user's happiness with a certain institution's goods, Liébana-Cabanillas et al. (2013) added to the satisfaction study area from the perspective of e-banking users. Martins et al. (2014) developed a conceptual model that combined the unified theory of acceptance and use of technology (UTAUT) with perceived risk to explain behavior intention and use behavior of Internet banking.

Other elements must be taken into account in addition to the functional features. Environmental sustainability is a key subject that has to be properly examined in the current situation. Environmental, economic, and social sustainability are the three pillars of environmental sustainability. Environmental sustainability has a significant impact on the acceptance of e-banking services by today's eco-conscious customer. Studies on topics like cybersecurity and environmental sustainability have yet to be carried out.

17.2.1 Hypothesis and Model Development

TAM claims that the user's desire to use Internet banking services is influenced by external factors. These findings would be interesting to see confirmed in a consumer-centric scenario, such as Internet banking uptake. We examined their mediation and moderation effects in our regression analysis with demographic covariates, rather than examining core hypotheses connected to PEOU and PU as per TAM. Our conceptual model is based on the theories listed below.

Trust

"Trust has been conceptualized as trustor's cognitive beliefs that results from observing the trustee's action, and attributing the cause of the behaviour to the trustee's internal trust-related characteristics (Kesharwani & Bisht, 2012)." Ngubelanga & Duffett (2021) mention that consumer trust in a business enhances the likelihood of a customer purchasing a service or product, resulting in increased customer loyalty and, eventually, repeat purchases. The perceived riskiness of transactions can be reduced to a large extent by increasing the customer's trust in the bank offering the online services (Vatnani & Verma, 2014). "Trust is a crucial construct in order to increase intention to use and happiness among mobile users when doing m-commerce and m-banking activities (Sharma & Sharma, 2019)." Liébana-Cabanillas et al. (2013) has hypothesized that "trust in the electronic banking service of a financial institution positively determines the usefulness of the service." Aboobucker and Bao (2018) has hypothesized that "the perceived trust is believed as a serious concern among Internet banking customers in Sri Lanka." Hence, we understand that trust has significant influence on customer's IU, so we hypothesize as follows:

H1: Trust in e-banking services has a significant impact on the adoption of e-banking services.

Social Influence

The impact of social influence on technology acceptability has long been recognized. Most of the previous works have been done to study the importance of social influence, but their results have been inconsistent. In Kesharwani and Bisht (2012), it is hypothesized that "social influences will affect the individual intention to use internet banking services." Ngubelanga and Duffett (2021) state that social influence has a positive influence on perceived usefulness due to mobile commerce applications. Chaouali et al. (2016) and Venkatesh et al. (2003) have emphasized on the essence of social influence and its role in technology acceptance behavior. Thus, we hypothesize as follows:

H2: Social influence has a significant impact on the adoption of e-banking services.

Security Concerns

The security concerns and perceived risk play an important role in many customer's intentions to perform banking transactions. There is a negative relationship between intentions and risk. Users are most likely to transact online if perceptions related to behavioral and environmental risks are high (Kesharwani & Bisht, 2012). Aboobucker and Bao (2018) have hypothesized that "the perceived risk is believed as a serious concern among Internet banking customers in Sri Lanka." Arif et al. (2020), George and Kumar (2013), Mortimer et al. (2015), and Suh and Han (2003) have also emphasized the importance of security concerns and perceived risk toward user's adoption of technology. Hence, we hypothesize as follows:

H3: Security concerns have a significant impact on the adoption of e-banking services.

Environmental Sustainability

The users are showing a shift in thinking during recent years, and the focus has shifted toward sustainable banking and matters concerning social, governance, and environmental impacts. It is seen that these factors influence the adoption intention of technology services and influence consumer trust. Previous studies have also observed the competitive advantage the firm gains by adopting environmental sustainability policies (Cantele & Zardini, 2018; Gupta & Gupta, 2021). Apart, it also directly or indirectly enhances the firm's overall performance (Büyüközkan & Karabulut, 2018; Gupta & Gupta, 2020). These factors must be considered to gauge the intention to use e-banking services in India.

Hence, we have added this construct in addition to the other TAM variables to study how the ESG impacts the customer's intentions to use e-banking services and thereby affects the adoption and customer satisfaction index. Hence, we have intended to establish how environmental sustainability factors impact the adoption of e-banking services and hypothesize as follows:

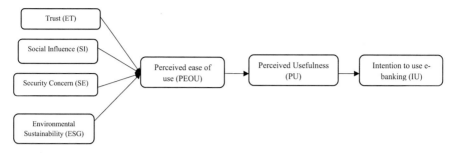

Fig. 17.1 Proposed theoretical model

H4: Environmental concerns positively and significantly impact the adoption of e-banking services.

17.2.2 Conceptual Model

The proposed model is a modified form of TAM (Fig. 17.1). TAM model is validated as a key influencing model to explain technology adoption by users in previous research as well (Davis, 1989; Venkatesh et al., 2003; Wang et al., 2003). Keeping the TAM proposed by Davis as a theoretical basis, an extended TAM incorporating environmental and sustainability-related factors for e-banking adoption is conceptualized. The study also builds in demographic factors—age, education level, and income ranges, how each of these acts as a moderator on the various factors on adoption of e-banking services. The research model broadens the scope of adoption decision of e-banking services basis additional factors of environmental sustainability along with trust, security, social influence, PEOU, and PU.

17.3 Methodology

Measure There were 7 constructs, i.e., Evaluation of trust, Evaluation of Social Influence, Evaluation of Security, PEOU, PU, Intention to Use, and Environmental Sustainability, in the study. Five items for Trust was adopted from Flavián et al. (2006); Kesharwani and Bisht (2012); Lu et al. (2011). Similarly, 5-item scale for Social influence, Security were adopted from Hsu & Lin (2016) and Kesharwani and Bisht (2012), respectively. Seven-item scale for environmental sustainability was adopted from Gupta and Gupta (2020, 2021). Five-item scale each of PEOU,

Table 17.1 Demographic profile

Gender	Frequency	Percent
Female	94	23.13%
Male	309	76.87%
Age	**Frequency**	**Percent**
21–30 years	140	34.83%
31–40 years	182	45.27%
41–50 years	45	11.19%
Above 51 years	28	8.71%
Education level	**Frequency**	**Percent**
Bachelor's degree or equivalent	175	43.53%
Doctoral	33	7.76%
Masters	156	38.81%
Professional qualification	38	9.45%
Duration of using banking services	**Frequency**	**Percent**
1–6 months	27	6.72%
6–12 months	36	8.96%
Less than a month	65	16.17%
More than a year	274	68.16%

PU was adopted from Chueh & Huang (2023). Finally, 5-item scale to measure intention to use e-banking was adopted from Song et al. (2023); Srivastava and Gupta (2022). The 7-point Likert scale was used to measure each of the 7 constructs ranging from 1 for strongly disagree to 7 for strongly agree.

Sampling Design The survey questionnaire was prepared online and was administered to random sample of 600 Indian banking users of all residential areas via Google form. Out of which 402 completed and valid responses were received with an acceptable response rate of 67%. Additionally, the demographic details (gender, age, education level, annual family income per annum, duration of using the bank's internet and mobile banking facilities) were also gathered through the survey. The demographic variables play an important role in the intention to use internet banking services. The demographic profile summary is shown in Table 17.1.

Data Screening Total responses collected was 402. The responses were checked for "missing values" and found "No missing values" in responses. The responses or questionnaire was tested for unengaged responses and for sensitivity with the questionnaire by estimating standard deviation, we end up removing 46 responses whose standard deviation was less than 0.4 (10% thumb rule) and we were left with 356 clean responses. The sample further were tested for multivariate outlier and normality using Mahalonabis distance (Mahalonabis, 1936). We end up removing 40 more responses, finally left with 316 clean data. Skewness and kurtosis were estimated for each observed (items) variables. The values were within ± 1.

17 Analysis of Customer Perception of E-banking Services in India

Table 17.2 Estimated values of Alpha, AVE, CR, MSV, and factor correlation

Variable	α	CR	AVE	MSV	ET	SI	SE	ESG	PEOU	PU	IU
ET	0.94	0.93	0.76	0.44	**0.87**						
SI	0.92	0.92	0.70	0.13	0.30	**0.84**					
SE	0.93	0.91	0.71	0.38	0.63	0.30	**0.85**				
ESG	0.99	0.99	0.92	0.63	0.52	0.30	0.49	**0.96**			
PEOU	0.97	0.97	0.85	0.63	0.66	0.27	0.62	0.69	**0.92**		
PU	0.98	0.98	0.90	0.52	0.66	0.31	0.59	0.79	0.78	**0.95**	
IU	0.96	0.94	0.80	0.52	0.51	0.36	0.55	0.72	0.63	0.70	**0.89**

17.3.1 Analysis

Scale Testing: Reliability and Validity

Reliability testing of the scales is by estimating Cronbach's alpha values for the individual constructs. The values are reported in Table 17.2. All values are more than 0.7 indicating the consistency of the items explaining the constructs. Thus are reliable (Cronbach, 1951; Hair et al., 2014).

Measurement model (Confirmatory factor analysis, CFA) is analyzed for checking the validity of the constructs. AVE, CR, and MSV values are estimated to check the requirement of convergent and discriminant validity. The fit indices of the measurement models estimated are: chisqr/df-: 2.1; CFI-0.96; TLI-0.96; GFI-0.92; RMSEA-0.057; and SRMR-0.045. The fit indices values reflect good fit model. The estimated AVE, CR, and MSV values are reported in Table 17.2. The values of CR and AVE for all constructs are greater than 0.7 and 0.5, respectively, confirming convergent validity, while MSV values are less than AVEs confirming discriminant validity (Hair et al., 2014).

17.3.2 Hypothesis Testing

After testing for measurement model which ensured the good model fit model as well as reliable and valid scale, covariance-based structural equation modeling was done for testing the hypothesis using JAMAVI 2.3.24 (Fig. 17.2).

17.3.2.1 Estimation of Direct Effects

The estimated values of the direct effects are tabulated in Table 17.3. The direct effect of ET ($\beta = 0.3$, p-value <0.01), SE ($\beta = 0.21$, p-value <0.01), and ESG ($\beta = 0.41$, p-value <0.01) on PEOU was significant.

Similarly, direct effect of PEOU ($\beta = 0.3$, p-value <0.01), ET ($\beta = 0.17$, p-value <0.01), and ESG ($\beta = 0.42$, p-value <0.01) on PU and direct effect of PU ($\beta = 0.19$,

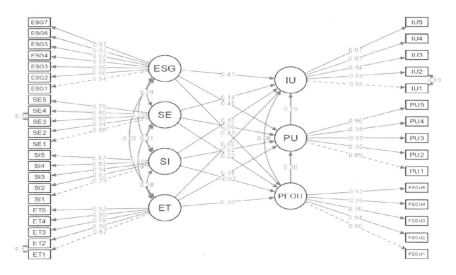

Fig. 17.2 Path diagram-structural equation modeling

Table 17.3 Estimated outcome of direct effects

Dep	Pred	Estimate	SE	β	z	p	Outcome	R-Square
PEOU	ET	0.30	0.05	0.30	5.65	<.001	Accept	0.605
PEOU	SI	−0.02	0.04	−0.02	−0.46	0.64	Failed	
PEOU	SE	0.21	0.05	0.22	4.14	<.001	Accept	
PEOU	ESG	0.41	0.05	0.43	9.01	<.001	Accept	
PU	PEOU	0.30	0.05	0.30	5.95	<.001	Accept	0.742
PU	ET	0.17	0.04	0.18	3.95	<.001	Accept	
PU	SI	0.02	0.03	0.02	0.67	0.50	Failed	
PU	SE	0.06	0.04	0.06	1.39	0.16	Failed	
PU	ESG	0.42	0.04	0.45	10.08	<.001	Accept	
IU	PEOU	0.07	0.07	0.08	1.13	0.26	Failed	0.573
IU	PU	0.19	0.08	0.19	2.42	0.02	Accept	
IU	ET	0.00	0.06	0.00	0.06	0.95	Failed	
IU	SI	0.09	0.04	0.10	2.36	0.02	Accept	
IU	SE	0.13	0.05	0.14	2.57	0.01	Accept	
IU	ESG	0.37	0.06	0.41	6.12	<.001	Accept	

p-value <0.05), SI (β = 0.09, p-value <0.05), SE (β = 0.13, *p*-value =0.01), and ESG (β = 0.37, *p*-value <0.01) on IU were also found significant. Thus, overall H2, H3, and H4 were accepted.

17.3.2.2 Estimation of Indirect Effect: Mediation Through PEOU and PU

Apart from direct effect of the exogenous variables, indirect effect toward intention to use the e-banking was also analyzed mediated through PEOU, PU, or both. Though study failed to establish the direct effect of ET on IU but ET do have significant indirect contribution in IU fully mediated through combined PEOU and PU ($\beta = 0.017$, p-value <0.05) and also through PU ($\beta = 0.034$, p-value <0.05). Thus, overall ET helps in generating the intension to use e-banking. Hence, H1 is also accepted.

Similarly, ESG and SE have direct effect as well as indirect effect on IU. SE has indirect effect ($\beta=0.012$, p-value <0.05) partially mediated through combined path of PEOU and PU. The ESG also has partially mediated indirect effect on IU through combined path of PEOU and PU ($\beta=0.023$, p-value <0.05) and PU ($\beta=0.079$, p-value <0.05). Thus, total effect of SE and ESG is TE (SE)=0.142 and TE (ESG)=0.472. SI does not have any significant indirect effect on IU.

17.4 Results, Conclusion, and Implications

The study focuses on the impact of antecedent like Trust, Social influence, security, and environmental sustainability, on the intention to use e-banking services. The study uses modified TAM model for testing and establishes the proposed theory. The study used covariance-based structural equation modeling for testing the hypotheses using JAMOVI 2.3.24.

The additional variable has added to the model's predictive power creating extended TAM model and has provided more consistent and conclusive results along with validating the core TAM hypothesis. The environmental sustainability, social influence, and perceived usefulness were identified as significant factors impacting the intention to use e-banking services in India.

The significant factors affecting intention to use e-banking services in India with more than or equal to 95% confidence interval were: Trust, Social influence, security and environmental sustainability, **PEOU (mediating), and PU (mediating)**.

This research could aid banks in better understanding the key elements that impact consumers and improving their service delivery model and policies to encourage customers to adopt e-banking services. Furthermore, switching from offline to online banking channels is in both the banks' and customers' interests in order to save money and increase productivity. This knowledge of such research outcomes can also help banks to increase customer penetration for usage of internet banking. The bank managers need to understand these factors and devise their customer targeting strategies keeping these research findings in mind. This study, thus, aims at filling literature gaps and, therefore, the study is quite important and contemporary from both academic and banking industry perspectives.

Description	Parameter	Estimate	SE	β	z	p	Outcome	Mediation-PEOU	Mediation-PU	Both
ET ⇒ PEOU ⇒ PU ⇒ IU	p38*p42*p48	0.017	0.008	0.017	2.103	0.036	Accept			Full
ET ⇒ PEOU ⇒ IU	p38*p47	0.022	0.02	0.023	1.107	0.268	Failed	No		
ET ⇒ PU ⇒ IU	p43*p48	0.032	0.016	0.034	2.066	0.039	Accept		Full	
SI ⇒ PEOU ⇒ PU ⇒ IU	p39*p42*p48	-0.001	0.002	-0.001	-0.454	0.65	Failed			No
SI ⇒ PEOU ⇒ IU	p39*p47	-0.001	0.003	-0.001	-0.428	0.668	Failed	No		
SI ⇒ PU ⇒ IU	p44*p48	0.004	0.006	0.004	0.646	0.518	Failed		No	
SE ⇒ PEOU ⇒ PU ⇒ IU	p40*p42*p48	0.012	0.006	0.013	1.981	0.048	Accept			Partial
SE ⇒ PEOU ⇒ IU	p40*p47	0.015	0.014	0.017	1.095	0.274	Failed	No		
SE ⇒ PU ⇒ IU	p45*p48	0.011	0.009	0.011	1.215	0.224	Failed		No	
ESG ⇒ PEOU ⇒ PU ⇒ IU	p41*p42*p48	0.023	0.01	0.025	2.192	0.028	Accept			Partial
ESG ⇒ PEOU ⇒ IU	p41*p47	0.03	0.027	0.033	1.123	0.262	Failed	No		
ESG ⇒ PU ⇒ IU	p46*p48	0.079	0.033	0.086	2.369	0.018	Accept		Partial	
PEOU ⇒ PU ⇒ IU	p42*p48	0.056	0.025	0.058	2.252	0.024	Accept		Full	

17.5 Future Scope

The sample of this study is concentrated or limited, and respondents were Indian internet banking users. This is not a longitudinal study, but it can be used to test for larger, worldwide acceptance in specific cultural contexts. This study does not consider demographic factors of language and region. So, location-specific factors, more latent variables, personal factors, and external variables can be studied in further studies. Additional constructs, such as familiarity with computers and new technologies, are not included in this study. Customer satisfaction may be influenced by familiarity, which is mediated via PU. So, there is future scope of study in these aspects.

References

Aboobucker, I., & Bao, Y. (2018). What obstruct customer acceptance of internet banking? Security and privacy, risk, trust and website usability and the role of moderators. *Journal of High Technology Management Research, 29*, 109. https://doi.org/10.1016/j.hitech.2018.04.010

Alsamydai, M. J. (2014). Adaptation of the technology acceptance model (TAM) to the use of Mobile banking services. *International Review of Management and Business Research, 3*, 2039–2051.

Arif, I., Aslam, W., & Hwang, Y. (2020). Barriers in adoption of internet banking: A structural equation modeling – Neural network approach. *Technology in Society, 61*, 101231. https://doi.org/10.1016/j.techsoc.2020.101231

Büyüközkan, G., & Karabulut, Y. (2018). Sustainability performance evaluation: Literature review and future directions. *Journal of Environmental Management, 217*, 253. https://doi.org/10.1016/j.jenvman.2018.03.064

Cantele, S., & Zardini, A. (2018). Is sustainability a competitive advantage for small businesses? An empirical analysis of possible mediators in the sustainability–financial performance relationship. *Journal of Cleaner Production, 182*, 166. https://doi.org/10.1016/j.jclepro.2018.02.016

Carranza, R., Díaz, E., Sánchez-Camacho, C., & Martín-Consuegra, D. (2021). e-Banking adoption: An opportunity for customer value co-creation. *Frontiers in Psychology*. https://doi.org/10.3389/fpsyg.2020.621248

Chaouali, W., Ben Yahia, I., & Souiden, N. (2016). The interplay of counter-conformity motivation, social influence, and trust in customers' intention to adopt Internet banking services: The case of an emerging country. *Journal of Retailing and Consumer Services, 28*, 209. https://doi.org/10.1016/j.jretconser.2015.10.007

Chueh, H. E., & Huang, D. H. (2023). Usage intention model of digital assessment systems. *Journal of Business Research, 156*, 113469. https://doi.org/10.1016/j.jbusres.2022.113469

Cronbach, L. J. (1951). Coefficient alpha and the internal structure of tests. *Psychometrika, 16*, 297. https://doi.org/10.1007/BF02310555

Davis, F. D. (1989). Perceived usefulness, perceived ease of use, and user acceptance of information technology. *MIS Quarterly: Management Information Systems, 13*, 319. https://doi.org/10.2307/249008

Flavián, C., Guinalíu, M., & Gurrea, R. (2006). The role played by perceived usability, satisfaction and consumer trust on website loyalty. *Information and Management, 43*, 1. https://doi.org/10.1016/j.im.2005.01.002

Fonchamnyo, D. C. (2012). Customers' perception of e-banking adoption in Cameroon: An empirical assessment of an extended TAM. *International Journal of Economics and Finance, 5*(1), pp 166–176.

George, A., & Kumar, G. S. G. (2013). Antecedents of customer satisfaction in internet banking: Technology acceptance model (TAM) redefined. *Global Business Review, 14*, 627. https://doi.org/10.1177/0972150913501602

Gupta, A. K., & Gupta, N. (2020). Effect of corporate environmental sustainability on dimensions of firm performance—Towards sustainable development: Evidence from India. *Journal of Cleaner Production, 253*, 119948. https://doi.org/10.1016/j.jclepro.2019.119948

Gupta, A. K., & Gupta, N. (2021). Environment practices mediating the environmental compliance and firm performance: An institutional theory perspective from emerging economies. *Global Journal of Flexible Systems Management, 22*, 157. https://doi.org/10.1007/s40171-021-00266-w

Hair, J. F., Black, W. C., Babin, B. J., & Anderson, R. E. (2014). Multivariate data analysis. In *Pearson new international* (7th ed.). Pearson Education. https://doi.org/10.1007/978-3-319-01517-0_3

Hsu, C. L., & Lin, J. C. C. (2016). Effect of perceived value and social influences on mobile app stickiness and in-app purchase intention. *Technological Forecasting and Social Change, 108*, 42. https://doi.org/10.1016/j.techfore.2016.04.012

Jibril, A. B., Kwarteng, M. A., Chovancova, M., & Denanyoh, R. (2020). Customers' perception of cybersecurity threats toward e-banking adoption and retention: A conceptual study. In *Proceedings of the 15th international conference on cyber warfare and security, ICCWS 2020*. https://doi.org/10.34190/ICCWS.20.020

Kesharwani, A., & Bisht, S. S. (2012). The impact of trust and perceived risk on internet banking adoption in India: An extension of technology acceptance model. *International Journal of Bank Marketing, 30*, 303. https://doi.org/10.1108/02652321211236923

Laukkanen, T. (2007). Internet vs mobile banking: Comparing customer value perceptions. *Business Process Management Journal, 13*, 788. https://doi.org/10.1108/14637150710834550

Liébana-Cabanillas, F., Muñoz-Leiva, F., & Rejón-Guardia, F. (2013). The determinants of satisfaction with e-banking. *Industrial Management and Data Systems, 113*, 750. https://doi.org/10.1108/02635571311324188

Lu, Y., Yang, S., Chau, P. Y. K., & Cao, Y. (2011). Dynamics between the trust transfer process and intention to use mobile payment services: A cross-environment perspective. *Information and Management, 48*, 393. https://doi.org/10.1016/j.im.2011.09.006

Mahalonabis, P. C. (1936). *On the generalised distance in statistics* (pp. 49–55). Proceedings of the National Institute of Science of India.

Martins, C., Oliveira, T., & Popovič, A. (2014). Understanding the internet banking adoption: A unified theory of acceptance and use of technology and perceived risk application. *International Journal of Information Management, 34*, 1. https://doi.org/10.1016/j.ijinfomgt.2013.06.002

Mortimer, G., Neale, L., Hasan, S. F. E., & Dunphy, B. (2015). Investigating the factors influencing the adoption of m-banking: A cross cultural study. *International Journal of Bank Marketing, 33*, 545. https://doi.org/10.1108/IJBM-07-2014-0100

Ngubelanga, A., & Duffett, R. (2021). Modeling mobile commerce applications' antecedents of customer satisfaction among millennials: An extended tam perspective. *Sustainability (Switzerland)*. https://doi.org/10.3390/su13115973

Raj, A., Dwivedi, G., Sharma, A., de Sousa, L., Jabbour, A. B., & Rajak, S. (2020). Barriers to the adoption of industry 4.0 technologies in the manufacturing sector: An inter-country comparative perspective. *International Journal of Production Economics, 224*, 107546. https://doi.org/10.1016/J.IJPE.2019.107546

Safeena, R., Date, H., Kammani, A., & Hundewale, N. (2012). Technology adoption and Indian consumers: Study on Mobile banking. *International Journal of Computer Theory and Engineering*. https://doi.org/10.7763/ijcte.2012.v4.630

Sathiyavany, N., & Shanmugathas, S. (2018). E-Banking service qualities, E-Customer satisfaction, and e-Loyalty: A conceptual model. *International Journal of Social Sciences and Humanities Invention*. https://doi.org/10.18535/ijsshi/v5i6.08

Selvanathan, M., Tan, P. J., Bow, T. F., & Supramaniam, M. (2016). The impact of cost, customer experience, ease of use, and trust towards adoption of online banking. *International Business Research, 9*, 235. https://doi.org/10.5539/ibr.v9n11p235

Sharma, S. K., & Sharma, M. (2019). Examining the role of trust and quality dimensions in the actual usage of mobile banking services: An empirical investigation. *International Journal of Information Management, 44*, 65. https://doi.org/10.1016/j.ijinfomgt.2018.09.013

Sinha, I., & Mukherjee, S. (2016). Acceptance of technology, related factors in use of off branch e-banking: An Indian case study. *Journal of High Technology Management Research, 27*, 88. https://doi.org/10.1016/j.hitech.2016.04.008

Song, J., Cai, L., Yuen, K. F., & Wang, X. (2023). Exploring consumers' usage intention of reusable express packaging: An extended norm activation model. *Journal of Retailing and Consumer Services, 72*, 103265. https://doi.org/10.1016/j.jretconser.2023.103265

Srivastava, V., & Gupta, A. K. (2022). Price sensitivity, government green interventions, and green product availability triggers intention toward buying green products. *Business Strategy and the Environment, 32*, 802. https://doi.org/10.1002/BSE.3176

Suh, B., & Han, I. (2003). The impact of customer trust and perception of security control on the acceptance of electronic commerce. *International Journal of Electronic Commerce*. https://doi.org/10.1080/10864415.2003.11044270

Vatnani, R., & Verma, S. (2014). Comprehensive framework for internet banking adoption: An empirical analysis in the Indian context. *International Journal of Business Information Systems, 15*, 307. https://doi.org/10.1504/IJBIS.2014.059753

Venkatesh, V., Morris, M. G., Davis, G. B., & Davis, F. D. (2003). User acceptance of information technology: Toward a unified view. *MIS Quarterly: Management Information Systems, 27*, 425. https://doi.org/10.2307/30036540

Wang, Y. S., Wang, Y. M., Lin, H. H., & Tang, T. I. (2003). Determinants of user acceptance of internet banking: An empirical study. *International Journal of Service Industry Management, 14*, 501. https://doi.org/10.1108/09564230310500192

Yu, C. S. (2012). Factors affecting individuals to adopt mobile banking: Empirical evidence from the UTAUT model. *Journal of Electronic Commerce Research, 13*, 104–121.

Chapter 18
Defense Spending and Economic Growth: An Empirical Investigation in the Case of Greece

Antonis Tsitouras, Nicholas Tsounis, and Harry Papapanagos

Abstract The existing empirical literature presents a limited number of country-specific studies that investigate the relationship between defense expenditures and economic growth. Despite the mounting concerns in Greece regarding the underwhelming economic growth of recent years and the persistent issue of excessive defense expenditures, no empirical study has yet investigated the effects of defense spending on economic growth in both the short and long run. The present study aims to address the aforementioned gaps in the literature by applying the autoregressive distributed lag (ARDL) bound testing approach to cointegration and analyzing the impact of defense spending, domestic investment, population growth, and literacy on economic growth in both the short and long term. The study employs the most up-to-date data available to ensure accuracy and relevance. The findings indicate that there is a positive impact of military expenditure on the economy's growth in the short term. Nonetheless, when considering a longer time period, the same factor exerts an adverse influence on the growth of the economy. The findings of our investigation indicate that excessive military expenditures have significant adverse impacts on important drivers of economic growth, such as domestic investment, literacy rates, and population expansion, among others.

Keywords Economic Growth · Defence Spending · Time Series Analysis · ARDL

JEL Classifications C22, H56, O11

A. Tsitouras (✉) · N. Tsounis
Department of Economics, University of Western Macedonia, Kastoria, Greece
e-mail: atsitouras@uowm.gr

H. Papapanagos
Department of Balkan, Slavic & Oriental Studies, University of Macedonia, Thessaloniki, Greece

© The Author(s), under exclusive license to Springer Nature Switzerland AG 2024
N. Tsounis, A. Vlachvei (eds.), *Applied Economic Research and Trends*, Springer
Proceedings in Business and Economics,
https://doi.org/10.1007/978-3-031-49105-4_18

18.1 Introduction

In the development economics literature, the impact of defense spending on economic growth is an important topic that has not yet been extensively studied. Notwithstanding the extensive empirical literature, it is still debatable whether defense spending leads to a lower or higher growth rate.

The notion of "defense expenditure" refers to all current and future costs associated with the military forces, including those for peacekeepers, defense ministries, and other governmental organizations working on defense-related initiatives. Furthermore, it may encompass paramilitary units deemed to possess the requisite training and equipment for military maneuvers, alongside military space endeavors (SIPRI, 1989).

The allocation of funds for military expenditures serves as an indicator of a nation's perception of potential security risks. The fact that a significant portion of the budget is allocated to military spending is not exclusively associated with emerging economies. Industrialized countries, including the United States, the United Kingdom, France, and Greece, also allocate significant resources to strengthening their military defense.

In the wake of the 2008 financial crisis and the ensuing imposition of austerity measures, further compounded by the recent pandemic crisis, several member states of North Atlantic Treaty Organization (NATO) have endeavored to curtail their spending on national defense. Greece is part of a distinguished group of economies, comprising the United States, the United Kingdom, France, and Turkey, which have consistently allocated more than 2% of their gross domestic product (GDP) toward military expenditures for the past four decades. Despite its economic and financial vulnerabilities, Greece continues to prioritize its military expenditures. Given this context and the anticipated economic recovery in Greece after a prolonged recession, concerns have arisen regarding the possibility of increasing defense spending. It is imperative to acknowledge that the procurement initiatives of the Hellenic Armed Forces (EMPAE) have encountered several setbacks in the years of crisis, thereby jeopardizing their effectiveness. Hence, it is crucial to enhance the procurement initiatives, particularly in light of Turkey's potential demand for a modification of the existing state of affairs in the Aegean and the Eastern Mediterranean region.

Governments frequently face competing demands to distribute resources toward expeditious development and economic growth, augmented social welfare provisions, enhanced educational opportunities, infrastructure, healthcare systems, elevated living standards, and ultimately heightened national security. Henceforth, it is crucial for the governmental entities to harmonize three goals: safeguarding the nation's defense and security, fostering economic expansion and advancement, and ensuring their political durability. The allocation of government budgets toward military expenditure is a critical subject matter that underscores the careful utilization of scarce resources. Several countries, such as Greece and Turkey, persist in allotting substantial portions of their fiscal resources to defense expenditures on a yearly basis, leading to the reallocation of resources from other civil expenditures, such as those related to healthcare and education.

Numerous studies have been carried out to investigate the relationship between defense expenditure and economic growth. The seminal work of Benoit in 1973 and 1978 established a positive correlation between these two variables. The adoption of a basic methodology and the existence of several related challenges led many scholars to reassess the above-mentioned association by utilizing more sophisticated techniques, alternate theoretical models, longer time periods, or broader cross-sectional investigations. Despite the considerable amount of empirical research that has been conducted subsequent to the Benoit study, a consensus regarding the influence of military expenditure on economic growth has not yet been attained. Dunne and Uye (2010) suggest that a multitude of factors may contribute to divergent outcomes, including but not limited to distinct theoretical frameworks, models and specifications, diverse estimation techniques, disparate nations, and varying time frames analyzed. The lack of consensus among academics, along with continuous progressions in econometric methodologies, has motivated scholars in this domain to persevere in their endeavors to establish a more robust and dependable correlation.

The current body of research posits that there exist two principal pathways by which military expenditures influence a country's economic development. Firstly, expanding military expenditures yields a beneficial effect on economic expansion by stimulating aggregate demand via increased employment and production. Moreover, it elevates the level of human capital through increased levels of education, technological training, and stable social and political environments.

On the contrary, empirical evidence suggests that augmented allocation of resources toward military expenditure has a detrimental effect on economic growth, as it leads to suboptimal allocation of resources. Lipow and Antinori (1995) have proposed that the crowd-out effect of private investment, along with the resulting displacement of civilian resource utilization, has the potential to impede economic growth.

The significance of this empirical paper is further supported by the contradiction of previously published findings. Several academic studies (Antonakis & Karavidas, 1990; Antonakis, 1997; Andreou et al., 2002) have demonstrated that there exists a negative correlation between military expenditure and economic growth in Greece. Nonetheless, a number of scholarly investigations, including Chletsos and Kollias' (1995) and Balfoussias and Stavrinos' (1996) researches, have reported a favorable influence. Finally a strand of literature includes empirical studies that reveal a neutral or insignificant relationship between military spending and economic growth in the case of Greece (see, Chletsos & Kollias, 1995; Kollias & Makrydakis, 2000; Dunne et al., 2001; Dritsakis, 2004; Dunne & Nikolaidou, 2005; Georgantopoulos, 2012; Manamperi, 2016; Nikolaidou, 2016).

Greece, a developed nation, faces severe economic issues, including huge deficits, a rapidly expanding public debt, and security concerns with Turkey. Greece's economic instability has been linked to growing military spending over the previous few decades. Thus, military spending's impact on Greece's economy needs to be examined.

The aim of this empirical study is to add to the literature on the impacts of defense spending on economic growth in several ways:

First, there is no consensus in the literature on the net effect of defense spending on economic growth. Therefore, our results may be relevant for developed countries such as Greece that have significant external security issues and diachronically increased military spending and are vulnerable to problems across the socioeconomic and political spectrum.

Second, there is an important reason to include more explanatory factors than military spending in the relative paradigm, since the process of determining economic growth is extremely complex and depends on numerous factors. We also include three more critical dynamics of economic growth: population growth, higher educational attainment, and domestic investment.

Thirdly, it has been observed that previous empirical research conducted on Greece lacks crucial details concerning the consequences of the recent economic crisis that occurred in the country's economy. The objective of the present study is to address the gap in empirical research.

Finally, this study employs the ARDL methodology for cointegration analysis to examine the short-term and long-term relationships among the variables under consideration. The ARDL estimation technique has been demonstrated to possess noteworthy advantages in comparison to traditional cointegration approaches, such as those formulated by Engle and Granger (1987) and Johansen and Juselius (1988). The ARDL methodology is utilized to investigate the existence of long-term relationships, irrespective of the integration order. It is considered to be more accurate, particularly for datasets with inadequate time series. The issue of endogeneity can be effectively addressed, and the coefficients of both short-term and long-term explanatory variables are dependable since they are concurrently estimated with a minor alteration (Pesaran et al., 1999; Pesaran et al., 2001).

18.2   Greek Defense Spending: An Overview

Over the course of time, Greece has dedicated significant human and material resources toward defense in the interest of national security. From a comparative standpoint, it can be argued that it exhibits the highest degree of militarization in NATO and the EU.

A comparative list of statistical data from important NATO countries such as the United States of America, Great Britain, France, and Turkey is presented in this analysis. Also examined are the cases of Spain and Portugal, with which Greece has economic similarities but significant differences in external security, which makes them an interesting object of examination.

In fact, Greece and Turkey are among the leading nations in terms of military expenditure as a proportion of their respective gross domestic products (GDP) within the North Atlantic Treaty Organization (NATO), alongside the United States of America and the United Kingdom. Over the course of the past 42 years, the United States of America and the United Kingdom have, respectively, allocated an average of 4.48% and 3.15% of their Gross Domestic Product toward military expenditures. Greece and Turkey allocated 3.42% and 3.07% of their respective gross domestic product (GDP) toward military expenditure. In contrast to other member states of the European Union and NATO, France, Spain, and Portugal recorded military expenditures as a percentage of GDP of 2.37%, 1.81%, and 1.61%, respectively.

Between 1980 and 1990, the United States of America and the United Kingdom allocated 6.11% and 4.87% of their respective gross domestic products (GDP) toward military expenditures. Throughout the aforementioned timeframe, Greece and Turkey sustained an average military expenditure as a proportion of their respective gross domestic products of 4.62% and 3.61% correspondingly. During the same time frame, France, Spain, and Portugal reported military expenditures as a percentage of their respective gross domestic products (GDP) as 3.10%, 2.63%, and 1.92%.

Between 1991 and 2000, there was a recorded decrease in military expenditures across all nations. The military expenditures as a percentage of GDP for the United States of America, the United Kingdom, Greece, and Turkey were 3.89%, 3.04%, 3.45%, and 3.85%, respectively. Within the identical temporal framework, France, Spain, and Portugal disclosed their military expenditures as a percentage of their gross domestic product (GDP) at levels of 2.46%, 1.89%, and 1.62%, respectively.

Between 2001 and 2009, an additional decline in military spending was observed across all countries except for the United States of America. The United States of America, the United Kingdom, Greece, and Turkey are countries that have demonstrated military expenditure as a percentage of their gross domestic product (GDP) at rates of 3.94%, 2.77%, 3.18%, and 3.34%, respectively. Within the identical chronological scope, France, Spain, and Portugal disclosed their military expenditures as a percentage of their gross domestic product (GDP) at levels of 2.25%, 1.55%, and 1.67%, respectively.

Since the financial crisis and up to the year 2021, there has been a consensus among economies to decrease military expenditures. The percentage of gross domestic product (GDP) allocated to military expenditure in the United States of America, the United Kingdom, Greece, and Turkey is 3.99%, 2.47%, 2.88%, and 2.79%, respectively. Within the identical chronological scope, France, Spain, and Portugal disclosed their military expenditures as a percentage of their gross domestic product (GDP) to be 2.02%, 1.42%, and 1.48%, respectively.

It is worth noting that Greece has experienced a significant rise in military spending in the years 2020 and 2021, amounting to 3.06% and 3.86% of the gross domestic product (GDP), respectively. By contrast, Turkey's military spending as a proportion of its Gross Domestic Product (GDP) experienced a decline, reaching 2.43% and 1.90% in 2020 and 2021, respectively.

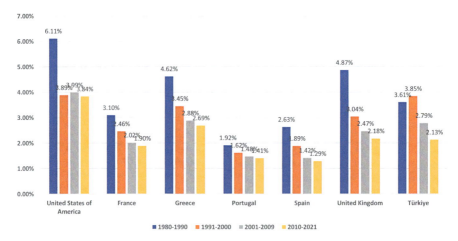

Fig. 18.1 Military expenditure by country as percentage of gross domestic product, 1980–2022. (Source: SIPRI Database (2023))

The examination of the structural allocation of military procurement expenditure between Greece and NATO provides insight into the rationale behind the elevated levels of spending, as depicted in Fig. 18.1.

A significant disparity exists between the allocation of funds toward personnel and equipment procurement when comparing Greece and the average of NATO. The focus of Greece is primarily on personnel expenditures, both in the military and civilian sectors. Conversely, NATO member countries on average allocate a significant portion of their budget toward the upkeep of modern weaponry, with over 20% of their budget being invested in armament purchases, research, and development. This investment is then utilized to produce new military weapons equipment and systems. It is indicative that the announcement of the purchase of three Belharra frigates was made in 2021 against the background of the signing of the Greece–France agreement on strategic partnership and cooperation in defense and security. It is recalled that Greece has agreed and has already begun receiving 24 Rafale fighter jets.

18.3 The Literature on Defense Spending and Economic Growth

The global allocation of resources to defense accounts for a significant proportion. Despite its considerable size, the economic consequences of this expenditure have only recently been studied in the context of economic theory. Four different schools of thought, namely Keynesian, Liberal, Marxist, and Neoclassical, engage in a scholarly discourse on the correlation between defense spending and economic progress within the existing literature review.

In the Keynesian framework, Dunne (1996) postulates that the national government displays assertiveness and interventionism by using military spending to increase output through multiplier effects in situations where aggregate demand is inefficient. According to Faini et al. (1984), in cases where aggregate demand is insufficient relative to expected supply, an increase in military spending can lead to an increase in capacity utilization, profits, investment, and ultimately economic growth. In empirical research, Keynesian demand models are often used to shed light on the relationship between economic growth and military spending. Within this demand-oriented framework, empirical research usually shows a negative correlation between military spending and economic growth, primarily due to the crowding out of savings or investment. The theoretical framework in question is inherently flawed as it focuses too much on the demand side, ignoring supply-side factors such as technological side effects and externalities. The inclusion of explicit production functions was first introduced by Smith and Smith (1980) to address the limitation of focusing exclusively on the demand side.

The Military–Industrial Complex (MIC) serves as a central element in a linked liberal or institutional framework that seeks to clarify the rationale for defense spending. The Military–Industrial Complex (MIC) is a significant interest group that benefits from defense spending, leading to a potential propensity to exaggerate global conflicts and hinder non-military conflict resolution efforts (Dunne, 1990).

The Marxist perspective views imperialism and military expenditure as a social phenomenon that has a historical dimension. In this framework, the sociopolitical and strategic dimensions of military expenditure are considered more important than the economic aspects. According to Dunne (1990), it is argued that defense spending can boost economic growth by serving as a means of conflict prevention or by acting as an implicit industrial strategy. An important role in military spending is played by a particular theoretical perspective within this academic discipline. Baran and Sweezy (2017) argue that in a capitalist economy, the available surplus exceeds the necessary level for consumption and investment as the economy becomes richer. Therefore, under the paradigm of underconsumption, military spending may prove beneficial to the growth of the economy in situations of disequilibrium.

In contrast, neoclassical theory relies exclusively on the fundamental role of aggregate supply. In terms of the neoclassical paradigm, an escalation in defense spending will ultimately lead to an increase in public spending, crowding out private investment. If taxes are used to increase military spending, this will lead to a crowding out of private investment. The expected result of the increased tax rate is a reduction in savings, which should lead to an escalation of the national interest rate. According to the neoclassical view, there is a negative correlation between economic growth and defense spending. The above approach has been used by several scholars, as shown by the work of Alexander (1990), Mintz and Stevenson (1995), Murdoch et al. (1997), and Sezgin (1997).

18.4 Defense Spending and Economic Growth in Greece: An Empirical Review

The existing empirical literature on the correlation between military spending and economic growth in Greece is insufficient but yields similarly inconclusive results as the global empirical studies. After a thorough examination of the significant empirical literature on Greece, some basic facts can be highlighted.

Several econometric studies have used panel data analysis in their samples and included Greece among other economies with different levels of economic development and notable differences in external security. The additional information resulting from these empirical works is useful in a virtual context. However, the aforementioned work has been insufficient to provide all-encompassing policy suggestions, as the variables that serve as either beneficial or detrimental catalysts for economic growth in an economy can vary considerably depending on the observable level of economic progress and the level of military spending.

Previous empirical research, with the exception of recent studies by Manamperi (2016), Nikolaidou (2016), and Paparas et al. (2016), has not included adequate data from the period of the Greek economic crisis to examine the impact of military spending on economic growth. The aim of this study is to contribute to the current empirical literature by filling the research gap mentioned above.

In the field of econometric methodology, it is noteworthy that a considerable part of the research effort has used the OLS cross-sectional analysis technique. However, given the non-stationarity of time series macro data, it is plausible that the results of their regression analyses could be biased. Therefore, it is imperative to identify cointegration relationships, as highlighted in various studies, including Antonakis (1997), Chletsos and Kollias (1995), Dunne and Nikolaidou (2001), and Nikolaidou (2016).

Table 18.1 presents the primary outcomes of previous empirical studies that have examined the impact of defense expenditures on the economic growth in the case of Greece or in the EU-15 countries.

Research on the impact of military spending on economic growth in Greece has produced three different categories of results. The first group of researchers observed a positive correlation between the two variables, while the second group found a negative correlation. The third group, on the other hand, found a neutral relationship between military spending and economic growth.

In fact, there are a considerable number of studies, indicating that defense spending has a positive impact on economic growth in the case of Greece (see Kollias, 1994, 1995; Balfoussias & Stavrinos, 1996; Kollias et al., 2013). For the EU-15, we can identify two studies (see Kollias et al., 2007; Malizard, 2016) that confirm a positive relationship between defense spending and economic growth.

On the other hand, we identified four studies (Antonakis, 1997, 1999; Dunne & Nikolaidou, 2001; Paparas et al., 2016) that confirm that military spending has a negative impact on economic growth. In addition, we identified two other studies (Mylonidis, 2008; Dunne & Nikolaidou, 2012) that applied econometric techniques

Table 18.1 List of variables and data sources

Variable	Label of variable	Unit of measurement	Source	Website
GDP per capita	GDP p.c.	Log of GDP per capita (constant 2015 US$)	World Bank	https://data.worldbank.org/indicator/NY.GDP.PCAP.KD
Military expenditure	MILI	Military expenditure (% of GDP)	SIPRI Military Expenditure Database	https://milex.sipri.org/sipri
Gross fixed capital formation	INVE	Gross fixed capital formation (% of GDP)	World Bank	https://data.worldbank.org/indicator/NE.GDI.FTOT.ZS
Educational attainment	EDUC	Percentage (%) of Total Educational attainment, at least completed short-cycle tertiary, population 25+	UNESCO Database	http://data.uis.unesco.org/Index.aspx
Population	POPU	Population growth (annual %)	World Bank	https://data.worldbank.org/indicator/SP.POP.GROW

with panel data in the case of the EU-15 economies and confirmed a negative relationship between the above variables. Finally, there is a study (see Stylianou, 2012) that applies the panel data method and confirms a negative relationship between military expenditure and economic growth in a sample consisting of data from Greece, Cyprus, and Turkey.

The third strand of literature comprises empirical studies that show a neutral or insignificant relationship between military spending and economic growth. This group of studies includes eight (8) empirical studies that have conducted time series analysis in the case of Greece (see Chletsos & Kollias, 1995; Kollias & Makrydakis, 2000; Dunne et al., 2001; Dritsakis, 2004; Dunne & Nikolaidou, 2005; Georgantopoulos, 2012; Manamperi, 2016; Nikolaidou, 2016). Similarly, we identified one (1) study (see Kollias & Paleologou, 2010) using data from EU-15 economies that showed that defense spending has no statistically significant impact on the economy.

18.5 Model Specification

Various growth models have been used in the defense economics literature, including Barro's (1990) model, which has been applied by scholars such as Aizenman and Glick (2003), Mylonidis (2008), and Pieroni et al. (2008).

Mankiw et al. (1992) introduced the extended Solow growth model, which was used to revise the study of the impact of military spending on economic growth. The Barro growth model proposed in 1990 includes different types of government spending financed by taxes, and their effects on output are determined by the production function. This argument assumes a nonlinear correlation between government spending and economic growth resulting from the interplay between the productivity-enhancing and tax-distorting effects of government spending, as suggested by Dunne and Perlo-Freeman (2005).

The complicated nature of the original Barro model forced economists to deal with potential exogenous variables when examining the impact of military spending on economic growth (Aizenman & Glick, 2003). In this study, a modified Barro model is used to identify the relevant variables when examining the impact of military spending on economic growth, building on the previous discourse (see Mylonidis, 2008; Manamperi, 2016).

Thus, we examine the following regression model econometrically in the case of Greece from 1980 to 2021 in Eq. 18.1.

$$\text{GDPpc}_t = \alpha_1 + \beta_1 \text{MILI}_t + \gamma_1 \text{INVE}_t + \delta_1 \text{EDUC}_t + \varepsilon_1 \text{POPU}_t + u_{1t} \qquad (18.1)$$

GDPpc_t denotes the Log of GDP per capita (constant 2015 US$) at time $t = 1, 2,...T$; MILI_t stands for the military expenditure as a % of GDP; INVE_t refers to the Gross fixed capital formation as a % of GDP; EDUC_t denotes the attainment rate of tertiary education in the population; and finally, $\alpha 1$ denotes a continuous parameter and $u1_t$ the normally distributed residual term.

18.6   Data

The present investigation uses a distinctive dataset comprising yearly observations for Greece spanning the period from 1980 to 2021, with the aim of achieving more resilient and enlightening findings.

The World Bank was the source of the data related to the logarithm of GDP per capita (constant 2015 US dollars), Gross fixed capital formation as a percentage of GDP, and annual population growth percentage. The information regarding the levels of tertiary education has been collected from UNESCO. The data regarding military expenditure as a percentage of gross domestic product (GDP) have been collected from the Stockholm International Peace Research Institute (SIPRI) database.

Table 18.1 presents comprehensive details regarding the variables utilized in this empirical investigation, and Table 18.2 provides descriptive statistics related to each of the significant variables employed in this research.

Table 18.2 Summary statistics of the key variables in Greece 1980–2021

	GDPpc_t	MILI_t	INVE_t	EDUC_t	POPU_t
Mean	9.78	3.41	20.37	18.83	0.27
Median	9.79	3.28	22.97	18.58	0.35
Maximum	10.09	5.74	30.66	35.00	1.21
Minimum	9.58	2.35	10.58	7.60	−0.72
Std. dev.	0.15	0.89	5.82	9.20	0.47
Skewness	0.48	0.98	−0.60	0.15	−0.34
Kurtosis	2.18	3.26	2.02	1.57	2.88
Observations	42	42	42	42	42

18.7 Methodology

In this study, a two-stage econometric approach is used. First, the unit root tests of Ng-Perron (2001) and DF-GLS (Elliott et al., 1996) are used to examine the level of integration of the variables. After confirming the order of integration, we then use the ARDL approach to examine the short- and long-term relationships between the variables.

To achieve this goal, we use the more robust approach of Pesaran et al. (2001), which incorporates a multivariate framework that accounts for all relevant variables in the empirical model presented in Eq. (18.1).

In the context of cointegration using the ARDL approach, the first stage involves a long-run analysis using an unconstrained error correction model. This model is an ARDL adjustment of the empirical model represented by Eq. (18.2).

$$\Delta \text{GDPpc}_t = \alpha_0 + \sum_{i=1}^{n} ai_{\text{GDPpc}} \Delta \text{GDPpc}_{t-i} + \sum_{i=1}^{n} ai_{\text{MILI}} \Delta \text{MILI}_{t-i}$$
$$+ \sum_{i=1}^{n} ai_{\text{INVE}} \Delta \text{INVE}_{t-i} + \sum_{i=1}^{n} ai_{\text{EDUC}} \Delta \text{EDUC}_{t-i} + \sum_{i=1}^{n} ai_{\text{POPU}} \Delta \text{POPU}_{t-i}$$
$$+ a_1 \text{PDPpc}_{t-1} + \beta_1 \text{MILI}_{t-1} + \gamma_1 \text{INVE}_{t-1} + \delta_1 \text{EDUC}_{t-1} + \varepsilon_1 \text{POPU}_{t-1} + u_{1t}$$

$$(18.2)$$

The symbol Δ is used to represent the first difference operator. The variable GDPpct represents the logarithm of GDP per capita, while MILIt represents military expenditure as a percentage of GDP. INVEt refers to gross fixed capital formation as a percentage of GDP, and EDUCt denotes the attainment rate of tertiary education within the population.

The F check was used to assess the long-term relationship between the variables based on the statistical significance of the variables' lagged levels.

According to Pesaran et al. (2001), the null hypothesis is characterized by the absence of a long-term co-integration relationship, indicating no co-integration, among the variables in Eq. (18.2), $H_0 = \alpha_1 = \beta_1 = \gamma_1 = \delta_1 = \varepsilon_1 = 0$ as opposed to the alternative hypothesis. $H_0 \neq \alpha_1 \neq \beta_1 \neq \gamma_1 \neq \delta_1 \neq \varepsilon_1 \neq 0$.

The F statistic is evaluated by comparing it with the critical values established by Pesaran et al. (2001) and the F non-standard test distribution. The authors established two critical limits, namely a lower and an upper limit. The determination of the lower critical values in the ARDL model is based on the assumption that all independent variables have the property of zero-order stationarity ($I(0)$), while the upper critical values are determined by the assumption that all variables have the property of one-order non-stationarity ($I(1)$). If the approximated value of the F-statistic exceeds the upper critical value, the null hypothesis of non-cointegration is rejected. Conversely, the null hypothesis is retained if it is not exceeded. If the predicted value of F is within the range of minimum and maximum values, the results are considered inconclusive.

In order to evaluate the enduring association between variables, it is imperative to verify the presence of cointegration. Subsequently, by utilizing Eq. (18.1) as a foundation, we can incorporate the error correction term (ECT_{t-1}) into our fundamental model, specifically the autoregressive distributed lag (ARDL) model. The present study showcases the incorporation of an error correction term into a basic causality examination.

$$\text{GDPpc}_t = \theta_1 + \varphi_1 \text{ECT}_{t-1} + \sum_{i=1}^{k} \eta_i \Delta \text{GDPpc}_{t-i} + \sum_{i=1}^{k} \kappa_i \Delta \text{MILI}_{t-i}$$

$$+ \sum_{i=1}^{k} \lambda_i \text{INVE}_{t-i} + \sum_{i=1}^{k} \mu_i \Delta \text{EDUC}_{t-i} + \sum_{i=1}^{k} \nu_i \text{POPU}_{t-i} + o_{it}$$

$$(18.3)$$

The symbol ECT represents the error correction term of the long-term cointegrating equation, where the difference operator is denoted by Δ. According to Eq. (18.3) of the simple Error Correction Model, both the residual term o ($i = 1$) and the constant term ($\theta 1$) follow a normal distribution.

The F-statistic or Wald test holds significant statistical value in detecting short-term Granger causality, whereas the t-test serves the purpose of confirming long-term Granger causality, as shown by the statistical importance of the lagged ECM term.

18.8 Findings

Time Series Unit Root Tests
The results of using the method proposed by Elliott et al. (1996) DF-GLS and the unit root test developed by Ng and Perron (2001) are shown in Table 18.3. The results show that the considered variables exhibit stationarity either at their level (POPU_t) or after one-time differentiation (GDPpc_t, MILI_t, INVE_t, and EDUC_t). The results show that all variables do not show integration at $I(2)$ and higher levels. Therefore, the ARDL bound test proposed by Pesaran et al. (2001) can be used to determine the presence of cointegration between variables.

Table 18.3 Results of the unit root tests

Variables	DF-GLS		Ng-Perron	
	Constant	Constant & trend	Constant	Constant & trend
At levels	Statistic	Statistic	Statistic	Statistic
$GDPpc_t$	−1.478 (2)	−2.136 (2)	−4.963 (2)	−13.423 (2)
$MILI_t$	−1.159 (0)	−1.321 (0)	−2.065 (0)	−5.633 (0)
$INVE_t$	−0.479 (0)	−1.983 (0)	−4.016 (0)	−7.974 (0)
$EDUC_t$	−0.337 (0)	−1.755 (0)	2.005 (0)	−3.515 (0)
$POPU_t$	−2.015 (2)**	−3.720 (1)**	−3.615 (1)	−25.736 (1)***
At first difference				
$GDPpc_t$	−3.779 (2)***	−3.723 (2)**	−14.837 (2)***	−32.360 (2)***
$MILI_t$	−2.221 (0)**	−3.811 (0)***	−7.423 (0)**	−20.733 (2)**
$INVE_t$	−4.922 (0)***	−5.370 (0)***	−18.732 (0)***	−18.198 (0)**
$EDUC_t$	−3.598 (1)***	−5.866 H180)***	−18.202 (0) ***	−30.268 (2)**
$POPU_t$	−3.560 (1)***	−4.400 (1)***	−23.677 (1) ***	−29.486 (1)***

Notes: The DF-GLS and Ng-P tests' optimal lag structures are determined using the Akaike information criterion (AIC) and are indicated in parentheses.

At the 1%, 5%, and 10% levels, respectively, ***, **, and * indicate rejection of the null hypothesis of a unit root.

	Critical values for the DF-GLS test		Critical values for the NP (MZa) test	
	Constant	Constant & trend	Constant	Constant & trend
1%	−2.627	−3.770	−13.800	−23.800
5%	−1.950	−3.190	−8.100	−17.300
10%	−1.611	−2.890	−5.700	−14.200

Table 18.4 The cointegration test results

Estimated model:	$GDPpc_t = f(MILI_t, INVE_t, EDUC_t, POPU_t)$
Lag order	(4, 2, 3, 4, 4)
F-static	10.02***
	Critical Values ($T = 38$)
Significance level	
Lower bounds I(0)	
1 percent level	5.06
2.5 percent level	4.49
5 percent level	4.01
10 percent level	3.52
Upper bounds I(1)	
1 percent level	3.74
2.5 percent level	3.25
5 percent level	2.86
10 percent level	2.45
Diagnostics	
Serial correlation:	$X^2 = 1.729\ (0.213)$
Functional form:	$X^2 = 2.675\ (0.102)$
Normality:	$X^2 = 0.474\ (0.688)$
Heteroscedasticity:	$X^2 = 1.128\ (0.408)$
ARCH:	$X^2 = 2.086\ (0.158)$
White	$X^2 = 0.937\ (0.563)$
Durbin Watson	2.583

Notes:

The Akaike information criterion (AIK) was used to pick the ARDL specification

Parentheses denote P-values

Eviews 12 was used to conduct the estimation and cointegration tests

**, ** and * indicate statistically significant results at 1%, 5% and 10%, correspondingly

Confidence intervals are obtained from Pesaran et al. (2001)

Time Series Cointegration Test

The estimates of the ARDL cointegration technique for Eq. (18.2) are shown in Table 18.4, while the critical values of the F statistic are given in panel A. The results show that the null hypothesis, which assumes the existence of a long-term relationship according to Eq. (18.1), is rejected at a statistical significance level of 1% because the calculated F value exceeds the upper critical threshold.

Moreover, the tests of the ARDL model for serial correlation and heteroskedasticity show negative results, as can be seen in the lower sections of Table 18.4.

The Evaluation of the Coefficients in the Short and Long Term

Having established long-run cointegration, we calculated the short-run and long-run effects of military spending, domestic investment, educational attainment, and population growth on per capita income. The results of the short-run dynamic variables associated with the long-run correlations from the ECM Eq. (18.3) are summarized in Table 18.5.

18 Defense Spending and Economic Growth: An Empirical Investigation... 313

Table 18.5 Short-run estimated coefficients

Variable	Coefficient	Standard error	T-ratio	Prob-value
ΔGDPpc$_t$	0.280	0.141	1.988	(0.064)
ΔGDPpc$_t$ (−1)	0.165	0.163	1.012	(0.326)
ΔGDPpc$_t$ (−2)	0.335	0.137	2.445	(0.026)
ΔMILI$_t$	0.020	0.014	1.442	(0.016)
ΔMILI$_t$ (−1)	0.059	0.014	4.225	(0.000)
ΔINVE$_t$	0.014	0.002	7.622	(0.059)
ΔINVE$_t$(−1)	−0.006	0.003	−2.036	(0.011)
ΔINVE$_t$(−2)	−0.007	0.003	−2.861	(0.000)
ΔEDUC$_t$	0.004	0.004	1.182	(0.254)
ΔEDUC$_t$(−1)	−0.021	0.004	−5.010	(0.000)
ΔEDUC$_t$(−2)	−0.022	0.004	−5.562	(0.060)
ΔEDUC$_t$(−3)	−0.025	0.004	−6.167	(0.000)
ΔPOPU$_t$	0.044	0.028	1.561	(0.138)
ΔPOPU$_t$ (−1)	−0.119	0.026	−4.498	(0.000)
ECTerm	−0.861	0.109	−7.915	(0.000)
Intercept	7.794	0.982	7.936	(0.000)

GDPpc$_t$ is the dependent variable
Notes: Δ indicates first differences. p-values are presented in parentheses
R-Squared $= 0.908$
Adjusted R-Squared $= 0.829$
S.E. of Regression $= 0.016$
F-Stat. $= 11.581***$
DW-statistic $= 2.583$
Akaike Info. Criterion $= -5.087$
Schwarz Bayesian Criterion $= -4.810$

A look at the short-run coefficients shows that military spending positively affects per capita income in the short run and is statistically significant at the 1% level. In terms of the distribution of defense funds, as shown in Fig. 18.2, this is not a surprising result. Indeed, Greece places great emphasis on personnel spending, which includes both the military and civilian sectors. In the context of Greece, the immediate positive impact on economic growth can be attributed to demand-stimulating effects resulting from wages paid to military and civilian personnel employed in the defense sector. This increase in aggregate demand in the economy leads to a subsequent increase in output and employment levels.

Of particular importance in the context of Greece is the observation that employees in the defense industry receive higher wages than their counterparts in the private sector of the economy. This phenomenon leads to an increase in aggregate demand, which in turn leads to an increase in employment. The argument assumes that socioeconomically disadvantaged populations who find employment in the armed forces would experience an improvement in their standard of living due to improved income distribution.

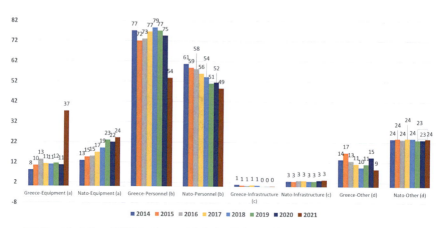

Fig. 18.2 Distribution of defense expenditure by main category—percentage of total defense expenditure. (Source: NATO Database (2023))

Regarding the impact of domestic investment variable on economic growth, we reveal that there is a rather neutral relationship between per capita income and the sum of lagged coefficients for the corresponding short-run changes. On the other hand, after examining the sum of the lagged coefficients for short-run changes in education levels and population growth, we conclude that increasing population and education levels take time to have a positive effect on economic growth.

The estimated lagged ECT has a negative sign and is statistically significant at the 1% level. The ECT is a measure of how quickly cointegrated parameters reach equilibrium in the short run once the relationship is broken (or deviates). The coefficient of the error correction term is 0.861, which means that 86.4% of the disequilibrium is corrected annually.

The long-term analysis is shown in Table 18.6. All long-run parameters are statistically significant and have the expected sign, suggesting that they have an impact on the dynamics of economic growth over time. In fact, our study clearly shows that long-term military spending has a negative impact on economic growth. This relationship is statistically significant at the 1% level. In fact, a 1% increase in military spending reduces economic growth by 0.071%, all other factors remaining unchanged. Thus, this study suggests that economic growth has a destabilizing effect and that, in the case of Greece, an increase in military spending can prevent economic growth. Overall, this finding supports the notion that the lack of allocation of resources for domestic production and maintenance of military equipment in Greece is a detrimental factor to economic progress in the long run, as evidenced by the country's military spending (see Fig. 18.2). More importantly, the Greek government's excessive military spending, narrowed the fiscal margins for other public expenditures considering the size of the budget. In brief terms, it can be posited that economies with elevated military expenditures may experience

18 Defense Spending and Economic Growth: An Empirical Investigation... 315

Table 18.6 Long-run estimated coefficients

Variable	Coefficient	Standard error	T-ratio	Prob-value
$MILI_t$	-0.071	0.009	-7.516	(0.000)
$INVE_t$	0.027	0.002	17.201	(0.000)
$EDUC_t$	0.024	0.002	9.669	(0.000)
$POPU_t$	0.109	0.048	2.257	(0.038)

$GDPpc_t$ is the dependent variable
R-Squared $= 0.993$
Adjusted R-Squared $= 0.984$
S.E. of Regression $= 0.018$
F-Stat. $= 112.099$***
DW-statistic $= 2.583$
Akaike Info. Criterion $= -4.876$
Schwarz Bayesian Criterion $= -3.928$
Notes: p-values are displayed in parentheses

a reduction in available resources for alternative social expenditures, such as healthcare and education, which could act more effectively as growth stimulators.

It is noteworthy that in the case of Greece, it has been observed that defense spending functions as unproductive spending in the long run. First, it is important to note that these expenditures have significant opportunity costs. Secondly, it was observed that they have the potential to crowd out investment. Overall, excessive Greek military spending and its structure have been found to act as an obstacle to economic growth by disrupting resource allocation and impeding progress.

Our findings are consistent with those of Antonakis (1997, 1999), Dunne and Nikolaidou (2001), and Paparas et al. (2016), who have shown that military spending and economic growth are negatively related in the case of Greece.

Moreover, domestic investment was found to increase economic growth, and this relationship was found to be statistically significant at the 1% level of significance. This suggests that the ability of the Greek government to promote economic growth while supporting investment programs (i.e., tax cuts, specific investment incentives) can lead to positive growth rates in the long run. Indeed, a 1% increase in domestic investment can lead to a 0.027% improvement in economic growth.

More importantly, the neoclassical approach can provide an explanation for the relatively modest positive impact of domestic investment on economic growth. According to this view, an increase in military spending can lead to a corresponding increase in government spending, which can ultimately crowd out private investment. In the case of an increase in military spending through taxation, private investment is crowded out. The increased tax rate leads to a reduction in savings and thus to an increase in the domestic interest rate. In line with the neoclassical approach, it is concluded that military expenditure has a negative impact on the economic growth of a given nation.

As for the influence of the two demographic factors, education level and population expansion were found to have a remarkable and statistically significant

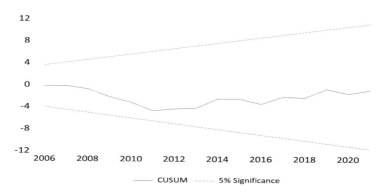

Fig. 18.3 Plot of cumulative sum of recursive residuals

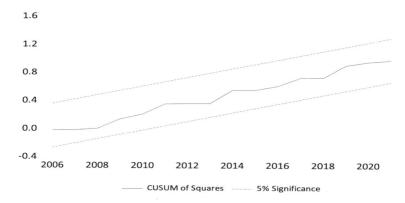

Fig. 18.4 Plot of cumulative sum of squares of recursive residuals

influence, with significance levels of 1% and 5%, respectively. The results of our study indicate that a 1% increase in the level of higher education and population expansion leads to a 0.024% and 0.109% increase in economic growth, respectively.

The relatively limited positive impact of the two demographic factors on economic growth is consistent with previous research studies, including Tsitouras et al. (2020) on Greece, Tsitouras et al. (2017) on European economies in transition, and Islam (2017) on Japan, all of which face comparable demographic obstacles.

Moreover, it is possible that there are structural breaks in the time series data due to the changes in the structure of the Greek economy that took place between 1980 and 2021. This study aims to test the accuracy of the short-run and long-run elasticities by using the cumulative sum (CUSUM) and cumulative sum of squares (CUSUMSQ) tests of Brown, Durbin and Evans (1975). Figures 18.3 and 18.4 illustrate the graphical representation of the CUSUM and CUSUMSQ test statistics, which show statistical significance at a 5% level. This ensures that the expected coefficients remain consistent over the required time intervals.

18.9 Conclusions

Economic growth and defense spending are rarely studied in the context of a single developed economy. Despite growing concerns in Greece about rising military spending, no previous study has attempted to empirically assess the impact of defense spending on short- and long-term economic growth using the most recent data available, which includes the period of the ongoing Greek crisis. This study makes an important contribution to filling these gaps.

This empirical study examined the long- and short-term effects of defense spending, domestic investment, population growth, and tertiary education levels on economic growth, using Greece as an example, using the ARDL bound testing approach to cointegration.

The findings validate the enduring correlation among the variables under examination. The findings suggest that military expenditures have a favorable effect on economic expansion in the short term. Nevertheless, over an extended period, the identical factor poses an adverse impact on the growth of the economy. The aforementioned incompatible finding can primarily be explained by the configuration of military expenditure in the context of Greece. It is expected that a significant proportion of defense expenditure is allocated toward the remuneration of military personnel. The demand-stimulating effects resulting from wages paid to military and civilian personnel employed in the defense sector lead to an increase in aggregate demand in the economy and thus to an increase in the level of output and employment, which ultimately leads to economic growth.

The long-term findings are consistent with the notion that Greece's lack of military funding for domestic production and maintenance of military equipment is a hindrance to long-term economic growth. It is evident that the Greek government has reduced the fiscal space for public spending such as health and education, which could potentially serve as more effective growth stimulants, by prioritizing military spending in recent decades.

The results of our study suggest that excess military spending has notable negative effects on important drivers of economic growth, including but not limited to domestic investment, literacy rates, and population growth. It is envisaged that the limited positive impact of the above-mentioned growth-enhancing factors can be counteracted by an increase in military spending, which could lead to a corresponding escalation in public spending, potentially crowding out private investment, especially in the context of Greece. In the scenario where military spending is increased through taxes, private investment is crowded out. The higher tax rate has a negative impact on savings, which in turn leads to an increase in the domestic interest rate. Overall, it can be deduced that military spending has a negative impact on a country's economic development in the long run, unless there is a reallocation of military spending in favor of more productive spending.

The empirical findings of our study have noteworthy policy implications. Given the defense challenges Greece faces and the ongoing potential for conflict from neighboring Turkey, it is extremely difficult for Greece to push through a significant reduction in its defense spending. Restructuring defense spending is crucial, with a focus on developing modern weapons and technological capabilities rather than relying exclusively on the most expensive options. It is also important to prioritize the continuous military training of the local population. It is recommended that this approach be pursued rather than engaging in excessive recruitment efforts for political gain. Finally, it is recommended for Greece to allocate a greater proportion of its resources toward enhancing the favorable and important determinants of economic growth, namely education, physical, and human capital.

References

Aizenman, J., & Glick, R. (2003). *Military expenditure, threats, and growth*. National Bureau of Economic Research. Working paper No. 9618

Alexander, W. R. J. (1990). The impact of defence spending on economic growth: A multi-sectoral approach to defence spending and economic growth with evidence from developed economies. *Defence and Peace Economics, 2*(1), 39–55.

Andreou, A. S., Parsopoulos, K. E., Vrahatis, M. N., & Zombanakis, G. A. (2002). Optimal versus required defence expenditure: The case of the Greek-Turkish arms race. *Defence and Peace Economics, 13*(4), 329–347.

Antonakis, N. (1997). Military expenditure and economic growth in Greece, 1960-90. *Journal of Peace Research, 34*(1), 89–100. https://doi.org/10.1177/0022343397034001007

Antonakis, N. (1999). Guns versus butter: A multisectoral approach to military expenditure and growth with evidence from Greece, 1960-1993. *Journal of Conflict Resolution, 43*(4), 501–520.

Antonakis, N., & Karavidas, D. (1990). *Defence expenditure and growth in LDCs. The case of Greece, 1950-1985*. Discussion Paper, Centre of Planning and Economic Research, Athens.

Balfoussias, A., & Stavrinos, V. (1996). The Greek military sector and macroeconomic effects of military spending in Greece. In N. P. Gleditsch et al. (Eds.), *The peace dividend* (pp. 191–213). North Holland Publications.

Baran, P. A., & Sweezy, P. M. (2017). *The age of monopoly capital: Selected correspondence of Paul M. Sweezy and Paul A. Baran, 1949-1964*. NYU Press.

Barro, R. J. (1990). Government spending in a simple model of endogeneous growth. *Journal of Political Economy, 98*(5, Part 2), S103–S125.

Benoit, E. (1973). *Defence and economic growth in developing countries*. Lexington Books.

Benoit, E. (1978). Growth and defense in developing countries. *Economic Development and Cultural Change, 26*(2), 271–280.

Brown, R. L., Durbin, J., & Evans, J. M. (1975). Techniques for testing the constancy of regression relationships over time. *Journal of the Royal Statistical Society: Series B: Methodological, 37*(2), 149–163.

Chletsos, M., & Kollias, C. (1995). Defense expenditure and growth in Greece 1974-90: Some preliminary econometric results. *Applied Economics, 27*(9), 883–890. https://doi.org/10.1080/00036849500000042

Dritsakis, N. (2004). Defense spending and economic growth: An empirical investigation for Greece and Turkey. *Journal of Policy Modeling, 26*(2), 249–264.

Dunne, J. P. (1990). *Using input-output models to assess the employment effects of military expenditure: A comparative assessment*. University of Cambridge Department of Applied Economics.

Dunne, J. P. (1996). Economic effects of military expenditure in developing countries: A survey. *Contributions to Economic Analysis, 235*, 439–464.

Dunne, P., & Nikolaidou, E. (2001). Military expenditure and economic growth: A demand and supply model for Greece, 1960–96. *Defence and Peace Economics, 12*(1), 47–67.

Dunne, J. P., & Nikolaidou, E. (2005). Military spending and economic growth in Greece, Portugal and Spain. *Frontiers in Finance and Economics, 2*(1), 1–17.

Dunne, J. P., & Nikolaidou, E. (2012). Defence spending and economic growth in the EU15. *Defence and Peace Economics, 23*(6), 537–548.

Dunne, J. P., & Perlo-Freeman, S. (2005). The demand for military spending in developing countries. *International Review of Applied Economics, 17*(1), 23–48.

Dunne, J. P., & Uye, M. (2010). *Military spending and development. The global arms trade: A handbook* (pp. 293–305). Routledge.

Dunne, P., Nikolaidou, E., & Vougas, D. (2001). Defence spending and economic growth: A causal analysis for Greece and Turkey. *Defence & Peace Economics, 12*(1), 5–26. https://doi.org/10.1080/10430710108404974

Elliott, G., Rothenberg, T. J., & Stock, J. H. (1996). Efficient Tests for an Autoregressive Unit Root. *Econometrica, 64*, 813–836.

Engle, R. F., & Granger, C. W. (1987). Co-integration and error correction: Representation, estimation, and testing. *Econometrica: Journal of the Econometric Society*, 251–276.

Faini, R., Annez, P., & Taylor, L. (1984). Defense spending, economic structure, and growth: Evidence among countries and over time. *Economic Development and Cultural Change, 32*(3), 487–498.

Georgantopoulos, A. G. (2012). A causal analysis of the defence-growth relationships: Evidence from the Balkans. *European Scientific Journal/April Edition, 8*(7).

Islam, M. R. (2017). Income inequality and economic growth nexus in Japan: A multivariate analysis. *The Ritsumeikan Economic Review: The Bi-Monthly Journal of Ritsumeikan University, 65*(4), 439–456.

Johansen, S., & Juselius, K. (1988). *Hypothesis testing for cointegration vectors: With application to the demand for money in Denmark and Finland (No. 88-05)*. University of Copenhagen. Department of Economics.

Kollias, C. (1994). The economic effects of defence spending in Greece 1963-90: Some preliminary econometric findings. *SPOUDAI-Journal of Economics and Business, 44*(3-4), 114–130.

Kollias, C. (1995). Country survey VII: Military spending in Greece. *Defence and Peace Economics, 6*(4), 305–319.

Kollias, C., & Makrydakis, S. (2000). A note on the causal relationship between defence spending and growth in Greece: 1955–93. *Defence and Peace Economics, 11*(1), 173–184.

Kollias, C., & Paleologou, S. M. (2010). Growth, investment and military expenditure in the European Union-15. *Journal of Economic Studies, 37*(2), 228–240.

Kollias, C., Mylonidis, N., & Paleologou, S. M. (2007). A panel data analysis of the nexus between defence spending and growth in the European Union. *Defence and Peace Economics, 18*(1), 75–85.

Kollias, C., Mylonidis, N., & Paleologou, S. M. (2013). Crime and the effectiveness of public order spending in Greece: Policy implications of some persistent findings. *Journal of Policy Modeling, 35*(1), 121–133.

Lipow, J., & Antinori, C. M. (1995). External security threats, defense expenditures, and the economic growth of less-developed countries. *Journal of Policy Modeling, 17*(6), 579–595.

Malizard, J. (2016). Military expenditure and economic growth in the European Union: Evidence from SIPRI's extended dataset. *The Economics of Peace and Security Journal, 11*(2).

Manamperi, N. (2016). Does military expenditure hinder economic growth? Evidence from Greece and Turkey. *Journal of Policy Modeling, 38*(6), 1171–1193.

Mankiw, N. G., Romer, D., & Weil, D. (1992). A contribution to the empirics of economic growth. *Quarterly Journal of Economics, 107*, 407–437.

Mintz, A., & Stevenson, R. T. (1995). Defense expenditures, economic growth, and the "peace dividend". A longitudinal analysis of 103 countries. *Journal of Conflict Resolution, 39*(2), 283–305.

Murdoch, J. C., Sandler, T., & Sargent, K. (1997). A tale of two collectives: Sulphur versus nitrogen oxides emission reduction in Europe. *Economica, 64*(254), 281–301. https://doi.org/10.1111/1468-0335.00078

Mylonidis, N. (2008). Revisiting the nexus between military spending and growth in the European Union. *Defence and Peace Economics, 19*(4), 265–272.

NATO Database. (2023). Available at: https://www.nato.int/cps/en/natohq/topics_49198.htm

Ng, S., & Perron, P. (2001). Lag length selection and the construction of unit root tests with good size and power. *Econometrica, 69*(6), 1519–1554.

Nikolaidou, E. (2016). The role of military expenditure and arms imports in the Greek debt crisis. *The Economics of Peace and Security Journal, 11*(1).

Paparas, D., Richter, C., & Paparas, A. (2016). Military spending and economic growth in Greece and the arms race between Greece and Turkey. *Journal of Economics Library, 3*(1), 38–56.

Pesaran, M. H., Shin, Y., & Smith, R. P. (1999). Pooled mean group estimation of dynamic heterogeneous panels. *Journal of the American Statistical Association, 94*(446), 621–634.

Pesaran, M. H., Shin, Y., & Smith, R. J. (2001). Bounds testing approaches to the analysis of level relationships. *Journal of Applied Econometrics, 16*(3), 289–326.

Pieroni, L., d'Agostino, G., & Lorusso, M. (2008). Can we declare military Keynesianism dead? *Journal of Policy Modeling, 30*(5), 675–691.

Sezgin, S. (1997). Country survey X: Defence spending in Turkey. *Defence and Peace Economics, 8*(4), 381–409.

SIPRI. (1989). Available at: https://www.sipri.org/yearbook/1989

SIPRI. (2023). Available at: https://www.sipri.org/databases/milex/sources-and-methods#definition-of-military-expenditure

Smith, D., & Smith, R. (1980). British military expenditure in the 1980s. *Protest and Survive*, 193–198.

Stylianou, T. (2012). *Economic growth and defense spending in Greece, Turkey and Cyprus: Evidence from cointegrated panel analysis.* Turkey and Cyprus: Evidence from Cointegrated Panel Analysis (June 1, 2012).

Tsitouras, A., Koulakiotis, A., Makris, G., & Papapanagos, H. (2017). International trade and foreign direct investment as growth stimulators in transition economies: Does the impact of institutional factors matter? *Investment Management and Financial Innovations, 14*(4), 148–170. https://doi.org/10.21511/imfi.14(4).2017.13

Tsitouras, A., Mitrakos, P., Tsimpida, C., Vlachos, V., & Bitzenis, A. (2020). An investigation into the causal links among FDI determinants: Empirical evidence from Greece. *Journal of East-West Business, 26*(1), 17–55.

Chapter 19
Quality of IFRS Reporting: Developed, Transitional, and Developing Economies

Patrik Svoboda and Hana Bohušová

Abstract This study aims to assess how listed companies in developed, transition, and developing countries comply with selected mandatory disclosure requirements under International Accounting Standards (IAS)/International Financial Reporting Standards (IFRS). Through methods for quantifying the quality of financial reporting as measured by the level of compliance with selected IAS/IFRS, particularly in the notes, the chapter aims to compare the quality of reporting in countries representative of these groups. To measure compliance with IAS/IFRS, the annual reports of non-financial companies traded on stock exchanges were examined. Cooke's (Account Bus Res 22:229–237, 1992) unweighted disclosure index (DI) was used. For the evaluation, selected standards used by all types of companies regardless of sector (IAS1, 2, 8, 10, 12, 16, 36, 37, 38, and 40) have been used. Compatibility assessments were also conducted within the selected industries. The main finding of our research was the relatively low difference in the quality of IAS/IFRS reporting between the countries studied. The average DI for Czech companies is 87.89%, 93.17%, and 83.52% for German and Ghanaian companies, respectively. The lowest DI levels are represented by IAS37 and IAS16, while the highest DI qualities are represented by IAS10 and IAS8. The findings from the survey conducted could serve existing and potential investors, as well as other users such as providers of loan capital, for their decision-making.

Keywords IFRS · Reporting · Notes · Disclosure index · Dichotomous method · Stock exchange

---

P. Svoboda
Department of Accounting and Taxes, Faculty of Business and Economics, Mendel University in Brno, Brno, Czech Republic
e-mail: patrik.svoboda@mendelu.cz

H. Bohušová (✉)
Department of Economics and Management, AMBIS University, Prague, Czech Republic
e-mail: hana.bohusova@ambis.cz

© The Author(s), under exclusive license to Springer Nature Switzerland AG 2024
N. Tsounis, A. Vlachvei (eds.), *Applied Economic Research and Trends*, Springer Proceedings in Business and Economics,
https://doi.org/10.1007/978-3-031-49105-4_19

19.1 Introduction

Financial statements provide information for evaluating the financial position and performance of companies. The accompanying notes to financial statements serve as a valuable source of information for financial decision-making. They provide details for analyzing variances from trends and assessing the company's performance, including identifying significant relationships. It is essential for the notes to adhere to the fundamental principles of financial reporting based on accounting theory.

One of the widely recognized reporting systems for financial statements is the International Financial Reporting Standards (IFRS). IFRS is used by listed companies in over 120 countries, ranging from developing to highly economically developed nations. However, the question remains whether the quality of financial statements prepared in accordance with IFRS is comparable across these countries. Research findings on this matter have been contradictory thus far. The objective of our research is to evaluate the quality of financial statements prepared according to IFRS in selected regions, representing different categories of economic development.

Several theories underpin the assessment of financial reporting quality for different user groups. The agency theory highlights the issue of information asymmetry between managers and shareholders. Managers, as agents, possess more information about the company compared to shareholders, the principals. This can create a conflict of interest, as agents may prioritize their own profit maximization over the interests of the principals. Managers can influence the financial information presented in the statements through earnings management. The agency theory is often applied in studies focusing on the quality of financial statement notes.

Another significant theory is the signaling theory, which explores how financial information disclosure adds value to a firm. Signaling theory examines how information presentation can portray an organization in a positive light. Additionally, the capital needs theory explains managers' incentives for financial information disclosure. It suggests that higher-quality information disclosure reduces information asymmetry, thus enabling firms to raise capital at lower costs, as there is a positive relationship between investor uncertainty and the cost of financing.

The quality of financial reporting can be assessed by analyzing the data presented in the individual reporting areas published in the notes. Entities are required to present the notes in a systematic manner, particularly for two key user groups: current and potential investors, and credit providers. These groups rely on relevant financial information to make informed decisions and facilitate the efficient functioning of the capital market. Relevant financial information should be accurate, comprehensive, comparable, and provided in a timely manner.

The term "disclosure quality" is commonly used to evaluate the level of reporting. Various approaches exist for assessing the quality of reporting, which can be classified based on the methodological procedures employed. Beattie et al. (2004) classified these methods into two main groups: subjective and semi-objective. Among the semi-objective methods, disclosure indexes are considered the most objective. Similarly, Scaltrito (2016) divides the approaches to evaluating disclosure quality into two groups: subjective and objective, with objective instruments including reporting frequency, textual analysis, and disclosure indexes.

Disclosure indexes are commonly used techniques in studies to assess financial reporting compliance. These indexes quantify the level of information provided by companies based on specific elements observed in their general-purpose financial statements. To develop a unified measure representing the quality of financial reporting, it is necessary to define the elements that are significant for external users' decision-making, regardless of whether the information is mandatory or voluntary. The disclosure index can be expressed in two ways: unweighted and weighted. The list of selected items serves as a checklist to evaluate the presence of reported and described items in the notes. Different scoring methodologies can be used to develop the final disclosure index, which acts as a proxy variable explaining the level of information provided by the company. The specialized literature presents three main approaches, as outlined by Beattie et al. (2004) and Ashton (2010): (1) dichotomous approach, (2) dichotomous and quantitative approach, and (3) score range approach. Ashton (2010) emphasizes the weaknesses of the weighted form of the disclosure index, as it can be influenced by subjective judgments regarding the relevance of individual items.

The research on financial reporting quality and compliance with IAS has been ongoing since the end of the last century. Pioneers in this field include Wallace (1988), Baiman and Verrecchia (1993), Zarzeski (1996), Street et al. (1999), and others. Baiman and Verrecchia (1993) emphasized that the quality of accounting disclosures can enhance the efficiency of the stock market. Healy and Palepu (2001) concluded that firm size, stock ownership, industry sector, stakeholder interests, international exposure, and investors' expectations are the main factors that can impact the quality of financial statements. There is evidence supporting the economic consequences of financial reporting quality, such as reducing the cost of capital and increasing the international mobility and efficiency of capital markets (Young et al., 2003; Sun, 2005; Bushman & Landsman, 2010). Numerous studies have examined the quality of IFRS or US GAAP disclosure in developed countries, including Glaum and Street in Germany (2003), Ball et al. (2003), Ball (2006), Boesso and Kumar (2007), and Scaltrito (2016).

With the accession of transition countries to the EU and the requirement for listed companies to report according to EU Regulation 1610 and IAS/IFRS, studies on reporting quality were also carried out in Eastern European countries. These studies included Slovenia, Croatia, Serbia, Montenegro, Bosnia and Herzegovina, Macedonia, Romania, the Baltic states, and Czechia.

Pervan et al. (2010) conducted an empirical analysis of financial reporting regulation and practice in selected Eastern European countries. Míková and Valášková (2013) examined the presentation of financial statements and segment reporting compliance among Czech companies traded on the Prague Stock Exchange, revealing significant differences in compliance levels across the areas. While the presentation of financial statements showed a high level of compliance, compliance with segment reporting was lower.

Čevela (2016) conducted research on companies traded on the Prague Stock Exchange and found that the majority of companies met almost 100% of the requirements. Karmo and Laidroo (2014) evaluated the level of disclosure compliance among corporations listed on Baltic stock exchanges and found higher disclosure quality compared to other Central and Eastern European peers. They concluded that the average disclosure compliance level of these corporations is significantly higher, by at least 30%, than that of Central European entities. However, they noted that disclosure compliance among companies listed on developed EU stock exchanges is slightly higher.

Also, Svoboda et al. (2020) proved that disclosure quality can be strongly influenced by country-specific and local factors, as observed in previous studies by Glaum and Street (2003) and Míková and Valášková (2013).

Baiman and Verrecchia (1993) highlighted the research gap regarding disclosure quality in developing countries with emerging stock markets. In recent years, several studies have addressed this gap, including those by Agyei-Mensah (2013), Abedana et al. (2016), Okpala (2012), and Bova and Pereira (2012). The findings of these studies are summarized below.

Agyei-Mensah (2013) examined the quality of financial reporting in Ghana; the study proved that the quality of financial reporting after adoption of IAS/IFRS increased by almost 30%. Similar conclusions were reached by Abedana et al. (2016), who analyzed the disclosure quality level of financial reports in Ghana before and after the adoption of IAS/IFRS (2006/2007 and 2007/2008, respectively). The study found an average disclosure quality level of 76.95% for the pre-adoption year and 95.13% for the post-adoption year, indicating a significant improvement in disclosure quality after the adoption of IAS/IFRS in Ghana. Mbawuni (2019) assessed the financial reporting quality of companies in Ghana after the adoption of IFRS; the study also found a significant increase in the quality of financial reporting after the adoption of IAS/IFRS.

Okpala (2012) investigated the impact of IAS/IFRS adoption on financial reporting quality in Nigeria and found that the adoption did not have a significant impact on financial reporting quality. According to Yusuf (2016), the adoption of IAS/IFRS in Nigeria has improved accounting information significantly among Nigerian firms. His findings, compared to similar studies conducted in developed and emerging economies, show an incremental increase in the value relevance of accounting information after IAS/IFRS adoption. Agbetunde et al. (2018) concluded in their study on reporting quality in Nigeria that financial reporting regulation has a significant impact on the quality of financial statements, indicating that financial reporting regulation can be used to enhance the quality of financial statements. Tawiah and Boolaky (2019) conducted research covering a three-year period in 205 non-financial institutions across 13 African countries. Their findings revealed an average compliance score of approximately 70% among the companies over the period, with a minimum score of 58.59% and a maximum of 83.55%. According the conclusion of this research, there are differences in compliance with individual standards. There is lower compliance with the most recent standards.

19.2 Materials and Methods

The objective of this study is to assess the compliance of financial statements prepared in accordance with International Accounting Standards/International Financial Reporting Standards (IAS/IFRS) in highly developed, transitional, and developing countries. The agency theory, which focuses on information asymmetry between external users (stakeholders, investors, and capital providers) and management, underscores the importance of high-quality financial information for informed financial decision-making worldwide. Our research was motivated by the varying conclusions reached by previous studies conducted by Abhimantra et al. (2013), Samaha and Khlif (2016), and Chamisa (2000).

Abhimantra et al. (2013) found no significant differences in the quality of financial statements prepared according to IAS/IFRS between developed and developing countries. However, Samaha and Khlif (2016) argued that the quality of financial reporting is linked to the effectiveness of monitoring and enforcement by institutional mechanisms. Conversely, Abdiel et al. (1993) asserted that the quality of reporting in developing countries is generally low.

Our research focuses on a sample comprising selected listed companies from Czech Republic, Germany, and Ghana. Germany represents highly developed countries, the Czech Republic represents transitional countries, and Ghana represents developing countries. This study builds upon the findings of a previous study conducted by Svoboda et al. (2020), which compared the financial reporting quality of developed and transitional countries.

19.2.1 The Companies Sample Description

The study focuses on companies that are listed on regulated stock exchanges within the European Union (EU) and are therefore obligated to publish consolidated financial statements in accordance with International Financial Reporting Standards (IFRS) since 2005. In the Czech Republic, this requirement applies to companies listed on the Prague Stock Exchange. The evaluation of the transitional country is based on a sample of 24 non-financial companies registered on the Prague Stock Exchange.

For the German sample, 35 companies traded on the Frankfurt Stock Exchange (Prime Standard) were selected. To ensure comparability with the Czech sample, the selection of companies considered the sector classification according to the NACE classification system.

In the context of Ghana, the study includes 17 companies that were chosen based on the selected sectors for the study. These companies are all listed and actively traded on the Ghana Stock Exchange, making them relevant for the research conducted in Ghana.

Table 19.1 Sample of researched companies by industry

Industry	No. of companies Czech Republic	No. of companies Germany	No. of companies Ghana
Manufacturing (C)	6	10	8
Electricity, gas, steam and air conditioning supply, water supply; (D)	9	7	3
Transporting and storage (H)	2	5	1
Information and communication (J)	4	7	2
Human health and social work activities (Q)	2	4	2
Arts, entertainment, and recreation (R)	1	2	1
Total	24	35	17

Source: own processing

By examining companies from these different countries and stock exchanges, the study aims to provide insights into the compliance and quality of financial reporting practices in highly developed, transitional, and developing countries, thereby contributing to the understanding of financial reporting practices in various market contexts (Table 19.1).

The authors of the research employed the EY disclosure checklist for annual financial statements as a basis for their study. This checklist served as a starting point and was subsequently modified for the specific purposes of their research. The authors evaluated the relevant paragraphs of each International Accounting Standards (IAS) issued by the International Accounting Standards Board (IASB) in order to develop a reduced checklist for assessing the quality of financial statements.

To ensure the checklist's effectiveness, it was compared with the information needs of different user groups such as stakeholders, potential investors, and banks. The authors then developed a questionnaire based on the checklist and distributed it using the Survio system. A total of 124 respondents participated in the survey.

For the research, only IAS standards were considered, as they were relevant for all surveyed entities and had not been replaced by newer International Financial Reporting Standards (IFRS) at the time. Certain standards, namely IAS 11 (Construction Contracts), IAS 18 (Revenue), and IAS 17 (Leases), were intentionally excluded from the study because they expired in 2017 (IAS 11 and IAS 18) or 2018 (IAS 17) and have since been replaced by IFRS 15 (Revenue from Contracts with Customers) and IFRS 16 (Leases). Therefore, assessing the quality of reporting in relation to these standards was deemed irrelevant for the purposes of the research.

The research focused on data that were not affected by the COVID-19 pandemic to ensure the accuracy and relevance of the conclusions drawn. The study encompassed 10 IAS standards, 38 paragraphs, and a total of 146 items for evaluation and analysis (Table 19.2).

Table 19.2 Final checklist

Standard	Paragraphs	No. of checked items
IAS 1	112, 117, 121, 122, 125, 134,135	13
IAS 2	36, 37	8
IAS 8	22, 28, 29, 31	17
IAS 10	19, 21	3
IAS 12	79, 80, 81	11
IAS 16	73, 74, 77, 79	24
IAS 36	126, 129, 130, 134	20
IAS 37	84, 85, 86, 89, 92	15
IAS 38	118, 122, 123, 126	19
IAS 40	74, 76, 79	16

Source: own processing

19.2.2 Disclosure Index Method

Disclosure indexes are commonly used in research studies as a proxy for evaluating the quality of disclosure. However, there is no standardized approach for designing these indexes.

In our research, we measure disclosure quality by constructing compliance scores based on the information provided in the annual financial statements of the companies. This approach aligns with the methodologies used by Devalle et al. (2016), Bova and Pereira (2012), and Santos et al. (2014). It allows for a more nuanced evaluation of disclosure quality.

An important consideration in analyzing compliance levels among companies is determining the relevance of specific IAS/IFRS standards to particular industries. Tawiah and Boolaky (2019) highlight the potential bias that can arise from generalizing compliance across all companies, as certain industries may naturally have higher scores due to specific disclosure requirements. In our study, we consider standards that are generally applicable to all companies, excluding banks and insurance companies.

We employ an unweighted index, where a binary variable is used for coding: 1 indicates that a company has disclosed the item, 0 indicates non-disclosure, and NA indicates that the item is required but not applicable to the company. In cases where a company provides partial information, values within the 0–1 range are used to express the level of compliance with the evaluated item, following Cook's theory (1992). However, it is worth noting that this methodology assigns equal weight to each item, potentially overlooking differences in importance between standards with varying numbers of disclosure items. We made a conscious decision to use an unweighted approach due to the subjective nature of determining the significance of individual information for different user groups. Additionally, our approach does not penalize companies for not disclosing non-applicable requirements, aligning with Cook's theory (1992).

Table 19.3 Average unweighted disclosure index

Companies	Average unweighted disclosure index %
Czech companies	87.89
German companies	93.17
Ghanaian companies	83.52

Source: own processing

$$\mathrm{CS}_j = \frac{T = \sum_{i=1}^{m} d_i}{M = \sum_{i=1}^{n} d_i} \tag{19.1}$$

where

CS_j is the total compliance score for each company, and $0 < CSj < 1$.
T is the total number of items disclosed (di) by company j, and $m < n$.
M is the maximum number of applicable items that company j is expected to disclose.

The hand-collected information of annual reports for the year 2017 of researched companies was the subject of the evaluation.

19.3 Results and Discussion

Using the checklist, we calculated unweighted disclosure indexes for each researched company individually. These indexes represent the level of compliance with IAS/IFRS disclosure requirements for each company.

To evaluate IAS/IFRS compliance on a country level, we calculated average comprehensive indexes for the Czech Republic, Ghana, and Germany, based on the indexes of the researched companies representing each country.

The results indicate that the comprehensive disclosure index for the Czech Republic and Ghana is below 90%, suggesting a lower level of compliance with IAS/IFRS requirements in these countries. On the other hand, German companies achieved a compliance level higher than 90%, but below 95%. This suggests a relatively higher level of compliance among German companies compared to the Czech Republic and Ghana, but there is still room for improvement (Table 19.3).

19.3.1 Results of Analysis in Particular Sectors

The evaluation of disclosure indexes was also conducted within individual sectors of the economy, as shown in Fig. 19.1. The analysis revealed that German companies achieved the highest level of compliance with IAS/IFRS, with a compliance rate of

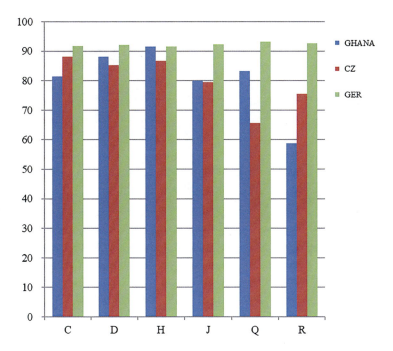

Fig. 19.1 Disclosure indexes by sectors. Manufacturing (C), Electricity, gas, steam and air conditioning supply, water supply; (D), Construction (F), Transporting and storage (H), Information and communication (J), Human health and social work activities (Q), Arts, entertainment and recreation (R)

over 90% in six sectors, showing relatively consistent performance. In the Czech Republic, there are noticeable differences among sectors, with the manufacturing, transport, and storage sectors reaching the highest level of compliance, while the health care, cultural, and entertainment sectors had the lowest level of compliance. Ghanaian companies demonstrated a solid level of disclosure quality, particularly in the transport and storage sector, with a compliance rate exceeding 90%. However, the sector categorized as "R – Arts, culture, and entertainment" showed very low compliance, with a rate below 60%.

Comparing these results to previous studies, the findings for the Czech Republic are similar to Čevela (2016), which reported an 87% compliance rate. However, the compliance rate for Germany, as reported by Akman (2011), was slightly higher at 78%. Akman's study focused on the change in disclosure levels after the mandatory adoption of IAS/IFRS and demonstrated an increase in disclosure quality over time. It is important to note that Akman's study specifically analyzed the year 2006.

Regarding Ghana, the disclosure index levels are similar to Agyei-Mensah (2013) at 87%, but lower than the results reported by Abedana et al. (2016) at 95%. These studies provide insights into the disclosure quality of Ghanaian companies and indicate variations in compliance levels.

Fig. 19.2 Unweighted disclosure IAS/IFRS in the Czech Republic, Germany, and Ghana

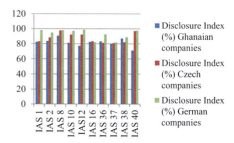

According to Fig. 19.2, the overall disclosure rate is lowest for Ghanaian companies, with 70% being the lowest rate among the researched sample. Czech companies also have a lower disclosure rate compared to German companies. When examining individual IAS standards, it is evident that German entities disclose a higher number of required items for almost all standards. The majority (90%) of standards are best presented by German companies, while only one standard is best presented by Ghanaian companies. The level of compliance with individual researched standards is over 90% for 70% of the evaluated standards and even above 95% for 60% of German companies.

The largest differences in reporting compliance between Czech, Ghanaian, and German companies were found in IAS 40—Investment property, with a difference of over 25% compared to Czech and German companies. Additionally, IAS 1 (15% and 15.5%) and IAS 36 (11.4% and 9.4%) showed significant differences in favor of German companies.

In the case of IAS 16, as shown in Fig. 19.2, there is a close compliance score among companies in all three countries. Ghanaian firms recorded a compliance rate as high as 82.6% for IAS 16. These firms provide sufficient details on the measurement, carrying amount, and gross value of the depreciated property, plant, and equipment. The qualitative description of revalued assets is also a focal point in their disclosure, as required by the standard. Although there have been limited studies conducted on a single country for the single standard IAS 16, Egbunike et al. (2018) conducted an investigation on cement manufacturing companies in Nigeria and achieved a 67.6% level of compliance for IAS 16. Marfo-Yiadom and Atsunyo (2014) reported a compliance level of 85.9% for IAS 16 in Ghana, indicating a high level of compliance with the standard in that context.

The overall quality of reporting according to IAS/IFRS is lower for Czech companies compared to German companies and slightly higher compared to Ghanaian companies. When comparing individual IAS standards, it is clear that German companies report a higher number of required items for the majority of standards. In the research sample, the quality of reporting for Czech companies is lower by more than 5% compared to German companies for half of the examined standards. Compared to Ghanaian companies, the quality of reporting is higher than 5% for 40% of the tested standards, while Ghanaian companies disclose a higher level of information for two standards.

A closer look at the compliance of requirements for individual IAS in the notes reveals that the lowest level of compliance is observed for IAS 37—provisions, contingent assets, and liabilities, with an overall compliance rate of approximately 81% for the researched sample. This is followed by IAS 16—property, plant, and equipment, with an approximate compliance rate of 82.8%.

In the analysis of individual requirements of each standard, the lowest value of the disclosure index is recorded for items related to more detailed data on contingent liabilities and assets and individual categories of provisions for all researched countries. Additionally, for IAS 16, entities often did not provide information about contractual obligations from the acquisition of property, plant, and equipment, book values, gross value of fully depreciated property, plant, and equipment, disposed property, plant, and equipment transferred to hold for sale. IAS 38—Intangible assets show a low level of disclosure for items requiring a description of reasons and factors considered in determining the useful life of intangible assets, especially regarding liens or restriction rights. There are also weaknesses in reporting contractual obligations to acquire intangible assets. IAS 2—Inventories show lower compliance as most entities did not disclose descriptive information about the factors leading to the reversal of write-down to net realizable value of inventories or the cost formula used in inventory valuation. Lastly, IAS 1, which sets out general rules for the preparation and disclosure of financial statements, has a lower level of disclosure index due to items related to the nature and extent of judgments and key assumptions made by management. The lower value of the disclosure index for IAS 8 is due to poor reporting of the effect of new standards as required by the standard.

In the Ghanaian context, the lowest recorded disclosure score was found for IAS 40, where a single firm failed to cover the reconciliation of the carrying amount at the start and end of the reporting period. IAS 38 had a lower disclosure index under German companies but was higher than Czech companies at 87.1% compliance. In contrast to both German and Czech firms, companies in Ghana were almost fully non-compliant with the disclosure of the amount of contractual commitment for the acquisition of intangible assets.

Among German companies, there are six standards with compliance rates between 95% and 100%. The disclosure index for IAS 37 is lower due to weaknesses in estimating future outflows from business entities. Similar situations were observed for Czech companies. Regarding IAS 36, the main weaknesses could be attributed to insufficient description of specific items. While German companies achieved a compliance rate of 98% for disclosure requirements of goodwill under IAS 36 and IAS 38, Czech companies had a lower compliance rate of 88%.

The results of the analysis demonstrate that Germany, as a representative of developed countries, achieved the highest level of IAS/IFRS compliance, followed by the Czech Republic as a representative of transition countries, and Ghana as a representative of developing countries. The compliance level for all evaluated standards is summarized in Table 19.4.

Table 19.4 Level of disclosure index for individual IAS/IFRS

Disclosure index	Number of IAS/IFRS		
	Czech Republic	Germany	Ghana
Over 95%	2	6	0
85–95%	3	2	2
Less than 85%	5	2	8

Source: own processing

19.4 Conclusion

The chapter is grounded in agency theory, which posits that high compliance with individual treatments of IAS/IFRS should lead to a reduction in information asymmetry between principals and agents. The analysis results depict the level of compliance of selected requirements of IAS/IFRS measured by disclosure indexes. Czech companies exhibit a compliance level of 87.89%, German companies show a compliance level of 93.17%, and Ghanaian companies demonstrate a compliance level of 83.52% (using the dichotomous method).

The average disclosure index of individual standards reveals that IAS 37 and IAS 16 have the lowest levels of DI, particularly due to inadequate presentation of contingent liabilities and assets, individual categories of provisions, and items related to contractual obligations from the acquisition of property, plant, and equipment. Additionally, insufficient disclosure of data such as book values, gross value of fully depreciated property, plant, and equipment, as well as disposed property, plant, and equipment transferred to held for sale, contributes to the lower DI for these standards across all researched countries. On the other hand, the highest quality of DI is observed for IAS 10 and IAS 8.

This research aligns with previous studies conducted by Paananen and Lin (2007), Galani et al. (2011), Pervan et al. (2010), Ionascu et al. (2014), Míková and Valášková (2013), Čevela (2016), Karmo and Laidroo (2014), Pivac et al. (2017), Agyei-Mensah (2013), and Okpala (2012) in specific areas. It encompasses EU countries, including representatives from advanced and transitioning economies, as well as a representative from the developing country category. The research utilizes data from 2017, enabling a comparison of changes in disclosure quality over time.

A surprising finding of this research is the relatively small differences between the reporting levels of developed and developing countries. This conclusion aligns with other studies that compare the quality of financial reporting in developed countries and transitioning economies, such as Pervan et al. (2010) and Pivac et al. (2017).

The research results should serve as an initial platform for further investigation into the relationship between a company's value and the quality of financial reporting, as well as the relationship between the cost of capital and the quality of financial reporting.

References

Abdiel, G., Abayo, C., Adams, A., & Roberts, C. B. (1993). Measuring the quality of corporate disclosure in less developed countries: The case of Tanzania. *Journal of International Accounting, Auditing and Taxation, 2*(2), 145–158. https://doi.org/10.1016/1061-9518(93)90003-C

Abedana, V., Omane-Antwi, K., & Oppong, M. (2016). Adoption of IFRS/IAS in Ghana: Impact on the quality of corporate financial reporting and related corporate tax burden. *Research Journal of Accounting and Finance, 7*(8), 10–25.

Abhimantra, A., Maulina, A. R., & Agustianingsih, E. (2013). *The comparison of IFRS implementation in developing and developed countries (Case Study: Europe)*, pp. 66–69.

Agbetunde, L., Anyahara, I., & Ajibade, T. (2018). Financial reporting regulation and quality and quality of financial statements in Nigeria. *Journal of Accounting and Management, 1*(1), 38–48.

Agyei-Mensah, B. K. (2013). Adoption of international financial reporting standards (IFRS) in Ghana and the quality of financial statement disclosures. *International Journal of Accounting and Financial Reporting, 3*(2), 269–286. https://doi.org/10.5296/ijafr.v3i2.4489

Akman, N. H. (2011). The effect of IFRS adoption on financial disclosure: Does culture still play a role? *American International Journal of Contemporary Research, 1*(1), 6–17.

Ashton, R. H. (2010). Quality, timing, and luck: Looking Back at Ashton (1974). *Auditing: A Journal of Practice & Theory, 29*(1), 3–13. https://doi.org/10.2308/aud.2010.29.1.3

Baiman, S., & Verrecchia, R. E. (1993). The relation between capital markets and financial disclosure, production efficiency and insider trading. *Journal of Accounting Research, 34*(1), 1–22. https://doi.org/10.2307/2491329

Ball, R. (2006). International Financial Reporting Standards (IFRS): Pros and cons for investors. *Accounting and Business Research, 36*(1), 5–27. https://doi.org/10.1080/00014788.2006.9730040

Ball, R., Robin, A., & Wu, S. (2003). Incentives versus standards: Properties of accounting income in four East Asian countries. *Journal of Accounting and Economics, 36*(1), 235–270. https://doi.org/10.1016/jjacceco.2003.10.003

Beattie, V., McInnes, W., & Fearnley, S. (2004). A methodology for analysing and evaluating narratives in annual reports: A comprehensive descriptive profile and metrics for disclosure quality attributes. *Accounting Forum, 28*(3), 205236. https://doi.org/10.1016/j.accfor.2004.07.001

Boesso, G., & Kumar, K. (2007). Drivers of corporate voluntary disclosure. A framework and empirical evidence from Italy and the United States. *Accounting, Auditing and Accountability Journal, 20*(2), 269–296.

Bova, F., & Pereira, R. (2012). The determinants and consequences of heterogeneous IFRS compliance levels following mandatory IFRS adoption: Evidence from a developing country. *Journal of International Accounting Research, 11*(1), 83–111. https://doi.org/10.2139/ssrn.1542240

Bushman, R. M., & Landsman, W. R. (2010). The pros and cons of regulating corporate reporting: A critical review of the arguments. *Accounting and Business Research, 40*(3), 1–38. https://doi.org/10.2139/ssrn.1574282

Čevela, D. (2016). Quality of information disclosed in annual reports of listed companies in the Czech Republic. *European Financial and Accounting Journal, 2016*(2), 21–36. https://doi.org/10.18267/j.efaj.155

Chamisa, E. (2000). The relevance and observance of the IASC standards in developing countries and the particular case of Zimbabwe. *The International Journal of Accounting, 35*(2), 267–286. https://doi.org/10.1016/S0020-7063(00)00049-2

Cooke, T. E. (1992). The impact of size, stock market listing and industry type on disclosure in the annual reports of Japanese listed corporations. *Accounting and Business Research, 22*, 229–237. https://doi.org/10.1080/00014788.1992.9729440

Devalle, A., Rizzato, F., & Busso, D. (2016). Disclosure indexes and compliance with mandatory disclosure-The case of intangible assets in the Italian market. *Advances in Accounting, 35*(C), 8–25. https://doi.org/10.1016/j.adiac.2016.04.003

Egbunike, P. A., Jesuwunmi, C. A., Adewoyin, A. O., & Ogunmeru, A. O. (2018). Empirical appraisal of IAS16 disclosures compliance level of listed cement manufacturing firms in Nigeria. *International Journal of Economics and Business Administration, 4*(2), 56–76.

Galani, D., Alexandridis, A., & Stavropoulos, A. (2011). The association between the firm characteristics and corporate mandatory disclosure the case of Greece. *International Journal of Economics and Management Engineering, 5*(5), 411–417.

Glaum, M., & Street, D. L. (2003). Compliance with the disclosure requirements of Germany's new market. *Journal of International Financial Management and Accounting, 14*, 64–100. https://doi.org/10.1111/1467-646X.00090

Healy, P. M., & Palepu, K. G. (2001). Information asymmetry, corporate disclosure, and the capital markets: A review of the empirical disclosure literature. *Journal of Accounting and Economics, 31*(1–3), 405–440. https://doi.org/10.1016/S0165-4101(01)00018-0

Ionascu, M., Ionascu, I., Sacarin, M., & Minu, M. (2014). *IFRS adoption in developing countries: The case of Romania*, pp. 311–350.

Karmo, I., & Laidroo, L. (2014). Baltic listed companies' disclosure quality – Far ahead or lagging behind? Discussions on Estonian Economic Policy: EU Member States After the Economic Crisis. 1. https://doi.org/10.15157/tpep.v22i1.1371

Marfo-Yiadom, E., & Atsunyo, W. (2014). Compliance with international financial reporting standards by listed companies in Ghana. *International Journal of Business and Management, 9*(10), 87–100. https://doi.org/10.5539/ijbm.v9n10p87

Mbawuni, J. (2019). Users' perception of financial reporting quality in Ghana. *Accounting and Finance Research, 8*(3), 187. https://doi.org/10.5430/afr.v8n3p187

Míková, T., & Valášková, M. (2013). Do listed companies in PSE meet IFRS disclosure requirements? *International Journal of Organizational Leadership, 2*(2), 52–61. https://doi.org/10.33844/ijol.2013.60437

Okpala, K. (2012). Adoption of IFRS and financial statements effects: The perceived implications on FDI and Nigeria economy. *Australian Journal of Business and Management Research, 7*(2), 76–83. https://doi.org/10.5901/mjss.2016.v7n2p99

Paananen, M., & Lin, C. (2007). The development of accounting quality of IAS and IFRS over time: The case of Germany. *Journal of International Accounting Research, 8*(1). https://doi.org/10.2139/ssrn.1066604

Pervan, I., Horak, H., & Vasilj, M. (2010). Financial reporting regulation for the listed companies: Analysis for selected Eastern European transitional countries in the process of EU enlargement. *Economic Thought and Practice, 19*, 277309.

Pivac, S., Vuko, T., & Čular, M. (2017). Analysis of annual report disclosure quality for listed companies in transition countries. *Economic Research-Ekonomska Istraživanja, 30*, 721–731. https://doi.org/10.1080/1331677X.2017.1311231

Samaha, K., & Khlif, H. (2016). Adoption of and compliance with IFRS in developing countries. *Journal of Accounting in Emerging Economies, 6*(1), 33–49. https://doi.org/10.1108/JAEE-02-2013-0011

Santos, E. S., Ponte, V. M. R., & Mapurunga, P. V. R. (2014). Mandatory IFRS adoption in Brazil index of compliance with disclosure requirements and some explanatory factors of firms reporting (2010). *Revista Contabilidade & Finanças, 25*, 161–176. https://doi.org/10.2139/ssrn.2310625

Scaltrito, D. (2016). Voluntary disclosure in Italy: Firm-specific determinants an empirical analysis of Italian listed companies. *EuroMed Journal of Business, 11*(2), 272–303. https://doi.org/10.1108/EMJB-07-2015-0032

Street, D. L., Gray, S. J., & Bryant, S. M. (1999). Acceptance and observance of International Accounting Standards: An empirical study of companies claiming to comply with IASs. *The International Journal of Accounting, 34*(1), 11–48.

Sun, K. (2005). Financial reporting quality, capital allocation efficiency, and financing structure: An international study. *SSRN Electronic Journal.* https://doi.org/10.2139/ssrn.816384

Svoboda, P., Poskočilová, B., & Bohušová, H. (2020). Financial reporting quality: The case of Czech and German listed companies. *International Journal of Monetary Economics and Finance, 13*(3), 235–243. https://doi.org/10.1504/IJMEF.2020.108822

Tawiah, V., & Boolaky, P. (2019). Determinants of IFRS compliance in Africa: Analysis of stakeholder attributes. *International Journal of Accounting & Information Management, 27*(4), 573–599.

Wallace, R. (1988). Corporate financial reporting in Nigeria. *Accounting & Business Research, 18*(72), 352–362. https://doi.org/10.1080/00014788.1988.9729382

Young, D., Guenther, D., & A. (2003). Financial reporting environments and international capital mobility. *Journal of Accounting Research, 41*(3), 553–579. https://doi.org/10.1111/1475-679X.00116

Yusuf, A. M. (2016). The value relevance of accounting disclosures among listed Nigerian firms: IFRS adoption. *Iranian Journal of Management Studies (IJMS), 9*(4), 707–740. https://doi.org/10.22059/IJMS.2017.59377

Zarzeski, M. T. (1996). Spontaneous harmonization effects of culture and market forces on accounting disclosure practices. *Accounting Horizons, 10*(1), 18–38.

Chapter 20
Influencer Marketing and Its Impact on Consumer Behavior: Case Study from Slovakia

Roman Chinoracky ⓘ**, Tatiana Corejova** ⓘ**, and Natalia Stalmasekova** ⓘ

Abstract Over time, the Internet has become a platform that has contributed to a new type of business—e-business. With the new type of e-business, the marketing of companies has changed. Internet marketing has become the new standard. Social media marketing has become a subset of it. Social media has created space for several influencers, people who can influence the opinions of other people. Many companies have responded to this trend and started promoting their products with the help of influencers. Given this fact, the aim of the article is to analyze the impact of influencers on consumers' shopping behavior. The analysis is carried out using primary research and a questionnaire on a selected sample of respondents (Slovaks) categorized by age and gender. Purchasing behavior is analyzed according to the see, think, do and care (STDC) model. The research results show how influencers affect consumers in the individual phases of the STDC model. The research concept presented in the article is intended for everyone who deals with the issue of consumer behavior research.

Keywords Internet marketing · Marketing on social media · Influencer marketing · Consumer behavior · STDC model

20.1 Introduction

The Internet, as a global information network, has become an inexhaustible source of information that people can turn to when solving any problem (Nashelsky, 1994; Vermaat et al., 2018; Urbinati et al., 2020). With all the possibilities that the Internet offers, many companies understood that this is a space, which represents an opportunity to buy and sell products. A new type of business is emerging, which we call electronic business or e-business for short.

R. Chinoracky · T. Corejova (✉) · N. Stalmasekova
University of Zilina, Zilina, Slovakia
e-mail: tatiana.corejova@uniza.sk

© The Author(s), under exclusive license to Springer Nature Switzerland AG 2024
N. Tsounis, A. Vlachvei (eds.), *Applied Economic Research and Trends*, Springer Proceedings in Business and Economics,
https://doi.org/10.1007/978-3-031-49105-4_20

While in a traditional business consumers obtained information from paper brochures or other tools of traditional marketing communication, in e-commerce the preferred form of information sharing is a website to which many e-businesses use various other forms of online marketing communication (Madleňák & Rostášová, 2015).

Marketing promotion is a well-known element of the marketing mix (4Ps— product, price, place, and promotion), which describes the set of tools that management can use to influence sales. The Internet offers a new alternative way of promotion and becomes a space for every form of communication that a company uses (Kotler et al., 2017; Kingsnorth, 2016).

Within the marketing mix, the Internet has the most visible influence on the company's communication policy. The importance of communication via the Internet is growing due to the constant changes and dynamism of the environment, globalization, but also the development and greater use of new technologies. The Internet offers a new alternative way of marketing promotion to inform about products and helps with purchasing decisions. Online marketing tools include websites (Duckett, 2011), internet (online) advertising (Madlenak & Madlenakova, 2015), online public relations (Phillips & Young, 2009), internet sales support (Olbrich et al., 2019; Terlutter & Capella, 2013), and online direct marketing (Madlenak et al., 2017; Hudak et al., 2017).

While the tools of classical marketing communication have been published on traditional media (television, newspapers, and radio), the tools of online marketing communication are published on internet social media (Kingsnorth, 2016; Kotler et al., 2017). Social media is the umbrella term for web-based software and services that allow users to come together online and exchange, discuss, communicate, and participate in any form of social interaction.

Social media marketing, as a subset of online marketing, serves as a communication tool through which the user creates their own content and presents it publicly among other users on the Internet. Social media users are the most important element of virtual communities; therefore, it is appropriate to define the typology and behavior of social media users (Constantinides, 2014; Rovnanova, 2018). There are many types of social media users—from active to passive users, spammers to activists, but one of these groups is specific and is called influencers.

The main goal of the article is to analyze the impact of influencer marketing on consumer shopping behavior in the Slovak environment. It is possible to say that influencer marketing has become the norm for today's businesses. In the Slovak environment, influencer marketing is regularly analyzed for consumer shopping behavior (Stankova, 2018; Gundova & Cvoligova, 2019; Nastišin, 2020). The research carried out is partial and does not examine the impact of influencer marketing on consumer behavior comprehensively. At the same time, current data from 2021 are missing. Therefore, the gap is the absence of research into the impact of influencer marketing on consumer shopping behavior in 2021.

20.2 Theoretical Background

Influencers can play various roles according to which they influence consumer behavior. These influencer roles do not describe types of influencers, but rather the roles that they may play. A single influencer may play several roles throughout one decision process or have a single impact at one point (Brown & Hayes, 2008). Theories in economics, and behavioral and social sciences suggest that product purchases featuring low degrees of consumer involvement are more likely to be influenced by external factors such as public opinion (Garbarova & Holla Bachanova, 2020). Such irrational factors may sow the seeds that quickly grow into purchasing items. By Brown and Hayes (2008), it is possible to show how the roles of influencers can change due to the involvement of decision-makers in the decision-making process.

Idea planters are the thinkers in the industry. They are the innovators and may be drawn from outside the normal industry boundaries. Predictors tell us what (they believe) will be adopted soon. Much of the origination of this kind of influence comes from the supplier community, which is essentially telling us what is next in their product pipeline. Trendsetters are the early adopters. They set themselves as reference points and create the direction for the rest of the market. They are important because they not only validate the market but also communicate success to the market. Some influencers just stand up and proclaim (and therefore be proclaimers) that the world will be how they want it to be. They mandate (as far as they can) what and how. They are able to be listened to and acted upon. One of the most important roles an influencer can play is that of information gatherer and disseminators (or aggregators/communicators). It is where the media and analysts get most of their influence: their knowledge of the detail of the market allows them power as to who has access to that knowledge (Brown & Hayes, 2008).

At some point, a definition of the decision to be taken must be made. That is the role of scoopers, to map out the limitations, parameters, and dimensions of the problem and its likely solutions. Recommenders suggest what you should do. They are sometimes, but not often, able to dictate a decision. Most often, they will make their professional judgment known and then leave the final decision up to the ultimate decision-maker. Persuaders tell you what you must do. They are not passive at all, conveying precise direction rather than advice. Negotiators, decide how and how much, advising on the financial elements of the deal, as well as the mechanics of how to construct a deal. Validators are the safety net for a decision-maker. The decision-maker is using the validator to prove to his/her superiors that the decision is low risk (Brown & Hayes, 2008).

Each of these roles of influencer is, of the term influencer, a precondition for influencer to be able to attract a certain audience whose opinions, attitudes, and preferences it influences. There are several opinions on how to categorize influencers according to their follower count on social media. There are specific groups of influencers differentiated by the follower-count like Santora (2023) who identified nano-influencers (from 1K–10K followers), micro-influencers (10K–

100K followers), macro-influencers (100K–1M followers), and mega or celebrity influencers (more than one million followers).

If a brand is collaborating with an online influencer to market one of its products or services, we talk about new form of online marketing and social media marketing—influencer marketing. Influencer marketing takes the idea of endorsement (by influencer) and places it into a modern-day content-driven marketing campaign (Geyser, 2023). By the Annual Marketing Reports (2021a, b) and State of Influencer Marketing 2021, the most used influencer platform is the media-sharing network Instagram, which use up to 89% of influencers worldwide. Most Instagram influencers focus on lifestyle theme. The second most used platform is YouTube, which use up to 70% of influencers worldwide. Influencers on YouTube fall into the category People and blogs. The third and fourth platform used for influencers is Facebook and the classic blog. Facebook uses 45% and the blog 44% of all influencers. Influencers tend to cover different shares of companies' marketing budgets. Worldwide, up to 38% of influencers cost companies from 10% to 20% of their marketing budget and even 11% of businesses that spend more than 40% of their marketing budget on influencers. Many companies are actively cooperating with influencers.

From the above, it follows that when investigating influencer marketing, attention is usually paid to the platforms used, budgets, and the degree of cooperation between companies and influencers. The influence of influencer marketing is a separate topic, while it is also important to evaluate the purchasing behavior of consumers and their preferences. The consumer perspective is the basis for evaluating the impact of influencer marketing and its effectiveness.

20.3 Research Framework

Consumer behavior can be analyzed according to consumer behavior models. There are several models of purchasing behavior and purchasing decisions. Our research examines consumers' shopping behavior according to what stage of the sales funnel consumers are involved. Therefore, the selected model of shopping behavior, according to which we determined consumer preferences, is the see, think, do and care (STDC) model. Google's digital marketing expert Avinash Kaushik (2015) and clusters consumers into four groups (Table 20.1) created STDC's purchasing behavior model.

Table 20.1 Audience clusters according to STDC model

Audience intent cluster	Audience
See	Largest addressable qualified audience (LAQA)
Think	LAQA with mild commercial intent
Do	LAQA that's ready to transact
Care	Repeat customers

20 Influencer Marketing and Its Impact on Consumer Behavior: Case Study... 341

The consumer is in the See phase when he first meets the brand. This means that for the first time, it consciously registers (and subconsciously) the company's logos, name, and products. At this stage, the consumer does not need the product and does not consider buying it. In the Think phase, the consumer knows what his need is, that a particular product or service will satisfy. This means that the consumer has decided to shop and decides which product will satisfy his need best and compares the products of different companies. The Do phase represents the purchase phase. The consumer is determined and knows exactly which product to buy. The Care phase is a post-purchase phase where the consumer, if satisfied with the product, repeats the purchase or recommends the product (or brand) to his acquaintances, either in person or via social media (Kaushik, 2015; Signal Fox, 2019).

According to the individual phases of the STDC model, we set four research goals that helped us solve the research problem and formulate ten research questions (see Table 20.2). The research objectives and research questions follow on from identifying the consumer perspective and perception of influencer marketing.

Table 20.2 Research goals and questions

Phase	Research goal	Research question
SEE	Finding out about influencers and their participation in cooperation with companies, from the consumer's point of view	How does the advertising campaign of your favorite brand affect you, whose main face of the campaign is a socially known influential person (so-called influencer)?
		Do you think that companies should establish cooperation with influencer?
		Do you follow any influencers through social media?
		What is the key content topic of influencers you follow?
THINK	Measuring consumers' willingness to buy a product based on influencer's recommendations	Which of the following factors is important to you when you are deciding to buy a product?
		Would you be willing to buy a product of a certain brand based on influencer recommendations?
		Would the possibility of getting a discount code provided by a given influencer play a role in your purchasing decision?
DO	Measuring the quantity and intensity of purchases of products promoted by influencers	When making a purchase, would you prefer a product of an unknown brand, or a product recommended by an influencer?
		Did you buy a product that was publicly promoted by influencer?
CARE	Finding out the willingness to recommend the product promoted by the influencer (Phase CARE)	Is the influence of the influencer in the advertising campaign one of the factors based, on which you would recommend the given brand or the influencer itself to your friends and family?

For fulfilling the research goals, we carried out primary research with the help of which we directly ascertained the preferences of consumers according to which we clustered them into individual groups of the STDC model. The primary was based on questionnaire. As already mentioned, such oriented research has not been carried out in Slovakia. Therefore, the questionnaire was distributed to Slovak citizens who are at the age at which we can consider them as potential consumers (age 16+). To generalize the findings obtained by the primary research and the questionnaire was representative, it was necessary to address 340 respondents. We set age and gender as the quota for the sample we set. The groups of respondents who had to addressed, according to the quota selection and the gender and age quotas set by us.

The questionnaire was distributed to respondents electronically by sharing it on the social network Facebook. Using the social network Facebook, certain Facebook groups were selected in which, due to their thematic focus, it was possible to obtain answers from a selected sample of respondents categorized according to quotas (Drengubiak, 2020).

20.4   Results

The answers of the respondents from the questionnaire are evaluated gradually according to the order of the questions stated in the questionnaire. Respondents completed the questionnaire, and the structure of the respondents' responses corresponds to the quotas according to which the minimum sample of respondents was set.

The purpose of the first question (Table 20.2) in the questionnaire was that we wanted to find out whether the respondents' register is affected by marketing campaigns that features influencers as persons promoting a certain good or service. Influencers are positively perceived by 22% of respondents and 35% of them perceive influencers positively depending on the specific influencer. This means that most respondents (a total of 57%) are to some extent positively affected by influencers. Regarding the gender of respondents, women are more inclined to influencers who can influence their shopping behavior. The difference between the positive and negative perceptions of influencers is smaller in the group of men than in the group of women. Unlike men, women are more prone to influencers and their shopping behavior potentially can lead to the purchase of certain goods or services due to influencer's recommendations.

Given that Slovakia is a relatively conservative country, older respondents (56+) do not perceive influencers as something negative. As could be assumed, with younger respondents, sympathy for influencers increases.

Based on the answers to second question, we wanted to find out the importance that respondents attach to advertising campaigns, the face of which can be influencers. In a clear majority (65% in total), respondents agree that influencers should be the faces of advertising campaigns. So, branding a particular product with influencer can positively affect the marketability of that product. From the point of view of the gender of the respondents, the situation is similar to a certain extent. Advertising influencer campaigns are more acceptable for women than for men.

Same situation as before applies for age. Older respondents (56–65 and 66+) are not inclined to advertising, the main character of which is influencer. On the other hand, younger generations support advertising campaigns that include well-known influencer. Interesting fact is that respondents from age group 46–55 view influencer advertising campaigns rather positively. Therefore, it is appropriate to segment marketing efforts, especially for the younger generation of consumers who decide to buy a particular product or service. Marketers should consider that well-targeted ads featuring influencers could persuade even mid-to-older generations (46–55) to buy certain products.

We wanted not only to know if respondents met influencers but also if they do follow influencers on social media. Almost half of the respondents do follow influencers, and other half does not follow any influencers on social media. Even though respondents know about them, they tend to not follow them on social media. If we analyze the responses by gender, again as in previous questions, more women follow influencers then men. According to the numbers that represent answers to this question, in contrast as many men follow influencers as women do not follow. When we look at age: youngest generation of consumers (16–25) do follow influencers on social media. Middle-aged groups of respondents differ. While 26–35-year-olds are almost split when we talk about if they follow any influencers on social media, respondents with age between 36 and 45 predominantly, do follow influencers on social media.

Older generations (56+) tend to not follow influencers on social media. We can assume that older generations are not present on newer generation of social media (YouTube, Instagram), which is often popular with today's generation of influencers.

When we knew which respondents do follow influencers on social media, we identified the key content topic of influencers to follow. In general, respondents follow influencers who publish lifestyle content on social media. As this was an open question respondents could mark other answers as well because often they follow more influencers. Other popular topics were sport, travel, and music. Interesting finding is that relatively small portion of respondents like to follow content, which is humorous in its nature. Women predominantly follow lifestyle influencers. This is since many lifestyle influencers are various makeup artists or healthy food enthusiasts. In many cases, these are women's favorite topics. That is why we can see high popularity of lifestyle content among respondents. In Slovakia, many lifestyle influencers go about these topics. For men, the most popular topic is sports. This is somewhat logical choice same as in the case of women choosing lifestyle.

From age perspective, clearly lifestyle influencers are most popular with younger (16–35) to mid generations (36–45). Again, this can be since in Slovakia there are many lifestyle influencers. Other popular choice for younger to mid generations was sport and travel. Older generations tend to steer from lifestyle influencers to the topics of sport and news (journalism).

Next, we examined the phase "Think" and the important factors for respondents when they are deciding to buy a product. Clearly, quality and price are top factors followed by availability of product (in shops), power of product brand, and discounts. Least marked answer was reviews from influencers. We can conclude that if respondents do follow influencers who do not mean that they predominantly view their opinion as a key factor that can influence their purchasing decision. The price and quality are most important factors influencing purchasing decision for both genders. Influencer's recommendations for both genders are last factor among others that they think can influence them to buy products.

Price and quality clearly dominated for younger generations (16–25 and 26–35) as well as for mid generation of 36–45-year-olds as a top factor influencing purchase. For next three generations of mid to older respondents, other factors are also important. Exception is influencers' recommendations (reviews) to buy a certain product. As influencers are most popular among 16–25-year-olds, their recommendation as a factor of purchase was mostly marked by these respondents. For other age groups, this factor was clearly least marked.

We also wanted to know how respondents view influencer's recommendations but this time not in the contrast with other known purchasing factors. More than half of respondents would not be willing to buy an influencer recommended product. On the other note, clear majority of respondents cannot directly say they would or would not buy a product that is recommended by influencer (they either somewhat agree or disagree with it). More men than women are rather conservative, and their purchasing decision would not influence influencers' recommendations. More women tend to somewhat agree with influencers' recommendations when deciding to buy a product. On other hand, more men somewhat disagree with reviews and recommendations influencers give to a product.

From age perspective, younger (16–25- and 26–35-year-olds) to mid and mid-older generations (36–45- and 46–55-year-olds) to some degree consider influencers' recommendations as a factor that can affect their purchasing decision. Older generations of respondents (55–65 and 66+ year-olds) do not acknowledge recommendations of influencers to buy a certain product as a factor that can influence them when they go shopping.

Discount codes are a popular tool of online sales support that is widely used on social media in Slovakia as a mean of companies' promotion. Take part in a survey or a contest, follow our Instagram profile, register to our newsletter, those are examples of activities in which we can take a part and because of it, we can get a discount. To gain attention, some activities that are associated with discount codes are often in the conditions of Slovakia promoted by influencers.

More than a half of respondents (62%) agree or somewhat agree, that discount codes provided by influencers would influence their decision to buy a product. This means that if influencers directly cannot affect purchasing decision, they can do it indirectly through the participation in activities in which a company gives away with influencers help to consumers (potential or current customers) a discount code or some other form of discount. When we look at this through the lenses of gender, more men and women agree or somewhat agree with the notion that after they would receive a discount code promoted by influencer their purchasing decision could be altered. Similarly, each age group with exception of older generation of 66+ year-olds, where more than half of them does not trust discount codes promoted by influencers as a mean of altering their purchasing decision.

The respondents are willing to buy a product recommended by influencer rather than a product of an unknown brand. This means that even if respondents do not attach some sort of importance to influencers, they are willing to consider recommendations of a known persona, which happens to be an influencer promoting certain product. Both gender and age groups are would rather buy a product recommended by influencer than buy a product of an unknown brand.

Close majority of respondents did buy a product that promote and recommend influencer. Relatively large group of respondents did not buy a product promoted by influencer, but this product attracted their attention. This means that these respondents in maybe near future can switch their opinion and buy a product that promote and recommend an influencer. A lot more women than men did buy a product recommended by an influencer. Men even marked a consideration of a survey of a product's properties after an influencer recommendation less then direct negative answer. This can mean that many men did not have a chance to meet a product that promote and recommend influencers, even though they have knowledge about influencers.

Purchase of a product by the recommendation of an influencer made more respondents from young to mid age groups. Least purchases made older generations of 56–65 and 66+ year-olds.

In previous research, we identified that many respondents would prefer products recommended by influencers. This would assume that respondents would potentially recommend these products to their family or friends. The opposite is true. Almost 58% of respondents would recommend product promoted by influencer. This may mean that many products promoted by influencers in Slovakia do not possess a certain quality that would encourage respondents to recommend these products to their family or friends. In the age groups, only 16–25 and 36–45 year old respondents are more inclined recommend products promoted by influencers. Every other age group had more respondents who would not recommend such products. The reason for this may lie in the already mentioned narrative that even though respondents potentially can be influenced in their purchasing decision-making by influencers, in reality, influencers in Slovakia do not promote quality products and therefore respondents would not recommend them.

20.5 Discussion and Conclusion

Based on the research, we can do several conclusions that point out how population of Slovaks perceives influencers in their purchasing intentions and decisions that may lead to a purchase of a product or a service.

The topic for discussion should certainly be the search for opportunities to carry out similar research over several times and not only in Slovakia but also other countries. In this way, we would be able to examine how consumers' preferences in time and space change regarding marketing activities whose faces are influencers.

Limits of our research are connected with the regional conditions of Slovakia, with the culture as well as the traditions in purchasing behavior. Similar survey in other countries can provide different results. Results can serve as a basis for activities a company can carry out if it wants to reach and gain new customers by the means of influencer marketing.

The STDC model, which was used to investigate the impacts of influencer marketing, provides a suitable framework. According to the individual phases of the STDC model, we can state the following conclusions about the impact of influencer marketing on the purchasing behavior of consumers:

- *Phase SEE*

Advertising featuring influencers positively affects respondents. Respondents state that companies should promote itself with the help of influencers. Half of respondents do, and half do not follow influencers on social media. Most popular topic of influencer's content is lifestyle and sport.

Women are more affected by ads featuring influencers, and they think companies should advertise themselves with help of influencers. More women than men follow influencers on social media. For men, popular are sports social media personalities that are influencers. Women tend to follow lifestyle influencers.

The younger the respondents were, the more eager they were to be affected by influencers. Certain gap in this statement is in the affection for influencers, which was measured for 66+ year old respondents. All age groups agree companies should advertise its product with help of influencers. Almost all respondents, from all age groups to a certain degree follow influencers. Exception is the age group of 66+ year old respondents. While younger generations follow lifestyle and sport influencers, older ones ten to follow more serious topics like journalism and news.

- *Phase THINK*

Key purchasing factor for respondents is price and quality. Recommendations (or reviews) of influencers are last. If we exclude factors from decision-making process, half of the respondents would not buy an influencer-recommended product. Regardless of this, more than half of the respondents is not certain and they somewhat agree or disagree with buying the product that is recommended or promoted by influencer. Large part of respondents would be affected to buy a product if they would get some sort of discount that is a part of give-away activities promoted by influencers.

For both women and men, price and quality are the key purchasing factor. Recommendations of influencers are for them last key factor that may influence their purchasing decision. More men than women would not buy a product that is associated with influencer. It applies for undecided respondents, a large portion of them are men. Both men's and women's shopping decision-making would be affected by discount that would be given to them by influencer.

Price and quality are key for young and mid-to-younger generations of respondents. Mid-to-older and old age groups of respondents perceive purchasing factors more evenly. Exception is recommendations of influencers. This factor is positively viewed only by youngest generation of respondents (16–25). Young to mid-young generations would buy products promoted or recommended by influencers. Older generations are more skeptical, and they would not buy such products. With the exception of the 66+ year-old group of respondents, each age group of respondents stated that they agreed that the discount given to them by influencers could positively change their consumer behavior.

- *Phase DO*

Unknown brands are not popular with respondents. They would more likely buy a product from a brand that is associated with an influencer. Majority of respondents did buy a product that promoted or recommended influencer.

Women and men predominantly would rather buy a product, which is associated with an influencer than an unknown product. More women than men did buy a product promoted or recommended by influencer.

All age groups would rather buy a product that is known because of influencer. Products of unknown brands are not popular with any age groups. Young to mid-young age groups (16–25 to 36–45) of respondents did buy more products promoted or recommended by influencers. Older age groups buy less influencer-recommended products.

- *Phase CARE*

More than a half of respondents would not recommend influencer-promoted products. More men than women would not recommend influencer-promoted products and in general, respondents of both gender groups would not incline to recommendation of such products. Except for two age groups (16–25 and 36–45), no age group of respondents would recommend influencer-promoted products.

Acknowledgments This research was supported by project VEGA 1/0011/21 Research on the interactions among new emerging technologies, the performance of enterprises and industries based on network technology infrastructure, the application of new business models and the institutional regulatory, environmental, and social environment.

References

Annual Marketing Report. (2021a). *State of influencer marketing 2021*. Available online: https://hypeauditor.com/whitepapers/state-of-influencer-marketing-2021. Accessed on May 17, 2023.
Annual Marketing Report. (2021b). *The state of influencer marketing 2021: Benchmark report*. Available online: https://influencermarketinghub.com/influencer-marketing-benchmark-report-2021/. Accessed on May 17, 2023.

Brown, D., & Hayes, N. (2008). *Influencer marketing: Who really influences your customers?* (1st ed., pp. 39–43). Butterworth-Heinemann.

Constantinides, E. (2014). Foundations of social media marketing. *Procedia Social and Behavioral Sciences, 148*, 40–57. https://doi.org/10.1016/j.sbspro.2014.07.016

Drengubiak, M. (2020). *The impact of influencer marketing on consumer shopping behaviour.* Bachelor Thesis, University of Žilina, Žilina, 79 p.

Duckett, J. (2011). *HTML & CSS: Design and build websites* (1st ed., pp. 1–4). John Wiley & Sons.

Garbarova, M., & Holla Bachanova, P. (2020). Purchaising behaviour of E-insurance consumers. In *Vision 2020: Sustainable economic development and application of innovation management from regional expansion to global growth* (pp. 3139–3152). ISBN 978-0-9998551-1-9. Norristown: International business information management association.

Geyser, W. (2023). *What is influencer marketing: An in depth look at marketing's next big thing.* Available online: https://influencermarketinghub.com/influencer-marketing/. Accessed on May 17, 2023.

Gundova, P., & Cvoligova, K. (2019). Impact of influencer marketing on consumer behavior. *Acta Academica Karviniensia, 19*(3), 31–41. https://doi.org/10.25142/aak.2019.018

Hudak, M., Kianicková, E., & Madlenak, R. (2017). The importance of E-mail marketing in E-commerce. *Procedia Engineering, 192*, 342–347. https://doi.org/10.1016/j.proeng.2017.06.059

Kaushik, A. (2015). *See, Think, Do, Care Winning Combo: Content + Marketing + Measurement!* Available online: https://www.kaushik.net/avinash/see-think-do-care-win-content-marketing-measurement/. Accessed on August 29, 2021.

Kingsnorth, S. (2016). *Digital Marketing Strategy: An integrated approach to online marketing* (1st ed., pp. 5–29). Kogan Page.

Kotler, P., Kartajaya, H., & Setiawan, I. (2017). *Marketing 4.0: Moving from traditional to digital* (1st ed., pp. 32–37). John Wiley & Sons.

Madlenak, R., & Madlenakova, L. (2015). *Marketing v elektronickom obchodovaní* (Bratislava, 1st ed., 154 p.). ISBN 978-80-8181-025-1. Dolis.

Madleňák, R., & Rostášová, M. (2015). *Marketing v elektronickom obchodovaní* (1st ed., pp. 11–27). Dolis.

Madlenak, R., Madlenakova, L., & Rudawska, A. (2017). Viral marketing as part of effective university marketing strategy. In *INTED 2017: 11th International technology, education and development conference 2017* (pp. 5629–5634). Valencia: Conference proceedings. ISSN 2340-1079. ISBN 978-84-617-8491-2. IATED Academy 2017.

Nashelsky, L. (1994). *Introduction to digital technology* (4th ed., pp. 3–4). Prentice-Hall.

Nastišin, L. (2020). Vnímanie influencer marketing ako efektívneho e-biznis nástroja na podporu marketingových aktivít spoločnosti. *Journal of Global Science, 2020*, 1–6.

Olbrich, R., Schultz, C. D., & Bormann, P. M. (2019). The effect of social media and advertising activities on affiliate marketing. *International Journal of Marketing and Advertising, 13*(1), 47–72. https://doi.org/10.1504/IJIMA.2019.10019165

Phillips, D., & Young, P. (2009). *Online public relations: A practical guide to developing an online strategy in the world of social media* (2nd ed., pp. 3–8). Kogan Page.

Rovnanova, A. (2018). Konkurenčná diferenciácia v digitálnom prostredí. In *PHD Progress: vedecký časopis študentov doktorandského štúdia Fakulty prevádzky a ekonomiky dopravy a spojov Žilinskej univerzity v Žiline.* ISSN 1339-1712. Roč. 6, č. 1 (2018), s. 78–83.

Santora, J. (2023). *12 Types of influencers you can use to improve your marketing.* Available online: https://influencermarketinghub.com/types-of-influencers/. May 17, 2023.

Signal Fox. (2019). *See – Think – Do – Care Model.* Available online: https://www.signalfox.org/see-think-do-model/. Accessed online on May 17, 2023.

Stankova, M. (2018). Impact of influencers on the purchasing behaviour of a specific target group of consumers. In *The Proceedings of the International Scientific Conference for PhD. Students and Young Scientists 2018* (pp. 168–182).

Terlutter, R., & Capella, M. L. (2013). The gamification of advertising: Analysis and research directions of in-game advertising, advergames, and advertising in social network games. *Journal of Advertising, 42*, 95–112. https://doi.org/10.1080/00913367.2013.774610

Urbinati, A., Chiaroni, D., Chiesa, V., & Frattini, F. (2020). The role of digital technologies in open innovation processes: An exploratory multiple case study analysis. *R&D Management – Special Issue: Open Innovation in the Digital Age, 50*(1), 136–160. https://doi.org/10.1111/radm.12313

Vermaat, M., Sebok, S., Freund, S., Campbell, J., & Frydenberg, M. (2018). *Discovering computers: Digital technology, data, and devices* (1st ed.). Cengage Learning.

Chapter 21
The Reflection of COVID-19 Pandemic in the State Budget of the Slovak Republic: Selected Problems

Janka Grofčíková and Katarína Izáková

Abstract The years 2020 and 2021 were statistically significant in terms of the unprecedented impact of the COVID-19 pandemic. There has been a sharp decline in economic and social activity, a decline in revenues going to the public administration budget, and an increase in public spending on support schemes and tools. The aim of the chapter is to examine the changes in the volume of income and expenditure of the state budget, as the most important part of the public administration balance sheet, during the period of the COVID-19 pandemic and to identify the causes of deviations in the cash flows of the state budget of the Slovak Republic. Changes in the volume of income and expenses were compared on a daily basis using the Wilcoxon signed-rank test. The monitored period is the years 2018 to 2021. Our findings point to strong financial support aimed at mitigating the consequences of the pandemic both at the national level and from the EU, which was statistically significantly reflected in the ongoing implementation of the state budget, specifically in the items of income from grants and transfers and in the total and current expenditures of the state budget.

Keywords State budget · Cash receipts and expenditures · Budget execution · COVID-19

JEL Codes H50, H60

21.1 Introduction

Since 2020, the global economy has been significantly affected by the impact of the COVID-19 pandemic. Governments around the world were adopting restrictions

---

J. Grofčíková (✉) · K. Izáková
Faculty of Ecomonics, Matej Bel University in Banská Bystrica, Department of Finance and Accounting, Banska Bystrica, Slovakia
e-mail: janka.grofcikova@umb.sk; katarina.izakova@umb.sk

© The Author(s), under exclusive license to Springer Nature Switzerland AG 2024
N. Tsounis, A. Vlachvei (eds.), *Applied Economic Research and Trends*, Springer Proceedings in Business and Economics,
https://doi.org/10.1007/978-3-031-49105-4_21

to prevent the spread of this disease, including lockdown. Due to state measures, many businesses were forced to close their operations and many companies had to temporarily suspend their activities. People stopped meeting, could not travel, working from home was introduced. EU Member States also had to deal with the emergency situation in the field of public health and at the same time to support the economy. Mitigating the impact of the COVID-19 pandemic on citizens and businesses and increasing the resilience of the EU, the European Council approved the Next-Generation EU instrument in the amount of EUR 750 billion for the years 2021–2026. Financial resources should be provided by means of seven programs in the form of loans of 360 billion EUR and grants of 390 billion EUR. Approximately 90% of funds from the NGEU will be allocated through the Recovery and Resilience Facility (RRF) from which EU Member States can apply for a loan of up to 6.8% of their gross national income in 2019 as part of submitting their plan of recovery and resilience (see Fig. 21.1). The distribution of 70% of the total package of financial resources is subject to an allocation mechanism, that takes into account: the number of inhabitants of the Member State; the inverse of the GDP per capita; and the average unemployment rate over the past 5 years (2015–2019) compared to the EU average, which subsequently affects the redistribution of the given funds (European Commission, 2022). From the point of view of the allocation of resources per capita, Greece has the highest allocation and Luxembourg the lowest (Pfeiffer et al., 2021).

Porcher (2023) confirms that European countries tend to implement indirect measures—such as credit guarantees or capital injections into companies. The author documents that the average total percentage of GDP allocated to fiscal expenditures, tax deferrals, and extra-budgetary measures is the highest in Europe

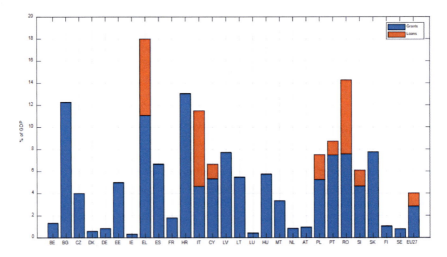

Fig. 21.1 Overview of assumed allocation grants to Member States from the Recovery and Resilience Support Mechanism (in 2018 prices) per capita for the years 2021–2023

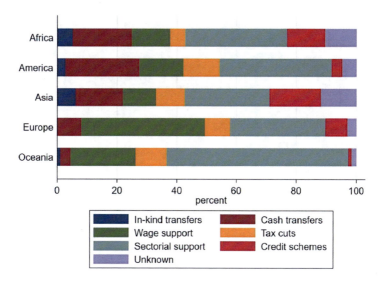

Fig. 21.2 Distribution of fiscal expenditures by continent as of June 2021

compared to other continents as of 1 June 2021, at around 7% of GDP, while in America it is below 3% of GDP (see Fig. 21.2).

In Africa and Asia, in-kind transfers are used relatively more. Cash transfers also have a high share of total spending in Africa, Asia, and the Americas (including South America). These observations are consistent with the idea that these regions mostly consist of developing countries where a large part of the economy is still informal. A broader support for wages is characteristic of Europe, whereas Oceania has a strong sectoral support (such as investments or increased budget for certain sectors) due to its relative isolation.

21.1.1 Pandemic State Budgets in the Slovak Republic

The Slovak economy, regulated by pandemic rules in 2020 and 2021, has resulted in a recession with high state budget deficits and subsequently increased government debt.

In the context of comparing public finance deficits with neighboring countries, as well as the EU and eurozone average, we can state that the deficit achieved in 2021 was the second highest among the V4 countries and was also above the EU and eurozone average (see Fig. 21.3).

The documented deficits were influenced by the measures taken by governments to reduce the negative effects of the lockdown, combined with the need to stimulate the economy and help vulnerable groups of the population.

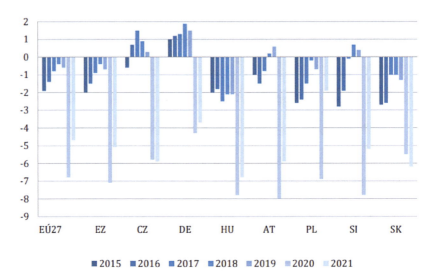

Fig. 21.3 Comparison of public finance deficits of selected eurozone (EZ) countries in % of GDP (2015–2021)

Such measures in Slovakia were, e.g., "First aid" projects that were taught to employers (and self-employed individuals) who had to close their operations or limit their activities, the state reimbursed 80% of the total cost of the work (with a maximum contribution of 1100 EUR per employee).

Subsequent claims were paid to employers depending on the decline in revenues, while employees were entitled to sick leave benefits from the first day of temporary incapacity for work in the amount of 55% of the daily assessment basis.

The "kurzarbeit" (short-time work) was also introduced. Employers could request the state to pay for the wage compensation during the time when the employer could not assign work to the employee due to an obstacle on the employer's side. These measures, including job support, social assistance, pandemic-related sick, and nursing leave benefits, as well as remission of taxes and levies represented the highest item of direct aid in the amount of 1.3 billion EUR, and the total expenditure on measures to combat the COVID-19 disease amounted to 4.6 billion EUR (5.1% of GDP) (Ministry of Finance of the Slovak Republic, 2022). The share of individual measures in the total combined expenses with the pandemic in 2021 is shown in Fig. 21.4.

A large part of the public sector, such as healthcare, education, and a portion of the economy (especially services), has been placed in hitherto unknown and qualitatively new situations that will likely be affected by their functioning in the future.

From the perspective of ministries during the years 2020–2021, financial aid to mitigate negative anti-pandemic measures was provided as follows:

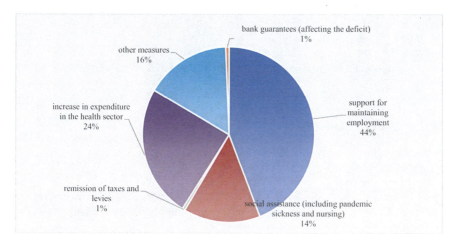

Fig. 21.4 The share of individual measures in the total combined expenses with the pandemic in 2021

Table 21.1 Development of the state budget of the Slovak Republic in the years 2018–2021 in millions EUR

	2018	2019	2020	2021
Total revenues	15,381	15,825	15,750	17,197
1. Tax	11,966	12,336	11,872	13,546
2. Non-tax	1211	1327	1289	1338
3. Grants and transfers	2203	2161	2588	2313
Total expenditures	16,563	18,027	23,509	24,211
Current expenditures	14,160	15,168	20,846	21,772
Capital expenditures	2402	2858	2662	2440
Deficit/surplus	−1182	−2201	−7758	−7014

- The Ministry of Labour, Social Affairs, and Family via the aforementioned "First Aid" and its variations, with a total amount of 2193.79 million EUR.
- The Ministry of Economy provided support to business entities in the field of culture and selected haulage contractors in the amount of 156.26 million EUR.
- The Ministry of Transport and Construction provided assistance to tourism and road transport in the total amount of 152.62 million EUR.
- The Ministry of Culture provided for the support of the cultural and creative industry in the total amount of 24.23 million EUR.

The state budget deficit in 2021 reached the value of 7 billion EUR and against the year 2020 decreased by 744 million EUR, mainly due to higher taxes incomes and lower expenditure growth (Ministry of Finance of the Slovak Republic, 2022) (Table 21.1).

We can observe a significant increase in tax revenues in the structure of tax revenues in 2021, as well as a decrease in revenues from grants and transfers.

We can observe a significant increase in the structure of tax revenues in 2021 and as well as a decrease in revenues from grants and transfers. The most significant portion of the item of grants and transfers is formed by the mentioned revenues from the EU budget, which reached a value of almost 2.6 billion EUR in 2020, with the highest volume allocated in the chapter of Sustainable Growth. The year 2021 confirms the persistent problems with the absorption of EU funds, where Slovakia is, in international comparison, at the bottom of the list as of the end of June 2021.

21.2 Literature Review

The economic downturn caused by the effects of the pandemic and emergency fiscal support manifested in a sharp increase in the deficit of public finances and public debt of the EU. Fiscal policy has shifted from being formally procyclical/acyclical before the COVID-19 period to countercyclical/countercyclical over the years of the pandemic.

These facts are confirmed by a study by Bökemeier and Wolski (2022), who document that the change in EU policy is due to public expenditures related to COVID-19, particularly in the areas of public health, economic affairs, and social protection. The effects of the ECB's unconventional monetary policy and the sustainable debt of the Eurozone are also addressed by Barbier-Gauchard et al. (2023). They also confirm that during the current recovery phase, it is necessary to properly manage the Cohesion Funds, which is a condition for meeting the expectations related to the programming period 2021–2027.

Italian authors Boffardi et al. (2022) focus on the EU's cohesion policy, in the case of export support at the time of COVID-19, and on the positive impact of the use of EU funds on regional export performance, perceived especially in the context of the new European strategy.

Similar messages are also interpreted by Bonadio et al. (2021), finding that adverse trade effects of the pandemic crisis were localized in regions more exposed to international global value chains and external demand shocks.

The scientific literature also tracks COVID-19 from the perspective of its impacts on financial markets, institutions, and the real economy. The findings of Tran and Uzmanoglu (2023) suggest that investors perceive lockdowns as negative financial events that may increase the borrowing costs of issuers in lockdown states. Gubareva (2021) analyzes the liquidity of emerging market bonds during the uncertainty caused by Covid-19. The results of Cox and Woods (2023) document that market structure and trading dynamics were significantly affected during the peak of the COVID-19 pandemic based on trading differences with stocks listed on the NYSE and NASDAQ.

21.3 Methodology

The aim of the chapter is to examine the changes in the volume of income and expenditure of the state budget during the period of the COVID-19 pandemic and to

21 The Reflection of COVID-19 Pandemic in the State Budget of the Slovak...

Table 21.2 Structure of revenues and expenditures of the Slovak Republic's state budget

Total income	1. Tax income	(a) Personal income tax
		(b) Corporate income tax
		(c) Income tax collected by withholding
		(d) VAT
		(e) Consumption taxes
	2. Non-tax income	
	3. Grants and transfers	Revenues from the EU budget
Total expenses	1. Current expenses	
	2. Capital expenditure	
Deficit/surplus		

identify the causes of deviations in the volume of cash flows of the state budget of the Slovak Republic. The material that forms the information base for our research consists of information on the Interim State budget execution on a cash basis as well as information from the State Closing Account, which are published on its website by the Ministry of Finance of the Slovak Republic, in the State reporting section (www.mfsr.sk). Since the published data is a cumulative value, for the needs of our research, we calculated the volume of daily increases and decreases in the volume of cash, broken down by individual items of the state budget. In order to achieve comparability of items in the entire monitored period, we examine the items of income and expenses in the breakdown shown in Table 21.2.

We monitor the total revenues of the state budget of the Slovak Republic broken down into (1) tax revenues, (2) non-tax revenues, and (3) revenues from grants and transfers. We examine tax revenues broken down into revenues (a) from personal income tax, (b) from corporate income tax, (c) revenues from withholding tax, (d) from value-added tax, and (e) revenues from consumption taxes. A more detailed breakdown of the daily increments of non-tax income is not publicly available. The largest share of income from grants and transfers is income from the EU budget. We do not examine other incomes in this income group.

Considering the availability of data, we can examine the structure of total expenses only by dividing them into current and capital income. The last item examined is the difference between income and expenditure shown in the item "Deficit/Surplus."

The monitored period is the years from 2018 to 2021. The years 2020 and 2021 are the period during which the COVID-19 pandemic was fully manifested at all levels of economic and social life. The years 2018 and 2019 serve to compare the changes that occurred in the volume and structure of income and expenses in the pandemic years compared to previous periods.

Changes in the volume of income and expenses on a daily basis will be compared on an interannual basis and statistically evaluated using non-parametric tests for two related samples, specifically using the Wilcoxon signed-rank test, which is considered a non-parametric equivalent of the paired-sample t-test. We formulate one-tailed hypotheses: H_0: There is no difference in the volume of cash flow between the two investigated periods (H_0: $\mu_0 = \mu_1$,), H_1: There is a difference in the volume of cash flow between the two compared periods (H_1: $\mu_0 < \mu_1$ or H_1: $\mu_0 > \mu_1$). We verify the hypotheses at the level of significance $\alpha = 0.05$.

21.4   Empirical Results and Discussion

The year 2020 was statistically significant in terms of the unprecedented impact of the COVID-19 pandemic. There was a strong decline in economic and social activity, a decline in revenues going to the public administration budget, an increase in public spending on support schemes and instruments, and an increase in unemployment and a "rewriting" of the budget assumptions for the following years. For this reason, the comparison of the public administration balance between 2019 and 2020 is strongly marked by non-standard economic development under the influence of external factors. The year 2021 was, like 2020, economically and socially demanding, the COVID-19 pandemic continued its negative impact on economic activity, the economy, travel, and the provision of public services. Governments have taken other measures to reduce the spread of the virus and mitigate the negative effects on citizens, employment, and living standards. To finance these needs, they used public administration resources as well as resources from the EU budget.

The most important part of the public administration balance sheet is the state budget, which is based on the cash principle. Figure 21.5 shows the sequence of real fulfillment of state budget revenues, broken down into total revenues, tax revenues, non-tax revenues, and revenues from grants and transfers by individual months (axis "x") from 2018 to 2021. Percentage shares (axis "y") indicate the share of the volume of monthly income to the volume of annual income in the given income category.

As can be seen from Fig. 21.5 (graph Total income), the measures to prevent the spread of the pandemic, which were adopted by the government in the tax area in 2020, affected the course of the real fulfillment of state budget income. While in 2018 and 2019 the percentage distribution of income in individual months is almost identical, in 2020 we observe a decrease in the share of monthly income, especially in the months immediately after the onset of the corona crisis. The critical period began with the declaration of a state of emergency from 12 March 2020 and the simultaneous adoption of a number of restrictive measures. The government of the Slovak Republic proceeded with a more significant relaxation of restrictions from 20 May 2020. In May 2020, the volume of tax revenues reached only 4.37% of annual revenues, while in the others three monitored years it was an average of 6.6%. In the following months, the situation improved, and by the end of the year, the state managed to get 110% of the total planned income into the state budget.

The most important component of the total revenues of the state budget is tax revenues. The share of tax revenues in the total revenues of the state budget was 78% in 2018 and 2019. In 2020, this share fell to 75%; in 2021 it rose again to 79%.

Fig. 21.5 Real fulfillment of state budget revenues in individual months of the year (share of monthly income in total annual income)

However, the decrease in the share of tax revenue in total revenue was the result of budget planning, as the actual tax revenue of the state reached 103% of the budgeted revenue in 2020, and in 2021, it was up to 115%. We can therefore conclude that the state managed to get money from taxpayers to finance its activities even during the pandemic years. However, in Fig. 21.5 (graph Tax income), we see that there was a clear decrease in the share of taxes received between March and May 2020. The situation also improved from the point of view of tax collection too from May 2020. By the end of 2020, the state managed to exceed the planned tax revenue by 3%.

We also see a lower monthly share of real income fulfillment in 2020 in the group of non-tax income (see Fig. 21.5, graph Non-tax income). Income from grants and transfers (see Fig. 21.5, graph Grant's and transfer's income) in January to August 2020 reached the approximate values of the other three monitored years, a more significant increase in the monthly share of income occurred by September 2020.

We verify changes in state budget revenues on a daily basis using the Wilcoxon signed-rank test. We present the test results in Table 21.3, where the values of the Z-score of the Wilcoxon signed-rank test are given, which are based on positive or negative differences in each monitored interannual period. If the Z-score is based on positive differences, it means that there was a year-on-year decrease in the volume of income to the state budget in the majority of days between the compared years. In the opposite case, when the Z-score is based on negative differences, the number of days with a year-on-year daily increases in the volume of income to the state budget prevailed between the monitored years. The table also contains one-tailed

Table 21.3 Test statistics

	Total income 2019 vs. 2018	Total income 2020 vs. 2019	Total income 2021 vs. 2020
Z	$-.174^-$	-1.105^+	$-.594^-$
Asymp. Sig. (1-tailed)	.431	.135	.276
	Tax income 2020 vs. 2018	Tax income 2019 vs. 2019	Tax income 2021 vs. 2020
Z	$-.232^-$	-1.233^+	-1.331^-
Asymp. Sig. (1-tailed)	.408	.109	.092
	Non-tax income 2019 vs. 2018	Non-tax income 2020 vs. 2019	Non-tax income 2021 vs. 2020
Z	-1.321^-	$-.638^+$	-1.597^-
Asymp. Sig. (1-tailed)	.093	.262	.055
	Grant's and transfer's income 2019 vs. 2018	Grant's and transfer's income 2020 vs. 2019	Grant's and transfer's income 2021 vs. 2020
Z	$-.454^-$	-1.915^-	$-.615^+$
Asymp. Sig. (1-tailed)	.325	*.028*	.269

Wilcoxon signed-rank test
$^-$Based on negative ranks
$^+$Based on positive ranks

Asymptotic Significance values. Values highlighted in italics are significant at the selected level of significance.

A statistically significant increase in state budget revenues in 2020 is found in the item revenues from grants and transfers, the actual amount of which reached 151% of the planned revenues of this category. A decisive part of these funds, both in the budget and in actual fulfillment, was made up of resources from the EU budget, allocated and drawn within the relevant program periods. Other income groups of the state budget (tax income, non-tax income) as well as total income recorded year-on-year decreases in most items on a daily basis, but these changes were not statistically significant and were based on a lower volume of budgeted amounts. We can conclude from this that the changes in the time distribution of income occurred only within the given calendar year; the annual amount of the actual fulfillment of these incomes reached or slightly exceeded its budgeted amount.

If we research more closely the individual tax revenue categories, we will find that there have been several statistically significant changes in the monitored years. Figure 21.6 shows the breakdown of tax revenue collection by individual subcategories during individual months in the years 2018 to 2021. We present the results of the Wilcoxon signed-rank test in Table 21.4.

Personal income tax is a shared tax, and the entire tax revenue is redistributed by a set mechanism between municipalities and higher territorial units. The share

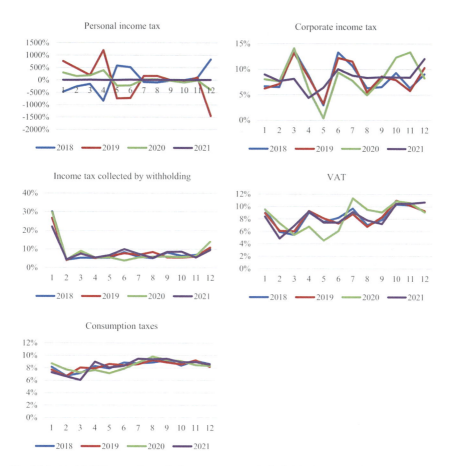

Fig. 21.6 Real fulfillment of state budget tax revenues in individual months of the year (share of monthly income in total annual income)

of municipalities in the revenue is 70%; the higher territorial total accounts for the remaining 30% of the revenue. Only parts of the tax revenue remain on the state budget account due to the shift between the tax being credited to the SR account and its transfer to municipalities and higher territorial units. In 2020, the income of the state budget from the personal income tax, taking into account the mentioned rules of fiscal decentralization, reached the value of −23,019 thousand EUR and reached 48% of the budgeted value. In addition to the decrease in economic activity, a 5.6% decrease in the number of self-employed persons and a 5.2% decrease in the number of natural persons—entrepreneurs contributed to the decrease in state budget revenues from personal income tax in 2020.

In 2020, the actual income from the implementation of the budget in the corporate income tax item reached 92.3%. Among other things, the cash yield was also reduced by measures to support businesses due to the economic downturn in the

Table 21.4 Test statistics

	Personal income tax 2019 vs. 2018	Personal income tax 2020 vs. 2019	Personal income tax 2021 vs. 2020
Z	-2.113^-	$-.293^+$	-1.039^+
Asymp. Sig. (1-tailed)	*.017*	.385	.149
	Corporate income tax 2019 vs. 2018	Corporate income tax 2020 vs. 2019	Corporate income tax 2021 vs. 2020
Z	$-.268^-$	-1.213^+	-3.342^-
Asymp. Sig. (1-tailed)	.394	.113	*.000*
	Income from withholding tax 2019 vs. 2018	Income from withholding tax 2020 vs. 2019	Income from withholding tax 2021 vs. 2020
Z	-4.578^-	-1.109^+	-6.055^-
Asymp. Sig. (1-tailed)	*.000*	.134	*.000*
	VAT 2019 vs. 2018	VAT 2020 vs. 2019	VAT 2021 vs. 2020
Z	$-.391^-$	$-.981^+$	$-.950^-$
Asymp. Sig. (1-tailed)	.348	.163	.171
	Consumption taxes 2019 vs. 2018	Consumption taxes 2020 vs. 2019	Consumption taxes 2021 vs. 2020
Z	-1.126^-	-2.851^-	-0.636^-
Asymp. Sig. (1-tailed)	.130	*.002*	.262

Wilcoxon signed-rank test
$^-$Based on negative ranks
$^+$Based on positive ranks

form of deferral of tax advances in 2020. The deferral of the payment of income tax advances could be used by enterprises whose turnover fell by 40% compared to the same period of the previous calendar year. These and other measures adopted by the Slovak government to prevent the spread of the pandemic and mitigate its effects were also reflected in the collection of taxes on the income of natural and legal persons. In 2020, the state collected 48% of the budgeted funds from personal income tax; in 2021, it was 158% of the budgeted value. The average fulfillment of income from personal income tax was at the level of 103% in the pandemic years. Based on the data presented in Table 21.4, we further identify:

- A statistically significant year-on-year increase (Z-score is based on negative rank) in the number of days with a higher volume of daily state budget income from personal income tax in 2019, in 2020 and 2021 the number of days with a lower amount of income prevails compared to the previous period (Z-score is based on positive rank),

- Interruption of increases in income from corporate income tax in 2020 compared to 2019, and a subsequent statistically significant increase in the number of days with an increase in these incomes in 2021 compared to 2020.

Revenues from taxes on goods and services make up an average of 76% of tax revenues of the state budget. These include value-added tax, consumption taxes, and taxes on use, on goods, and on activity permits and other taxes. The decisive part of this group of taxes consists of VAT and consumption taxes. Actual VAT collection in 2020 at the level of 106.8% of the budgeted amount stemmed from stable household consumption and maintaining the success of tax collection. The collection of consumption taxes exceeded the budgeted amount of 2020 by 3% and achieved a statistically significant increase (Sig. = 0.002). This was mainly related to higher economic growth and household consumption compared to conservative assumptions due to the unpredictable impact of the pandemic. The biggest difference was in the tax on mineral oils, alcohol, and tobacco products.

While we did not identify statistically significant changes in the volume of total revenues of the state budget in the years under review (see Table 21.3), we identified significant changes in expenditures. In Table 21.5, we present the results of the Wilcoxon signed-rank test, where we compared the volume of daily real state budget expenditures, broken down by economic classification into current and

Table 21.5 Test statistics

	Total expenses 2019 vs. 2018	Total expenses 2020 vs. 2019	Total expenses 2021 vs. 2020
Z	-1.237^-	-3.810^-	-1.623^-
Asymp. Sig. (1-tailed)	.108	*.000*	.052
	Current expenses 2019 vs. 2018	Current expenses 2020 vs. 2019	Current expenses 2021 vs. 2020
Z	-1.195^-	-4.226^-	-1.809^-
Asymp. Sig. (1-tailed)	.116	*.000*	*.035*
	Capital expenditure 2019 vs. 2018	Capital expenditure 2020 vs. 2019	Capital expenditure 2021 vs. 2020
Z	$-.998^-$	-1.334^+	-1.433^+
Asymp. Sig. (1-tailed)	.159	.091	.076
	Deficit/surplus 2019 vs. 2018	Deficit/surplus 2020 vs. 2019	Deficit/surplus 2021 vs. 2020
Z	$-.553^+$	-2.984^+	$-.276^+$
Asymp. Sig. (1-tailed)	.290	*.001*	.391

Wilcoxon signed-rank test
$^-$ Based on negative ranks
$^+$ Based on positive ranks

capital expenditures. The results of the test show a statistically significant growth of total state budget expenditures in 2020 (Sig. $= 0.000$) and current expenditures in both 2020 and 2021 (Sig. < 0.05). The growth of state expenditures also affected the size of the state budget deficit, which statistically significantly increased in 2020.

The amendment to the State Budget Act for 2020 approved 33.4% higher expenditures compared to the first version of the Act. Realized expenses were 11% lower than the approved budget. Compared to 2019, however, they were 30% higher. The main reason for the increase in expenses in a year-on-year comparison was to cover the needs caused by the COVID-19 pandemic.

One of the items of current state budget expenses related to covering the needs caused by the pandemic was salary expenses intended for rewards for employees performing tasks within the "Shared responsibility" action, as well as funds intended for the rehabilitation of expenses directly implied by the emergence of a pandemic related to the disease COVID-19, respectively expenses related to the fulfillment of the Regulations of the Government of the Slovak Republic. In 2020, the most funds were spent in the item general and special material, where real expenses exceeded the budgeted amounts by 85%. In addition to financing the normal operation of individual budgetary organizations, the funds were mainly used for the purchase of personal protective equipment in connection with the COVID-19 pandemic, the purchase of disinfectants and cleaning agents, tests for the coronavirus, medical certificates, and other medical materials.

Current expenses include current transfers, which also exceeded their budgeted amount by 37.4% in 2020. These funds were aimed, among other things, at subsidizing state financial assets for the purpose of implementing measures to mitigate the impact of the pandemic, at financial stabilization of medical facilities, financial assistance aimed at ensuring liquidity and maintaining employment and operations of small- and medium-sized enterprises, creating space for providing returnable resources for self-government.

Capital expenditure consists of expenditure on the acquisition of tangible and intangible assets, including expenditure related to the acquisition of such assets, and capital transfers, which include payments made to enable the recipient to acquire capital assets or to compensate for their damage or destruction. Real capital expenditures in 2020 exceeded the budgeted value by 64%. However, their volume constituted only 93% of capital expenditures in 2019. Based on the results of the Wilcoxon signed-rank test and Z-score based on positive differences in 2020 and 2021 (see Table 21.5), we can conclude that in these years, they were realistic that capital expenditures of the state budget are lower on most days of the year compared to the previous period. The increased volume of capital expenditures was concentrated in a lower number of days, but these changes were not statistically significant (Sig. > 0.05).

21.5 Conclusion

As part of the reallocation of resources to eliminate the effects of the COVID-19 pandemic, a total of 1105 million EUR was allocated, mainly to areas aimed at supporting the maintenance of employment (410.26 million EUR), supporting the health care system (204 million EUR), supporting micro-, small-, and medium-sized enterprises (330.2 million EUR), further supporting the components of the integrated rescue system (51 million EUR), and other measures to mitigate the impacts of COVID-19 (109.3 million EUR). The funds were provided within the relevant operational programs of the EU. From the total reallocation of resources intended to eliminate the impacts of COVID-19, 342.96 million EUR were spent from EU resources at the national level as of 31 December 2020, which represented 31.04% of the transferred resources. As of 31 December 2021, it was 794.01 million EUR, which represents 71.85% of transferred EU resources.

As a response to the negative effects of the pandemic, the European Commission proposed using the full potential of the EU budget. Its proposals are based on the Next-Generation EU instrument and the strengthened multiannual financial framework for the years 2021 to 2027. The Next-Generation instrument entered into force in February 2021 with funds in the amount of 806.9 billion EUR, expressed in current prices. It is a one-time emergency instrument intended to provide the EU budget with the additional capacity needed to respond decisively to the most urgent challenges. Funds from it will be provided through programs aimed at supporting recovery and resilience with an emphasis on strengthening the single market, intensifying cooperation in the field of healthcare, crisis management, supporting green and digital transformation, and building a fairer and more resilient economy. The economy and society of every European country needs these funds. It is to be hoped that they will be used to the greatest possible benefit of all of us. Ensuring the effective use of these funds will be the task of all of us, including researchers, who are opening up space for further research in this area.

Acknowledgments This chapter has been supported by the Scientific Grant Agency of Slovak Republic under project VEGA No. 1/0579/21 "Research on Determinants and Paradigms of Financial Management in the context of the COVID-19 Pandemic." The authors would like to express their gratitude to the Scientific Grant Agency of the Ministry of Education, Science, Research, and Sport of the Slovak Republic for financial support of this research and publication.

References

Barbier-Gauchard, A., Ligonnière, S., & Saadaoui, J. (2023). The European economy in the time of Covid-19: Towards a new dawn? *International Economics, 174*(2023), 1–3. https://doi.org/10.1016/j.inteco.2023.02.002

Boffardi, R., Di Caro, P., & Arbolino, R. (2022). Making the EU cohesion policy work to support exports at time of Covid-19: Evidence on the Italian regions. *International Economics, 172*(2022), 190–202. https://doi.org/10.1016/j.inteco.2022.09.008

Bökemeier, B., & Wolski, M. (2022). This time is different: Fiscal response to the COVID-19 pandemic among EU countries. *International Economics, 172*(2022), 217–226. https://doi.org/10.1016/j.inteco.2022.10.001

Bonadio, B., Huo, Z., Levchenko, A., & Pandalai-Nayar, N. (2021). Global supply chains in the pandemic. *Journal of International Economics, 133*, 103534. https://doi.org/10.1016/j.jinteco.2021.103534

Cox, J., & Woods, D. (2023). COVID-19 and market structure dynamics. *Journal of Banking & Finance, 147*(2023), 106362. https://doi.org/10.1016/j.jbankfin.2021.106362

European Commission. (2022). *Recovery fund: The EU delivers.* Retrieved from https://www.consilium.europa.eu/sk/infographics/recovery-fund-eu-delivers/

Gubareva, M. (2021). The impact of Covid-19 on liquidity of emerging market bonds. *Finance Research Letters, 41*(2021), 101826. https://doi.org/10.1016/j.frl.2020.101826

Ministry of Finance of the Slovak Republic. (2022). *State final account of the Slovak Republic 2022.* Retrieved from https://www.mfsr.sk/sk/financie/statne-vykaznictvo/klucove-dokumenty-uctovne-zavierky/statny-zaverecny-ucet-sr/

Pfeiffer, P., Varga, J., & Veld, J. (2021). *Quantifying spillovers of next generation EU investment.* European Commission. Directorate-General for Economic and Financial Affairs. Retrieved from https://economy-finance.ec.europa.eu/system/files/2021-07/dp144_en.pdf

Porcher, S. (2023). A dataset of governments' economic responses to COVID-19. *Data in Brief, 47*(2023), 109021. https://doi.org/10.1016/j.dib.2023.109021

Tran, N., & Uzmanoglu, C. (2023). Reprint of: COVID-19, lockdowns, and the municipal bond market. *Journal of Banking & Finance, 147*(2023), 106758. https://doi.org/10.1016/j.jbankfin.2023.106758

Chapter 22
Role of Information Technology in the Efficiency of HR Processes in Educational Institutions: A Case Study of Greece

Olympia Papaevangelou ⓘ, **Stavros Kalogiannidis** ⓘ, **Dimitrios Syndoukas, Zacharias Karantonis, and Despoina Savvidou**

Abstract The objective of this study is to determine the role of Information technology (IT) in the efficiency of HR processes in educational institutions. The major focus was on how utilizing information technology in human resource management can help to enhance efficiency of HR planning, selection and recruiting of employees, and evaluation and compensation in education institutions. The study used an exploratory research design. A systematic questionnaire was answered by a sample of 120 management, senior, junior, and contract employees from four educational institutions in Greece. The findings indicate a strong positive correlation between the use of IT and general efficiency of HR processes that include: selection and recruiting, human resource planning, assessment, and remuneration. This demonstrates how well Information and Communication Technology (ICT) is used in business human resource management. It is important for education institutions in Greece to enhance routine utilization of information systems to enable proper interactions between human resources and the various departments, which could increase organizational efficiency. The use of ICT ensures the effectiveness of human resource management.

Keywords Information technology · Efficiency of HR processes in educational institutions · HR evaluation and compensation · recruitment and selection · and HR planning

---

O. Papaevangelou · S. Kalogiannidis (✉) · D. Syndoukas
Department of Business Administration, University of Western Macedonia, Kozani, Greece
e-mail: dba00021@uowm.gr; aff00056@uowm.gr; dsyndoukas@uowm.gr

Z. Karantonis
Secondary & Postsecondary Educator, Ministry of Education, Rhodes, Greece

D. Savvidou
Department of Mineral Resources Engineering, University of Western Macedonia, Kozani, Greece
e-mail: aff00722@uowm.gr

© The Author(s), under exclusive license to Springer Nature Switzerland AG 2024
N. Tsounis, A. Vlachvei (eds.), *Applied Economic Research and Trends*, Springer Proceedings in Business and Economics,
https://doi.org/10.1007/978-3-031-49105-4_22

22.1 Background to the Study

The role of Information technology (IT) in the efficiency of HR processes in educational institutions has been studied by Ali Quaosar and Rahman (2021) where they found that research suggests that Information technology can improve the efficiency of HR processes in educational institutions. They posit that this is because it provides more transparency and less biased decision-making. This can help to facilitate performance evaluations, promotion, and termination and compensation adjustments so that the universities are more efficient. HR process relates to different activities, steps taken, and procedures that are necessary for an organization to function. These procedures involve ensuring that human resources functions such as recruitment, training, administrative processes, and leave management are done efficiently and timely (Bulmash, 2009; Gardner et al., 2003; UNESCO, 2020). Information and Communication Technology (ICT) is a rapidly expanding field, and it offers a wide range of potential applications for the HR function in educational institutions. ICT has an important role to play in the general efficiency of different practices or processes of HRM. It can be used to share information about students with schools across different countries or cities or even different educational institutions if necessary (Mutahi & Busienei, 2015).

Traditional HRM encompassed excessive amount of paperwork and protracted administrative processes, which largely slowed down the entire HR processes. According to Mitu (2016), the capacity of a company to carry out its operations more quickly and inexpensively is referred to as HRM efficiency. Due to today's demands, there is more emphasis on HRM to support strategic goals and focus on value-adding activities, which has altered the nature of the work and increased expectations for human resource (HR) professionals (Fabiana Meijon Fadul, 2019). One of these shifts is the widespread, modern use of IT to assist diverse HR operations in education institutions. Additionally, analysts anticipate that the expanding use of information technology will boost HR professionals' effectiveness and encourage them to participate in internal consulting projects for businesses (Bhalakrishnan, 2020; Papapolychroniadis et al., 2017).

The usage of ICT is seen in modern HRM as a driver for operational efficiency. This viewpoint has been reinforced by the steadily rising investment in ICT-related management tools made in emerging nations (Najeeb, 2013). As a result, there is little to no space for debate over the idea that "people" are one of the primary factors influencing an organization's success or failure, and as a result, the significance of these individuals' knowledge, abilities, attitudes, and behaviors for the advancement of an organization (Nadarajah et al., 2012; Selase, 2018). The main resource that may contribute to an organization's growth and development is its people. Although a business does not have complete control over this asset, it may utilize specific tools and strategies to significantly affect how they function in order to further the organization's objectives. Due to the digital revolution, corporations have used information technology to enhance HR processes or services as a tool to influence the performance and behavior of the people they depend on to succeed in business

(De Alwis et al., 2022; Gardner et al., 2003). It is no surprise that over the past 20 years, information technology has been playing an increasing role in reducing the workload and cost of day-to-day paperwork. In fact, while today most of us use our phone as a calculator, it would be unimaginable to do so forty years ago. However, what is a little less obvious is IT's effects on the field of Human Resources. This study focuses on ICT's effect on HR processes in educational institutions with focus on the Greece education sector.

22.1.1 Problem Statement

In the last decade, IT has finally made its way into the job market and has now been one of the most sought after skill sets. This is not surprising, given that schools are increasing their investments on IT. In 2016, it was estimated that nearly £1.7 billion was spent by Greece further education providers on Information technology (IT) (Piabuo et al., 2017; Sirajuddin & P, 2021). And despite this progress, there are still many misconceptions about what IT really entails. Significant disparities were discovered when some writers sought to compare the roles of IT in process-oriented and services-oriented companies. Alami et al. (2016) examined the influence of ICT on HRM practices, and both studies have confirmed how IT impacts HR processes. This research aims to add to the body of literature by examining how ICT affects HRM effectiveness. Moreover, the organizational changes and employee recruitment or compensation effects of IT have received minimal academic attention, notably in Greece (Ali Quaosar & Rahman, 2021). As a result, the main goal of this paper is to provide empirical evidence about the influence of ICT on the effectiveness of HRM functions in Greek educational institutions (Gangl et al., 1978). The introduction of computers and the internet considerably expanded the effect of technology, which has profoundly altered the corporate sector throughout the information age. Technology affects almost every business area, including human resources, and technology continues to have an impact on HR practices (Hassanzada & Chatterjee Rao, 2020; Selase, 2018). Less attention has been paid to the links between utilizing E-HRM and the effectiveness of HRM. The importance of learning more and investigating how this prolonged use affects HRM effectiveness has increased (Al Qalhati et al., 2020). This research aims to fill this gap in the body of knowledge on E-HRM by determining the role of IT in the efficiency of HR processes in educational institutions.

22.1.2 Purpose of the Study

This study sought to establish the role of Information technology in the efficiency of HR processes in educational institutions using Greece as the case study.

22.1.3 Objectives of the Study

1. To establish the role of Information technology in planning with regard to efficiency of HR processes in educational institutions.
2. To find out the relationship between ICT-based recruitment and selection and efficiency of HR processes in educational institutions.
3. To establish how IT in HR evaluation and compensation influences efficiency of HR processes in educational institutions.

22.1.4 Research Questions

1. What is the role of Information technology in planning in regard to efficiency of HR processes in educational institutions?
2. What is the relationship between ICT-based recruitment and selection and efficiency of HR processes in educational institutions?
3. How does IT in HR evaluation and compensation influence efficiency of HR processes in educational institutions?

22.1.5 Research Hypotheses

H1: Information technology in planning positively influences efficiency of HR processes in educational institutions.
H2: There is a significant relationship between ICT-based recruitment and selection and efficiency of HR processes in educational institutions.
H4: IT in HR evaluation and compensation positively influences efficiency of HR processes in educational institutions.

22.1.6 Contribution of the Study

This study contributes greatly to the area of human resource management and information technology most especially in regard to IT in HR evaluation and compensation, IT-based training and development, ICT-based recruitment and selection, and Information technology in planning.

22.2 Literature Review

22.2.1 Theoretical Review

The Technology Acceptance Model was the most popular theory in E-HRM (TAM). In order to forecast and analyze ICT usage patterns, i.e., what makes future adopters decide whether or not to utilize technology, two theoretical notions in TAM that serve as the main predictors of system usage as well as attitudes toward utilizing the system, or the user's willingness to do so, are perceived utility and ease of use (Carli et al., 2019). The phrase "degree to which a person believes that using a particular system would enhance his or her job performance" is used to describe perceived usefulness, while "degree to which a person believes that using a particular system would be free of effort" is used to describe perceived ease of use (Kanungo & Mendonca, 1988). DeLone and McLean published a complete taxonomy of factors affecting the performance of information systems in 1992 after reviewing past work (Indjejikian, 1999). After reading the literature on Information Systems (IS) performance, the authors categorized success measures into six main categories: system quality, information quality, utilization, user satisfaction, individual impact, and organizational effect. These areas, which are interrelated and dependent on one another, give a comprehensive view of information system success. The model is meant to guide further research projects. The Technology Acceptance Model emphasizes the fact that ICT by alone cannot provide an improvement in organizational production. Other human qualities like skills, a worker's unique ability, leadership, and an upbeat attitude should be added to it. Therefore, the only way to guarantee an increase in production is by combining these traits with ICT. The definition of human resources management (HRM) was recently updated by Gonzalez et al. (2020) to include a "strategic, integrated, and cohesive approach to the employment, development, and well-being of the people working in businesses." Strategic human resource management, HR processes, corporate responsibility, knowledge management, organizational growth, and resourcing (human resource planning, recruiting and selection, as well as employee remuneration) are some of the topics covered.

22.2.2 Information Systems in HR Management

In general, information systems have a significant influence on human resource management because they change how businesses gather, store, utilize, and distribute information (I. Nikolaou, 2021; Wang & Ma, 2021). The Human Resource Management Information System seeks to improve both the effectiveness of HRM and the quality of work in the public sector. HR quality is a crucial success element for firms in the public sector. The social, economic, technical, political, and legal environments must be examined and taken into consideration when planning human resources for the public sector. Therefore, employees should participate in the definition of strategies and the development of programs to build corporate human capital (World Economic Forum, 2012).

De Alwis et al. (2022) indicate that the mission of the human resources industry is to recruit, choose, inspire, and keep competent workers in the workplace, where technology has changed how businesses manage human resource operations and gather, store, utilize, and communicate information about human resources. Through better recruitment techniques, organizational communication, employee participation, and improved human resources management abilities, information systems have boosted HRM efficiency. The most suitable technical solutions should be used to connect various aspects of human resource management to human capital initiatives (Bhalakrishnan, 2020; Gonzalez et al., 2020; Lousã et al., 2020).

Through the use of ICTs, people's sense of self is increasingly generating a shared sense of experience outside of the bounds of physical location (Rohilla, 2017). Through ICTs, we are exposed to external factors more often and these factors have a significant effect on people's behavior (Gangl et al., 1978). The Information Age has a significant influence on identities and imagination via the media and pictures it produces, which change our lives, communities, countries, and governments. There are constant cultural exchanges between industrialized and developing nations in all directions (Vyzirgiannakis, 2018). The conversations that take place via these channels often reach much larger audiences since they do expand beyond their original medium through other channels. Both in wealthy and developing nations, the information included in internet conversations has the power to go back and forth between the real and virtual worlds (Carli et al., 2019).

Recent empirical data from developing nations, however, revealed that greater HR performance is not always the result of increased ICT investment (Ali Quaosar & Rahman, 2021; Barisic et al., 2019). Many businesses continue to use outdated techniques, and they will not switch to ICTs unless the advantages outweigh the costs of initial investment and ongoing maintenance. The strategic goals should be the main focus of the human resource processes. These strategies culminate in the development of a strategic IT plan, which in turn yields a suitable IT human resource strategic plan (Carli et al., 2019). Therefore, it is still evident that for technology to assist successful management of HRM performance in companies, it must be able to provide access to both written information and, more crucially, knowledge held by people who are the organization's key resources (Koldewijn, 2009; Vyzirgiannakis, 2018). In addition to increasing the visibility and traceability of such information, technology needs to work toward facilitating cooperation and knowledge dissemination among its holders both inside and across enterprises (Bhalakrishnan, 2020; Mitu, 2016).

According to Long (2009), even if there are many reasons why ICT and efficiency do not correlate (including the difficulty of assessing costs and benefits), it is crucial for businesses to fully utilize ICT if they have complementary resources. We think the advantages of using ICT will be larger if it is combined with suitable organizational resources and competencies, notably employees' credentials, proactive direction, and innovative culture, taking use of complementarities.

22.2.3 Role of IT in Efficiency of HR Processes

In the contemporary era, the quick growth of IT has had a significant impact on the quick growth of human resources. Since there are numerous issues confronting the public sector's human resources right now and modern society is defined by a high degree of technological advancement, it is crucial to train public employees on how to utilize the facilities and information technology devices. As a result, one of the most crucial components of all human activity is information technology (Selase, 2018; Vyzirgiannakis, 2018). An environment built on information and real-time communication was made possible by the growth of IT. Automated employee registration has given way to increasingly sophisticate reporting and decision-making processes in personnel information systems. Information and communication technology (ICT), such as the Internet, mobile technology, and new media in human resources, have been shown to facilitate the implementation of an organization's personnel policy (Reija, 2018; Wang & Ma, 2021).

Organizations today realize that using IT is necessary for effective recruiting. Online job boards are being used by businesses to identify the best candidates for available positions. The procedure has been enhanced by the use of the internet since more people are aware of the offer, increasing their chances of being employed as successful employees (Omran & Anan, 2018; Papapolychroniadis et al., 2017). Technology has altered how managers and workers access HR data, assisting employees in all HR operations today, including recruitment, selection, formation and development, and retirement. Due to its complexity, information technology is currently a difficult tool to utilize in human resources, but when used effectively, these kinds of technology may help businesses save time and money while completing tasks (Bulmash, 2009; Nikolaou, 2018).

22.2.3.1 Information Technology in Planning

Bartlett and Bartlett (2013) indicate that when it comes to HR planning, e-HR, especially the features of Employee and Manager Self-Service Applications, has helped in employee data updates, personnel changes, and job requests or applications. This indicates that because workers have the option to update their personal data, HR recordkeeping becomes more accurate and data quality improves (Piabuo et al., 2017; Selase, 2018). A high degree of dedication to converting HRM duties, especially administrative ones, to the electronic form has a large probability of altering the emphasis to one that is more strategically oriented (Johnson & Gueutal, 2017; Mitu, 2016).

The number of businesses embracing E-HRM and the breadth of applications inside firms are both steadily increasing, according to HR specialists. Just recently have businesses begun to employ IT to provide improved HRM services (Bhalakrishnan, 2020). In the past, HR practitioners acted as administrative specialists and employee advocates, but with the implementation of E-HR, HR's emphasis shifted from operational HR to becoming a more strategic partner to the enterprise (Al Qalhati et al., 2020; Indjejikian, 1999). Numerous studies conducted globally have stressed how crucial technology developments are in transforming the HR department's function from one of administrative to one of strategic (Bartlett & Bartlett, 2013; Ekwoaba et al., 2015).

Optimizing the use of web-based, technology-based channels, electronic human resource management (E-HRM) is a way for applying HR methodologies, policies, and practices in enterprises (Calenda, 2016; Mutahi & Busienei, 2015). A portal created by e-HRM technology allows practitioners, staff members, and HR professionals to see, retrieve, and edit data needed for managing HR processes. E-HRM, according to (Khera, 2012), is the use of information technology to support at least two individual or collective actors in collaborating to carry out HRM activities. Surveys reveal that the number of businesses embracing E-HRM is rising, as is the variety of uses for it inside those businesses.

22.2.3.2 ICT-Based Recruitment and Selection and Efficiency of HR Processes in Educational Institutions

One of the aspects of e-HR that is most often mentioned is the practice of online recruiting. Online hiring entails publishing job opportunities on a business website or the website of an online recruiting vendor and allowing applicants to electronically submit their resumes by email or another electronic format (Galanaki, 2002). The prospect of recruiting passive job searchers online has generated a lot of discussion as a novel approach. Online hiring also has significant advantages in terms of cost, time, applicant pool, and response quality (Bulmash, 2009). However, there is always the risk of resume overload, in addition to the doubtful efficacy for senior executive roles and the poor reputation and performance of numerous websites and databases (Faroque, 2016; Mutahi & Busienei, 2015). The sorting and contacting of prospects may both be made better with the help of technology. The Internet may make hiring easier, particularly when there are significant distances involved. For example, online exams and video conferencing have been widely employed in the first phases of the hiring process and have the potential to save both money and time (Piabuo et al., 2017; UNESCO, 2020).

It is projected that modern HR professionals would be more strategic, adaptive, cost-conscious, and customer-focused. Even though it now aspires to incorporate all operational HRM operations, E-HRM first concentrates on the recruiting, selection, compensation, and assessment procedures (Mamoudou & Joshi, 2014; Omran & Anan, 2018). Even though it now aspires to incorporate all operational HRM operations, E-HRM first concentrates on the recruiting, selection, as well as compensation procedures. Nevertheless, the new E-HRM can sometimes be challenging for the HR profession, especially in instances where E-HRM responsibilities are similar to those of traditional HRM, such as creating organizations and jobs for people, acquiring HRs. This however does not take away the fact that IT in is very important boosting employee motivation and maintaining HR processes (*Concept of Information Communication Technology*, 2012).

22.2.3.3 IT in HR Evaluation and Compensation

E-HR is important in evaluating the human resources and enables the completion of the whole performance assessment (PA) online using the company intranet interface. This indicates that the manager and employees are able to electronically submit performance information to the HR department (Ali Quaosar & Rahman, 2021; Fabiana Meijon Fadul, 2019). Despite criticism for the absence of written documentation, this technique lowers paperwork and, if read receipts are utilized for both the supervisor and the supervised, it may significantly cut down on time and expenses for the HR department. Managers may input performance results right away using the self-service tool, and workers can manage their performance objectives, outcomes, and plans on their own HR pages (Indjejikian, 1999; Martin, 1994; Vyzirgiannakis, 2018). Additionally, it may provide managers details on how to perform a PA, the precise standards and benchmarks for a certain job or function, and illustrations and models of successful evaluations (Indjejikian, 1999; Nadarajah et al., 2012).

Mishra and Akman (2010) revealed that information technology is vital in facilitation of human resources rewards. Employee self-service eases the strain on the HR department by allowing workers to electronically input their benefit selection choices. Experience has shown that even when a self-service employee benefits system is put in place, workers may still contact with benefit-related inquiries, bewildered by their options, and unable to comprehend a wider incentives perspective (Alami et al., 2016; Mutahi & Busienei, 2015). Web-delivered employee benefits, on the other hand, are thought to result in significant cost-savings for the HR division if effectively implemented. Through manager self-service, the manager can also accept raises and incentives. The IT applications frequently notify managers of decisions they must make or request that they ratify the employee incentive plans (Bhalakrishnan, 2020; Jahanian et al., 2012).

22.2.4 Related Studies

According to Mutahi and Busienei (2015), E-HRM components have a positive effect on organizational growth. E-recruitment was found to have the greatest impact on organizational growth, followed by e-selection, e-training, e-development, and e-compensation. E-recruitment as well as e-selection of employees in educational institutions has a substantial influence on the development of the institution. Al Shobaki et al. (2017) showed that the main factors influencing the uptake of e-HRM in organizations are majorly the different perceptions of ease of use among employees or management, attitude, as well as communication in the organization.

Shobaki et al. (2017) further revealed that perceived risk, system security, and resource availability have less of an effect on the adoption of e-HRM technology.

According to Faroque (2016), IT is an effective way to characterize a computer system that is used to gather, alter, store, analyze, retrieve, and disseminate data on human resources. It also consists of people, forms, rules, processes, and data in addition to hardware and software. Most HR planning tasks may now be automated, which can benefit organizations. Information technology turns as a very important strategic tool since it collects, manages, and provides information for decision-making. A properly integrated organizational HRIS should interface with other systems, such as the payroll and accounting systems, to facilitate and consequently enhance departmental collaboration. When transmitting information, data security should be assured because HRIS deals with sensitive employee data.

Panayotopoulou et al. (2007) showed that an HRIS has the ability to produce reports, evaluate expenses, discover trends, and compare the organization to other businesses. As new HRIS trends integrate new technology with organizational goals and objectives, they seem to have a significant impact on HR planning. When combined with the HRIS subsystem, the enterprise resource planning system (ERP) gives an organization a definite edge over rivals. HRIS are divided into two categories, "advanced" and "unsophisticated," according to how they are used (Mamoudou & Joshi, 2014; Najeeb, 2013).

According to Mishra and Akman (2010), HRIS has grown in significance for the effective execution of business strategy. Information system strategies may result from in-depth research and careful planning, or they may arise from creative, irrational, or unplanned thinking. The corporate strategy and other internal activities may be in alignment with the HR strategy (Furtmueller et al., 2011; Jahanian et al., 2012). The medium- to long-term strategic objectives of education institutions may be accomplished with the help of HR strategy.

22.3 Methodology

22.3.1 Research Design

A cross-sectional survey research design was used based on a quantitative research methodology. This research design was associated with collected data using quantitative tools and statistically evaluating a particular phenomenon based on current trends, current occurrences, and current interconnection between the different aspects of IT in HR evaluation and compensation, IT-based training and development, ICT-based recruitment and selection, and Information technology in planning. The cross-sectional survey design helped the researcher to generalize the different findings of the study to a larger population education institutions in Greece that provided data about the topic of study.

22.3.2 Target Population

The study targeted the different accessible public limited companies in Greece. The population was based on to establish the suitable sample for the study. The study targeted public limited companies of Greece since this would help to obtain a more representative sample of people with good knowledge on how the various aspects of IT in HR evaluation and compensation, IT-based training and development, ICT-based recruitment and selection, and Information technology in planning.

22.3.3 Sample Size

The study utilized a sample of 120 study participants who were sampled from the different selected professionals in the Greece educational sector.

22.3.4 Sampling Technique

Probability sampling methodologies called stratified and simple random sample were used in the investigation. In this case, the aim sample was obtained by stratified sampling and the final sample was drawn from the strata using a straightforward random sampling technique. The advantage of simple random sampling is that it yields samples that are quite representative of the population. However, working with huge samples might make it time-consuming.

22.3.5 Data Collection

An online questionnaire was used to gather information from the chosen managers, directors, or staff members at the chosen professionals in the Greece educational sector. One of the simplest and most popular methods for collecting data is via a survey questionnaire. This is because it is less expensive since a large number of respondents are surveyed quickly, and it allows respondents to openly express their opinions on delicate subjects without worrying about the researcher's approval or disapproval. The link between the various features of IT in HR evaluation and compensation, IT-based training and development, ICT-based recruitment and selection, and Information technology in planning was studied using an online survey questionnaire.

22.3.6 Data Analysis

For each of the study's questions, frequencies, percentages, standard deviations, and means were used to arrange, categorize, and evaluate the quantitative data scores from the questionnaire. To examine associations with a 99% level of confidence, Pearson's correlation statistics were used. To determine the overall predictive potency of the various independent factors on the study's dependent variable, regression analysis was carried out. The multiple regression model in eq. 1 greatly helped in the general estimation of different predictive values for this study based on the independent variables.

$$Y = \beta_0 + \beta_1 X_1 + \beta_2 X_2 + \beta_3 X_3 + \varepsilon \qquad (22.1)$$

where

Y = Efficiency of HR processes
β_0 = constant (coefficient of intercept)
X_1 = Information technology in HR planning
X_2 = ICT based recruitment and selection
X_3 = IT in HR evaluation and compensation
ε = Represents the error term in the multiple regression model

$\beta 1 \ldots \beta 3$ = represents the independent variables' regression coefficient and their impact on figuring out how much of an impact they have. Based on the assumption that there was no autocorrelation, the error term in this research investigation was assumed to be independent across observations. Therefore, the autocorrelation factor was not taken into account in this research investigation. The study's hypotheses were tested at the 5% level of significance (0.05).

22.3.7 Ethical Considerations

The researcher made sure that respondents gave their informed permission by providing them with information about the study's specifics, after which the researcher evaluated their desire to participate. Additionally, the management of the information gathered from respondents was done while maintaining a high standard of secrecy and privacy.

22.4 Results

This chapter presents the different results of the study and their interpretation.

22 Role of Information Technology in the Efficiency of HR Processes... 379

Table 22.1 Background characteristics of the study participants

Item	Categories	Frequency	Percent (%)
Gender	Male	84	70.0
	Female	36	30.0
Age bracket	26 years and below	10	8.4
	27–37 years	76	63.3
	38–48 years	21	17.5
	49–59 years	13	10.8
Level of education	Certificate	8	6.7
	Diploma	10	8.3
	Bachelor's degree	62	51.7
	Master's	31	25.8
	PhD	9	7.5
Experience	Below 1 year	11	9.2
	Between 2 and 4 years	37	30.9
	Between 4 and 7 years	58	48.3
	Over 7 years	14	11.6
	Total	120	100

Source: Primary data (2023)

22.4.1 Background Characteristics

The results on characteristics of the study participants are presented in Table 22.1.

Results of the study in Table 22.1 revealed that more than half of the participants were males 84 (70%) and only 36 (30.0%) were females. Majority of the study participants (63.3%) were in the age bracket of 27–37 years followed by 15.7% in the bracket of 38–48 years and the least number (4.3%) were on the age bracket of 49–59 years. In regard to the time spent in the education sector, majority (48.3%) had between 4 and 7 years of experience and only 11.6% had over 7 years of experience.

22.4.2 Descriptive Statistics

Descriptive results for each aspect of variables are: Information technology in planning, ICT-based recruitment and selection, and IT in HR evaluation and compensation.

Table 22.2 IT in selection and recruitment in educational institutions

	SD	D	NS	A	SA
IT helps to ensure accuracy of information during selection and recruitment	2.9	10.0	5.7	55.7	25.7
Many educational institutions are struggling to recruit competent staff due to lack of IT professionals and systems	5.7	25.7	14.3	48.6	5.7
Psychometric and personality tests are very important in the recruitment process	5.7	20.0	14.3	52.9	7.1
IT can enhance the job search and application process for candidates and improve the hiring system for a school	2.9	22.9	12.9	55.7	5.7
The fast-paced, fascinating field of IT recruiting links hiring managers with the best technical talent.	2.9	10.0	15.7	61.4	10.0

22.4.2.1 Results for IT in Selection and Recruitment in Educational Institutions

IT in selection and recruitment in educational institutions was studied using five items, and the results on the same are presented in Table 22.2.

The results in Table 22.2 show that majority of the study participants (55.7%) agreed that IT helps to ensure accuracy of information during selection and recruitment. Concerning whether many educational institutions are struggling to recruit competent staff due to lack of IT professionals and systems, 48.6 agreed and only 5.7% strongly disagreed. Also 52.9% agreed that psychometric and personality tests are very important in the recruitment process. Furthermore, 52.9% agreed that IT can enhance the job search and application process for candidates and improve the hiring system for a school. Finally, 55.7% agreed that the fast-paced, fascinating field of IT recruiting links hiring managers with the best technical talent.

22.4.2.2 Results for IT in HR Planning

Results about IT in HR planning are presented in Table 22.3.

The results in Table 22.3 show that 42.9% of the participants disagreed with the notion that the Internet is effectively used in HR planning to organize and manage human resources. It was agreed upon by 41.4% respondents that ICT technologies are used throughout the HR planning process to manage employee retirement, weekly and monthly activities, and other tasks. Also half of the participants (50%) agreed that HR planning enables education institutions to get the right amount of employees and generate the enough revenue for the institution. Furthermore, 48.6% agreed that proper planning for HR processes allows companies to guarantee a steady stream of skilled or competent staff. Finally, more than half of the participants (68.6%) agreed that IT expedites and improves HR planning at educational institutions.

22 Role of Information Technology in the Efficiency of HR Processes... 381

Table 22.3 Results for IT in HR planning

	SD	D	NS	A	SA
Internet is effectively used in HR planning to organize and manage human resources	14.3	42.9	17.1	22.9	2.9
ICT technologies are used throughout the HR planning process to manage employee retirement, weekly and monthly activities, and other tasks	5.7	27.1	18.6	41.4	7.1
HR planning enables education institutions to get the right amount of employees and generate enough revenue for the institution	4.3	14.3	22.9	50.0	8.6
Proper planning for HR processes allows companies to guarantee a steady stream of skilled or competent staff	5.7	25.7	14.3	48.6	5.7
IT expedites and improves HR planning at educational institutions	4.3	1.4	5.7	68.6	20.0

Source: Primary data (2023)

Table 22.4 Results on IT-based HR evaluation and compensation

Statement	SD	D	NS	A	SA
A computerized and systematic evaluation/assessment of worker's performance is essential in educational institutions	0.0	15.7	17.1	55.7	11.4
Computers help in effective recording of salary situation of workers in schools	2.9	8.6	18.6	61.4	8.6
Internet can be used in the general evaluation and reward management in education sector	1.4	21.4	11.4	57.1	8.6
By using technology for pay management, HR and the employee's manager may avoid making impulsive judgments that could be expensive for the business	2.9	5.7	8.6	61.4	21.4
A compensation management system's data allows for a rapid comparison of an employee's pay to that of the rest of his or her team, peers, and industry standards	2.9	30.0	11.4	44.3	11.4
By automatically deducting taxes and benefits from employee pay, an HRIS may help employers save time and reduce the risk of error	1.4	28.6	11.4	50.0	8.6

Source: Primary data (2023)

22.4.2.3 Results on HR Evaluation and Compensation

The results about HR evaluation and compensation are presented in Table 22.4.

The results in Table 22.4, majority of the study participants (55.7%) agreed that a computerized and systematic evaluation/assessment of worker's performance is essential in educational institutions. Concerning whether computers help in effective recording of salary situation of workers in schools, 61.4% agreed and only 8.6% disagreed. Concerning whether internet can be used in the general evaluation and reward management in education sector, 57.1% agreed and only 1.4 strongly disagreed. It was agreed upon by 61.4% of respondents that by using technology for

Table 22.5 Aspects of Efficiency of HR processes in education institutions

Statement	SD	D	NS	A	SA
An HR department plays a significant role in the efficiency process of an education institution	2.9	18.6	28.6	42.9	7.1
Many education institutions are not fully considering the efficiency of their HR processes	5.7	28.6	17.1	43.0	5.6
The methods used for recruitment and retention are changing, along with the understanding that HR employees need to take an active role in retaining students and staff members	1.4	32.9	22.9	35.7	7.1
HR efficiency relates to how well an HR process achieves its objectives in relation to the time, expense, and inputs involved	0.0	7.1	28.6	45.7	18.6
Efficiency relates to the amount of resources used by HR programs, such as cost-per-hire	5.7	22.9	21.4	34.3	15.7

Source: Primary data (2023)

pay management, HR and the employee's manager may avoid making impulsive judgments that could be expensive for the business. Furthermore, 44.3% agreed that a compensation management system's data allows for a rapid comparison of an employee's pay to that of the rest of his or her team, peers, and industry standards. Finally, 50.0% agreed that by automatically deducting taxes and benefits from employee pay, an HRIS may help employers save time and reduce the risk of error.

22.4.2.4 Aspects of Efficiency of HR Processes in Education Institutions

The results about aspects of Efficiency of HR processes in education institutions are presented in Table 22.5.

The results in Table 22.5 show that majority of the respondents (42.9%) agreed that an HR department plays a significant role in the efficiency process of an education institution. Also 43% agreed that many education institutions are not fully considering the efficiency of their HR processes. Furthermore, most respondents (35.7%) agreed that the methods used for recruitment and retention are changing, along with the understanding that HR employees need to take an active role in retaining students and staff members. Concerning whether HR efficiency relates to how well an HR process achieves its objectives in relation to the time, expense, and inputs involved, 45.7% agreed and only 7.1% disagreed. Finally, 34.3% of respondents agreed that "the amount of resources used by HR programs, such as cost-per-hire," constitutes efficiency.

22.4.3 Correlation Analysis

		Efficiency of HR processes in education institutions	IT in HR evaluation and compensation	IT-based training and development	Information technology in HR planning
Efficiency of HR processes in education institutions	Pearson correlation	1	0.250	0.352	0.770
	Sig. (2-tailed)		0.007	0.000	0.000
	N	120	120	120	120
IT in HR evaluation and compensation	Pearson correlation	0.750	1	0.092	0.068
	Sig. (2-tailed)	0.007		0.317	0.461
	N	120	120	120	120
ICT-based recruitment and selection	Pearson correlation	0.452	−0.092	1	0.249
	Sig. (2-tailed)	0.000	0.317		0.006
	N	120	120	120	120
Information technology in HR planning	Pearson correlation	0.770	0.068	0.249	1
	Sig. (2-tailed)	0.000	0.461	0.006	
	N	120	120	120	120

Source: Computed by author using SPSS version 20

The results show a positive correlation between IT in evaluation or compensation and efficiency of HR processes in education institutions ($r = 0.750$), which is significant at 0.05. There was a positive correlation between ICT-based recruitment and selection and efficiency of HR processes in education institutions ($r = 0.452$), significant at 0.05. This shows that schools, universities, or any other education institutions are able to hire competent and skilled staff through utilizing available information systems. Information technology in HR planning gave a positive correlation with efficiency of HR processes in education institutions ($r = 0.770$), showing that utilizing different aspects of IT in human resource planning helps to enhance the different activities performed by HR managers in the education institutions.

22.4.4 Regression Analysis

Regression analysis helped to see how each of the independent variables in this study affects the dependent variable. The outcomes of the regression are shown in Table 22.5 whereby the coefficient of determination (R square) is 0.825, indicating that the independent variables account for 82.5% of efficiency of HR processes. This demonstrates how well this regression model fits the data and how the independent variables account for the data. The findings also demonstrate that the model is fit or globally appropriate based on the fact that the critical value of our F-statistics is substantially higher than that in the table of t-statistics, demonstrating the model's global suitability.

Coefficients						
		Unstandardized coefficients		Standardized coefficients	t	Sig.
Model		B	Std. error	Beta		
1	(Constant)	3.734	0.176		21.244	0.000
	IT in HR evaluation and compensation	0.184	0.059	0.091	3.102	0.002
	ICT-based recruitment and selection	0.380	0.062	0.203	6.145	0.014
	Information technology in planning	0.958	0.050	0.593	19.063	0.000
	R-square	0.825				
	Adjusted R Square	0.820				
	Sig.	0.000				
	n	120				

Source: Computed by author using SPSS version 20

The regression table illustrates how IT in HRM can enhance the efficiency of HR processes. Concerning evaluation and compensation, a unit change in IT usage results in an improvement in efficiency of the HR processes evaluation and compensation by 0.184, which is substantial at the 5% level. This is due to the fact that a computerized method of review reduces partiality and tribalism in evaluation since well-kept records are readily analyzed, and choices can be made fast. IT in HR evaluation and compensation is also significantly related to Efficiency of HR processes ($P = 0.002 < 0.05$) which led to the acceptance if hypothesis one (*H1*) that, *Information technology in planning positively influences efficiency of HR processes in educational institutions.*

HR is much more effective when they utilize an online platform for recruiting. It enables the HR managers in education institutions to have access to the greatest job candidates and assists them in choosing and hiring the best employees. Because of this, the link is substantial at the 1% level; as a result, a change of one unit in the usage of an online platform for recruiting would result in a change of 0.380 units in HR efficiency. Therefore, hypothesis H2 was accepted, indicating that *there is a significant relationship between ICT-based recruitment and selection and efficiency of HR processes in educational institutions.*

The use of computers to schedule operations on a weekly basis ensures effective follow-up and overall HR efficiency. Consequently, a unit change in the use of IT in HR planning causes an improvement in efficiency of HR processes by 0.958 points, and this equally significant at the 5% level of significance ($P = 0.000$). This led to acceptance of hypothesis H4 that *IT in HR evaluation and compensation positively influences efficiency of HR processes in educational institutions.*

22.5 Discussion

This study assessed the role of Information technology in the efficiency of HR processes in educational institutions. Even the most crucial source of an organization, its human resources have not been impacted by the influence of Information technology's penetration into every aspect of the business today, which has led to growth and productivity. Organizations' relative effectiveness has decreased as a result of Information technology; thus, their resources, particularly their human resources, should be extensive and complete. By using this approach, it is feasible to provide workers more power and all the knowledge they need to accomplish their duties or work for the firm to the best of their abilities (Alami et al., 2016). The need for coordinated planning in efficiently using human resources as the most important strategic resource of any organization, creating appropriate information system, on the other hand, calls for expanding the activities and duties of managers in the field of human resource management. These activities also interact continuously (Jahanian et al., 2012; Nadarajah et al., 2012). This information is current, and it has made the system necessary in big businesses. Information technology, in the eyes of human resource managers, facilitates decision-making that results in the success of the whole business and aids in its expansion and productivity. Accordingly, many facets of human resource management (recruitment, employment, promotion, education, and development) may make use of Information technology, or an electronic HRMS (Gardner et al., 2003; Mitu, 2016). Even today, information technology has impacted every aspect of the business, including its most valuable resource: its people resources. All firms now have a thorough and full understanding of their resources, notably their human resources, thanks to informed information technology. On the other hand, many theorists consider the effect of Information technology on human resource management to be the shift in an organization's approach to human resource management and its alignment with the organization's strategic objectives (Nadarajah et al., 2012). The utilization of fresh and applied information is the axis of human resource growth, but information in a logical process known as information technology may build and develop significant capacities in human resource support. IT improves efficiency of human resource management and adapts it to the organization's strategy in order to boost the effect of technology, the degree of acceptance, and the outcome of innovation and change (Nikolaou, 2018; Wang & Ma, 2021).

The process of selecting teachers and professional staff is changing, with a shift from interviews to evidence-based practices. There has been a significant rise in the use of psychometric and personality tests as part of the recruitment process (Al Shobaki et al., 2017; Jahanian et al., 2012). In educational institutions, where these tests are increasingly being used in selection and recruitment, there is an opportunity for learning through self-reflection on the part of all stakeholders involved. Discussions around technology-enhanced assessments and their effectiveness across contexts can be informed by evidence-based practices in selection (Calenda, 2016). Many large corporations have vast infrastructures that rely upon IT as an essential part of their operations. Under these circumstances, it is crucial that HR management evaluations make sense in light of the corporation's investments and resources assigned to these areas (Lousã et al., 2020; Sirajuddin & P, 2021). In spite of this, many companies still employ an outdated evaluation process that relies heavily on subjective factors such as personality assessments or performance-based ratings (Furtmueller et al., 2011; Gonzalez et al., 2020). By turning to high-tech tools such as cloud software, recruitment prediction systems and more, HR professionals can be better able to assess and integrate technology into their compensation packages for its employees with greater accuracy and efficiency than ever before (Lousã et al., 2020). It is still clear that for technology to assist the efficient management of HRM performance in businesses, it must be able to allow access to both written information and, more crucially, knowledge held by people who represent the organization's primary resources (Alami et al., 2016; Piabuo et al., 2017). The advantages of IT in HR processes will be larger if ICT is utilized in conjunction with the appropriate organizational resources and skills, notably employees' credentials, proactive direction, and creative culture, taking use of complementarities (Al Qalhati et al., 2020; Piabuo et al., 2017).

22.6 Conclusion

The study established the level to which IT helps to improve the efficiency of different HR processes in education institutions. The dependability and stability of the organization's human resources are increased through valuable information. Information technology is being used in companies to gather, process, and store information. In the past, there have been more papers with information accessible. As a result, it could only be disclosed and supplied to a certain individual at one location. Since planning, organizing, leading, and controlling are managerial tasks that are essential to an organization's success, and carrying out these tasks effectively also requires access to the right information, an organization cannot advance without information tools and without developing the skills required to use Information technology. By using Information technology in education institutions, it is possible to provide workers more power and equip them with accurate information that will enable them to carry out the organization's tasks and function in the most effective manner. Finally, it can be said that the enormous process of Information technology necessitates new human resource management techniques that require individuals to be thoroughly knowledgeable about information systems and how to best utilize them. Additionally, as information technologies adapt to new and flexible structures, the environment will experience significant changes in their traditional structures.

22.6.1 Recommendations

The following recommendations are given in light of prior debates and the research's findings:

It is very important for managers in education institutions to change the cultural and social background of their institutions before introducing Information technology into all fields of public employment via public planning and private employment through the media, education, and other professions.

Eliminating unfavorable Information technology attitudes impacts the development and effectiveness of companies via the use of human resources in the public realm of work and employment through cultural planning by public and private organizations.

Since this study concentrated on the general efficacy impacts of Information technology on human resource management especially in education institutions, it is very important to do a comparable study that rather focuses on Information technology practitioners.

22.6.2 Areas for Future Research

Future research in this field should concentrate on a range of topics, since this study lays the groundwork for such research. The function of E-HRM in companies should first and foremost be studied in more detail with a bigger sample size. They also recommend that future researchers use quantitative methodologies to support their studies.

References

Al Qalhati, N., Karim, A. M., Al Mughairi, B., Al Hilali, K., & Hossain, M. I. (2020). Technology and HR practices in educational sector in Sharqiya Governate of Oman. *International Journal of Academic Research in Business and Social Sciences, 10*(10). https://doi.org/10.6007/ijarbss/v10-i10/7956

Al Shobaki, M. J., Naser, S. S. A., El Talla, S. A., Amuna, Y. M. A., Abu, Y. M., & Hrm, A. (2017). HRM University systems and their impact on e-HRM. *Hal.Archives-Ouvertes.Fr, 6*(3), 5–27. https://hal.archives-ouvertes.fr/hal-01567728/

Alami, R., Hashemi Gorji, O., Shokri Asrami, M., Rasouli Saravi, H., Jafari Soteh, M., & Rajabi Ahangari, F. (2016). The role of information technology (IT) in development and increase of the efficiency of human resources. *Journal of Social Science Studies, 3*(2), 188. https://doi.org/10.5296/jsss.v3i2.8602

Ali Quaosar, G. M. A., & Rahman, M. S. (2021). Human resource information systems (HRIS) of developing countries in 21st century: Review and prospects. *Journal of Human Resource and Sustainability Studies, 09*(03), 470–483. https://doi.org/10.4236/jhrss.2021.93030

Barisic, A. F., Poor, J., & Pejic Bach, M. (2019). The intensity of human resources information systems usage and organizational performance. *Interdisciplinary Description of Complex Systems, 17*(3), 586–597. https://doi.org/10.7906/indecs.17.3.15

Bartlett, B. J. E., & Bartlett, M. E. (2013). Integrating a human resource information system : A module with case. *Society for Human Resource Management, 42.* https://www.shrm.org/academicinitiatives/universities/teachingresources/Documents/08-0882_Integrating_HR_Info_Sys.pdf

Bhalakrishnan, H. (2020). *A study on performance appraisal of management teachers., 19*(3), 1–14. https://doi.org/10.17051/ilkonline.2020.03.735581

Bulmash, J. (2009). *Human resource management and technology.* Managing Human Resources.

Calenda, D. (2016). *Case studies in the international recruitment of nurses: Promising practices in recruitment among agencies in the United Kingdom, India, and The Philippines edited by Davide Calenda.* In International Labour Organization. www.ilo.org/publns

Carli, G., Maria, D., & Benfatto, C. (2019). Libera Università degli Studi Sociali human resource information systems and the performance of the human resource function. *Concept of Information Communication Technology, 1997,* 1–94.

De Alwis, A. C., Andrlić, B., & Šostar, M. (2022). The influence of E-HRM on modernizing the role of HRM context. *Economies, 10*(8), 1–13. https://doi.org/10.3390/economies10080181

Ekwoaba, J. O., Ugochukwu, U., & Ikeije, N. U. (2015). The impact of recruitment and selection criteria on organizational performance. *Global Journal of Human Resource Management, 3*(2), 22–33. https://doi.org/10.1017/CBO9781107415324.004

Fadul, F. M. (2019). *Artificial intelligence (AI) in employee selection: How algorithm-based decision aids influence recruiters' decision-making in resume screening.* August.

Faroque, O. (2016). Usage and acceptance level of ICT in human resource management and development by private and government institutions in Bangladesh. *The International Journal of Business & Management, 4*(6), 248–257.

Furtmueller, E., Wilderom, C., & Tate, M. (2011). Managing recruitment and selection in the digital age: E-HRM and resumes. *Human Systems Management, 30*(4), 243–259. https://doi.org/10.3233/HSM-2011-0753

Galanaki, E. (2002), The decision to recruit online: a descriptive study. *Career Development International, 7*(4), 243–251. https://doi.org/10.1108/13620430210431325

Gangl, K., Hofmann, E., Hartl, B., & Kirchler, E. (1978). E-HR adoption and the role of HRM: Evidence from Greece. September, 1–33.

Gardner, S. D., Lepak, D. P., & Bartol, K. M. (2003). Virtual HR: The impact of information technology on the human resource professional. *Journal of Vocational Behavior, 63*(2), 159–179. https://doi.org/10.1016/S0001-8791(03)00039-3

Gonzalez, R., Gasco, J., & Llopis, J. (2020). Information and communication technologies and human resources in hospitality and tourism. *International Journal of Contemporary Hospitality Management, 32*(11), 3545–3579. https://doi.org/10.1108/IJCHM-04-2020-0272

Hassanzada, F., & Chatterjee Rao, A. (2020). Information technology impact on human resource management from growth and effectiveness points of view. *European Journal of Molecular & Clinical Medicine, 7*(6), 2020.

Indjejikian, R. J. (1999). Performance evaluation and compensation research: An agency perspective. *Accounting Horizons, 13*(2), 147–157. https://doi.org/10.2308/acch.1999.13.2.147

Jahanian, R., Nav, Z. N., & Asadi, A. (2012). The impact of information technology and communication training on the performance of human resources in educational organizations. *World Applied Sciences Journal, 16*(6), 850–855. https://www.idosi.org/wasj/wasj16(6)12/13.pdf

Johnson, R. D., & Gueutal, H. G. (2017). *SHRM Foundation's Effective Practice Guidelines Series The Use of E-HR and HRIS in Organizations Transforming HR Through Technology.* www.shrm.org/foundation.

Kalogiannidis, S., Kalfas, D., & Chatzitheodoridis, F. (2022a). The impact of collaborative communication on the physical distribution service quality of soft drinks: A case study of beverage manufacturing companies in Greece. *Beverages, 8*, 47. https://doi.org/10.3390/beverages8030047

Kalogiannidis, S., Loizou, E., Melfou, K., & Papaevangelou, O. (2022b). Assessing relationship between entrepreneurship education and business growth. In P. Sklias, P. Polychronidou, A. Karasavvoglou, V. Pistikou, & N. Apostolopoulos (Eds.), *Business development and economic governance in southeastern Europe. Springer proceedings in business and economics.* Springer. https://doi.org/10.1007/978-3-031-05351-1_10,183-194

Kalogiannidis, S., Savvidou, S., Papaevangelou, O., & Pakaki, F. (2022c). Role of management in optimising the quality of education in educational Organisations. In N. Tsounis & A. Vlachvei (Eds.), *Advances in quantitative economic research. ICOAE 2021. Springer proceedings in business and economics.* Springer. https://doi.org/10.1007/978-3-030-98179-2_21

Kalogiannidis, S., Kontsas, S., Konteos, G., & Chatzitheodoridis, F. (2022d). Investigation of the redesigning process of the development identity of a local government regional unit (City): A case study of Kozani regional unit in Greece. In N. Tsounis & A. Vlachvei (Eds.), *Advances in quantitative economic research. ICOAE 2021. Springer proceedings in business and economics.* Springer. https://doi.org/10.1007/978-3-030-98179-2_20

Kalogiannidis, S., Kalfas, D., Chatzitheodoridis, F., & Kontsas, S. (2022e). The impact of digitalization in supporting the performance of circular economy: A case study of Greece. *Journal of Risk and Financial Management, 15*(8), 349. https://doi.org/10.3390/jrfm15080349

Kanungo, R. N., & Mendonca, M. (1988). Evaluating employee compensation. *California Management Review, 31*(1), 23–39. https://doi.org/10.2307/41166536

Khera, D. S. N. (2012). Human resource information system and its impact on human resource planning: A perceptual analysis of information technology companies. *IOSR Journal of Business and Management, 3*(6), 6–13. https://doi.org/10.9790/487x-0360613

Koldewijn, R. (2009). The role of IT in HR policies convergence, divergence, crossvergence: A process model based on evidence from the Middle East. *August*.

Long, Y. (2009). The impact of information technology on the HR function transformation. *Business Administration HRM*, 1–81.

Lousã, E. P., Rodrigues, A. C., & Pinto, E. M. (2020). How do HRM practices relate to innovation performance in information technology firms. *IBIMA Business Review, 2020*, 1. https://doi.org/10.5171/2020.306950

Mamoudou, S., & Joshi, G. (2014). Impact of information technology in human resources management. *Global Journal of Business Management and Information Technology., 4*(1), 33–41.

Martin, P. (1994). The use of performance appraisal and compensation systems in total quality management.

Mishra, A., & Akman, I. (2010). Information technology in human resource management: An empirical assessment. *Public Personnel Management, 39*(3), 271–290. https://doi.org/10.1177/009102601003900306

Mitu, C. P. (2016). Implementating information technology in E-human resource management. *Ovidius University Annals: Economic Sciences Series, XVI*(1), 386–390.

Mutahi, N., & Busienei, J. R. (2015). Effect of human resource management practices on performance of public universities in Kenya. *International Journal of Economics, Commerce and Management, III*(10), 696–736.

Nadarajah, S., Kadiresan, V., Kumar, R., Kamil, N. N. A., & Yusoff, Y. M. (2012). The relationship of HR practices and job performance of academicians towards career development in Malaysian private higher institutions. *Procedia – Social and Behavioral Sciences, 57*, 102–118. https://doi.org/10.1016/j.sbspro.2012.09.1163

Najeeb, A. Z. (2013). *The impact of training and information and communication technology on employees performance: An empirical study on pharmaceutical manufacturing companies in Amman*. Middle East University. https://pdfs.semanticscholar.org/8cfc/5ecb0bc4626593b8b9d529861a277863cbf2.pdf

Nikolaou, I. (2021). What is the role of technology in recruitment and selection? *Spanish Journal of Psychology, 24*(February). https://doi.org/10.1017/SJP.2021.6

Nikolaou, P. (2018). Munich personal RePEc archive effective strategies for human resource management in educational organizations. Conflict management case studies effective strategies for human resource management in educational organizations. Conflict management case studies. *Journal of Contemporary Education, Theory & Research, 2*(2), 30–34.

Omran, K., & Anan, N. (2018). Studying the impact of using E-HRM on the effectiveness of HRM practices: An exploratory study for the internet service providers (ISP) in Egypt. *International Journal of Academic Research in Business and Social Sciences, 8*(4), 454–486. https://doi.org/10.6007/ijarbss/v8-i4/4026

Panayotopoulou, L., Vakola, M., & Galanaki, E. (2007). E-HR adoption and the role of HRM: Evidence from Greece. *Personnel Review, 36*(2), 277–294. https://doi.org/10.1108/00483480710726145

Papapolychroniadis, I., Rossidis, I., & Aspridis, G. (2017). Comparative analysis of recruitment systems in the public sector in Greece and Europe: Trends and outlook for staff selection systems in the Greek public sector. *Academic Journal of Interdisciplinary Studies, 6*(1), 21–30. https://doi.org/10.5901/ajis.2017.v6n1p21

Piabuo, S. M., Piendiah, N. E., Njamnshi, N. L., & Tieguhong, P. J. (2017). The impact of ICT on the efficiency of HRM in Cameroonian enterprises: Case of the Mobile telephone industry. *Journal of Global Entrepreneurship Research, 7*(1), 1–18. https://doi.org/10.1186/s40497-017-0063-5

Reija, O. (2018). New technology-based recruitment methods CORE view metadata, citation and similar papers at CORE. *May*

Rohilla, J. (2017). Role of information technology in human resource management. *International Journal of Advance Research, Ideas and Innovations in Technology, 3*(2), 566–569.

Selase, A. E. (2018). The impact of recruitment and selection criteria on organizational performance. GN Bank, Greater Accra region of Ghana as the Mirror. *Journal of Public Administration and Governance, 8*(3), 283. https://doi.org/10.5296/jpag.v8i3.13637

Sirajuddin, M., & P, J. (2021). Information technology and human resources management: An overview of developing countries. *Helix, 11*(2), 1–5. https://doi.org/10.29042/2021-11-2-1-5

UNESCO. (2020). The role of education management information systems in supporting progress towards SDG 4 recent trends and international experiences.

Vyzirgiannakis, D. (2018). Public sector e-recruitment practices in Greece: The case of the Supreme Council for Civil Personnel Selection (Asep) Website. *SSRN Electronic Journal.*, September. https://doi.org/10.2139/ssrn.3119937

Wang, J., & Ma, H. (2021). Application of information technology in human resource management. *Journal of Physics: Conference Series, 1881*(2), 1034–1038. https://doi.org/10.1088/1742-6596/1881/2/022091

World Economic Forum. (2012). *The global information technology report 2012 living in a hyperconnected world.* In Forum American Bar Association.

Chapter 23
US Museums: Digitization, Social Media Engagement, and Revenue Diversification in the Pandemic

Angela Besana, Martha Friel, Enrico Giorgio Domenico Crisafulli, and Cristina Rossi

Abstract During the pandemic, US museums had to cope with stringency and lockdown. The impact of the pandemic was very different in the US states as for timing and policies, and the cultural and creative industries were tremendously affected.

The sustainability of museums was granted by their digitization as for contents, communication, social media marketing, and fundraising. Digitization became a crucial factor in the development of activities inside and outside museums. Information Technology (IT) was accentuated, and the effort was reinforced to adapt and advance offline collections and exhibitions to virtual audiences, whose profiling can today better framed thanks to big data and artificial intelligence. Accounting of expenses and revenues changed, as well as the approach to bidirectional and social media networking and engagement.

Considering a very deep analysis of the academic literature about digitization in museums, the aim of the paper is the regression of accounting data of 2020s 990 Forms for revenues (contributions and program service), advertising expense, fundraising, and IT ones, so that, thanks a stepwise, multiple, and linear regression, it can be detected how much communication efforts and concerning expenses impacted on revenues in such an extraordinary contingency. Results provide evidence of the highest and positive correlation between contributions and IT expense as well as program service revenues. With the approach of behavioral economics, the focus on some case histories will disclose how much the digitization changed relationships with visitors thanks to edutainment and social media.

A. Besana (✉) · C. Rossi
Department of Business, Law, Economics and Consumer Behaviour "Carlo A. Ricciardi", IULM University, Milan, Italy
e-mail: angela.besana@iulm.it; cristina.rossi26@studenti.iulm.it

M. Friel · E. G. D. Crisafulli
Department of Humanities, IULM University, Milan, Italy
e-mail: martha.friel@iulm.it; enricogiorgiodomenico.crisafulli@studenti.iulm.it

© The Author(s), under exclusive license to Springer Nature Switzerland AG 2024
N. Tsounis, A. Vlachvei (eds.), *Applied Economic Research and Trends*, Springer Proceedings in Business and Economics,
https://doi.org/10.1007/978-3-031-49105-4_23

Keywords US art museums · Pandemic · Digitization · Marketing · Fundraising · Social media · Performances · Behavioral economics

23.1 US Museums in a Turbulent *Landscape*

The pandemic was a *trauma* for the cultural and creative industries worldwide. Reaching and engaging new audiences has been a real challenge for galleries, museums, libraries, and archives. Museums have always been a place for visitors to come in touch with artworks. Due to the pandemic and prevention measures, many museums had to close, reinventing their identity as hybrid entities between the real and the online world (Sweeney & Dressel, 2022).

Born mainly as a method for preserving and making artwork and artifacts available online for the public and the next generations, digitization has also acquired the significant role of creating a link between cultural entities and the public, a role that has reached a relevant boost during the pandemic, as also underlined by UNESCO that has defined the growing importance of digital technology in cultural institutions (UNESCO, 2021).

In fact, digitization has become a crucial factor in the development of activities inside and outside museums. Many digital experiences, such as virtual tours and online activities, have been realized to engage the public in innovative ways. Only to quote some examples between hundreds of museums around the world that allow following virtual tours of their collections: in the USA, there is the Smithsonian National Museum of Natural History, the Metropolitan Museum of Art, the Guggenheim, and the MoMA in New York, and the J. Paul Getty Museum in Los Angeles.

Also, social media platforms have become increasingly important: Facebook, Twitter, and Instagram are increasingly used to promote museums' activities and engage the public in fundraising and crowdfunding campaigns. Counting all the social media pages, the USA has the most followed museum in the world, the Museum of Modern Art, with more than 13 million followers around the world and distributed on different platforms, such as TikTok, Instagram, and Facebook. In the top ten list of Museums per number of followers, the USA counts the Metropolitan Museum of Art of New York, with 10.4 million, second-ranked museum worldwide, and the Guggenheim, with almost seven million, fifth-ranked worldwide (Dawson, 2022).

As quoted by Catton and Smith (2021), the French former Ministry of Culture André Marlaux's idea of a "museum without a wall," theorized in 1947, could be the origin of a new concept for what it is called "museum." Thanks to new technologies, virtual exhibitions have taken place during the pandemic and they are still going on, allowing both the availability of works of art online and the engagement of the online public. In this sense, it can be said that the pandemic has contributed to developing a new idea of participation in cultural heritage, which can be literally co-created by the public according to their expectations, experiences, tastes, and needs.

This idea of participative culture is not new, and it was shown since the 2010s how Web 2.0 has accelerated and facilitated the contributions made by users in designing encyclopedic collaborative projects, non-profit crowdsourcing projects, and sharing knowledge or digital content (Giaccardi, 2012). This process has been increasingly developed, and in Web 4.0, users can experience immersive works of art and museum tours.

Previous studies had underlined how museums have been increasingly using digital technologies to reach new audiences and create more engaging and personalized visitor experiences (Allen-Greil et al., 2011), as well as the potential for increased access and engagement with collections, while also noting challenges related to funding, sustainability, and preservation (Manžuch et al., 2005).

American museums have faced a challenging problem during the pandemic since they had to intensify revenue diversification to survive and thrive. They had also adapted to new revenue channels, innovative platforms such as Kickstarter (Cobley et al., 2020; Reynolds, 2020).

The focus on US museums depends on their mature adoption of digitization and social media. Above all, after the full recovery from previous crisis, the pandemic differently impacted as concerns time and geography of US museums, so that they represent a multifaceted sample, which has not been so far investigated for revenue diversification and ICT expense in the pandemic. As this paper will show, many strategies have been developed thanks to digitization during the pandemic, which had represented a significant challenge on one side and an accelerant for finding new solutions in participative initiatives and revenue diversification on the other.

Through a very deep analysis of the very latest academic literature, the second paragraph will describe how much digital technologies affected the supply and the communication in museums, above all social media marketing and fundraising. Museum sustainability has been granted by this strategic (r)evolution, and digital technologies allow museums to collect big data, whose strategic implications and impact on economic performances are still to be wholly detected thanks to the algorithms of artificial intelligence. As a matter of fact, as long as digital technologies revolutionize their cultural and creative supply, pricing can change, and additional revenues can derive. The third paragraph will be the empirical reply to the research question about how much the pandemic was a constraint for US museums to develop digitization and a different communication, inclusive of online marketing and fundraising thanks to social media and IT, Information Technology (IT). This constraint impacted on their economics performances. For the sample of the 100 biggest US Art museums, the highest share of their revenues being contributions, it will result that 2020 contributions are mostly connected to the IT expense. The significant, multiple, linear, and stepwise regression will give evidence of coefficients for program service expense, fundraising expense, and advertising expense, too. The fourth paragraph will explore examples of best practices for some of these museums, whose managers support digital edutainment to share positive experiences, relief, well-being in social media networking, and the maintenance of the status-quo of museums as engaging and stimulating locations, offline, and online ones. The approach of these activities can be framed according to behavioral economics.

23.2 Marketing, Fundraising, and Social Media for Museums Sustainability

Due to rapid technological advancements, museums have undergone significant transformations in the past few decades. The rise of digitization has impacted how museums preserve and exhibit their collections, their marketing and management strategies, and revenue generation streams.

On the one hand, considering outward-oriented digitization, this can enrich museums" service offerings using a human-centered design approach to improve accessibility and encourage participation from relevant constituencies (Garcia Carrizosa et al., 2020; Palumbo, 2022).

Digital technology has become an integral part of the museum experience today, with institutions worldwide using it to enhance online and on-site visitor engagement, improve accessibility, and streamline operations (Giannini & Bowen, 2019; Hossaini & Blankenberg, 2017). Many studies have analyzed how introducing technological tools in museums, such as touchscreens, augmented reality, and interactive exhibits, can enhance visitor experiences and increase engagement with museum collections (Pantano, 2011; Jung & tom Dieck, 2017; Errichiello et al., 2019). Literature has proven how augmented reality (AR) and virtual reality (VR) in museums can significantly enhance visitor experiences and generate interest in the institution (Chung et al., 2015; Kim, 2018). By using these technologies, museums" educational and transformational purposes can also be merged with entertainment activities, leading to richer and more meaningful exchanges with visitors and increasing their organizational appeal to current and prospective customers (Palumbo, 2022; Trunfio et al., 2022).

Moreover, digital technologies can provide incredible opportunities for cultural institutions to make accessible their collections and exhibitions for people who may not be able to physically visit the museum due to distance, cost, or other constraints. This has led to museums adopting digital strategies such as virtual exhibitions and online collections to reach wider audiences (Proctor, 2011).

On the communication front too, museums have shifted from traditional, passive strategies toward more proactive, audience-centered approaches (Falk & Dierking, 2016). In the last two decades, museums have increased their use of social media platforms to engage with audiences, sharing images, videos, and other content related to their collections and exhibitions. The outcomes of those strategies have been widely analyzed by academic literature, suggesting that museums can leverage user-generated content and social sharing to optimize their online presence creating interest and engagement (Marty, 2008; Vassiliadis & Belenioti, 2017).

In this framework, social media platforms have become integral to museum marketing and fundraising efforts, providing new avenues for audience engagement and community building (Fletcher & Lee, 2012; Vassiliadis & Belenioti, 2017). User-generated content, such as visitor reviews and social media posts, has been shown to impact museum attendance, reputation, and museum strategies (Waller & Waller, 2019; Zafiropoulos et al., 2015). Furthermore, social media influencers can significantly promote museum exhibitions and events (Trombin & Veglianti, 2020).

On the other hand, when looking at inward-oriented digitization, many opportunities emerge here too. Digitization has changed how museums collect and manage data for operational efficiency, leading to more informed decision-making and personalized visitor experiences.

Bertacchini and Morando (2013), for example, highlighted the challenges and strategies for museums in managing the access and use of their digital collections showing how the shift to digitization and digital networks transforms the way physical collections are produced and managed by museums and users. More recently, studies have highlighted the interesting prospects of using artificial intelligence (AI). AI can be used to help museums both for enhancing visitor experiences (Ioannakis et al., 2020) and to catalog their collections more efficiently and accurately. By analyzing images and other data, AI algorithms can help identify and classify objects, reducing the need for manual cataloguing and freeing up time for curators to focus on other tasks (Villaespesa & Murphy, 2021).

Many museums have invested on all these fronts and have been proactive for decades before 2020. However, there is no doubt now that the COVID-19 pandemic has accelerated the adoption of digital technology even in those museums, which were further behind due to their size or lack of resources.

Forced to close their doors to the public for extended periods, museums turned to digital technologies to continue engaging with their audiences and sharing their collections (de las Heras-Pedrosa et al., 2022; Raimo et al., 2022). Many museums created virtual exhibitions that could be accessed online, allowing visitors to explore their collections from the comfort and safety of their homes. They began hosting online events, such as lectures, workshops, and performances, providing new ways for audiences to interact with and learn about their collections; museums also began offering virtual tours of their galleries and exhibits, providing an immersive experience that could be accessed from anywhere in the world (UNESCO, 2021).

The COVID-19 pandemic has therefore accelerated the digital transformation of museums, forcing them to adapt to new ways of engaging with audiences and sharing their collections.

Interestingly, museums have also reinforced and multiplied online revenue generation strategies in this process, such as e-commerce, crowdfunding, and digital membership programs (Alshawaaf & Lee, 2021; Borowiecki & Navarrete, 2017; Navarrete, 2013).

Already in 2008, Marty highlighted the importance of museums embracing digitization not only for operational efficiency but also for survival in a highly competitive cultural market. In 2011 Proctor (Proctor, 2011) highlighted the potential of digital merchandising as a new source of income. Moreover, digital memberships and subscriptions were also analyzed as becoming increasingly popular in generating recurring revenue (Kidd, 2011) and crowdfunding, which leverages online platforms to raise funds from many donors, also emerged as an interesting fundraising tool for museums (Riley-Huff et al., 2016).

The pandemic has prompted museums to better focus on these strategies and to review them, thanks to an update and strengthening of digital strategies. Many museums have organized themselves to capitalize on the virtual exhibition trend, offering online access to exclusive content for a fee. Recent research has also shown how loyalty and identification derived from such digital experiences and social media activities cause tech-savvy visitors to be more willing to support digital museums economically (Zollo et al., 2022).

However, digitization also presents several challenges for museums, which often struggle with issues such as funding, skills, and infrastructure when implementing digital strategies. The pandemic has demonstrated the need for museums to promote digital literacy skills, increase their investment in digital technologies, and develop the digital strategies they will need to respond to future crises and to survive in an increasingly competitive environment (Marty & Buchanan, 2022).

Digital technologies, therefore, are reshaping the museum value chain, offering numerous opportunities to engage with audiences, enhance visitor experiences, improve primary production processes, and generate additional revenues (Simone et al., 2021).

This paper contributes to the current knowledge as for the research of economic performances of digitization thanks to the analysis of revenues and costs, among them IT expense, fundraising, and advertising ones. The current gap in the field is the measurement of performances, though the accounting rows can only give evidence of revenues and expenses, while time-consuming digitization and social media cannot find their whole metrics in accounting. Besides, a new metrics will hopefully match economic data, IT, and social media effectiveness thanks to new parameters and feedbacks.

23.3   Revenues and IT Expense in the Pandemic. The Sample of US Art Museums, the Method, and Results

If turbulent times are a constraint, they can commit museums to revolutionize their supply and communication thanks to IT and social media. Strategic implications for marketing and fundraising can be multiple as previously emphasized. Pricing of new activities can generate additional revenues. Fundraising can evolve thanks to digital memberships and platforms. In 2020, how much were revenues of US museums affected by information technology efforts and expense? Can expense and revenue accounting give evidence of the US museums digital revolution?

Multiple data were selected and collected at www.guidestar.org and https://www.causeiq.com/ from 990 Forms as regards the "Art Museum" activity and for the US biggest museums according to 2020s Total Revenues. A second selection criterion was the relevance of the Guidestar metrics according to platinum, gold, silver, and bronze seals. The seals metrics can rank nonprofit organizations for increasing transparency, and it is not only a matter of sharing (with different stakeholders) accounting data from assets to revenues and gains but also the availability and disclosure of performances of websites and social media.

The here investigated sample refers to the biggest (for total revenues) 100 US Art Museums, 95% with previously mentioned Guidestar seals in 2020. As reported in the 990 Form Glossary, revenues can include *Direct public support*: contributions, gifts, grants, and bequests received directly from the public. It refers to amounts received from individuals, trusts, corporations, estates, foundations, public charities or raised by an outside professional fundraiser, and *Government contributions or grants* which are payments from the Government to a nonprofit organization to further the organization's public programs. Direct public support, Government contributions, and grants are summed up, to estimate 2020s *Contributions*. The other main revenue category is *Program service revenues* which are fees and other monies received by an organization for services rendered.

If contributions (69.40%) and program service revenues (7.77%) are more than 75% of the sample revenues, ancillary revenues are derived from *Interest on savings and temporary cash investments* (the amount of interest income from savings and temporary cash), *Dividends and interests from securities* (the income from equities and securities), *Rental income* (net of costs) which are received from investment property, and *Other investment income*. These categories are summed up in the *Investment Income*. The total amount of Investment Income is 877,838,357 $ in 2020.

Marginal revenues can include revenues from *Fundraising (Special) Events* (net of costs), revenues from *Sales of assets* (items owned by the organization) and *Sales of inventory*; and *other revenues* (revenues not previously counted). These categories are usually summed up in *Other Revenues*.

The revenue diversification will be here investigated only for the following main categories: *Contributions* with the target of the willingness-to-donate and *Program Service Revenue* with the target of willingness-to-pay.

Expense categories include *Program Service Expense* related to the production of the core business, *Fundraising Expense, Management and General Expense*, and miscellaneous costs that are not related to previous accounting lines. According to 990 Form standards, the *IT, Information Technology Expense,* the *Fundraising expense,* and the *Advertising* expense can be separately reported and counted from any other expense.

Next to revenue and expense categories, the *(Net) Gain or Loss of the year* is the difference—positive or negative—between revenues and costs. Though 50 museums are affected by a loss in 2020, the net gain of the whole sample is 440,123,994 $. *Net Assets* and *Total assets* are not deeply investigated and commented here. These data are here important to signal the size of the sample, though the analysis will be concentrated on revenues and expenses. Their total amounts sum up to

Table 23.1 Descriptive statistics for the sample of the biggest US museums, 2020

	Mean	Std. Deviation
CONTRIBUTIONS	30114087.31	133404559.064
PROGRAM SERVICE REV	3373653.88	8795886.827
ADVERTISING EXPENSE	571963.22	1685722.967
IT EXPENSE	1635284.19	9991352.958
FUND RAISING EXPENSE	5516534.81	36162993.344

Source: elaboration with SPSS Statistics

30,458,602,387 $ for Total Assets and 25,306,839,596 $ for Net Assets, so that these data give evidence of an *impressive* solvency.

Table 23.1 shows average amounts and standard deviations for investigated rows of revenues and expenses. Standard deviations are significant for the size variety of the investigated sample: from the smallest museums like Fitchburg Art Museum, O'Keefe Museum of Art, Butler Institute of American Art, Fort Wayne Museum of Art, Plains Art Museum and St. Louis Contemporary Art Museum to the biggest ones like Whitney Museum, Los Angeles County Museum of Art, Houston Museum of Fine Arts, Boston Museum of Fine Arts, New York, the Met and the Smithsonian.

Table 23.2 shows significant correlations for Contributions and Program Service Revenues. Besides, IT Expense is highly correlated with both and main revenue sources. A very modest correlation results for contributions and the fundraising expense. It might be that the pandemic caused the slow-down of most of fundraising events.

According to the most significant correlations, a stepwise multiple and linear regression was implemented for the 2020s data *contributions* as dependent variable of *program service revenues*, the very next and alternative revenue source from marketing, *advertising expense*, as a "proxy" of the marketing expense, the *IT expense* for the impact of digitization during the pandemic and the *fundraising expense*, as supposed for the main cause and "enabler" of increasing contributions. Only some outputs of the comprehensive analysis with SPSS Software will be here commented.

In Table 23.3, all main R and F tests are summarized and Model 4 is selected and here commented for all variables, as it is the most significant (R, R Square, Adjusted R Square), though the very modest difference for R and F change, among the third and the fourth ones.

In Table 23.4, ANOVA results consistent for all models, though the fourth was selected for all investigated predictors.

Table 23.5 comments for standardized coefficients.

If as concerns Pearson, IT Expense is highly correlated with both and main revenue sources, this expense shows the highest and positive coefficient. If as concerns Pearson, the lowest correlation results for contributions and the fundraising expense, here it will result for a negative coefficient.

The highest and positive coefficient refers to IT Expense, and this can be evidence that contributions were solicited and collected thanks to digitization of contents,

Table 23.2 Correlations, 2020's data

		Contributions	Program service rev	Advertising expense	IT expense	Fundraising expense
Pearson correlation	CONTRIBUTIONS	1.000	0.804	0.301	0.573	0.120
	PROGRAMSERVICEREV	**0.804**	1.000	0.247	0.528	0.178
	ADVERTISINGEXPENSE	0,301	0.247	1.000	0.144	0.071
	IT EXPENSE	**0.573**	**0.528**	0.144	1.000	0.872
	FUNDRAISINGEXPENSE	0.120	0.178	0.071	0.872	1.000
Sig. (1-tailed)	CONTRIBUTIONS		0.000	0.001	0.000	0.117
	PROGRAMSERVICEREV	0.000		0.007	0.000	0.038
	ADVERTISINGEXPENSE	0.001	0.007		0.077	0.243
	IT EXPENSE	0.000	0.000	0.077		0.000
	FUNDRAISINGEXPENSE	0.117	0.038	0.243	0.000	

Source: elaboration with SPSS Statistics

Table 23.3 The model summary

Model summary

Model	R	R square	Adjusted R square	Std. error of the estimate	Change statistics				
					R square change	F change	df1	df2	Sig. F change
1	0.804[a]	0.647	0.643	79707180.820	0.647	179.320	1	98	0.000
2	0.823[b]	0.677	0.671	76550594.388	0.031	9.249	1	97	0.003
3	0.968[c]	0.937	0.935	33926884.455	0.260	397.834	1	96	0.000
4	0.976[d]	0.952	0.950	29881335.406	0.015	28.754	1	95	0.000

Source: elaboration with SPSS Statistics
[a]Predictors: (Constant), PROGRAMSERVICEREV
[b]Predictors: (Constant), PROGRAMSERVICEREV, IT EXPENSE
[c]Predictors: (Constant), PROGRAMSERVICEREV, IT EXPENSE, FUNDRAISINGEXPENSE
[d]Predictors: (Constant), PROGRAMSERVICEREV, IT EXPENSE, FUNDRAISINGEXPENSE, ADVERTISINGEXPENSE

Table 23.4 ANOVA[a]

Model		Sum of squares	df	Mean square	F	Sig.
1	Regression	11392638634552000000.000	1	11392638634552000000.000	179,320	<.001[b]
	Residual	6226169980780900000.000	98	63532346742662200.000		
	Total	17618808615332900000.000	99			
2	Regression	11934614919168200000.000	2	5967307459584080000.000	101,831	<.001[c]
	Residual	5684193696164710000.000	97	58599935012200730.000		
	Total	17618808615332900000.000	99			
3	Regression	16513816466071900000.000	3	5504605488690650000.000	478,232	<.001[d]
	Residual	1104992149260920000.000	96	11510334888134660.000		
	Total	17618808615332900000.000	99			
4	Regression	16770559119986600000.000	4	4192639779996640000.000	469,556	<.001[e]
	Residual	848249495346316000.000	95	8928942056627701.000		
	Total	17618808615332900000.000	99			

Source: elaboration with SPSS Statistics

[a]Dependent Variable: CONTRIBUTIONS

[b]Predictors: (Constant), PROGRAMSERVICEREV

[c]Predictors: (Constant), PROGRAMSERVICEREV, IT EXPENSE

[d]Predictors: (Constant), PROGRAMSERVICEREV, IT EXPENSE, FUNDRAISINGEXPENSE

[e]Predictors: (Constant), PROGRAMSERVICEREV, IT EXPENSE, FUNDRAISINGEXPENSE, ADVERTISINGEXPENSE

Table 23.5 Coefficients[a]

Model		Unstandardized coefficients		Standardized coefficients	t	Sig.	95,0% confidence interval for B		Correlations			Collinearity statistics	
		B	Std. error	Beta			Lower bound	Upper bound	Zero-order	Partial	Part	Tolerance	VIF
4	(Constant)	9962763.157	3450323.457		2.887	0,005	3113005.051	16812521.262					
	PROGRAMSERVICEREV	1.630	0.555	**0.107**	2.936	0.004	0.528	2.733	0.804	0.288	0.066	0,378	2,645
	IT EXPENSE	23.266	0.967	**1.743**	24.058	0.000	21.346	25.186	0.573	0.927	0.542	0,097	10,352
	FUNDRAISINGEXPENSE	−5.264	0.231	**−1.427**	−22.817	0.000	−5.722	−4.806	0.120	−0.920	−0.514	0,130	7717
	ADVERTISINGEXPENSE	9,866	1.840	**0.125**	5.362	0,000	6.213	13.519	0.301	0.482	0.121	0,938	1067

Source: elaboration with SPSS Statistics

[a]Dependent Variable: CONTRIBUTIONS

communication, memberships, and platforms. The positive correlation concerns the advertising expense, too. This results as a matching and cause-related effect for both marketing and fundraising purposes, which cannot be excluded in a unique spot, technique, or advertising (virtual) event during such an extraordinary time. The positive correlation with program service revenues is contradicting the usually commented trade-off of cultural organizations, whose boards and employees would be constrained to manage scarce resources and to choose between marketing and fundraising, program service revenues, and contributions (Besana et al., 2023; Camarero et al., 2023). The negative correlation of contributions and the fundraising expense is confirming that such an extraordinary contingency caused the failure of fundraising events and techniques, whose audiences and stakeholders were probably targeted by other calls for actions and funds. Culture might not be the most beloved and nonprofit mission for philanthropists, donors, and sponsors during the pandemic.

Who are the big spenders for Information Technology? These are the museums, whose 2020's IT expense was between 82 million $ and 728,000 $. San Francisco of Modern Art, the Smithsonian Institution, The MET Metropolitan Museum of Art, the New York MOMA, the Los Angeles County Museum of Art, the Boston Museum of Fine Arts, the Houston Museum of Fine Arts, the Detroit Institute of Arts, the Asian Art Museum in San Francisco, the New Museum of Contemporary Art in New York, and the Solomon R. Guggenheim Foundation are the biggest IT spenders of the sample in 2020. These giant museums have implemented the virtual version of their exhibitions, works of arts, events, and media for at least two decades. The contemporary collection of the San Francisco MOMA is a differentiated and versatile opportunity for offline and online visitors, and the list of stories through "watch, read, listen, and learn" is a matter of engaged communities, multicultural dialogue, and multi-sensory education. The Smithsonian is such a giant *Educator*, who could not avoid the availability of the American heritage offline and online, above all, during the pandemic. The immersive Houston Museum of Fine Arts is a melting pot of online and offline events, from tours to digital archives of exhibitions, films, edutainment, and learning programs for different audiences. The collection is available online with all works. The Museum supplies a wide range of lectures, conversation on arts, concerts, readings, performances, symposia, films, workshops, with event archive at https://www.mfah.org/programs/adults/conversations-about-art/

If the pandemic was a disruptive event, these museums were mature and they were ready to engage with online visitors. Digital technologies have adapted them to a supply, whose offline and digital features have been continually optimized. Digital technologies have stimulated their marketing for contents and pricing and their fundraising for memberships and platforms, whose fringe, collateral implications, and benefits can evolve on a new path. Revenues are still listed in ordinary accounting lines, and additional revenues are expected to be summed up after the full recovery from the pandemic.

23.4 Focus and Clarification on Featured Case Studies

Even more than a decade ago, social media proved to be a very important vehicle for American museums. On this topic, in 2012, a study collected 315 online surveys. These showed how important American museum professionals consider social media engagement to be (Fletcher & Lee, 2012). Until recently, the use of social networks by museums was more unidirectional (list of events, reminders, promotional messages) through a prevalent use of Facebook and Twitter (Fletcher & Lee, 2012).

During the pandemic, there was a change from unidirectional to bidirectional. In fact, there were many initiatives that involved people taking an active part in online events promoted by museums (Massi & Turrini, 2020). Many of these have made their collections available online, launching a series of digital initiatives (Burke et al., 2020). As a result, social media seem to have strengthened visitor communities (Massi & Turrini, 2020). This allowed museums to show their content and to stay in touch with their audience, as well as to reach new potential visitors.

Some initiatives have mobilized home visitors as creative contributors to the museum. The most illustrative case was promoted in California by the Getty Museum, which launched a social media challenge to recreate its artwork from objects people had at home. The "Getty Museum Challenge" prompted thousands of people to recreate works of art from the museum and post the photos on social media (Twitter, Facebook and Instagram). The Getty provided links to its collection online. Participants showed creativity and fun during the lockdown (Burke et al., 2020).

Another initiative was promoted by Dan Hicks, professor of contemporary archaeology at Oxford University and curator of the Pitt Rivers Museum, who launched #MuseumsUnlocked. Each day of #MuseumsUnlocked, which lasted 100 days, had a different theme that ranged from various museums, places, objects, and themes. Every day, hundreds of contributions with photos and descriptions of museums and cultural sites visited in the past were sent in by visitors (Burke et al., 2020). Similarly, the hashtag #MuseumsFromHome encouraged Twitter users to interact with collections from their homes. Indeed, during the lockdown, some museum institutions launched contemporary collecting projects, that is, a collection of photos, objects, websites, and diaries on the pandemic (Massi & Turrini, 2020).

One of the participants in the #MuseumsFromHome initiative is the Akron Art Museum in Ohio. This has promoted several online games, such as crosswords and puzzles, based on the museum"s cultural offerings (O'Neill, 2023). The initiatives developed by museums during the spread of the pandemic demonstrate the growing importance of digital transformation and value co-creation.

From what does the success of these initiatives derive?

According to Daniel Kahneman, the human mind performs two types of thinking: rational and intuitive. Rational thinking works slowly, while intuitive thinking is fast, effortless, and automatic (Kahneman & Egan, 2011). There are mental pathways that allow us to immediately come to conclusions and thus make choices. These are the heuristics or mental shortcuts. Heuristics can often produce cognitive bias (Kahneman & Egan, 2011). In a crisis, our brain refers to situations already experienced, resulting in a belief bias (Lechanoine & Gangi, 2020). These may have played an important role in the success that social initiatives had during the pandemic. Some of them will be listed below.

Self-enhancement transmission bias (SET) is the tendency to describe oneself more positively than a normative criterion would predict (Han & Hirshleifer, 2015). People like to share their most positive aspects with others (Krueger, 1998) and wish to create and maintain a positive self-concept (Wojnicki & Godes, 2008).

People share more positive experiences. Museums on social have offered ways to promote themselves positively, such as the Getty Challenge, where participants had the opportunity to showcase their art in recreating certain works.

Another determining factor can be attributed to In-group bias: we tend to trust, defend, and consider better people who we perceive to be members of our own group (Lindholm & Christianson, 1998). During the lockdown, social media was one of the only tools available to interact with a group. In this sense, museum visitors may have felt like a group of people with common interests. In addition, some research has examined how specific social networking sites promoted well-being; for example, active use of Instagram has been linked to both greater life satisfaction (Masciantonio et al., 2020; Fritz et al., 2023; Felbermayr & Nanopoulos, 2016).

A final fundamental bias to consider in this analysis concerns the status quo. This is the marked tendency to prefer the status quo in making one's decisions (Samuelson & Zeckhauser, 1988). One of the reasons why it took some time for people to adapt to the recent pandemic is that they wanted to remain as they were before in their lives (Ozdinc, 2021). Therefore, the tendency of the audience to continue to visit a museum, despite the different online form, may have been caused at times by the status quo bias.

In any case, these new dynamic ways of interacting with a museum institution proved to be engaging and stimulating. Thanks to the sharing processes, new products have emerged in the history of memory institutions and their digital offerings (Samaroudi et al., 2020).

23.5 Conclusions

The strategic importance of digitization and social media marketing is quite mature in the biggest US museums, and this is a first and pilot study about the impact of pandemic on their economic performances, considering how much digitization changed their approach to supply, stakeholders, marketing, and fundraising. The paper outlines a framework to better understand how much these organizations might cope with extraordinary contingencies with marketing, applied economics, and behavioral economics approaches. This integration of different literature and evidence—the fourth paragraph—can be considered an academic challenge and a cross-sectional evaluation of both strategic implications and measurements. This paper remains a pilot study for the extraordinary performances of a sample of US museums during the pandemic 2020 year.

The significant regression of the here investigated sample of US museums shows the highest and positive correlation with the Information Technology Expense. The positive correlation is also significant for the advertising expense. US museums emphasized their supply and communication efforts through the web and social media. When meant as offline and events, fundraising was not efficient and the negative coefficient is here extraordinarily meaning that the pandemic impacted on traditional fundraising.

The pandemic has demonstrated the need for museums to promote digital literacy skills, increase their investment in digital technologies, and develop the digital strategies they will need to respond to future crises and to survive in an increasingly competitive environment.

However, as the sector continues to evolve, further research is needed to understand the long-term implications and performances of digitization on museums and their marketing and revenue strategies. This research is willing to feel the gap with the current literature, which is stressing the importance of digitization for multiple stakeholders' engagement, and which is giving multiple examples of applications both for marketing and fundraising, but which is not considering economic performances, also considering the very latest and here discussed approach of behavioral economics. By adopting audience-centered marketing approaches, building solid relationships with donors, and leveraging the power of social media, museums can enhance their financial stability, community engagement, and overall sustainability. To do so, museums must also develop new marketing approaches and revenue models to ensure long-term sustainability.

Economic performances can be considered limited evidence of digitization and strategic implications. A new metrics must be found for the matching of economic data, IT, and social media effectiveness. A pilot study on only one year (of the pandemic) is an evident limit of this research.

Academic research has provided valuable insights into best practices and emerging trends, which can inform museum professionals" efforts to ensure the continued success of their institutions. Practical implications of this research concern the reinforcement of IT and social media roles and employees in museums, also considering the separation of goals as concerns marketing and fundraising. This study may also inspire European museums, though governances and teams do not often and clearly separate marketing officers from fundraisers. Nevertheless, further research is needed to better understand on a long-term basis how much these organizations might cope with extraordinary contingencies by refining their digital strategies.

References

Allen-Greil, D., Edwards, S., Ludden, J., & Johnson, E. (2011). Social media and organizational change. In J. Trant & D. Bearman (Eds.), *Museums and the web 2011: Proceedings* (pp. 101–112). Archives & Museum Informatics.

Alshawaaf, N., & Lee, S. H. (2021). Business model innovation through digitisation in social purpose organisations: A comparative analysis of Tate Modern and Pompidou Centre. *Journal of Business Research, 125*, 597–608.

Bertacchini, E., & Morando, F. (2013). The future of museums in the digital age: New models for access to and use of digital collections. *International Journal of Arts Management, 15*(2), 60–72.

Besana, A., Esposito, A., & Vannini, M. C. (2023). It is not only a matter of masterpieces. Masters of economic performances in US art museums' thanks to relationship marketing. *International Journal of Small Business and Entrepreneurship, 48*(1), 27–38.

Borowiecki, K. J., & Navarrete, T. (2017). Digitization of heritage collections as indicator of innovation. *Economics of Innovation and New Technology, 26*(3), 227–246.

Burke, V., Jørgensen, D., & Jørgensen, F. A. (2020). Museums at home: Digital Initiativesin response to COVID-19. *Norsk museumstidsskrift, 6*(2), 117–123.

Camarero, C., Garrido, M.-J., & Vicente, E. (2023). Social and financial signalling to increase fundraising revenue in museums. *Journal of Nonprofit & Public Sector Marketing, 35*(2), 144–164.

Catton, F., & Smith, L. M. (2021). Museums without walls: A temporal analysis of virtual exhibitions in GLAM institutions. *A Canadian Journal for Information Science Students and Early Career Professionals, 2*(2), 72–85.

Chung, N., Han, H., & Joun, Y. (2015). Tourists' intention to visit a destination: The role of augmented reality (AR) application for a heritage site. *Computers in Human Behavior, 50*, 588–599.

Cobley, J., Gaimster, D., So, S., Gorbey, K., Arnold, K., Poulot, D., & Jiang, M. (2020). Museums in the pandemic: A survey of responses on the current crisis. *Museum Worlds, 8*(1), 111–134.

Dawson, A. (2022). World's major museums resist TikTok surge – with a few notable exceptions, *The Art Newspaper, Visitor Figures 2021* (last accessed on 5th May 2023, https://www.theartnewspaper.com/2022/03/28/worlds-major-museums-resist-tiktok-surge).

de las Heras-Pedrosa, C., Iglesias-Sánchez, P. P., Jambrino-Maldonado, C., López-Delgado, P., & Galarza-Fernández, E. (2022). Museum communication management in digital ecosystems. Impact of COVID-19 on digital strategy. *Museum Management and Curatorship*, 1–23.

Errichiello, L., Micera, R., Atzeni, M., & Del Chiappa, G. (2019). Exploring the implications of wearable virtual reality technology for museum visitors' experience: A cluster analysis. *International Journal of Tourism Research, 21*(5), 590–605.

Falk, J. H., & Dierking, L. D. (2016). *The museum experience revisited*. Routledge.

Felbermayr, A., & Nanopoulos, A. (2016). The role of emotions for the perceived usefulness in online customer reviews. *Journal of Interactive Marketing, 36*, 60–76.

Fletcher, A., & Lee, M. J. (2012). Current social media uses and evaluations in American museums. *Museum Management and Curatorship, 27*(5), 505–521.

Fritz, M. M., Margolis, S., Radošić, N., Revord, J. C., Rosen, K. G., Nieminen, L. R. G., Reece, A., & Lyubomirsky, S. (2023). Examining the social in the prosocial: Episode-level features of social interactions and kind acts predict social connection and well-being. *Emotion, 23*(8), 2270–2285.

Garcia Carrizosa, H., Sheehy, K., Rix, J., Seale, J., & Hayhoe, S. (2020). Designing technologies for museums: Accessibility and participation issues. *Journal of Enabling Technologies, 14*(1), 31–39.

Giaccardi, E. (2012). *Heritage and social media: Understanding heritage in a participatory culture*. Routledge.

Giannini, T., & Bowen, J. P. (2019). *Museums and digitalism* (pp. 27–46). Museums and Digital Culture: New Perspectives and Research.

Han, B. & Hirshleifer, D.A. (2015). *Self-enhancing transmission bias and active investing* (May 2015). Available at SSRN: https://ssrn.com/abstract=2032697 or https://doi.org/10.2139/ssrn.2032697

Hossaini, A., & Blankenberg, N. (2017). *Manual of digital museum planning*. Rowman & Littlefield.

Ioannakis, G., Bampis, L., & Koutsoudis, A. (2020). Exploiting artificial intelligence for digitally enriched museum visits. *Journal of Cultural Heritage, 42*, 171–180.

Jung, T. H., & tom Dieck, M. C. (2017). Augmented reality, virtual reality and 3D printing for the co-creation of value for the visitor experience at cultural heritage places. *Journal of Place Management and Development, 10*(2), 140–151.

Kahneman, D., & Egan, P. (2011). *Thinking, fast and slow* (Vol. 1). Farrar, Straus and Giroux.

Kidd, J. (2011). Enacting engagement online: Framing social media use for the museum. *Information Technology & People, 24*(1), 64–77.

Kim, S. (2018). Virtual exhibitions and communication factors. *Museum Management and Curatorship, 33*(3), 243–260.

Krueger, J. (1998). Enhancement bias in descriptions of self and others. *Personality and Social Psychology Bulletin, 24*(5), 505–516.

Lechanoine, F., & Gangi, K. (2020). COVID-19: Pandemic of cognitive biases impacting human behaviors and decision-making of public health policies. *Frontiers in Public Health, 8*, 613290.

Lindholm, T., & Christianson, S. A. (1998). Intergroup biases and eyewitness testimony. *The Journal of Social Psychology, 138*(6), 710–723.

Manžuch, Z., Huvila, I., & Aparac-Jelušić, T. (2005). Digitization of cultural heritage. In L. Kajberg & L. Lorring (Eds.), *European curriculum reflections on library and information science education* (pp. 37–64). Royal School of Library and Information Science.

Marty, P. F. (2008). Museum websites and museum visitors: Digital museum resources and their use. *Museum Management and Curatorship, 23*(1), 81–99.

Marty, P. F., & Buchanan, V. (2022). Exploring the contributions and challenges of museum technology professionals during the COVID-19 crisis. *Curator: The Museum Journal, 65*(1), 117–133.

Masciantonio, A., Bourguinon, D., Bouchat, P., Balty, M., & Rime, B. (2020). Don't put all social network sites in one basket: Facebook, Instagram, Twitter, TikTok and their relations with well-being during the COVID-19 pandemic. *PsyArxiv*. https://psyarxiv.com/82bgt/

Massi, M., & Turrini, A. (2020). Virtual proximity or physical distance? Digital transformation and value co-creation in COVID-19 times. *Il Capitale Culturale*, 177–195.

Navarrete, T. (2013). Digital cultural heritage. In *Handbook on the economics of cultural heritage* (pp. 251–271). Edward Elgar Publishing.

O'Neill, J. (2023). *The Akron Art Museum's #museumfromhome strategy: Collaborative cross-words, American Alliance of Museums*. Available at: https://www.aam-us.org/2020/03/23/akron-art-museums-museumfromhome-strategy-collaborative-crosswords/ (Accessed: 13 May 2023).

Ozdinc, F. (2021). Behavioral economics insights to Covid-19 pandemic. *Journal of Financial Economics and Banking, 2*(2), 11–14.

Palumbo, R. (2022). Enhancing museums' attractiveness through digitization: An investigation of Italian medium and large-sized museums and cultural institutions. *International Journal of Tourism Research, 24*(2), 202–215.

Pantano, E. (2011). Virtual cultural heritage consumption: A 3D learning experience. *International Journal of Technology Enhanced Learning, 3*(5), 482–495.

Proctor, N. (2011). The Google art project: A new generation of museums on the web? *Curator: The Museum Journal, 54*(2), 215–221.

Raimo, N., De Turi, I., Ricciardelli, A., & Vitolla, F. (2022). Digitalization in the cultural industry: Evidence from Italian museums. *International Journal of Entrepreneurial Behavior & Research, 28*(8), 1962–1974.

Reynolds, A. (2020). Crowdsourcing and crowdfunding. In L. Perez Gonzalez, M. Baker, B. B. Blaagaard, & H. Jones (Eds.), *Routledge encyclopedia of citizen media*. Routledge.

Riley-Huff, D. A., Herrera, K., Ivey, S., & Harry, T. (2016). Crowdfunding in libraries, archives and museums. *The bottom line, 29*(2), 67–85.

Samaroudi, M., Rodriguez, E. K., & Perry, L. (2020). Heritage in lockdown: Digital provision of memory institutions in the UK and US of America during the COVID-19 pandemic. *Museum Management and Curatorship, 35*, 337–361.

Samuelson, W., & Zeckhauser, R. J. (1988). Status quo bias in decision making. *Journal of Risk and Uncertainty, 1*, 7–59.

Simone, C., Cerquetti, M., & La Sala, A. (2021). Museums in the Infosphere: Reshaping value creation. *Museum Management and Curatorship, 36*(4), 322–341.

Sweeney, L., & Dressel, J. (2022). *Art Museum director survey 2022: Documenting change in museum strategy and operations*. Ithaka S+R. Available at https://sr.ithaka.org/publications/art-museum-director-survey-2022/ (Last accessed on 8th May 2023).

Trombin, M., & Veglianti, E. (2020). Influencer marketing for museums: A comparison between Italy and The Netherlands. *International Journal of Digital Culture and Electronic Tourism, 3*(1), 54–73.

Trunfio, M., Lucia, M. D., Campana, S., & Magnelli, A. (2022). Innovating the cultural heritage museum service model through virtual reality and augmented reality: The effects on the overall visitor experience and satisfaction. *Journal of Heritage Tourism, 17*(1), 1–19.

UNESCO (2021, April). *Museums around the world in the face of Covid-19*. Available at https://unesdoc.unesco.org/ark:/48223/pf0000376729_eng (Last accessed on 11th May 2023).

Vassiliadis, C., & Belenioti, Z. C. (2017). Museums & cultural heritage via social media: An integrated literature review. *Tourismos, 12*(3), 97–132.

Villaespesa, E., & Murphy, O. (2021). This is not an apple! Benefits and challenges of applying computer vision to museum collections. *Museum Management and Curatorship, 36*(4), 362–383.

Waller, D. S., & Waller, H. J. (2019). An analysis of negative reviews in top art museums' Facebook sites. *Museum Management and Curatorship, 34*(3), 323–338.

Wojnicki, A.C., & Godes D. (2008). Word-of-mouth as self-enhancement. HBS *Marketing Research Paper* No. 06-01. New York: ACM.

Zafiropoulos, K., Vrana, V., & Antoniadis, K. (2015). Use of twitter and Facebook by top European museums. *Journal of Tourism, Heritage & Services Marketing (JTHSM), 1*(1), 16–24.

Zollo, L., Rialti, R., Marrucci, A., & Ciappei, C. (2022). How do museums foster loyalty in tech-savvy visitors? The role of social media and digital experience. *Current Issues in Tourism, 25*(18), 2991–3008.

Chapter 24
Understanding Customer Perception and Brand Equity in the Hospitality Sector: Integrating Sentiment Analysis and Topic Modeling

T. D. Dang and M. T. Nguyen

Abstract This study integrates sentiment analysis and topic modeling techniques to investigate customer perception and brand equity within the hospitality sector. Drawing upon data from Booking.com in Ho Chi Minh City, Vietnam, an array of machine learning (ML) and deep learning (DL) models, including logistic regression (LR), random forest (RF), multinomial Naive Bayes (NB), Dense, long short-term memory (LSTM), and convolutional neural network (CNN), were employed. Notably, the Dense model exhibited a notable degree of accuracy, with the best-performing model achieving an accuracy rate of 0.95. Furthermore, the Dense model showcased an impressive F1-score of 0.97, underscoring its efficacy in sentiment classification. Using latent Dirichlet allocation (LDA), topic modeling analysis identified significant themes encompassing noise levels, room conditions, facilities, staff performance, and location advantages. These findings enhance our comprehension of the variables that shape brand equity and provide tangible implications for hotel managers seeking to enhance service quality, elevate customer satisfaction, and fortify their brand's competitive position. Overall, this study highlights the effectiveness of data-driven approaches in attaining insights into customer perceptions and serves as a guiding resource for future research endeavors in hospitality.

T. D. Dang (✉)
Eastern International University, Thu Dau Mot City, Binh Duong Province, Vietnam

Ho Chi Minh City University of Technology (HCMUT), Vietnam National University Ho Chi Minh City (VNUHCM), Ho Chi Minh City, Vietnam
e-mail: doan.dang@eiu.edu.vn; dtdoan.sdh221@hcmut.edu.vn

M. T. Nguyen
Ho Chi Minh City University of Technology (HCMUT), Vietnam National University Ho Chi Minh City (VNUHCM), Ho Chi Minh City, Vietnam
e-mail: n.m.tuan@hcmut.edu.vn

© The Author(s), under exclusive license to Springer Nature Switzerland AG 2024
N. Tsounis, A. Vlachvei (eds.), *Applied Economic Research and Trends*, Springer Proceedings in Business and Economics,
https://doi.org/10.1007/978-3-031-49105-4_24

Keywords Customer perception · Brand equity · Sentiment analysis · Topic modeling · Hospitality sector · Machine learning

24.1 Introduction

The hospitality sector is pivotal in global economies, contributing to employment, economic growth, and tourism experiences (Sheehan et al., 2018; Raguseo et al., 2017). In an increasingly interconnected world, the influence of customer perception and brand equity has become critical for businesses operating in the hospitality industry (Sürücü et al., 2019). Understanding customer sentiments and preferences has become paramount for organizations to effectively manage their brand reputation and enhance customer satisfaction (Serra-Cantallops et al., 2020). With the emergence of social media platforms and online review platforms like Booking.com, Agoda.com, and Airbnb.com, today, customers are able to publish their thoughts, opinions, and experiences about products and services online either by directly emailing the organization concerned or by writing reviews in an online platform (Raguseo et al., 2017; Chaw & Tang, 2019). User-generated content (UGC) has become an abundant source of data that holds significant value for businesses in understanding customer perceptions. Sentiment analysis and topic modeling have emerged as powerful techniques to unlock the insights hidden within this vast textual data (Chaw & Tang, 2019; Blasco-Arcas et al., 2022).

Sentiment analysis, also known as opinion mining, enables the extraction of personal information from UGC by classifying sentiments into positive, negative, or neutral categories (Kirilenko et al., 2018). It gives businesses a quantitative understanding of customer attitudes toward specific attributes such as staff performance, facilities, cleanliness, and location. In addition to sentiment analysis, topic modeling techniques have gained traction in uncovering latent themes and topics prevalent within UGC (Sürücü et al., 2019; Blasco-Arcas et al., 2022; Kirilenko et al., 2018). One such technique is LDA, a probabilistic model that identifies underlying topics by analyzing word co-occurrence patterns (Blei et al., 2003). By applying LDA to customer reviews, businesses can gain a qualitative understanding of customer interests, concerns, and preferences (Blasco-Arcas et al., 2022; Albalawi et al., 2020).

This study aims to contribute to the existing literature by integrating sentiment analysis and topic modeling techniques to comprehensively understand customer perception and brand equity in the hospitality sector. Leveraging a dataset of 31,989 customer reviews from Booking.com in Ho Chi Minh City, Vietnam, this research employs a range of ML and DL models, including RF, LR, NB, LSTM, CNN, and FNN (Blasco-Arcas et al., 2022; Essien & Chukwukelu, 2022). Through the combination of sentiment analysis and topic modeling using LDA (Blei et al., 2003), the study aims to identify underlying patterns, evaluate their impact on brand equity, and provide valuable insights for hospitality managers to enhance service quality, improve customer satisfaction, and strengthen their brand's competitive position.

This research contributes to academic theory and practical managerial decision-making in the hospitality sector by harnessing the power of sentiment analysis and topic modeling. The findings from this study will inform the development of effective marketing strategies and assist hospitality managers in making data-driven decisions to meet and exceed customer expectations. Furthermore, this research sets the stage for future investigations in the domain of customer perception and brand equity, emphasizing the need to explore novel approaches to UGC analysis and address the challenges faced by the industry in an ever-evolving digital landscape.

24.2 Literature Review

24.2.1 Customer Perception and Brand Equity

Branding plays a vital role in services, and customer perception plays a crucial role in shaping brand equity in the hospitality sector (Sürücü et al., 2019; Iglesias et al., 2019). Positive customer experiences and favorable perceptions contribute to developing a solid brand reputation, increased customer loyalty, and higher customer satisfaction (Liat et al., 2014). Understanding customer perceptions enables businesses to tailor their offerings, improve service quality, and create targeted marketing strategies (Sheehan et al., 2018; Blasco-Arcas et al., 2022).

On the other hand, brand equity encompasses the intangible assets associated with a brand, including customer perceptions, brand awareness, brand loyalty, and brand associations (Brahmbhatt & Shah, 2017). Customer perceptions directly impact brand equity, as positive perceptions enhance brand value and competitive advantage (Martínez & Nishiyama, 2019). Studies have shown that a positive online reputation from customer reviews and sentiments strongly correlates with higher brand equity (Sürücü et al., 2019; Iglesias et al., 2019; Brahmbhatt & Shah, 2017; Martínez & Nishiyama, 2019).

24.2.2 User-Generated Content Data

The emergence of online platforms and social media has revolutionized how customers share their experiences and opinions (Lamberton & Stephen, 2016). UGC has become a valuable source of information for businesses in various industries, including the hospitality sector (Ye et al., 2011). UGC encompasses customer reviews, ratings, and feedback on TripAdvisor, Yelp, and Booking.com (Mariani & Borghi, 2020). These platforms provide a wealth of data that reflects customer experiences, preferences, and sentiments. Researchers have recognized the significance of UGC data in understanding customer perceptions, identifying trends, and informing decision-making processes (Chaw & Tang, 2019; Essien & Chukwukelu, 2022; Ye et al., 2011; Mariani & Borghi, 2020).

24.2.3 Sentiment Analysis and Topic Modeling

Sentiment analysis, or opinion mining, utilizes ML and DL algorithms to extract and quantify subjective information from text data. ML and DL models like LR, RF, NB, LSTM, Dense, and CNN have been widely employed for sentiment analysis in the hospitality sector (Ye et al., 2011; Abkenar et al., 2021; Debortoli et al., 2016; Zarezadeh et al., 2022). These algorithms classify sentiments into positive, negative, or neutral categories, providing valuable insights into customer attitudes toward different attributes. Deep learning algorithms like LSTM and CNN capture sequential and local patterns in text, while LR, RF, and NB leverage statistical relationships to classify sentiments accurately (Ullah et al., 2020).

Topic modeling techniques, such as LDA (Blei et al., 2003), non-negative matrix factorization (NMF) (Lee & Seung, 2000), and latent semantic analysis (LSA) (Landauer et al., 1998), uncover latent themes and topics within textual data. LDA, the most commonly used algorithm, identifies underlying topics by analyzing word co-occurrence patterns. NMF and LSA factorize matrices to extract topics and semantic structures from the text. These algorithms assist in understanding customer interests, concerns, and preferences in the hospitality sector. Key topics identified through topic modeling include noise levels, room conditions, facilities, staff performance, and location advantages (Albalawi et al., 2020).

Integrating sentiment analysis and topic modeling enables researchers and businesses to gain comprehensive insights into customer perceptions and brand equity (Sürücü et al., 2019; Brahmbhatt & Shah, 2017; Martínez & Nishiyama, 2019). By applying sentiment analysis, businesses can understand sentiment distribution toward different attributes, while topic modeling allows for identifying key topics prevalent in customer reviews (Martínez & Nishiyama, 2019; Abkenar et al., 2021; Zarezadeh et al., 2022; Ullah et al., 2020). These insights help businesses identify areas for improvement, align their services with customer preferences, and make data-driven decisions to enhance customer satisfaction and strengthen their brand's competitive position in the hospitality sector. These models facilitate a deeper understanding of customer sentiments and preferences, aiding businesses in improving service quality, enhancing customer satisfaction, and effectively managing brand equity (Mustak et al., 2021).

24.3 Methodology

24.3.1 Framework for Analyzing UGC

This research uses a framework for analyzing UGC from Booking.com to understand customer preferences and enhance experiences in the tourism sector (Abkenar et al., 2021; Zarezadeh et al., 2022). The process comprises three stages: data

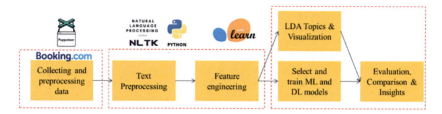

Fig. 24.1 Summary flow uses ML and DL for analytics

collection and organization, data preparation, sentiment classification, and topic modeling (Essien & Chukwukelu, 2022). For details, see Fig. 24.1.

Data from Booking.com concerning hotels in Ho Chi Minh City, Vietnam, was collected in February 2023 using Node.js and Puppeteer (Chang, 2022). The dataset included over 156,256 records and was preprocessed using Python libraries, retaining only English comments for uniform analysis. The data was cleaned, encoded, and explored to identify patterns and insights, laying the foundation for further steps; final dataset comprised 31,989 records. Finally, ML and DL models were evaluated and tuned for sentiment classification and topic modeling. The model's performance was assessed by testing data with metrics like accuracy, precision, and recall. LDA was used for topic modeling.

24.3.2 ML and DL Models for Sentiment Analysis

The study utilized six different algorithms to classify sentiments expressed in comments, comprising three traditional ML algorithms (RF, LR, and NB) (Ullah et al., 2020; Salmony & Faridi, 2021) and three DL models (Dense, LSTM, and CNN) (Abid et al., 2020). The inclusion of traditional ML algorithms allowed leveraging established methods widely used in sentiment analysis; DL models, on the other hand, offer the ability to capture complex patterns and dependencies in data (Mehraliyev et al., 2022). By incorporating DL models alongside traditional ML algorithms, the study sought to evaluate their respective effectiveness in sentiment analysis. This comprehensive approach provides insights into the strengths and limitations of both ML and DL techniques for sentiment classification tasks (Albalawi et al., 2020; Mustak et al., 2021).

24.3.3 Topic Modeling

Furthermore, the research used LDA for topic modeling, helping identify underlying themes in hotel reviews by analyzing word frequencies. LDA's generative probabilistic model estimated latent topics and word distributions, providing deeper insights into review sentiment.

> *Step 1: Preprocess the text data (remove stopwords, tokenize, and others.).*
> *Step 2: Create a document-term matrix to represent the frequency of terms in each document.*
> *Step 3: Initialize LDA model parameters (number of topics, alpha, beta, and others).*
> *Step 4: Train the LDA model on the document-term matrix.*
> *Step 5: Extract the top words for each topic and assign a label to each topic based on the top words.*
> *Step 6: Analyze and interpret the resulting topics to gain insights into the underlying themes in the text data.*

24.3.4 Model Evaluation

Model performance was assessed using accuracy, precision, recall, and F1-score metrics (see Table 24.1). The research used these metrics to evaluate six ML and DL algorithms on the hotel reviews dataset, providing insights into their predictive power and areas for improvement (Ullah et al., 2020; Hossin & Sulaiman, 2015).

Table 24.1 Classification performance metrics

Performance metric	Description	Formula
Confusion matrix	It is a 2×2 table that includes true positive (TP), false positive (FP), false negative (FN), and true negative (TN) metrics	
Accuracy	It measures the proportion of correct predictions made by the model	$Accuracy = (TP + TN)/(TP + TN + FP + FN)$
Precision	It measures the fraction of positive predictions	$Precision = TP / (TP + FP)$
Recall	It measures the fraction of actual positive instances correctly predicted by the model	$Recall = TP/(TP + FN)$
F1-score	The harmonic means of precision and recall	$F1\text{-score} = 2 \times (precision \times recall)/(precision + recall)$

24.4 Experiment Results

24.4.1 Data Collection and Preprocessing

The crawler gathered hotel names, star ratings, locations, addresses, and UGC-like reviews and ratings (see Fig. 24.2). After collecting, only English reviews with complete attribute values were retained and then encoded for machine readability (Ullah et al., 2020).

Before analyzing the dataset, crucial preprocessing techniques were implemented on the textual data to guarantee precise and significant outcomes (Kirilenko et al., 2018; Puh & Bagić Babac, 2022). These techniques encompassed converting all text to lowercase to ensure consistency and prevent duplication based on case sensitivity. Tokenization was performed to split the text into individual words or tokens, while stopwords, commonly uninformative words, were removed. Additionally, lemmatization was applied to reduce words to their base or dictionary form (Bird, 2006). These preprocessing steps were vital in preparing the text data for subsequent sentiment and topic modeling analysis by reducing noise, improving interpretability, and optimizing algorithmic efficiency (Debortoli et al., 2016). The "sentiment" attribute was created for sentiment analysis, classifying reviews into three categories representing positive, negative, and neutral customer experiences (Puh & Bagić Babac, 2022). The top popular words extracted from comments are shown in Fig. 24.3.

24.4.2 Sentiment Analysis

The study aimed to classify sentiments expressed in comments using six different algorithms, three of which were traditional ML algorithms RF, LR, and NB (Ullah et al., 2020; Salmony & Faridi, 2021), and the other three were DL models: Dense, LSTM, and CNN (Ullah et al., 2020; Abid et al., 2020). The objective was to develop models that could automatically analyze the textual content of comments

Fig. 24.2 Sample of review

Fig. 24.3 The word cloud summary

Table 24.2 Summary classification performance metrics

Model	Accuracy	Precision			Recall			F1 score		
		Neg	Neu	Pos	Neg	Neu	Pos	Neg	Neu	Pos
NB	0.88	0.97	0.00	0.88	0.05	0.00	1	0.10	0.00	0.94
RF	0.90	0.96	0.94	0.90	0.22	0.20	1	0.36	0.34	0.95
LR	0.94	0.85	0.88	0.95	0.65	0.34	0.99	0.74	0.50	0.97
LSTM	0.93	0.66	0	0.96	0.76	0	0.99	0.71	0	0.97
CNN	0.94	0.75	0.67	0.96	0.74	0.30	0.99	0.75	0.41	0.98
Dense	0.95	0.83	0.97	0.96	0.76	0.43	0.99	0.79	0.60	0.97

Note: *RF* Random forest, *LR* logistic regression, *NB* multinomial Naive Bayes, *LSTM* long short-term memory, *CNN* convolutional neural network

and accurately predict the corresponding sentiment category. The performance metrics of the classification models are summarized in Table 24.2. The table presents accuracy, precision, recall, and F1 score for each sentiment category (negative, neutral, and positive) across the different models.

NB (multinomial Naive Bayes) achieved an accuracy of 0.88 with high precision for the negative sentiment category while having low precision and recall for the neutral and positive categories. RF (random forest) achieved an accuracy of 0.90 with balanced precision, recall, and F1 scores for all sentiment categories. LR (logistic regression) achieved an accuracy of 0.94 with relatively high precision, recall, and F1 scores across all sentiment categories. The deep learning models also performed well. LSTM achieved an accuracy of 0.93, CNN achieved an accuracy of 0.94, and Dense achieved the highest accuracy of 0.95. These models showed competitive precision, recall, and F1 scores for all sentiment categories, indicating their effectiveness in sentiment classification tasks.

24.4.3 Topic Modeling

The LDA algorithm was used on the Booking.com data to identify ten topics related to customer perception in the hospitality industry.

> *Topic #1: noisy, noise, good, room, hear, sound, location, night, door, staff*
> *Topic #2: room, good, location, water, bathroom, shower, bed, dirty, bad, old*
> *Topic #3: hotel, check, room, good, pool, staff, airport, breakfast, stay, time*
> *Topic #4: pool, breakfast, good, location, great, rooftop, room, bar, staff, nice*
> *Topic #5: good, location, staff, great, wonderful, clean, friendly, room, nice, exceptional*
> *Topic #6: good, breakfast, room, hotel, location, staff, great, slow, nice, stay*
> *Topic #7: room, hotel, good, great, staff, location, stay, breakfast, nice, bed*
> *Topic #8: exceptional, great, staff, clean, nice, location, place, good, stay, friendly*
> *Topic #9: hotel, staff, room, stay, booking, good, great, time, location, exceptional*
> *Topic #10: location, good, walking, market, near, hotel, distance, close, restaurant, city*

These topics were condensed into five main themes:

- Room Quality and Cleanliness (#2, #5): Includes water supply, bathroom quality, bed comfort, and overall cleanliness.
- Hotel Facilities and Services (#3, #4): Focuses on amenities, check-in/out processes, pool availability, staff interactions, breakfast offerings, and overall satisfaction.
- Location and Convenience (#10): Evaluate the hotel's proximity to attractions, markets, restaurants, and the city center, considering convenience and accessibility.
- Staff Friendliness and Service (#7, #8, #9): Assesses staff friendliness, exceptional service, professionalism, and overall experience during the hotel stay.
- Overall Experience and Satisfaction (#1, #6): Reflects on room quality, noise levels, breakfast experience, and overall satisfaction.

These themes highlight the critical dimensions of customer perception in the hospitality industry, covering room quality, cleanliness, hotel facilities, services, location, staff friendliness, and overall satisfaction. Utilizing these insights, hotel managers can identify areas for improvement and enhance the overall customer experience.

24.5 Discussion and Implication

The sentiment analysis and topic modeling findings hold significant implications for understanding customer perception and its impact on brand equity in the hospitality sector. The sentiment analysis results revealed that LR, Dense, and CNN models demonstrated high accuracy, precision, recall, and F1 scores, indicating their effectiveness in sentiment classification. Employing the LDA algorithm, the topic modeling results identified five critical themes related to customer perception in the hospitality industry. These themes included Room Quality and Cleanliness, Hotel Facilities and Services, Location and Convenience, Staff Friendliness and Service, and Overall Experience and Satisfaction (Topic #1–10).

Theoretically, these findings align with established models such as the SERVQUAL and brand equity pyramid (Macieira et al., 2020). These models emphasize the importance of service quality, customer experience, and brand perception in shaping customer satisfaction and brand equity (Górska-Warsewicz & Kulykovets, 2020). Theoretical implications suggest the significance of adopting customer-centric strategies in the hospitality industry. Understanding and addressing customer preferences, needs, and perceptions are vital for maintaining a competitive advantage and fostering long-term customer relationships. By tailoring services to meet customer expectations, hotels can create positive experiences, enhance brand loyalty, and strengthen brand associations (Lee & Chuang, 2022).

Practically, these findings provide actionable insights for hotel managers aiming to enhance customer satisfaction and improve brand equity. Emphasizing room quality, cleanliness, and overall experience is crucial for meeting customer expectations and fostering positive perceptions. By maintaining high standards in these areas, hotels can consistently deliver quality experiences, resulting in increased customer satisfaction and loyalty. Investing in hotel facilities, services, and staff interactions is crucial for shaping customer perceptions. Providing superior amenities, streamlining check-in/out processes, and cultivating friendly and professional staff interactions contribute to positive customer experiences and enhance brand equity (Sürücü et al., 2019; Zarezadeh et al., 2022; Parzych & Brkić-Vejmelka, 2020).

Moreover, the location and convenience of a hotel play a significant role in customer satisfaction. Hotels strategically located near attractions, markets, restaurants, and city centers provide added value and convenience, contributing to positive customer perceptions and enhancing brand equity (Topic #10) (Hanaysha, 2016).

24.6 Limitations and Future Works

This study, while insightful, is limited by its focus on data from Booking.com and from a single city, Ho Chi Minh, which may not fully represent the diversity of customer perceptions across different platforms and regions. Additionally, using only six ML and DL models and LDA for topic modeling may overlook particular complex sentiments or themes in customer reviews. Other attributes from UGC data should combine with text data to make the most sense.

For future work, expanding data sources, incorporating diverse geographies, and deploying advanced sentiment analysis and topic modeling techniques can improve our understanding of customer perceptions. Also, examining the impact of temporal factors on customer sentiments can yield further insights. Continued research in this direction can enhance the reliability of findings and contribute to better practices in hospitality management.

24.7 Conclusion

This study demonstrates the potential of sentiment analysis and topic modeling in understanding customer perception and brand equity in the hospitality sector. Using ML and DL techniques on Booking.com data, we identified vital aspects impacting customer satisfaction. While the study is limited to one city and a specific set of models, it underscores the power of data-driven approaches in enhancing customer experience and brand equity. Future research could expand on this foundation, encompassing a broader geographical scope and leveraging various analytical tools, ultimately striving to improve the quality of hospitality services.

Acknowledgments The authors would like to thank Eastern International University, Binh Duong Province, Vietnam, funding this research.

References

Abid, F., Li, C., & Alam, M. (2020). Multi-source social media data sentiment analysis using bidirectional recurrent convolutional neural networks. *Computer Communications, 157*, 102–115.

Abkenar, S. B., Kashani, M. H., Mahdipour, E., & Jameii, S. M. (2021). Big data analytics meets social media: A systematic review of techniques, open issues, and future directions. *Telematics and Informatics, 57*, 101517.

Albalawi, R., Yeap, T. H., & Benyoucef, M. (2020). Using topic modeling methods for short-text data: A comparative analysis. *Frontiers in Artificial Intelligence, 3*, 42.

Bird, S. (2006). NLTK: the natural language toolkit. In *Proceedings of the COLING/ACL 2006 interactive presentation sessions* (pp. 69–72). Association for Computational Linguistics.

Blasco-Arcas, L., Lee, H.-H. M., Kastanakis, M. N., Alcañiz, M., & Reyes-Menendez, A. (2022). The role of consumer data in marketing: A research agenda. *Journal of Business Research, 146*, 436–452.

Blei, D. M., Ng, A. Y., & Jordan, M. I. (2003). Latent dirichlet allocation. *Journal of Machine Learning Research, 3, no. Jan*, 993–1022.

Brahmbhatt, D., & Shah, J. (2017). Determinants of brand equity from the consumer's perspective: A literature review. *IUP Journal of Brand Management, 14*(4), 33–46.

Chang, Z. (2022). A Survey of Modern Crawler Methods. In *The 6th International Conference on Control Engineering and Artificial Intelligence* (pp. 21–28).

Chaw, L. Y., & Tang, C. M. (2019). Online accommodation booking: What information matters the most to users? *Information Technology & Tourism, 21*(3), 369–390.

Debortoli, S., Müller, O., Junglas, I., & Vom Brocke, J. (2016). Text mining for information systems researchers: An annotated topic modeling tutorial. *Communications of the Association for Information Systems (CAIS), 39*(1), 7.

Essien, A., & Chukwukelu, G. (2022). Deep learning in hospitality and tourism: A research framework agenda for future research. *International Journal of Contemporary Hospitality Management, no. ahead-of-print*, 4480.

Górska-Warsewicz, H., & Kulykovets, O. (2020). Hotel brand loyalty—A systematic literature review. *Sustainability, 12*(12), 4810.

Hanaysha, J. (2016). Restaurant location and price fairness as key determinants of brand equity: A study on fast food restaurant industry. *Business and Economic Research, 6*(1), 310–323.

Hossin, M., & Sulaiman, M. N. (2015). A review on evaluation metrics for data classification evaluations. *International Journal of Data Mining & Knowledge Management Process, 5*(2), 1.

Iglesias, O., Markovic, S., Singh, J. J., & Sierra, V. (2019). Do customer perceptions of corporate services brand ethicality improve brand equity? Considering the roles of brand heritage, brand image, and recognition benefits. *Journal of Business Ethics, 154*, 441–459.

Kirilenko, A. P., Stepchenkova, S. O., Kim, H., & Li, X. (2018). Automated sentiment analysis in tourism: Comparison of approaches. *Journal of Travel Research, 57*(8), 1012–1025.

Lamberton, C., & Stephen, A. T. (2016). A thematic exploration of digital, social media, and mobile marketing: Research evolution from 2000 to 2015 and an agenda for future inquiry. *Journal of Marketing, 80*(6), 146–172.

Landauer, T. K., Foltz, P. W., & Laham, D. (1998). An introduction to latent semantic analysis. *Discourse Processes, 25*(2–3), 259–284.

Lee, S., & Chuang, N.-K. (2022). Applying expanded servicescape to the hotel industry. *Journal of Hospitality & Tourism Research, 46*(4), 771–796.

Lee, D., & Seung, H. S. (2000). Algorithms for non-negative matrix factorization. *Advances in Neural Information Processing Systems, 13*, 25.

Liat, C. B., Mansori, S., & Huei, C. T. (2014). The associations between service quality, corporate image, customer satisfaction, and loyalty: Evidence from the Malaysian hotel industry. *Journal of Hospitality Marketing & Management, 23*(3), 314–326.

Macieira, F., Oliveira, T., & Yanaze, M. (2020). Models of satisfaction antecedents: A brief review. An integrative literature review of the most discussed satisfaction models in marketing studies. *International Journal of Services and Operations Management, 36*(3), 348–359.

Mariani, M., & Borghi, M. (2020). Environmental discourse in hotel online reviews: A big data analysis. *Journal of Sustainable Tourism, 29*(5), 829–848.

Martínez, P., & Nishiyama, N. (2019). Enhancing customer-based brand equity through CSR in the hospitality sector. *International Journal of Hospitality & Tourism Administration, 20*(3), 329–353.

Mehraliyev, F., Chan, I. C. C., & Kirilenko, A. P. (2022). Sentiment analysis in hospitality and tourism: A thematic and methodological review. *International Journal of Contemporary Hospitality Management, 34*(1), 46–77.

Mustak, M., Salminen, J., Plé, L., & Wirtz, J. (2021). Artificial intelligence in marketing: Topic modeling, scientometric analysis, and research agenda. *Journal of Business Research, 124*, 389–404.

Parzych, K., & Brkić-Vejmelka, J. (2020). Guests' assessment of hotel facilities and services: Zadar case study. *European Journal of Tourism, Hospitality and Recreation, 10*(3), 241–250.

Puh, K., & Bagić Babac, M. (2022). Predicting sentiment and rating of tourist reviews using machine learning. *Journal of Hospitality and Tourism Insights, 6*, 1188.

Raguseo, E., Neirotti, P., & Paolucci, E. (2017). How small hotels can drive value their way in infomediation. The case of 'Italian hotels vs. OTAs and TripAdvisor'. *Information & Management, 54*(6), 745–756.

Salmony, M. Y. A., & Faridi, A. R. (2021). Supervised sentiment analysis on amazon product reviews: A survey. In *2021 2nd international conference on intelligent engineering and management (ICIEM)* (pp. 132–138). IEEE.

Serra-Cantallops, A., Ramon Cardona, J., & Salvi, F. (2020). Antecedents of positive eWOM in hotels: Exploring the relative role of satisfaction, quality and positive emotional experiences. *International Journal of Contemporary Hospitality Management, 32*(11), 3457–3477.

Sheehan, M., Grant, K., & Garavan, T. (2018). Strategic talent management: A macro and micro analysis of current issues in hospitality and tourism. *Worldwide Hospitality and Tourism Themes, 10*, 28.

Sürücü, Ö., Öztürk, Y., Okumus, F., & Bilgihan, A. (2019). Brand awareness, image, physical quality and employee behavior as building blocks of customer-based brand equity: Consequences in the hotel context. *Journal of Hospitality and Tourism Management, 40*, 114–124.

Ullah, M. A., Marium, S. M., Begum, S. A., & Dipa, N. S. (2020). An algorithm and method for sentiment analysis using the text and emoticon. *ICT Express, 6*(4), 357–360.

Ye, Q., Law, R., Gu, B., & Chen, W. (2011). The influence of user-generated content on traveler behavior: An empirical investigation on the effects of e-word-of-mouth to hotel online bookings. *Computers in Human Behavior, 27*(2), 634–639.

Zarezadeh, Z. Z., Rastegar, R., & Xiang, Z. (2022). Big data analytics and hotel guest experience: A critical analysis of the literature. *International Journal of Contemporary Hospitality Management, 34*, 2320.

Chapter 25
Business Ethics and Green Taxonomy in an Era that Energy Consumption and Prices Are Defined by a War: An Empirical Study in Western Macedonian Enterprises

A. Metsiou, G. Broni, E. Papachristou, M. Kiki, and P. Evangelou

Abstract The concept of business ethics refers to the principles and standards guiding the behavior of individuals and organizations in the business world, including ethical principles such as honesty, integrity, fairness, and responsibility. Companies which adhere to strong ethical standards are more likely to earn the trust and respect of their customers, thus achieving long-term success and sustainability. Therefore, in order to comply with the concept of ethics in business and relationships between national companies, laws apply in the term of the international trade.

In this framework, green taxonomy collaborates with the business's successful appearance, by referring to a classification system for sustainability and investments. Green taxonomy provides a framework for companies to identify and categorize their economic activities that promote their contribution to environmental objectives, such as reducing greenhouse gas emissions, conserving natural resources, and promoting sustainable development while helping investors to decide where to direct their resources and investments.

This paper examines the presence of business ethics and green taxonomy in the region of Western Macedonia. The collection of primary data for conducting the quantitative survey was achieved using a structured closed-ended questionnaire. Descriptive statistics and frequencies were applied to answer the research questions.

The survey provides valuable insights into the current state of green policy adoption among enterprises in Western Macedonia and highlights the potential for these businesses to adopt more sustainable practices. It seems that there is still a significant gap between the certification of ISO standards and the implementation of green policies in the surveyed enterprises in Western Macedonia. However, the

---

A. Metsiou (✉) · G. Broni · E. Papachristou · M. Kiki · P. Evangelou
University of Western Macedonia, IEES, Kozani, Greece
e-mail: diees00004@uowm.gr

© The Author(s), under exclusive license to Springer Nature Switzerland AG 2024
N. Tsounis, A. Vlachvei (eds.), *Applied Economic Research and Trends*, Springer
Proceedings in Business and Economics,
https://doi.org/10.1007/978-3-031-49105-4_25

results also highlight the potential for these enterprises to adopt green policies and contribute to sustainable business practices.

Keywords Business ethics · Green taxonomy · Times of crisis · Investments · Global economy

25.1 Introduction

The concept "green taxonomy" refers to a classification system that defines and categorizes economic activities based on their environmental sustainability, by providing a framework that identifies the environmentally sustainable activities. Therefore, its importance lies in several key aspects, such as providing certain criteria and definitions that offer clarity and consistency in assessing and labeling environmentally sustainable activities (Kharchenko & Illiashenko, 2017). It also helps the enterprises to identify potential environmental risks and assess their exposure to these risks and therefore align their activities with the "green taxonomy." "Green taxonomy" can also play an important role in enabling enterprises to access green finance, such as "green" bonds, and "green" loans, and also by positioning as environmentally responsible, enterprises can acquire a share of the expanding green market (Debbarma & Choi, 2022). Overall, the adaptation of the "green taxonomy" demonstrates an enterprise's commitment to environmental sustainability and can enhance the company's reputation and helps to build trust among stakeholders and strengthen the enterprise's relationships with its customers, employees, investors, and communities. All in all, it provides a structured approach for enterprises to transit to a sustainable future.

25.2 Literature Review

25.2.1 Business Ethics

Nowadays, the concepts of "ethics" and "responsibility" are concepts inextricably linked to progress and civilization in every field of human activity. Therefore, these concepts are also equally linked to the business field. After all, entrepreneurship is a field of human activity which plays an important role in guarding human responsibility, economic development, and social cohesion (Advantage, 2020). Indeed, in the times we live in, times that are characterized by rapid technological developments and the strengthening of globalization, a new business model has emerged, enhanced by the concepts of corporate social responsibility and business ethics, which play an important role in the development of a business. Business ethics contribute to maintaining social cohesion and achieving the well-being of a society and, in addition, it gives the company high added value by integrating into the company's development actions of various dimensions of a social, environmental, and cultural nature, contributing to the sustainable development of the company providing ecological, economic, and sociocultural foundations (Sternberg, 2000).

Business ethics include the principles and values that should guide business decisions and behavior. It involves treating customers, employees, business partners, and the public with respect, honesty, and transparency. Therefore, business ethics are an important factor in the long-term success of a business, as a company that focuses on business ethics is more likely to establish stable and long-term relationships with its customers, employees, and associates. According to Kirrane (1990), the main principles of business ethics include:

- Transparency and integrity in communication and business relationships.
- Transparency and integrity in business relationships and business dealings.
- Competitive behavior with respect for the competitors.
- Compliance with laws and regulations.
- Commitment to sustainability, as business ethics and sustainability are intricately linked and are important factors for the long-term success of a business.

Sustainability refers to the ability of a business to create value for future generations while maintaining its ability to grow and generate profits. This means that the business must take into consideration the social, environmental, and economic factors and act in coherence with them (Turner et al., 1994; Jones et al., 2005).

According to Thiroux and Krasemann (1980) and Mazza and Furlotti (2019), business ethics as a term also involve treating customers, employees, associates, and the public with respect, honesty, and transparency, as a company that focuses on business ethics is more likely to establish stable and long-term relationships with its customers, employees, and partners. Today, due to the global economic crisis, the need to develop new forms of responsibility that contribute to maintaining the competitiveness of a company is becoming increasingly urgent. This occurs because of factors such as the globalization of the markets, the ways in which available economic resources are distributed on a global scale, the concerns about changing environmental conditions, such as climate change, and the achievements in the field of modern technologies (Clegg et al., 2007).

The growth policies pursued by governments and businesses in previous decades have led to the current economic recession. Now the common goal of all businesses and organizations, both private and public, is Sustainable Development, defined as the purpose to improve the quality of life through the development and adoption of policies that protect the environment. The path to Sustainable Development can be successful only when driven by ethical ways so that society can see far ahead (Rozuel & Kakabadse, 2010).

Sustainable Development is possible in a society when businesses:

25.2.2 Maximize the Capabilities of Their People in an Effective and Efficient Manner

- Maximize the planet's ability to sustain and renew its capacity to provide sustainable life.
- Improve society's own ability to sustain itself and solve its own problems.
- Increase the usefulness of their existence through innovation, available resources, and focusing on all stakeholders.
- Focus on recycling during all the production process stages, from the design of the product or service to the recycling of the final product itself, when it is no longer useful or usable.

Overall, business ethics can play a key role in the well-being of the company as well as society and enhance sustainable development (White, 2001).

25.2.3 Ethics in Times of Economic and Social Crises

The presence of ethics is particularly important in times of crisis, as it represents a key principle that can help address the challenges people face. Crises can cause great stress, uncertainty, and insecurity and can cause significant changes in people's lives. Ethics can provide a guiding principle for the decisions people make during times of crisis (Brans, 2002). During these periods, the need for solidarity and cooperation between people is greater than ever before. Ethics invites all to consider the best practice of action to address these crises (Chouliaraki, 2017). Moreover, ethics can help maintain trust and solidarity in society during challenging times, and the presence of ethics is most important during times of crisis, as it represents a fundamental principle that can help address the challenges the society faces (Balmer et al., 2007).

Moreover, ethics can provide a guiding principle for the decisions people, governments, and companies make during periods of crisis, as ethics calls everyone to examine the best possible practical course of action to address these crises. In addition, the presence of ethics can help society maintain trust and solidarity, which are essential values that can help people come together and support each other through challenging times. Furthermore, by upholding ethical principles, people can foster a sense of mutual respect and understanding that can help everyone navigate through crises (Baxi & Ray, 2012).

In conclusion, ethics is even more important in times of crisis, whether it is a financial, health, or other forms of crisis and ethics should not be considered a secondary issue, and although business decisions are made primarily based on economic consequences and profits, ethics as well must remain a focus during these times (Ellis, 2022). By dealing with challenges, companies can demonstrate their ethical values which will have a positive impact on the business's credibility and reputation. Moreover, business ethics during a crisis can help to bring about new opportunities for the company, as it has been shown on many occasions and Covid-19 and the Russian–Ukrainian war have surfaced the matter (Svensson & Wood, 2008).

25.2.4 Energy Consumption and Prices Due to the Russian–Ukrainian War

The Russian–Ukrainian war has had a significant impact on energy consumption and prices, particularly in Europe. As known, Russia is one of the world's largest energy producers and a major supplier of natural gas to Europe and the war between Russia and Ukraine has disrupted the energy supplies, particularly concerning the natural gas supplies. That is because Ukraine is a country that serves as a key transit country for Russian gas exports to Europe (Sauvageot, 2020). The problem of energy consumption due to the conflict between the two countries has been present back from the year 2014 when people were concerned about whether Russia would cut off gas supplies to Ukraine. That incident would have caused multiple effects on gas supplies and energy consumption and a rise in processes in the European countries. A great fear was caused for a potential energy crisis, and some countries have taken measures to reduce their reliance on Russian gas. A great concern had been raised as well about energy supplies and the possible impact on energy prices due to the conflict. In these times, back in 2014 were the early stages of the conflict that ultimately led to a war, there was a sharp increase in oil and gas prices, but they have been stabilized over the years. In 2022, the problem resurfaced as the two countries engaged in war and it has highlighted the importance of energy security, particularly for countries that rely mostly on imports of natural gas and other fossil fuels (Kiki et al., 2023).

Moreover, the war, as well as the Western sanctions on Russia, has led to major increases concerning the prices of many important goods such as wheat and energy and that has fueled both a coming food crisis and an inflationary wave in the global economy. It is well known that Russia is not only an oil exporter but also the major one after Saudi Arabia. Furthermore, Russia is the world's leading exporter of natural gas, wheat, and nitrogen fertilizers; therefore, it has not been a surprise that the war led to the rise of international oil prices to their highest levels since the record highs of 2008. There have been efforts by the countries to reduce their dependence on Russian oil, gas, and petroleum products, or even to cap their prices, but with no impressive results. More importantly, the efforts have been intensified after Russia cut off gas flows through the Nord Stream 1 gas pipeline to Germany, wholesale gas prices soared in Europe. A fear has arisen that a complete cutoff would plunge the Eurozone into recession, with a sharp contraction in both Germany and Italy, according to Goldman Sachs. One of the priority steps taken by the European states was to intervene in their energy markets. Governments intervened in the markets as they began campaigns for a reduction in energy consumption (Uma et al., 2022).

Among the measures the governments took was the nationalization of the energy companies. Germany, in particular, is considering bailing out Uniper, one of the world's largest importers of natural gas, after it was struck by a great reduction in imports due to Russian gas (Silvester, 2021). The tumultuous developments triggered by the Ukrainian war leads to the conclusion that there has now been a new era for international relations, the global economy, and political affairs. It is still not clear what the exact nature of this new era will be. However, we can fairly assert that even when this war is over there might be no return to the previous situation, as the war seems to guide the world through a historic turning point (Prusko & Ehmke, 2023).

One of the areas where the situation has changed completely is the field of energy, as Russia is the main supplier of gas and oil to the European Union. Therefore, EU leaders have already taken the political decision to decouple Russia regarding the energy field. However, it has repeatedly been shown that there is a long distance between making a decision and its implementation. And as the energy sector is concerned, the situation is more complicated due to the economic demands, the timelines, and the raw materials' availability.

25.2.5 Green Taxonomy

The term "green taxonomy" refers to a type of tax levied on greenhouse emissions and other environmental activities. It is imposed to promote sustainability and environmental protection, as green taxation can act as an incentive for businesses and consumers to reduce their use of energy and products that emit greenhouse gases. In particular, green taxonomy involves increasing the prices of products that cause pollution or sufficient energy use, such as fuel and electricity. Green taxonomy can generate additional revenue for the state, which can be used to finance environmental projects and initiatives, such as the development of renewable energy sources and the enhancement of sustainability in industry and agriculture (Alessi et al., 2019).

According to Sikora (2021), the severe impacts and changes caused to the environment and climate by the irresponsible exploitation and use of natural resources and carbon dioxide emissions have led to the need to adopt practices and policies worldwide to mitigate them and achieve the sustainability of the planet. Besides, it is a known fact that the earth is facing significant risks, such as the depletion of natural and water resources, global warming, and other serious effects of human greed. Green taxonomy is a measure taken to enhance the protection of the environment.

At a European Union level, the Green Deal (Tutak et al., 2021) aims to make Europe a climate-neutral continent, through what has been set out in the European

Green Deal. More specifically, the objective is to transform the EU into a "modern, resource-efficient, and competitive economy" based on three goals:

- Achieving zero net greenhouse gas emissions by 2050.
- Achieving decoupling of economic growth from resource use.
- Fully addressing the marginalization of every person and every region.

In order to define common policies and common actions to secure the objectives of the European Green Deal, a long period of planning and adjustment has been required, and the principles and regulations that have finally been established with regard to green taxonomy correspond to a major challenge for investors and financial funds of companies, public organizations, as well as the design and implementation of financial investment programs to support companies and organizations (Elkerbout et al., 2020; Tsiropoulos et al., 2022).

The purpose of the EU Green Taxonomy is to create a more transparent structure on which green investments will be based, aiming to facilitate and encourage investment by all stakeholders and interested parties in practices that can be described as sustainable. The economic activities that can make the greatest contribution to achieving the two environmental objectives of climate change mitigation and adaptation to climate change have been identified by the European Parliament and the European Council as a top priority.

Alessi and Battiston (2022) state that as green taxonomy focuses on climate objectives, it includes activities that aim to reduce greenhouse gas emissions and improve climate resilience and therefore includes the sectors with the largest contribution to CO_2 emissions, as well as activities that allow their transformation, as the transformation of activities in these sectors is essential to achieve the EU's climate objectives. Through the climate delegated act, the EU Green Taxonomy criteria cover the economic activities of around 40% of listed companies, in sectors responsible for almost 80% of Europe's direct greenhouse gas emissions. Through this coverage, the EU Green Taxonomy can significantly increase the potential of green finance to support the transition, in particular for high carbon-emitting sectors.

Overall, green taxonomy is a tax policy that seeks to influence the behavior of people and businesses by encouraging environmental protection and sustainability. It involves imposing taxes on activities that cause pollution and greenhouse gas emissions, while providing tax reductions to businesses and individuals for activities that promote sustainability and environmental protection, such as the use of renewable energy or recycling. Green taxonomy is considered to be an effective way to achieve environmental objectives and ensure sustainable development (Shafi et al., 2023).

25.3 Methodology

25.3.1 *Aim and Research Questions*

This paper aims to investigate the willingness and preparation of enterprises based in Western Macedonia, Greece to adopt "green" policies that will help their transition to the green economy standards according to the EU Green Deal objective for sustainable development. The secondary purpose is to examine the degree of influence that green actions implemented by the enterprises of Western Macedonia have on their performance in the aspects of operational efficiency, relational efficiency, and business allowances. The study population consists of enterprises operating in the Region of Western Macedonia being active for at least a year during the time of the research.

Based on the stated aim of the research, the main research question was formulated as follows:

"In what degree have the enterprises of Western Macedonia adopted green policies?"

Secondary research questions that emerged from the aim and the secondary purpose of this research were formulated as follows:

"In what degree are the enterprises of Western Macedonia willing to adopt green policies/more green policies (if they are already applying any)?"
"In what degree do the enterprises of Western Macedonia apply actions in line with green policies?"
"In what degree do the green actions implied by the enterprises of Western Macedonia influence their operational efficiency?"
"In what degree do the green actions implied by the enterprises of Western Macedonia influence their relational efficiency?"
"In what degree do the green actions implied by the enterprises of Western Macedonia influence their business allowances?"

25.3.2 *Type of Research*

To answer the research questions posed and since the aim of this research was to investigate measurable and, thus, quantitative parameters, we used a structured questionnaire adapted from previous research contacted by Lee et al, (2012). The primary data that were collected were statistically analyzed with the use of IBM SPSS 20.0. Descriptive statistics were used to derive answers to our research questions, as it is a fundamental approach when examining a current situation, as stated by Finlay et al. (2013).

25.3.3 Data Collection—Measurement Tool

A structured closed-ended questionnaire[1] was used to collect primary data in the scope of quantitative research. The questions included were adopted from the questionnaire used in previous research regarding green supply chain management and organizational performance, contacted by Lee et al. (2012). The mandatory criterion for the completion and submission of the questionnaire was the implementation of any of the EU green policies by the company.

The questionnaire consisted of a total of 41 questions, divided into four sections. The first section included only one question, to ensure that the enterprises already implemented at least one of the EU green policies. The second section included five questions regarding the enterprises' characteristics. The third section consisted of one question of multiple possible choices regarding the green policies the enterprise implemented. Finally, the fourth section consisted of statements to which were given five choices of agreement (Likert scale) regarding the areas of application of green policies. This section is divided into two categories. In the first category, the questions focus on four factors: Internal Environmental Management (EIM—with five sub-questions), Green Markets (GM—with four sub-questions), Cooperation with Customers (CC—with four sub-questions), and Eco-Design (ED—with five sub-questions). In the second category, the questions focus on three factors related to internal operations, efficiency, and performance of the firm as follows: Operational Efficiency (OE—with six sub-questions), Relational Efficiency (RE—with six sub-questions), and Business Performance (BP—with four sub-questions).

The questionnaire was developed in electronic form using Google Forms and distributed to businesses operating in the Region of Western Macedonia. The questionnaire was distributed via email, after the researchers have communicated personally with the entrepreneurs, and during this communication, they were informed about the purpose and importance of the survey, as well as the preservation of anonymity and sensitive information about the business, while the necessary clarifications were given and it was underlined that their participation was voluntary, with no consequences in case of refusal. The questionnaire that was distributed online was active for a three-month period (January 10 to April 10, 2023). Fifty-six questionnaires were fully answered and submitted. Statistical analysis was contacted using the statistical program IBM SPSS Statistics 20.0. Descriptive statistics and frequencies were applied to answer the research questions.

---

[1] The questionnaire is available at: https://forms.gle/A13SGqNmzrbhrWex9

Table 25.1 Reliability Analysis (Cronbach's Alpha)

Factors	Cronbach's Alpha
Internal environmental management (EIM)	0.857
Green markets (GM)	0.787
Cooperation with customers (CC)	0.964
Eco-design (ED)	0.909
Operational efficiency (OE)	0.823
Relational efficiency (RE)	0.972
Business performance (BP)	0.818
Total	0.931

Table 25.2 Enterprises' years of operation—frequencies table

Years of operation	n	%
<5	6	10.7
5–10	9	16.1
11–15	20	35.7
>15	21	37.5
Total	56	100.0

25.3.4 Reliability Analysis

The reliability of the questionnaire was tested using the coefficient Cronbach's Alpha consistency on each factor (dimension) of the questionnaire, as presented in Table 25.1. The analysis showed high internal consistency for all the factors considered.

25.4 Results and Discussion

25.4.1 Sample Description

Of the 56 enterprises sampled in the survey, 21 (37.5%) have been operating for more than 15 years and 20 (35.7%) have been operating for more than 11 but less than 15 years (see Table 25.2). The vast majority (78.6%) of the enterprises that participated in the research were small-sized businesses (<50 employees) (see Table 25.3). The main economic sector that the enterprises sell their products or services is the wholesale and retail sector (41.1%) (see Table 25.4), while most enterprises (51.8%) are active in the Secondary Economy Sector (see Table 25.5). The total amount (100.0%) of the enterprises that participated in the survey act as secondary business suppliers (see Table 25.6).

25 Business Ethics and Green Taxonomy in an Era that Energy Consumption...

Table 25.3 Number of enterprises' employees (size of the enterprise)—frequencies table

Number of employees	n	%
<50	44	78.6
50–100	10	17.9
101–200	2	3.6
Total	56	100.0

Table 25.4 Enterprises' main costumers—frequencies table

Main costumers	n	%
Primary economy sector	5	8.9
Secondary economy sector	20	35.7
Wholesale and retail sector	23	41.1
Tourism and accommodation	6	10.7
Sector of the catering industry	2	3.6
Total	56	100.0

Table 25.5 Enterprises' main activity—frequencies table

Main enterprises' activity	n	%
Primary economy sector	3	5.4
Secondary economy sector	29	51.8
Wholesale and retail	9	16.1
Tourism and accommodation	3	5.4
Sector of the catering industry	12	21.4
Total	56	100.0

Table 25.6 Enterprises' position in the supply chain—frequencies table

Enterprises' Position in the Supply Chain	n	%
Main business supplier	0	0.0
Secondary business supplier	56	100.0
Main supplier to government agencies	0	0.0
Secondary supplier to government agencies	0	0.0
Total	56	100.0

25.4.2 Degree of Green Policies' Adoption

In the question regarding the green policies adopted by the enterprises of Western Macedonia by the period of this survey, most businesses (87.5%) answered that they are ISO certified. Nevertheless, the percentage of application of green policies is very low (3.6–14.3%) with the sole exception of the case of Environment, Health, and Safety (EHS) policies that 30.4% of the sampled enterprises have already adopted (see Table 25.7, Fig. 25.1).

Table 25.7 Green policies adopted by the enterprises of Western Macedonia—frequencies table

Green policies/Quality Standard	Yes		No	
	n	%	N	%
Electronic product environmental assessment tool (EPEAT)	7	12.5	49	87.5
EU eco-management and audit scheme (EU EMAS)	2	3.6	54	96.4
European union voluntary label for environmental excellence (EU eco-label)	7	12.5	49	87.5
Environment, health, and safety (EHS)	17	30.4	39	69.6
Life-cycle assessment (LCA)	8	14.3	48	85.7
ISO	49	87.5	7	12.5

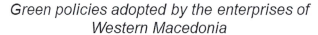
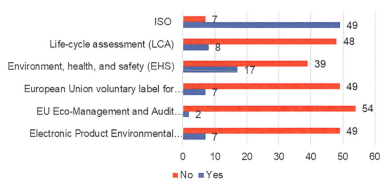

Fig. 25.1 Green policies adopted by the enterprises of Western Macedonia

25.4.3 Green Policies' Actions Adoption

The choices given to the statements that aimed to measure the implementation of actions in line with green policies or the intention of the enterprises to adopt certain green policies soon showed that most of the sample is planning to consider implementing green actions, though they have not started any actions yet. The only cases in the answers that showed a trend of green policy adoption were the cases regarding ISO certification (either for the enterprise or for their suppliers and customers) as well as in the answers given for the Cooperation with Clients section (see Table 25.8).

25.4.4 Enterprises' Performance

Responses on the current performance of the business and the influence of green actions on it show that the actions in question affect their operational efficiency

Table 25.8 Percentages of implementation of actions in line with green policies

Green actions	Implementation not currently considered (1)	Planning to consider implementation (2)	Implementation is under planning (3)	Started implementation proceedings (4)	Already implementing (5)	Mean
Internal environmental management (IEM) [(GSCM)]	3.6	62.5	12.5	16.1	5.4	2.57
Internal environmental management (IEM) [GSCM support]	3.6	66.1	17.9	8.9	3.6	2.43
Internal environmental management (IEM) [cooperation]	3.6	58.9	19.6	8.9	8.9	2.61
Internal environmental management (IEM) [compliance-audit]	5.4	55.4	16.1	12.5	10.7	2.68
Internal environmental management (IEM) [ISO]	3.6	10.7	7.1	53.6	25.0	3.86
Green markets (GM) [eco labeling]	3.6	55.4	14.3	16.1	10.7	2.75
Green markets (GM) [suppliers]	1.8	48.2	21.4	17.9	10.7	2.88
Green markets (GM) [suppliers auditing]	5.4	50.0	21.4	10.7	12.5	2.75
Green markets (GM) [suppliers - ISO]	3.6	17.9	8.9	50.0	19.6	3.64
Cooperation with clients (CC) [environmentally friendly design]	1.8	35.7	50.4	21.4	35.7	3.54
Cooperation with clients (CC) ["clean" production]	1.8	37.5	7.1	19.6	33.9	3.46
Cooperation with clients (CC) ["green" packaging]	3.6	37.5	10.7	16.1	32.1	3.36
Cooperation with clients (CC) [environmentally friendly products]	1.8	33.9	12.5	19.6	32.1	3.46
ECO DESIGN (ED) [raw materials/energy]	1.8	51.8	17.9	16.1	12.5	2.86
ECO DESIGN (ED) [reusable components]	7.1	50.0	26.8	8.9	7.1	2.59
ECO DESIGN (ED) [hazardous substances]	1.8	46.4	28.6	12.5	10.7	2.84
ECO DESIGN (ED) [disassembly]	10.7	46.4	26.8	12.5	3.6	2.52
ECO DESIGN (ED) [LCA]	8.9	46.4	23.2	12.5	8.9	2.66

significantly, although there is a moderate impact in the aspect of turnover reduction and operating costs reduction. The sections regarding relational efficiency and business allowances seemed to be even more influenced (see Table 25.9).

25.4.5 Discussion

The statistical analysis of the answers given during the survey revealed that most of the participating enterprises were active in their respective economic sectors for more than 11 years, which shows that they have gained a certain position in the market. The vast majority (78.6%) are small enterprises with less than 50 employees, which is in line with the general picture of enterprises in the survey area. The main economic sector to which the sampled enterprises sell their products or services is the wholesale and retail sector, which is in accordance with the present situation in Western Macedonia, where most businesses operate as retailers as it is shown by the data of registered businesses in the local chambers of commerce. Nevertheless, most of the enterprises that participated in the survey stated that they operate in the Secondary Economy Sector, while they mostly act as secondary business suppliers.

The survey results indicate that the majority of enterprises (87.5%) in Western Macedonia are ISO certified. However, the implementation of green policies is low, with only 3.6–14.3% of enterprises adopting such policies, except for the case of Environment, Health, and Safety (EHS) policies, where 30.4% of enterprises have already adopted them. The responses of the surveyed enterprises regarding the implementation of actions in line with green policies show that most of them are planning to adopt green actions, but they have not started any actions yet.

The survey also revealed that ISO certification and cooperation with clients were the only factors that showed a trend of green policy adoption. The results suggest that the adoption of green policies is influenced by factors such as certification and cooperation with clients. Additionally, the responses on the current performance of the business and the influence of green actions on it show that green actions significantly affect the operational efficiency of enterprises, although there is a moderate impact on reducing turnover and operating costs.

The survey results indicate that green policies have a more significant impact on relational efficiency and business allowances. Relational efficiency refers to the ability of enterprises to build and maintain relationships with suppliers and customers. The survey results suggest that green policies have a positive impact on the relational efficiency of enterprises. Business allowances refer to financial incentives provided by governments to encourage the adoption of green policies. The results of the survey show that green policies have a significant impact on business allowances, indicating that enterprises are more likely to adopt green policies if they receive financial incentives.

The survey results suggest that the adoption of green policies in Western Macedonia is still in its infancy. The results highlight the importance of factors such

25 Business Ethics and Green Taxonomy in an Era that Energy Consumption. . .

Table 25.9 Enterprises' performance and green actions influence

Green actions	Strongly disagree (1)	Disagree (2)	Neither Agree/Nor Disagree (3)	Agree (4)	Strongly agree (5)	Mean
Operational efficiency (OE) [turnover reduction]	17.9	44.6	17.9	16.1	3.6	2.43
Operational efficiency (OE) [operating costs reduction]	28.6	51.8	10.7	8.9	0.0	2.00
Operational efficiency (OE) [product quality improvement]	3.6	1.8	42.9	33.9	17.9	3.61
Operational efficiency (OE) [customer service improvement]	1.8	0.0	44.6	37.5	16.1	3.66
Operational efficiency (OE) [time reduction]	3.6	12.5	58.9	14.3	10.7	3.16
Operational efficiency (OE) [customer value]	1.8	1.8	7.1	53.6	35.7	4.20
Relational efficiency (RE) [respect]	1.8	0.0	7.1	19.6	71.4	4.59
Relational efficiency (RE) [sincerity]	1.8	1.8	14.3	8.9	73.2	4.50
Relational efficiency (RE) [information exchange]	1.8	0.0	8.9	17.9	71.4	4.57
Relational efficiency (RE) [working relationship]	1.8	0.0	7.1	19.6	71.4	4.59
Relational efficiency (RE) [commitment]	1.8	0.0	5.4	16.1	76.8	4.66
Relational efficiency (RE) [productive relations]	1.8	0.0	10.7	16.1	71.4	4.55
Business allowances (BA) [better use of assets]	0.0	3.6	5.4	69.6	21.4	4.09
Business allowances (BA) [competitive positioning]	0.0	3.6	50.0	26.8	19.6	3.63
Business allowances (BA) [improved profitability]	3.6	5.4	57.1	21.4	12.5	3.34
Business allowances (BA) [overall improved organizational performance]	0.0	3.6	8.9	55.4	32.1	4.16

as ISO certification and cooperation with clients in promoting the adoption of green policies. The survey also shows that green policies have a significant impact on the operational efficiency of enterprises, as well as on relational efficiency and business allowances. Therefore, it is essential for enterprises in Western Macedonia to adopt green policies to ensure sustainable business practices and contribute to addressing the global challenge of climate change.

25.5 Conclusions

The statistical analysis of the survey results revealed that the participating enterprises have been active in their respective economic sectors for more than 11 years, indicating that they have gained a certain position in the market. Moreover, the majority of the sampled enterprises (78.6%) are small enterprises with less than 50 employees, which is in line with the general picture of businesses in the survey area. The main economic sector to which the sampled enterprises sell their products or services is the wholesale and retail sector, reflecting the current situation in Western Macedonia, where most businesses operate as retailers, as shown by the data of registered businesses in the local chambers of commerce.

Interestingly, most of the enterprises that participated in the survey stated that they operate in the Secondary Economy Sector, while they mostly act as secondary business suppliers. This indicates that there is potential for these enterprises to shift toward more sustainable practices and adopt green policies, which could not only benefit their own businesses but also contribute to the overall sustainability of the region.

According to the survey results, the degree of green policy adoption among the enterprises of Western Macedonia is quite low, with only 3.6–14.3% of businesses applying green policies, except for Environment, Health, and Safety (EHS) policies, which were adopted by 30.4% of the sampled enterprises. However, the survey also found that most of the sampled enterprises are planning to consider implementing green actions soon.

The degree of willingness to adopt green policies among the enterprises of Western Macedonia was quite high, with most of the sampled enterprises expressing a desire to adopt green policies soon. The survey results revealed that the only cases in the answers that showed a trend of green policy adoption were the cases regarding ISO certification (either for the enterprise or for their suppliers and customers) as well as in the answers given for the Cooperation with Clients section.

The degree to which the enterprises of Western Macedonia apply actions in line with green policies is very low, except for EHS policies. Most of the sampled enterprises stated that they have not started any green actions yet, although they are planning to consider implementing them soon.

The survey results suggest that the green actions implied by the enterprises of Western Macedonia have a significant impact on their operational efficiency, although there is a moderate impact on turnover reduction and operating costs reduction. Furthermore, the sections regarding relational efficiency and business allowances seemed to be even more influenced by the implementation of green policies.

The survey provides valuable insights into the current state of green policy adoption among enterprises in Western Macedonia and highlights the potential for these businesses to adopt more sustainable practices. It seems that there is still a significant gap between the certification of ISO standards and the implementation of green policies in the surveyed enterprises in Western Macedonia. However, the results also highlight the potential for these enterprises to adopt green policies and contribute to sustainable business practices. Nevertheless, the findings of the survey suggest that while there is still a long way to go in terms of green policy adoption, there is a willingness among businesses to consider implementing green policies and practices, which is a positive step toward more sustainable economic growth in the region.

As a next step, it would be valuable to explore further the reasons why enterprises in Western Macedonia have been slow to adopt green policies and develop strategies to overcome these barriers. By doing so, the region can move toward more sustainable economic growth, which benefits both the enterprises and the environment.

References

Advantage, C. (2020). Corporate social responsibility. In *CSR and socially responsible investing strategies in transitioning and emerging economies* (Vol. 65). IGI Global.

Alessi, L., & Battiston, S. (2022). Two sides of the same coin: Green taxonomy alignment versus transition risk in financial portfolios. *International Review of Financial Analysis, 84*, 102319.

Alessi, L., Battiston, S., Melo, A., & Roncoroni, A. (2019). *The EU sustainability taxonomy: A financial impact assessment. European Commission.* Available at: https://ec.europa.eu/jrc/en/publication/eusustainability-taxonomy-financial-impact-assessment

Balmer, J. M., Fukukawa, K., & Gray, E. R. (2007). The nature and management of ethical corporate identity: A commentary on corporate identity, corporate social responsibility and ethics. *Journal of Business Ethics, 76*(1), 7–15.

Baxi, C. V., & Ray, R. S. (2012). *Corporate social responsibility.* Vikas Publishing House.

Brans, J. P. (2002). Ethics and decision. *European Journal of Operational Research, 136*(2), 340–352.

Chouliaraki, L. (2017). Suffering and the ethics of solidarity. In *Alleviating world suffering* (pp. 49–60). The Challenge of Negative Quality of Life.

Clegg, S., Kornberger, M., & Rhodes, C. (2007). Business ethics as practice. *British Journal of Management, 18*(2), 107–122.

Debbarma, J., & Choi, Y. (2022). A taxonomy of green governance: A qualitative and quantitative analysis towards sustainable development. *Sustainable Cities and Society, 79*, 103693.

Elkerbout, M., Egenhofer, C., Núñez Ferrer, J., Catuti, M., Kustova, I., & Rizos, V. (2020). The European green deal after Corona: Implications for EU climate policy. *CEPS Policy Insights, 6*, 1–12.

Ellis, J. E. (2022). *Feeling accountable: Affect and embodied ethics in times of crisis* (p. 17438721221089822). Law, Culture and the Humanities.

Finlay, I., Sheridan, M., Coburn, A., & Soltysek, R. (2013). Rapid response research: Using creative arts methods to research the lives of disengaged young people. *Research in Post-Compulsory Education, 18*(1–2), 127–142.

Jones, C., Parker, M., & Ten Bos, R. (2005). *For business ethics*. Routledge.

Kharchenko, V., & Illiashenko, O. (2017). Concepts of green IT engineering: Taxonomy, principles and implementation. In *Green IT Engineering* (pp. 3–19). Concepts, Models, Complex Systems Architectures.

Kiki, M., Metsiou, A., Papachristou, E., Migkos, S., & Manios, S. (2023). Possible social, political, and economic implications of major events. The collapse of financial institutions, the Covid-19 pandemic, and the Russian-Ukrainian war. *International Journal of Research Publication and Reviews*.

Kirrane, D. E. (1990). Managing values: A systematic approach to business ethics. *Training & Development Journal, 44*(11), 52–60.

Lee, S. M., Kim, S. T., & Choi, D. (2012). Green supply chain management and organizational performance. *Industrial Management & Data Systems, 112*(8), 1148–1180.

Mazza, T., & Furlotti, K. (2019). Quality of code of ethics: An empirical analysis on the stakeholder employee. *Social Responsibility Journal, 16*(8), 1377–1402.

Prusko, W., & Ehmke, D. (2023). Restructuring lessons from the Covid pandemic: Bail-out vs. Market approach: Country view: Germany. *European Business Organization Law Review, 24*, 1–23.

Rozuel, C., & Kakabadse, N. (2010). Ethics, spirituality and self: Managerial perspective and leadership implications. *Business Ethics: A European Review, 19*(4), 423–436.

Sauvageot, E. P. (2020). Between Russia as producer and Ukraine as a transit country: EU dilemma of interdependence and energy security. *Energy Policy, 145*, 111699.

Shafi, M., Ramos-Meza, C. S., Jain, V., Salman, A., Kamal, M., Shabbir, M. S., & Rehman, M. U. (2023). The dynamic relationship between green tax incentives and environmental protection. *Environmental Science and Pollution Research, 30*(12), 32184–32192.

Sikora, A. (2021). European green deal–legal and financial challenges of the climate change. In *Era forum* (Vol. 21, No. 4, pp. 681–697). Springer.

Silvester, C. (2021). Portfolio optimisation in Uniper. *Impact, 2021*(1), 46–50.

Sternberg, E. (2000). *Just business: Business ethics in action*. Oxford University Press.

Svensson, G., & Wood, G. (2008). A model of business ethics. *Journal of Business Ethics, 77*(3), 303–322.

Thiroux, J. P., & Krasemann, K. W. (1980). *Ethics: Theory and practice* (p. 480). Glencoe Publishing Company.

Tsiropoulos, I., Siskos, P., & Capros, P. (2022). The cost of recharging infrastructure for electric vehicles in the EU in a climate neutrality context: Factors influencing investments in 2030 and 2050. *Applied Energy, 322*, 119446.

Turner, G. B., Taylor, G. S., & Hartley, M. F. (1994). Ethics policies and gratuity acceptance by purchasers. *International Journal of Purchasing and Materials Management, 30*(2), 42–47.

Tutak, M., Brodny, J., & Bindzár, P. (2021). Assessing the level of energy and climate sustainability in the European union countries in the context of the European green deal strategy and agenda 2030. *Energies, 14*(6), 1767.

Umar, M., Riaz, Y., & Yousaf, I. (2022). Impact of Russian-Ukraine war on clean energy, conventional energy, and metal markets: Evidence from event study approach. *Resources Policy, 79*, 102966.

White, G. W. (2001). Business ethics. *Journal of Business & Finance Librarianship, 6*(4), 49–49.

Chapter 26
Economics and Marketing of Skills. *Pass the Point of No Return* in Arts and Tourism

Angela Besana, Annamaria Esposito, Chiara Fisichella, and Maria Cristina Vannini

Abstract After the pandemic, universities *pass the point of no return* toward the supply of skills, arts, and tourism are in the need after the pandemic. Jobs *evolve* together with curricula. University stakeholders look for students and young employees, who can approach both the online and the offline customer and who can be resilient in the competitive landscape.

In Milan and during the pandemic, IULM University, one of the most leading Italian universities for arts and tourism curricula in Italy, experienced lock-down with remote activities and virtual relations with firms, whose boards constantly paid attention to young students and provided them with valuable internships, typical and atypical collaborations. Soon after the pandemic, this university had an immediate and prompt recovery. In 2022, students were ready for their professional experiences in *alive* event organization, front and back office of hotels and cultural organizations, fundraising for culture and creativity, support to destination management, and social media marketing. What was needed, as concerns a mixture of prepandemic and postpandemic skills.

The aim of this paper is to estimate how much skills evolved and changed because of the pandemic and how much the satisfaction of students and entrepreneurs (stage tutors) is, today and after the pandemic, concerning a new match of competences in arts and tourism.

The methodology includes a stepwise multiple regression of the satisfaction of students and tutors for stages in arts and tourism. Students' and tutors' satisfaction is here estimated for main items of standard questionnaires, considering that satisfying training attracts students and employees.

A. Besana (✉) · A. Esposito · C. Fisichella
Business, Law, Economics and Consumer Behavior "Carlo A. Ricciardi" Department, IULM University, Milan, Italy
e-mail: angela.besana@iulm.it; annamaria.esposito@iulm.it; chiara.fisichella@iulm.it

M. C. Vannini
Maria Cristina Vannini, Soluzionimuseali- ims sas, Milano, Italy
e-mail: cristina.vannini@soluzionimuseali.com

© The Author(s), under exclusive license to Springer Nature Switzerland AG 2024
N. Tsounis, A. Vlachvei (eds.), *Applied Economic Research and Trends*, Springer Proceedings in Business and Economics,
https://doi.org/10.1007/978-3-031-49105-4_26

Keywords Economics · Marketing · University · Stage · Satisfaction · Arts · Tourism

26.1 *Passed the Point of No Return*, Economics of Skills for Arts and Tourism Education

The pandemic was a sort of *trauma* for universities. Though their efforts to retain their education, research standards, and live experiences, universities had to replace most of their offline activities with online ones (Benner et al., 2022; Reimers & Marmolejo, 2021). Their curricula had to adapt and change after years of maturation according to the ordinary life cycles for industries and markets like culture, tourism, creativity, and any other competitive landscape, where their laureates were foreseen as employees (Lv et al., 2022; Besana et al., 2022; Besana & Esposito, 2017). Connecting with their stakeholders like corporate partners, public administrations, local associations, and foundations, they had to decide for different frameworks, partnerships, and locations for internships and stages, while internships remained the essential and first step of professionalization of their students. Competences and skills were revolutionized for the extraordinary needs and economic contingencies of the pandemic (Besana et al., 2023; Tanase et al., 2022; Toklucu et al., 2022; Bayerlein et al., 2021). Above all, in art and tourism markets, where businesses suffered by a complete stop of their activities.

First, most of stages were online and telematic.

Second, most of competences and skills, whose design had been specifically trained and ready for the tourism supply chain, for events, from visual to performing ones, had to stop and to be redesigned for online and streaming. Some of specific competences for culture, tourism, and creativity disappeared and changed in online marketing and fundraising, virtual and crisis communication, budgeting and monitoring of extraordinary accountability, health management, human resources management in crisis (Shtembari & Feridun Elgün, 2023; Briant & Crowther, 2020; Bilsband et al., 2020).

In Milan and during the pandemic, IULM University, which is one of the most leading universities for arts and tourism curricula in Italy, experienced lockdown with remote activities and virtual relations with firms. Corporate boards had constantly paid attention to young students and had provided them with valuable internships and collaborations, which could be framed not only into stages (workshops, project works, creative labs, and projects in the fields).

Soon after the pandemic, this university had an immediate and prompt recovery. In 2022, all activities fully restarted in IULM buildings. Students were ready for their professional experiences in alive event organization, front and back office of hotels and cultural organizations, fundraising for culture and creativity, support to destination management and promotion, social media marketing, and what was needed as a mixture of prepandemic and post-pandemic skills.

The aim of this paper is to estimate how much skills evolved and changed because of the pandemic and how much the satisfaction of students and entrepreneurs (stage tutors) is, today and after the pandemic, concerning a new match of competences in arts and tourism. If competences and skills were specific and detailed by professional standards before the pandemic, they were extraordinary designed during the pandemic. It might be that needs for standardized and ad hoc competences and ad hoc knowledge of arts and tourism are not more claimed by corporate tutors for staging students, who must be flexible and able to adapt in a new competitive landscape, whose structure and strategies must be renewed and fitted to different businesses after the pandemic (Besana et al., 2023; Volkov et al., 2022; Bilsland et al., 2020).

The methodology includes a stepwise multiple regression of the satisfaction of students and tutors for stages in arts and tourism. Students' and tutors' satisfaction is here estimated for main items of standard questionnaires. If skills change, the satisfaction may depend on specific knowledge, expertise, and know-how, students like to show and improve, and it may not depend on these standards for stage tutors, who look for basic competences, commitment, and adaptability.

26.2 Universities, Stages, and Satisfaction

Universities' purpose is to increase the level of students' education for knowledge improvement, employability, and contribution to the human and economic development of society (Vittadini, 2004). Three goals that are experience goods (Aitkin & Longford, 1986; Gori, 1992; Stiefel, 1999; Gori & Vittadini, 1998) and can be assessed ex-post, at different time intervals from the end of the service provision (Vittadini, 2004).

Stage or internship, it is an opportunity to evaluate *in itinere* if these three goals are reached or nearly to be reached, evaluating, for example, if there is a gap between theory and practice (Fox, 2001). In fact, internship permits to test skills, interests, and career choices in real working situations, providing a transition from "classroom to job" (Coco, 2000). Benefits of it are, for instance: ability to relate classroom concepts to practical applications; improved knowledge of industry career paths; crystallization of interests and career ambitions; reduced shock upon entering the workplace; and faster advancement (Coco, 2000). Benefit for the employer is, for example, the opportunity to "try before they buy" students they might wish to recruit (Neuman, 1999).

Jung and Lee (2016) studied the effect of short-term internship experience and find it shortened the duration to find a job and enhanced wages and job satisfaction. More, Prianto et al. (2017) found that being involved in internship program have a significant effect on the quality-of-life skills—abilities for adaptive and positive behavior—of the graduates and on the readiness to work.

Considering satisfaction as important factor of this process, Paulins (2008) suggested that students with satisfying internship experiences will have more positive feelings toward their career search process and university. In the hospitality sector, Ko (2008) demonstrated that training satisfaction is important for students to remain in it. This dynamic is termed the affective occupational commitment (Koo et al., 2016). More, Putra and Pubra (2020) observed that the greater the satisfaction with the internship experience at a company, the higher the conversion intention to remain in that company.

Which are the variables that influence a satisfying internship experience? Nelson (1994) reported that students had higher levels of satisfaction if they had supportive mentors during their internships. However, Gupta et al. (2010) indicated that students' assessment of their internships is not unidimensional, but instead arises from several factors as for example the comfort with the with the work environment. D'Abate et al. (2009) indicated that characteristics of the job (specifically, task significance and feedback) and characteristics of the work environment (in particular, learning opportunities, supervisor support, and organizational satisfaction) were the best predictors of internship satisfaction.

Parameters, variables, and estimates are, therefore, multidimensional and, according to national standards, this research will investigate a sample of internships, whose satisfaction is estimated both for students and for corporate tutors or employers with a multidimensional approach. This research will therefore concern the literature gap of the current emphasize on only one of the internship sides, either students or firms. This research will focus on the work environment and team, them confirming among the best predictors for students' satisfaction. This research will confirm how much adaptation and commitment are significant skills, too.

26.3 University Stakeholders and Students After the Pandemic: It Is Not Only a Matter of Stages

The COVID-19 pandemic has reshaped the landscape of internships, presenting both opportunities and challenges for students, employers, and universities. As for the transition to a post-pandemic world, it is crucial to explore the implications of this global crisis on internships and understand how stakeholders can adapt to create meaningful and impactful internship experiences.

The post-pandemic internship scenario is characterized by emerging trends that stress the importance of fostering innovation in internship programs and highlight the importance of adaptability, digital literacy, and remote collaboration skills. Traditional internship models have evolved, remote internships, and hybrid formats have gained prominence, enabling organizations to continue providing valuable learning experiences while adapting to remote work arrangements. These models have expanded access to internships, allowing students to engage with companies globally and fostering a diverse and inclusive internship environment.

Nowadays, employers are looking for candidates with resilience, problem solving skills, and the ability to navigate virtual workspaces (Irwin et al. 2022; Gill, 2020). Therefore, post-pandemic internships must emphasize developing these skills, preparing students for the changing demands of the workforce, and equipping them with the tools to thrive in the digital era.

From a network perspective, the pandemic has left a positive legacy as it has reshaped networking and mentoring opportunities for interns. Virtual networking events, online mentorship programs, and digital platforms have emerged as essential components of post-pandemic internships. These platforms facilitate connections between interns, professionals, and alumni, providing opportunities for mentorship, career guidance, and expanding professional networks. At the same time, they bring out new marketing strategies, new perspectives, and new trends.

Universities have been challenged to first adapt and then navigate these rapid changes and choose the right strategies to stay connected with stakeholders and achieve one of their most important educational goals: ensuring students transition from the classroom to the workplace developing students' capacity for work-related skills, enhancing job placement opportunities (Odlin et al., 2022; Besana & Esposito, 2017), and developing students' problem-solving, communication, and human relations skills.

Universities have been challenged to adapt to these rapid changes and to choose the right relationship marketing approaches (Varsha et al., 2022) and new communication tools—i.e., social media—in order to keep in touch with their stakeholders, including students, alumni, faculty, staff, and the public (Besana et al., 2023; Khashab et al., 2020; Kumar & Nanda, 2020). Furthermore, social media networking has had a significant impact on various aspects of communication and engagement for universities, offering a positive influence on university operations and brand building. These platforms facilitate real-time communication, feedback, and dialogue, fostering a sense of community and connection, providing universities with new avenues for relationship marketing aimed at building and nurturing relationships with stakeholders, increasing loyalty, support, and engagement with the universities (Besana et al., 2023).

In addition, universities can utilize social media to share news, updates, events, research findings, and other relevant information, as these platforms serve as effective channels for disseminating information to a wider audience, including prospective students and stakeholders, offering universities opportunities to enhance their value proposition (Papademetriu et al., 2022).

From an employment perspective, professional networks like LinkedIn enable universities to connect with employers, alumni, and industry professionals (Chala et al., 2021). This facilitates career development, job placement, and networking opportunities for students and alumni.

The emerging trends in post-pandemic internships have created unique opportunities for research and innovation, allowing interns to contribute to projects that foster creativity, critical thinking, and problem-solving skills.

At IULM University in Milan (Italy), innovation has been adopted as a recovery strategy, leading to the emergence of new internship formats such as project work, workshops, and creative work. A brief description of each format is provided below.

Workshops are research projects or professional training courses proposed by professors within the faculty. These workshops involve students and are designed to be consistent with the training courses offered by the degree programs. Students participate in these workshops to gain research experience and further their understanding of specific topics.

Project works are professional training projects carried out in collaboration with a company or cultural institution that has an agreement with the university. The project work is approved by the Faculty Council and a professor from the degree course manages the relationship with the company/institution. The professor together with the company representative prepare the project brief and they oversee the development of the design work, ensuring its relevance to the student's educational path and professional opportunities.

Creative works involve innovation of contents and processes based on the teachings and testimonies of established professionals in a specific sector. The creative work is coordinated by a professional with teaching experience who organizes a series of testimonials and defines an assignment brief for the participants. The topics covered in the testimonials align with the professional opportunities of the degree course. Creative work can also be interdisciplinary, embracing multiple productive sectors.

The experiences of these alternative internship models enable students to practice their learning and skills in a professional-like environment, providing insight into different area of expertise (Hergert, 2009). This experiential learning can be considered a useful mechanism for developing student work readiness (Kapareliotis et al., 2019) and testifies a changing internship landscape as well as a new range of stakeholders.

The emergence of these alternative, typical and atypical internship models reflects the evolving internship landscape. Universities are recognizing the need to offer flexible and innovative internship opportunities that respond to industry needs and equip students with skills and abilities adapted to the needs of the labor market. The post-pandemic internship landscape presents a transformative opportunity for stakeholders to redefine internship programs and adapt to the changing needs of scenario and work as well. By embracing remote, hybrid and innovative models, prioritizing skills for the future, fostering virtual networking and adaptability, internship programs can continue to provide valuable student experiences. Collaborative partnerships between employers and universities will be key to designing and delivering internships that prepare students for the challenges and opportunities of the post-pandemic era. As the world rebuilds, internships serve as a bridge connecting academic knowledge with practical skills, enabling students to excel and contribute to an innovative future workforce.

The here investigated sample is strictly related to internships. Nevertheless, the research will confirm how much firms and employers are looking for flexibility and adaptation, in order to cope with arts and tourism after the pandemic in the digital and social media age.

26.4 The Analysis of IULM Students' and Corporate Stakeholders' Satisfaction in 2022

The dataset refers to 281 students' questionnaires (116 for tourism and 165 for arts curricula) and 214 tutors' questionnaires (85 for tourism and 129 for arts stages or internships). These questionnaires concern 2022's satisfaction, the post pandemic year.

According to the National Agency *Almalaurea* standards, students can estimate their satisfaction for following items: coherence with the degree program, basic skills, expertise and know-how for arts and tourism, hardware and software skills, foreign languages, adaptability, working for goals, problem solving, team building, workspace and tools, relationship within the team, and relationship with the tutor and comprehensive satisfaction.

Corporate tutors (employers) can estimate similar items: basic competences, expertise and know-how for arts and tourism, hardware and software skills, adaptability, problem solving, team building, and commitment. The goal achievement—and not "working for goals"—can be counted for their satisfaction.

Every item can be estimated from 1 (minimum) to 5 (maximum).

Two analyses were implemented for separate sides of the internship: one on students' satisfaction and the other one on tutors' satisfaction.

Stepwise multiple regression was implemented for students with the "comprehensive satisfaction" as dependent variable from coherence with the degree program, basic skills, expertise and know-how for arts and tourism, hardware and software skills, adaptability, working for goals, problem solving, team building, workspace (characteristics of the work environments) and tools, relationship within the team, and relationship with the tutor. As foreign languages can be differently relevant in firms within either tourism or art businesses and either national or international relations, this variable was excluded.

Only some outputs of the comprehensive analysis with SPSS Software will be here commented.

Table 26.1 is the summary of Pearson correlations.

As concerns students' satisfaction, Pearson correlations are very significant for the relationship within the team and with the tutor, for the expertise and specific know-how, adaptability, and working for goals. During stages, students look for interaction, inspiration from mentors and employers and the opportunity to show their specific competences for arts and tourism. Working for goals means adaptability. After the pandemic, they estimate marginal risks, being determined to goals and being flexible.

In Table 26.2, all tests are summarized, and the Model 5 is the most efficiently implemented, as it is significant (R, R Square, Adjusted R Square, and Durbin-Watson), though it must be considered the very modest difference for F change and Sig. F Change. Model 5 includes five predictors out of nine: relationship within the team, relationship with the tutor, expertise and know-how for arts or

Table 26.1 Pearson correlations for students' questionnaires

Correlations

		Satisfaction	Coherence with degree programme	Expertise and know-how for arts or tourism	Hardware and software skills	Adaptability	Problem solving	Working for goals	Work space and tools	Relationship within the team	Relationship with the tutor
Pearson correlation	Satisfaction	1000	0,466	**0,696**	0,454	**0,554**	0,485	**0,525**	0,480	**0,783**	**0,671**
	Coherence with degree programme	0,466	1000	0,376	0,323	0,283	0,305	0,214	0,330	0,415	0,411
	Expertise and know-how for arts or tourism	0,696	0,376	1000	0,621	0,565	0,546	0,623	0,421	0,639	0,504
	Hardware and software skills	0,454	0,323	0,621	1000	0,463	0,438	0,418	0,416	0,406	0,252
	Adaptability	0,554	0,283	0,565	0,463	1000	0,596	0,484	0,328	0,530	0,319
	Problem solving	0,485	0,305	0,546	0,438	0,596	1000	0,512	0,331	0,540	0,324
	Working for goals	0,525	0,214	0,623	0,418	0,484	0,512	1000	0,359	0,504	0,385
	Work space and tools	0,480	0,330	0,421	0,416	0,328	0,331	0,359	1000	0,549	0,476
	Relationship within the team	0,783	0,415	0,639	0,406	0,530	0,540	0,504	0,549	1000	0,754
	Relationship with the tutor	0,671	0,411	0,504	0,252	0,319	0,324	0,385	0,476	0,754	1000

Source: Own elaboration with SPSS

Table 26.2 Summary for five models

Model Summary[a]

Model	R	R Square	Adjusted R Square	Std. error of the estimate	Change statistics					Durbin-Watson
					R Square change	F change	df1	df2	Sig. F change	
1	,783[b]	0,613	0,611	0,574	0,613	441,175	1	279	0,000	
2	,823[c]	0,677	0,675	0,525	0,065	55,835	1	278	0,000	
3	,831[d]	0,691	0,687	0,515	0,013	12,028	1	277	0,001	
4	,836[e]	0,700	0,695	0,508	0,009	8120	1	276	0,005	
5	,842[f]	0,709	0,704	0,502	0,009	8656	1	275	0,004	1931

Source: Own elaboration with SPSS

[a] Dependent Variable: Satisfaction

[b] Predictors: (Constant), Relationship within the team

[c] Predictors: (Constant), Relationship within the team, expertise and know-how for arts or tourism

[d] Predictors: (Constant), Relationship within the team, expertise and know-how for arts or tourism, coherence with degree programme

[e] Predictors: (Constant), Relationship within the team, expertise and know-how for arts or tourism, coherence with degree programme, relationship with the tutor

[f] Predictors: (Constant), Relationship within the team, expertise and know-how for arts or tourism, coherence with degree programme, relationship with the tutor, adaptability

tourism according to the different curriculum and industry, coherence with the degree program and adaptability.

With focus on standardized coefficients, the overall satisfaction grows with relationship within the team, expertise and know-how for arts or tourism, relationship with the tutor, adaptability, and coherence with the degree program. The relationship is essential to inspire and strengthen advocacy and skills. Students want to show their competences, specifically for arts and tourism. They have experienced the pandemic and the stringency, and they know that flexibility can be an added value and priority soon after the pandemic.

For data in Table 26.3, the human interaction and the willingness to demonstrate a specific knowledge and professional skills lead students' satisfaction.

For corporate tutors (employers), it is a different matter.

Table 26.4 shows Pearson correlations for main items: goal achievement is here meant as the dependent variable, for a tutor who is fully satisfied when goals are achieved thanks to very committed and flexible students.

After the pandemic, tutors look for committed, flexible students, whose basic competences can paradoxically be more significant than the specific expertise and know-how. In a post-pandemic year, businesses can be quite more diversified than before the pandemic, with new trends for contents and media, offline and online supplies, so that their competitive landscapes are not more focused only on tourism and arts. Gains and solvency are granted in a diversified landscape, where the specific expertise can be an added value. Nevertheless, basic competences can be enough and in professionalizing experiences like internships, while specific skills are built according to needs and markets. Tutors' satisfaction can estimate and appreciate a collection of "general" skills in students, who can grow and mature their competences towards a versatile profile and strategy mix.

This is confirmed for models in Table 26.5. In Table 26.5, all tests are summarized, and the Model 5 results as the most efficiently implemented, as it is significant (R, R Square, Adjusted R Square), though it must be considered the very modest difference for R Square Change, F change, and Sig. F Change.

The Durbin Watson test is significant, and the model includes five independent variables out of seven.

Model 5 is here chosen with goal achievement depending on commitment, adaptability, hardware and software skills, basic competences, and problem solving. The specific expertise and know-how for arts or tourism is not here a significant predictor. Table 26.6 shows coefficients.

Tutors' satisfaction is significantly depending on commitment and adaptability. No matter for specific skills and after extraordinary contingencies, which have left entrepreneurs with the need for a restart and total rethinking of their businesses in order not to *return to economic slow-down and lock-down of the pandemic*, tutors appreciate students for their commitment and for their flexibility together with hardware and software skills for offline and online businesses, basic competences, and problem solving.

Table 26.3 Coefficients in the Model 5

Coefficients[a]

Model	Unstandardized coefficients		Standardized coefficients	t	Sig.	95,0% confidence interval for B		Correlations			Collinearity statistics	
	B	Std. error	Beta			Lower bound	Upper bound	Zero-order	Partial	Part	Tolerance	VIF
5 (constant)	−0,766	0,257		−2979	0,003	−1272	−0,260					
Relationship within the team	0,434	0,067	**0,379**	6449	0,000	0,302	0,567	0,783	0,362	0,210	0,307	3261
Expertise and know-how for arts or tourism	0,250	0,044	**0,258**	5650	0,000	0,163	0,337	0,696	0,323	0,184	0,507	1972
Coherence with degree programme	0,123	0,042	**0,106**	2884	0,004	0,039	0,206	0,466	0,171	0,094	0,784	1275
Relationship with the tutor	0,182	0,054	**0,172**	3367	0,001	0,075	0,288	0,671	0,199	0,110	0,406	2464
Adaptability	0,175	0,059	**0,122**	2942	0,004	0,058	0,291	0,554	0,175	0,096	0,612	1635

Source: Own elaboration with SPSS

[a]Dependent Variable: Satisfaction

Table 26.4 Pearson correlations for tutors' questionnaires

Correlations

		Goal achievement	Basic competences	Expertise and know-how for arts or tourism	Commitment	Hardware and software skills	Adaptability	Problem solving	Team building
Pearson correlation	Goal achievement	1000	**0,630**	0,575	**0,704**	0,613	**0,699**	**0,645**	0,550
	Basic competences	0,630	1000	0,561	0,575	0,476	0,665	0,509	0,608
	Expertise and know-how for arts or tourism	0,575	0,561	1000	0,776	0,579	0,583	0,553	0,449
	Commitment	0,704	0,575	0,776	1000	0,590	0,643	0,659	0,501
	Hardware and software skills	0,613	0,476	0,579	0,590	1000	0,534	0,531	0,401
	Adaptability	0,699	0,665	0,583	0,643	0,534	1000	0,665	0,570
	Problem solving	0,645	0,509	0,553	0,659	0,531	0,665	1000	0,618
	Team building	0,550	0,608	0,449	0,501	0,401	0,570	0,618	1000

Source: Own elaboration with SPSS

Table 26.5 Summary for five models (tutors' goals achievement)

Model Summary[a]

Model	R	R Square	Adjusted R Square	Std. error of the estimate	Change statistics					Durbin-Watson
					R Square change	F change	df1	df2	Sig. F change	
1	,704[b]	0,496	0,494	0,407	0,496	208,901	1	212	0,000	
2	,774[c]	0,599	0,596	0,364	0,103	54,266	1	211	0,000	
3	,792[d]	0,628	0,623	0,352	0,029	16,156	1	210	0,000	
4	,802[e]	0,643	0,636	0,345	0,015	8765	1	209	0,003	
5	,807[f]	0,651	0,643	0,342	0,008	5048	1	208	0,026	1957

Source: Own elaboration with SPSS

[a]Dependent Variable: Goal achievement

[b]Predictors: (Constant), Commitment

[c]Predictors: (Constant), Commitment, adaptability

[d]Predictors: (Constant), Commitment, adaptability, hardware and software skills

[e]Predictors: (Constant), Commitment, adaptability, hardware and software skills, basic competences

[f]Predictors: (Constant), Commitment, adaptability, hardware and software skills, basic competences, problem solving

Table 26.6 Coefficients in the Model 5 for tutors' goal achievement

Coefficients[a]

Model		Unstandardized coefficients		Standardized coefficients	t	Sig.	95,0% confidence interval for B		Correlations			Collinearity statistics	
		B	Std. error	Beta	t	Sig.	Lower bound	Upper bound	Zero-order	Partial	Part	Tolerance	VIF
5	(Constant)	0,398	0,264		1509	0,133	−0,122	0,918					
	Commitment	0,228	0,055	**0,262**	4189	0,000	0,121	0,336	0,704	0,279	0,171	0,429	2333
	Adaptability	0,251	0,072	**0,229**	3490	0,001	0,109	0,392	0,699	0,235	0,143	0,389	2573
	Hardware and software skills	0,128	0,037	**0,183**	3430	0,001	0,054	0,201	0,613	0,231	0,140	0,592	1690
	Basic competences	0,220	0,074	**0,170**	2984	0,003	0,075	0,365	0,630	0,203	0,122	0,515	1943
	Problem solving	0,102	0,045	**0,136**	2247	0,026	0,012	0,191	0,645	0,154	0,092	0,457	2190

Source: Own elaboration with SPSS
[a]Dependent Variable: Goal achievement

26.5 What Kind of Skills After the Pandemic from Universities to Work Environments

The results as concerns the IULM sample are confirming that COVID-19 stimulated and accelerated an innovation path both for the working process and the role of digitization.

The forced closure of the *cultural industries production system* (Pratt, 1997) and of the tourism sector in Italy was justified considering their products and services *"non-essential structures and activities"* (Agostino et al., 2020). Some authors have recently argued that this approach stems from the omission of cultural rights from the body of third-generation rights listed in the Italian Constitution (Amari, 2023), and this has generated a general disregard about the contribution that cultural and creative industries (CCIs) and their workers provide to society.

This time of unprecedented crisis has created some positive outcomes and new opportunities in terms of increased adaptability and accelerated innovation (Crooke, 2020). To this regard, COVID-19 acted as a significant path disrupter, altering policy paradigms, practices, behaviors, and set of values across countries and sectors (Eurofound, 2022; Capano et al., 2022). In Italy, the lockdown promoted the acceleration of the digital transformation of the working process whose most popular outcome has been the transformation of social media from communication tools into content distribution channels (Samaroudi et al., 2020).

At the same time, COVID-19 had a twofold impact on universities. On the one hand, universities had to learn how to establish a new relation with the students and quickly develop efficient platforms and professors' technological skills. On the other side, universities faced the need to create new curricula focused on the new employability set of values requirements.

In fact, work environments and skills required by the job market have been transformed toward an increasingly hybrid form of technological applications and skill development related to content design (Banks, 2020) and design thinking practices (Johansson-Sköldberg et al., 2013), confirming the trend set by the European Commission with the Erasmus+ project to connect STEM (Science, Technology, Engineering, Mathematics) with artistic and cultural skills (STEAM). In this perspective and as the empirics here confirms, on the one hand, there has been the emergence of values strictly connected to emotional behaviors, such as empathy (Villari, 2021), mediation, social support, curiosity, willingness to collaborate, and organizational participation and commitment—attitudes leading to the democratization of the decision-making process (Arnaboldi & Coget, 2016). At the same time, the demand of skills in work management has increased such as the ability to complete tasks in scheduled time and to deal with complexity, organization of the workflow, autonomy, flexibility, and willingness to learn (Van Houten et al., 2020; Karseth & Solbrekke, 2010).

Two dimensions seem to have gained primacy in the new service-oriented work practices—in which IULM University has its share as previously investigated—art and creativity (Papademetriu et al., 2022) and analysis, the latter more visibly than the former but both equally requested. In the current *normalized time*, every productive sector is concentrated on contextualization of data analysis and on content creation sense-making to respond in an agile and, possibly, more ethical and sustainable way to novel societal, technical, and economic contexts, trying to keep the pace with the ever-evolving and hard competing changes of the globalized arena (Verma & Gustafsson, 2020).

Universities find their competitive ground in constructing educational and professional paths that enable students to build on these skills.

26.6 Conclusion

In 2023, IULM entered the World University Rankings by Subject compiled by the international education agency Quacquarelli Symonds (QS). The subject area featured is "Hospitality & Leisure Management." If the QS ranking classifies universities according to 5 different broad subject areas and 54 narrow subject areas, based on criteria such as Academic Reputation, Employer Reputation and Research, weighted differently depending on the subject areas and disciplines, for "Hospitality & Leisure Management," the score is concerning 95% the reputational component (45% Academic Reputation and 50% Employer Reputation) and 5% research.

This result is here confirming the choice of one of the most leading university for tourism and arts curricula in Italy, as a substantial sample for the investigated satisfaction on both sides of the internship, students and tutors (employers).

Hospitality means tourism and leisure includes arts. If the here investigated sample is confirming the *mitigation* between specific and basic skills, IULM has given evidence of QS ranking for industries, where students are motivated for specific interests, skills, and professionalization (tourism, events, performing and visual arts, fairs, journey agencies, etc.). Nevertheless, corporate stakeholders ask for basic competences, commitment, and adaptability for stages and internships, where professionalization is granted by appreciated and valuable employers, work environments, and relationships, which can grant the growth from basic to specific skills.

As the empirics here confirms, in working environments satisfying experiences depend on emotional behaviors, empathy, mediation, social support, curiosity, willingness to collaborate, commitment—attitudes leading to the democratization of the decision-making process. It is also confirmed the increase as for the demand of skills such as the ability to complete tasks in scheduled time and to deal with complexity, organization of the workflow, autonomy, flexibility, and willingness to learn and lifelong learning.

If satisfaction depends on standardized Almalaurea items, learning and professionalizing experiences can be framed as for stages and internships. This framework is today broadening to workshops, creative and project works, whose satisfaction parameters must be conceptualized and/or adapted from Almalaurea items. Universities are therefore diagnosing and investing in the need to offer flexible and innovative opportunities that respond to stakeholders' needs and equip students with skills and abilities for this transformative scenario.

After the pandemic, corporate stakeholders are flexible and ready for the evolution of markets and industries, considering how much the pandemic affected the strategic and competitive landscape and their performances, in a digital landscape too. With antibodies these internship tutors developed during the pandemic, they can now appreciate skills of students and young professionals. Nevertheless, they have learnt, and they must cope with an unforeseeable, unpredictable, and very next future, considering economic crises like the very latest inflationary one. Theaters and museums are now finding recovery and stability after the pandemic in Italy. Hotels are rethinking their teams with crisis managers and health monitoring applications and employees. Hardware, software, digitization, and social media skills are always searched, together with a general commitment, adaptability, and team working.

Theoretical implications are therefore suggesting that literature and research should always focus on both sides of internships with a multidimensional approach to parameters, typical and atypical frameworks, and different visions between students and corporate stakeholders. Practical implications derive for both universities and stakeholders for flexible programs and curricula, which can focus on industries, whose boards and corporate tutors can enable and mediate for employability in different markets, where adaptability and commitment are priorities apart from core businesses.

Further research will investigate if the pandemic might cause either the full-stop of internships abroad or the recovery for international experiences is stabilized. If information technology, streaming, and social media are leading the skills change, further research will also concern the metrics and performances of social media, platforms, and technologies, whose results are not always affordable and clear, and whose benchmarks are difficult to derive. Collaborative partnerships between employers and universities will be key to designing and delivering internships and bridging opportunities, whose flexible framing can prepare students for the challenges and opportunities of the post-pandemic era. The very next research will also concern how to estimate satisfaction of workshops, project, and creative works, when standardized students' and tutors' questionnaires may be modified in order to better focus and discriminate as for outputs, which can be different from an internship or stage experience.

References

Agostino, D., Arnaboldi, M., & Lampis, A. (2020). Italian state museums during the COVID-19 crisis: From onsite closure to online openness. *Museum Management and Curatorship, 35*(4), 362–372.

Aitkin, M., & Longford, N. (1986). Statistical modelling issues in school effectiveness studies. *Journal of the Royal Statistical Society, Series A, 149*(1), 1–43.

Amari, M. (2023). *Elogio dei diritti e dei doveri culturali*. Rubbettino.

Arnaboldi, M., & Coget, J. F. (2016). Social media and business. We've been asking the wrong question. *Organizational Dynamics, 45*, 47–54.

Banks, S. (2020). *Ethics and values in social work*. Bloomsbury Publishing.

Bayerlein, L., et al. (2021). Developing skills in higher education for post-pandemic work. *Labour & Industry, 31*(4), 418–429.

Benner, M., Grant, J., & O'Kane, M. (2022). *Crisis response in higher education how the pandemic challenged university operations and organisation* (p. 2022). Springer International Publishing AG.

Besana, A., & Esposito, A. (2017). Tourism curricula, entrepreneurial engagement and stakeholders' satisfaction: Economics and relationship marketing of universities. *Eurasian Business Review, 7*(3), 375–388.

Besana, A., Esposito, A., Fisichella, C., & Vannini, M. C. (2022). On the stage of pandemic times. When cultural organizations and universities valorize their collaborations. In E. Borin (Ed.), *Internationalization in focus: Theoretical, strategic, and management perspectives in education, research, policy and practice*. ENCATC.

Besana, A., Esposito, A., & Fisichella, C. (2023). Staging though the pandemic: Evaluation and communication in the university. In N. Tsounis & A. Vlachvei (Eds.), *Advances in empirical economics research*. Springer Nature.

Bilsland, C., Nagy, H., & Smith, P. (2020). Virtual internships and work-integrated learning in hospitality and tourism in a post-COVID-19 world. *International Journal of Work-Integrated Learning, 21*(4), 425–437.

Briant, S., & Crowther, P. (2020). Reimagining internships through online experiences: Multidisciplinary engagement for creative industries students. *International Journal of Work-Integrated Learning, 21*(5), 617–628.

Capano, G., Howlett, M., Jarvis, D. S. L., & Ramesh, M. (2022). Long-term policy impacts of the coronavirus: Normalization, adaptation, and acceleration in the post-COVID state. *Policy and Society, 41*(1), 1–12.

Chala, N., Pichyk, K., Voropai, O., & Bilovodska, O. (2021). Customer engagement with universities' social media after COVID-19: EaP countries case. In *International scientific and practical conference "sustainable development in the post-pandemic period"*. SDPPP.

Coco, M. (2000). Internships: A try before you buy arrangement. *SAM Advanced Management Journal, 65*(2), 41–47.

Crooke, E. (2020). Communities, change and the Covid-19 crisis. *Museum and Society, 18*(3), 305–310.

D'Abate, C. P., Youndt, M. A., & Wenzel, K. E. (2009). Making the most of an internship: An empirical study of internship satisfaction. *Academy of Management Learning & Education, 8*(4), 527–539.

Eurofound-ETF. (2022). *Living, working and COVID-19 in the European Union and 10 EU neighbouring countries*. Publications Office of the European Union.

Fox, T. (2001). A sense of place. *Caterer and Hotelkeeper, 189*, 4160.

Gill, R. J. (2020). Graduate employability skills through online internships and projects during the COVID-19 pandemic: An Australian example. *Journal of Teaching and Learning for Graduate Employability, 11*(1), 146–158.

Gori, E. (1992). *La valutazione dell'efficienza ed efficacia dell'istruzione, Atti della XXXVI Riunione Scientifica della Società Italiana di Statistica* (pp. 223–230). CEDAM.

Gori, E., & Vittadini, G. (1998). La valutazione dell'efficienza ed efficacia dei servizi alla persona: impostazioni e metodi. In *Relazione presentata al Seminario su "Progetto strategico CNR – Misure e parametri per la politica economica e sociale"* (pp. 29–30). tenutosi presso l'ISTAT.

Gupta, P., Burns, D. J., & Schiferl, J. S. (2010). An exploration of student satisfaction with internship experiences in marketing. *Business Education & Administration, 2*(1), 27–37.

Hergert, M. (2009). Student perceptions of the value of internships in business education. *American Journal of Business Education, 2*(8), 9–14.

Irwin, A., Perkins, J., Hillari, L. L., & Wischerath, D. (2022). Is the future of internships online? An examination of stakeholder attitudes towards online internships. *Higher Education, Skills and Work-Based Learning, 12*(4), 629–644.

Johansson-Sköldberg, U., Woodilla, J., & Çetinkaya, M. (2013). Design thinking: Past, present and possible futures. *Creativity and Innovation Management, 22*(2), 121–146.

Jung, J., & Lee, S. J. (2016). Impact of internship on job performance among university graduates in South Korea. *International Journal of Chinese Education, 5*, 250–284.

Kapareliotis, I., Voutsina, K., & Patsiotis, A. (2019). Internship and employability prospects: Assessing student's work readiness. *Higher Education, Skills and Work-Based Learning, 9*(4), 538–549.

Karseth, B., & Solbrekke, T. D. (2010). Qualifications Frameworks: The avenue towards the convergence of European higher education? *European Journal of Education, 45*(4), 563–57.

Khashab, B., Gulliver, S. R., & Ayoubi, R. M. (2020). A framework for customer relationship management strategy orientation support in higher education institutions. *Journal of Strategic Marketing, 28*(3), 246–265.

Ko, W. (2008). Training, satisfaction with internship programs, and confidence about future careers among hospitality students: A case study of universities in Taiwan. *Journal of Teaching in Travel & Tourism, 7*(4), 1–15.

Koo, G. Y., Diacin, M. J., Khojasteh, J., & Dixon, A. W. (2016). Effects of internship satisfaction on the pursuit of employment in sport management. *Sport Management Education Journal, 10*(1), 29–42.

Kumar, V., & Nanda, P. (2020). Social Media in Higher Education: A framework for continuous engagement. *International Journal of Information and Communication Technology Education, 15*(1), 109–120.

Lv, X., et al. (2022). Impacts of university lockdown during the coronavirus pandemic on college students' academic achievement and critical thinking: A longitudinal study. *Frontiers in Psychology, 13*, 995784.

Nelson, A. A. (1994). Hospitality internship: The effects of job dimensions and supportive relationships on student satisfaction. *Dissertation Abstracts International, 56*(2), 62.

Neuman, H. (1999). Internships. *Career World, 27*(6), 16.

Odlin, D., Benson-Rea, M., & Sullivan-Taylor, B. (2022). Student internships and work placements: Approaches to risk management in higher education. *Higher Education, 83*(6), 1409–1429.

Papademetriou, C., Anastasiadou, S., Konteos, G., & Papalexandris, S. (2022). COVID-19 pandemic: The impact of the social media technology on higher education. *Education Science, 12*(261), 1–26.

Paulins, V. A. (2008). Characteristics of retailing internships contributing to students' reported satisfaction with career development. *Journal of Fashion Marketing and Management, 12*(1), 105–118.

Pratt, A. C. (1997). The cultural industries production system: A case study of employment change in Britain, 1984–91. *Environment and Planning, 29*(11), 1953–1974.

Prianto, A., Asmuni, A., & Firman, M. S. (2017). The effect of academic performance and involvement in the internship program toward life skills and work readiness of university graduates in East Java Indonesia. *International Journal of Business and Management Invention, 6*(8), 41–55.

Putra, I., & Purba, D. (2020). Effects of satisfaction, subjective norms, and selfefficacy on job application intentions of student interns. *Psychological Research on Urban Society, 3*(2), 9.

Reimers, F. M., & Marmolejo, F. J. (2021). *University and school collaborations during a pandemic sustaining educational opportunity and reinventing education.* Springer International Publishing AG.

Samaroudi, M., Rodriguez, E. K., & Perry, L. (2020). Heritage in lockdown: Digital provision of memory institutions in the UK and US of America during the COVID-19 pandemic. *Museum Management and Curatorship, 35*(4), 337–361.

Shtembari, E., & Feridun Elgün, F. (2023). Generation Z 'life skills' acquired and enhanced through internships before and during COVID-19 pandemic. *Administrative Sciences, 13*(2), 38.

Stiefel, L. (1999). *The Measurement of Output Quality in US Nonprofit Organizations.* In Italian Statistical Association.

Tănase, F.-D., et al. (2022). Online education in the COVID-19 pandemic—Premise for economic competitiveness growth? *Sustainability, 14*(6), 3503.

Toklucu, E., et al. (2022). The effects of the crisis management skills and distance education practices of universities on student satisfaction and organizational image. *Sustainability, 14*(10), 5813.

Van Houten, G., Russo, G., & Eurofound. (2020). *European company survey 2019 – Workplace 561 practices unlocking employee potential.*

Varsha, J., Mogaji, E., Sharma, H., & Babbili, A. S. (2022). A multi-stakeholder perspective of relationship marketing in higher education institutions. *Journal of Marketing for Higher Education, 25,* 1–19.

Verma, S., & Gustafsson, A. (2020). Investigating the emerging COVID-19 research trends in the field of business and management: A bibliometric analysis approach. *Journal of Business Research, 118,* 253–261.

Villari, B. (2021). Community-centered design: A design perspective on innovation in and for places. *The International Journal of Design in Society, 16*(1), 47–58.

Vittadini, G. (2004). *Linee guida per la valutazione dell'efficienza esterna della didattica mediante il Capitale Umano, Atti del convegno "Le strategie metodologiche per lo studio della transizione Università-Lavoro", a cura di Enrica Aureli Cutillo* (pp. 375–395). CLEUP.

Volkov, A., et al. (2022). Using digital tools to teach soft skill-oriented subjects to university students during the COVID-19 pandemic. *Education Sciences, 12*(5), 335.

Chapter 27
Risk-Taking Behavior and Effects of Framing in Group and Individual Decisions: Evidence from Chamas and Student Subjects in Kenya

Mercy Inyangala Kano, Gülnur Muradoğlu, and John Olukuru

Abstract This study investigates risk-taking behavior in the context of group and individual decisions among chamas (informal savings and investment groups) and students in Kenya. Moreover, by comparing two presentation formats, we explore how framing techniques impact decision-making processes for these two populations. The study adopts an experimental approach with subjects selected from chamas and students in Kenya, representing different decision-making contexts. Subjects are presented with lottery choice tasks, where decisions and risk preferences are observed at the individual and group level. Chamas display significantly greater risk aversion than students in both formats of the lottery choice task and at both the individual and group level. Additionally, both at the individual and group levels, we find evidence of framing effects for chama decisions. However, the study found no significant evidence of framing effects for student decisions at the group level, but it did find evidence for framing effects for student decisions at the individual level. The findings contribute to understanding the role of information framing in financial decision-making and have practical implications for organizations, policymakers, and financial institutions. This study also highlights the importance of cultural considerations in examining risk-taking behavior. By conducting the research in Kenya with chamas, we provide valuable insights into decision-making in a specific cultural context, broadening the generalizability of findings.

Keywords Framing effects · Group risk taking behavior · Chamas in Kenya · Informal savings and investment groups

---

M. I. Kano (✉) · J. Olukuru
Strathmore University Institute of Mathematical Sciences, Nairobi, Kenya
e-mail: mkano@strathmore.edu

G. Muradoğlu
School of Business and Management, Queen Mary University of London, London, UK

© The Author(s), under exclusive license to Springer Nature Switzerland AG 2024
N. Tsounis, A. Vlachvei (eds.), *Applied Economic Research and Trends*, Springer
Proceedings in Business and Economics,
https://doi.org/10.1007/978-3-031-49105-4_27

27.1 Introduction

The decision to invest has major repercussions for people, groups, and society, and risk-taking behavior is a vital component of financial decision-making (Campbell et al., 2002; Malkiel, 2021). Many such financial decisions that involve risk taking are made by teams or groups, such as management boards, committees, families, or couples, rather than by individuals. For instance, in Kenya and several other African nations, savings and investment groups are a common method of achieving financial objectives (Redford et al., 2022).

The term "chamas" is commonly used in Kenya to refer to a particular kind of informal savings and investment group that is well liked by people, particularly women, who desire to pool their resources to attain shared financial goals (FSD Kenya, 2015). Each chama member normally makes a specific financial contribution on a weekly or monthly basis. The donations are then used to finance different investments or savings objectives, such as buying land, starting a business, or saving for a child's education. Chamas may also participate in other activities like social gatherings, charitable donations, and fundraising initiatives. Individuals that join a chama have a mutual social connection such as friendship, membership in the same church, neighbors, or schoolmates (Mathuva, 2022). The chama model has gained appeal due to its potential to promote financial inclusion and entrepreneurship, particularly among low-income groups, according to the report by CBK et al. (2021).

Individuals' risk preferences might change as a result of group decision-making, as they may become more or less risk seeking. This phenomenon, known as choice shift, is well documented in the literature (Stoner, 1961; Stoner, 1968). Several studies have investigated how risk-taking behavior differs between group decisions and individual decisions based on the risk attitude elicitation tool by (Holt & Laury, 2002). According to some studies, groups were found to be more risk averse than individuals (Ambrus et al., 2015; Baker et al., 2008; Masclet et al., 2009). Other studies found no significant difference in risk preferences of individuals and groups (Brunette et al., 2015; Deck et al., 2012; Harrison et al., 2012). These studies that compared risk-taking in group and individual decisions have yielded inconsistent and inconclusive findings, leaving a gap in our understanding of this phenomenon. In addition, most of this prior research has mainly relied on lottery choice tasks with university students as subjects to measure risk preferences, who could not truly represent actual investors.

This study addresses these gaps in the literature by comparing risk-taking behavior in group versus individual decisions using chamas and student subjects in Kenya to evaluate variations in risk-taking behavior. This is the first study of its kind to compare risk-taking behavior across these two groups. Our findings aim to shed light on decision-making in group settings, helping investors and researchers alike to make informed decisions and develop more robust models of investor behavior. The results of this study will inform strategies for promoting financial inclusion and entrepreneurship among low-income communities where chama system is more prevalent in Kenya. In addition, we examine framing effects at both the individual and group level based on two presentation formats for a lottery choice task. Understanding the influence of presentation formats on decision-making can be useful for developing effective communication strategies and understanding how different framing techniques influence risk perceptions and decision outcomes.

27.2 Related Literature

27.2.1 Choice Shift

The term "choice shift" describes a phenomena in which the collective decision of the group shifts from the individual decisions of the members made before the group discussion to either a more risky or a more risk averse alternative. In other words, compared to the average individual decision, the group decision is more extreme or polarized (Eliaz et al., 2006).

Diffusion of responsibility, familiarity, and groupthink are just a few of the social psychology theories that explain why choice shift may happen in group decisions. Diffusion of responsibility happens when people may feel less responsible for their actions in a group context, which promotes more risk-taking behavior (Wallach et al., 1964). Individuals may believe that the risk is shared by the group while making decisions in a group, which might lessen their perception of personal risk. Another element that may impact choice shift is familiarity. Group discussions and consensus-building can lead to greater familiarity with the problem at hand, which may reduce the perception of risk associated with a particular decision (Bateson, 1966). This might encourage groups to take more risks. An alternative view is that groupthink may be to blame for choice shift in group decisions when people fail to consider all available options out of a desire to keep the group together. This results in poor decision-making (Janis, 1972). For instance, in cohesive groups where the leader is more assertive and a risk taker, the decisions made by the group may be riskier.

Other alternative explanations of choice shift is social influence as advanced by Sanders and Baron's (1977) Social Comparisons Theory (SCT) and Burnstein and Vinokur's (1977) Persuasive Arguments Theory (PAT). These theories both suggest that people are influenced by their peers though the theories differ in their explanation of how this social influence occurs. SCT posits that choice shift occurs in group decisions because people seek social approval and try to avoid social disapproval. Group discussions reveal which risk preferences are socially acceptable, so group members change their risk-taking behavior in the direction of the group to gain approval with the group. PAT, on the other hand, is based on the concept of group polarization that is said to occur when individuals in a group setting engage in more extreme decisions than their original private decisions (Moscovici & Zavalloni, 1969). Group members polarize their risk preferences during group discussion as they exchange arguments for their preferences and end up with even stronger arguments in favor of their risk preferences after the group discussion. Overall, both theories suggest that social influence can occur through the process of comparison and persuasion. However, they differ in their emphasis on the importance of comparison versus persuasion in the process of social influence.

Economic theories to explain choice shifts in group risk preferences were advanced by Eliaz et al. (2006), Roux and Sobel (2015), and Jouini et al. (2013). The economic theory of choice shifts developed by Eliaz et al. (2006) is based on the diffusion of responsibility in group decisions under risk. According to Eliaz et al. (2006), group decisions involve both information and preference aggregation. They predict that even when group members have access to all relevant information, their individual preferences may still change simply as a result of the group decision-making process. In contrast, Roux and Sobel's (2015) economic model that is based on PAT predicts that groups will make more extreme judgments as a result of better information in situations when group members share similar preferences but have access to diverse information. Nevertheless, because Roux and Sobel's (2015) approach assumes homogeneous preferences, it does not take into consideration the situation of people with heterogeneous preferences. Jouini et al.'s (2013) collective risk aversion model with heterogeneous risk preferences predicts that groups will be more risk averse than their individual members in low stakes lotteries and that groups will be less risk averse than their individual members in high stake lotteries. Based on these economic theories of choice shift (Eliaz et al., 2006; Jouini et al., 2013; Roux & Sobel, 2015), we predict that when individuals make joint decisions as members of groups, there may be a choice shift simply because the decision was made as a group.

27.2.2 Risk Preferences in Group Versus Individual Decision-Making

Research on risk-taking behavior in group versus individual decisions has been carried out in various fields, including psychology, economics, and finance. Early studies in social psychology such as (J. A. F. Stoner, 1961) and (Wallach et al., 1964) found that groups were more risk seeking than individuals. Recent investigations, however, have produced conflicting results. For instance, some studies have found that groups are more risk averse than individuals (Ambrus et al., 2015; Baker et al., 2008; Masclet et al., 2009; Shupp & Williams, 2008), while other studies have found no significant differences in risk-taking behavior between groups and individuals (Brunette et al., 2015; Deck et al., 2012; Harrison et al., 2012; Keck et al., 2014). In these studies, the researchers conduct experimental studies to compare risk preferences revealed by groups of three to five persons to individuals in lottery choice tasks. With the exception of Masclet et al. (2009) where subjects included people from the working class in France, the studies used student subjects from universities in the USA and France. Subjects were asked to choose between safe and risky lotteries and their risk preferences were inferred from a variety of measures such as the mean number of safe choices, probability of safe choice and certainty equivalent ratios.

Studies explicitly looking at investment decisions have generally supported the idea that groups exhibit more risk-taking behavior than individuals. For example, Sutter (2009) and Bougheas et al. (2013) conducted experiments using student subjects at German and UK universities, respectively, where subjects had to decide on the amount to be invested in a risky gamble in each of nine rounds with three treatments; individual decisions, individual decisions with salient group membership and group decisions. The findings from Sutter (2009) and Bougheas et al. (2013) were consistent where a comparison of the average amount invested in each round by individuals and groups revealed that groups invested significantly higher amounts than individuals and hence took higher risks than individuals.

A key issue in past research is that, with the exception of Masclet et al. (2009), most of the studies only included student participants, whose risk preferences may vary from those of seasoned investors, thus limiting generalizability of findings. In a few of the studies (Brunette et al., 2015; Harrison et al., 2012; Masclet et al., 2009), student participants are chosen at random and placed in anonymous groups. Group members are prohibited from discussing with one another, and the group decision is reached by applying the majority rule or voting continuously until a unanimous decision is reached. Even though (Masclet et al., 2009) include real people, not simply students, in their experiments, they nevertheless place the subjects in anonymous groups for the group decisions. Investor groups, which are made up of acquainted individuals who have previously made decisions together, are not typically like this. In this study we compare risk-taking tendencies of both endogenously created groups of real investors (chamas) and randomly formed student groups.

27.2.3 Framing Effects

Framing effects is a phenomenon that describes how people's decisions are affected by the way information is presented to them. (Tversky & Kahneman, 1981) conducted an influential study on this subject. In their study, they gave participants a hypothetical scenario involving an outbreak of a deadly disease in Asia. Participants were asked to choose between two treatment options for the hypothetical Asian disease problem. The programs are described in terms of their effectiveness as a means of saving lives.

In one version of the Asian disease problem, the options are presented to participants in a positive frame and are quantified in terms of the number of lives that can be saved. Participants in this situation are typically risk averse and favor the safer program that ensures saving a specific number of lives. Another version involves giving participants a negative frame and framing the options in terms of the number of lives that will be lost. Participants in this situation are typically risk seekers and favor the riskier program, even though it increases the likelihood of saving no lives at all. The findings revealed that, despite the two treatments being mathematically equal, participants were more likely to select the one that was expressed in terms of lives saved. The framing effect showed that people's preferences and decisions can be influenced by the way information is presented, resulting in differing decisions in decision scenarios that are otherwise identical.

The seminal study by (Tversky & Kahneman, 1981) paved the way for further research on framing effects and emphasized the importance of taking into account how options are framed when examining how individuals make choices and judgments. The way information is framed can change how people understand it and can have an impact on their attitudes and behaviors. For instance, how an investment opportunity is presented—as "low risk" versus "high potential gain"—can affect whether a potential investor is more inclined to take a chance. Alternatively, presenting"a political issue as a "public health crisis" as opposed to a "violation of individual rights" may affect how individuals view the problem and their opinions of potential policy remedies. Thus, the framing effect covers a wide range of presentations, such as positive and negative framing as well as other presentational styles that may affect how individuals interpret information and come to judgments (Levin et al., 1998).

There is a lot of research on framing effects. The findings from prior studies that have replicated the Asian disease problem or a variation have generally found that framing effect is universal (Im & Chen, 2022), although the size of the effect varies depending on the assessment methods used (Diederich et al., 2018; Druckman, 2001; Kühberger, 1998). Most of these earlier investigations into framing effects, assessed through lotteries, have primarily involved student subjects and with the exception of (Paese et al., 1993), they all involve individual decisions. Although Paese et al. (1993) investigate framing effects at the group level, the study assigns student subjects randomly into groups of three which may not be representative of endogenously formed decision-making groups found in real life.

This study advances our knowledge of risk-taking behavior and effects of framing, both at the individual and group levels, by investigating shifts in risk preferences in a lottery choice task employing two distinct formats across two different populations: chamas and student subjects. Although framing effects on risk preferences have been well studied in the past (Druckman, 2001; Im & Chen, 2022; Kühberger, 1998; Paese et al., 1993; Wang & Johnston, 1995), few studies have investigated the variations in responses between students and chamas (informal savings groups) at the individual and group level. Our study seeks to address this gap by contrasting the risk attitudes produced by two formats of a lottery choice task for both chamas and student subjects. By doing this, we hope to shed light on the influence of social dynamics on decision-making and reveal potential differences in framing effects among different populations. The results of this study may have significant ramifications for our comprehension of the variables influencing risk attitudes in various circumstances and offer insightful information for financial education and policy making.

27.3 Methodology

We use an overall research design that consists of two sessions to address our research objective of examining risk-taking behavior and effects of framing at the individual and group level. The first session involved students and was held in May 2022, while the second session held in November 2022 involved self-employed people, salaried workers, casual workers, and retired workers who were members of savings and investment groups popularly known as chamas in Kenya. Each session lasted approximately 2 hours.

We recruited a total of 264 participants for the experiments. The university students were recruited from undergraduate courses at Strathmore University. We sent an email invitation to the students inviting them to participate in the experiments. A total of 129 students (63.5% female and 46.5% male) responded and participated in the experiment. We recruited 135 participants from chamas (83.5% female and 16.5% male) with the help of the Kenya National Chamber of Commerce and Industry (KNCCI) Nairobi County. The high proportion of women compared to men in our chama sample is representative of the overall chama membership in Kenya, which is characterized predominantly by women (Gugerty, 2007; Mathuva, 2022).

Each of the experimental sessions with students and chamas involved individual and group decision-making stages. At each stage, participants completed two lottery choice tasks, utilizing a within subjects design, wherein the same individuals completed identical lottery choice tasks during both the individual and group decision stages. We point out that this within subjects design might produce an order effect, where the presentation of the treatments in a particular order may have an impact on the dependent variable. This could be due to learning effects, which may lead to an improvement in performance in the second treatment, or fatigue effects, which may result in a reduction in performance in subsequent treatments (Cozby & Bates, 2014). As shown in Table 27.1, roughly half of the participants were randomized to the individual-group order, while the other half were randomized to the group-individual order, in order to account for these order effects as in Deck et al. (2012).

Both the individual and group decision stages involved the same tasks. During the group stage, the group members were required to carry out face-to-face discussions and arrive at a consensus on the group's decision. The participants completed

Table 27.1 Decision stages and sample sizes

Participants	Decision order	Stage 1	Stage 2	Number of groups	Number of participants
Students	Individual—Group	Individual	Group	21	63
	Group—Individual	Group	Individual	22	66
Chamas	Individual—Group	Individual	Group	23	69
	Group—Individual	Group	Individual	22	66

a post-experiment survey to provide demographic and other background data at the conclusion of the experiments. Every participant in the experiments received compensation totaling Ksh500 (\$5) for their participation.

We employ the Holt and Laury's (2002) lottery choice task to elicit risk attitudes of individuals and groups. This method has been used most frequently in prior studies to measure risk attitudes of groups and individuals (Ambrus et al., 2015; Baker et al., 2008; Deck et al., 2012; Keck et al., 2014; Masclet et al., 2009). Ten lottery selection options, each with a safe lottery A or a risky lottery B, are shown to the participants. The payoffs for safe lottery A are Ksh400 and Ksh320 with a minor difference between the low and high payoffs, whereas the payoffs for risky lottery B are Ksh770 and Ksh20 with a wider disparity between the low and high payoffs. While the payoffs in the ten lottery selection decisions remain constant, the probabilities of the high payoffs grow progressively by 10% from the first 10% to 100% in the last decision. Participants were asked if they would want to play Lottery A or Lottery B.

To investigate framing effects, we present the participants with two versions of the lottery choice task, one in a tabular format and another in a graphical pie-chart format employing a within subject's design. Table 27.2 represents the tabular format of the lottery choice task.

We focus on switching points, which are the moments when people change their preference between the two lotteries, in order to analyze the risk attitude of participants. We infer participant's risk attitudes from the total number of safe lottery A choices made by the participant before switching to risky lottery B. Only a very high risk taker would choose lottery B in the first choice because both lotteries' high payoffs have a low probability of 10%. The expected payoff for lottery A is higher than that of lottery B by Ksh233 as shown in Table 27.3. As the probability of the higher payoff increases moving down toward the tenth decision, a person should cross over to lottery B. Basically, a participant is considered risk neutral if they choose four safe lottery A options before moving to risky lottery B. A participant is categorized as risk averse if they make more than four safe lottery A selections and risk seeking if they make fewer than four safe lottery A selections. However, even the most risk averse participant should switch over to lottery B at the tenth decision on the bottom row since lottery B has a higher sure payoff than lottery A.

Figure 27.1 displays the lottery options in the lottery choice task in a graphical pie-chart format. Participants complete the graphical lottery choice task after finishing the tabular lottery choice task.

Our analysis involves a comparison of risk aversion of groups and individuals from the tabular and graphical lottery choice tasks. To determine whether there are significant differences in risk preferences of participants in the individual and group stages and in the two lottery choice tasks we perform Wilcoxon signed-rank tests and three-way ANOVA tests. We also analyze the risk preference classifications for participants in the two lottery choice tasks based on constant relative risk aversion (CRRA) characterization of risk attitudes. We extend the analysis by conducting ordered probit and random effects interval regressions.

Table 27.2 Tabular lottery choice task

Decision	Lottery A				Lottery B				Choice	
	Probability (p)	Payoff Ksh	Probability (1-p)	Payoff Ksh	Probability (p)	Payoff Ksh	Probability (1-p)	Payoff Ksh		
1	10%	400	90%	320	10%	770	90%	20	A	B
2	20%	400	80%	320	20%	770	80%	20	A	B
3	30%	400	70%	320	30%	770	70%	20	A	B
4	40%	400	60%	320	40%	770	60%	20	A	B
5	50%	400	50%	320	50%	770	50%	20	A	B
6	60%	400	40%	320	60%	770	40%	20	A	B
7	70%	400	30%	320	70%	770	30%	20	A	B
8	80%	400	20%	320	80%	770	20%	20	A	B
9	90%	400	10%	320	90%	770	10%	20	A	B
10	100%	400	0%	320	100%	770	0%	20	A	B

Adapted from Holt and Laury (2002) and Masclet et al. (2009)

Table 27.3 Tabular lottery choice task with expected values

Decision	Lottery A				Lottery B				EV^A	EV^B	Difference
	Prob. (p)	Payoff (Ksh)	Prob (1 − p)	Payoff (Ksh)	Prob. (p)	Payoff (Ksh)	Prob (1 − p)	Payoff (Ksh)			
1	10%	400	90%	320	10%	770	90%	20	328	95	233.00
2	20%	400	80%	320	20%	770	80%	20	336	170	166.00
3	30%	400	70%	320	30%	770	70%	20	344	245	99.00
4	40%	400	60%	320	40%	770	60%	20	352	320	32.00
5	50%	400	50%	320	50%	770	50%	20	360	395	−35.00
6	60%	400	40%	320	60%	770	40%	20	368	470	−102.00
7	70%	400	30%	320	70%	770	30%	20	376	545	−169.00
8	80%	400	20%	320	80%	770	20%	20	384	620	−236.00
9	90%	400	10%	320	90%	770	10%	20	392	695	−303.00
10	100%	400	0%	320	100%	770	0%	20	400	770	−370.00

Lottery Decision 1

Please decide which lottery A or B you would prefer by selecting your choice.

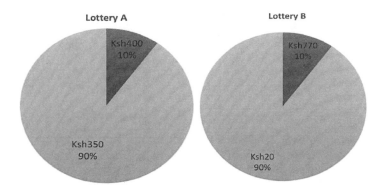

Lottery Decision 2

Please decide which lottery A or B you would prefer by selecting your choice.

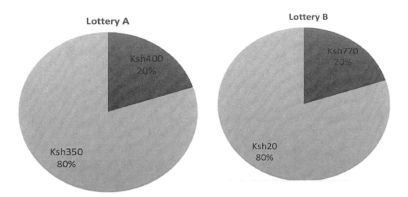

Fig. 27.1 Graphical lottery choice task

27.4 Experimental Results

First, we present the preliminary analysis results of the comparison of risk aversion of groups and individuals from the tabular and graphical lottery choice tasks as measured by the number of safe choices (Sect. 27.4.1). Second, we present the results of the risk preference classifications for participants in the two lottery choice tasks based on constant relative risk aversion (CRRA) characterization of risk attitudes (Sect. 27.4.2). Finally, we extend the analysis by conducting ordered probit and interval regressions and present the results in Sect. 27.4.3.

Table 27.4 Risk aversion—number of safe choices in lottery choice tasks

Lottery choice task	Individuals		Groups	
	Tabular format	Graphical format	Tabular format	Graphical format
Students				
Mean	5.05	4.86	5.05	4.95
Standard deviation	1.28	1.29	1.15	1.27
Maximum	8	8	6	6
Minimum	2	4	4	3
N	105	105	39	37
Chamas				
Mean	5.58	5.38	5.86	5.68
Standard deviation	2.49	2.95	2.72	3.12
Maximum	9	9	10	9
Minimum	1	0	0	0
N	92	79	35	25

Note: Excludes inconsistent responses. Inconsistent refers to a participant with multiple switch points where they switch back and forth between the safe lottery A and the risky lottery B

27.4.1 Risk Aversion—Number of Safe Choices in Lottery Choice Tasks

Table 27.4 presents the summary statistics of the results for the number of safe choices by groups and individuals in the two lottery choice tasks. Analysis of the data demonstrates that on average, chama participants were significantly more risk averse in both the tabular and graphical lottery choice tasks than student participants. The Wilcoxon rank-sum tests conducted for the tabular and the graphical lottery choice task, respectively, show that the null hypothesis that the student and chama distributions are equal is rejected in both cases ($p = 0.003$ and $p = 0.004$).

An analysis of the data for effects of framing on risk preferences in the two lottery choice tasks reveals that on average, at the individual decisions stage, student participants were slightly risk averse in the tabular lottery choice task (M = 5.05; SD = 1.28) and risk neutral in the graphical lottery choice task (M = 4.86; SD = 1.29). The Wilcoxon signed-rank test was performed to evaluate whether the distributions of the number of safe choices by students in the two lottery choice tasks were equivalent. The results indicate that the null hypothesis was rejected ($p = 0.025$) thus indicating the presence of framing effects. Individual stage decisions for chama participants indicate that they were risk averse in both the tabular lottery choice task (M = 5.58; SD = 2.49) and the graphical lottery choice task (M = 5.38; SD = 2.95). Results from the Wilcoxon signed-rank test revealed that the distributions of the number of safe choices made by chama individuals in the two lottery choice tasks were equal ($p = 0.417$) indicating absence of framing effects.

27 Risk-Taking Behavior and Effects of Framing in Group and Individual... 477

Turning to the group stage decisions, the results indicate that student groups were slightly risk averse in the tabular lottery choice task (M = 5.05; SD = 1.15) and slightly risk neutral in the graphical lottery choice task (M = 4.95; SD = 1.27). Results from the Wilcoxon signed-rank test revealed that the distributions of the number of safe choices made by student groups in the two lottery choice tasks were equal ($p = 0.626$). In line with the findings at the individual stage, chama groups were risk averse in both the tabular lottery choice task (M = 5.86; SD = 2.72) and the graphical lottery choice task (M = 5.68; SD = 1.27). Results from the Wilcoxon signed-rank test revealed no significant differences in the distributions of the number of safe choices made by chama groups in the two lottery choice tasks ($p = 0.946$).

When we analyze the individual and group outcomes of the lottery choice tasks, we find that there are generally no significant differences between the distribution of the number of safe choices for individual and group decisions for both students and chamas. In both the individual and group stages of the tabular lottery choice task, students made an average of 5.05 safe selections. For the graphical lottery choice tasks, although Wilcoxon rank-sum tests did not find a significant difference between the distributions of the number of safe choices at the individual and group stages ($p = 0.797$), the number of safe choices made by chamas at the individual stage (4.86) was lower than that for the group stage (4.95). In line with student findings, the results from Wilcoxon rank-sum tests show that there were also no significant differences in the number of safe choices made by chamas at the individual and group stages for both the graphical and lottery choice tasks, respectively ($p = 0.498$ and $p = 0.581$).

We also perform a three-way factorial ANOVA to analyze the effect of type of decision maker (students or chamas), decision stage (individual or group), and lottery choice task format (tabular or graphical) on the number of safe choices. Simple main effects analysis shows that the type of decision maker (students or chamas) had a statistically significant effect on number of safe choices, $F (1, 507) = 10.01$, $p = 0.0017$. Both the decision stage (individual or group), $F (1, 507) = 0.62$, $p = 0.43$, and the lottery choice task format (tabular or graphical) $F (1, 507) = 0.52$, $p = 0.47$ are not statistically significant.

We plot the predictive margins for the interaction between decision maker and decision stage and interaction between decision maker and lottery choice task format. These results are presented in the graph in Fig. 27.2, which indicates that both students and chamas displayed a lower level of risk aversion, making fewer safe choices during the individual stage compared to the group stage. However, the ANOVA analysis results suggest that this difference is not statistically significant ($p = 0.6823$). The graph also shows that chamas were more risk averse than students, making significantly more safe choices ($p < 0.05$) regardless of the lottery choice task format presented to them.

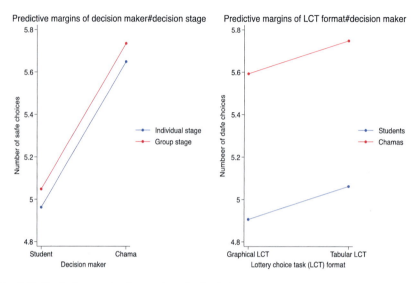

Fig. 27.2 Predictive margins for number of safe choices

27.4.2 Risk Preference Classification Based on CRRA Intervals

For a more precise characterization of the risk attitude, we assume a power utility function where $U(x) = x^{(1-r)}/(1-r)$ for $x > 0$ and r is the constant relative risk aversion (CRRA) coefficient (Brunette et al., 2015; Masclet et al., 2009). Thus, positive values of r indicate risk aversion, negative values indicate risk loving, while a value of 0 indicates risk neutrality. The switching point in the lottery decisions is used to infer the range of the CRRA coefficient.

The results of this risk preference classification for students and chamas (excluding inconsistent responses with multiple switch points) show that at the individual level, 66% of the student subject choices in the tabular lottery choice task and 56% of the choices in the graphical lottery choice task fell at the interval of [5, 9] safe choices. At the group level, 64% of the student choices in the tabular lottery choice task and 59% of the choices in the graphical lottery choice task fell within the range of [5, 9] safe choices. In comparison, for chamas, 52% of their choices in the tabular lottery choice task and 42% of their choices in the graphical lottery choice task fell at the interval of [5, 9] safe choices at the individual stage. At the group decision stage, 54% of the chamas choices in the tabular lottery choice task and 32% of the choices in the graphical lottery choice task fell at the interval of [5, 9] safe choices. Tables 27.5 and 27.6 present these findings. Thus, though the results show that on average chamas were more risk averse that student subjects based on the mean number of safe choices, we see that a smaller proportion of chama choices falls within the range of [5, 9] safe choices than that for students in both lottery choice tasks.

Table 27.5 Risk aversion classifications based on lottery choices for students

Number of safe choices	Implied range of CRRA for $U(x) = x^{(1-r)}/(1-r)$	Risk preference classification	Proportion of choices (%)							
			Individuals				Groups			
			Lottery task—tabular format		Lottery task—graphical format		Lottery task—tabular format		Lottery task—graphical format	
			All	Excluding Inconsistent	All	Excluding Inconsistent	All	Excluding Inconsistent	All	Excluding Inconsistent
0–1	$r < -0.95$	Extremely risk loving	1.53%	1.9%	2.29%	1.89%				
2	$-0.95 < r < -0.49$	Highly risk loving	0.76%	0.95%	2.29%	1.89%				
3	$-0.49 < r < -0.15$	Risk loving	3.82%	1.9%	7.63%	7.55%			6.98%	8.11%
4	$-0.15 < r < 0.15$	Risk neutral	24.43%	28.57%	30.53%	32.08%	30.23%	33.33%	27.91%	29.73%
5	$0.15 < r < 0.41$	Slightly risk averse	38.93%	39.05%	30.53%	29.25%	41.86%	46.15%	37.21%	37.84%
6	$0.41 < r < 0.68$	Risk averse	13.74%	12.38%	12.98%	13.21%	9.3%	10.26%	18.6%	16.22%
7	$0.68 < r < 0.97$	Very risk averse	9.16%	10.48%	6.87%	8.49%	4.65%	5.13%	2.33%	2.7%
8	$0.97 < r < 1.37$	Highly risk averse	4.58%	3.81%	5.34%	4.72%	2.33%	2.56%	4.65%	2.7%
9–10	$1.37 < r$	Extremely risk averse	3.05%	0.95%	1.53%		2.33%	2.56%	2.33%	2.7%
N			**131**	**105**	**131**	**106**	**43**	**39**	**43**	**37**
Risk-averse frequency (5–9 safe choices)			66%	66%	56%	56%	58%	64%	63%	59%

Note: Inconsistent refers to a participant with multiple switch points where they switch back and forth between the safe lottery A and the risky lottery B

Table 27.6 Risk aversion classifications based on lottery choices for chamas

Number of safe choices	Implied range of CRRA for $U(x)=x^{(1-r)}/(1-r)$	Risk preference classification	Proportion of choices (%)							
			Individuals				Groups			
			Lottery task—tabular format		Lottery task—graphical format		Lottery task—tabular format		Lottery task—graphical format	
			All	Excluding inconsistent	All	Excluding inconsistent	All	Excluding inconsistent	All	Excluding inconsistent
0–1	$r < -0.95$	Extremely risk loving	6.67%	8.70%	10%	15.19%	6.52%	8.57%	8.7%	16%
2	$-0.95 < r < -0.49$	Highly risk loving	2.5%	1.09%	5.83%	1.27%				
3	$-0.49 < r < -0.15$	Risk loving	2.5%	3.26%	3.33%	2.53%				
4	$-0.15 < r < 0.15$	Risk neutral	11.67%	11.96%	17.5%	16.46%	8.7%	11.43%	8.7%	16%
5	$0.15 < r < 0.41$	Slightly risk averse	40%	32.61%	20%	16.46%	26.09%	34.29%	10.87%	20%
6	$0.41 < r < 0.68$	Risk averse	9.17%	9.78%	13.33%	10.13%	13.04%	17.14%	4.35%	8%
7	$0.68 < r < 0.97$	Very risk averse	8.33%	9.78%	10%	8.86%	2.17%	2.86%	2.17%	4%
8	$0.97 < r < 1.37$	Highly risk averse	0.83%		5%	6.33%				
9–10	$1.37 < r$	Extremely risk averse	18.33%	22.83%	15%	22.78%	19.57%	25.71%	19.57%	36.00%
N			**120**	**92**	**120**	**79**	**46**	**35**	**46**	**25**
Risk-averse frequency (5–9 safe choices)			58%	52%	48%	42%	41%	54%	17%	32%

Note: Inconsistent refers to a participant with multiple switch points where they switch back and forth between the safe lottery A and the risky lottery B

27.4.3 Ordered Probit and Interval Regression Results

Table 27.7 provides the results of ordered probit regressions with the implied range of CRRA as the dependent variable for the tabular lottery choice task and the graphical lottery choice task. According to the results of the ordered probit regressions, the significant positive coefficient for the chama variable for both the tabular and graphical lottery choice tasks indicates that being a chama participant versus a student increases the likelihood of being in the higher ranges of CRRA intervals. This finding is in line with the findings from the preliminary analysis in that chama participants are more inclined than students to choose the safe option, making them perhaps more risk averse. In both the graphical and tabular lottery choice tasks, group decision-making does not appear to significantly affect the likelihood of selecting the safe option. Choosing a safe option was less likely for participants who made decisions first individually, then in a group, as opposed to those who did it the other way around. However, this effect was nonsignificant ($p > 0.05$) for both lottery choice tasks.

Table 27.7 also contains the findings from random effects interval regressions for the tabular and graphical lottery choice tasks. It is clear from the chama variable's statistically significant positive coefficients that chamas tended to make significantly more safe choices. These outcomes are consistent with those of the ordered probit regressions.

27.5 Discussion

In this study, we examine the risk-taking behavior and effects of framing in individual and group decisions of students and chamas (informal savings and investments groups) in Kenya. By comparing two presentation formats for a lottery choice task, we explore how framing techniques impact decision-making processes for these two populations.

On one hand, choice shift theories predict that when people discuss and make decisions as a group, they often end up adopting risk preferences that are more extreme or different from their initial individual risk preferences. Our data show that neither students' nor chamas' risk preferences significantly differ because of group discussion, in contrast to what choice shift theories predict. This conclusion also contrasts with those of (Ambrus et al., 2015; Baker et al., 2008; Masclet et al., 2009) who found that groups are more risk-averse than individuals, but it is in line with those of (Brunette et al., 2015; Deck et al., 2012; Harrison et al., 2012). Studies utilizing a within-subjects design, such those by Brunette et al. (2015), Deck et al. (2012), and Harrison et al. (2012), do not seem to find evidence of choice shift. However, studies with a between subjects design, where different participants are used in each condition of the independent variable—like those by Ambrus et al. (2015), Baker et al. (2008), and Masclet et al. (2009)—have shown that groups are

Table 27.7 Probit and interval regression models

	(1)	(2)	(3)	(4)
	CRRA range Tabular LCT	CRRA range Graphical LCT	CRRA tabular LCT	CRRA graphical LCT
1.Chama	0.687***	1.104***	0.225***	0.307***
	(0.134)	(0.146)	(0.078)	(0.097)
1.Group	− 0.075	0.162	0	0.056
	(0.14)	(0.146)	(0.085)	(0.107)
1.Individual to group	− 0.004	− 0.123	− 0.068	− 0.263***
	(0.132)	(0.136)	(0.078)	(0.096)
Constant			0.335***	0.334***
			(0.067)	(0.079)
/cut1	− 0.531***	− 0.373***		
	(0.122)	(0.118)		
/cut2	− 0.491***	− 0.266**		
	(0.121)	(0.117)		
/cut3	− 0.465***	− 0.241**		
	(0.121)	(0.118)		
/cut4	0.503***	0.425***		
	(0.12)	(0.116)		
/cut5	0.813***	0.765***		
	(0.123)	(0.117)		
/cut6	1.085***	0.976***		
	(0.124)	(0.118)		
/cut7	1.141***	1.097***		
	(0.121)	(0.118)		
/cut8	1.684***	1.497***		
	(0.154)	(0.144)		
/var.(cons[indiv_id])			0.221	0.295
			(3.856)	(3.847)
/var.(e.crra)			0.141	0.195
			(3.856)	(3.847)
Log-likelihood	− 456.968	− 473.134	− 514.003	− 482.574
Observations	265	265	248	227
Pseudo R^2	0.029	0.065		

Note: (1) and (2) are the ordered probit regression results for the tabular and graphical lottery choice tasks (LCT) where the dependent variable is the implied range of the CRRA based on the participants' switching points in the LCTs. Regressions (3) and (4) are random effects interval regressions for the tabular and graphical LCT, where the dependent variable is the lower and upper limit of the implied range of the CRRA based on the participants' switching points in the lottery choice tasks

Standard errors are in parentheses
***p < 0.01, **p < 0.05, *p < 0.1

more risk averse than individuals. From this, one may conclude that whether a study used a between- or within-subjects design may have an impact on whether choice shift occurs, which provides a basis for further research.

On the other hand, the theory on framing effects suggests that the way information is presented or framed can significantly influence decision-making and judgments. Subtle changes in the way the lottery choice task is presented may result in shifts in risk preferences of individuals and groups. Our study found evidence of framing effects for the students but not for chama subjects. On average, students were risk averse when presented with the tabular lottery choice task but were risk neutral in the graphical lottery choice task at both the individual and group levels. There was no significant difference in risk preferences of the chama subjects in the two lottery choice tasks. Chama subjects were risk averse in both the tabular and graphical lottery choice tasks. This result is contrary to the findings by (Kühberger, 1998) who concluded from their meta-analysis of prior research that most studies found no differences in framing effects for students and target populations.

Interestingly, the results show that chamas were significantly more risk averse than students in both formats of the lottery choice task. This points to possible differences in risk preferences of students and chama subjects. Except for (Masclet et al., 2009) most of the previous studies on risk preferences as evaluated from lotteries only involved student subjects. Our findings indicate that students as study subjects may behave differently from other target populations which is in contrast with the findings by (Kühberger, 1998). This suggests that context and participant characteristics play a role in evaluating risk-taking behavior.

This study has several implications. First implication is that participant characteristics and cultural considerations have a role to play in assessment of risk preferences. Conducting the study in Kenya with chamas, which are informal savings and investment groups prevalent in many African countries, provides cultural context and expands the generalizability of findings. The study's findings highlight the importance of considering cultural and contextual factors when examining risk-taking behavior.

Second, investigating framing effects at both the individual and group levels in the context of lottery choice tasks provides insights into the impact of presentation formats on decision-making. This knowledge can be valuable for designing effective communication strategies and understanding how different framing techniques influence risk perceptions and decision outcomes.

Third, the findings from this study can have practical implications for organizations, policymakers, and financial institutions. Understanding risk-taking behavior and framing effects can help in designing better investment strategies, risk management approaches, and financial education programs tailored to specific cultural and group contexts.

Finally, this study's findings have some economic implications. The study highlights the presence of framing effects in chama decisions at both the individual and group levels. This implies that the way financial information is presented can influence decision-making. Policymakers and financial institutions can leverage framing techniques to better communicate financial information and influence risk perceptions and behavior. In addition, the findings of the study underscore the need for improved financial education and literacy among both chamas and students. Enhancing financial knowledge and understanding risk-reward trade-offs can help individuals make informed decisions and manage their financial risks effectively.

Overall, this study provides valuable insights into risk-taking behavior, framing effects, and context considerations in financial decision-making. The implications suggest potential areas for policy interventions, product design, and financial education initiatives to promote better financial outcomes and risk management.

References

Ambrus, A., Greiner, B., & Pathak, P. A. (2015). How individual preferences are aggregated in groups: An experimental study. *Journal of Public Economics, 129*, 1–13.

Baker, R. J., Laury, S. K., & Williams, A. W. (2008). Comparing small-group and individual behavior in lottery-choice experiments. *Southern Economic Journal, 75*(2), 367–382.

Bateson, N. (1966). Familiarization, group discussion, and risk taking. *Journal of Experimental Social Psychology, 2*(2), 119–129.

Bougheas, S., Nieboer, J., & Sefton, M. (2013). Risk-taking in social settings: Group and peer effects. *Journal of Economic Behavior & Organization, 92*, 273–283. https://doi.org/10.1016/j.jebo.2013.06.010

Brunette, M., Cabantous, L., & Couture, S. (2015). Are individuals more risk and ambiguity averse in a group environment or alone? Results from an experimental study. *Theory and Decision, 78*(3), 357–376.

Burnstein, E., & Vinokur, A. (1977). Persuasive argumentation and social comparison as determinants of attitude polarization. *Journal of Experimental Social Psychology, 13*(4), 315–332.

Campbell, J. Y., Viceira, L. M., & Viceira, L. M. (2002). *Strategic asset allocation: Portfolio choice for long-term investors*. Clarendon Lectures in Economic.

CBK, KNBS, & FSD Kenya. (2021). 2021 FinAccess Household Survey. Central Bank of Kenya, Kenya National Bureau of Statistics, Financial Sector Deepening Kenya. https://www.knbs.or.ke/wp-content/uploads/2021/12/2021-Finaccess-Household-Survey-Report.pdf

Cozby, P., & Bates, S. (2014). Methods in Behavioral Research. McGraw-Hill Education.

Deck, C., Lee, J., Reyes, J., & Rosen, C. (2012). Risk-taking behavior: An experimental analysis of individuals and dyads. *Southern Economic Journal, 79*(2), 277–299.

Diederich, A., Wyszynski, M., & Ritov, I. (2018). Moderators of framing effects in variations of the Asian Disease problem: Time constraint, need, and disease type. *Judgment and Decision Making, 13*(6), 529–546.

Druckman, J. N. (2001). Evaluating framing effects. *Journal of Economic Psychology, 22*(1), 91–101.

Eliaz, K., Ray, D., & Razin, R. (2006). Choice shifts in groups: A decision-theoretic basis. *American Economic Review, 96*(4), 1321–1332.

FSD Kenya. (2015, August 12). *Explainer: Savings groups in Kenya*. Financial Sector Deepening Kenya. https://www.fsdkenya.org/finaccess/explainer-savings-groups-in-kenya/

Gugerty, M. K. (2007). You can't save alone: Commitment in rotating savings and credit associations in Kenya. *Economic Development and Cultural Change, 55*(2), 251–282.

Harrison, G. W., Lau, M. I., Rutström, E. E., & Tarazona-Gómez, M. (2012). Preferences over social risk. *Oxford Economic Papers, 65*(1), 25–46.

Holt, C. A., & Laury, S. K. (2002). Risk aversion and incentive effects. *American Economic Review, 92*(5), 1644–1655.

Im, H., & Chen, C. (2022). To save or lose? A cross-national examination of the disease risk framing effect and the influence of collectivism. *Journal of Behavioral Decision Making, 35*(4), e2276.

Janis, I. L. (1972). Victims of groupthink: A psychological study of foreign-policy decisions and fiascoes. Houghton Mifflin.

Jouini, E., Napp, C., & Nocetti, D. (2013). Collective risk aversion. *Social Choice and Welfare, 40*(2), 411–437.

Keck, S., Diecidue, E., & Budescu, D. V. (2014). Group decisions under ambiguity: Convergence to neutrality. *Journal of Economic Behavior & Organization, 103*, 60–71.

Kühberger, A. (1998). The influence of framing on risky decisions: A meta-analysis. *Organizational Behavior and Human Decision Processes, 75*(1), 23–55. https://doi.org/10.1006/obhd.1998.2781

Levin, I. P., Schneider, S. L., & Gaeth, G. J. (1998). All frames are not created equal: A typology and critical analysis of framing effects. *Organizational Behavior and Human Decision Processes, 76*(2), 149–188.

Malkiel, B. (2021). *A random walk down wall street the time-tested strategy for successful investing*. WW Norton&Company Ltd..

Masclet, D., Colombier, N., Denant-Boemont, L., & Loheac, Y. (2009). Group and individual risk preferences: A lottery-choice experiment with self-employed and salaried workers. *Journal of Economic Behavior & Organization, 70*(3), 470–484.

Mathuva, D. (2022). Savings groups in Kenya: A Contextualised literature review on savings groups in Kenya. In D. T. Redford & G. Verhoef (Eds.), *Transforming Africa* (pp. 163–178). Emerald Publishing Limited. https://doi.org/10.1108/978-1-80262-053-520221013

Moscovici, S., & Zavalloni, M. (1969). The group as a polarizer of attitudes. *Journal of Personality and Social Psychology, 12*(2), 125.

Paese, P. W., Bieser, M., & Tubbs, M. E. (1993). Framing effects and choice shifts in group decision making. *Organizational Behavior and Human Decision Processes, 56*(1), 149–165. https://doi.org/10.1006/obhd.1993.1049

Redford, D. T., Verhoef, G., Peprah, J. A., Muruka, G., Biche, L., Wolf, C., Rickard, K., Ali, S. D., Siembou, S., & Onomo, C. M. B. (2022). *Transforming Africa*. Emerald Publishing Limited.

Roux, N., & Sobel, J. (2015). Group polarization in a model of information aggregation. *American Economic Journal: Microeconomics, 7*(4), 202–232.

Sanders, G. S., & Baron, R. S. (1977). Is social comparison irrelevant for producing choice shifts? *Journal of Experimental Social Psychology, 13*(4), 303–314.

Shupp, R. S., & Williams, A. W. (2008). Risk preference differentials of small groups and individuals. *The Economic Journal, 118*(525), 258–283.

Stoner, J. A. (1968). Risky and cautious shifts in group decisions: The influence of widely held values. *Journal of Experimental Social Psychology, 4*(4), 442–459.

Stoner, J. A. F. (1961). *A comparison of individual and group decisions involving risk* [Massachusetts Institute of Technology]. http://dspace.mit.edu/handle/1721.1/11330

Sutter, M. (2009). Individual behavior and group membership: Comment. *The American Economic Review, 99*(5), 2247–2257.

Tversky, A., & Kahneman, D. (1981). The framing of decisions and the psychology of choice. *Science, 211*(4481), 453–458.

Wallach, M. A., Kogan, N., & Bem, D. J. (1964). Diffusion of responsibility and level of risk taking in groups. *The Journal of Abnormal and Social Psychology, 68*(3), 263.

Wang, X. T., & Johnston, V. S. (1995). Perceived social context and risk preference: A re-examination of framing effects in a life-death decision problem. *Journal of Behavioral Decision Making, 8*(4), 279–293. https://doi.org/10.1002/bdm.3960080405

Chapter 28
Empirical Study on the Role of Cultivation in the Acceptance of ICT Technologies in the Agricultural Sector of Kozani

Deligiannis Dimitrios, Saprikis Vaggelis, Avlogiaris Giorgos, and Antoniadis Ioannis

Abstract This chapter presents the factors that impact the agricultural sector of the Kozani region to use Information and Communication Technologies (ICT) as well as the crops to which they are applied. The area under consideration is the largest prefecture in the region of Western Macedonia which is currently in the status of "Just Development Transition" due to the region's dependence on the production of the fossil fuel Lignite. In this survey data from 100 farmers of the region collected via a convenience sample procedure. The results reveal that a large part of Kozani's population has moved to the agricultural sector in the last decade and a significant part of it is women. It also shows the tendency of young farmers for higher value-added crops and the number of crops chosen by the users of ICT technologies. At the same time, the paper greatly reveal the need to better inform farmers in the area as well as mobilize experts to ensure that new technologies and skills are transferred in an appropriate manner to the stakeholders.

Keywords ICT · Kozani region · Agriculture · Technology adoption

D. Dimitrios (✉) · S. Vaggelis · A. Ioannis
Department of Management Science and Technology, School of Economic Sciences, University of Western Macedonia, Kozani, Greece
e-mail: mpp00012@uowm.gr; esaprikis@uowm.gr; iantoniadis@uowm.gr

A. Giorgos
Department of Statistics and Insurance Science, School of Economic Sciences, University of Western Macedonia, Grevena, Greece
e-mail: gavlogiaris@uowm.gr

© The Author(s), under exclusive license to Springer Nature Switzerland AG 2024
N. Tsounis, A. Vlachvei (eds.), *Applied Economic Research and Trends*, Springer Proceedings in Business and Economics,
https://doi.org/10.1007/978-3-031-49105-4_28

28.1 Introduction

Kozani is located in Western Macedonia in Greece and is the only region in Greece that does not have access to the sea. Until 1959, its economic model was based on the primary agricultural sector and livestock farming. The creation of the first power plant in 1959 boosted the service sector and improved the living standards of the inhabitants. The Paris Agreement on Climate Change in 2015 (United Nations, 2015) and the subsequent Green European Agreement (Commission, 2019) require the decoupling of electricity generation from the fuel lignite, which is largely utilized by the region's power plants. Decisions to close local plants have already brought about changes in the local economy.

Radulov et al. (2019) report that the contribution of factories to the region's GDP is 45%, while the agricultural sector contributes only 6%. One of the challenges of the current period is the utilization of local resources so that the rural population becomes a new driving force of the local economy. The introduction of Information and Communication Technologies (ICT) in the agricultural sector has been intensively studied. The evolution of the technology, the possibility of collecting more data and the ever-increasing demands in their use require additional skills, and the absence of which contributes to the so-called "Digital Divide" (Botsiou et al., 2018).

This article aims to capture the use of ICT by farmers in the region, the challenges for digital and green transition, and the crops where new techniques and technologies are applied. The survey findings are expected to provide important insights regarding the level of readiness for digital transition, the reasons for ICT use, and how these technologies affect farmers and their communities.

In specific, the objectives of this empirical study are:

- To help managers better understand the expectations and aspirations of farmers in the region and.
- document the crops in which farmers use ICTs.

This chapter is structured in seven sections. Section 28.1 presents the extant international and domestic literature, Sect. 28.2 analyzes the research methodology, and Sect. 28.3 presents the study's results. Then, Sect. 28.4 describes the results of the research. Section 28.5 presents conclusions, and finally Sect. 28.6 presents limitation and future recommendations.

28.2 Literature Review

Increasing productivity in the agricultural sector to meet the need for food sufficiency is a global concern, especially in the context of increasing consumption trends and the global food distribution crisis (World Food Programme, 2022; FAO & ITU, 2022). ICT in the agricultural sector is seen as an innovation by a large part of the rural population (Kountios et al., 2023). According to Rogers (1962), the stages of innovation acceptance are knowledge, persuasion, decision, implementation, and confirmation. In Greece, there are a large number of organizations and enterprises whose aim is to encourage the use of new technologies (HAICTA, 2023), research and disseminate new technologies and techniques (Gaiasense, 2023), and create new innovative tools and services with the aim of smart agriculture (ITHACA, 2023).

The need to identify the factors influencing farmers' attitudes and ICT use in Greece has been the focus of several studies focusing on the specific local characteristics (Botsiou et al., 2018; Michailidis et al., 2008) and the need for training and use of these technologies (Kountios & Papadavid, 2022). The main reasons for using new technologies are mainly "Ease of Use", "Perceived Usefulness" (Davis, 1989), "Social Influence" (Venkatesh & Davis, 2000), age (Ali, 2012; Agwu et al., 2008; Tamirat et al., 2018; Barnes et al., 2019), "experience" (Alambeigi & Ahangari, 2016), "farm size" (Barnes et al., 2019; Smith et al., 2004), and "type of crops".

The relationship between "Experience" and "Acceptance/Use" has been confirmed in an inverted U-shaped curve (Ainembabazi & Mugisha, 2014). Less experience with a particular crop indicates lower acceptance of new technologies. As experience increases, adoption of ICT increases, but as farmers gain higher levels of experience, adoption decreases. This finding indicates the need for retraining and continued adoption of new ICTs. Farm size and type was also identified as an important factor for ICT adoption in the work of Hall et al. (2003) on cattle farmers and peanut producers.

28.3 Research Methodology

The present study is part of a larger survey in the region of Western Macedonia which was conducted from August 2022 to October 2022. To reveal the factors and the way of acceptance and use of specific technologies, a questionnaire was structured that included two parts: the assessment of demographic data in the first part and the interpretation of factors of the Unified Theory of Acceptance and Use of Technology 2 (UTAUT2) model (Venkatesh et al., 2012), utilizing the Likert scale in the second part.

In (2003), Venkatesh, et al. compared the results of eight preexisting adoption models of technology acceptance and use in order to identify the optimal one. Taking data from these models, they formulated a new theory, which in practice outperformed the results of the previous ones that explained from 17% to 53% of the technology acceptance and use factors. The new model, Unified Theory of Acceptance and Use of Technology—UTAUT, interpreted 70%.

In 2012, a new modified model was published to overcome criticisms that its application was industry-only and new factors were added. The new model UTAUT2 (Venkatesh et al., 2012) was shown to be applicable to consumers by adding its factors Hedonic Motivation, Price value, Facilitating Conditions and Habit.

The first part of the survey consisted of 18 demographic characteristics questions, while the second part contained 30 questions related to the factors of Performance Expectancy, Expected Effort, Social Influence, Facilitating Conditions, Hedonic Motivation, Perceived Value (Venkatesh et al., 2012), Self-confidence Factor (Adrian et al., 2005), Perceived Cost, Behavioral Intention, and ICT Usage.

A pilot study took place first. Specifically, the questionnaire was initially completed by 16 respondents, including farmers, mathematicians, and engineers, to test the completion time and ease of understanding the questions. Their responses are not included in the sample. Most of the questionnaire was completed by the researcher through face-to-face meetings and where impossible it was sent via Google Forms, after prior communication and briefing. The results of the questionnaire were processed using the statistical package IBM SPSS version 20. Descriptive statistics was applied for the analysis of the data gathered.

28.4 Results

This section presents the findings of the survey and the related analysis using descriptive statistics.

Age The sample consisted of 100 farmers in Kozani region, and 71% of them were male. The age of the sample was mainly ranged from 25 up to 54 years (70%). Traditionally, the age of farmers appear to be much higher in the agricultural sector. However, the survey was conducted in a period when there were restrictions due to the COVID-19 pandemic. Thus, the older farmers were reluctant to face-to-face meetings. Moreover, they did not have the necessary knowledge, skills, and possibly the technology to complete the online form.

Experience The scale chosen to capture the experience of the sample was structured in 5-year increments. In this way, 6 groups were created that included both young farmers and farmers close to retirement. The analysis showed that 46% of the sample has up to 10 years of experience, which reflects the political will to introduce young farmers into the productive sector. At the same time, almost one-fourth of the farmers have 26 or more years of experience and are close to retirement. The data are presented in Table 28.1.

Table 28.2 shows the analysis of experience by gender. The results are in accordance to the results of the Women's Entrepreneurship Policy, both the ESPA (2023) and Public Employment Service programs.

It is worth noting that in recent years even more women have been entering a sector that traditionally employed mainly by men. According to Maghsoudi et al. (2012), rural women can benefit from business training and support to maximize commercial opportunities for greater economic growth and development of local communities.

28 Empirical Study on the Role of Cultivation in the Acceptance of ICT... 491

Table 28.1 Experience

Experience in Years	Frequency	Percent
1–5	18	18,0
6–10	28	28,0
11–15	10	10,0
16–20	10	10,0
21–25	11	11,0
Over 26	23	23,0
Total	100	100,0

Table 28.2 Years of experience per gender

Gender	Years of experience						Total
	1–5	6–10	11–15	16–20	21–25	Over 26	
Woman	9	8	2	1	3	6	29
Man	9	20	8	9	8	17	71
Total	18	28	10	10	11	23	100

Table 28.3 Reasons for ICT usage

	Frequency	Valid percent	Cumulative percent
Increase productivity	31	52,5	52,5
Cost reduction	9	15,3	67,8
More effective protection against risks	11	18,6	86,4
Reduction of environmental impact	1	1,7	88,1
Other	7	11,9	100,0
Total	59	100,0	

ICT Usage Factors

The main reasons for ICT technology usage were as follows: (1) increase productivity, (2) reduce costs, (3) more effective protection against hazards, and (4) reduce environmental impact. There was also the option (5) "other". The respondents mentioned that they utilize new technologies in their production process in a percentage of 59%. The results are presented in Table 28.3.

Respondents were asked to indicate the most predominant reason, having only one option to choose from. Increasing productivity was the most dominant one (52.5%), followed by being more effective protection from risks (18.6%). This was followed by reducing production costs (15.3%), while only 1.7% chose that they use new technologies to reduce environmental impact.

The closed question format did not allow to capture a large percentage (11.9%) who indicated another reason. The "other reasons" were mainly related to the mandatory nature of specific techniques and technologies in order farmers join National and Community Support and Subsidy Programmes. Another influential factor is the acquisition of similar technologies by acquaintances or other important persons related to them (social influence).

The devices used by the research sample are presented in Table 28.4:

Table 28.4 Device used per selection factor of ICT

	Device used		
	Smartphone	Tablet	Laptop/PC
Increase productivity (n = 31)	30	15	20
Cost reduction (n = 9)	9	2	8
More effective protection against risks (n = 11)	8	5	9
Reduction of environmental impact (n = 1)	1	1	1
Other (n = 7)	6	3	4

Table 28.5 ICT usage options

	App used	
	Yes	No
Mobile application	26	33
Ground sensors	4	55
Production management application on PC or laptop	7	52
Application for recording cultivation work	14	45
Satellite images	15	44
Agricultural automation system	6	53
Use of agrometeorological station	11	48
GPS on agricultural machinery	16	43
Individual consulting services for the management of cultivation operations	9	50
Integrated advisory service/smart farming systems for the overall management of the farm	2	57
Drones (for taking aerial photographs)	0	59
Drones (for spraying)	0	59
Electrically powered agricultural machinery	0	59
Automation and robotics in production	0	59

The options available in order to identify the purpose of ICT use and exploitation are presented in Table 28.5:

Based on Table 28.5 results, it is depicted that most ICT application is focused on simple recording of basic tasks or weather monitoring, rather than on their effective application to tasks used in Precision Agriculture or Intelligent Agriculture. The 41% of the sample stated that they do not utilize any of the aforementioned technologies. Respondents were allowed to indicate more than one factor in this question. Table 28.6 shows the reasons that they indicated as inhibitors:

Lack of awareness of the benefits of technology (26.9%) and lack of funding (20.22%) are the most important inhibitors. The inability to connect and transfer

Table 28.6 Reasons for non-use

	Frequency	Valid percent
Lack of funding	18	20,22%
Lack of resources—It is costly	16	17,98%
Lack of information/knowledge about the benefits of technology	24	26,97%
Lack of advice from an agricultural advisor	11	12,36%
I do not have the technical capabilities required	9	10,11%
I have a negative view of the technology	4	4,49%
I am intimidated by new technologies in my work	2	2,25%
Other	4	4,49%
Don't know/Don't answer	1	1,12%
Total	89	100%

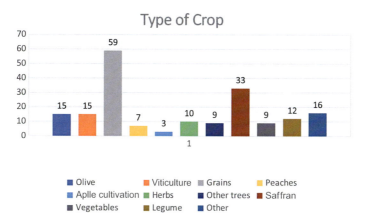

Fig. 28.1 Type of Crops

data between different vendors is an issue that limits utility and increases dependencies and costs when interested farmers seek to use other companies' applications.

Crops Using ICT

One of the main objectives of the study was to identify the crops for which farmers in the Kozani region use ICT technologies. Figure 28.1 shows the crops and the percentage of the sample using them. The total number of crops is 188 which indicate that farmers in Kozani are not limited to only one crop, but for each farmer there are 1.88 crop types. The most popular crops are grains and saffron. It is also important to note, however, the tobacco cultivation, which is included under "other crops". In the past, tobacco cultivation provided employment for a large part of the rural population. Nowadays, tobacco crops are excluded from subsidies and farmers do not choose to engage in this product. Nevertheless, a part of the population still supports it. Peach growers are also an important factor, but as mentioned above, they did not participate, with the exception of a few, as the survey period coincided with the harvest period.

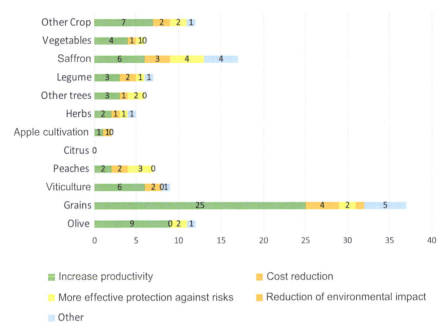

Fig. 28.2 Type of crops within ICT usage

Table 28.7 Saffron and Herbs total Experience

	Experience in Years						
	1–5	6–10	11–15	16–20	21–25	Over 26	Total
Saffron	15,15%	42,42%	12,12%	3,03%	15,15%	12,12%	100,00%
Herbs	40,00%	30,00%	10,00%	10,00%	0,00%	10,00%	100,00%

The survey focused more on the crops of the 59% of the sample, which use ICT technologies. Interestingly, this sample utilizes 2.3 types of crops, significantly higher than the overall average. This leads us to conclude that farmers who are utilizing ICTs are considering additional solutions through different crops and show more potential than those who choose not to use them. Figure 28.2 shows the types of crops in the sample that utilize ICTs.

The main reason for producers to adopt new technologies is to increase productivity. It is worth noting that "Other Reasons" account for more than 20% in Saffran and Herbs. The latter finding is consistent with the forced introduction of technology through funding programs. Table 28.7 shows the experience of these farmers. 57.58% of Saffron farmers and 70% of Herbs farmers have less than 10 years of experience and belong to the category of "New Farmers".

Experience Curve and Use of ICT Technologies

The relationship between "Experience" and "ICT Utilization" reported in the literature by Ainembabazi and Mugisha (2014) is presented in Fig. 28.3. It is

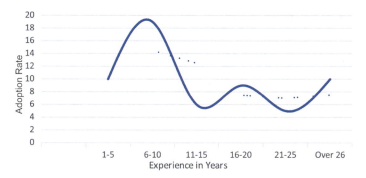

Fig. 28.3 Experience curve

observed that in the case of the rural population of Kozani, the relationship is also shown in the form of an inverted U. The moving average is shown with a dotted line, from which the relevant information is gathered.

The relative need for information about the benefits of Technology, which is one of the most important reasons for "Non-Use," is also explained in this curve.

28.5 Conclusions

This part makes a first attempt to identify the reasons why farmers in the Kozani region use ICT technologies. It, then, lists the crops to which they are applied. The results show that the main reason for ICT use is to increase productivity. It is also important to mention that producers using ICT decide to diversify risk by investing in more crops, while reducing their exposure from a single crop production.

The findings also reflect the increased participation of women in agricultural production over the last decade. In addition, a large part of the rural population, also in the last decade, has shifted to cultivation of aromatic plants and herbs. In the traditional Saffran crop, it was observed that a remarkable entry of new farmers took place in the five-year period 2012–2017, accounting for 42.4% of the sample of this crop.

Both the perception that farmers are not aware of the benefits of new technology in their fields and the inverted U-shaped curve depicted in Fig. 28.3 demonstrate the need for continued awareness. Farmers gain knowledge and experience through continuous employment, but fail to combine it with the new technologies and techniques that are constantly being discovered. Michailidis et al. (2008) concluded that farmers in the region of Kozani did not understand the benefits of ICT use. The fact that farmers are focusing on monitoring rather than production-oriented technologies such as precision agriculture and smart farming should be of concern to the relevant stakeholders and industry professionals.

28.6 Limitations and Future Research

The first limiting factor comes from the dates the survey lasted, as it coincided with the peach fruit harvest season, which acted as a deterrent to holding meetings with the specific producers. The second restriction comes from the restrictive measures that were in place to limit the COVID-19 pandemic but also from the cautious attitude of older people in particular regarding their social interactions. This is also the reason why the specific sample shows a relatively low average age of farmers.

As already mentioned, this article is the first part of an ongoing research aimed at identifying and creating groups of farmers with similar characteristics across the region of Western Macedonia. In the future, the study aims to investigate the factors contributing to the adoption and use of new ICT technologies, based on models of diffusion and adoption of ICT technologies, such as UTAUT2.

References

Adrian, A. M., Norwood, S. H., & Mask, P. L. (2005). Producers' perceptions and attitudes toward precision agriculture technologies. *Computers and Electronics in Agriculture, 48*(3), 256–271.

Agwu, A. E., Ekwueme, J. N., & Anyanwu, A. C. (2008). Adoption of improved agricultural technologies disseminated via radio farmer programme by farmers in Enugu State, Nigeria. *African Journal of Biotechnology, 9*, 1277–1286.

Ainembabazi, J. H., & Mugisha, J. (2014). The role of farming experience on the adoption of agricultural technologies: Evidence from smallholder farmers in Uganda. *Journal of Development Studies, 5*, 666–679.

Alambeigi, A., & Ahangari, I. (2016). Technology acceptance model (TAM) as a predictor model for explaining agricultural experts behavior in acceptance of ICT. *International Journal of Agricultural Management and Development (IJAMAD), 6*(2), 235–247.

Ali, J. (2012). Factors affecting the adoption of information and communication technologies (ICTs) for farming decisions. *Journal of Agricultural & Food Information, 13*(1), 78–96.

Barnes, A. P., et al. (2019). Exploring the adoption of precision agricultural technologies: A cross regional study of EU farmers. *Land Use Policy, 80*, 163–174.

Botsiou, M., Dagdilelis, V., & Koutsou, S. (2018). The Greek farmers' ICT skills and the intra-rural digital divide formation. *Agricultural Economics Review, 19*(1), 52–68.

Commission, E. (2019). *The European green deal.* Available at: https://eur-lex.europa.eu/legal-content/EN/TXT/?qid=1588580774040&uri=CELEX:52019DC0640. Accessed 2 Apr 2022.

Davis, F. D. (1989). Perceived usefulness, perceived ease of use, and user acceptance of information technology. *MIS Quarterly, 13*(3), 319–340.

ESPA. (2023). *espa.gr.* Available at: https://www.espa.gr/el/Pages/ProclamationsFS.aspx?item=5688. Accessed 12 May 2023.

FAO and ITU. (2022). *Status of digital agriculture in 47 sub-Saharan African countries publication* (p. 364). Food and Agriculture Organization.

Gaiasense. (2023). *Gaiasense.* Available at: https://www.gaiasense.gr/en/gaiasense. Accessed 5 May 2023.

HAICTA. (2023). *HAICTA.* Available at: https://www.haicta.gr/aims-and-objectives.html. Accessed 5 May 2023.

Hall, L., Dunkleberger, J., Ferreira, W., & Prevatt, W. J. (2003). Diffusion-adoption of personal computers and the Internet in farm business decisions: Southeastern beef and peanut farmers. *Journal of Extension, 41*(3), 8.

ITHACA. (2023). *Internet of things & applications lab – Home page.* Available at: https://ithaca.ece.uowm.gr/. Accessed 5 May 2023.

Kountios, G., & Papadavid, G. (2022). The adoption of information and communication technologies in farmers and the emerging need for an integrated system of agricultural advisory and training. *HAICTA 2022, 09*, 418–421.

Kountios, G., Konstantinidis, C., & Antoniadis, I. (2023). Can the adoption of ICT and advisory services be considered as a tool of competitive advantage in agricultural holdings? *Agronomy, 13*(2), 530.

Maghsoudi, T., Hekmat, M., & Davodi, H. (2012). Supporting the entrepreneurship development in the agriculture production cooperatives. *African Journal of Business Management, 6*(10), 3639–3647.

Michailidis, A., et al. (2008). *Adoption of information and communication technologies among farmers in the region of West Macedonia.* AWICTSAE.

Radulov, L., et al. (2019). *Report on the current role of coal mining and related policies in the TRACER.* Black Sea Energy Research Center.

Rogers, E. M. (1962). *Diffusion of innovations* (p. 367). The Free Press of Glencoe.

Smith, A., Morrison Paul, C. J., Goe, R. W., & Kenney, M. (2004). Computer and internet use by Great Plains farmers. *Journal of Agricultural and Resource Economics, 29*, 481.

Tamirat, T. W., Pedersen, S. M., & Lind, K. M. (2018). Farm and operator characteristics affecting adoption of precision agriculture in Denmark and. *Acta Agriculturae Scandinavica, Section B — Soil & Plant Science, 68*(4), 349–357.

United Nations. (2015). *Adoption of the Paris agreement – Paris agreement text English.* Available at: https://unfccc.int/sites/default/files/english_paris_agreement.pdf. Accessed 15 May, 2023.

Venkatesh, V., & Davis, F. D. (2000). A theoretical extension of the technology acceptance model: Four longitudinal field studies. *Management Science, 46*(2), 186–204.

Venkatesh, V., Morris, M. G., Davis, G. B., & Davis, F. D. (2003). User acceptance of information technology: Toward a unified view. *MIS Quarterly, 27*(3), 425–478.

Venkatesh, V., Thong, J. Y. L., & Xu, X. (2012). Consumer acceptance and use of information technology: Extending the unified theory of acceptance and use of technology. *MIS Quarterly, 36*(1), 157–178.

World Food Programme. (2022). *Globlal report on food crises.* Available at: https://www.fao.org/3/cb9997en/cb9997en.pdf. Accessed 4 May 2023.

Chapter 29
How Has the COVID-19 Pandemic Affected the Utilization of the Company's Working Capital?

Janka Grofčíková

Abstract Industrial production has long been among the dominant sectors of Slovakia's economy. Its share in the creation of GDP is an average of 17%. As a result of the adopted government measures related to the spread of the COVID-19 pandemic, industrial production in Slovakia fell by 26.7% in April 2020 compared to March 2020, which was reflected in several financial and economic characteristics of individual enterprises. The aim of this article is to investigate the changes in the management of working capital items in industrial production enterprises in Slovakia caused by the COVID-19 pandemic. We examine changes in working capital management using selected activity ratios, specifically using the asset turnover ratio, the inventory turnover period, the short-term receivables turnover period, the short-term liabilities turnover period, and the cash conversion cycle. We conduct research on a sample of 3541 enterprises of all size categories between 2017 and 2021. We evaluate changes in the inter-annual values of selected activity indicators by calculating growth rates and averages, verifying the statistical significance of changes using the Wilcoxon signed-rank test at a significance level of 5%. The results show a decrease in the turnover of assets in 2020, an increase in the turnover period of inventories, receivables and liabilities, and a decrease of the cash conversion cycle.

Keywords Activity utilization ratios · COVID-19 · Industrial production · Slovakia

---

J. Grofčíková (✉)
Department of Finance and Accounting, Faculty of Ecomonics Matej Bel University in Banská Bystrica, Banská Bystrica, Slovakia
e-mail: janka.grofcikova@umb.sk

© The Author(s), under exclusive license to Springer Nature Switzerland AG 2024 499
N. Tsounis, A. Vlachvei (eds.), *Applied Economic Research and Trends*, Springer Proceedings in Business and Economics,
https://doi.org/10.1007/978-3-031-49105-4_29

29.1 Introduction

The industry of Slovakia is divided according to NACE Rev. 2 to these industries: (B) mining and quarrying, (C) manufacturing, (D) electricity, gas, steam, and air conditioning supply, and (E) water supply, sewerage, waste management, and remediation activities. The industry of Slovakia (B+C+D+E) belongs together with the sectors (G) wholesale and retail trade and repair of motor vehicles and motorcycles, (H) transportation and storage, and (I) accommodation and food services activities, in terms of their share in the creation of GDP among, to the most important sectors. The average share of industry in the creation of GDP in the years 2017–2022 (1.Q-3.Q) was 22.26%, sectors G – I created an average of 17.37% of GDP. The share of industries in industry sales, expressed in current prices, is shown in Table 29.1.

Manufacturing (C) accounts for an average of 85% of industry's contribution to GDP creation. The same average share is occupied by industrial production in total sales for own services and goods in industry. Among the most important industries of manufacturing in Slovakia is manufacture of transport equipment, which accounted for an average of 34.3% of the industry's sales. The second in order, in terms of the sector's share of industry sales, is manufacture of basic metals and fabricated metal products, except machinery and equipment, its share is 15.7% on average. Other industries of manufacturing participate in the creation of sales by less than 10%.

Manufacturing enterprises, together with wholesale, retail trade, transportation and storage enterprises, accommodation, and food service enterprises, are among the most important employers in Slovakia. Industry employed a total of 23.7% in 2021, and the transportation, storage, accommodation, and food service sectors a

Table 29.1 The share of selected industries in sales in industry

	2018	2019	2020	2021	2022
	1.Q.−4.Q.	1.Q.−4.Q.	1.Q.−4.Q.	1.Q.−4.Q.	1.Q.−3.Q.
B, C, D, E Industry together (in thousands €, current prices)	99,914,398	100,157,533	91,977,447	106,172,814	100,982,748
B Mining and quarrying	0.60%	0.59%	0.62%	0.57%	0.44%
C Manufacturing	85.32%	85.58%	84.47%	84.47%	80.30%
D Electricity, gas, steam and air-conditioning supply	12.81%	12.47%	13.47%	13.46%	17.93%
E Water supply, sewerage, waste management and remediation	1.28%	1.36%	1.45%	1.50%	1.33%

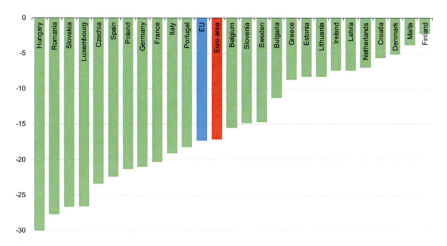

Fig. 29.1 Industrial production in April 2020 (% change compared with March 2020)

total of 23.3% of the employed population. Manufacturing accounted for 21.3% of total employment. Of the total number of active business entities in 2021, micro-, small-, and medium-sized enterprises with a maximum number of employees of up to 250 people made up 99.8% of them, micro-enterprises made up 97.5% of them. A total of 13.4% of active SMEs operated in the industry sector.

The measures to prevent the spread of the COVID-19 disease, which Slovakia introduced in March 2020, also had a significant impact on industrial production. According to Eurostat (2020), seasonally adjusted EU industrial production fell by 17.3% in April 2020 compared to March 2020. In April 2020, compared to April 2019, the decline in EU industrial production was −27.2%. These were the largest annual decreases recorded since April 2009. The largest decrease between March and April 2020 was recorded in the production of consumer durables (−27.8%), capital goods (−27.3%), intermediate products (−14.9%), short-term consumer goods (−10.7%), and energy (−5%). Industrial production fell in all member countries for which data were available (see Fig. 29.1).

The highest decline was recorded in Hungary (−30.5%) and Romania (−27.7%) and Slovakia had the third highest decline in industrial production (−26.7%).

According to the report of the Ministry of Economy of the Slovak Republic (Industrial production, 2018), unlike the EU average, where industry contributed 15.5% to the total GDP in 2012, the industry of the Slovak Republic provided 23.9% of GDP in the mentioned period, the share of industrial production alone was 18.9% of GDP of Slovakia. In 2017, it already made up 24.1% of Slovakia's GDP.

The above proves that the Slovak industry, especially industrial production, is a long-term dominant economic sector. Any disruption of industrial production disrupts the stability and performance of Slovakia's economy in its foundations.

29.2 Literature Review

All changes in the activities of enterprises are inevitably reflected in all items of assets and sources of its financing. The basic structure of the company's property consists of its fixed and current assets, the sources of financing the assets can be divided into equity and liabilities. Items of short-term assets and short-term liabilities, which are also called the working capital of the company, are most often affected by the company's operational activity. We generally define the working capital of a company as short-term assets, which include money, receivables, and inventories. Net working capital is determined by deducting short-term liabilities from short-term assets.

In general, the role of working capital management is to make decisions in relation to the management of the company's short-term assets and ensuring their financing from short-term liabilities. According to Nimalathasan (2010), the goal of working capital management is to ensure that the company will be able to carry out its operational activities without interruption and that it will have enough cash to cover its short-term debts and operating expenses. The importance of working capital management is confirmed by its time-consuming nature, the share of working capital items in the total invested capital of the company, but also the fact that working capital is necessary to ensure the company's growth. Non-systemic measures and nonconceptual management by the macro-environment, which we witnessed during individual waves of the corona crisis, only further confirm the importance of working capital management at the corporate level.

In addition to profitability, the company's working capital policy has an impact on its liquidity and financial health, which is also confirmed by Kipronoh and Mweta (2018). It also includes a spectrum of tools that allow the company to continuously monitor and evaluate the situation in the area of working capital. They also include activity indicators that allow the company to measure how effectively it manages its assets. If a company has more assets than is appropriate, it incurs unnecessary costs and thus a low profit. Conversely, if a business is short of assets, it risks having to forego potentially profitable business opportunities and thus lose the revenue it could have earned. According to Mansoori and Muhammad (2012), an appropriate assessment of working capital and identification of its basic components can help financial managers make decisions about the company's operations efficiently and effectively and can help them effectively manage working capital in a way that balances liquidity and profitability while helping them achieve set goals.

Several authors have devoted themselves to the research of working capital management and its management tools. The impact of working capital management on corporate performance and efficiency was also investigated by Rahemann et al. (2010), Samiloglu and Demirgunes (2008), Zariyawati et al. (2009), Shin and Soenen (1998), Padachi (2006), Nimalathasan (2010), and Banos-Caballero (2012). Research on the effect of working capital efficiency on the financial performance of the firm was also conducted by Prasad et al. (2019), and their goal was to introduce a working capital efficiency multiplier that would serve as a direct measure of the profitability of working capital management. The relationship between CCC and company profitability was investigated by several authors, and some identified a positive relationship (Mathuva, 2009; Dong & Su, 2010; Banos-Caballero et al., 2012; Rahemann et al., 2010), others found a negative relationship (Deloof, 2003; Wang, 2002; Falope & Ajilore, 2009).

The impact of the COVID-19 pandemic on the working capital management practices of companies operating in the financial sector was investigated by Hamshari et al. (2022). They consider selected indicators, namely quick ratio, financial liquidity, short-term liability turnover ratio, short-term receivables turnover ratio, cash conversion cycle and inventory turnover ratio, to be critical metrics of the working capital management strategy. Using the multiple regression model, they identified a negative impact on working capital management.

Zimon and Tarighi (2021) investigate the impact of the COVID-19 pandemic on working capital management policy in Polish SMEs. Their results show that businesses have adopted moderately conservative strategies for managing their working capital. Companies that achieved high liquidity and turnover cycle of money, in an effort to attract new customers and thus increase their sales, began to increase the maturity of receivables. At the same time, they reduced the turnover of liabilities, which enabled them to cooperate with several suppliers on the market.

29.3 Methodology

The aim of this chapter is to investigate the changes in the management of working capital items in industrial production enterprises in Slovakia caused by the impact of the disruption of the business environment due to the spread of the COVID-19 pandemic. We examine changes in working capital management using selected activity indicators, specifically using the asset turnover ratio, the inventory turnover period, the short-term receivables turnover period, the short-term liabilities turnover period, and the cash conversion cycle. When calculating the indicators, we used the following relationships:

$$\text{Asset turnover} = \frac{\text{total sales}}{\text{total assets}}, \qquad (29.1)$$

$$\text{Days inventory held} = \frac{\text{inventory}}{\text{total sales}} \times 360, \qquad (29.2)$$

$$\text{Days accounts receivable outstanding} = \frac{\text{accounts receivable}}{\text{total sales}} \times 360, \qquad (29.3)$$

$$\text{Days accounts payable outstanding} = \frac{\text{accounts payable}}{\text{total sales}} \times 360, \qquad (29.4)$$

and

$$\text{Cash conversion cycle} = \text{Days inventory held} + \text{Days accounts receivable}$$
$$\text{outstanding} - \text{Days accounts payable outstanding.} \tag{29.5}$$

These are activity ratios that allow the company to evaluate the degree of utilization of its assets and working capital in the operational process. We obtained the information necessary for the calculation of the examined indicators of the company's activity from the database of financial statements, which was provided to us for a fee by the company CRIF—Slovak Credit Bureau, LC which operates the CRIBIS.sk Universal Register and calculates average values for individual sectors of the economy on an annual basis. The procedure for calculating the indicators should be adjusted with respect to the depth and accuracy of the analysis. The indicators we use in our contribution correspond to the methodology of calculating the mean values of selected indicators for industries.

We are conducting research in the period from 2017 to 2021. The years 2020 and 2021 are the period during which the COVID-19 pandemic was fully manifested at all levels of economic and social life. The years 2017–2019 constitute the period before the start of the spread of the pandemic and will serve to compare the situation. The sample set consists of a total of 3541 randomly selected companies operating in the industrial production sector in Slovakia. Considering the formulated aim of the paper, we needed to select companies that performed their operational activities in the monitored period. Therefore, we first selected from the available database those enterprises that, during the monitored periods, reported the following items in their financial statements in a value higher than zero: income from economic activity, consumption of materials and energy and consumption of services. Subsequently, we selected for the research companies, for which we had available all the indicators that are the subject of our research between 2018 and 2021. We also cleaned the dataset from extreme values. In terms of size structure, our sample consists of a total of 2417 micro enterprises (68%), 722 small enterprises (20%), 316 medium enterprises (9%), and 86 large enterprises (2%).

We will compare the changes in the value of the selected indicators on an annual basis using indexes, and we will statistically evaluate them using non-parametric tests for two dependent samples, specifically using the Wilcoxon signed-rank test, which is considered a non-parametric equivalent of the paired-sample t-test. We formulate 1-tailed hypotheses: H_0: There is no difference in the value of the selected indicator between the two investigated periods (H_0: $\mu_0 = \mu_1$), H_1: There is a difference in the value of the selected indicator between the two compared periods (H_1: $\mu_0 < \mu_1$ resp. H_1: $\mu_0 > \mu_1$). We verify the hypotheses at the level of significance $\alpha = 0.05$.

We perform the Wilcoxon signed-rank test using SPSS. The output tables of the test show the value of the Z-score of the Wilcoxon signed-rank test, which is based on positive or negative differences in each monitored interannual period. If the Z-score is based on positive differences, it means that most of the subjects recorded a year-on-year decrease in the value of the investigated indicator during the given investigated period. In the opposite case, when the Z-score is based on negative differences, in a given year the number of subjects that recorded a year-on-year increase in the indicator prevailed.

29.4 Empirical Results and Discussion

29.4.1 Asset Turnover Ratio

The asset turnover ratio is a financial metric that measures a company's efficiency in generating revenue from its assets. It is calculated by dividing the company's sales or earnings by its total assets. The ratio indicates how efficiently a company uses its assets to generate sales revenue and is often used to evaluate operational efficiency and business performance. A higher asset turnover ratio generally means better asset utilization and revenue generation. It means that the business can expand without increasing its sources of financing. The indicator is also used for spatial comparison. When calculating it at the company level, it is appropriate to assess the impact of the used asset valuation method and depreciation methods.

Table 29.2 shows the results of the average value of turnover of assets of industrial enterprises in Slovakia, broken down by size into micro, small, medium, and large enterprises. The indicator indicates the number of monetary units corresponding to one monetary unit of the company's assets. If the value of the indicator grows, it signals the ability of the company to better use its assets with the operational process. From the results of the research, we see the best use of assets in micro-enterprises, where the average asset turnover in each of the monitored years is higher than the overall average for all enterprises. We find the lowest ability to use their assets to generate income in the group of small businesses, with the exception of 2018. Comparing the turnover of assets before and during the COVID-19 pandemic, we find a decrease in the use of assets in all size groups, the most significant decrease occurred in large enterprises (-8.64%) and in micro enterprises (-7.51%).

Table 29.2 Mean value of asset turnover ratio

	2017	2018	2019	2020	2021	Average 2017–2019	Average 2020–2021	Difference of Avg.	Change of Avg.
Micro	1.901	1.970	1.974	1.766	1.839	1.948	1.802	−0.146	−7.51%
Small	1.342	1.371	1.358	1.243	1.290	1.357	1.266	−0.091	−6.68%
Middle	1.376	1.364	1.386	1.258	1.322	1.375	1.290	−0.085	−6.19%
Large	1.499	1.444	1.481	1.345	1.349	1.475	1.347	−0.127	−8.64%
Together	1.732	1.781	1.784	1.604	1.669	1.766	1.636	−0.130	−7.35%

Table 29.3 Interannual changes in asset turnover ratio

	18/17	19/18	20/19	21/20	21/17	19/17	21/19
Micro	3.65%	0.20%	−10.57%	4.13%	−3.28%	3.86%	−6.88%
Small	2.11%	−0.93%	−8.49%	3.80%	−3.91%	1.16%	−5.01%
Middle	−0.92%	1.62%	−9.21%	5.10%	−3.93%	0.68%	−4.58%
Large	−3.71%	2.55%	−9.14%	0.28%	−10.03%	−1.25%	−8.89%
Together	2.82%	0.17%	−10.12%	4.06%	−3.67%	2.99%	−6.47%

Table 29.4 Test statistics[a] of asset turnover ratio

	2018/2017	2019/2018	2020/2019	2021/2020
Z	−4.276[b]	−.363[c]	−20.255[c]	−7.608[b]
Asymp. Sig. (1-tailed)	0.000	0.358	0.000	0.000

[a]Wilcoxon signed-rank test
[b]Based on negative ranks
[c]Based on positive ranks

By comparing the year-on-year percentage changes in asset turnover (see Table 29.3), we found the most significant decline in asset turnover in 2020. However, companies record a decline in asset turnover over a longer period of time. However, with the onset of the pandemic, this decrease is more pronounced. This is also documented by the results of the Wilcoxon signed-rank test, which confirmed the statistical significance of the decline in asset turnover in 2020 (the Z-score is based on positive differences, which means a higher number of subjects with a year-on-year decline in asset turnover) and subsequently a statistically significant growth in 2021 (Sig. = 0.000, see Table 29.4), in which the value of the Z-score is based on negative differences, which indicates that in the monitored interannual period, more entities recorded an increase in the value of the asset turnover indicator.

29.4.2 Inventory Turnover Days

The inventory turnover indicator indicates the number of days during which the inventory is tied up until the time of its consumption (in the case of stocks of raw materials and materials) or until the time of their sale (in the case of stocks of self-produced products) in the business. A lower number of days indicates better inventory management and faster inventory turnover. A higher number of days signals increased demands on financing resources necessary for tying up cash in the company's inventory. In the case of inventories of products and goods, this indicator is also an indicator of liquidity, as it indicates the number of days during which inventories are converted into cash or receivables. It is generally defined as the ratio of average inventory level to daily sales. It can also be calculated for individual types of stock.

The metric is inversely proportional to the company's inventory turnover, which measures the intensity of the company's inventory utilization. Inventory turnover ratio indicates how many times an item of inventory is sold and restocked during each year. It is calculated as the ratio of inventory to sales. In order to obtain a more realistic picture of the situation in the company, it is more appropriate to use the average inventory in the denominator of the indicator and the cost of goods sold in the numerator. When evaluating the use of the company's inventory, it is appropriate to compare the results with industry values. If the rated company has a higher inventory turnover compared to the industry, it signals that the company does not have excess illiquid assets that would require excess financing, and the inventory turnover period is short. In the opposite case, when inventory turnover is low, the company cannot convert inventory into cash quickly enough, which also lengthens inventory turnover time. A part of such low liquid stocks can also be non-saleable stocks, which tie up cash that the company cannot release from these stocks with the required profitability. This is reflected in low stock turnover, high current liquidity and a subsequent decrease in the company's solvency and profitability.

In Table 29.5, we present the average values of inventory turnover time expressed in the number of days in industrial production enterprises. With the onset of the COVID-19 pandemic, we see an increase in inventory turnover time in every size group of industrial production companies. We found the highest increase between the average stock turnover time before the pandemic (average 2017–2019) and the pandemic period (average 2020–2021) in the group of micro enterprises (an average increase of 14.38 days, i.e., 23.97%). During the pandemic, many businesses had to stop their business activities or to limit, and as a result of the global reduction in economic activity, they increased the volume of their inventories, reduced their sales, which was subsequently reflected in a decrease in the turnover of inventories and an increase in the time that money is tied up in inventories.

The negative impact of the government's measures to prevent the spread of the pandemic was also manifested at the company level in the stock turnover indicator, which, based on the comparison between the pre-pandemic and pandemic periods, increased by 20%, i.e., on average by 12.85 days. This is confirmed by the results of the comparison of interannual changes of the indicator using indexes (see Table 29.6), as well as the results of the Wilcoxon signed-rank test (see Table 29.7).

29.4.3 Days Accounts Receivable Outstanding

Trade receivables represent a large part of the assets of businesses around the world. The receivables turnover period expresses how long the company's assets are in the form of receivables on average per year, or the average number of days the company needs to receive payment from its customers after making a sale. It is calculated by dividing average receivables by average daily sales and multiplying the result by the number of days in a given period. This metric provides an overview of the efficiency of the company's credit and collection processes.

Table 29.5 Mean value of inventory turnover time in days

	2017	2018	2019	2020	2021	Average 2017–2019	Average 2020–2021	Difference of Avg.	Change of Avg.
Micro	60.045	59.012	60.987	71.375	77.423	60.015	74.399	14.384	23.97%
Small	75.142	79.381	86.630	87.770	98.025	80.384	92.897	12.513	15.57%
Middle	61.662	69.253	63.987	62.577	74.448	64.968	68.513	3.545	5.46%
Large	42.457	48.183	47.192	49.818	54.919	45.944	52.368	6.424	13.98%
Together	62.804	63.816	66.148	73.409	80.811	64.256	77.110	12.854	20.00%

Table 29.6 Interannual change in inventory turnover time in days

	18/17	19/18	20/19	21/20	21/17	19/17	21/19
Micro	−1.72%	3.35%	17.03%	8.47%	28.94%	1.57%	26.95%
Small	5.64%	9.13%	1.32%	11.68%	30.45%	15.29%	13.15%
Middle	12.31%	−7.60%	−2.20%	18.97%	20.74%	3.77%	16.35%
Large	13.49%	−2.06%	5.56%	10.24%	29.35%	11.15%	16.37%
Together	1.61%	3.65%	10.98%	10.08%	28.67%	5.32%	22.17%

Table 29.7 Test statistics[a] of inventory turnover time

	2018/2017	2019/2018	2020/2019	2021/2020
Z	−1.342[b]	−.824[b]	−9.518[b]	−8.701[b]
Asymp. Sig. (1-tailed)	0.090	0.205	0.000	0.000

[a]Wilcoxon signed-rank test
[b]Based on negative ranks

The indicator can be used as a guideline for managing receivables and checking compliance with the company's business policy. However, it is necessary to use the indicative value of the indicator with caution. A decrease in receivables turnover time does not necessarily mean that the company is paying receivables faster. In conditions of oscillating sales, this indicator changes even without changing the payment behavior of customers. This deficiency can be eliminated by switching to shorter intervals for monitoring the development of sales and receivables.

As can be seen in Tables 29.8 and 29.9, comparing the maturity period of receivables between 2019 and 2020, there was an increase in all size groups. The increase in the period of tying up funds in receivables is also evident from the average maturity period for the years 2017–2019 compared to the average for the years 2020 and 2021. In this case, the highest increase occurred in the group of micro enterprises (12.84%).

The results of the Wilcoxon signed-rank test also confirm statistically significant changes in the average time of debt collection in all monitored periods (see Table 29.10). While in the years 2017–2019, companies managed to reduce the average time of collection of their receivables and thereby speed up their turnover, in 2020 and 2021, in most companies, the management allowed the extension of the maturity period of the collection of receivables. It was of course caused by the influence of external factors, among which the extraordinary situation in connection with the COVID-19 pandemic prevailed.

29.4.4 Days Accounts Payable Outstanding

Account payables usually represent a large portion of firms' liabilities. Accounts payable turnover ratio is a financial metric that allows you to find out the average

Table 29.8 Mean value of days accounts receivable outstanding

	2017	2018	2019	2020	2021	Average 2017–2019	Average 2020–2021	Difference of Avg.	Change of Avg. (%)
Micro	73.619	72.767	71.827	76.445	87.716	72.738	82.081	9.343	12.84%
Small	88.331	85.340	81.687	85.764	90.741	85.119	88.252	3.133	3.68%
Middle	88.973	102.786	90.155	96.105	98.843	93.971	97.474	3.503	3.73%
Large	79.482	79.937	75.143	82.472	88.424	78.187	85.448	7.261	9.29%
Together	78.079	78.184	75.554	80.246	89.343	77.272	84.794	7.522	9.73%

Table 29.9 Interannual change in days accounts receivable outstanding

	18/17	19/18	20/19	21/20	21/17	19/17	21/19
Micro	−1.16%	−1.29%	6.43%	14.74%	19.15%	−2.43%	22.12%
Small	−3.39%	−4.28%	4.99%	5.80%	2.73%	−7.52%	11.08%
Middle	15.52%	−12.29%	6.60%	2.85%	11.09%	1.33%	9.64%
Large	0.57%	−6.00%	9.75%	7.22%	11.25%	−5.46%	17.67%
Together	0.13%	−3.36%	6.21%	11.34%	14.43%	−3.23%	18.25%

Table 29.10 Test statistics[a] of days accounts receivable outstanding

	2018/2017	2019/2018	2020/2019	2021/2020
Z	−5.576[b]	−5.437[b]	−5.866[c]	−1.802[c]
Asymp. Sig. (1-tailed)	0.000	0.000	0.000	0.036

[a]Wilcoxon signed-rank test
[b]Based on positive ranks
[c]Based on negative ranks

number of days during which the company draws trade credit provided by its suppliers. It also measures the average number of days that elapse until the company pays its suppliers or vendors for the goods or services received. The metric reflects the efficiency of the company's payment procedures and its ability to manage working capital. A higher number of accounts payable days indicate that the company is taking longer to pay its creditors, which may mean better cash flow management or negotiating more favourable payment terms. Extending the maturity period of liabilities also means for the company that it has the funds of its business partners at its disposal for a longer time, which it can use to finance its own needs.

The average maturity period of liabilities of industrial enterprises (see Table 29.11) exceeds the maturity period of receivables by approximately two times. Between 2019 and 2020, the maturity period of liabilities also increased. Suppliers therefore had to wait longer for their money. From the results of the analysis of the growth rate (see Table 29.12), we see the highest year-on-year increase in the maturity of the liabilities of industrial enterprises in 2020 and 2021. We note the biggest changes again in the group of micro enterprises, which before the pandemic, between 2017 and 2019, had an average maturity of liabilities of 169 days, during the pandemic, the maturity period of liabilities increased to 206.8 days, which is an increase of 37.7 days (22.32%) on average.

We detect statistically significant changes using the Wilcoxon signed-rank test (see Table 29.13) between 2018 and 2020, with the fact that there was a change in development in 2020. While in 2018 and 2019, companies statistically significantly reduced the maturity period of liabilities, in 2020 it increased significantly.

By comparing the maturity period of liabilities and the maturity period of receivables, we can find out whether companies are more likely to provide or draw trade loans. Based on the results of our analysis, we can confirm that companies operating in the industrial production sector in the Slovak Republic are more

Table 29.11 Mean value of days accounts payable outstanding

	2017	2018	2019	2020	2021	Average 2017–2019	Average 2020–2021	Difference of Avg.	Change of Avg. (%)
Micro	168.940	170.014	168.202	194.417	219.141	169.052	206.779	37.727	22.32%
Small	171.962	175.002	171.257	173.722	192.492	172.741	183.107	10.367	6.00%
Middle	131.299	167.568	143.902	147.364	175.436	147.590	161.400	13.810	9.36%
Large	118.457	139.846	126.250	127.968	135.780	128.184	131.874	3.690	2.88%
Together	165.016	170.080	165.637	184.384	207.782	166.911	196.083	29.172	17.48%

Table 29.12 Interannual change in days accounts payable outstanding

	18/17	19/18	20/19	21/20	21/17	19/17	21/19
Micro	0.64%	−1.07%	15.59%	12.72%	29.71%	−0.44%	30.28%
Small	1.77%	−2.14%	1.44%	10.80%	11.94%	−0.41%	12.40%
Middle	27.62%	−14.12%	2.41%	19.05%	33.62%	9.60%	21.91%
Large	18.06%	−9.72%	1.36%	6.10%	14.62%	6.58%	7.55%
Together	3.07%	−2.61%	11.32%	12.69%	25.92%	0.38%	25.44%

Table 29.13 Test statistics[a] of days accounts payable outstanding

	2018/2017	2019/2018	2020/2019	2021/2020
Z	−4.868[b]	−4.218[b]	−8.459[c]	−.652[c]
Asymp. Sig. (1-tailed)	0.000	0.000	0.000	0.257

[a] Wilcoxon signed-rank test
[b] Based on positive ranks
[c] Based on negative ranks

inclined to draw trade loans. The difference in the average maturity of receivables and payables is presented in Table 29.14.

Micro-enterprises are among those that tend to draw business credit to the highest extent. We found the lowest difference between the maturity periods in the group of large companies, which is also understandable considering their capital equipment. If the difference between the turnover period of liabilities and receivables is very high, it may also signal initial insolvency of the company. In the case of the opposite relationship, which we do not identify in the Slovak industrial enterprises, there would be a threat of secondary insolvency, which arises as a result of the inability of the enterprise to collect its receivables, which subsequently causes its inability to pay its own obligations.

29.4.5 Cash Conversion Cycle

The cash conversion cycle is a financial indicator that quantifies the time it takes for a company to convert its investments in raw materials and inventory into cash flows from sales. It is a complex indicator that takes into account the entire operating cycle of the company, including the time needed to sell inventory, collect receivables, and pay liabilities. The cash conversion cycle is calculated by subtracting the average payables maturity period from the sum of the average inventory holding period and the average receivables collection period. It also shows the number of days the business needs to finance its operating activities from sources other than accounts payable to its suppliers.

The cash conversion cycle reflects the efficiency of a company's working capital management and provides insight into its ability to generate cash flow from operating activities. A shorter cash conversion cycle indicates more efficient use

Table 29.14 The difference between the turnover period of liabilities and turnover period of receivables

	2017	2018	2019	2020	2021	Average 2017–2019	Average 2020–2021	Difference of Avg.	Change of Avg. (%)
Micro	95.321	97.247	96.374	117.972	131.425	96.314	124.698	28.384	29.47%
Small	83.631	89.662	89.570	87.959	101.751	87.621	94.855	7.234	8.26%
Middle	42.326	64.782	53.747	51.258	76.593	53.618	63.926	10.307	19.22%
Large	38.976	59.909	51.107	45.496	47.356	49.997	46.426	−3.571	−7.14%
Together	86.937	91.896	90.083	104.138	118.440	89.639	111.289	21.650	24.15%

of working capital, faster inventory turnover, faster collections from customers, and longer payment terms with suppliers. Conversely, a longer cash conversion cycle indicates potential liquidity problems and less effective working capital management.

The results of the analysis of the cash conversion cycle of industrial production enterprises expressed in the number of days are shown in Table 29.15. Positive values of the indicator indicate the number of days of the operating cycle that enterprises need to finance from long-term liabilities or equity. The negative values of the indicator point to a certain financial reserve, which the companies managed to obtain by appropriate setting of payment conditions and measures to rationalize the length of the production cycle. From the results, we see that mainly micro and small businesses are in a situation where the maturity period of their short-term liabilities exceeds the period of commitment of funds in the operating process. By comparing the situation before the pandemic and during its duration, we find that companies extended the maturity of their short-term receivables by an average of 8.8 days compared to the length of the operating cycle. Micro enterprises (14 days) and medium enterprises (6.7 days) contributed the most to this. With the onset of the pandemic, small- and medium-sized enterprises were more likely to find themselves in a situation where the need to obtain additional funding sources needed to supplement the operating cycle increased.

We present the analysis of the interannual growth rates of the cash conversion cycle indicator in Table 29.16.

We present the results of the Wilcoxon signed-rank test in Table 29.17. Statistically significant year-on-year changes in the indicator are identified in 2018, 2019, and 2021. In all these years, there was a significant increase in the value of the indicator, which for the company means an increase in the need for financing operating activities from additional resources.

29.5   Conclusion

The aim of this chapter was to investigate the changes in the management of working capital items in industrial production enterprises in Slovakia caused by the impact of the disruption of the business environment due to the spread of the COVID-19 pandemic.

The results of the analysis point to the fact that companies also used components of working capital to ensure their survival and relative stabilization of their financial situation. A company's working capital consists of its inventory, receivables, and cash. Net working capital is created by the difference between the company's short-term assets and its short-term liabilities. In order to analyse the effectiveness of the use of working capital, we used selected indicators of the company's activity in our contribution, namely the asset turnover ratio, inventory turnover time, short-term receivables and short-term liabilities, and the cash conversion cycle.

Table 29.15 Mean value of cash conversion cycle in days

	2017	2018	2019	2020	2021	Average 2017–2019	Average 2020–2021	Difference of Avg.	Change of Avg. (%)
Micro	−35.276	−38.234	−35.388	−46.597	−54.002	−36.299	−50.299	−14.000	38.57%
Small	−8.489	−10.281	−2.941	−0.188	−3.727	−7.237	−1.958	5.279	−72.95%
Middle	19.337	4.471	10.240	11.319	−2.144	11.349	4.587	−6.762	−59.58%
Large	3.482	−11.726	−3.915	4.321	7.563	−4.053	5.942	9.995	−246.61%
Together	−24.133	−28.080	−23.936	−30.729	−37.628	−25.383	−34.179	−8.796	34.65%

29 How Has the COVID-19 Pandemic Affected the Utilization...

Table 29.16 Interannual change in cash conversion cycle

	18/17	19/18	20/19	21/20	21/17	19/17	21/19
Micro	8.39%	−7.45%	31.67%	15.89%	53.08%	0.32%	52.60%
Small	21.12%	−71.40%	−93.59%	1878.42%	−56.10%	−65.36%	26.73%
Middle	−76.88%	129.02%	10.53%	−118.95%	−111.09%	−47.04%	−120.94%
Large	−436.80%	−66.61%	−210.38%	75.02%	117.23%	−212.44%	−293.19%
Together	16.36%	−14.76%	28.38%	22.45%	55.92%	−0.82%	57.21%

Table 29.17 Test statistics[a] of cash conversion cycle

	2018/2017	2019/2018	2020/2019	2021/2020
Z	−3.530[b]	−2.554[b]	−.436[b]	−5.271[b]
Asymp. Sig. (1-tailed)	0.000	0.005	0.331	0.000

[a]Wilcoxon signed-rank test
[b]Based on negative ranks

We found out that the industrial production enterprises, which as a result of the adopted government measures had to limit their operational activities, also changed the way of managing their working capital. With the onset of the pandemic in those companies, there was a statistically significant increase in the inventory turnover time, an increase in the collection time of receivables and the maturity of liabilities. In this case, it was not possible to find out from the data we had available whether it was a modification of the contractual terms of the companies, or a breach of the contractual terms and a delay in payment and direct debits. However, by comparing the maturity period of liabilities and the period of collection of receivables, we found that the maturity of liabilities increased at a higher rate than the period of collection of receivables, as a result of which companies created a certain package of hidden reserves that could be used to financially cover necessary needs.

The cash conversion cycle indicator had a negative average value in the individual monitored years. This indicates the creation and existence of certain hidden reserves of operating cycle financing since enterprises have sources of financing in the form of short-term liabilities available for a longer period than the average duration of the operating cycle.

Acknowledgments This paper has been supported by the Scientific Grant Agency of Slovak Republic under project VEGA No. 1/0579/21, "Research on Determinants and Paradigms of Financial Management in the context of the COVID-19 Pandemic." The authors would like to express their gratitude to the Scientific Grant Agency of The Ministry of Education, Science, Research and Sport of the Slovak Republic for financial support of this research and publication.

References

Banos-Caballero, S., García-Teruel, P. J., & Martinez-Solano, P. (2012). How does working capital management affect the profitability of Spanish SMEs. *Small Business Economics, 39*(2), 517–529.

CRIBIS.sk Univerzálny register. CRIF – Slovak Credit Bureau, s.r.o., Available at: https://www3.cribis.sk/

Deloof, M. (2003). Does working capital management affect profitability of Belgian firms? *Journal of Business Finance and Accounting, 30*(3/4), 573–588.

Dong, H. P., & Su, J. T. (2010). The relationship between working capital management and profitability: A Vietnam case. *International Research Journal of Finance and Economics, 49*, 62–71.

Eurostat. (2020). *Industrial production down by 17.1% in euro area and 17.3% in EU.* News Release Euro Indicators. 92/2020. Available on: https://ec.europa.eu/eurostat/documents/2995521/10294900/4-12062020-AP-EN.pdf/93c51a4c-e401-a66d-3ab3-6ecd51a1651f

Falope, O. I., & Ajilore, O. T. (2009). Working capital management and corporate profitability: Evidence from panel data analysis of selected quoted companies in Nigeria. *Research Journal of Business Management, 3*(3), 73–84.

Hamshari, Y. M., et al. (2022). The impact of the corona epidemic on working capital management for Jordanian companies listed on the Amman stock exchange. *Cogent Economics & Finance, 10*, 2157541. https://doi.org/10.1080/23322039.2022.2157541

Kipronoh, P., & Mweta, T. (2018). Overview of working capital management: Effective measures in managing working capital components to entrepreneurs. *European Journal of Business and Management, 10*, 7.

Mansoori, E., & Muhammad, J. (2012). The effect of working capital management on firm's profitability: Evidence from Singapore. *Interdisciplinary Journal of Contemporary Research in Business, 4*, 5.

Mathuva, D. (2009). The influence of working capital management components on corporate profitability: A survey on Kenyan listed firms. *Research Journal of Business Management, 4*(1), 1–11.

Ministerstvo hosporástva SR. (2018). *Priemyselná výroba a jej postavenie v hospodárstve SR.* Industrial production and its position in the Slovak economy. Available at: https://www.economy.gov.sk/uploads/files/ezNh8gXF.pdf

Nimalathasan, B. (2010). Working capital management and its impact on profitability: A study listed manufacturing companies in Sri Lanka. *Journal of Management, 8*(1), 76–83.

Padachi, K. (2006). Trends in working capital management and its impact on firms' performance: An analysis of Mauritian small manufacturing firms. *International Review of Business Research Papers, 2*(2), 45–58.

Prasad, P., Sivasankaran, N., Paul, S., & Kannadhasan, M. (2019). Measuring impact of working capital efficiency on financial performance of a firm: An alternative approach. *Journal of Indian Business Research, 11*(1), 75–94. https://doi.org/10.1108/JIBR-02-2018-0056

Rahemann, A. A., Qayyum, T., & Bodla, M. A. (2010). Working capital management and corporate performance of manufacturing sector in Pakistan. *International Research Journal of Finance and Economics, 47*(1), 156–169.

Samiloglu, F., & Demirgunes, K. (2008). The effect of working capital management on firm profitability: Evidence from Turkey. *The International Journal of Applied Economics and Finance, 2*(1), 44–50. https://doi.org/10.3923/ijaef.2008.44.50

Shin, H. H., & Soenen, L. (1998). Efficiency of working capital management and corporate profitability. *Financial Practice and Education, 8*(2), 37–45.

Wang, Y. J. (2002). Liquidity management, operating performance, and corporate value: Evidence from Japan and Taiwan. *Journal of Multinational Financial Management, 12*(2), 159–169.

Zariyawati, M. A., Annuar, M. N., Taufiq, H., & Abdul Rahim, A. S. (2009). Working capital management and corporate performance: Case of Malaysia. *Journal of Modern Accounting and Auditing, 5*(11), 47–54.

Zimon, G., & Tarighi, H. (2021). Effects of the COVID-19 global crisis on the working capital management policy: Evidence from Poland. *Journal of Risk and Financial Management, 14*, 169. https://doi.org/10.3390/jrfm1404016

Chapter 30
Trainer's Characterization of Entrepreneurs to Reduce Unemployment Gap, Lambayeque

Vidal Taboada Silvia Lourdes, Guillermo Segundo Miñan Olivos,
Jairo Jaime Turriate Chávez, Luis Alberto Vásquez Caballero,
Mercedes Alejandrina Collazos Alarcón,
and Mónica del Pilar Pintado Damián

Abstract This research is carried out due to an economic problem, unemployment, which is common in countries of the region and does so much damage to economies and their inhabitants; this is the reason it seeks to present how entrepreneurship is a strategy that is generating very good results in the countries that are being promoted. However, it is important to recognize that the entrepreneurs trainer has an important role for the closure of this gap. It is a basic research, quantitative approach, non-experimental design, transactional-descriptive level; a validated instrument was applied to a sample population of 48 professors from Lambayeque, with a reliability level of 0.92 of Cronbach's Alpha. The achieved results are very satisfactory because they cover the necessary competencies such as knowledge, skills, role, motives, and values for this entrepreneur's training.

Keywords Professor characterization · Entrepreneurship · Unemployment

30.1 Introduction

As per the United Nations (United Nations, 2021), there is 24% youth unemployment in just the first quarter; hence, it is considered that they are a generation without possibilities of education or work, which will affect their economy and

---

V. T. S. Lourdes
Universidad Cesar Vallejo, Chiclayo, Peru
e-mail: vtaboadas@ucvvirtual.edu.pe

G. S. M. Olivos (✉) · J. J. T. Chávez · L. A. V. Caballero · M. A. C. Alarcón ·
M. del Pilar Pintado Damián
Universidad Tecnológica del Perú, Chimbote, Peru
e-mail: c20342@utp.edu.pe; E20207@utp.edu.pe; C18580@utp.edu.pe; C24133@utp.edu.pe; mpintado@utp.edu.pe

© The Author(s), under exclusive license to Springer Nature Switzerland AG 2024
N. Tsounis, A. Vlachvei (eds.), *Applied Economic Research and Trends*, Springer
Proceedings in Business and Economics,
https://doi.org/10.1007/978-3-031-49105-4_30

social life. Therefore, adequate measures are required to reduce the effect that the pandemic has had. Likewise, ECLAC (Economic Commission for Latin America and the Caribbean, 2022) estimates that unemployment will be 11.5% for women and 8% for men, in both cases it has increased in relation to 2019, which was 9.5% and 6.8%, respectively. On the other hand, according to the World Bank (2020), unemployment increased from May to July in Peru. Also, those who kept their jobs had the characteristics of belonging to large companies with a good educational level, and a higher percentage of men kept their jobs compared to women.

Youth unemployment is a global problem, so the creation of small business units and medium-sized enterprises in a sustainable way is the solution to this situation. The research is based in Morocco, which is a country in the Arab world with the highest unemployment, and it is recommended to take advantage of the attractions that Morocco has, as well as the agreements with the United States and Europe, so you should invest in this country. According to Reyes (2022), informality in Mexico is more than 50% of economic activity and stable jobs have precarious conditions. The Latinobarometro survey in 2018 shows the fear that people have of being fired and this has been constant since the 1990s and who are most vulnerable to layoffs are young people of low economic situations with family burdens. Currently, in Colombia, the time for a young person to leave unemployment is doubled and there is a lower possibility of finding employment for a woman. The restrictions of the quarantine were shown in the mobility of workers generating more unemployment. It is concluded that this will last for 18 months from the moment of confinement (Mora, 2021).

Jinchuña et al. explain that the pandemic in Peru had significantly hit people in their economy. The result of this research shows that families with high incomes were affected by 30%; however, families with low incomes were affected by 100% and the restriction measures affected jobs by 49% and 92% of the income received by families and have the perception that there will be 50% unemployment. In Lambayeque – Peru, there are 200,000 unemployed people, which represents 80% of microenterprises. There is a competitiveness plan, with the purpose of formalizing companies, encouraging youth employment, and helping the sectors most exposed to unemployment. It also seeks to train people between 30 and 50 years old who are unemployed and who have completed secondary school. In Spain, the constant changes and the general perspective point out that entrepreneurship is the new way to achieve optimal models in the media and that it should start from the university, so it is necessary to assess the consequences that entrepreneurship brings. Qualitative research was carried out through interviews. There are good results when training is provided in entrepreneurship in business areas, but it is also suggested that the training has a practical aspect, which adapts to reality and has a relationship with the business world and also university (Aceituno-Aceituno et al., 2018).

In Colombia, entrepreneurship is the way to achieve progress and economic advancement locally, departmentally, and at the national level. We sought to identify the most outstanding features of the professor who trains university entrepreneurs. Therefore, the quantitative approach, non-experimental descriptive research of transitional design was used. It is recommended that these professors work in networks with the presence of the state, business, professionals, and the community, to enrich the enterprises (Mosquera-Carrascal et al., 2020).

It is necessary to train entrepreneurs because they will contribute to employment and improve the living situation at the economic, social, business, and educational levels. That is why it is important to educate and train them to achieve innovative and creative traits as an entrepreneur so that they can be productive and competitive and can create companies and innovate according to the needs of the existing ones (Murgueitio et al., 2019). The active participation of universities in the process of training entrepreneurs in the social, economic, and business context is transcendent. In this research, we want to characterize the traits of vocation and training to be able to set up companies with university students in Ecuador. We work in a field study with a multivariate statistical analysis to capture strategies from the university for the training of entrepreneurial students, who can create companies. The results explain that the strategy of the Ecuadorian university is the execution of business plans, but they must be constantly improved (Guachimbosa et al., 2019).

Research in Mexico seeks to determine the relationship between business training and the performance that companies may have. Information was obtained through a questionnaire applied to companies and exploratory factor analysis and linear regressions. It was demonstrated that such a relationship exists and it is recommended to work with continuous strategies in intellectual capital to take advantage of opportunities and this will provide better results (Ibarra-Cisneros & Hernández-Perlines, 2019). In the same way, it seeks to show that there is a relationship between entrepreneurship training in master's degrees with the desire to undertake. The research is quantitative and descriptive. Additionally, the results showed the importance of training in business plans to start undertakings. The practice together with the theory helped in the desire to undertake and those who did not is because they have a fixed income and a stable job (Sepúlveda-Calderón & Zapata-Cuervo, 2019).

Midolo Ramos et al. (2021) seek to identify the capacity to undertake to compare it with the GEM of Peru. It uses a descriptive, observational, and cross-sectional approach, applying a survey questionnaire. It was determined that 53% of university students have the desire and attitude to undertake and this characteristic is in both sexes of the student population in a university in Arequipa-Peru. Villalobos Rodríguez et al. (2021) introduce how important it is to promote entrepreneurship because it is a fundamental basis through which it is possible to provide employment, innovation, progress, and economic prosperity in the economies of a region; especially among young people. That is why this research seeks options to generate employment and this contributes to better conditions. A documentary review was conducted. It is concluded that entrepreneurship counteracts unemployment and ensures that young people have an income adequate for the situation they live. Additionally, Rodriguez Piña et al. (2019) propose to create a business incubator with the aim to develop creativity and innovation, using Information and Communication Technologies (ICTs) and this will allow sustainability in entrepreneurship.

Blanchard (2017) explains that the level of unemployment occurs when an individual does not have a job or is looking for one, and Valderrama (2021) explains Okun's Law, which establishes the relationship between unemployment and production, and to this law, in the econometric approach, the variable underemployment is added so that jobs that do not have the right conditions are identified and better explain Peruvian reality. Because of this, the growth of the economy is recommended.

According to Hilarión (2014), there are factors of success in entrepreneurship, which consist of identifying what are the personal characteristics that the entrepreneur must have: independence, adventure, risk, and constantly having the knowledge and surrounding yourself with the experiences that other entrepreneurs have; have goods and services that are demanded by many customers; have a business plan to guide you in the market that is and sustain over time; and count on enough resources for the process of entering the market and remaining in it.

The types of entrepreneurship began to develop in the 1970s and administrative entrepreneurs who grow with the companies where they work providing innovation and self-employed entrepreneurs who create and manage their own companies are presented. Also in 1974, four types of entrepreneurs were presented, namely, the manager or the innovator, who seeks changes; the growth-oriented entrepreneur, to advance the company; the efficiency-oriented entrepreneur, who achieves what is proposed; and the artisan entrepreneur, who seeks to enter the market. However, in 1989 four types of entrepreneurs were presented in Spain and are characterized by the desires they want to achieve, represented in the artisan; the risk-oriented entrepreneur; the family-oriented entrepreneur; and the manager.

The concept of entrepreneurship was explained for the first time in Schumpeter's theory and it was argued that to achieve economic advancement or progress, the role of the entrepreneur is needed because it contributes to this progress. The entrepreneur must create and make innovations, and based on that the following situations occur: enter a new product or service; enter a new form of production; enter a new market; and identify a new source of inputs or semi-finished goods (Carter & Jones-Evans, 2012).

Through the iceberg model proposed by Spencer and Spencer, it is explained that the knowledge that the trainer has to carry out the activities with the entrepreneurs is necessary. In addition, the skills developed to achieve what was planned with them and these competencies are located in the visible part of the iceberg, while in the non-visible part is the social role that is required for this task, such as the image you have about yourself, the traits of different situations, and motives and values you have to do something. It is important to see that the visible part of the iceberg can be worked on in professor training, but it is the non-visible part that significantly influences the visible part (Spencer and Spencer 1993, as cited by Rojas et al., 2019).

According to Romaní et al. (2021), both the GEM and GUESSS provide us with information about entrepreneurship in the world and especially in Latin America. The GEM gives us information on entrepreneurship activity, making comparisons internationally and its relationship with the growth that can be achieved, in the same way, entrepreneurs know how the entrepreneurial activity of their area is and will allow a clear perspective of advantages and disadvantages that can be given. Likewise, they provide governments with information for good decision-making in public policies that contribute to entrepreneurship. GUESSS allows participants to gain clear insights into entrepreneurship in general and learn how entrepreneurship is at the university level. This involves universities, politicians, academics, and students from their context. Both GEM and GUESSS have the challenge of continuing to expand their reach and achieve a greater presence in the countries of the region. However, the GEM must be maintained in the participating countries and ensure that those who do not participate are incorporated. For this reason, the participation of government, multilateral organizations, and country associations is sought.

30.2 Material and Method

For the development of this research, a quantitative approach was used because a statistical analysis was performed; it is deductive-sequential and has precision. Its scope is descriptive because a phenomenon and its components are studied (Hernández-Sampieri & Mendoza, 2018). The validated instrument of Instrument to Identify Personal and Didactic Characteristics Used by Professors in the Training of Entrepreneurs was used, which was composed of 6 dimensions and 28 items (Rojas et al., 2019). The population and the sample coincide, and there are 48 professors who work with entrepreneurs in Lambayeque, who have experience. The general objective of this research was to characterize the professor trainer of entrepreneurs to reduce the unemployment gap in Lambayeque, the specific ones to identify the characterization of the professor trainer of entrepreneurs, analyze unemployment in recent years, and finally analyze the importance of entrepreneurship to reduce the unemployment gap. The technique used is the survey questionnaire; the information was processed in Excel and organized into tables and figures. The discussion was carried out taking into account the background and theoretical framework.

30.3 Results and Discussion

The results of the survey applied to professors' trainers of entrepreneurs are presented, as well as their analysis with which we can discuss the proposal of this research.

A sample of 48 professors was analyzed, and it can be identified that only 4% of the respondents are in the age range of 31–35 years; however, 50% represented an age range of 46 years and older. And it can be identified that professor trainers are mostly male, represented by 67%, compared to females (Table 30.1).

Table 30.2 shows that there is a good assessment of knowledge with 92% in TA and 8% EA, as well as for reasons with 85% of BP and 14% EA, the same happens

Table 30.1 Distribution of the population sample according to social characteristics

Indicator	Description	Frecuence	Frecuence%
Age	De 31 a 35	2	4%
	De 36 a 40	14	29%
	De 41 a 45	8	17%
	De 46 a más	24	50%
	Total	48	100%
Sex	Masculino	32	67%
	Femenino	16	33%
	Total	48	100%

Table 30.2 Summary of dimension results

Assessment	TA F%	EA F%	NEND F%	ED F%	TD F%
Knowledge	92%	8%	0%	0%	0%
Skills	76%	22%	2%	0%	0%
Social net	83%	17%	0%	0%	0%
Character traits	82%	16%	2%	0%	0%
Values	60%	33%	5%	2%	0%
Reasons	85%	14%	1%	0%	0%

with social networks and character traits with 83% and 82%, respectively. But in terms of skills, 76% are visualized in TA and 22% in EA, and this is because it is the dimension that has the most indicators and the perspectives of professors are diversified in values if 60% is registered in TA and 33% in EA with an NEND of 5% and ED of 2%. If the indicators of tolerance, respect, and responsibilities are considered, then measures must be taken to improve this situation so that the results are optimal.

Table 30.3 shows that the ratings of the indicators are high percentages and are framed in a TA and EN, and in some cases, there is a minimum valuation in NEND. It is observed that in ED and TD it has no valuation whatsoever. But it seeks to achieve the optimum of the valuations and must work in that perspective. It can be analyzed that the professor trainer has the knowledge and wants to know more, however, skills need to be developed for the benefit of entrepreneurs.

In Fig. 30.1, the valuation of the variable studied higher represents 98% in good and only 2% in "Regular," and 0% in "Very Bad," and "Bad," but the ideal would be to have a percentage in "Very Good," so that there is a gap that must be improved and must be articulated according to the needs of entrepreneurs. Because of this, the characterization of professor trainers for the training of entrepreneurs is important.

It is important to recognize the professor's traits that form entrepreneurs: knowledge is also necessary, skills that are part of the iceberg that is visualized, but it is also necessary to the social role of the professor, the image the professor projects, the traits that identify him, the reasons and values he has, which must be taken into consideration in order to carry out strategies (Rojas et al., 2019) that contribute to employment and improve living conditions (Mosquera-Carrascal et al., 2020; Guachimbosa et al., 2019).

Table 30.3 Summary of indicator results

item	TA F%	EA F%	NEND F%	ED F%	TD F%
I recognize and understand who an entrepreneur is and what he does	88%	12%	0%	0%	0%
I enable the participation of all students in all activities and tasks, establishing the basis for the development of the project to be based on cooperation strategies.	85%	15%	0%	0%	0%
I promote in the student the search for various alternatives for the solution of a given problem	88%	12%	0%	0%	0%
I identify the student's expectations, both from the academic perspective and from the perspective of entrepreneurship.	60%	38%	2%	0%	0%
My students explain how what they learn at the University relates to the real world	81%	17%	2%	0%	0%
I have the ability to put myself in the place of the students and understand their motives	83%	17%	0%	0%	0%
I investigate, I look for information, and I have permanent concern to know more.	94%	6%	0%	0%	0%
I propose and find new and effective ways to facilitate student learning	90%	10%	0%	0%	0%

Fig. 30.1 Description of the variable characterization of professor entrepreneurs' trainer

Unemployment in recent years has increased in the countries of the region, as indicated by the United Nations (2021) and ECLAC (2022). In Morocco, Mexico, and Colombia, the same reality is observed (Reyes, 2022; Mora, 2021 argue it, respectively). In Peru, unemployment has grown and those who have retained employment are those who work in large companies and have a good educational level (World Bank, 2020). In Lambayeque, there is high unemployment and corresponds to microenterprises, there is a lot of informality as indicated by Industry.

Entrepreneurship is important because it will allow economic progress to be achieved as explained by Mosquera-Carrascal et al. (2020), Villalobos Rodríguez et al. (2021), and Murgueitio et al. (2019). The participation of the universities in entrepreneurs' training is therefore important because theory together with practice helps to undertake as stated by Sepúlveda-Calderón and Zapata-Cuervo (2019). In a Peruvian university, there is 53% of university students who wish to undertake this as stated by Midolo Ramos et al. (2021). That is why it is necessary to characterize

Table 30.4 Estimating the impact of entrepreneurship on the unemployment gap

High	Use media, Tics from the university Teachers must work with networks with the support of the state. Active participation of universities. Create business incubators to develop creativity and innovation.	Economic progress: local, departmental, and national. It contributes to employment increase. Quality life improvement of entrepreneurs.
Impact	Dismiss	Mitigating Actions
Low	Strategies without clear and defined goals by universities.	Entrepreneurs must be identified: as being independent, adventurous, risky, and constant; get the knowledge and surround yourself with the experiences that other entrepreneurs have; get goods and services that are demanded by many customers; count on a business plan to guide you in the market that is and sustain over time; get enough resources for entering the market process and remaining in it.
	Low **Feasibility** High	

professors who train entrepreneurs so that they have all the necessary skills to identify difficulties they may have to improve them and achieve the objective set with entrepreneurs so that entrepreneurship is the means to generate business and reduce the unemployment gap.

Table 30.4 shows an estimate of the possible impact of entrepreneurship on the unemployment gap.

30.4 Conclusions

The characterization of professor trainers of entrepreneurs covers knowledge, skills, roles, reasons, and values, which they must develop in order to achieve the goal because this preparation helps people generate to their own employment, as well as the employment for people around them. Therefore, they will improve their living conditions and improve the social and economic region and country conditions.

In these years, unemployment has grown and with pandemic restrictions, it has become more accentuated. This macroeconomic phenomenon affects all countries in the region, generating informality, few development opportunities, inequality, and an economy in recession.

It is important to highlight that entrepreneurship at the international, national, and local levels is generating jobs and has managed to reduce the existing unemployment gap. Because of this, the state, university, business community, and community must be organized to encourage entrepreneurship, which would clearly contribute to region and country development.

References

Aceituno-Aceituno, P., Casero-Ripollés, A., Escudero-Garzás, J.-J., & Bousoño-Calzón, C. (2018). University training on entrepreneurship in communication and journalism business projects. *Comunicar, 26*(57), 91–99. Scopus. https://doi.org/10.3916/C57-2018-09

Banco Mundial. (2020). *Coronavirus increased inequalities in Peru.* World Bank. https://www.bancomundial.org/es/news/press-release/2020/09/08/crisis-por-el-coronavirus-aumento-las-desigualdades-en-el-peru

Blanchard, O. (2017). *Macroeconomy (Séptima).* Pearson.

Carter, S., & Jones-Evans, D. (2012). Enterprise and small business: Principles. *Practice and Policy (Tercera), 6.* Pearson. https://www.emerald.com/insight/content/doi/10.1108/ijebr.2000.6.3.177.1/full/html

Economic Commission for Latin America and the Caribbean. (2022, January 12). *Latin America and the Caribbean will slow its growth to 2.1% in 2022 amid significant asymmetries between developed and emerging countries [Text].* CEPAL. https://www.cepal.org/es/comunicados/america-latina-caribe-desacelerara-su-crecimiento-21-2022-medio-importantes-asimetrias

Guachimbosa, V., Lavín, J. M., & Santiago, N. (2019). University for entrepreneurship. Professional training profile and vocation to create companies. Technical University of Ambato, Ecuador. *Venezuelan Journal of Management, 24*(85), 31–47. https://doi.org/10.37960/revista.v24i85.23827. Scopus.

Hernández-Sampieri, R., & Mendoza, C. (2018). *Research methodology. The quantitative, qualitative and mixed routes | RUDICS.* McGraw Hill. https://virtual.cuautitlan.unam.mx/rudics/?p=2612

Hilarión, J. (2014). *Entrepreneurship and innovation design and plan your business.* Cengage Learning. https://libgen.is/search.php?req=emprendimiento&lg_topic=libgen&open=0&view=simple&res=25&phrase=1&column=def

Ibarra-Cisneros, M. A., & Hernández-Perlines, F. (2019). The influence of intellectual capital on the performance of Mexico's small and medium-sized manufacturing enterprises: The case of Baja California. *Innovar, 29*(71), 79–96. https://doi.org/10.15446/innovar.v29n71.76397

Midolo Ramos, W. R., Cornejo Condori, Y. M., & Ayala Cochón, F. F. (2021). Entrepreneurial capacity at the National University of San Agustín de Arequipa-2019. *Revista Venezolana de Gerencia, 26*(Special Issue 5), 261–275. Scopus. https://doi.org/10.52080/rvgluz.26.e5.18

Mora, J. J. (2021). Analysis of unemployment and employment after a strict COVID-19 confinement policy in Cali. *Lecturas de Economia, 94*, 165–193. Scopus. https://doi.org/10.17533/UDEA.LE.N94A342002

Mosquera-Carrascal, A., Vergel-Quintero, D., & Bayona-Trillos, R. A. (2020). Entrepreneurial profile: Strategic competence of university professors in Colombia. *Revista Venezolana de Gerencia, 25*(4), 97–114. Scopus.

Murgueitio, M., Burbano, E. L., & Moreno, E. (2019). Education and formative research in the training of entrepreneurs. Application of PBL problem-based learning. *Revista ESPACIOS, 40*(09). https://www.revistaespacios.com/a19v40n09/19400905.html

Naciones Unidas. (2021). *The COVID-19 pandemic wreaks havoc on youth employment in Latin America.* https://news.un.org/es/story/2021/08/1495432

Reyes, C. M. (2022). Perception of the risk of unemployment in Mexico. A quantitative study. *Revista de Ciencias Sociales, 28*(1), 90–105. Scopus. https://doi.org/10.31876/rcs.v28i1.37682

Rodriguez Piña, R. A., Ramos, R. A., Barahona Avecilla, F. R., Inca, F. F., & Gómez Carrión, S. C. (2019). Design and procedural implementation to create incubator of ideas in university subjects. Case study. *Espacios, 40*(5). Scopus.

Rojas, G. Y., Pertuz, V., Navarro, A., Quintero, L. T., Rojas, G. Y., Pertuz, V., Navarro, A., & Quintero, L. T. (2019). Instrument to identify personal and didactic characteristics used by professors in the training of entrepreneurs. *Formación Universitaria, 12*(2), 29–40. https://doi.org/10.4067/S0718-50062019000200029

Romaní, G., Martins, I., Varela, R., & Pombo, C. (2021). New trends on entrepreneurship research in Latin America and Caribbean countries: Evidence from GEM and GUESSS projects – An analytical editorial. *Academia Revista Latinoamericana de Administracion, 34*(3), 329–342. Scopus. https://doi.org/10.1108/ARLA-09-2021-364

Sepúlveda-Calderón, P., & Zapata-Cuervo, N. (2019). Influence of entrepreneurship courses on the intention and action of undertaking in master's students. *Espacios, 40*(19). https://www.revistaespacios.com/a19v40n19/a19v40n19p02.pdf

Valderrama, E. S. (2021). A review for Peru of the relationship among unemployment, underemployment and production. *Revista Finanzas y Politica Economica, 13*(2), 473–511. Scopus. https://doi.org/10.14718/revfinanzpolitecon.v13.n2.2021.8

Villalobos Rodríguez, G., Moraga López, G., Guevara Portuguez, M. J., & Luis, A.-C. (2021). Evidence of the contribution of entrepreneurship to the reduction of youth unemployment. *Revista Venezolana de Gerencia, 26*(95), 758–775. Scopus. https://doi.org/10.19052/rvgluz.27.95.20

Chapter 31
LNG Carriers' Discharge Waiting Time and Energy Inflation

Stavros Karamperidis, Nektatios A. Michail, and Konstantinos Melas

Abstract In this study, we examine the relationship between the port congestion of the LNG carriers at European ports and energy inflation in the euro area. Given the fact that energy inflation is affecting not only companies but households as well, in our research, we provide an additional measure that adds to the shortcomings of the event. Our findings give further insights into the relationship between the shipping industry and its impact on the real economy and strengthen the argument that the industry per se is a leading indicator of the real economy.

Keywords Liquefied Natural Gas · European Union · Inflation · Energy Inflation · VAR model

The shipping industry contributes 85% of global trade, thus its importance in the world economy is widely documented (UNCTAD, 2021). Nevertheless, the industry per se has been highly affected the recent years by a range of external effects. On the one hand, the pandemic crisis (Michail & Melas, 2020) and, on the other hand, the geopolitical tensions are two predominant factors that have disrupted the global supply chains and as a consequence have pushed governments to adopt forms of protectionism that are inhibitory factors in international trade (Michail & Melas, 2022). Both conditions have been documented in the shipping context by the extent of port congestion (Komaromi et al., 2022; Steinbach, 2022). In general, port congestion captures the delay that vessels face between the time that they arrive at the anchorage points of the port, and the berthing of the vessel for loading or unloading cargo (berth-related congestion). Port congestion will eventually have an

S. Karamperidis
Plymouth Business School, Plymouth, UK

N. A. Michail
Central Bank of Cyprus, Nicosia, Cyprus

K. Melas (✉)
Department of Economics, University of Western Macedonia, Kastoria, Greece

© The Author(s), under exclusive license to Springer Nature Switzerland AG 2024
N. Tsounis, A. Vlachvei (eds.), *Applied Economic Research and Trends*, Springer
Proceedings in Business and Economics,
https://doi.org/10.1007/978-3-031-49105-4_31

economic impact for the shipowners, the charters of the vessels, and the economy as a whole leading to higher product costs (Steinbach, 2022).[1]

Various papers have been published recently on the effects of port congestion on global trade (Komaromi et al., 2022), the US economy (Steinbach, 2022), and the by-products of petroleum (Bai et al., 2021). Nevertheless, despite the current energy crisis that has erupted due to the Russia–Ukraine war, little research has been conducted on liquefied natural gas (LNG, thereafter) congestion that was one of the main commodities that have been affected significantly by the event mentioned above (Hudecova & Rajcaniova, 2023) and lead to a substantial price increase. The latter is of great importance given the energy transition that the EU countries have been pushing forward for the usage of natural gas given the better environmental profile compared to oil products (Zachmann, 2008) and the sustainability that natural gas provides (Al-Yafei et al., 2021).

In this study, we examine the relationship between the port congestion of the LNG carriers at European ports and energy inflation in the euro area. Given the fact that energy inflation is not only affecting negatively companies (Bean, 2006) but households as well (Breitenfellner et al., 2015), in our research, we provide an additional measure that adds to the shortcomings of the event. Our findings give further insights into the relationship between the shipping industry and its impact on the real economy (Kilian, 2009) and strengthen the argument that the industry per se is a leading indicator of the real economy (see Kilian, 2019; Michail et al., 2022).

By measuring port congestion via the use of data for all the LNG vessels that discharged in euro area ports over the January 2018–December 2022 period, we observe an increase in discharge delays when demand rises or when port issues occur. Overall, congestion appears to have an effect on both natural gas prices as well as energy inflation, with the latter's reaction standing at 0.1% per 1% shock in port congestion.

31.1 Data and Methodology

Limited by data availability, we collected data from January 2018 until December 2022 for all LNG vessels trading around the world (29,468 voyages in total) from the AXSMarine database. The variables collected include the discharge wait duration (in days), the size of the vessel (in Deadweight tons – DWT), and the country of discharge. Based on the country of discharge, we narrowed our selection to vessels trading within the euro area waters, leading to an examination of 3254 voyages from January 2018 until December 2022.

---

[1] The estimated trade effects related to port congestions only for the USA correspond to $15.7 billion in export losses for the period May to November 2021.

31 LNG Carriers' Discharge Waiting Time and Energy Inflation

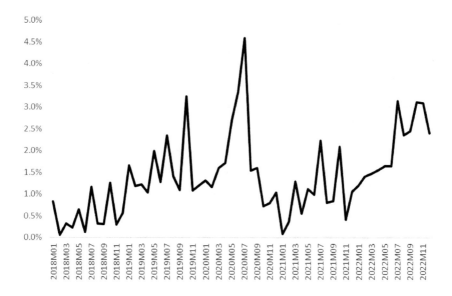

Fig. 31.1 Euro area LNG Port Congestion Index

To obtain a metric of port congestion, we have used the sum of the discharge wait duration multiplied by the vessel size, over the total vessel size multiplied by the total days of trading in the month over that particular period. This allows us to create a Port Congestion Index for LNG carriers, which is presented as a share of all vessels, weighted by their size and number of days in wait. This intuitive measure offers us insights into how port issues as well as increased demand can potentially affect the flow of LNG in the euro area.

Figure 31.1 depicts said index. As expected, and as suggested by the literature (Gui et al., 2022), port congestion rose during the pandemic, as a result of the lockdowns and social distancing protocols that constricted port traffic. Following the first pandemic wave in 2020, congestion eased but started to climb up again in early 2022, when Europe started distancing itself from Russia, and cut down on pipeline imports, focusing on imports using LNG carriers. This increase in demand resulted in a larger number of vessels being in the euro area ports and thus contributed to higher port congestion.

While the index itself does provide an intuitive view with regard to how port congestion is affected by macroeconomic and geopolitical developments, our main point of interest is how congestion can potentially affect the euro area economy. To assess this, we propose the use of a vector autoregression (VAR) model with euro area variables and the Port Congestion Index. Formally, the VAR model can be expressed by the following system of linear equations:

$$X_t = a_0(t) + \sum_{i=1}^{k} \beta_i X_{t-i} + u_t.$$

where X_t is a matrix of endogenous variables, which have been selected to test the relevant hypothesis. $A_{0i}(t)$ is a vector of constants and $A_i(l)$ is a polynomial in the lag operators. Finally, i denotes the respective lag used, while t represents the time period.

The main variable of interest over the period has been energy inflation, which marked the highest increases since the first compilation of data for the euro area. However, to avoid issues relating to taxation easing, which took place during the COVID-19 pandemic, we employ the constant tax series, as obtained by Eurostat. To isolate the congestion effects, we also control for the impact of energy prices. Given that the vast majority of electricity generation in Europe uses natural gas, we use the Dutch TTF price to account for the price increases.[2] Finally, to proxy for macroeconomic developments as well as expectations about the economy, we also use the Eurostoxx index. In robustness checks, we have also included the euro area unemployment rate to capture the prevalent labor conditions and hence the relevant domestic price pressures. The Eurostoxx index was obtained from the European Central Bank's Statistical Data Warehouse, while the other variables were obtained from Eurostat. The data range from January 2018 to December 2022 limited by the availability of the vessel data.

Estimation-wise, the VAR model uses two lags on the basis of the Akaike and Schwarz information criteria. The estimated VAR passes all the normality, autocorrelation, and heteroscedasticity tests, which are available upon request. As previously suggested, the main focus of this study relates to the effects of port congestion (i.e., discharge delay) on inflation and energy prices. Hence, the presentation of the estimates will be limited to these effects, which are presented via impulse response functions (IRFs) in the following section. The rest of the impacts are available upon request.

31.2 Empirical Estimates

Figure 31.2 presents the impulse response functions from the VAR model, as specified in the previous section. As suggested, to conserve space, we only present the most relevant responses, while the rest are available upon request. As evidenced from the responses, following a 15% shock in discharge delay (disch_delay), we observe an increase in energy inflation of around 1.5% at around 3 months following

---

[2] Oil is also an important determinant, given its use as a transport fuel. However, natural gas and oil have a very strong positive correlation (higher than 80%), thus making the use of both redundant. In the robustness check, using the oil price made no qualitative difference in the conclusions reached.

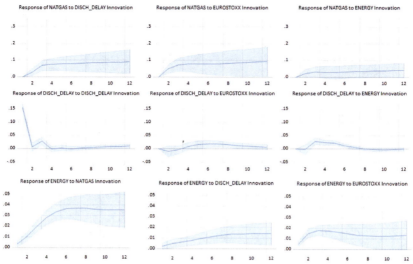

Fig. 31.2 VAR impulse response functions. Notes: the figure shows the impulse responses from a VAR model with two lags. Shaded areas represent the 68% confidence interval. For example, "Response of ENERGY to DISCH_DELAY" shows how energy inflation is expected to react following a shock that increases port congestion (discharge delay)

the shock (i.e., 0.1% per 1% shock). This is mainly driven by the increase in natural gas (natgas) prices observed over the same period, by around 9%.

While the above exercise appears to be straightforward, its policy implications are quite significant: in particular, it highlights the case the delays in vessel discharge, commonly viewed as "port congestion," can have an economically meaningful effect on energy prices. With the pass-through of energy prices to headline inflation standing at around 60% in the first 9 months of 2022 (Corsello & Tagliabracci, 2023), the policy implications suggest that the significant increase in inflation over the year can be also attributed to port issues.

As per a variance decomposition of our VAR model, around 70% of the energy inflation variance is a result of natural gas prices, while another 10% stems from discharge delay. Given the effort to move away from Russian gas imports via pipelines, and the use of LNG carriers to import gas in Europe, one can expect that, in a heavy winter, port congestion is likely to increase, with a potentially significant effect on energy inflation.

31.3 Conclusions

This study offers the first examination of how port congestion for LNG carriers affects euro area energy inflation. Our measure of port congestion, created using data for all the LNG vessels that discharged in euro area ports over the January 2018–December 2022 period, shows increases when demand rises or when port issues occur. Overall, this appears to have an effect on both in natural gas prices as well as energy inflation, with the latter's reaction standing at 0.1% per 1% shock in port congestion.

References

Al-Yafei, H., Aseel, S., Kucukvar, M., Onat, N. C., Al-Sulaiti, A., & Al-Hajri, A. (2021). A systematic review for sustainability of global liquified natural gas industry: A 10-year update. *Energy Strategy Reviews, 38*. https://doi.org/10.1016/J.ESR.2021.100768

Bai, X., Jia, H., & Xu, M. (2021). Port congestion and the economics of LPG seaborne transportation. *Maritime Policy and Management*. https://doi.org/10.1080/03088839.2021.1940334

Bean, C. R. (2006). *Globalisation and inflation*. Bank of England Quarterly Bulletin 2006 – Q4, London.

Breitenfellner, A., Crespo Cuaresma, J., & Mayer, P. (2015). Energy inflation and house price corrections. *Energy Economics, 48*, 109–116. https://doi.org/10.1016/J.ENECO.2014.08.023

Corsello, F., & Tagliabracci, A. (2023). Assessing the pass-through of energy prices to inflation in the euro area. *SSRN Electronic Journal*. https://doi.org/10.2139/SSRN.4350522

Gui, D., Wang, H., & Yu, M. (2022). Risk assessment of port congestion risk during the COVID-19 pandemic. *Journal of Marine Science and Engineering, 10*. https://doi.org/10.3390/jmse10020150

Hudecova, K., & Rajcaniova, M. (2023). Geopolitical risk and energy market. *Peace Economics, Peace Science and Public Policy*. https://doi.org/10.1515/PEPS-2022-0033/MACHINEREADABLECITATION/RIS

Kilian, L. (2009). Not all oil price shocks are alike: Disentangling demand and supply shocks in the crude oil market. *American Economic Review, 99*, 1053–1069. https://doi.org/10.1257/aer.99.3.1053

Kilian, L. (2019). Measuring global real economic activity: Do recent critiques hold up to scrutiny? *Economics Letters, 178*, 106–110. https://doi.org/10.1016/j.econlet.2019.03.001

Komaromi, A., Cerdeiro, D., & Liu, Y. (2022). *Supply chains and port congestion around the world* (No. 2022/059). International Monetary Fund, Washington DC.

Michail, N. A., & Melas, K. D. (2020). Shipping markets in turmoil: An analysis of the Covid-19 outbreak and its implications. *Transportation Research Interdisciplinary Perspectives, 7*, 100178. https://doi.org/10.1016/j.trip.2020.100178

Michail, N. A., & Melas, K. D. (2022). Geopolitical risk and the LNG-LPG trade. *Peace Economics, Peace Science and Public Policy, 0*. https://doi.org/10.1515/peps-2022-0007

Michail, N. A., Melas, K. D., & Cleanthous, L. (2022). The relationship between shipping freight rates and inflation in the Euro Area. *International Economics, 172*, 40–49. https://doi.org/10.1016/j.inteco.2022.08.004

Steinbach, S. (2022). Port congestion, container shortages, and U.S. foreign trade. *Economics Letters, 213*, 110392. https://doi.org/10.1016/J.ECONLET.2022.110392

UNCTAD. (2021). *Review of maritime transport*, New York.

Zachmann, G. (2008). Electricity wholesale market prices in Europe: Convergence? *Energy Economics, 30*, 1659–1671. https://doi.org/10.1016/j.eneco.2007.07.002

Chapter 32
Big Data Analytics in Management Reporting: A Systematic Literature Review

Simon Luca Kropf

Abstract Data are sometimes referred to as the new oil (Humby & Palmer, 2006) since it is assumed to have similar characteristics. Its value is particularly connected to its refinement as, otherwise, data cannot be used effectively. In principle, this is like crude oil, a commodity that must be refined into gas, chemicals, plastic, or similar outputs of higher value. Data must similarly be broken down and transferred to create a valuable output as well (Palmer M, Data is the new oil. ANA Marketing Maestros. https://ana.blogs.com/maestros/2006/11/data_is_the_new.html, 2006). The reference of data to oil is also mentioned in practice in the context of its overall value in the economy, whereby digital data are characterized as the most valuable resource (Economist, The world's most valuable resource is no longer oil, but data. The Economist. https://www.economist.com/leaders/2017/05/06/the-worlds-most-valuable-resource-is-no-longer-oil-but-data, 2017). Also, the availability of data for analysis is expected to show strong growth in the future, thanks to advances in technology and data-gathering techniques, which are applied across a diverse range of industries. This development is particularly driven by the large growth of data segments, especially in connection to social media as well as to data from applications in the realm of the Internet of Things. Currently, data growth is expected to exceed the growth in data storage capacity, as stated by the International Data Corporation or IDC (Hariri RH, Fredericks EM, Bowers KM, J Big Data 6(44):1–16, 2019; IDC, Data creation and replication will grow at a faster rate than installed storage capacity. According to the IDC Global DataSphere and StorageSphere Forecasts. https://www.idc.com/getdoc.jsp?containerId=prUS47560321, 2021). Given the increase in the availability of large amounts of data, the data analytics market revenue is also projected to show strong growth in the near future as well (Statista, Big data analytics market global revenue 2025. Statista. https://www.statista.com/statistics/947745/worldwide-total-data-market-revenue/, 2020). As a result of advancing digitization, a very large

---

S. L. Kropf (✉)
Faculty of Business and Economics, Mendel University in Brno, Brno, Czech Republic
e-mail: xkropf@mendelu.cz

© The Author(s), under exclusive license to Springer Nature Switzerland AG 2024
N. Tsounis, A. Vlachvei (eds.), *Applied Economic Research and Trends*, Springer Proceedings in Business and Economics,
https://doi.org/10.1007/978-3-031-49105-4_32

basic spectrum for data-driven decisions of all kinds has been created. In addition, the storage of data has become very cost-effective with the current state of the art. Coupled with today's vast amount of data, there is enormous potential for companies to transform data into information to generate significant competitive advantages and build valuable knowledge that can support companies. This implies that data management and decision support systems are of great importance to corporate management and corporate management reporting, and this importance can be expected to grow in future (Seufert A, Treitz R, von Dacke M, Control Mag 07/08:48–53, 2017).

Keywords Big data · Big data analytics · Management reporting · Explorative data modelling

JEL Codes M15, M40, O32

32.1 Introduction

Generally, the application of big data analytics is complex, and using it successfully requires the handling of numerous challenges. These include, in particular, issues on data acquisition and data management but also issues in connection to data access and its processing as well. In addition, the data need to be properly analyzed using suitable mathematical and statistical methods that lead to an understanding of the information contained within the data. Additionally, specific applications need to be correctly designed (Shi, 2022, p. 16). The complexity of the analytical approach can differ as well. Specifically, analytics can be classified into three different layers of complexity: descriptive analytics, predictive analytics, and prescriptive analytics (Akerkar, 2019, p. 64).

Applying big data analytics also has implications for a variety of fields or different organizational functions. One of the many fields for application is management reporting. That term refers to the task of providing the management of organizations with useful information. Taschner (2013, pp. 33–35) emphasizes the role of management reporting as a part of the company-wide information systems environment that reports to the leadership. However, there is also a bridge between the external and the internal accounting of a firm. Independent from the focus, management reporting requires data to be gathered, processed, and adequately communicated in order to provide information that is useful for management decision-making. The potential receivers of the information provided by the management reporting function or the management reporting system are of a relatively broad nature and can include internal and external receivers of the information (Schön, 2018, p. 18).

The characteristics of management reporting make it useful to address this theme within the novel context of big data analytics. By applying big data techniques, management reporting can provide more useful information (Weichel & Herrmann, 2016), so that it becomes possible to create more value for the firm (Buschbacher,

2016). Big data analytics can also enable many novel applications as well such as sustainable supply chain management (Mageto, 2021).

32.2 Theoretical Background

32.2.1 *Big Data and Big Data Analytics*

Big data analytics has gained a lot of attention in the last couple of years from both the academic sector and private industry. It is strongly aligned with other technological developments like in relation to networks, sensors, or other fields in the realm of internet technology such as social media or smart applications. These have facilitated the gathering and storage of large amounts of data typically on an enormous scale and from many different sources. As such, big data analytics is based on a massive amount of information, employing sophisticated techniques not only for data analysis but also for the prediction of future outcomes and developments. The overall goal of big data analytics is to provide support for advanced decision-making capabilities (Hariri et al., 2019; Mikalef et al., 2018). Data provide the basis of information and can be understood as a syntactically logical combination of chars that can be transformed into information by a relationship-dependent situation. Information should especially be available as required by the task or the process (Appelfeller & Feldmann, 2018, pp. 140–141). Thus, information is a collection of data that triggers relevant processes in the decision-making process depending on the situation. Information is not generally applicable and can only be used depending on the situation. Information is also often classified as a resource that affects a company's products and services (Seufert et al., 2017). In the context of big data applications, the mining of big data from various sources potentially helps to uncover useful information and obtain valuable knowledge, which can subsequently be used to derive further insights and to guide business actions (J. Souza et al., 2020, p. 669). It can be mentioned that the amount of data that is potentially available for big data applications is currently rising at an exponential rate, while simultaneously being strongly connected to cloud technology as well (Hashem et al., 2015). Semantically, the term *big data analytics* can be divided into two sub-terms *big data* and *analytics,* with the latter referring to data analytics. It is also frequently connected to Moore's law of the successive increase in the speed of information technology processes (Moore, 1965). To approach a holistic definition of big data analytics, the term big data will be defined first. Generally, there are many definitions of big data available in the academic literature that refer to a variety of different dimensions of this broad concept. An overview of existing definitions is, for example, provided by De Mauro et al. (2016), who compare the definitions according to their relation to the dimensions of information, technology, methods, and impact. From that, the authors work out the following consensual definition of big data, pointing to three different definitions features:

Big Data represents the Information assets characterized by such a High Volume, Velocity and Variety to require specific Technology and Analytical Methods for its transformation into Value. (De Mauro et al., 2016, p. 133)

This definition particularly emphasizes the idea of the importance of the 3 Vs: volume, velocity, and variety. These have already been mentioned for quite some years in the context of big data like, for example, by Laney (2001). It is also part of the commonly used definition from Gartner, who also emphasizes that big data demands innovative and effective forms of processing information for obtaining value in the form of process automation, decision-making, and knowledge generation (Gartner, 2017). Having mentioned the 3 Vs as central to the definition of big data, these attributes shall be introduced below in more detail:

Data *Volume*

The feature data volume refers to the sheer volume of the data available for the analysis, coupled with some part of variety within the data. For example, a large database of only structured data does not qualify as belonging to the realm of big data, irrespective of its size as claimed by Dorschel and Dorschel (2015, p. 7). Irrespective of the volume of data, which is often measured in petabytes, the size of the data available is clearly a central component of big data analytics, from which intelligence is derived in order to obtain superior knowledge for competitive advantage (McAfee et al., 2012). Therefore, volume refers to the size and the scale of the dataset as well, whereby borders that define a necessary size are typically not provided (Gandomi & Haider, 2015; Hariri et al., 2019).

Data *Velocity*

Furthermore, data velocity needs to be mentioned as a characteristic of big data. This concept refers to the frequency in which the data are generated and also the speed that defines how fast data is available to serve a particular analytical application (McAfee et al., 2012; Russom, 2011, p. 7). Furthermore, an important attribute of data velocity is the tight connection of velocity with the volume attribute of big data (W. Dorschel & Dorschel, 2015, p. 7). Data velocity can potentially refer to real-time data or streaming data, which can be sourced, for example, from applications in the context of IoT (Hariri et al., 2019).

Data *Variety*

Data variety was mentioned already together with data volume, where it was considered a necessary feature. The variety attribute refers to the degree of structure within the data. There are several forms possible within a dataset, which can range from structured data to semi-structured and even unstructured data. Variety also refers to different data types or formats as well like text, multimedia content, or other data (Hariri et al., 2019). Other forms can include positioning data, data from sensors, or large amounts of data from social media sources (McAfee et al., 2012). For analytical purposes, it is obvious that data analysis techniques need to be applied that take the requirements of the dataset into account. Some techniques, for example, require a particular data format or cannot be applied to incomplete data (Tsai et al., 2015).

The 3 Vs can be understood as a very basic conception of big data with the attributes of (1) volume, (2) velocity, and (3) variety being very important for a dataset to be classified as belonging to the realm of big data. However, there are additional attributes of data that provide further dimensions to the concept of big data. The expansion by two additional attributes into 5 Vs is mentioned, for example, by the information technology firm IBM. The 5 Vs of big data refer to the original 3 Vs concept but add additional dimensions to it (Hariri et al., 2019; Jain, 2016). These two additional attributes are mentioned below:

Data *Value*

The results that are generated by using big data technologies should lead to added value in the form of insights from the data that provide some utility to the user. Otherwise, investments in big data technology, infrastructure, or knowledge must be questioned on their economic value (Jain, 2016). Applied to management reporting, this notion is obvious, as value from reporting is of paramount importance for the leadership of companies (Taschner, 2013, p. 33).

Data *Veracity*

Veracity needs to be mentioned as another feature, which is connected to the reliability, completeness, and accuracy of the data. The attribute of veracity is particularly relevant for some selected types of data in the case that it is at first not quite clear if the analysis may lead to valuable insight and applicable results like, for example, in the analysis of data from social media platforms. These can be subjective or need to be carefully evaluated within the proper context and time (W. Dorschel & Dorschel, 2015, p. 8). It can be argued that veracity is highly connected to the issue of dealing with uncertainty, particularly in reducing its potentially negative impact.

Apart from the features of big data that have been mentioned so far, it should be noted that some researchers to include additional attributes into the definition of big data (Seddon & Currie, 2017). These additional dimensions of the concept should not further be explored at this point. Nevertheless, the existence of these additional features shows clearly how multi-faceted big data can be. Also, depending on the application and the practical use of data analysis techniques, these also need to be considered, depending on the context.

Having stated the concept of big data thus far, it is now possible to define and conceptualize the understanding of big data analytics. Generally, big data analytics refers to analytic methods, which are applied to datasets that qualify as belonging to big data. However, in practice, the term is sometimes not mentioned or used by those applying big data analytics techniques (Russom, 2011, p. 8). This conceptualization shows a rather broad approach to understanding the concept, which is further made more difficult or complex as big data analytics is also mentioned in the context of business intelligence applications as well. Nevertheless, it can be pointed out that big data analytics mainly refers to explorative methods of analyzing data

(Dorschel & Dorschel, 2015, p. 75). Technically, and with respect to the methods available for such an explorative analysis within the field of big data analytics, other technologies are strongly connected. These include several types of techniques within the field of artificial intelligence (AI), machine learning (ML), data mining, natural language processing (NLP), and computational intelligence (CI). These technologies, furthermore, contain methods or algorithms that are designed and able to provide solutions for big data analytic purposes. This is mostly due to the inherent characteristics of these technologies, especially related to the high speed, accuracy, and precision of using large and unstructured sets of data (Chen et al., 2014). As a result of the use of applications related to the technologies mentioned, big data analytics technologies can gain valuable insight into several types of data and derive business value from it. This is being performed by discovering hidden patterns, unknown correlations, or other information from the big sets of various forms of data (Tsai et al., 2015). Technologies in the realm of data analytics do not primarily focus on the question "What have we done?" but rather on "How should we do that in the future?." This is an important point, as the key contribution of big data analytics can be found in future-oriented analyses or predictions. It is, thereby, possible to perform sophisticated predictions based on historical data or even real-time data (Akerkar, 2019). Current reporting systems have so far mainly built on the analysis of structured and mainly numerical data; semi-structured and unstructured data have been largely neglected. However, the demand to use such type of data is increasing as well as demand regarding a higher speed in data availability and analysis with respect to the use of real-time data. This will require an information technology infrastructure that is able to gather, store, and analyze unstructured datasets as well (Seufert, 2014, p. 27). The applications of big data analytics are plentiful. Analytical concepts in the context of big data are of universal nature and can potentially be used across many domains like healthcare, where big data technology shows many possibilities for applications (Galetsi & Katsaliaki, 2020; Miah et al., 2022). Therefore, the potential of big data analytics is not restricted to solving economic and business questions but transfers to many other areas as well. With the introduction and the use of big data analytics, other questions arise that refer to domains like regulation as well. While in practice, the role of data is clearly acknowledged with respect to its value to the overall economy or businesses, there are still some risks to be mentioned because of it. Here, the importance of large firms in the digital realm like Alphabet, Amazon, Microsoft, or Apple is mentioned. By doing so, implications for issues concerning antitrust rules and regulations are stated due to the power that powerful digital companies have on the flow of data (Economist, 2017). Firms need to evaluate these concerns carefully and must prepare for potential risks not only due to market concentration power but also due to regulatory provisions as well.

32.2.2 Management Reporting

Management reporting is a part of the firm's information management system. The main purpose of management reporting is to provide management with the relevant information to make accurate and timely decisions on issues regarding the firm's leadership (Taschner, 2013, p. 33). Companies require an efficient and effective management reporting system to establish competitive advantages for the company. By combining an analysis of external and internal information that influence the business, it is possible to design a management reporting system that enables holistic business management of the company. Management reporting should, therefore, be considered in an overall economic context and not exclusively in an internal company cosmos. This is difficult to address, as management reporting has a clear focus on the internal perspective. However, corporate reports in general can have external and internal addressees. The target group is, therefore, not limited to internal groups of a company (Gleich et al., 2008, p. 19). However, despite their clear internal focus regarding the addressees of the reports (Taschner, 2013, p. 3), management reporting systems can be used for the purpose of providing information to internal and external receivers with relevant information (Schön, 2018, p. 18). Due to its focus on management, management reporting has a strong role in fulfilling organizational goals by mobilizing adequate resources. Management reporting, therefore, has a key function for planning, steering, and controlling a firm's business results and decision quality by providing adequate information (Gleich et al., 2008, p. 19). It can, therefore, be defined as.

> *Management Reporting is the part of business reporting that has the function of providing the executives of a company with information. The information is distributed using reports and is intended to support management in the context of the planning and steering process.* (Gleich et al., 2008, p. 20)

Given the role of management reporting in the provision of relevant information for managing the firm, it is necessary to provide sophisticated analysis for decision support. If managers are not provided with such type of analysis, decisions cannot be made on the basis of relevant facts and analysis, which in turn will lead to lower quality decision-making and inferior economic results for the firm (Kroll & Kittelberger, 2014, p. 189). Given the advance of innovative analytical methods like, for example, in the field of big data analytics, it is currently of high interest to practitioners to investigate the use of such techniques for management reporting systems. The goal is to improve the quality of information provision as a precursor to superior decision-making and value-creation (Weichel & Herrmann, 2016; Buschbacher, 2016). In order to adapt information systems adequately to their purposes, they also need to be designed in a way so that they can support the needs of the respective industry, the business unit, or segments (Kroll & Kittelberger, 2014, p. 189). Sophisticated analytical methods like big data analytics can hereby help to the necessary tools for this task (Mageto, 2021).

32.3 Research Methodology

To achieve the stated purpose of the research in this paper, a thorough investigation of the academic literature is required. This will be performed methodologically by carrying out a systematic literature review. The methodology of the systematic literature review can be described as a procedure that is characterized by its rigorously structural approach in the process of searching and selecting literature sources. This begins with a carefully stated procedure in the process of selecting the literature before the actual search process is carried out. Typically, this is stated and documented with the help of a review protocol, which contains the distinctive steps in the literature search. This makes the systematic literature review a specific type of literature review, which needs to be mentioned separately from the methodology of other forms of literature reviews as well (Denyer & Tranfield, 2009; Kitchenham et al., 2009). Systematic literature reviews are used across a diverse range of disciplines, including reviews connected to themes in the context of big data analytics as well (Galetsi & Katsaliaki, 2020; Mikalef et al., 2018). The basic principle of the selection process is shown in Fig. 32.1.

The identification of the need for carrying out a systematic review of the literature is the first step in the process of conducting the review. This can be performed with a short scoping study on the debates within the field, which can include theoretical, methodological, and practical themes (Tranfield et al., 2003, p. 214). For this paper, the motivation for carrying out the review was already performed, and it was stated that no research on the theme of big data analytics in the field of management reporting has so far been published. Given this motivation for

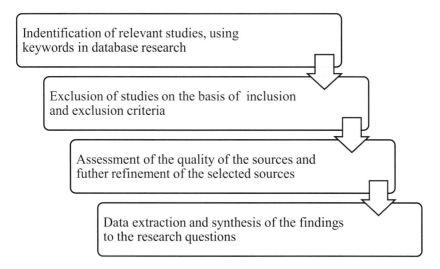

Fig. 32.1 Stages in the process of the systematic literature review. (Source: Own presentation based on Mikalef et al. (2018))

undertaking the review, the definition of appropriate research questions can be mentioned as the first central element in a systematic review of the literature. Questions need to be carefully formulated, and they must consider the needs of the addressees of the review. Therefore, depending on the context of the review, questions can be formulated inside teams of researchers and with the potential involvement of stakeholders as well (Denyer & Tranfield, 2009, pp. 681–682). In the context of this paper, this might theoretically involve practitioners who may be interested in a particular sub-theme of big data analytics within their specific management reporting system. However, for the purpose of this paper, an approach is performed, whereby the application of big data analytics is addressed toward management reporting in its general form. Therefore, no limiting or restraining elements are considered at this stage that would potentially lead to the exclusion of valuable findings. The research questions are stated as:

RQ1: What is the current state of research on the application of big data analytics in the field of management reporting?
RQ2: Which methods and techniques can be identified in current academic research on Big Data Analytics in Management Reporting?

After having stated the research questions, the next step in the systematic literature review is to define an appropriate search process, so that studies or research material can be identified and selected. The search process also includes the relevant points not only for evaluating quality but also for data extraction and synthesis (Tranfield et al., 2003, p. 214). The search process can be performed differently regarding the selection of studies. Typically, database research or a similar approach is used. However, manual selection or hand-searching of relevant journals is possible (Denyer & Tranfield, 2009, p. 683; Kitchenham et al., 2009, p. 8). These methods for identifying sources can optionally be expanded or partly substituted by backward and forward search as well, where references from existing articles are evaluated or citing sources are used (Brocke et al., 2009, p. 10). In the case of this paper, a keyword-based method is applied to scientific databases.

To apply this approach to big data analytics in management reporting, it is necessary to first determine the relevant keywords. The problem with using the search term *big data analytics* is that users do not necessarily refer to the term in practice, albeit methods of big data analytics are used (Russom, 2011, p. 8). This may also have implications for the determination of search terms. For example, an article on the use of data mining techniques in the field of management reporting might qualify as a useful source for the investigation in this paper, albeit it is not necessarily technically connected to the search term *big data analytics*, which in this case would be a category into which data mining would fall into. That, in turn, might lead to the problem that such a publication will not be found. A possible solution is to refer to similar keywords, especially to the term *business intelligence*, which is commonly associated with the use of big data for various purposes of providing information and associated analyses within firms (Seufert, 2014, p. 26). However, despite the issues in using the term *management reporting* when carrying out the

Table 32.1 Overview of key search terms

First search string	Boolean	Second search string
Big data analytics	AND	Management reporting
Machine learning		
Artificial intelligence		
Data mining		
Predictive analytics		

Source: Own presentation

search, the term does, at least, provide a narrow focus that is not provided when using *business intelligence*, which is a much broader concept as it also relates to non-management decision areas. From this conclusion, the best course of action is deemed to stick to *management reporting* as a key search term for systematic literature research. However, another issue arises when trying to determine the keywords for the analysis, which is related to the use of *management reporting* as a keyword for the search. It can similarly be argued that by using the term *big data analytics*, a publication may be suitable for inclusion, while not containing the term either in the metadata of the publication (as a keyword) or within the title, abstract, or even in the text. Given the many different areas of information systems within a company that may be a part of the overall management reporting system, it is necessary to use a more inclusive approach to the search. This can include terms that refer to some of the main areas for enterprise information systems, for example, customer relationship management, enterprise resource planning, or contract management (Akerkar, 2019, p. 65). However, it is also not feasible to use an extensive list of potential search terms from various company information systems that are deemed relevant for the analysis in this paper. In addition, such an analysis might also need to take into account at least some of the specifics in relation to different industries as well. A possible solution to this challenge is to focus on key areas, or fundamental elements within a business model that can be transferred across industries, e.g., customers, channels, and resources (Morabito, 2015, p. 66). Nevertheless, this would provide rather numerous combinations of keywords that are much too broad, and it would necessitate further manual work for determining the inclusion and exclusion of the sources. It is, therefore, considered best to use an indirect approach, where potential areas for big data analytics with relevance to management reporting are not searched for directly but are later determined based on the search results. The search was conducted within the databases Business Source Complete via EBSCOhost, ScienceDirect, and JSTOR. Selection criteria and quality issues in relation to the search are stated in the next paragraph. The following Table 32.1 provides an overview of the keywords used for the database research.

In conducting a systematic review of the literature, it is necessary to clearly state the selection criteria, including the operators and the details on the keyword combination characteristics and details used when conducting the search in databases (Denyer & Tranfield, 2009, p. 684). This will be stated here with respect to the individual databases, as different criteria can be used in the search procedure, depending on the provider. Using the keyword combinations, a first search was conducted with Business Source Complete. The search results were limited to academic journals, while the password combinations shown in Table 32.1 were applied. A similar procedure was then applied in the ScienceDirect database as well, which has led to many results. The search terms have then been put into quotation marks to get more refined results. These have then been further refined by including only results from the subject area *Business, Management, and Accounting*, which is a defined criterion of the database information provider information. A selection by year was not performed. However, the search was restricted to review and research articles, while other types such as books have been excluded. A similar procedure was carried out by using the JSTOR database, where the same keyword combinations[1] were used. Here, the subject area was restricted to the theme defined by the data provider as *Management & Organizational Behavior*. The search results were also limited to include only results in English. Furthermore, only results from journals have been included as well. The list of results that have been obtained with the procedure described above was then subject to further inspection and evaluation to ensure a qualitatively high level of the body of literature for inclusion in the analysis. Duplicates have been eliminated from the findings. An assessment was made as to whether a particular result is able to provide a contribution to the research on the use of big data analytics in the realm of management reporting. This was performed by analyzing the contents outlined in the abstract of the publication. Due to the selection method, the use of quality checklists was deemed to be unnecessary, albeit recommended as far as it is applicable in systematic literature reviews (Denyer & Tranfield, 2009, p. 685). Also, no reference to journal rankings was performed, which is another potential criterion for quality in such types of reviews (Markoulli et al., 2017, p. 376). Generally, it can be stated that sources perceived as having a lower formal level of quality (e.g. ranking) can be included in a review if such a publication can contribute to answering the research questions and if existing quality issues are dealt with critically (Denyer & Tranfield, 2009, p. 685).

32.4 Results and Discussion

Based on the approach or protocol for the systematic literature review, described in the preceding paragraph, a selection process was performed where the total number of results was reduced based on applicable criteria for the inclusion and exclusion of studies to the analysis. The approach is thereby similar to the approach used by Mikalef et al. (2018). The process is shown below in Table 32.2 with the

---

[1] Quotation marks have not been applied uniformly with JSTOR as this has shown to narrow the results too much for the purpose of the review in the case of the term *big data analytics*. However, quotation marks have been used for *"machine learning," "artificial intelligence," "data mining," and "predictive analytics."*

Table 32.2 Steps in literature selection based on defined inclusion and exclusion criteria

	Inclusion/Exclusion criteria	Total articles
Stage 1	Identification of relevant articles based on the defined keywords within the databases JSTOR, ScienceDirect, and business source complete	n = 619
Stage 2	Exclusion of duplicates and exclusion of studies based on the titles	n = 96
Stage 3	Exclusion based on the abstract of the article	n = 76
Stage 4	Quality evaluation of remaining articles[a]	n = 76

Source: Own presentation
[a]No quality issues have been detected that would consider an article as having not enough quality to be included in the body of literature

corresponding criteria that have been applied, which has led to the final body of literature selected for the review and for the identification of themes in the context of big data analytics and management reporting:

32.4.1 RQ1: Current State of Research

In this paragraph, the current state of research will be pointed out to provide an answer to the first research question. This will be performed by clearly showing how the field has developed and how the current state of research is to be evaluated.

Generally, an intelligent way of using data for management decision-making is not a new field of research. As Beged-Dov et al. (1967, p. 829) point out, even the use of real-time monitoring of operating activities and results enables management to make superior decisions. Therefore, decision-making based on historical reporting cycles is not encouraged. It is encouraged to have decision-makers finding mechanisms so that decision-making can be more generalized and lessons from one situation to another can be more easily transferred (Howard & Morgenroth, 1968, p. 427). Also, technologically oriented management information systems were formed, beginning in the 1960s with firm departments such as marketing having encouraged the use of such systems by customizing the systems to the specific demands. With changes in business environments and business activities such as in electronic commerce, information systems have also changed accordingly, e.g., through the use of novel data such as on digital channels on data derived from customer experiences (Li et al., 2001, p. 307; Morgan et al., 2022, p. 462). These findings provide arguments for a strong motivation toward the usage of new technologies such as big data analytics, which is clearly recognizable in more historical sources on management information systems and reporting.

In addition to the relevance of using technology-assisted data processing in management decision-making, which is to be found in relatively historic sources from the late 1960s (Beged-Dov et al., 1967; Howard & Morgenroth, 1968), approaches for aligning computer programs with human decision-making came up on the academic managerial literature (Bouwman, 1983, p. 653). Also, approaches can be found in the literature to implement new technology and knowledge-based systems in decision-making. These have originally occurred within professions such as medicine or geology. The use of expert systems for decision-making is encouraged in the realm of marketing as well (Blanning, 1984, p. 311). An example of an area for applying new types of information technology is the field of manufacturing (Carrie & Banerjee, 1984, p. 251). Also, within the hospitality sector, applications of knowledge systems for management have been discussed as well (Nissan, 1987, p. 199). Furthermore, research suggests that the utilization of big data analytics for decision-making in the fields of accounting and finance is poised to have a transformative impact on routine business within organizations (Janvrin & Watson, 2017; Vasarhelyi et al., 2015; Warren et al., 2015).

Generally, a strong role in the development of measurement-based models regarding operational processes in the context of decision-making and management science was identified quite early in the academic literature (Little, 1986, p. 1). The implications of management information systems are plentiful and require a careful analysis and understanding of the nature of human behavior, organizational reality, as well as processes of information management and problem-solving (Preston, 1991, p. 43). It is presumed that inexpensive software development tools have a growing impact on knowledge-management systems that support management decision-making (May et al., 1991, p. 177).

Based on this state of knowledge, research attempts have been made towards developing ideas for knowledge-based systems in different fields of application. Indications for such empirical work were found in the body of literature from the review, beginning in the 1990s. These refer mainly to the development of so-called knowledge-based systems for which some authors came up with ideas for prototypes. Some examples from that research are listed below:

Development of a concept and prototype of an assistant to a brand manager that works as a knowledge-based system. The system is designed to support the brand management function (McCann et al., 1991, p. 51).

Prototype development of a knowledge-based support system in the context of a manufacturing company. The system is designed to aid in providing diagnostics and in the resolution of various problems within production environments. Also, the function includes the collection and storage of information to support management decision-making as well (May et al., 1991, p. 177).

Modeling framework for a knowledge management expert system that can be used for project evaluation such as in new product development for facilitating processing time and flexibility (M. J. Liberatore & Stylianou, 1995, p. 1296).

The examples mentioned as cases of expert knowledge management systems are not mentioned as examples of big data analytics, as the term has evolved later. Similarly, Nord & Nord (1995, p. 95) mention the term executive information systems, referring hereby to information or reporting systems that can be used by executives on-demand with the help of computers or with other digital devices in order to support aid strategic planning. Therefore, both terms – knowledge management systems and executive information systems – can be used similarly while both terms also show stark similarities and are in principle equal in the sense that computer or digital technology is involved that uses and processes data in order to support business decisions. There is a large variability regarding the use of the term big data itself (Russom, 2011, p. 8). As such, it can be argued that the examples pointed out above show how the entire field of research has logically evolved into a more sophisticated and technologically complex state.

One of the steps toward this current state is the integration of visual or graphical elements from diverse sets of data into management reporting. An example of such research, which shows how visualization is increasingly used for management reporting, is provided by Leece (1999, p. 267). The author applies different techniques within the field of knowledge discovery and databases coupled with data visualization for identifying relevant clusters regarding the ownership of risky financial assets. Thereby, relationships between variables like age, individual income, and financial wealth are shown with respect to concentrations or clusters.

It can be stated that the use of graphical information has been encouraged in the empirical academic literature on management information systems. For example, an experimental study has shown that the use of graphical information is beneficial as it coincides with increased forecasting abilities when compared to the use of only numerical information (Carey & Kacmar, 2003, pp. 444–445). With increases in technological possibilities, the way how information can be presented has reached unprecedented options that have not yet been available so far. Currently, internet-of-things technology enables, for example, the integration of different types of media in order to enrich corporate communication via digital reporting (Valentinetti & Flores Muñoz, 2021, p. 549).

With advances in academic research on the use of technology in management reporting, several distinctive approaches were subsequently made regarding the application of different techniques to numerous fields. Examples like the use of artificial neural networks, guided by genetic algorithms for household profiling information in marketing (Kim et al., 2005, p. 264) or a study on the impact of technological advancement on the management of lodging operations (Singh & Kasavana, 2005, p. 24), show an increased level of specialization in the academic literature as articles on very different fields of applications were published. Other examples of a specific nature are the use of data analytics for acquiring donors (Ryzhov et al., 2016, p. 849) or the application of analytics to perform other operations such as power grid optimization (Rudin et al., 2014, p. 364).

It is evident that these publications show mostly an indirect relationship toward management reporting, as the applications are generally concerned with improving specific operations. Nevertheless, operations are clearly part of the realm of management reporting and must be considered in the leadership of firms. It is thereby important that information is relevant and of subjective utility to the recipient of management reporting information (Taschner, 2013, p. 20). Especially given that big data analytics in business and accounting is one of the most valuable and underutilized resources for organizations. Failure to heed this knowledge can therefore imply enormous risks (Alharthi et al., 2017; Pappas et al., 2018; Sheng et al., 2019).

Despite these advances in research, it is mentioned in the literature that theories and methods within management accounting information systems are in need of further expansion of research activities so that complex relationships are better understood, and technology can be designed effectively and customized to the needs of practice (Granlund, 2011, p. 3). In order to facilitate further research, there are even articles that provide a case study on failed decision-support systems, aiming at improving such applications (Gorman, 2016, p. 183). Generally, there is still some lack of knowledge in some areas mentioned in the current literature (Ibrahim et al., 2021, p. 1; Rikhardsson & Yigitbasioglu, 2018, p. 37; Sivarajah et al., 2017, pp. 279–280; Chapman & Kihn, 2009; Davenport, 1998; Granlund & Malmi, 2002; Rom & Rohde, 2007).

32.4.2 RQ2: Methods and Techniques in Academic Research on Big Data Analytics in Management Reporting

It is mentioned in the literature that different types of methods or techniques within the realm of machine learning can be used for reporting purposes. Berkin et al. (2023, p. 1) evaluate five different techniques including logistic regression analysis, naïve Bayes, support vector machines, random forests, and decision tree analysis. The authors find that for the purpose of classifying information, support vector machine analysis shows the best results. However, the study of Berkin et al. (2023) does not focus specifically on management reporting but rather on corporate reporting. Further analysis is, therefore, required if the results are applicable to specific fields or areas of management reporting.

Also, early work in the field of data mining like, for example, the study of Cohen et al. (2001, p. 109) shows solutions regarding decision-support systems by employing web-enabled software. This is applied with real case study firms for optimization purposes; for example, in the context of production and distribution problems or in project management and statistical control functions of large industrial firms. This points to a twofold function of techniques in big data analytics where one function is to provide optimization solutions, while another function is to inform management adequately on important issues to the business. Web-based data mining techniques are also applied to other areas such as healthcare (Wilson, 2006, p. 475).

It can, therefore, be stated that the available number and the sophistication of methods and techniques have largely increased. This is particularly visible when comparing modern approaches of big data analytics such as predictive analytics (Mookherjee et al., 2016, p. 49) or quantitative textual information processing (e.g. Bao & Datta, 2014, p. 1371; Dyer et al., 2017, p. 221) with early methods and techniques within the realm of knowledge management such as scoring models, logic tables, or similar approaches, which are stated by Liberatore and Stylianou (1995, p. 1296).

Furthermore, it must be emphasized that there is typically a realm of different types of techniques for solving a specific problem within a given context. For example, Holland et al. (2020, p. 54) provide an overview of possibilities for evaluating the online performance of airlines. These can include several types of descriptive techniques but also time series and regression analysis or methods in the realm of predictive analytics as well. Managers at firms are, therefore, challenged to implement a suitable solution for which a variety of different analytical approaches exist.

Finally, the initial findings confirm the existence of many different types and techniques available, as supported by the results of the systematic review. An overview of the techniques that have been mentioned in the body of articles that have been reviewed shows this. Such an overview is provided below in Table 32.3:

In addition, Grolinger et al. (2014); Dean & Ghemawat (2008); Condie et al. (2010); and Sagiroglu & Sinanc (2013) engaged in generic analytics modeling. Neumeyer et al. (2010); Cherniack et al. (2003); and Stonebraker et al. (2005) examined stream analytical modeling. Malewicz et al. (2010); Lumsdaine et al. (2007); and Salihoglu & Widom (2013) explore graph analytical modeling.

32.5 Conclusion

Regarding the systematic research performed in this paper, several limitations can be mentioned. For example, due to the large number of publications in the field, displaying a comprehensive overview is challenging. It is particularly worthwhile noting that it is possible that relevant content may not be identified, which would have enriched the topic further. This is possibly based on two reasons. First, a restriction was made regarding the search process, especially with respect to the selection of keyworks but also regarding the limitation toward literature for the subject area of business, management, and accounting. Second, by evaluating the inclusion of an article from the literature based on the abstract, it is possible that some relevant content may not be identified. However, it must be mentioned that the chosen way for inclusion procedure is an established method, used by other researchers as well (Mikalef et al., 2018; Sivarajah et al., 2017, p. 267; Zuiderwijk et al., 2021, p. 5). In addition, as already stated, much of the literature is of a relatively broad nature. While the selected sources show applicability to the area of management reporting, there is a lack of in-depth research on the topic, making it more difficult to draw meaningful conclusions on the subject. However, this is mentioned in the literature as a relatively common issue with AI-related terminology, as their use is superficially applied and dedicated, and focused research is actually scarce (Zuiderwijk et al., 2021, p. 15). As a result, there is some level of subjective interpretation of the sources regarding their applicability to management reporting.

32 Big Data Analytics in Management Reporting: A Systematic Literature Review 553

Table 32.3 Overview of methods and techniques mentioned in the reviewed literature

Technology	Examples from literature
Artificial neural networks	Classification of households for marketing objectives Kim et al. (2005, p. 264)
Big data analysis	Profitability analysis of projects in the construction industry Bilal et al. (2019, p. 1)
Textual information processing	Evaluation of accounting information Dyer et al. (2017, p. 221) Quantification of types of risk from textual disclosures Bao and Datta (2014, p. 1371).
Support vector machines	Improving management information with respect to fraud detection Cecchini et al. (2010, p. 1146)
Data mining techniques	Several different applications of web-based data mining are possible Cohen et al. (2001, p. 109) Specific applications of web-based data mining in healthcare Wilson (2006, p. 475).
Sentiment analysis	Application of sentiment analysis in the context of false online information Lian et al. (2020, p. 1).
Internet-of-things	Enriching corporate reporting methods with different media content Valentinetti and Flores Muñoz (2021, p. 549).
Predictive analytics	End-to-end predictive analytics and optimization are applied to marketing Mookherjee et al. (2016, p. 49). Predictive data analysis for reducing food waste at supermarkets Bell et al. (2021, p. 453) Prescriptive methods for measuring marketing success based on diverse metrics Gubela and Lessmann (2021, p. 1).
Mixed methods	Exploratory data analysis using text mining techniques applied to corporate reports Parra et al. (2017, p. 106) Promotion of UN Sustainability Goals via Internet-of-things technology that feeds information into blockchain de Villiers et al. (2021, p. 598) Use of cloud technology, augmented reality, blockchain, and deep learning algorithms in the information processing of firm processes Brock and Kohli (2023, p. 1).

Source: Own presentation

References

Akerkar, R. (2019). *Artificial intelligence for business.* Springer. https://doi.org/10.1007/978-3-319-97436-1

Alharthi, A., Krotov, V., & Bowman, M. (2017). Addressing barriers to big data. *Business Horizons, 60*(3), 285–292. https://doi.org/10.1016/j.bushor.2017.01.002

Appelfeller, W., & Feldmann, C. (2018). *Die digitale transformation des Unternehmens.* Springer. https://doi.org/10.1007/978-3-662-54061-9

Bao, Y., & Datta, A. (2014). Simultaneously discovering and quantifying risk types from textual risk disclosures. *Management Science, 60*(6), 1371–1391.

Beged-Dov, A. G., Ehrenfeld, S., & Summer, C. E. (1967). An overview of management science and information systems. *Management Science, 13*(12), B817–B837.

Bell, D., Lycett, M., Marshan, A., & Monaghan, A. (2021). Exploring future challenges for big data in the humanitarian domain. *Journal of Business Research, 131*, 453–468. https://doi.org/10.1016/j.jbusres.2020.09.035

Berkin, A., Aerts, W., & Van Caneghem, T. (2023). Feasibility analysis of machine learning for performance-related attributional statements. *International Journal of Accounting Information Systems, 48*(100), 597. https://doi.org/10.1016/j.accinf.2022.100597

Bilal, M., Oyedele, L. O., Kusimo, H. O., Owolabi, H. A., Akanbi, L. A., Ajayi, A. O., Akinade, O. O., & Davila Delgado, J. M. (2019). Investigating profitability performance of construction projects using big data: A project analytics approach. *Journal of Building Engineering, 26*(100), 850. https://doi.org/10.1016/j.jobe.2019.100850

Blanning, R. W. (1984). Management applications of expert systems. *Information & Management, 7*(6), 311–316. https://doi.org/10.1016/0378-7206(84)90026-0

Bouwman, M. J. (1983). Human diagnostic reasoning by computer: An illustration from financial analysis. *Management Science, 29*(6), 653–672.

Brock, J. K.-U., & Kohli, A. K. (2023). The emerging world of digital exploration services. *Journal of Business Research, 155*(113), 434. https://doi.org/10.1016/j.jbusres.2022.113434

Brocke, J., Simons, A., Niehaves, B., Niehaves, B., Reimer, K., Plattfaut, R., & Cleven, A. (2009). Reconstructing the giant: On the importance of rigour in documenting the literature search process. In *ECIS 2009 proceedings* (pp. 1–14).

Buschbacher, F. (2016). Wertschöpfung mit big data analytics. In U. Schäffer & J. Weber (Eds.), *Controlling & management review sonderheft 1–2016: Big data—zeitenwende für controller* (pp. 40–45). Springer. https://doi.org/10.1007/978-3-658-13444-0_5

Carey, J. M., & Kacmar, C. J. (2003). Toward a general theoretical model of computerbased factors that affect managerial decision making. *Journal of Managerial Issues, 15*(4), 430–449.

Carrie, A., & Banerjee, S. (1984). Approaches to implementing manufacturing information systems. *Omega, 12*(3), 251–259. https://doi.org/10.1016/0305-0483(84)90020-3

Cecchini, M., Aytug, H., Koehler, G. J., & Pathak, P. (2010). Detecting management fraud in public companies. *Management Science, 56*(7), 1146–1160.

Chapman, C. S., & Kihn, L. A. (2009). Information system integration, enabling control and performance. *Accounting, Organizations and Society, 34*(2), 151–169. https://doi.org/10.1016/j.aos.2008.07.003

Chen, M., Mao, S., & Liu, Y. (2014). Big data: A survey. *Mobile Networks and Applications, 19*(2), 171–209. https://doi.org/10.1007/s11036-013-0489-0

Cherniack, M., Balakrishnan, H., Balazinska, M., Carney, D., Cetintemel, U., Xing, Y., & Zdonik, S. B. (2003). Scalable distributed stream processing. In *CIDR* (Vol. 3, pp. 257–268).

Cohen, M.-D., Kelly, C. B., & Medaglia, A. L. (2001). Decision support with web-enabled software. *Interfaces, 31*(2), 109–129.

Condie, T., Conway, N., Alvaro, P., Hellerstein, J. M., Elmeleegy, K., & Sears, R. (2010). MapReduce online. In *Nsdi* (Vol. 10(4), pp. 20–33).

Davenport, T. H. (1998). Putting the enterprise into the enterprise system. *Harvard Business Review, 76*(4), 121–131. https://hbr.org/1998/07/putting-the-enterprise-into-the-enterprise-system

De Mauro, A., Greco, M., & Grimaldi, M. (2016). A formal definition of big data based on its essential features. *Library Review, 65*(3), 122–135. https://doi.org/10.1108/LR-06-2015-0061

de Villiers, C., Kuruppu, S., & Dissanayake, D. (2021). A (new) role for business – Promoting the United Nations' sustainable development goals through the internet-of-things and blockchain technology. *Journal of Business Research, 131*, 598–609. https://doi.org/10.1016/j.jbusres.2020.11.066

Dean, J., & Ghemawat, S. (2008). MapReduce. *Communications of the ACM, 51*(1), 107–113.

Denyer, D., & Tranfield, D. (2009). Producing a systematic review. In *The Sage handbook of organizational research methods* (pp. 671–689). Sage.

Dorschel, W., & Dorschel, J. (2015). Einführung. In J. Dorschel (Ed.), *Praxishandbuch big data: Wirtschaft – Recht – Technik* (pp. 1–13). Springer. https://doi.org/10.1007/978-3-658-07289-6_1

Dyer, T., Lang, M., & Stice-Lawrence, L. (2017). The evolution of 10-K textual disclosure: Evidence from latent Dirichlet allocation. *Journal of Accounting and Economics, 64*(2), 221–245. https://doi.org/10.1016/j.jacceco.2017.07.002

Economist. (2017). The world's most valuable resource is no longer oil, but data. *The Economist.* https://www.economist.com/leaders/2017/05/06/the-worlds-most-valuable-resource-is-no-longer-oil-but-data

Galetsi, P., & Katsaliaki, K. (2020). A review of the literature on big data analytics in healthcare. *Journal of the Operational Research Society, 71*(10), 1511–1529. https://doi.org/10.1080/01605682.2019.1630328

Gandomi, A., & Haider, M. (2015). Beyond the hype: Big data concepts, methods, and analytics. *International Journal of Information Management, 35*(2), 137–144. https://doi.org/10.1016/j.ijinfomgt.2014.10.007

Gartner. (2017). *Definition of big data—Gartner information technology glossary.* Gartner. https://www.gartner.com/en/information-technology/glossary/big-data

Gorman, M. F. (2016). From magnum opus to mea culpa: A cautionary tale of lessons learned from a failed decision support system. *Interfaces, 46*(2), 183–195.

Granlund, M. (2011). Extending AIS research to management accounting and control issues: A research note. *International Journal of Accounting Information Systems, 12*(1), 3–19. https://doi.org/10.1016/j.accinf.2010.11.001

Granlund, M., & Malmi, T. (2002). Moderate impact of ERPS on management accounting: A lag or permanent outcome? *Management Accounting Research, 13*(3), 299–321. https://doi.org/10.1006/mare.2002.0189

Grolinger, K., Hayes, M., Higashino, W. A., L'Heureux, A., Allison, D. S., & Capretz, M. A. (2014). Challenges for mapreduce in big data. In *2014 IEEE world congress on services* (pp. 182–189). IEEE.

Gubela, R. M., & Lessmann, S. (2021). Uplift modeling with value-driven evaluation metrics. *Decision Support Systems, 150*(113), 648. https://doi.org/10.1016/j.dss.2021.113648

Hariri, R. H., Fredericks, E. M., & Bowers, K. M. (2019). Uncertainty in big data analytics: Survey, opportunities, and challenges. *Journal of Big Data, 6*(44), 1–16. https://doi.org/10.1186/s40537-019-0206-3

Hashem, I. A. T., Yaqoob, I., Anuar, N. B., Mokhtar, S., Gani, A., & Ullah Khan, S. (2015). The rise of "big data" on cloud computing: Review and open research issues. *Information Systems, 47*, 98–115. https://doi.org/10.1016/j.is.2014.07.006

Holland, C. P., Thornton, S. C., & Naudé, P. (2020). B2B analytics in the airline market: Harnessing the power of consumer big data. *Industrial Marketing Management, 86*, 52–64. https://doi.org/10.1016/j.indmarman.2019.11.002

Howard, J. A., & Morgenroth, W. M. (1968). Information processing model of executive decision. *Management Science, 14*(7), 416–428.

Humby, C., & Palmer, M. (2006). *Data is the new oil.* https://ana.blogs.com/maestros/2006/11/data_is_the_new.html

Ibrahim, A. E. A., Elamer, A. A., & Ezat, A. N. (2021). The convergence of big data and accounting: Innovative research opportunities. *Technological Forecasting and Social Change, 173*(121), 171. https://doi.org/10.1016/j.techfore.2021.121171

IDC. (2021). *Data creation and replication will grow at a faster rate than installed storage capacity, According to the IDC global datasphere and storagesphere forecasts.* https://www.idc.com/getdoc.jsp?containerId=prUS47560321

Jain, A. (2016). *The 5 V's of big data.* Watson Health Perspectives. https://www.ibm.com/blogs/watson-health/the-5-vs-of-big-data/

Janvrin, D. J., & Watson, M. W. (2017). "Big Data": A new twist to accounting. *Journal of Accounting Education, 38*, 3–8. https://doi.org/10.1016/j.jaccedu.2016.12.009

Kim, Y., Street, W. N., Russell, G. J., & Menczer, F. (2005). Customer targeting: A neural network approach guided by genetic algorithms. *Management Science, 51*(2), 264–276.

Kitchenham, B., Pearl Brereton, O., Budgen, D., Turner, M., Bailey, J., & Linkman, S. (2009). Systematic literature reviews in software engineering – A systematic literature review. *Information and Software Technology, 51*(1), 7–15. https://doi.org/10.1016/j.infsof.2008.09.009

Kroll, K., & Kittelberger, D. (2014). Management reporting – Konsequente Ausrichtung auf die Unternehmensstrategie und Branchenspezifika. In F. Keuper & R. Sauter (Eds.), *Unternehmenssteuerung in der produzierenden Industrie: Konzepte und Best Practices* (pp. 187–199). Springer. https://doi.org/10.1007/978-3-658-02142-9_9

Laney, D. (2001). *3D data management: Controlling data volume, velocity, and variety.* META Group. https://www.bibsonomy.org/bibtex/742811cb00b303261f79a98e9b80bf49

Leece, D. (1999). Applying data visualization and knowledge discovery in databases to segment the market for risky financial assets. *Managerial and Decision Economics, 20*(5), 267–280.

Lian, Y., Liu, Y., & Dong, X. (2020). Strategies for controlling false online information during natural disasters: The case of Typhoon Mangkhut in China. *Technology in Society, 62*(101), 265. https://doi.org/10.1016/j.techsoc.2020.101265

Liberatore, M. J., & Stylianou, A. C. (1995). Expert support systems for new product development decision making: A modeling framework and applications. *Management Science, 41*(8), 1296–1316.

Li, E. Y., McLeod, R., & Rogers, J. C. (2001). Marketing information systems in Fortune 500 companies: A longitudinal analysis of 1980, 1990, and 2000. *Information & Management, 38*(5), 307–322. https://doi.org/10.1016/S0378-7206(00)00073-2

Little, J. D. C. (1986). Research opportunities in the decision and management sciences. *Management Science, 32*(1), 1–13.

Lumsdaine, A., Gregor, D., Hendrickson, B., & Berry, J. (2007). Challenges in parallel graph processing. *Parallel Processing Letters, 17*(01), 5–20.

Mageto, J. (2021). Big data analytics in sustainable supply chain management: A focus on manufacturing supply chains. *Sustainability, 13*(13), 13. https://doi.org/10.3390/su13137101

Malewicz, G., Austern, M. H., Bik, A. J., Dehnert, J. C., Horn, I., Leiser, N., & Czajkowski, G. (2010). Pregel: A system for large-scale graph processing. In *Proceedings of the 2010 ACM SIGMOD international conference on management of data* (pp. 135–146). ACM..

Markoulli, M. P., Lee, C. I. S. G., Byington, E., & Felps, W. A. (2017). Mapping human resource management: Reviewing the field and charting future directions. *Human Resource Management Review, 27*(3), 367–396. https://doi.org/10.1016/j.hrmr.2016.10.001

May, J. H., Spangler, W. E., Wendell, R. E., & Zaun, H. U. (1991). A knowledge-based approach for improving information and decision making in a small business. *Information & Management, 21*(3), 177–189. https://doi.org/10.1016/0378-7206(91)90063-8

McAfee, A., Brynjolfsson, E., Davenport, T. H., Patil, D. J., & Barton, D. (2012). Big data: The management revolution. *Harvard Business Review, 90*(10), 60–68.

McCann, J. M., Lahti, W. G., & Hill, J. (1991). The brand manager's assistant: A knowledge-based system approach to brand management. *International Journal of Research in Marketing, 8*(1), 51–73. https://doi.org/10.1016/0167-8116(91)90007-T

Miah, S. J., Camilleri, E., & Vu, H. Q. (2022). Big data in healthcare research: A survey study. *Journal of Computer Information Systems, 62*(3), 480–492. https://doi.org/10.1080/08874417.2020.1858727

Mikalef, P., Pappas, I. O., Krogstie, J., & Giannakos, M. (2018). Big data analytics capabilities: A systematic literature review and research agenda. *Information Systems and E-Business Management, 16*(3), 547–578. https://doi.org/10.1007/s10257-017-0362-y

Mookherjee, R. R., Mukherjee, J., Martineau, J., Xu, L., Gullo, M., Zhou, K., Hazlewood, A., Zhang, X., Griarte, F., & Li, N. (2016). End-to-End predictive analytics and optimization in ingram micro's Two-Tier distribution business. *Interfaces, 46*(1), 49–73.

Moore, G. E. (1965). Cramming more components onto integrated circuits. *Electronics, 38*(8), 114–117.

Morabito, V. (2015). *Big data and analytics: Strategic and organizational impacts.* Springer International Publishing. https://doi.org/10.1007/978-3-319-10665-6

Morgan, N. A., Jayachandran, S., Hulland, J., Kumar, B., Katsikeas, C., & Somosi, A. (2022). Marketing performance assessment and accountability: Process and outcomes. *International Journal of Research in Marketing, 39*(2), 462–481. https://doi.org/10.1016/j.ijresmar.2021.10.008

Neumeyer, L., Robbins, B., Nair, A., & Kesari, A. (2010). S4: Distributed stream computing platform. In *2010 IEEE international conference on data mining workshops* (pp. 170–177). IEEE.

Nissan, E. (1987). Knowledge-based computer systems for tasks in hospitality management or related areas: Accommodation (lodging, alimentation) and leisure. *International Journal of Hospitality Management, 6*(4), 199–202. https://doi.org/10.1016/0278-4319(87)90030-2

Nord, J. H., & Nord, G. D. (1995). Executive information systems: A study and comparative analysis. *Information & Management, 29*(2), 95–106. https://doi.org/10.1016/0378-7206(95)00013-M

Palmer, M. (2006). *Data is the new oil.* ANA Marketing Maestros. https://ana.blogs.com/maestros/2006/11/data_is_the_new.html

Pappas, I. O., Mikalef, P., Giannakos, M. N., Krogstie, J., & Lekakos, G. (2018). Big data and business analytics ecosystems: Paving the way towards digital transformation and sustainable societies. *Information Systems and e-Business Management, 16*(3), 479–491. https://doi.org/10.1007/s10257-018-0377-z

Parra, C. M., Tremblay, M. C., Paul, K., & Castellanos, A. (2017). Exploratory content analysis using text data mining: Corporate citizenship reports of seven US companies from 2004 to 2012. *The Journal of Corporate Citizenship, 66*, 106–151.

Preston, A. M. (1991). The "problem" in and of management information systems. *Accounting, Management and Information Technologies, 1*(1), 43–69. https://doi.org/10.1016/0959-8022(91)90012-4

Rikhardsson, P., & Yigitbasioglu, O. (2018). Business intelligence & analytics in management accounting research: Status and future focus. *International Journal of Accounting Information Systems, 29*, 37–58. https://doi.org/10.1016/j.accinf.2018.03.001

Rom, A., & Rohde, C. (2007). Management accounting and integrated information systems: A literature review. *International Journal of Accounting Information Systems, 8*(1), 40–68. https://doi.org/10.1016/j.accinf.2006.12.003

Rudin, C., Ertekin, Ş., Passonneau, R., Radeva, A., Tomar, A., Xie, B., Lewis, S., Riddle, M., Pangsrivinij, D., & McCormick, T. (2014). Analytics for power grid distribution reliability in New York City. *Interfaces, 44*(4), 364–383.

Russom, P. (2011). Big data analytics. *TDWI Best Practices Report, 19*, 1–38.

Ryzhov, I. O., Han, B., & Bradić, J. (2016). Cultivating disaster donors using data analytics. *Management Science, 62*(3), 849–866.

Sagiroglu, S., & Sinanc, D. (2013). Big data: A review. In *Collaboration technologies and systems (CTS), 2013 international conference on* (pp. 42–47). IEEE.

Salihoglu, S., & Widom, J. (2013). GPS: A graph processing system. In *Proceedings of the 25th international conference on scientific and statistical database management* (p. 22). ACM.

Schön, D. (2018). *Planung und reporting im BI-gestützten controlling.* Springer. https://doi.org/10.1007/978-3-658-19963-0

Seddon, J. J., & Currie, W. L. (2017). A model for unpacking big data analytics in high-frequency trading. *Journal of Business Research, 70*, 300–307.

Seufert, A. (2014). Das Controlling als Business Partner: Business Intelligence &Big Data als zentrales Aufgabenfeld. In *Controlling und big data* (pp. 23–46). Haufe.

Seufert, A., Treitz, R., & von Dacke, M. (2017). Information als strategische Ressource. *Controller Magazin, 07/08*, 48–53.

Sheng, J., Amankwah-Amoah, J., & Wang, X. (2019). Technology in the twenty-first century: New challenges and opportunities. *Technological Forecasting and Social Change, 143*, 321–335. https://doi.org/10.1016/j.techfore.2018.06.009

Shi, Y. (2022). Big data and big data analytics. In Y. Shi (Ed.), *Advances in big data analytics: Theory, algorithms and practices* (pp. 3–21). Springer. https://doi.org/10.1007/978-981-16-3607-3_1

Singh, A. J., & Kasavana, M. L. (2005). The impact of information technology on future management of lodging operations: A Delphi study to predict key technological events in 2007 and 2027. *Tourism and Hospitality Research, 6*(1), 24–37.

Sivarajah, U., Kamal, M. M., Irani, Z., & Weerakkody, V. (2017). Critical analysis of big data challenges and analytical methods. *Journal of Business Research, 70*, 263–286. https://doi.org/10.1016/j.jbusres.2016.08.001

Souza, J., Leung, C. K., & Cuzzocrea, A. (2020). An innovative big data predictive analytics framework over hybrid big data sources with an application for disease analytics. In L. Barolli, F. Amato, F. Moscato, T. Enokido, & M. Takizawa (Eds.), *Advanced information networking and applications* (Vol. 1151, pp. 669–680). Springer. https://doi.org/10.1007/978-3-030-44041-1_59

Statista. (2020). *Big data analytics market global revenue 2025.* Statista. https://www.statista.com/statistics/947745/worldwide-total-data-market-revenue/

Stonebraker, M., Çetintemel, U., & Zdonik, S. (2005). The 8 requirements of real-time stream processing. *ACM SIGMOD Record, 34*(4), 42–47.

Taschner, A. (2013). *Management reporting.* Springer. https://doi.org/10.1007/978-3-8349-3823-7

Tranfield, D., Denyer, D., & Smart, P. (2003). Towards a methodology for developing evidence-informed management knowledge by means of systematic review. *British Journal of Management, 14*(3), 207–222. https://doi.org/10.1111/1467-8551.00375

Tsai, C.-W., Lai, C.-F., Chao, H.-C., & Vasilakos, A. V. (2015). Big data analytics: A survey. *Journal of Big Data, 2*(1), 21. https://doi.org/10.1186/s40537-015-0030-3

Valentinetti, D., & Flores Muñoz, F. (2021). Internet of things: Emerging impacts on digital reporting. *Journal of Business Research, 131*, 549–562. https://doi.org/10.1016/j.jbusres.2021.01.056

Vasarhelyi, M. A., Kogan, A., & Tuttle, B. M. (2015). Big data in accounting: An overview. *Accounting Horizons, 29*(2), 381–396. https://doi.org/10.2308/acch-51071

Warren, J. D., Moffitt, K. C., & Byrnes, P. (2015). How big data will change accounting. *Accounting Horizons, 29*(2), 397–407. https://doi.org/10.2308/acch-51069

Weichel, P., & Herrmann, J. (2016). Wie controller von big data profitieren können. In U. Schäffer & J. Weber (Eds.), *Controlling & management review Sonderheft 1–2016: Big data—Zeitenwende für Controller* (pp. 8–14). Springer. https://doi.org/10.1007/978-3-658-13444-0_1

Wilson, J. L. (2006). Developing a web-based data mining application to impact community health improvement initiatives: The Virginia Atlas of community health. *Journal of Public Health Management and Practice, 12*(5), 475–479.

Zuiderwijk, A., Chen, Y.-C., & Salem, F. (2021). Implications of the use of artificial intelligence in public governance: A systematic literature review and a research agenda. *Government Information Quarterly, 38*(3), 1–19. https://doi.org/10.1016/j.giq.2021.101577

Chapter 33
Using Enterprise Social Media Networks to Foster Team-Level Collaboration in a Project Organization

Thomas Ruf

Abstract This study investigates how to enhance collaboration within a project organization through the implementation of an enterprise social network (ESN). The theoretical framework employed is the adaptive structuration theory (AST), which incorporates the concept of stable appropriation. The study utilizes a structural equation model to examine the impact of ESN on project success and customer satisfaction. By promoting collaboration through the use of ESN, organizations can benefit from improved communication, knowledge sharing, and coordination among team members. The AST framework provides a theoretical lens to understand the social dynamics and interactions within a project-based setting.

Furthermore, the study explores the concept of stable appropriation, which refers to the consistent and effective utilization of ESN tools and features. The structural equation model is employed to analyze the influence of stable appropriation on project success and customer satisfaction. The findings suggest that fostering collaboration through ESN and promoting stable appropriation positively affects project success and customer satisfaction. Effective utilization of ESN tools facilitates efficient project management, enhances team productivity, and contributes to higher levels of customer satisfaction. These findings provide valuable insights for organizations seeking to improve collaboration within a project-based context. By implementing an ESN and promoting stable appropriation, companies can leverage the benefits of enhanced collaboration, ultimately leading to improved project outcomes and increased customer satisfaction.

Keywords Big data analytics · Management reporting · Explorative data modelling

---

T. Ruf (✉)
Faculty of Business, Mendel University in Brno, Brno, Czech Republic

© The Author(s), under exclusive license to Springer Nature Switzerland AG 2024
N. Tsounis, A. Vlachvei (eds.), *Applied Economic Research and Trends*, Springer
Proceedings in Business and Economics,
https://doi.org/10.1007/978-3-031-49105-4_33

559

33.1 Introduction

In recent years, social media applications have found broad applications in the corporate context under the heading of digital workplace. The new social media enables new forms of cooperation and communication between all players within the company or beyond company boundaries between companies, customers, and partners. The use of social media has been accelerated by the increasing spatial and temporal decoupling of collaboration, working in virtual teams, and working in agile organizational forms.

The use of social media technologies in companies is often referred to as enterprise social network (ESN) in the literature and publications.

As a definition for enterprise social media, numerous literature cites Leonardi (2014):

> Web-based platforms that allow workers to communicate messages with specific co-workers or broadcast messages to everyone in the organization; explicitly indicate or implicitly reveal particular co-workers as communication partners; post, edit, and sort text and files linked to themselves or others; and view the messages, connections, text, and files communicated, posted, edited and sorted by anyone else in the organization at any time of their choosing.

Modern, integrated enterprise social network platforms combine three technology areas: collaboration, communication, and transaction. They thus offer advantages in collaboration, innovation, knowledge management, information dissemination and exchange, networking, and leadership (Turban et al., 2011). Due to their broad applications, ESNs offer various research perspectives.

The main point of this research is whether ESNs have a positive impact on the success of project work and increase customer satisfaction. Due to the increasing importance of ESN in business practice, there is a need for action to examine how these technologies can be instrumentalized to increase efficiency and effectiveness from a theoretical and practical economic perspective.

The Corona pandemic has further increased spatial decoupling, reducing direct physical interaction within teams. An empirical study examining the use of social media applications to promote team-level collaboration makes a timely scientific contribution and provides new insights.

The goal of this paper is to help fill scientific gaps related to the use of enterprise social media to increase team efficiency. To this end, a theory-led and hypothesis-testing study will be conducted to conceptualize and operationalize the use of enterprise social media applications to promote collaboration at the team level.

The focus of this work is the question of how social media applications can be used in the company and at the team level to promote cooperation between all players. Another point of investigation is the impact of the commitment from the point of view of employees and management. To this end, situational factors are also taken into account in the investigation.

The following questions are derived for the study:

• What are the benefits of using enterprise social media networks at the team level?

- How does the use of enterprise social media networks affect project success?
- How can the use of enterprise social media networks to drive team-level performance be conceptualized and operationalized?

The focus of this work is on the third question, which is the conceptualization and operationalization of the use of social media applications. This is based on the basic hypothesis that the use of social media applications to promote collaboration can be described as a complex, multidimensional construct. The measurement of such constructs requires conceptualization and operationalization (Homburg & Giering, 1996). Conceptualization here means the acquisition of the construct dimensions and the subsequent development of the measuring instrument as operationalization (Homburg & Giering, 1996).

33.2 Literature Review

In the private sphere, the use of social networks, such as Twitter, Facebook, LinkedIn, and Instagram, is widespread.

Today's employees expect to find the technologies in the company that they are familiar with from their private environment. From the company's point of view, it is, therefore, advisable to follow this wish in order to be attractive as an employer and to increase employee commitment. Enterprise social networks (ESN) have become established in the corporate context (Wehner et al., 2017). Therefore, enterprise social networks could provide new insights for collaboration, communication, and knowledge management with the goal of increasing employee performance and engagement and intensifying knowledge building and sharing within the organization. Many organizations are now using social features on the intranet to improve their operations (Suh & Bock, 2015). Social technologies are now an accepted concept as more and more companies recognize the potential of an ESN.

Key ESN functionalities include collaboration, content, communication, and transaction. Collaboration facilitates the exchange and distribution of information between employees across the different ESN channels synchronously or asynchronously (Kuegler et al., 2015). The ESN supports the sharing of images, videos, blogs, wikis, and documents that can be collaborated on. Chat, comments, and video conferencing are available for communication (Kim, 2018). The above functions are only a selection of the common functions of an ESN. Analogous to social networks in a non-commercial setting, an organization can create profiles and blogs in the ESN for managers and employees to facilitate the identification of people and know-how within the organization in a simple but effective way (Kuegler et al., 2015).

Employee networking through ESN increases individual performance, knowledge sharing, and collaboration. (Bhandari & Yasunobu, 2009). Social networking is responsible for positive personal performance development.

An ESN that connects teams significantly influences employee innovation while promoting cross-team collaboration (Risius & Beck, 2014). Therefore, it would be recommendable that an organization adopt the most effective tool, like ESN, that could assist in maintaining employee collaboration to boost their productivity (Chin et al., 2015). In large companies, company-wide projects are regularly carried out, which require extensive and effective participation of employees. In addition to the individual work experience with which tasks are effectively performed, teamwork is a more fundamental factor in achieving the strategic goals set when implementing such projects in a company (Richter & Riemer, 2009). Adopting ESN will be the best option to make positive achievements in collaboration in a project team in an organization.

Especially in international and/or large companies, collaboration is a fundamental factor for achieving goals that must be taken into account and ensured. Many studies have looked at collaboration, but social networks have hardly been considered. Therefore, the study examines the influence of ESN on collaboration in team projects.

Enterprise social networks have become very important in the organizational context, especially in large internationally operating companies. Many publications and contributions at conferences covering a wide range of topics underline the relevance of theory and practice. Some literature has developed various focuses concerning the influence of ESN on the collaboration in teams in a large organization. For instance, Wehner et al. (2017) developed literature supporting research and practice and defined a framework for classification into three levels to structure the focus of the different publications. First is the technical focus, which refers to the software in particular technical aspects and functionalities, the user experience or employee experience, and questions about the implementation and introduction of the software. Second is the individual focus which concentrates on the employees and their immediate environment. The personal focus has typical questions about employees' benefits and motivation to use ESN. The third is the organizational focus, which is also the focus of this thesis on examining short- and long-term effects from a company perspective.

The focus is on the categories of performance enhancement, collaboration, and knowledge management, which corresponds to the classification organizational focus. Extended search for relevant literature for the topic used the Bielefeld Academic Search Engine (BASE, basesearch.net), the metasearch Google Scholar (scholar.google.com), and the research network Research Gate (research-gate.Net). For instance, Azaizah et al. (2018), while focusing on social network analysis, found that improved communication and knowledge sharing within and between organizations' units can be achievable through ESN implementation. Good communication is the basis under which collaboration is feasible, with knowledge sharing ensuring a high level of cooperation. Bertin et al. (2020) also say that the same leads to better access to shared information within teams. Furthermore, new cross-organizational informal connections will be developed and foster cohesion. The authors also claim that implementing ESN will ensure information access in a single source, most relevant for new employees or team members. Bertin et al. (2020) further say that developing a central point where the workforce or relevant actors can access information is critical for collaboration because it ensures that the employees access the same information relevant to a specific project.

Bertin et al. (2020) insist that the social culture that ESN creates ensures improved information flow, which guarantees increased collaboration efficiency. The formation of a shared vision and creation of the basis of trust are possible with the support of ESN. The technology also promotes the development of knowledge networks, which positively affects the solution of problems and thus influences work performance. Ellison et al. (2015) also weigh on the same about the impact of ESN on team collaboration in large organizations, arguing that the technology promotes internal knowledge sharing, especially in distributed organizations. Caron-Fasan et al. (2020) hold the same opinion claiming that large organizations can rely on ESN to ensure project teams' success because it promotes knowledge spread among team members. Besides creating functional knowledge markets within the case method company, experts become visible within the company.

Kuegler et al. (2015), in their explanatory factor analysis, identified that ESN promotes networking among employees, which positively influences knowledge sharing, individual performance, and collaboration. They insist that positive personal performance development is promoted through social connectedness. According to Kuegler et al. (2015), an enterprise social network that connects teams has a powerful effect on employee innovation and positively impacts cross-team collaboration. They insist that improving the coordination processes in the group is also another benefit to large organizations for project teams associated with ESN. Lal (2016) says that the effect is pronounced explicitly in temporarily and geographically dispersed teams. He says that employees can overcome temporal and geographical separations to develop social bonds more quickly than conventional digital media.

Moreover, Mäntymäki and Riemer (2014) suggest that ESN implementation positively influences work processes; enterprise social network platforms play a vital role in information gathering and sharing among employees. According to Rahman et al. (2020), ESNs promote social capital formation by fostering networking among employees and forming shared views and beliefs. Such facilitates knowledge transfer, which, in turn, impacts work performance. Seebach (2012) gives an opinion on the same stating that ESN increases bonding strength between employees and within teams. Positive support in the search for knowledge and experts. Collaboration among team members is fundamental since it impacts performance and productivity. Therefore, a company must identify the most effective and relevant strategy to promote positive engagement among its workforce (Mäntymäki & Riemer, 2014). The best approach should be reliable, efficient, adaptive, and responsive to change since change is inevitable. Therefore, ESN is a recommendable solution to challenges in team collaboration in an organization.

According to Rahman et al. (2020), ESN could be responsible for new insights into cooperation, communication, and knowledge creation to enhance employee performance and engagement and improve organizational knowledge-creation activities. Many organizations are now using social features on the intranet to improve their operations. ESN can help employees to quickly and easily find colleagues with specific skills, share knowledge and collaborate on a project. Using social tools has much potential value in enhancing collaboration, knowledge sharing, and communication within and across the organization.

Full implementation of social technologies provides the opportunity of improving employee productivity. More efficient and effective collaboration within and outside an organization ensures the realization of more value (Seebach, 2012). Social networks promote improved access to valuable information within the team. Networking among employees is useful because an ESN promotes positively influencing individual performance, knowledge sharing, and collaboration. An ESN that connects teams significantly affects employee innovation while promoting cross-team collaboration (Mäntymäki & Riemer, 2014). Therefore, it would be recommended that an organization adopt the most effective tool, like an ESN, that could assist in maintaining employee collaboration to boost their productivity.

The research object is the company's internal social media application, hereinafter referred to as the Enterprise Social Network, which is used for the study.

The enterprise social network is an integrated social media platform based on the Jive software (www.jivesoftware.com). The main goal for the use of this software is the networking of employees nationally and internationally. The enterprise social network was launched in February 2013. Currently, it has approximately 110,000 (as of March 2018) registered users and, with a total workforce of 220,000, has achieved a relatively high level of penetration in the company or organization. The launch of the enterprise social network was accompanied by internal communication measures.

The integrated social media platform provides employees with a range of functionalities based on other social networks such as Facebook or Google Currents.

During registration, the software generates a profile of the employee. In addition to the general information such as contact data with a photo, the employee can also add personal information such as qualifications, interests, and projects. All information is voluntary. Access to the contents of the enterprise social network without registration is not possible. Open and closed groups can be formed for collaboration, which are created and managed independently by the employees. Numerous communities have formed in everyday organizational life. To create content, the user can use functions such as blogs, status messages, wikis, and simple document management. The content can be rated, shared, and commented on by the community. Current events and new activities are represented on the enterprise social network by the "Activity Stream." The "Activity Stream" represents an aggregation of all new activities from groups or persons. If you join or "follow" a group, its activities appear in the personal "Activity Stream." The term "follow" here means that you subscribe to the content of a person or group and would like to be informed about new activities. In a volatile medium, such as a social network, there is a risk that updated information in the activity stream will flow unread in the current. The activity stream cannot be edited; it is not possible to manipulate prominent contributions.

The enterprise social network represents management as a medium for increasing locomotion and cohesion. In the pool or project organization under consideration, a closed group is used in the enterprise social network. In this group, employees are informed about organizational topics such as events, guidelines, and best practices. This information is provided by the pool management or by the employees themselves.

The adaptive structuration theory (Desanctis & Poole, 1994), AST, was chosen as the theoretical basis for the study. The AST is a well-known theoretical framework developed by sociologist Anthony Giddens in the field of organizational studies. It is not directly comparable to the usual technology acceptance models because its focus is broader, and it examines the relationship between technology and social structures within organizations. It goes beyond individual-level factors to examine the complex interplay between technology, social structures, agency, power, and control.

With regard to the successful use of technology, the adaptive structuration theory uses the concept of stable appropriation that reflects a holistic understanding of the use of social media applications. Stability is a social process that is formed by the factors of consensus, faithful commitment, and attitude of users. The more positive these three factors are in the group, the more successfully the team uses the technology in their work environment.

Thus, for the use of social media applications, a stable appropriation must be brought about, so that the management and group processes can run successfully and purposefully. The adaptive structuration theory with the postulate of stable appropriation thus has high relevance for the problem of this work. The measurement of the values is interpreted as the degree of maturity of appropriation.

33.3 Methods and Data

Based on the construct of stable appropriation and desired economic effects, the following research model was derived (Fig. 33.1):

From the research model, the hypotheses can be formulated:

H1: The construct "Stable Appropriation of the Enterprise Social Network in Teamwork" is a formative construct and shows the four dimensions of consensus, faithful use, attitude, perceived intensity of use, and media competence.
H2: The more stable the appropriation of the ESN, the higher the customer satisfaction.
H3: The more stable the appropriation of the ESN, the higher the compliance with project objectives.
H4: The more stable the appropriation of the ESN, the higher the improvement of project quality.
H5: The more stable the appropriation of the ESN, the better the achievement of cost targets.

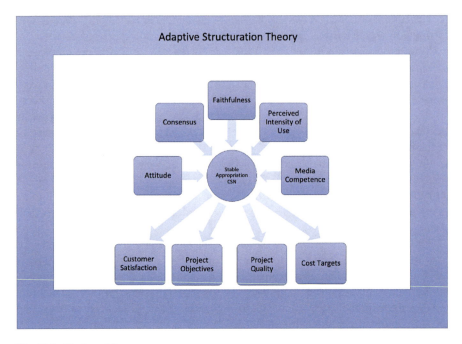

Fig. 33.1 Final model

I used partial least squares structural equation modeling (PLS-SEM) and Smart-PLS 3.0 software (Ringle et al., 2015) to estimate our model. According to Chin (1998), PLS estimation provides several benefits when compared to covariance-based methods, especially when testing complex structural models (Hair et al., 2017). Among other benefits, PLS maximizes explained variances and therefore increases prediction accuracy and does not make strict distributional assumptions. Furthermore, our research objective is exploratory, in which there is no clear consensus about the relationships that exist among the variables. PLS-SEM is primarily used to develop theories in exploratory research (Hair et al., 2017). Moreover, mediation, moderation, and multigroup analysis can be performed using PLS-SEM.

In order to validate the model outlined, this study conducts an empirical analysis based on an online survey of experts after the introduction and implementation of a social media platform. The respondents were employees of a company.

The written, standardized survey as a data collection method was preferred to the interview because of the homogeneous target group.

The survey tool Surveymonkey (www.surveymonkey.com) was used for the survey.

The respondents were employees of the studied company and project organization. The respondents are older than 21 and younger than 60 years. The data were collected in 2021. The survey was coordinated with the management of the field.

Respondents were sent the link to the survey via email to their company account. A window of 4 weeks was given for responses. The responses from the survey were anonymized in order to comply with data protection guidelines.

All employees of the corporate communications project organization were surveyed a total of 137 people (as of the 2020 survey). The response rate was 67.15% ($n = 92$), which is very satisfactory.

In the age structure of the respondents, the baby boomer generation of the last century still represents a significant group. In the distribution, the strongest group is Generation X, followed by Generation Y.

The questionnaire was divided into the following sets of questions:

- Agreement on a deployment (consensus)
- Meaningful use
- Attitude of the team members
- Intensity of use
- Media competence
- Influence on project efficiency and project effectiveness

33.4 Results and Discussion

The classical structural equation model consists of a measurement model and a structural equation between latent variables. Factors generate the measurements that reflect the latent constructs. The direction of relationships and their causality is either in an effect (reflective) or in a cause (formative) model (Bollen & Lennox, 1991; Wilcox et al., 2008). Consensus, attitude, faithfulness, identity, and media competence are reflective with respect to their indicators. Each indicator represents an error-afflicted measurement of the latent variable. The direction of causality is from the construct to the indicators, and observed measures are assumed to reflect variation in latent constructs. Altering the construct is, therefore, expected to manifest in changes in all the multi-item scale indicators.

Stable appropriation, however, is generated by the latent variables as a linear combination of consensus, attitude, faithfulness, identity, and media competence plus a disturbance term (Diamantopoulos & Siguaw, 2006). If any one of these measures decreases, the stable appropriation would decline. A formative measurement model happens when the measured variables are considered to be the cause of the latent variable. Here, stable appropriation is determined only by the five constructs consensus, attitude, faithfulness, identity, and media competence. No factor could be exchanged by another factor without changing the latent variable stable appropriation. This argumentation would lead to a formative measurement model for the HOC stable appropriation.

So the first hypothesis could be explained descriptively (Figs. 33.2 and 33.3).

I chose a reflective-formative model for the HOC. The arrows of the constructs point to the HOC to be formative because the constructs form the HOC stable

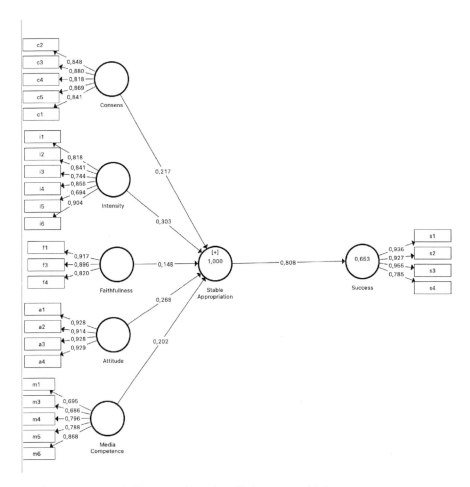

Fig. 33.2 Tested model (first step) with path coefficient resp. weightings

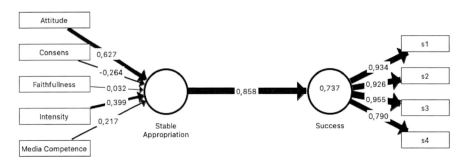

Fig. 33.3 Tested model (second step) with path coefficient resp. weightings

appropriation. Thus, the arrows represent the weights. In a formative model, the loss of a construct (indicator) can change the meaning of the model. If attitude, consensus, faithfulness, intensity, or media competence are replaced by another construct, the meaning of HOC (stable appropriation) changes as well (Hair et al., 2017).

The numbers on the arrows indicate the path coefficients or weightings. By comparing the relative sizes of significant path coefficients, statements can be made about the relative importance of the exogenous constructs for the prognosis of the endogenous constructs. The relationships between the reflective construct and measured indicator variables are called outer loadings, whereas the relationships between formative constructs and indicator variables are considered outer weights.

Within the second step of estimation, all weights with respect to the HOC stable appropriation are positive and significant (see Table 33.1). Attitude, media competence, and faithfulness showed the highest weights on stable appropriation. Consensus shows a positive weight on stable appropriation of 0.607 ($p < .001$). Stable appropriation shows a significant positive effect on success (loading $l = 0.858$; $p < 0.001$).

The effect size $f^2 = [R^2(\text{included}) - R^2(\text{excluded})]/1 - R^2(\text{included})$ for success is 2.796, which shows a large effect size (see Hair et al., 2017, p. 173).

The number in the circle indicates the determination coefficient R^2. R^2 is between 0 and 1. 1 means that the entire data spread may be explained by the constructs. The R^2 value indicates the proportion of variance of the endogenous construct explained by all predecessor constructs associated with the endogenous construct. For example, 73.7% of the variance of success is explained by the HOC stable appropriation ($R^2 = 0.737$). This implies that 26.3% of the variance is not explained. As a rule of thumb, $R^2 \geq 0.67$ shows a good fit, and $R^2 \geq 0.33$ shows a moderate fit (Chin, 1998).

Before testing the structural model, fit adjustment with standardized root mean square residual (SRMR) value was evaluated. SRMR is defined as the square root of the difference between the residuals of the sample covariance matrix and the hypothesized model. SRMR <0.08 indicates a good model fit (Henseler & Sarstedt, 2013). The result was 0.046, which indicated a good fit adjustment.

Bootstrapping was performed to provide a significance level for each hypothesized relationship; parameter settings for bootstrapping included no sign changes and 300 samples.

According to the results, stable appropriation, with its dimensions of faithfulness, consensus, attitude, intensity, and media competence, predicts significant success. All results are summarized in Table 33.2.

Table 33.2 shows that all hypotheses can be confirmed.

Stable appropriation shows a loading of 0.858 to success ($p < 0.001$). Item 1 (s1), customer satisfaction shows a loading of 0.934 ($p < 0.001$) to success. As both paths are significant with a positive loading, hypothesis 2 can be confirmed: The more stable the appropriation of the ESN, the higher the customer satisfaction.

Also for Item 2 (s2), compliance with project objectives, a positive loading of 0.926 ($p < 0.001$), can be obtained.

Table 33.1 Path coefficients and effect sizes (f^2)

	Path coefficients/loadings/weight	T Statistics	P values	Bias-corrected Bootstrap interval		f^2
				2.5%	97.5%	
Attitude → Stable Appropriation	0.940	26.382	<0.001	0.872	0.982	
Consensus → Stable Appropriation	0.607	6.102	<0.001	0.399	0.761	
Faithfulness → Stable Appropriation	0.733	7.130	<0.001	0.513	0.889	
Intensity → Stable Appropriation	0.932	24.288	<0.001	0.854	0.980	
Media Competence → Stable Appropriation	0.810	9.553	<0.001	0.630	0.940	
Stable Appropriation→ Success	0.858	35.833	<0.001	0.801	0.893	2.796

Table 33.2 Summary of hypotheses testing

Path	Beta coefficient/loading	t-value	p-value	Result
Stable appropriation → success	0.858	35.003	<0.001	Confirm
H2: Success → s1	0.934	72.569	<0.001	Confirm
H3: Success → s2	0.926	7.421	<0.001	Confirm
H4: Success → s3	0.955	104.377	<0.001	Confirm
H5: Success → s4	0.790	13.343	<0.001	Confirm

Confirm Note: Standardized root mean square residual = 0.046; Chi-square = 34.758

Together with the positive significant loading of stable appropriation to success ($l = 0.858$; $p < 0.001$), hypothesis 3 can be confirmed: The more stable the appropriation of the ESN, the higher the compliance with project objectives.

For item 3 (s3), improvement of project quality a significant positive loading to success could be observed ($l = 0.955$; $p < 0.001$).

So hypothesis 4 can be confirmed: The more stable the appropriation of the ESN, the higher the improvement of project quality.

Item 4 (s4), achievement of cost targets, shows a loading of 0.790 ($p < .001$) to success. Thus, hypothesis 5 can be confirmed: The more stable the appropriation of the ESN, the better the achievement of cost targets.

All five hypotheses of the study were confirmed, even if to varying degrees.

The theoretical basis of the study is AST with its central construct of stable appropriation, which has a direct influence on the degree of success effect in the use of collaboration systems. Group processes are very important for structure formation when using IT collaboration platforms, as they regulate the use of the platform and facilitate group collaboration. The definition of clear processes and rules for the use of the platform should prevent the platform from not being used in a meaningful way and affecting collaboration.

Processes can define, for example, how tasks and projects are organized within the group, how decisions are made, and how communication and collaboration should proceed. A clear definition of processes and rules can help users use the platform more effectively and avoid problems. It is also important that the processes are regularly reviewed and adjusted to ensure that they meet the needs of the group and that the use of the platform is optimized. In the target group studied, a project organization, the basic understanding of the relevance of processes is strong.

Other factors that contribute to stable appropriation from the user's perspective include:

1. Clear goals and requirements: It is important that the goals and requirements of the platform are clearly defined and communicated from the outset to enable effective use.
2. Ease of use: a user-friendly interface and intuitive navigation facilitate successful use of the platform.

3. Training and support: it is important that users are informed and trained about the functionality and possibilities of the platform in order to avoid problems and optimize use.
4. Availability of resources: it is important that the necessary resources, such as hardware, software, and network connections, are available to enable smooth use of the platform.
5. Feedback and adaptation: the platform should be regularly monitored and adapted to meet users' needs and solve problems.

Particularly noteworthy is the increase in customer satisfaction through the use of ESN. Enterprise social networks improve communication between customers and stakeholders by providing a quick and easy way to share information and collaborate. ESNs enable team members to share project documents and information, delegate tasks, and provide feedback. They also facilitate collaboration with external partners and customers by providing a common platform for communication and collaboration. A key factor is increasing transparency for all project participants as well as customers, partners, and suppliers.

The use of enterprise social networks (ESNs) can help meet project quality, budget, and schedule goals by improving communication and collaboration within the project team and with stakeholders. ESNs enable people to quickly and easily share information, delegate tasks, and provide feedback, which can help resolve issues faster and complete projects faster. They can also help meet budgets by, for example, reducing the need for physical meetings and travel.

All these aspects are interesting approaches for studies to investigate how the Corona pandemic changed collaboration with its facets such as the use of ESNs.

In the post-pandemic phase, it is becoming apparent that the hybrid working model will prevail and continue to exist in companies. This suggests that demand for virtual collaboration and communication tools will remain high even after the pandemic, as many companies have realized that they can work successfully without a physical presence.

The hybrid work model will be critical to the evolution of enterprise social networks. Thus, the functionalities and the way enterprise social networks are used in the company will change to better meet the needs of remote teams and hybrid models. Accompanying studies could make an important contribution here to analyzing requirements and potential and taking them to the next level of innovation.

In conclusion, it can be postulated that the study of enterprise social networks continues to be a very extensive research field that is not only limited to collaboration in enterprises.

References

Azaizah, N., Reychav, I., Raban, D. R., Tomer, S., & Roger, M. (2018). Impact of ESN implementation on communication and knowledge-sharing in a multi-national organization. *International Journal of Information Management, 43*, 284–294. https://doi.org/10.1016/j.ijinfomgt.2018.08.010. ISSN 0268-4012.

Bertin, E., Colléaux, A., & Leclercq-Vandelannoitte, A. (2020). Collaboration in the digital age: From email to enterprise social networks. *Systèmes d'information & management, 25*, 7. https://doi.org/10.3917/sim.201.0007

Bhandari, H., & Yasunobu, K. (2009). What is social capital? A comprehensive review of the concept. *Asian Journal of Social Science.* https://doi.org/10.1163/156853109X436847

Bollen, K., & Lennox, R. (1991). Conventional wisdom on measurement: A structural equation perspective. *Psychological Bulletin, 110*(2), 305–314.

Caron-Fasan, M. L., Lesca, N., Perea, C., & Beyrouthy, S. (2020). Adoption of enterprise social networking: Revisiting the IT innovation adoption model of Hameed et al. *Journal of Engineering and Technology Management, 56.* https://doi.org/10.1016/j.jengtecman.2020.101572

Chin, W. (1998). The partial least squares approach to structural equation modeling. In G. A. Marcoulides (Ed.), *Modern methods for business research* (pp. 295–298). Lawrence Erlbaum.

Chin, C. P.-Y., Evans, N., & Choo, K. M.-R. (2015). Enterprise social networks: A successful implementation within a telecommunication company. In *Conference: 21st Americas conference on information systems (AMCIS).*

Desanctis, G., & Poole, M. S. (1994). *Capturing the complexity in advanced technology use: Adaptive structuration theory* (Vol. 5). Organization Science.

Diamantopoulos, A., & Siguaw, J. A. (2006). Formative versus reflective indicators in organizational measure development: A comparison and empirical illustration. *British Journal of Management, 17*, 263–282. https://doi.org/10.1111/j.1467-8551.2006.00500

Ellison, N., Gibbs, J., & Weber, M. (2015). The use of enterprise social network sites for knowledge sharing in distributed organizations: The role of organizational affordances. *American Behavioral Scientist, 59*(1), 103–123. https://doi.org/10.1177/0002764214540510

Hair, J., Hult, T., Ringle, C., Sarstedt, M., Richter, N., & Hauff, S. (2017). *Partial Least Squares Strukturgleichungs-modellierung (PLS-SEM).* Vahlen Verlag. ISBN 9783800653607.

Henseler, J., & Sarstedt, M. (2013). Goodness-of-fit indices for partial least squares path modeling. *Computational Statistics, 28*(2), 565–580. https://doi.org/10.1007/s00180-012-0317-1

Homburg, C., & Giering, A. (1996). *Konzeptualisierung und Operationalisierung komplexer Konstrukte.* Marketing/ZFP/Journal of Research and Management. ISSN 0344-1369.

Kim, H.-Y. (2018). Effects of social capital on collective action for community development. *Social Behaviour and Personality, 46*(6), 1011–1028. https://doi.org/10.2224/sbp.7082

Kuegler, M., Smolnik, S., & Kane, G. (2015). What's in IT for employees? Understanding the relationship between use and performance in enterprise social software. *The Journal of Strategic Information Systems, 24*(2), 90–112., ISSN 0963-8687. https://doi.org/10.1016/j.jsis.2015.04.001

Leonardi, P. (2014). Social media, knowledge sharing, and innovation: Toward a theory of communication visibility. *Information Systems Research, 25*(4), 796–816. https://doi.org/10.1287/ISRE.2014.0536

Mäntymäki, M., & Riemer, K. (2014). *Information, Ideas and Input: The Value of Enterprise Social Networks.* Australasian Conference on Information Systems (ACIS). https://doi.org/10.13140/2.1.2868.1282

Rahman, I., Othman, A., Cruz, M., & Aziz, A. (2020). The implications of social media use on employee performance. *International Journal of Entrepreneurship and Management Practices, 3*, 22–33. https://doi.org/10.35631/IJEMP.311003

Richter, A., & Riemer, K. (2009). Corporate social networking sites—Modes of use and appropriation through co-evolution. In *20th Australasian conference on information systems.*

Ringle, C. M., Wende, S., & Becker, J.-M. (2015). *SmartPLS 3.* SmartPLS. Retrieved from http://www.smartpls.com

Risius, M., & Beck, R. (2014). You reap what you sow? How knowledge exchange effectiveness is affected by different types of communication in enterprise social media. In *47th Hawaii international conference on system science.* https://doi.org/10.1109/HICSS.2014.74

Seebach, C. (2012). Searching for answers—Knowledge exchange through social media in organizations. In *2012 45th Hawaii international conference on system sciences* (pp. 3908–3917). https://doi.org/10.1109/HICSS.2012.514

Suh, A., & Bock, G.-W. (2015). The impact of enterprise social media on task performance in dispersed teams. In *2015 48th Hawaii international conference on system sciences* (pp. 1909–1918). https://doi.org/10.1109/HICSS.2015.229

Turban, E., Bolloju, N., & Liang, T.-P. (2011). Enterprise social networking: Opportunities, adoption, and risk mitigation. *Journal of Organizational Computing and Electronic Commerce, 21*, 202–220. https://doi.org/10.1080/10919392.2011.590109

Wehner, B., Ritter, C., & Leist, S. (2017). Enterprise social networks: A literature review and research agenda. *Computer Networks, 114*(2017), 125–142. https://doi.org/10.1016/j.comnet.2016.09.001

Wilcox, J. B., Howell, R. D., & Breivik, E. (2008). Questions about formative measurement. *Journal of Business Research, 61*(12), 1219–1228. https://doi.org/10.1016/j.jbusres.2008.01.010

Chapter 34
Bankruptcy Prediction Using Machine Learning: The Case of Slovakia

Hussam Musa, Frederik Rech, Zdenka Musova, Chen Yan, and Ľubomír Pintér

Abstract This research paper develops bankruptcy prediction models using machine learning techniques, specifically logistic regression and neural networks. Analyzing a dataset of 8159 companies from the Slovak Republic, the study highlights the superior performance of neural networks over logistic regression in terms of classification accuracy. Neural networks capture intricate patterns and relationships within the data, leveraging their flexibility and adaptability to achieve higher precision in predicting bankruptcies. Despite COVID-19 challenges, the models perform well due to early containment measures and support for small- and medium-sized companies. However, methodological limitations hinder individual bankruptcy identification, relying on financial metrics. The global impact of the COVID-19 pandemic, energy crisis, Ukrainian conflict, and high inflation persists. Future research should incorporate these factors into bankruptcy models, not only for the Slovak Republic but also for other transitioning economies. This exploration will enhance the understanding and accuracy of bankruptcy predictions.

Keywords Bankruptcy prediction · Logistic regression · Neural networks · COVID-19 pandemic

34.1 Introduction

The emergence and disappearance of businesses are much more common now than they used to be. Corporate failures and bankruptcies have become more prevalent

---

H. Musa (✉) · Z. Musova · Ľ. Pintér
Faculty of Economics, Department of Finance and Accounting, Matej Bel University in Banská Bystrica, Banská Bystrica, Slovakia
e-mail: hussam.musa@umb.sk; zdenka.musova@umb.sk; lubomir.pinter@umb.sk

F. Rech · C. Yan
Department of Accounting, Dongbei University of Finance and Economics, Dalian, China
e-mail: frederikrech@gmail.sk; chenyan2001@136.com

© The Author(s), under exclusive license to Springer Nature Switzerland AG 2024
N. Tsounis, A. Vlachvei (eds.), *Applied Economic Research and Trends*, Springer
Proceedings in Business and Economics,
https://doi.org/10.1007/978-3-031-49105-4_34

and pronounced in quantitative terms (in terms of assets) due to globalization and the interdependence of national economies. The economies of individual nations no longer operate in isolation; they have become increasingly tied to one another. Because the economies of individual countries are increasingly dependent on each other, a financial crisis that starts in one country will spread to others almost immediately and become global (Klieštik et al., 2018). The COVID-19 pandemic, energy crisis, raging war in Ukraine, high inflation, the 2011 Great East Japan Earthquake, and the 2008 financial crisis are just a few recent examples of crises that have spread from their origin countries to the rest of the world in an alarming rate, reaching global scale.

In contrast to the localized origin of the 2008 financial crisis, the COVID-19 pandemic had immediate global implications. The pandemic-induced flash crash caused disruptions in company operations, ranging from temporary slowdowns to complete closures (Musa et al., 2022), with considerable heterogeneity among firms (Christine et al., 2020). Companies worldwide faced challenges such as folding or operating below normal capacities, and some even went out of business entirely (Afolabi et al., 2021). The implementation of social distancing measures proved challenging for certain companies, while remote work was not feasible for all. Consequently, unemployment rates surged, particularly among young individuals who were twice as likely to lose their jobs compared to their older counterparts (Lambovska et al., 2021). Additionally, companies faced obstacles such as insufficient capital to sustain operations, limited financial means for purchasing necessary materials, increased procurement costs, and inadequate access to loans or credit facilities (Afolabi et al., 2021). Consequently, companies experienced a significant decline in their ability to generate value (Mitan et al., 2021). These challenges were not evenly distributed globally, with emerging countries suffering more severe effects from the COVID-19 pandemic than developed nations. Smaller, fast-growing companies in emerging markets were particularly impacted due to their greater financial constraints (Christine et al., 2020). Unlike the 2008 global financial crisis, swift responses from central banks and substantial fiscal stimulus packages aided in the faster recovery from the COVID-19 pandemic (Harjoto & Rossi, 2021).

The presented research paper focuses on developing bankruptcy prediction models using machine learning techniques, specifically logistic regression and neural networks. The study specifically examines the context of the Slovak Republic, covering the period from 2018 to 2020. The research encompasses companies of all sizes and most industries within the region. To conduct the analysis, a dataset comprising 8159 companies was extracted from the Orbis database. The entire research process, including data analysis and model creation, was carried out using RStudio (R Core Team, 2022).

34.2 Literature Review

Over the last four decades, the application of bankruptcy prediction models has gained widespread popularity in advanced economies, particularly in the western regions. This trend can be traced back to the pioneering study conducted by Fitzpatrick (1932). Initially, bankruptcy prediction models were characterized by their simplicity and static nature. However, as the field progressed, the second stage of development introduced the incorporation of multiple indicators and innovative methods for multi-criteria evaluation.

Currently, there is a widespread interest in developing country- or industry-specific bankruptcy prediction models and carefully selecting the suitable methodology for their creation, as well as comparing them with other approaches, including both traditional and artificial intelligence methods. The underlying theme in these endeavors is to demonstrate that a model tailored to a specific country's macroeconomic environment or industry possesses superior predictive capabilities compared to a universal model. This assertion has been supported by numerous studies conducted in this field (Sponerová, 2021).

According to Kovacova and Kliestik (2017), in Slovakia, bankruptcy prediction gained prominence following the successful transition of the country in 1995, which triggered a robust institutional evolution. Initially, there were only a few studies focused on bankruptcy prediction during that period (see: Chrastinová, 1998; Gurčík, 2002). However, after the onset of the global financial crisis in 2008, there was a significant increase in attention toward this issue. Slovak companies, like their counterparts in other economies, had to grapple with various financial difficulties due to deepening globalization and increasing interdependence across markets (Kovacova & Kliestik, 2017).

The following researchers conducted their work on bankruptcy prediction within the context of the Slovak Republic. Svabova et al. (2018) present a model using linear discriminant analysis to predict financial difficulties in small companies in the Slovak Republic. The model, based on 24 financial ratios, achieves a high classification accuracy of 93.1% in the test sample and 93% in the training sample. It offers valuable insights for proactive measures and future research can focus on validating and improving the model with up-to-date data. Kovacova and Kliestik's (2017) study employed and evaluated the logit and probit models, comparing their classification accuracies. The findings indicate that the logit model exhibits slightly better classification accuracy compared to the probit model. Bod'a and Úradníček (2016) evaluate Altman's "Z-score model" in the context of Slovak corporate practice and confirm its usefulness in predicting bankruptcy. They compare three variants of the model, including the original and revised versions, and find that Altman's formula applies well in the Slovak setting. The original and revised versions of the model are particularly recommended for accurate classification. Similarly, Adamko and Svabova (2016) focused on evaluating the predictive power of Altman's global model using a dataset of companies from Slovakia. Štefko et al. (2020) compare bankruptcy prediction methods, specifically the Additive Data Envelopment Analysis (DEA) model (ADD model) and the Logit model, using a sample of 343 stable businesses in Slovakia's heating industry. It concludes that the DEA method is a reliable predictor of business failure, providing insights for enhancing financial health and competitiveness. Mihalovič (2018) developed a hybrid model using a genetic algorithm and neural network with data from 2014 to 2017, including healthy and bankrupt firms. Comparative analysis demonstrates the superior predictive capability of the developed model. Further studies on bankruptcy prediction in the Slovak Republic can be found in Lesáková et al. (2020), Horváthová and Mokrišová (2020), Sponerová (2021) and Vavrek et al. (2021), etc.

34.3 Methodology and Data

34.3.1 Data Sample

In order to create the bankruptcy prediction models, the financial data of the Slovak Republic companies from the Orbis database were used. The created set contains financial data from 8159 small, middle-sized, and large companies for the period 2018–2020. Due to the large number of businesses, we work with, it is not possible to determine individually how many overdue financial obligations each has, for how long it has them as well as determine the exact number of their creditors and it cannot be ascertained directly from the financial statements. Therefore, the following conditions will be used to categorize companies as bankrupt or non-bankrupt:

$$\text{assets} - (\text{liabilities} + \text{accrued liabilities}) < 0 \qquad (34.1)$$

and

$$\text{profit after taxes} \leq 0 \qquad (34.2)$$

The businesses that will be identified as non-bankrupt are those that meet one of the above-mentioned conditions.

34.3.2 Variable Selection

During the process of creating the models, 22 variables were taken into consideration, consisting of 21 financial variables and 1 categorical variable. The final selection of variables included in each individual model was determined using the outlined stepwise methodological processes (Table 34.1).

34.3.3 Methodology of Research

The following section describes the methodological steps involved in the creation of the econometric models for bankruptcy prediction in the Slovak Republic. As the

34 Bankruptcy Prediction Using Machine Learning: The Case of Slovakia

Table 34.1 Selected financial indicators

Indicator	Calculation algorithm
X01	Short-term assets/short-term liabilities
X02	Sales/total assets
X03	Net income/equity
X04	Working capital/total assets
X05	Net income/total assets
X06	(Long-term + short-term liabilities)/total assets
X07	Short-term assets/total assets
X08	Operating profit/total assets
X09	Cash and cash equivalents/total assets
X10	Short-term liabilities/total assets
X11	Short-term assets/sales
X12	Inventories/sales
X13	Long-term liabilities/total assets
X14	Net income/sales
X15	Cash and cash equivalents/short-term liabilities
X16	Working capital/sales
X17	Return on assets (profit before tax/total assets)
X18	(short-term assets—Inventory)/short-term liabilities
X19	Equity/(long-term + short-term liabilities) * 100
X20	Profit before tax/operating income
X21	Working capital
Size	

Source: Variables selected based on Bellovary et al. (2007) and Ravi Kumar and Ravi (2007); and data availability

main objective of this research is to create a bankruptcy prediction model, we will present a step-by-step approach for successfully creating such an application.

Microsoft Excel was used for variable ratio calculation and visualization. To perform the analysis, RStudio was utilized (R Core Team, 2022), which features the statistical programming language R.

34.3.3.1 Multiple Discriminant Analysis Methodological Steps

Using logistic regression, a bankruptcy prediction model for the Slovak Republic will be created. The following is an orderly description of the methodological process:

I. In the first step, companies are categorized into two groups: (1) bankrupt and (2) non-bankrupt. The criteria for this categorization are outlined above.
II. The next step is deciding on the variables to use in model creation. Here, a common approach in the field of bankruptcy prediction models is used:

examining past research articles and choosing the variables they use most frequently.

III. Following the categorization process, it was revealed that 66.44% of the companies are categorized as non-bankrupt, while 33.56% as bankrupt. Using this dataset to create a logistic regression model would result in a model with an almost 100% Type II error rate, meaning bankrupt companies would be wrongly classified as non-bankrupt. To prevent this and create a model with high overall classification and low Type I and Type II errors, it is imperative to create a balanced dataset comprising 50% bankrupt and 50% non-bankrupt companies.

IV. After loading the new balanced dataset into RStudio, a generalized linear model will be fit using the function <glm> from the stats package (R Core Team, 2022), with a specified family, which links the binomial error distribution and the logistic regression function (Campbell & Dobson, 1991).

V. When fitting the <glm> function in RStudio, a warning message may appear that says "glm.fit: fitted probabilities numerically 0 or 1 occurred." This warning is not an error and typically arises when outliers are present in the data. The recommended solution is to ignore the variables where the score cannot be calculated, instead of removing the outliers. It's important to keep the data as authentic as possible, and removing outliers is generally not considered good practice. Therefore, it is possible that the total number of predictions will be lower as compared to the number of inputs.

VI. To perform stepwise selection in RStudio, the function <step> from the stats package (R Core Team, 2022) is used with the backward direction specified. This function performs a stepwise algorithm to select the model with the highest explanatory power based on the AIC (Akaike information criterion). The process involves initially, including, all explanatory variables and then step-by-step excluding them (Hastie & Pregibon, 1992). Overfitting can cause the stepwise model to assign excessive weights to certain insignificant variables in some instances. To prevent overfitting, it is necessary to manually remove certain variables.

VII. The significance of each explanatory variable is determined by using a statistical test known as Wald's Z (Fahrmeir et al., 2013), and the final model is completed when most of the remaining variables are found to be significant at = 0.05. The iteration procedure can be extracted from the <step> function by calling out the ANOVA.

VIII. To verify the improvements in the new model as compared to the base model, the Omnibus test of model coefficients was used. Since RStudio lacks a dedicated output or function for this task, it was necessary to manually compute these values. The computation utilized inputs from the outputs of stepwise logistic regression, specifically null deviance and residual deviance, which are basically the chi-sq statistic values for the null model and final model, respectively. To calculate the improvements made by the new model relative to the null model, the difference between null deviance and residual deviance is computed. On the other hand, the improvements made within the last step of the iteration are determined by calculating the difference between the residual deviances of the two most recent steps. The p-value of the chi-sq statistics was calculated with the function <pchisq> from the stats package (R Core Team, 2022).

IX. Logistic regression analysis lacks a universally accepted analogous measure to assess goodness of fit, which represents the proportion of variance in the criterion explained by the predictors. However, there are multiple competing measures available, each with their own limitations, such as Cox and Snell and Nagelkerke's statistics (Cohen et al., 2014). In RStudio, it is possible to obtain the Cox and Snell and Nagelkerke's pseudo R-squared values by utilizing the <nagelkerke> function from the rcompanion package (Mangiafico, 2021), which provides both the pseudo R-squared and the log-likelihood value for the final model.

X. Once the creation process stops, the logistic regression output is displayed. Then the classification accuracy of the created model is assessed.

34.3.3.2 Neural Networks Methodological Steps

Using neural networks, bankruptcy prediction models will be developed for the Slovak Republic. The methodological process for creating these models is outlined as follows:

I. The first two steps are identical to the logistic regression approach.

II. Next, it is necessary to normalize data, which entails scaling the data to a uniform range, allowing for accurate comparisons between predicted and actual values. Neglecting to normalize the data can lead to the prediction value remaining constant across all observations, irrespective of input values. The method employed for normalization was max-min normalization. The corresponding RStudio code follows this structure:

```
<function(x) { return ((x - min(x)) / (max(x) - min(x)))>.
```

III. In the next step, the dataset will be randomly divided into two groups of companies—that is, the training file (neural networks are trained on it to achieve the best possible results)—it will be 20% of the data, the test file (the success of the classification of trained neural structures is determined)—80% of the data.

IV. To train the neural networks in RStudio, the function <neuralnet> from the neuralnet package (Fritsch et al., 2019) was used. This function allows flexible settings through custom-choice of activation function and algorithm. We will utilize the sigmoid activation function in combination with the resilient backpropagation with the weight backtracking algorithm. The architecture of the model consists of a single hidden layer containing 12 neurons. To train the neural networks, the maximum number of iterations will be limited to 100,000, and the threshold for the partial derivatives of the error function is 1. The number of iterations was set to 200. The code used in RStudio is as follows:

```
<modelSK = neuralnet(
  Bankrupt~.,
```

```
data=train.data,
stepmax = 100000,
rep = 200,
lifesign = "full",
hidden=c(12,1),
threshold = 1,
algorithm = "rprop+",
act.fct = "logistic",
linear.output = FALSE)>
```

V. The main focus is ex ante predictions and therefore the criterion for model selection will be based on out-of-sample classification accuracy for 2019. The selected model will be the one producing the highest classification accuracy with the lowest Type I and Type II errors, simultaneously.
VI. Once the algorithm successfully converged and the NN model was created, the classification accuracy of the created model is assessed.

34.4 Results

34.4.1 Logistic Regression

The first methodological approach used in this paper is logistic regression. First, the dataset had to be balanced in order not to overfit the model to type I error. This was achieved by balancing the dataset which now includes 50% bankrupt and 50% of non-bankrupt models. Next, training and testing datasets (80% and 20%, respectively) were created for the model fitting and validation procedures. It is important to note that not all outputs will be of the same count as the original dataset as some companies' scores cannot be estimated by logistic regression (due to the outlined warning). Nevertheless, the amount lost by the warning message is usually small and therefore will be ignored.

After balancing the dataset, it contains a total count of 5482 companies, with 2741 classified as bankrupt and 2741 classified as non-bankrupt. To construct a bankruptcy predictive model using logistic regression, the backward stepwise regression method was utilized. This method helped identify the coefficients of the selected explanatory variables, which were then incorporated into the final logistic regression model (Table 34.2).

In the 14th iteration step, the final model was created, which consisted of a constant and 9 explanatory variables. Among them, all were explanatory variables, and no artificial DUMMY variables were selected.

To evaluate the impact of individual variables on the dependent variable in the logistic regression model, Wald's Z test statistic was used. The results showed that all explanatory variables in the resulting model were statistically significant at the significance level of $\alpha = 0.05$, except for X20. Despite this, they were still included in the final model.

Table 34.2 Variables included in the final model for the Slovak Republic

	Coefficients	Estimate	Std. error	Wald test	p-Value
Step 14	(Intercept)	1.9990	0.1776	11.256	.000
	X05	−51.9200	6.3470	−8.18	.000
	X06	−0.5654	0.2852	−1.982	.047
	X07	−8.4160	0.3072	−27.396	.000
	X09	−2.3460	0.4573	−5.131	.000
	X10	7.6100	0.3686	20.644	.000
	X11	0.0467	0.0151	3.096	.002
	X15	0.0397	0.0155	2.57	.010
	X18	25.4100	5.1850	4.901	.000
	X20	−0.0001	0.0001	−1.337	.181

Source: Own processing

The final logistic regression equation that represents the global bankruptcy prediction model for the Visegrad Group companies, and defines the likelihood of an enterprise being bankrupt or non-bankrupt, is expressed by the following relationship:

$$\text{logit}(p)_{V4} = \ln\left(\frac{p}{1-p}\right) = 1.999 - 51.92X_{05} - 0.5654X_{06}$$
$$- 8.416X_{07} - 2.346X_9 + 7.61X_{10} + 0.0467X_{11} \tag{34.3}$$
$$+ 0.0397X_{15} + 25.41X_{18} - 0.0001X_{20}$$

where

X05 Net income/total assets
X06 (long-term + short-term liabilities)/total assets
X07 short-term assets/total assets
X09 Cash and cash equivalents/total assets
X10 Short-term liabilities/total assets
X11 Short-term assets/sales
X15 Cash and cash equivalents/short-term liabilities
X18 Return on assets (profit before tax/total assets)
X20 Equity/(long-term + short-term liabilities) * 100

To assess the quality of the explanatory power of the logistic regression-based prediction model, it is necessary to evaluate it using appropriate characteristics. The created model's iteration process is illustrated in Table 34.3, indicating a gradual improvement based on the individual step chi-square as well as the resulting model chi-square value (Resid. Deviance). The individual step chi-square values were statistically not significant meaning that variables were excluded from the model due to multicollinearity issues. The AIC value also indicates a gradual improvement in the estimated prediction error, id. est the relative quality of the model.

Table 34.3 Procedure of the iteration in the backward selection logistic global model for the Slovak Republic

| Step | Step | | | Model | | | AIC |
	Chi-Sq	df	p-Value	Resid. deviance	df	p-Value	
	NA	NA	NA	2781.726	1	.000	2827.726
-X08	0.0019	1	0.966	2781.728	2	.000	2825.728
-X12	0.0087	1	0.926	2781.736	3	.000	2823.736
-X13	0.0741	1	0.786	2781.81	4	.000	2821.81
-Size	0.0749	1	0.784	2781.885	5	.000	2819.885
-X04	0.1245	1	0.724	2782.01	6	.000	2818.01
-X22	0.1354	1	0.713	2782.145	7	.000	2816.145
-X03	0.3736	1	0.541	2782.519	8	.000	2814.519
-X02	0.6522	1	0.419	2783.171	9	.000	2813.171
-X17	1.1263	1	0.289	2784.297	10	.000	2812.297
-X14	0.2433	1	0.622	2784.54	11	.000	2810.54
-X21	1.4415	1	0.230	2785.982	12	.000	2809.982
-X19	1.6506	1	0.199	2787.633	13	.000	2809.633
-X01	0.0881	1	0.767	2787.721	14	.000	2807.721

Table 34.4 Omnibus test of model coefficients[a]

		Chi-square	df	p-Value
Step 14[b]	Step	−0.0881	1	.767
	Model	3288.4	9	.000

[a]Performed on training data
[b]The chi-square value is negative because it indicates the decrease in the chi-square value from the previous step

The Omnibus test of model coefficients in Table 34.4 confirms that the new model created after the 14th step is better at predicting bankruptcies than the base model which includes all the variables, and the new model signifies the final iteration of the backward selection logistic model. The chi-square value of the last iteration step indicates an increase of 0.088 compared to the previous step. The stepwise selection process excludes variables not only due to their lack of increase in the resulting classification but also due to multicollinearity. Based on the high p-values, it is likely that all variables were excluded due to the violation of multicollinearity. Based on the chi-square value for the model and its p-value, the stepwise selection model classification ability improved.

The model's explanatory power or pseudo R-squared is measured by Cox and Snell as well as Nagelkerke's statistics. According to the statistics, the model accounts for 52.8% and 70.4% of the dependent variable's variability, respectively (refer to Table 34.5).

The model validation relied on a threshold of 0.5, as the model was trained on a balanced dataset and the goal was to assess its predictive performance within the sample.

34 Bankruptcy Prediction Using Machine Learning: The Case of Slovakia 585

Table 34.5 Characteristic of the logistic regression model for the Slovak Republic

Model	Log likelihood differentiation	Cox and Snell R squared	Nagelkerke R squared
	−1646.3	.528	.704

Based on training data

Table 34.6 Classification table for the training data in the logistic regression model

		Reality	
		0	1
Prediction	0	1858 (87.97%)	254 (12.03%)
	1	334 (14.71%)	1937 (85.29%)

The overall predicting ability of the model is 86.58%

Table 34.7 Classification table for the testing data in the logistic regression model

		Reality	
		0	1
Prediction	0	462 (87.5%)	66 (15.14%)
	1	86 (12.50%)	482 (84.86%)

The overall predicting ability of the model is 86.13%

Table 34.8 The Slovak Republic logistic regression model classification accuracy results

	Correctly classified non-bankrupt	Correctly classified bankrupt	Type I error	Type II error	Overall classification
Training data					
2018	87.97%	85.29%	12.03%	14.71%	86.58%
Testing data					
2018	87.5%	84.86%	12.5%	15.14%	86.13%
Ex-ante prediction					
1 year	89.04%	68.53%	10.96%	31.47%	80.95%
2 years	86.23%	60.46%	13.77%	39.54%	76.07%

Source: own processing

The logistic regression model created for the Slovak Republic was divided into an 80% training sample (for classification results refer to Table 34.6) and a 20% testing sample for validation purposes (for classification results refer to Table 34.7).

The model's overall prediction accuracy remained stable on the testing data with small changes. Both type I and type II errors also remained stable near the values from the training data. However, it is important to note that this discriminant ability is overestimated as the same dataset was used for both model construction and verification. The ex-ante predictions are displayed in Table 34.8.

Interestingly, the model's ex ante predictions for correctly classifying non-bankrupt companies showed a slight improvement. This improvement can be attributed to the utilization of an unbalanced dataset for ex ante predictions, where the number of non-bankrupt companies increased.

The correct classification rate for bankrupt companies 1 year before bankruptcy was 68.53%, and for 2 years before bankruptcy, it was 60.46%. Overall, the model achieved a correct classification rate of 80.95% and 76.07% for companies 1 and 2 years before bankruptcy, respectively.

The 2 years before bankruptcy prediction covers the initial year of the COVID-19 pandemic, namely, 2020. The slight decline in prediction accuracy suggests that the pandemic was not a substantial exogenous factor contributing to the reduced accuracy of the created bankruptcy models. Furthermore, the exclusion of the control variable size from the model reinforces the indication that the COVID-19 pandemic did not affect the evaluated companies asymmetrically. This might be due to the prompt action taken by the Slovak government to swiftly implement early containment measures, coupled with the substantial financial support and subsidies allocated to small- and medium-sized enterprises during the COVID-19 pandemic. These measures enabled businesses that would have otherwise faced immediate bankruptcy to maintain their operations.

34.4.2 Neural Networks

The second methodological approach used was neural networks. As outlined above, the learning process of neural networks was capped at 100,000 steps with 200 repetitions. The threshold of the error improvements was set at 1. When constructing the model, all variables were included, and the model included a single hidden layer consisting of 12 neurons.

Neural networks are well known for overfitting problems. Although they can achieve superior results in training and testing datasets, the results frequently fall short when subjected to out-of-sample validation. The algorithm's convergence is achieved by meeting the minimum error improvement within 100,000 steps. However, the lowest error rate might not be an optimal criterion for selecting the best model as it only reflects the classification accuracy within the sample. Therefore, the selection process among the 200 repetitions will be based on out-of-sample validation, specifically the classification accuracy in 2019. Nonetheless, we will also present the within-sample classification accuracy.

The algorithm for the Slovak Republic neural network model achieved convergence successfully on 189 occasions but failed to meet the minimum improvement threshold within 100,000 steps 11 times, resulting in the absence of 11 models. Out of the 189 models, the model generated in the 86th repetition had the highest out-of-sample classification accuracy for the year 2019, with an estimated sum of squared error of 151.3065. Figure 34.1 illustrates the neural network architecture of the model produced in the 86th repetition.

34 Bankruptcy Prediction Using Machine Learning: The Case of Slovakia

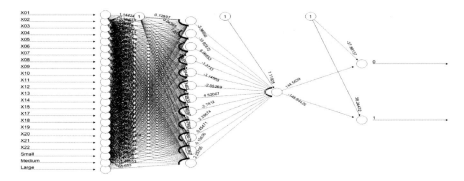

Fig. 34.1 Neural network architecture for the Slovak Republic. (Note: 11th repetition)

Table 34.9 Classification table for the 2019 data

		Reality	
		0	1
Prediction	0	5320 (98.23%)	96 (1.77%)
	1	2.793 (8.06%)	2.522 (91.94%)

The overall predicting ability of the model is 96.11%

Table 34.10 Neural network classification results

	Correctly classified non-bankrupt	Correctly classified bankrupt	Type I error	Type II error	Overall classification
Training data					
2018	99.20%	94.34%	0.8%	5.66%	97.56%
Testing data					
2018	97.88%	92.87%	2.12%	7.13%	96.20%
Ex ante predictions					
1 year	90.16%	76.49%	9.84%	23.51%	85.56%
2 years	85.34%	69.31%	14.66%	30.69%	80.18%

Source: Own processing

Upon validation with the 2019 dataset, the resulting model attained an overall classification rate of 96.11%, accurately classifying 98.23% of non-bankrupt and 91.94% of bankrupt companies. The rate of type I error was 1.77% and the type II error rate was 8.06% (Table 34.9).

The model was created on the training data where it achieved an overall classification accuracy of 97.56%, with correctly classifying 99.20% of non-bankrupt companies and 94.34% of bankrupt ones. Upon model validation on testing data, the classification accuracy slightly deteriorated in both type I and II error terms (Table 34.10).

The model achieved a classification accuracy of 90.16% for non-bankrupt companies and 76.49% for bankrupt companies when predicting bankruptcy 1 year in advance. However, when predicting bankruptcy 2 years in advance, the classification accuracy slightly declined. Both Type I and Type II errors increased by approximately 6 percentage points. Nevertheless, the model retained high overall classification rates in both cases.

Just like the logistic regression model, the neural network also did not exhibit a significant decline in prediction accuracy attributed to the COVID-19 pandemic. This finding further strengthens the notion that the pandemic did not play a substantial exogenous role in reducing the accuracy of the model.

34.5 Conclusion

This research paper has successfully focused on the development of bankruptcy prediction models using machine learning techniques, with a specific emphasis on logistic regression and neural networks. The study has provided valuable insights within the context of the Slovak Republic, covering the period from 2018 to 2020, and has encompassed companies of various sizes and industries within the region. The analysis was conducted using a dataset containing 8159 companies extracted from the Orbis database. Throughout the research process, including data analysis and model creation, RStudio (R Core Team, 2022) served as the primary tool.

Based on our analysis and evaluation, it becomes evident that neural networks exhibited superior performance compared to logistic regression in all aspects examined. The advantage of neural networks was apparent not only in terms of minimizing Type I and Type II errors but also in their ability to make accurate ex ante predictions for both 1 and 2 years before bankruptcy.

Neural networks demonstrated their strength by outperforming logistic regression in terms of classification accuracy, capturing more nuanced patterns and relationships within the data. Their ability to leverage complex architectures and learn from large amounts of data allowed them to better capture the intricate dynamics that contribute to bankruptcy outcomes. This flexibility and adaptability of neural networks proved invaluable in achieving higher accuracy and precision in the bankruptcy prediction task.

Moreover, the models' performance, although experiencing a slight deterioration in predictive ability, remained commendable even when faced with the unprecedented disruptions caused by the COVID-19 pandemic. Despite the challenges posed by the uncertain economic landscape and the unique circumstances brought about by the pandemic, both neural networks and logistic regression models were able to correctly classify a significant portion of companies. The swift response of the Slovak government in implementing early containment measures, along with the substantial financial support and subsidies provided to small and medium-sized companies during the COVID-19 pandemic, may account for this outcome. Thanks to these measures, businesses that would otherwise have been at risk of immediate bankruptcy were able to sustain their operations.

Nonetheless, the decline in classification accuracies could be attributed to methodological limitations, which may also serve as constraints within this study. Given the extensive number of companies encompassed in the dataset, it becomes impractical to identify bankrupt companies on an individual basis. Consequently, the study relies on financial metrics that indicate potential bankruptcies. Although these metrics offer utility, they do not provide definitive measurements of bankruptcies. It is conceivable that a company may appear bankrupt in 1 year but non-bankrupt in the following year due to slight improvements in its financial metrics.

The repercussions of the COVID-19 pandemic, energy crisis, ongoing conflict in Ukraine, and effects of high inflation continue to have a global impact. In future research, researchers could incorporate these factors into model constructions to explore their influence on bankruptcies. This analysis could extend beyond the Slovak Republic to encompass other transitioning economies as well.

Acknowledgments This paper has been supported by the Scientific Grant Agency of the Slovak Republic under project VEGA No. 1/0579/21 "Research on Determinants and Paradigms of Financial Management in the Context of the COVID-19 Pandemic." The authors would like to express their gratitude to the Scientific Grant Agency of the Ministry of Education, Science, Research and Sport of the Slovak Republic for the financial support of this research and publication.

References

Adamko, P., & Svabova, L. (2016). Prediction of the risk of bankruptcy of Slovak companies. In *8th international scientific conference managing and modelling of financial risks*.

Afolabi, K. B., Tijani, A. A., Osagie, R. O., & Afolabi, K. B. (2021). Effect of strategic alliance and partnership on the survival MSMEs post COVID-19 pandemic. *Ekonomicko-Manazerske Spektrum, 15*, 126–137.

Bellovary, J. L., Giacomino, D. E., & Akers, M. D. (2007). A review of bankruptcy prediction studies: 1930-present. *Journal of Financial Education, 33*(Winter). https://doi.org/10.1017/CBO9781107415324.004

Boďa, M., & Úradníček, V. (2016). The portability of Altman's Z-score model to predicting corporate financial distress of Slovak companies. *Technological and Economic Development of Economy, 22*(4), 532–553. https://doi.org/10.3846/20294913.2016.1197165

Campbell, M. J., & Dobson, A. J. (1991). An introduction to generalized linear models. *Biometrics, 47*(1), 347. https://doi.org/10.2307/2532526

Chrastinová, Z. (1998). *Methods of evaluating the economic creditworthiness and predicting the financial situation of agricultural enterprises* (Metódy hodnotenia ekonomickej bonity a predikcie finančnej situácie poľnohospodárskych podnikov) (pp. 34). VÚEPP Bratislava.

Christine, M., Besart, A.-A., Cirera, A. X., Cruz, M., Davies, E., Grover, A., Iacovone, L., Kilinc, U., Medvedev, D., Maduko, F. O., Poupakis, S., Torres, J., & Tran, T. T. (2020). *Unmasking the impact of COVID-19 on businesses firm level evidence from across the world*. http://www.worldbank.org/prwp

Cohen, P., Cohen, P., West, S. G., & Aiken, L. S. (2014). Applied multiple regression/correlation analysis for the behavioral sciences. In *Applied Multiple regression/correlation analysis for the behavioral sciences*. https://doi.org/10.4324/9781410606266

Fahrmeir, L., Kneib, T., Lang, S., & Marx, B. (2013). Regression: Models, methods and applications. In *Regression: Models, methods and applications* (Vol. 9783642343339). https://doi.org/10.1007/978-3-642-34333-9

Fitzpatrick, P. J. (1932). A comparison of ratios of successful industrial enterprises with those of failed firms. *Certified Public Accountant, 6*, 727–731.

Fritsch, S., Guenther, F., & Wright, M. (2019). Neuralnet: Training of neural networks. *R Package Version, 1*(44), 6. https://Github.Com/Bips-Hb/Neuralnet

Gurčík, Ľ. (2002). G-index—A method of predicting the financial status of agricultural enterprises (G-index—metóda predikcie finančného stavu poľnohospodárskych podnikov). *Agricultural Economics, 48*(8), 373–378.

Harjoto, M. A., & Rossi, F. (2021). Market reaction to the COVID-19 pandemic: Evidence from emerging markets. *International Journal of Emerging Markets, 18*, 173. https://doi.org/10.1108/IJOEM-05-2020-0545

Hastie, T. J., & Pregibon, D. (1992). Generalized linear models. In *Generalized linear models*. Wadsworth & Brooks/Cole.

Horváthová, J., & Mokrišová, M. (2020). Comparison of the results of a data envelopment analysis model and logit model in assessing business financial health. *Information (Switzerland), 11*(3), 1–20. https://doi.org/10.3390/info11030160

Klieštik, T., Klieštiková, J., Kováčová, M., Švábová, L., Valášková, K., Vochozka, M., & Oláh, J. (2018). *Prediction of financial health of business entities in transitioning economies*. Addleton Academic Publishers.

Kovacova, M., & Kliestik, T. (2017). Logit and probit application for the prediction of bankruptcy in Slovak companies. *Equilibrium. Quarterly Journal of Economics and Economic Policy, 12*(4), 775–791. https://doi.org/10.24136/eq.v12i4.40

Lambovska, M., Sardinha, B., & Belas, J. (2021). Impact of the COVID-19 pandemic on youth unemployment in the european. *Ekonomicko-Manazerske Spektrum, 15*(1), 55–63.

Lesáková, Ľ., Gundová, P., & Vinczeová, I. (2020). The practice of use of models predicting financial distress in Slovak companies. *Journal of Eastern European and Central Asian Research, 7*(1), 123–136. https://doi.org/10.15549/jeecar.v7i1.369

Mangiafico, S. S. (2021). rcompanion: Functions to support extension education program evaluation. In *Buildings*. The Comprehensive R Archive Network.

Mihalovič, M. (2018). The use of scoring models in predicting the default of economic entities in the Slovak Republic (Využitie skóringových modelov pri predikcii defaultu ekonomických subjektov v Slovenskej republike). *Politicka Ekonomie, 66*(6), 689–708. https://doi.org/10.18267/J.POLEK.1226

Mitan, A., Siekelova, A., Rusu, M., & Rovnak, M. (2021). Value-based management: A case study of Visegrad Four countries. *Ekonomicko-Manazerske Spektrum, 15*(2), 87–98.

Musa, H., Rech, F., Yan, C., & Musova, Z. (2022). The deterioration of financial ratios during the Covid-19 pandemic: Does corporate governance matter? *Folia Oeconomica Stetinensia, 22*(1), 219–242. https://doi.org/10.2478/FOLI-2022-0011

R Core Team. (2022). *R: A language and environment for statistical computing*. R Foundation for Statistical Computing. https://www.r-project.org/

Ravi Kumar, P., & Ravi, V. (2007). Bankruptcy prediction in banks and firms via statistical and intelligent techniques—A review. *European Journal of Operational Research, 180*(1), 1–28. https://doi.org/10.1016/J.EJOR.2006.08.043

Sponerová, M. (2021). Bankruptcy prediction: The case of The Czech Republic and Slovakia. *Selected Papers (Part of ITEMA Conference Collection)*, 65–71. https://doi.org/10.31410/itema.s.p.2021.65

Štefko, R., Horváthová, J., & Mokrišová, M. (2020). Bankruptcy prediction with the use of data envelopment analysis: An empirical study of Slovak businesses. *Journal of Risk and Financial Management, 13*(9), 212. https://doi.org/10.3390/JRFM13090212

Svabova, L., Durica, M., & Podhorska, I. (2018). Prediction of default of small companies in the Slovak Republic. *Economics and Culture, 15*(1), 88–95. https://doi.org/10.2478/JEC-2018-0010

Vavrek, R., Gundová, P., Vozárová, I. K., & Kotulič, R. (2021). Altman model verification using a multi-criteria approach for slovakian agricultural enterprises. *E a M: Ekonomie a Management, 24*(1), 146–164. https://doi.org/10.15240/TUL/001/2021-1-010

Chapter 35
Value Creation in Automotive Industry in Slovakia

Ľuboš Elexa

Abstract Analytical and methodological instruments evaluating the performance of companies have a long history and are rich in quantity. Each one has its pros and cons, many are frequently criticized, or are more or less suitable just for research or practical evaluation. In the context of new environmental or innovation challenges the automotive production faces, this paper aims to analyze the added value created in the automotive industry in Slovakia at the level of final assembly in the long-term run, including its structure and deviations and to identify main differences between individual producers. The paper focuses on final car producers in Slovakia in the period from 2009 to 2021 and compares them according to generated accounting value-added, its dynamics and structural components, main identified factors, productivity measures, and according to the economic value-added (EVA) ZERO threshold. The results brought many specific details of long-term production, in which individual companies differ, specifics hidden behind them and the effectiveness, by which these companies have achieved their production and financial success.

Keywords Value · Economic value added · Automotive industry · Final assembly

35.1 Introduction

The concept of value creation and its gradual distribution out of the company became an integral part (and factor) in the process of building competitive business strategies (Di Gregorio, 2013). As a result, value gained a significant impact on all business areas, which has manifested in an effort to understand the stages of its generation and key creators, both in daily management on the corporate level (Coff,

---

Ľ. Elexa (✉)
Faculty of Economics, Matej Bel University in Banská Bystrica, Banská Bystrica, Slovakia
e-mail: lubos.elexa@umb.sk

© The Author(s), under exclusive license to Springer Nature Switzerland AG 2024
N. Tsounis, A. Vlachvei (eds.), *Applied Economic Research and Trends*, Springer
Proceedings in Business and Economics,
https://doi.org/10.1007/978-3-031-49105-4_35

2010) or in specific functional areas such as financial-economic (Chatain & Zemsky, 2011), entrepreneurial-innovative (Hitt et al., 2011), or in marketing (Johansson et al., 2012). Despite the relatively simple basic definition of value, for example, through the individual price or total sales, its diverse quantitative definition, as well as permanent subjective perception, make the value a much more multidisciplinary object of study and a multi-layered construct that cannot be perceived unilaterally. This is also the reason why there is essentially no unified definition of value (Gallarza et al., 2011) and its measurement is also individualized (Grönroos, 2008). In the creation and distribution of value, two principles have been met: the principle of merit, which defines value in relation to the sources that contributed to its generation, and the principle of fulfillment/responsibility toward stakeholders. This is further differentiated according to the levels where distribution (reward) takes place (Lepak et al., 2007). The intra-organizational level includes so-called internal subjects (employees, managers, owners) with different degrees of risk, legitimacy, authority, and power. The inter-organizational (inter-company) level is primarily represented by suppliers (inputs), competitors (inspiration, threat), and customers (earnings), to a lesser extent also by the state and its institutions (public goods, services). Since merit does not automatically lead to a fair distribution, the interaction of heterogeneous groups leads to potential conflicts and consequent financial and non-financial problems within them (or even between them). Basically, the value of an enterprise and the values it creates are defined in various ways, the opinions on their significance and the procedure of their quantification subjectively differ, although they cannot be fully separated from each other.

35.2 Financial and Accounting Value – The Value for Owners and Investors

Profit is an economic and financial result needed for the existence and development of companies, but also a generator and source of other values with very diverse forms of expression. Its distribution or use expresses the company's level of social responsibility too, although from an accounting perspective. Increasing the value of owners through improving the quality of services and products and increasing the efficiency of employees' work became the basis of efficient and effectiveness management at the end of the twentieth century. It was named value management or management according to the values (Sledzik, 2013). It focuses less on financial goals and brings to the forefront the value offered to customers; thus, it makes financial results a secondary effect of such a relationship with customers.

The specific criteria used within value-oriented approaches vary significantly, with some regard to geographical routines (e.g., internal and external corporate governance systems), company size, capital market development, owners' preferences, or external pressures to prioritize other financial or non-financial goals. Grant and Fabozzi (2011) divide similar criteria/indicators into traditional and value-based groups and assign them different metrics. According to them, the traditional ones include areas of financial analysis, but from the perspective of the owner/investor primarily focus on profitability combined with other value indicators (e.g., growth in values, share price/earnings per share, share price/earnings per share, share price/cash flow, share price/book value per share, dividend yield, etc.). Value-oriented metrics are defined in the form of residual income, its range, economic added value, its range, market-added value, or cash flow return on investment. The relationship between accounting and market values gained greater importance and received more attention based on Ohlson's research (1995), which confirmed the earnings and the book value of equity as key determinants in market valuation (Abuzayed et al., 2009). Chen and Wang (2004) confirmed the significant role of operating earnings as factors in creating value in business and emphasized the factors involved in its generation, as based on its dynamics they more realistically explain the ability of companies to generate future profits and ensure their long-term sustainability. Brown et al. (1999), on the other hand, confirmed the gradual decline in the importance of profit orientation and similarly, Quinn et al. (1996) questioned the meaning of exclusively accounting information in knowledge economy, especially in companies with a high degree of innovation and rapid technological development. Despite this, they are not ignored as they are still an important criterion of business performance and in an undeveloped capital market they are the only (public) source of data. Moreover, they are directly involved in the quantification of other market-oriented metrics which are partly described in Table 35.1.

One- and two-dimensional metrics are based on financial accounting, which makes them regularly and quickly available, although relevant mostly for private companies (Merchant & van der Stede, 2017). Despite numerous criticisms, several studies (Maditinos et al., 2009) confirmed their persistent significance, demonstrating a stronger dependency even in the case of publicly traded companies, where the

Table 35.1 Reclassification of traditional and market criteria (Foulquier et al., 2019)

One-dimensional measurement	Two-dimensional measurement	Three- and multidimensional measurement
Gross margin	ROA	Net present value
EBITDA margin	ROE	Internal rate of return
EBIT margin (EBT)	ROI	EVA
NOPAT margin	ROCE	EVA momentum
Net margin	Profitability break down	REVA
Cash flow	Earnings per share	CFROI
Operating CF margin		Total shareholder return
Contributory profit margin		Marris' Q
		Return on risk-weighted capital (RORAC, RAROC)
		Value creation models

correlation between stock prices and the earnings per share indicator was higher than with ROE, ROI, or EVA. Three- and multi-dimensional metrics, or value creation models, go beyond the boundaries of financial accounting and consider also future expectations. Many of these metrics aim to evaluate residual income (e.g., economic one in the case of EVA) and explicitly target owners in an effort to retain them or attract investors. They are frequently suitable only for publicly traded companies.

The value-added indicators are relatively well known and easily quantifiable criteria, although not so frequently utilized in small businesses. Lesáková et al. (2007) categorize the value-added indicator as a reduced type, which expresses the individual contribution of a specific company (or industry) to the value created within the relevant supply or value chain that also reflects results "without some distortions made by the work of supplying companies." Rutherford (1977) refers to this value as the company's contribution to the prosperity generated within the economy, a portion distributed outside the company to various stakeholders (regardless of how they understand the benefit).

The value-added indicator is fundamentally formed by two generating factors (sales margin and production) and one consuming factor (production consumption), primarily covering material and energy consumption, and purchased services, as indicated in Table 35.2.

Retroactively, value-added can be defined also as the contribution of employees (wages, insurance, or social costs), machinery and production capacity (depreciation), and utilized capital (profit, interests, dividends, taxes), thereby allocating value-added more or less to individual production factors (or stakeholders) that were used in the production of goods, provision of services, or sale of merchandise. Bao and Bao (1998) offered a similar alternative based on the contribution of various stakeholders/factors:

$$Value - added = profit + depreciation + wages + social\ insurance + interests$$
$$+ dividends + income\ taxes$$

Table 35.2 Structure and model of value-added (Profit statement, 2022)

Category	Relation	Factor
A. Trade margin	−	Revenue from the sale of goods
		Cost of goods sold
B. Production	++	Revenue from the sale of own products and services
		Change in interdepartmental inventories
		Activation of internal services
C. Consumption	+	Material, energy, and other consumption
		Services
Added value	=	(A + B − C)

Dormagen (1991) calls these two approaches the dichotomy of value-added, which includes the first approach known as the "difference method" and the second approach called the "additive method," which according to Haller and Stolowy (1998) includes undistributed profit too. In general, it is also referred to as gross value-added, from which net value-added is derived by subtracting depreciation. According to some authors (Haller & van Stadden, 2014), it exhibits the characteristics of both a measure of firm performance and a measure of its social responsibility. Value-added has become a symbol of core business value, mainly because it reflects the interests of other stakeholders and provides additional information with higher explanatory power in relation to market risk compared to focusing solely on financial results or cash flow (Pong & Falconer, 2005). The mentioned social dimension allows companies to emphasize their relationships with other actors, particularly in terms of corporate culture and community development and has a significant PR importance as well.

The significance of value-added lies not only in expressing the contribution to individual recipients or quantifying the main sources that shaped business productivity. Absolute values are comparable between companies just with a certain degree of abstraction and with no relationships (e.g., in relation to company size, activity, industry characteristics, production homogeneity). They are objectified only when they are combined with other variables (production factors, other outputs, a comparable base, or a structural unit) and the influence of partial variables could be relativized. This allows us to compare heterogeneous activities (companies) under similar conditions.

The Economic Value Added (EVA[®]) as an additional indicator was developed to eliminate the shortcomings associated with traditional accounting-oriented indicators/methods (mainly subjectivity and retrospection) and the need to consider also factors representing managerial decision-making (Bromwich & Walker, 1998). EVA is a registered trademark of Stern Stewart & Co., although similar concepts of result objectification were known long before, as Alfred Marshall already used the concept of economic profit long ago (Morard & Balu, 2009). Pavelková and Knápková (2010) classified the economic value-added indicator as a part of the "fourth generation," which corresponds to an ownership or investment perspective. However, its use by external stakeholders (including investors) is significantly influenced by the availability of information or the ability to "understand" its features as the time, risks, or alternative opportunities. Although there are multiple approaches to calculating EVA (Kijewska, 2016; Rylková, 2016; Sabol & Sverer, 2017), the primary factor for determining its value is net operating result decreased by cost of capital or net operating assets (Blendinger & Michalski, 2018). These factors are quite dependable on many partial items, including influences that distort the information value provided by financial accounting. Stern Stewart & Co. identified up to 160 potential adjustments that need to be made (Bernier & Mouelhi, 2012) when adjusting operating profit, capital, or operating assets. This also brings a certain subjectivity as the indicator is calculated in multiple ways. Therefore, Shil (2009) considered each indicator as a so-called modified EVA since each company must create its own definition adapted to its organizational structure, product mix, strategy, and accounting practices, which optimally consider the trade-off between simplicity and accuracy.

The consideration of costs related to ordinary corporate activities, both operating and financial ones, is a fact that makes EVA different from other indicators (EPS, EBITDA, ROIC) (Daraban, 2017). The traditional approach to cost calculation is based on a weighted average considering the proportion of individual capital resources and their price (partial or opportunity costs). While the quantification of external capital costs is based on more explicit data, for the cost of equity it is necessary to consider a variety of variables that reflect, among other things, the level of risk. According to some authors (Markham & Palocsay, 2006; Chang & Dasgupta, 2011), it requires considering the probability and uncertainty of their variability. The high variability of the items used or considered (country, region, industry, company size, value development, forecast, risk, capital structure, alternative appreciation) means that their application requires a sensitive approach considering possible changes in time, but also the elimination of subjective approach of the user. The objections in the case of performance and the choice of indicators or usage of EVA do not relate only to the application of different methods in the selected enterprises. Critical studies are devoted to the use (Chen & Dodd, 1997; Holler, 2008), storytelling ability (Kaur & Narang, 2009), or the relationship of indicators with market value (Tortella & Brusco, 2003). It implies that the results of such application depend significantly on the conditions, as other studies carried out in different sectors, legislative frameworks, or markets found the opposite, i.e., even the positive impact of EVA on its explanatory power (Forker & Powell, 2008). As a reaction to similar reproaches and questioned accuracy, Bacidore et al. (1997) proposed a redefined EVA value (REVA) based on the market values of assets and the market value of the cost of capital, and some later studies confirmed a higher informative power of REVA (Yan & Wang, 2016) or MVA (Moghaddam & Shoghi, 2012) versus EVA. Regardless, REVA has received considerably less attention, even though the importance of various forms of market expression of equity or owner's value is constantly growing in practice. Similar research overwhelmingly try to reflect the value of owners in the case of publicly traded companies, mainly due to the effort to use the share price as a dependent variable. Other alternatives to the EVA indicator are also relative EVA (Mařík & Maříková, 2005), EVA momentum, or cash value added (Zavorotniy, 2014). Šrenkel and Smorada (2014) used the so-called EVA ZERO indicator as an expression of its relative value, which is calculated as follows (NOPAT represents net operating profit after taxes, C_d costs of debt, and E equity):

$$r_e \ (\text{EVA zero}) = \frac{\text{NOPAT} - C_d}{E}$$

The resulting value represents the "break-even," i.e., the relative value of the cost of equity, at which the amount of economic value added is zero. An alternative explanation is that with an equity cost lower than EVA ZERO, the enterprise creates additional value for its owners. However, since individual aspects of value cannot be expressed just by a single indicator, as it is part of a large system, it must be considered as a criterion and part of the strategic scope for the purpose of long-term value creation (Lueg & Schäffer, 2010; Dekker et al., 2012; Burkert, Lueg, 2013), also due to the diversity of stakeholders and the responsibility of businesses toward them. In addition, time and risk are factors that distinguish between owners the so-called group of investors, speculators, or "gamblers," who differ in behavior, length of ownership, objectives, economic benefits (Arthur et al., 2016), and these groups also develop their own value system and criteria based on which they decide on the allocation of capital. Although in the case of private companies, the ownership gambling is less relevant or none (in terms of limited number of owners and the dynamics of equity), profit-oriented business does not exclude speculative and risky behavior in terms of specific business ideas. The frequency of ownership changes in publicly traded companies is significantly higher, which is due, among other things, to more scattered ownership, a shorter investment period, and a higher openness of the company to a capital market.

The variety of methods used in expressing value at the corporate level (general value, added, economic) brought a large variability of measures, but also, unfortunately, the possibility of very heterogeneous objectives. This is one of the reasons why conflict situations arise between these groups, or why the interests of internal and external entities are often contradictory. The same applies to differences of interest within the groups themselves. Such conflicts undermine the value and performance (Attig, 2007), they also lead to different satisfactions of owners (fulfilled or unfulfilled expectations) and thus to variability of their structure and investments (Iturriaga & Crisóstomo, 2010). Fernandez (2002) therefore proposed a system of benchmarks that prove when a company creates or liquidates value for its owners. The most preferred comparative criteria are shown in Table 35.3.

Positive value symbolizes an increase in the value of ownership over time, although it does not explicitly respond to either inflation or the cost of capital. Added value and extra value are differentiated because they exceed the valuation expected at the beginning, so it is an "additional" remuneration provided as a result of the development of the economy, industry, specific market growth, excellence in management, lack of competition, as well as possible coincidence or a whole series of specific circumstances. The industry or market is an ideal criterion when considering investments. Such results are often applied to internal stakeholders, to

Table 35.3 Comparative value criteria for owners (Fernandez, 2002)

	Benchmark	Return higher than the benchmark
Return for owners	Zero	Added value for owners
	Yield on bonds	Additional return corresponding to the level of risk
	Required return on equity	Created extra value
	Return in companies of the same industry	Returns outpace industry performance
	Market return	Return outperforms market performance

owners as recipients of values, and to management as their co-creator, administrator, and partial distributor.

35.3 Methodology

The quantitative and qualitative analysis of value-added was based on financial data (financial statements) available under the Finstat database (2022) and from companies' annual reports. Data for the profitability of the parent companies were drawn for each stock exchange from the investment portal www.investing.com. Used data compared the development of added values among the biggest car producers in Slovakia in the period from 2009 to 2021, except indicators where the data were not available.

The analytical methods were used in the form of classification, causal, relational, and correlation analysis (Pearson's r), followed by comparison, induction, and deduction. In the identification, evaluation, and implications arising from the interrelations of financial data and their synergy with the development of production, inputs, and other outputs, the content-causal method was used and the generalization for the whole automotive industry in the final synthesis was applied. Regarding the influence of the size of analyzed companies on the amount of their inputs and outputs, absolute values of added value were considered just as a starting point, respectively, as a basis for further analysis of development trends. The structural analysis focused on components that drained added value for the benefit of individual stakeholders. Productivity in value-added used data on employment and wage and/or personnel costs. The analysis of economic added value used the innovative EVA ZERO indicator to set the threshold of equity costs. In comparisons, the relative values were preferred. Median values were used for industrial/holding comparisons within the SK NACE 29 industry. For the purpose of determining the impact of inflation on the development of selected absolute values, the inflation calculator INEKO was used (2021).

35.4 Analysis of Value-Added in Automotive Production in Slovakia

The automotive industry became the backbone of the Slovak economy, creating interesting business opportunities but great dependability as well. The positive case of Volkswagen's development (it started in 1991) attracted other final producers (PSA in 2003, Kia in 2004, Jaguar in 2015), most recently Volvo with an expected starting of the production in 2026. Total production grew from 575,776 cars in 2008 to 990,000 in 2020 (SARIO, 2022). Employment in final production went up in Volkswagen by 61%, in PSA by 53%, and in Kia by 20% between 2010

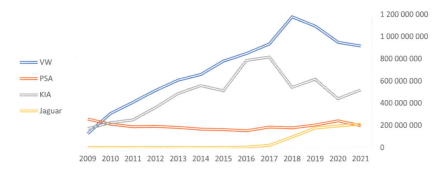

Fig. 35.1 Development of gross value-added of final car manufacturers 2009–2019 (in €)

and 2021 (Finstat, 2022) but with significant fluctuations in recent years and huge induced employment in supplying sectors (16.2% in the automotive industry in total) (ACEA, 2022). Gross value added (VA) in industry has changed fundamentally over the last decade, as is presented in Fig. 35.1. Its amount has doubled in the SK NACE 29 division since 2009. However, as was already indicated, it was affected by the number of companies involved, so more individual demonstration is needed. Its development in individual car manufacturers has been considerably more heterogeneous than suggested by the sector. While gross value-added at Volkswagen was significantly multiplied (from €124 million to €914 million), in Kia it tripled (from €169 million to €519 million), but in PSA its absolute value fell by 23% (from €255 million to €197 million). Given Jaguar Land Rover's short history, Fig. 35.1 reports its development only since 2016.

The main causes of such development can be found in the economy and structure of the individual value chain, also influenced by different external factors (e.g., tax and insurance policy, wage development, COVID), volume of cars produced, their structure (modes, brands, and classes), and by competitors (including internal). While in the luxury class (VW, Porsche, Audi) competition was lower and elasticity of demand more resistant to price changes, in the middle and lower classes, the intensity of competition increased due to a wider range of comparable cars.

With almost the equivalent volume of cars produced (VW 378000, PSA 371000), the value-added at VW was more than five times higher. It means that the typology of cars produced had a significant impact on value-added. The correlation (Pearson's r) between the development of value-added and the development of production volumes confirmed a stronger linear dependence for VW and Kia ($r = 0.74$ and $r = 0.84$, respectively), while for PSA there was a moderate negative impact ($r = -0.41$). Figure 35.2 shows the relationship between value-added and the volume of cars produced by individual manufacturers.

The correlation between the value-added and the revenues from the sale of own products and services turned out to be similar. While in Volkswagen and Kia there was a strong direct dependence ($r = 0.97$, respectively $r = 0.9$), in the case of PSA it was a very weak indirect dependence ($r = -0.16$). Both comparisons showed that only in PSA the growth in the number of cars produced and consequently

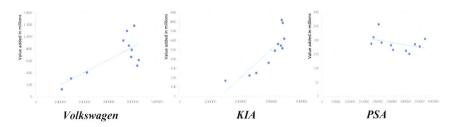

Fig. 35.2 Development of value-added depending on the number of cars produced (Volkswagen, Kia, PSA)

Table 35.4 Absolute and relative changes between 2009 and 2021 (in mil. €; coef. below)

	VW	KIA	PSA	Jaguar[a]
Value added	+789,987,36	+349,83,07	−58,260,77	+114,92,21
Revenue from the sale of goods and services	+6583,13,24	+3854,73,29	+1420,11,76	+104,81,56
Material consumption	+5471,12,94	+3133,53,28	+1617,42,07	+11,81,7
Purchase of services	+214,93,01	+371,43,64	−46,121,31	−21,90,49

[a]In Jaguar Land Rover covering just the period of 2018–2021

the growth of sales did not lead to a proportional increase in value-added. The alternative justification in the form of exports of work in progress is undermined by the fact that changes in intra-organizational inventories, which also affect the value-added, amounted to values below 1% of production and could not (in case of negative development) compensate the year-on-year growth in production or sales. These differences in the generation of value-added at the level of final producers were then made primarily due to the structure of their production portfolio, pricing policy, and cost structure.

It was already clear from Fig. 35.1 that companies did not show exactly similar growth rates of value-added. Production developed differently in 2008 and partly in 2009, when, for example, PSA increased production by 10% in 2008, while Volkswagen lost 20% due to the different impacts of the financial crisis on global demand, in this case mainly due to its orientation on SUV production for the American markets (Jesný & Kukučka, 2009). While Volkswagen's value-added grew then by around €817 million in 10 years (3.97 times the value of 2009), in Kia by €447 million (3.63 times), in PSA it fell by €52.4 million (20%). Even if the value-added was converted to constant prices in 2009, it would grow 3.1 times in Volkswagen, so it could be stated that the amount of value-added has evolved significantly. The individual components of value-added and their changes in absolute (mil. €) and relative expression (coefficient) are shown in Table 35.4.

Table 35.5 presents the development of added value per production unit. It offers generalized insight since the production of components (engines, transmissions, differentials, etc.) or tools contributes very heterogeneously to the overall outputs of individual manufacturers as well (and its value is confidential in

35 Value Creation in Automotive Industry in Slovakia

Table 35.5 Development of value-added per produced cars

	2021	2020	2019	2018	2017	2016
VW	2958, 38	3063, 19	2893, 06	2886, 86	2581, 24	2197, 33
KIA	1687, 74	1634, 89	1791, 18	1628, 74	2428, 95	2309, 20
PSA	624, 99	711, 97	548, 02	502, 13	550, 87	478, 52
	2015	**2014**	**2013**	**2012**	**2011**	**2010**
VW	1961, 89	1670, 36	1425, 38	1228, 08	1930, 98	2118, 36
KIA	1515, 68	1723, 55	1556, 14	1229, 57	985, 18	971, 46
PSA	533, 19	644, 13	729, 36	888, 37	1051, 05	1128, 24

value). Paradoxically, however, available synthetic data from annual reports showed that the largest ancillary production is provided by Volkswagen (4.6% of total sales) and Kia (by 26% more engines produced than cars).

The year 2009 is worth mentioning as well, when the added value per one car in Volkswagen amounted to 1010 €, in PSA 1247 €, and in Kia 1128.7 €. Here, can be seen another effect of the short-lived reduction in production (after the crisis in 2008). It showed how a temporary loss in sales can affect capacity utilization and the resulting value creation, profitability, and the entire supply chain efficiency. When quantifying the share of stakeholders in the value created, it should be noted that such "draining" of values for various reasons (historical retained earnings, financial activity) does not correspond to 100% of the amount of value-added but is considered just as a reward for the use of factors of production (capital, fixed assets, labor) and contribution to the financing of certain public goods and services (through taxes, insurance). Therefore, it is not always a real outflow of (financial) values, but a theoretical one since depreciation does not represent a current expense, but a potential amortization fund for the restoration of fixed assets in the future. Alternatively, they can be understood as an accounting expression of wear and tear in relation to historical cost. Net profit represents a prospective entitlement to remuneration of owners, but it does not have to be paid in full, and its further prospective increase/usage is expected due to retained earnings of previous periods or unpaid loss. On the other hand, these bonuses do not cover some other types of (mainly non-financial) benefits that the owner or employees receive, and the consumption of some production factors is underestimated in terms of their contribution (renting, outsourcing of services, use of fully depreciated assets) or may be partially negated (state support).

For Volkswagen, distributed values in 2021 were 16.8% higher than value-added generated (12.4% in 2009), in PSA were 16% lower (5.6% lower in 2009), and in Kia lower by 0.13% (11.7% higher in 2009). Fig. 35.3 shows the different drawdowns/distributions in relation to each other, i.e., not as a share of value-added but as a proportion of the total distribution in 2021. Kia achieved the highest share of profit (owners' point of view), while the highest share of wages (employees) was achieved in PSA. It partly clarifies the nature of the activities and the working claims laid upon the workforce, but it reflects the profitability as well. On the other hand, it certainly does not correspond to the demands on the technologies used, given

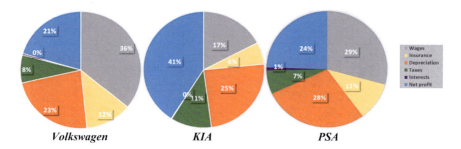

Fig. 35.3 How added value was used for stakeholders in Volkswagen, Kia, and PSA in 2021

the different depreciation and investment policy, production life cycle, and burden (e.g., in PSA, there was a one-third higher depreciation in 2009 than in 2019). While Volkswagen grew the most in 10 years in profit (7.3 times) and payable income taxes (3.9 times), in Kia it was slightly higher growth in profit (7.4 times) and taxes (5.8 times), but in PSA consumption and wages grew the most (107% and 55%), taxes fell by half (−49.6%), and profit by 3%.

For the sake of completeness, it should be added that the above-mentioned shares correspond to the dynamic assessment between 2009 and 2021 when necessary influence was made also due to the retained earnings as historical results. In 2021 Volkswagen's net profit (€447.5 million) was just 15% of retained earnings, compared with 19.2% in Kia and 99.1% in PSA, reflecting a higher or smaller rate of payouts/distribution of profit in the companies. The companies' annual reports showed dividends of €173.3 million in VW in 2019 (€447.5 million proposed for 2020), €57.2 million in Kia, and €37.04 million in PSA. Therefore, these dividends are another drawdown following Fig. 35.3, which, however, varied considerably from year to year depending on profitability, planned investments, or the development of the production program (so dynamic nowadays).

While value-added in volume, its components, and other determining factors reflect the size of an enterprise and, over time the dynamics of its development, its relative definition eliminates the problem of the impact of the scale of economic activity. In this way, the volume of added value could be put in a different light using various relative indicators. Sales at Volkswagen increased significantly over 10 years, employment grew less intensively (in VW only 1.8 times and personnel costs 3.07 times), while value-added increased 3.97 times. Depreciation and profit could be considered as relatively variable items (despite depreciation as a fixed cost) that are somehow substitutable (a decrease in depreciation while maintaining production capabilities creates room for increasing profits), this is less visible in the development of personnel costs. In the period under review, they had a significantly increasing trend, which exceeded employment growth, thus indicating an increase in other induced and social costs. Nevertheless, labor productivity measured by the number of employees can be assessed highly positively, as its value per employee has more than doubled in 10 years. This was also the case of wage productivity,

35 Value Creation in Automotive Industry in Slovakia

Table 35.6 Value-added based ratios

| | Volkswagen | KIA | | | PSA | Jaguar | |
	2009	2021	2009	2021	2009	2021	2021
VA/sales	0,1072	0,096	0,1005	0,094	0,1362	0,0599	0,719
Personnel cost/VA	0,5334	0,492	0,2785	0,245	0,2431	0,4899	0,505
Depreciation/VA	0,4251	0,237	0,4602	0,255	0,4093	0,2811	0,475
Profit/VA	0,1348	0,21	0,1537	0,427	0,2335	0,2447	0,0289
Tax/VA	0,0103	0,079	neg.	0,114	0,056	0,0789	0,0416
VA/employment	43,958	81,413	77,172	150,043	69965[a]	52,014	46,571
VA/wages	2603	2,71	4,85	5528	4114	2,84	2818

[a]Calculated from employment in 2010 due to the availability of the exact number of employees, while in 2009 only a broad interval of employment was available

where €1 of wages paid generated €2.6 of value-added in 2009 and €2.71 in 2021. All these comparisons are available in Table 35.6.

Based on the calculations it can be concluded that from the point of view of the owners, the share of profit in value-added developed positively and increased from 13.48% to almost 21%, despite the personnel costs. Their share decreased from 53.3% to 49.2%. Of course, the whole effect of personnel costs growth contributed not only to the benefit of employees but also to the benefit of the state in terms of insurance and other payments. In this sense, the state also gained, thanks to the growth of income taxes, which in 2009, also due to a radical decrease in profitability, significantly fell and their share in value-added reached only 1.03% then and 7.9% in 2021. Overall, the value-added (VA) in sales decreased from 10.72 to 10.5%.

Employment at KIA grew slowly (by 25%) but with more than tripled revenue, a 270% increase in personnel costs and almost 8.6 times higher profit. On the other hand, this development was reflected in a significantly higher value-added ratio per employee or in relation to wages paid. Changes over time were dynamic, which also had positive consequences for the development of added value. It was a change (decrease) in the share of personnel expenses and depreciation in value-added or, conversely, a significant increase in the profit share, which was subsequently reflected in the development of income tax (negative in 2009). KIA achieved the highest values in most ratios in 2021. On the other hand, the value-added in sales decreased from 10.05% to 9.4% as a result of the post-pandemic slowdown.

At PSA, employment grew by 56% with a 67% increase in sales, a 79% increase in personnel costs, and a 9.4% increase in profit. It should be noted that the development of total value-added did not grow in proportion with the increase in individual items and rather stagnated. This also had an impact on the development of the economic results and, in a way, on expenses. This was mainly due to a decrease in depreciation and an increase in personnel costs. As a result, the share of value-added in sales also decreased from 13.62% in 2009 to 5.99% in 2021. The high growth in personnel costs and the high share of these costs in total costs were also reflected in the fact that labor productivity in value-added and the productivity of wages paid gradually declined (opposite compared to competitors). Jaguar Land

Table 35.7 Economic value-added and modified "market value" indicators in %

	VW		KIA		PSA		Jaguar
	2009	2021	2009	2021	2009	2021	2021
EVA ZERO	1.69	15.22	Neg.	22.12	40.09	23.19	1.72
ROE (SK)	2.07	13.5	5.51	13.6	34.36	28.8	0.9
ROE (global)	–	7.67	–	8.5	–	26.27	−11.37
Payout ratio	N/A	38.72**	0	17.95**	0	60.37**	N/A

**2019 data

Rover is provided as an illustration, as its activity partially reflected the initial production stage, which can also be seen, for example, in higher depreciation values and low profitability (including tax duties).

However, economic value identified that differences between companies (visible in the case of financial results) are narrowing, in some aspects even the opposite results were found. For evaluating economic added value, so-called EVA ZERO was used to avoid subjective determination of the cost of equity. Thus, in this case, the EVA ZERO indicator indicated a hypothetical threshold, the break-even point of exceeding the maximum cost of equity. Up to this threshold, the subjective cost of equity attributed to an enterprise brought "positive" economic benefit or an extra value created for owners. For this reason, ROE is simultaneously presented as a benchmark, both for Slovak companies and global owners.

The data in Table 35.7 show that the relatively low EVA values in 2009 increased significantly by 2021. PSA was an exemption, as there the development was the opposite. The results of 2009 were influenced by several factors that affected the values above as well. First of all, companies did not have significant differences in their financial profits (€26–59 million) in absolute terms as they had later. However, the levels of capital employed or indebtedness varied significantly, which had an impact on the level of external capital costs (price for debt) or on the structure and value of financial activities. At the same time, the structure of indebtedness differed, in 2021 mainly in the form of the presence (PSA) or absence (KIA) of liabilities to parent companies and subsidiaries. While PSA was more indebted at a lower cost of debt, Kia's 24 million cost interests caused its negative EVA ZERO in 2009. Gradual growth and differences in profits from ordinary economic activity (€65–447 million) increased the level of EVA ZERO in Volkswagen and Kia, while in PSA reflected a stagnant economic results and fell down, although still reaching very positive numbers. And paradoxically, with a relatively high level of return on equity (ROE). ROE indicator (net profit to equity) served as a basis for comparison with EVA ZERO, although it also considered retained earnings from the past. At the same time, it served as a symbolic alternative to market value (even though the equity has in this case rather accounting value). The value of ROE in PSA was at 28.8%, as the share of equity to liabilities in this company was significantly lower than in other companies (in the case of ROA it would be 6.9%). Although the individual cost of equity is not discussed (as it is a matter of owners' consideration mostly), below presented EVA ZERO levels indicate the break-even, up to which

35 Value Creation in Automotive Industry in Slovakia

such considerations might go according to risks and potential future expectations. Specifically, in the case of PSA, the EVA ZERO fell below the values of ROE. On the other hand, it may be seen that the ROE of every company in Slovakia was higher than the same indicator for its global mother company.

The payout ratio was used as a supplementary indicator of market value, albeit cumulatively for the aggregate profit paid to the sole shareholder. It is therefore not a true market-based expression of value. However, it turned out (not surprisingly) that in the first years companies rather reinvested their profits, while nowadays dividends are paid (the proposal for the distribution of the financial result in 2020 in Volkswagen Slovakia was 100%).

35.5 Discussion and Conclusion

The simplicity of one- and two-criterion metrics, together with their quick availability, makes them ideal for everyday use, although with many objections. Inputs and outputs may not always be compared in the same period, they overlap multiple subperiods, which distort the data and limit their understanding. This is more pronounced in companies with long production cycles and, conversely, in the case of services and production with flexible finalization, the problem is less pronounced. The annual data provided by synthetic accounting documents partially eliminate this problem, but the length of the evaluation period limits the operability of decisions and the practicality of day-to-day management. Another possible problem, which was also highlighted by the European Central Bank (2010), is precisely that of business-to-business comparisons. Differences in conditions and other externalities of an economic and legislative nature may affect the understanding of efficiency. This is specifically relevant for international businesses, generally due to different tax and dividend policies, depreciation, prices, costs, interest rates, or exchange rates.

Standard financial health criteria are frequently criticized, and many of the criticisms against traditional indicators can also be applied to modern methods, including value- or market-oriented ones. If the problem in the case of profit is its possible manipulation, the same problem applies to future profits, and the same argument applies to potential time discrepancies between profit and cash flows. Any plan for future income and expenses is largely an estimation exposed to a variety of risks due to unforeseen circumstances to managers' optimism or manipulation efforts. Even after the inevitable transformations in the EVA calculation, operating profit does not cover various other benefits that managers, owners, or employees can receive. Benefits that are more hidden and individual, as the number of owners or the size of the business decreases. An objective calculation of the cost of equity (especially in the case of fragmented ownership) is problematic and, given the variety of methods, the objectivity of some of them is also questionable. Therefore, trying to use this indicator as a measure of appreciation of investment (real or opportunity) would be more suitable for larger entities, especially companies traded on creditworthy and dynamic markets. As it is an indicator of short-term performance (despite attempts to extrapolate its development into the future), it is not suitable for start-ups or companies that, for various reasons, invest larger amounts of capital in certain periods. Then EVA proves destructive rather than constructive in terms of creating value for owners, especially if the results of a given activity are to become apparent only after certain time (Daraban, 2017).

Basically, although the highest amount of value-added was created at Volkswagen, the relativization of absolute indicators showed that from a qualitative point of view, the creation of added value was more efficient at KIA. This was proved by the share of added value in the revenues generated from the sale of own products and services, as well as almost doubled the productivity of employees compared to Volkswagen and almost three times that of PSA. Labor productivity was also significantly higher than that of other companies. KIA achieved the highest share of profit in value-added (from the point of view of owners and tax due). Volkswagen and Kia's sales had a strong influence on the development of value-added, which drove value-added upwards, in contrast to PSA, where both production and sales growth acted reversely (the influence of the production of cheaper models and the influence of lower prices). This was also reflected in the lower value-added per car produced, which was the highest in PSA in 2009 but now stands at less than a quarter of the value at Volkswagen.

Employment grew significantly in all companies, which confirmed their importance for the Slovak economy. At the same time, however, the share of wages in value-added showed that at Volkswagen employees are better paid, but at Kia, they achieve much better productivity (both per person and wage paid). Kia is also the most profitable in terms of profit volume, but thanks to higher indebtedness, PSA has the highest return on equity. All three companies have a relatively high threshold of equity costs, which leaves them a lot of room to create additional economic value for owners. This is also reflected in the fact that over time, the volumes of distributed profit reached values approaching 100% (mainly VW).

In the case of foreign investments, it is always questionable how efficient the state support is. Mostly, when huge investing incentives are provided. Added value is not a perfect indicator, it has many disadvantages (as well as other indicators), but it also allows us to directly compare how stakeholders benefit from the company's story. In relation to state support, it is difficult to express its total volume over so many years of operation (as it comes from a variety of sources), but only Volkswagen paid in income taxes for the analyzed years an amount equal to 24% of its 2021 assets (Kia 22%); in the case of personnel costs, it has the value 1.65 times higher than the size of assets (Kia 44%), so just for these two stakeholders such investment seems efficient. Of course, for more accurate data, it is necessary to work more with inflation, specifically in the case of annual comparisons and also to take the whole supply chain into account.

Acknowledgments This article is a result of the research project VEGA 1/0290/22 "Regional investment as as a determinant of the development of enterprises and regions in the Slovak Republic" funded by the Scientific Grant Agency of the Ministry of Education, Science, Research and Sport of the Slovak Republic.

References

Abuzayed, B., Molyneux, P., & Al-Fayoumi, N. (2009). Market value, book value and earnings: Is bank efficiency a missing link? *Managerial Finance, 35*(2), 156–179. https://doi.org/10.1108/03074350910923491

ACEA. (2022). *Share of direct automotive employment in the EU by country.* https://www.acea.auto/figure/share-of-direct-automotive-employment-in-the-eu-by-country/. Accessed 31 May 2023.

Arthur, J., Williams, R., & Delfabbro, P. (2016). The conceptual and empirical relationship between gambling, investing, and speculation. *Journal of Behavioral Addictions, 5*(4), 580–591. https://doi.org/10.1556/2006.5.2016.0

Attig, N. (2007). Excess control and the risk of corporate expropriation: Canadian evidence. *Canadian Journal of Administrative Sciences, 24*(2), 94–106. https://doi.org/10.1002/cjas.10

Bacidore, J., Boquist, J., Milbourn, T., & Thakor, A. (1997). The search for the best financial performance measure. *Financial Analysts Journal, 53*(3), 11–20. https://doi.org/10.2469/faj.v53.n3.2081

Bao, B. H., & Bao, D. H. (1998). Usefulness of value added and abnormal economic earnings: An empirical examination. *Journal of Business Finance and Accounting, 25*(1–2), 251–265. https://doi.org/10.1111/1468-5957.00186

Bernier, G., & Mouelhi, C. (2012). Dynamic linkages between MVA and internal performance measures: A panel cointegration analysis of the U.S. insurance industry. *Insurance and Risk Management, 79*(3–4), 223–250. https://doi.org/10.2139/ssrn.1421599

Blendinger, G., & Michalski, G. (2018). Long-term competitiveness based on value added measures as part of highly professionalized corporate governance management of German DAX 30 corporations. *Journal of Competitiveness, 10*(1), 5–20. https://doi.org/10.7441/joc.2018.02.01

Bromwich, M., & Walker, M. (1998). Residual income past and future. *Management Accounting Research, 9*(4), 391–419. https://doi.org/10.1006/mare.1998.0091

Brown, S., Lo, K., & Lys, T. (1999). Use of R2 in accounting research: Measuring changes in value relevance over the last four decades. *Journal of Accounting and Economics, 28*(2), 83–115. https://doi.org/10.1016/S0165-4101(99)00023-3

Burkert, M., & Lueg, R. (2013). Differences in the sophistication of value-based management – The role of top executives. *Management Accounting Research, 24*(1), 3–22. https://doi.org/10.1016/j.mar.2012.10.001

Chang, X., & Dasgupta, S. (2011). Monte Carlo simulations and capital structure research. *International Review of Finance, 11*(1), 19–55. https://doi.org/10.1111/J.1468-2443.2011.01126.X

Chatain, O., & Zemsky, P. (2011). Value creation and value capture with frictions. *Strategic Management Journal, 32*(11), 1206–1231. https://doi.org/10.1002/SMJ.939

Chen, S., & Dodd, J. L. (1997). Economic value added (eva®): An empirical examination of a new corporate performance measure? *Journal of Managerial Issues, 9*(3), 318–333. ISSN: 2328-7470.

Chen, S., & Wang, Y. (2004). Evidence from China on the value relevance of operating income vs. below-the-line items. *International Journal of Accounting, 39*(4), 339–364. https://doi.org/10.1016/J.INTACC.2004.06.012

Coff, R. (2010). The coevolution of rent appropriation and capability development. *Strategic Management Journal, 31*(7), 711–733. https://doi.org/10.1002/SMJ.844

Daraban, M. (2017). Economic value added – A general review of the concept. Ovidius university annals. *Economic Sciences Series, 17*(1), 168–173. ISSN: 2393-3127.

Dekker, H. C., Groot, T., Schoute, M., & Wiersma, E. (2012). Determinants of the use of value-based performance measures for managerial performance evaluation. *Journal of Business Finance & Accounting, 39*(9–10), 1214–1239. https://doi.org/10.1111/JBFA.12004

Di Gregorio, D. (2013). Value creation and value appropriation: An integrative, multi-level framework. *Journal of Applied Business and Economics, 15*(1), 39–53. ISSN: 1857-8721.

Dormagen, J. C. (1991). Analyse de la valeur ajoutée. *Revue Fiduciaire Comptable, 164*, 24–32. ISSN: 0396-3640.

European Central Bank. (2010). *Beyond roe – How to measure bank performance. Appendix to the report on EU banking structures* (p. 44). ECB.

Fernandez, P. (2002). *A definition of shareholder value creation. Research paper no. 448.* https://core.ac.uk/download/pdf/6536328.pdf. Accessed 18 Mar 2023.

Finstat (2022). *Database of economic results of Slovak companies.* https://finstat.sk/databaza-financnych-udajov. Accessed 18 Apr 2023.

Forker, J., & Powell, R. (2008). A comparison of error rates for EVA, residual income, GAAP-earnings and other metrics using a long-window valuation approach. *European Accounting Review, 17*(3), 471–502. https://doi.org/10.1080/09638180802172420

Foulquier, P. et al. (2019). *Performance 21. Handbook of business performance and value creation in the 21st century.* https://www.edhec.edu/sites/www.edhec-portail.pprod.net/files/ebook_performance21.pdf. Accessed 21 Oct 2022.

Gallarza, M., Gil-Saura, I., & Holbrook, M. B. (2011). The value of value: Further excursions on the meaning and role of customer value. *Journal of Consumer Behaviour, 10*(4), 179–191. https://doi.org/10.1002/CB.328

Grant, J. L., & Fabozzi, F. J. (2011). Equity analysis using traditional and value-based metrics. In F. J. Fabozzi & H. M. Markowitz (Eds.), *Equity valuation and portfolio management.* Wiley.

Grönroos, C. (2008). Service logic revisited: Who creates value? And who co-creates? *European Business Review, 20*(4), 298–314. https://doi.org/10.1108/09555340810886585

Haller, A., & Stolowy, H. (1998). Value added in financial accounting: A comparative study between Germany and France. *Advances in International Accounting: A Research Annual, 11*, 23–51. ISSN: 0897-3660.

Haller, A., & van Staden, C. J. (2014). The value added statement – Appropriate instrument for integrated reporting. *Accounting, Auditing & Accountability Journal, 27*(7), 1190–1216. https://doi.org/10.1108/AAAJ-04-2013-1307

Hitt, M. A., Ireland, R. D., Sirmon, D. G., & Trahms, C. A. (2011). Strategic entrepreneurship: Creating value for individuals, organizations and society. *Academy of Management Perspectives, 25*(2), 57–75. https://doi.org/10.5465/amp.25.2.57

Holler, A. (2008). Have earnings lost value-relevance? Revisiting latest evidence on EVA. *Business Review Journal, 10*(2), 245–254. ISSN: 1553-5827.

Iturriaga, F., & Crisóstomo, V. (2010). Do leverage, dividend payout, and ownership concentration influence Firms' value creation? An analysis of Brazilian firms. *Emerging Markets Finance & Trade, 46*(3), 80–94. https://doi.org/10.2753/REE1540-496X460306

Jesný, M., Kukučka, J. (2009). *Automobilky opäť pomôžu ekonomike.* https://www.trend.sk/biznis/automobilky-opat-pomozu-ekonomike. Accessed 22 Feb 2023.

Johansson, M., Hallberg, N., Hinterhuber, A., Zbaracki, M., & Liozu, S. (2012). Pricing strategies and pricing capabilities. *Journal of Revenue and Pricing Management, 11*(1), 4–11. https://doi.org/10.1057/rpm.2011.42

Kaur, M., & Narang, S. (2009). Shareholder value creation in India's most valuable companies: An empirical study. *IUP Journal of Management Research, 8*(8), 16–42. ISSN: 0974-0287.

Kijewska, A. (2016). Causal analysis of determinants influencing the economic value added (EVA) – A case of polish entity. *Journal of Economics and Management, 26*(26), 52–70. https://doi.org/10.22367/jem.2016.26.03

Lepak, D. P., Smith, K. G., & Taylor, M. S. (2007). Value creation and value capture: A multilevel perspective. *Academy of Management Review, 32*(1), 180–194. https://doi.org/10.5465/AMR.2007.23464011

Lueg, R., & Schäffer, U. (2010). Assessing empirical research on value-based management: Guidelines for improved hypothesis testing. *Journal für Betriebswirtschaft, 60*(1), 1–47. https://doi.org/10.1007/s11301-009-0055-9

Maditinos, D., Sevic, Z., & Theriou, N. (2009). Performance measures: Traditional accounting measures vs. modern value-based measures. The case of earnings and EVA in the Athens stock exchange (ASE). *International Journal of Economic Policy in Emerging Economies, 2*(4), 323–334. https://doi.org/10.1504/IJEPEE.2009.030935

Mařík, M., & Maříková, P. (2005). *Moderní metody hodnocení výkonnosti a oceňování podniku* (1st ed.). Ekopress.

Markham, I. S., & Palocsay, S. W. (2006). Scenario analysis in spreadsheets with Excel's scenario tool. *INFORMS Transactions on Education, 6*(2), 23–31. https://doi.org/10.1287/ited.6.2.23

Merchant, K. A., & Van Der Stede, W. (2017). *Management control systems: Performance measurement, evaluation and incentives* (4th ed.). Financial Times/Prentice Hall.

Moghaddam, A. G., & Shoghi, H. (2012). A study of refined economic value added explanatory power associated with MVA & EPS in Tehran stock Exchange.Interdisciplinary journal of contemporary research. *Business, 3*(9), 403–412. ISSN: 2073-7122.

Morard, B., & Balu, F. O. (2009). Developing a practical model for calculating the economic value added. *Economic Computation and Economic Cybernetics Studies and Research, 43*(3), 107–122. ISSN: 1842-3264.

Ohlson, J. (1995). Earnings, book values, and dividends in equity valuation. *Contemporary Accounting Research, 11*(2), 661–687. https://doi.org/10.1111/j.1911-3846.1995.tb00461.x

Pavelková, A., & Knápková, D. (2010). *Finanční analýza*. Grada.

Pong, C., & Falconer, M. (2005). Accounting for A disappearance: A contribution to the history of the value added statement in the UK. *Accounting Historians Journal, 32*(2), 173–199. ISSN: 0148-4184.

Quinn, J., Anderson, P., & Finkelstein, S. (1996). Leveraging intellect. Academy of management. *Perspective, 10*(3), 7–27. https://doi.org/10.5465/ame.1996.9704111471

Rutherford, B. A. (1977). Value added as a focus of attention for financial reporting: Some conceptual problems. *Accounting and Business Research, 7*(27), 215–220. https://doi.org/10.1080/00014788.1977.9728707

Rylková, Ž. (2016). Economic value added in managerial economics. *Scientific papers of the University of Pardubice. Series D, 23*(38), 117–128. ISSN: 1211-555X.

Sabol, A., & Svere, F. (2017). A review of the economic value added literature and application. *Journal of Economics. Special Issue, 8*(1), 19–27. ISSN: 1857-6982.

SARIO. (2022). *Automotive sector in Slovakia*. https://sario.sk/sites/default/files/sario-automotive-sector-in-slovakia-2022-09-23.pdf. Accessed 22 May 2023.

Shil, N. C. (2009). Performance measures: An application of economic value added. *International Journal of Business and Management, 4*(3), 169–177. https://doi.org/10.5539/ijbm.v4n3p169

Sledzik, K. (2013). Financial and non-financial value drivers in shareholder value creation process. In Hittmar, Š. (Ed.). *Young Scientists Revue, 2013*, 89–95. https://doi.org/10.2139/ssrn.2257767

Šrenkel, Ľ., & Smorada, M. (2014). EVA ZERO – skutočná relatívna EVA. *Finančný manažér, 14*(1), 15–21. ISSN: 1335-5813.

Tortella, B., & Brusco, S. (2003). The economic value added (EVA): An analysis of market reaction. *Advances in Accounting, 20*, 265–280. https://doi.org/10.1016/S0882-6110(03)20012-2

Yan, Q., & Wang, Y. (2016). REVA-based value analysis on listed companies of power industry. In *International conference on modeling, simulation and optimization technologies and applications* (p. 2016). IEEE.

Zavorotniy, R. (2014). Cash value added as an indicator of efficiency of issuer's development in crisis economic environment. *Journal of International Studies, 7*(3), 44–54. ISSN: 2306-3483.

Lesáková, Ľ., et al. (2007). *Finančno-ekonomická analýza podniku*. Univerzita Mateja Bela v Banskej Bystrici.

Chapter 36
Does German Hospital Financing Lead to Distorted Incentives in the Billing of Intensive Care Ventilation Therapy?

Peter Kremeier

Abstract *Introduction:* In the German statutory health insurance system, hospitals are reimbursed according to the services provided. One important variable in the calculation of reimbursements is the hours of mechanical ventilation provided in the course of intensive care treatment. The amount of compensation is directly proportional to the number of hours of ventilation and increases when certain thresholds are reached (96, 250, 500, and 1000 h of ventilation). From an economic point of view, this is an incentive structure toward prolonged ventilation regardless of medical implications in order to increase the amount of compensation received.

Methods: In this study, the frequency of ventilation hours at and shortly after the critical thresholds were examined for anomalies in all cases billed to health insurers from 2009 to 2019. It was examined whether a significant accumulation of ventilation hours could be observed at and shortly after a threshold was reached.

Results: Descriptive analysis of the data showed that the mean values of ventilation hours around the critical thresholds (96, 250, 500, and 1000) are higher than before the critical thresholds for most years. Accordingly, the rates of change at and shortly after critical thresholds are also higher than otherwise. Statistical analysis was used to examine the differences in rates of change between critical and non-critical thresholds. It was shown that the median and mean rates of change are significantly higher for critical thresholds than for non-critical thresholds. Therefore, the null hypothesis that there is no difference in the rates of change between the critical and non-critical thresholds can be rejected. Application of the bootstrap test confirmed the robustness of these results.

Conclusions: The results at the descriptive, exploratory and inductive levels showed a clear trend toward increased ventilation hour frequency at critical thresholds. The results of this study may help to develop strategies to lower the frequency of ventilation hours and thereby reduce overall healthcare costs.

P. Kremeier (✉)
Simulationszentrum für klinische Beatmung, Karlsruhe, Germany
e-mail: pk@respicode.de

© The Author(s), under exclusive license to Springer Nature Switzerland AG 2024
N. Tsounis, A. Vlachvei (eds.), *Applied Economic Research and Trends*, Springer Proceedings in Business and Economics,
https://doi.org/10.1007/978-3-031-49105-4_36

Keywords Critical care · Healthcare cost · Mechanical ventilation · Cost analysis · Diagnosis related groups · Case-based flat rates · DRG-based reimbursement

36.1 Introduction

Health expenditure makes up a considerable proportion of economic output in modern industrialized countries. In 2018, healthcare costs accounted for 11.2% of the gross national product in Germany, ranking third after the United States with 16.9% and Switzerland with 12.2% (German Federal Statistical Office 2021). Depending on the healthcare system of a country, these costs are financed by tax (health insurance) contributions from the population or a combination of these financial sources. The problem of rising healthcare costs, in Germany as well as in other countries, is primarily attributed in absolute and relative terms to the "cost explosion" in the hospital sector (Handelsblatt, 2021). The reasons for this development are complex, but modern intensive care medicine is a particularly high-cost area. With the establishment of Diagnosis Related Groups (DRG) in the years 2003–2004, health insurance companies and politicians hoped to have found a solution to counter the rising cost of healthcare (Geissler et al., 2012). Billing according to DRG instead of the length of stay was intended to enable performance-based reimbursement and control increasing costs (Geissler et al., 2012). DRG-based payment systems are currently used in most European countries, especially in acute care settings (France, Germany, Austria, England, Sweden, Poland, Ireland, Estonia, Portugal, Spain, etc.). DRG systems are used for three main reasons:

- Increasing the transparency of services provided in hospitals through patient classification and measurement of hospital performance.
- Creating incentives for efficient use of resources in hospitals by basing payment on the number and type of cases treated.
- Ensuring and improving the quality of care through a combination of increased transparency and efficient use of resources (Geissler et al., 2012).

Before the introduction of the DRG system, hospitals had the distorted incentive to keep patients in hospital as long as possible because remuneration was based on the length of hospital stay. The full implementation of the DRG system (in other countries, the DRG system is only partially used) created an incentive to treat patients in a more process-optimized manner and, thus, to reduce the length of hospital stay. Average length of stay is one of the most important indicators because shorter hospital length of stay is associated with a reduction in direct treatment costs and indirect costs (Bremer, 2021).

With the introduction of a new hospital financing system based on flat rates per case, requirements for securing revenue in intensive care units have changed. Treatment methods or medications that are more costly than average are usually covered by additional charges or so-called "complicated procedures." The most important single treatment in intensive care units is ventilation therapy, which is billed on an hourly basis. Certain threshold values ensure an increase within the remuneration group, which is determined by the discharge diagnosis. The basis for billing is the medical documentation. An example of such threshold values are 96, 250, 500, and 1000 ventilation hours. If these values are exceeded, a case is assigned to the next higher remuneration group. To each remuneration group, a point value with a monetary value is assigned.

One could argue that this system created an incentive to ventilate patients longer than necessary without any medical indication for doing so. It could be expected that if this is the case, ventilation would be terminated more often shortly after reaching a revenue-relevant threshold value. Therefore, there would be more ventilation cases around the revenue-relevant ventilation thresholds than would be expected according to the distribution function.

36.2   Methods

A multi-step analysis was used to investigate the issue of distorted incentives in the billing of intensive care ventilation therapy. The initial starting point of this research was the case-based hospital statistics (DRG statistics) of the Federal Statistical Office. These statistics include all operations and procedures of full inpatients in hospitals up to the codable endpoint of a year. To answer the research question, extensive data sets for the years 2009–2019 were extracted. The data sets included information on the various hours of ventilation required by patients and the associated frequency of patients ventilated for any given duration. In order to facilitate correlation analysis, a new assessment metric was introduced, namely, the rate of change in ventilation frequency. This metric indicates the percentage change in the frequency of ventilated patients for a given number of ventilation hours in comparison with the frequency of previous ventilation hours and allows the comparison of different ventilation hours in the data set. To test correlation in the data sets, a three-step analysis was performed:

- Descriptive statistical analysis
- Exploratory statistical analysis
- Inductive statistical analysis

Descriptive statistics describe data using measures such as means, standard deviations, and histograms. In contrast, exploratory statistics are used to identify and investigate unknown structures, relationships, or patterns in data, whereas inductive statistics aim to draw conclusions that are generalizable. At this point, hypotheses are developed and their validity is tested by statistical tests. The goal is to make generally applicable statements about a population or process based on the data drawn from the sample.

Descriptive statistics are often the first step in data analysis to better understand and structure the data. Exploratory statistics are then used to uncover new relationships that were not apparent in descriptive statistics. Finally, inductive statistics is the tool used to draw statistically significant conclusions about a population or process based on the results of the previous steps.

36.3 Results

36.3.1 Ventilation Data for the Years 2009–2021

First, all cases of intensive care ventilation were extracted from the DRG statistics for the years 2009–2021. All cases with invasive ventilation via endotracheal tube or tracheal cannula as well as cases with non-invasive ventilation via mask were extracted and summed up for the respective accounting year. As a next step, all ventilation cases that were billed and their respective ventilation duration were taken from the statistics. Subsequently, the number of ventilation cases per accounting year and the number of ventilation hours per year were calculated (Fig. 36.1).

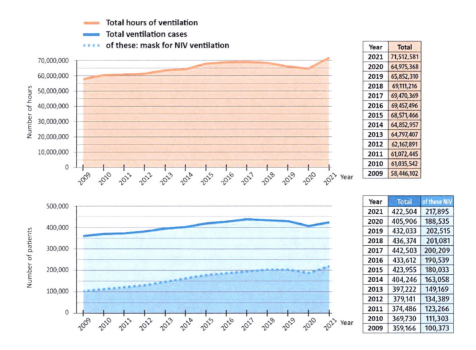

Fig. 36.1 Number of ventilation hours and ventilation cases per year

In order to avoid statistical artifacts due to the COVID-19 pandemic (Busse et al., 2021), the accounting years 2020 and 2021 were excluded.

36.3.2 Descriptive Statistical Analysis

In the descriptive part of this study, the data sets were examined for their distribution. In addition to the classical statistical position and dispersion measures, the absolute ventilation hours at the critical thresholds of 96, 250, 500, and 1000 h were examined. The evaluation showed that increased rates of change and absolute ventilation hour frequencies occurred after the critical thresholds were reached across all years examined (Fig. 36.2).

Although this is not always the case in every year for all thresholds, the prevalence of these findings indicates the increased occurrence of frequencies of ventilation hours after revenue-relevant thresholds are not stochastic in nature (Fig. 36.3).

36.3.3 Exploratory Statistical Analysis

In the exploratory analysis, two different statistical methods were used to examine the relationship between the frequency of ventilation hours and the critical thresholds. The first method was the "Cullen and Frey" graph (Xu et al., 2017), which was used to obtain an approximation of the distribution function. This method showed a negative binomial distribution. To confirm the association between the frequency of ventilation hours and the critical thresholds, regression analysis was performed in the inductive statistics part of this research (Fig. 36.4).

The second method consisted of dividing the ventilation hours from 2009 to 2019 into two groups by binary coding in order to then examine the association between each group with the rates of change in ventilation hour frequency. All ventilation hours that coincided with a threshold to the next higher remuneration level (96, 250, 500, and 1000 ventilation hours) were grouped into the critical ventilation hour group (dummy coding = 1). All other ventilation hours that did not correspond to a monetary threshold were assigned to the non-critical ventilation hour group (dummy coding = 0). For visualization and analysis of the group differences, several graphical representations were used, such as a scatterplot with a regression line (Sarikaya & Gleicher, 2017), a boxplot (Krzywinski & Altman, 2014), and a comparison of mean and median values (Fig. 36.5).

The graphical representations clearly show that when the rates of change in ventilation hour frequencies are grouped by critical and non-critical values, the mean and median values are higher for critical values than for non-critical values.

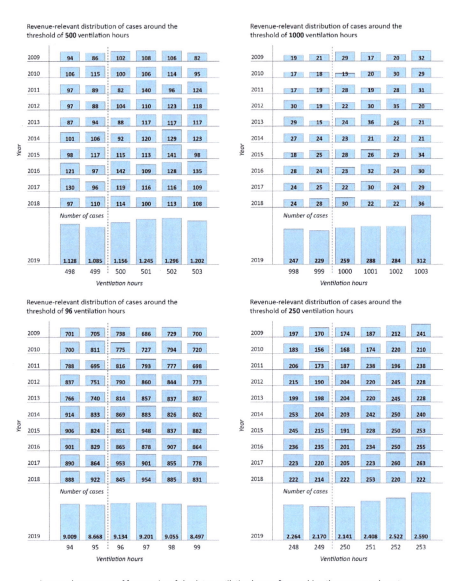

Fig. 36.2 Increased occurrence of frequencies of absolute ventilation hours after reaching the revenue-relevant thresholds

These results suggest that there is a systematic variation in the frequency of critical ventilation hours. Thus, around the critical values, there is a systematic increase in the rates of change (positive growth) (Figs. 36.6 and 36.7).

36 Does German Hospital Financing Lead to Distorted Incentives in the...

		96 hours			250 hours			500 hours			1000 hours	
	Year	Before the threshold	p-values**	After the threshold	Before the threshold	p-values	After the threshold	Before the threshold	p-values	After the threshold	Before the threshold	p-values	After the threshold
Mean growth rates	2009	-0.8 %	0.047	17.9 %	-0.1 %	0.714	-3.6 %	0.6 %	0.285	12.6 %	4.1 %	0.143	54.5 %
	2010	-1.1 %	0.333	4.7 %	-1.2 %	0.285	2.4 %	-1.5 %	0.190	18.6 %	7.1 %	0.238	38.1 %
	2011	-0.1 %	0.619	-4.4 %	-1.3 %	0.285	7.7 %	0.6 %	0.904	-13.0 %	2.5 %	0.892	-27.8 %
	2012	-1.3 %	0.047	17.4 %	-0.9 %	0.285	8.1 %	1.0 %	0.667	-7.9 %	5.0 %	0.143	47.4 %
	2013	-0.9 %	0.190	5.2 %	-0.8 %	0.333	4.7 %	0.5 %	0.143	18.2 %	2.2 %	0.204	15.8 %
	2014	-1.0 %	0.047	10.0 %	-1.5 %	0.380	3.0 %	0.2 %	0.850	-6.4 %	3.6 %	0.142	60.0 %
	2015	-1.2 %	0.190	4.3 %	-0.4 %	0.533	-0.5 %	-0.2 %	0.952	-13.2 %	4.4 %	0.570	-4.2 %
	2016	-1.3 %	0.285	3.3 %	-1.1 %	0.810	-11.2 %	1.4 %	0.597	-1.7 %	3.0 %	0.282	-13.6 %
	2017	-1.4 %	0.142	4.3 %	-0.8 %	1.000	-14.5 %	0.4 %	0.047	46.4 %	4.2 %	0.467	6.7 %
	2018	-1.4 %	0.047	9.3 %	-1.2 %	0.762	-7.3 %	-2.3 %	0.010	19.3 %	-2.3 %	0.718	-13.6 %
	2019	-1.1 %	0.952	-9.1 %	-1.2 %	0.380	3.6 %	-1.2 %	0.530	3.5 %	-2.3 %	0.467	6.7 %
	2009-2019	-1.2 %	0.047	5.4 %	-1.1 %	0.570	-1.3 %	-0.5 %	0.047	6.5 %	-0.2 %	0.190	13.1 %

Fig. 36.3 Inductive assessment: differences in growth rates* of ventilation hour lengths before and when revenue-relevant thresholds are reached *Values before reaching the thresholds are the mean values of the relative growth rates (growth rate in relation to the previous ventilation duration frequency) of the ventilation hours up to 10 h before the respective revenue-relevant thresholds **P-values are taken from one-sided Wilcoxon tests, which examine the difference in growth rates before thresholds are reached and once thresholds are reached. For a P-value ≤0.05, the growth rate upon reaching the threshold value is significantly larger than before reaching it

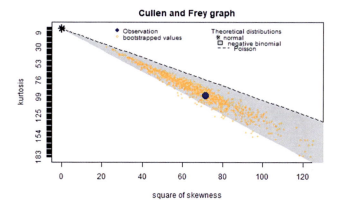

Fig. 36.4 Indication of negative binomial distribution of ventilation hour frequencies. (Cullen and Frey methodology)

36.4 Inductive Statistical Analysis

Inductive analysis was based on the exploratory analysis previously performed (distribution function and rate of change).

Building on the first exploratory method, in which a negative binomial distribution of ventilation hour frequency was found, fitting regression estimation according to a "generalized linear model" (Nelder & Welderburn, 1972) was performed. The estimated regression equation was used to examine the relationship between ventilation hour frequency and ventilation hour length. The result of the estimation

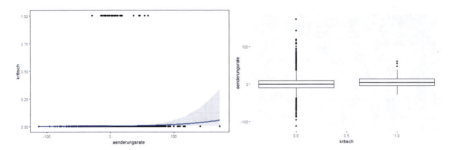

Fig. 36.5 Analysis of differences between critical and non-critical values—scatterplot (left) and boxplot (right)

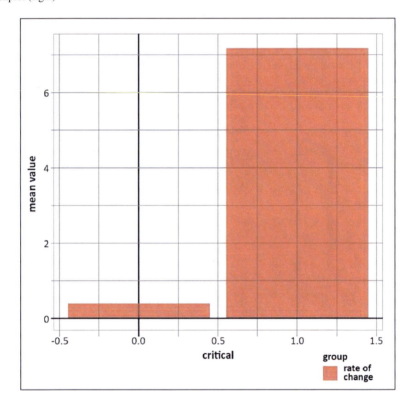

Fig. 36.6 Mean comparison between critical and non-critical values

was statistically significant, indicating that the longer the hours of ventilation, the lower the frequency. Estimates for each individual ventilation hour, including 95% confidence intervals, could be generated based on the derived distribution. However, the inspection of the estimates revealed that the precision of the estimates and confidence intervals were not sufficiently accurate to reliably represent the real frequency of ventilation hours. Hence, the effectiveness of the regression approach

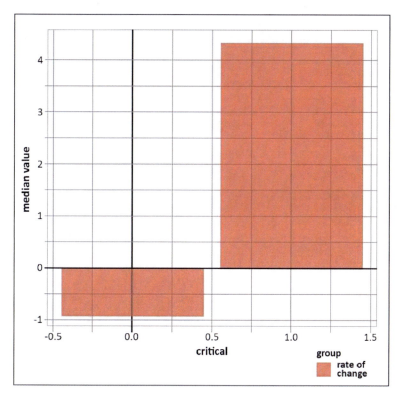

Fig. 36.7 Median comparison between critical and non-critical values

was limited to the significant negative effect of ventilation hour duration on the frequency of ventilation hours (Fig. 36.8).

Building on the second exploratory method regarding rates of change, a two-tailed t-test (Kim, 2015) and a Wilcoxon Rank Sum test (Rosner et al., 2003) were performed. This allowed examination of the means and medians of ventilation hour frequency based on the two different ventilation hour groups. In view of the p-values found, the null hypothesis of no difference in the rates of change in ventilation hour frequency between critical and non-critical thresholds could be provisionally rejected (Verhulst, 2016). A p-value below 5% was considered statistically significant. The results showed that the rates of change for the critical thresholds were statistically significantly higher at the median and mean values than for the non-critical thresholds. This suggests that the observed differences in mean values between critical and non-critical ventilation hours are not random but follow a statistical pattern. Bootstrap analysis further confirmed this, indicating the robustness of the results (Hesterberg, 2015). For bootstrap analysis, the critical groups were expanded to include the hours of ventilation shortly after the critical threshold. The same statistically significant results were found (Fig. 36.9).

```
## 
## Call:
## glm(formula = df_alle$Anzahl ~ df_alle$Beatmungsstunden, family = Gamma(link = "log"))
## 
## Deviance Residuals:
##     Min       1Q   Median       3Q      Max
## -0.7287  -0.4082  -0.1748   0.1168   4.3847
## 
## Coefficients:
##                              Estimate Std. Error t value Pr(>|t|)
## (Intercept)                 9.646e+00  5.123e-02  188.28   <2e-16 ***
## df_alle$Beatmungsstunden   -4.590e-03  8.788e-05  -52.23   <2e-16 ***
## ---
## Signif. codes:  0 '***' 0.001 '**' 0.01 '*' 0.05 '.' 0.1 ' ' 1
## 
## (Dispersion parameter for Gamma family taken to be 0.6611226)
## 
##     Null deviance: 2348.40  on 1008  degrees of freedom
## Residual deviance:  251.72  on 1007  degrees of freedom
## AIC: 16047
## 
## Number of Fisher Scoring iterations: 11
```

Fig. 36.8 Relationship between ventilation hour length and frequency using the GLM regression equation

```
## 
##  Bootstrap Welch Two Sample t-test
## 
## data:  df_zusammen$aenderungsrate[df_zusammen$kritisch == 1] and df_zusammen$aenderungsrate[df_zusa
mmen$kritisch == 0]
## bootstrap p-value = 0.006
## bootstrap difference of means (SE) = 6.902874 (2.755658)
## 95 percent bootstrap percentile confidence interval:
##    2.084777 12.490566
## 
## Results without bootstrap:
## t = 2.4256, df = 43.342, p-value = 0.01952
## alternative hypothesis: true difference in means is not equal to 0
## 95 percent confidence interval:
##    1.148537 12.461619
## sample estimates:
## mean of x mean of y
## 7.1938224 0.3887446
```

Fig. 36.9 *T*-test and Bootstrap *t*-test

36.5 Results

The available data indicate that there are significant differences in the frequency of ventilation hours related to revenue-relevant thresholds. Descriptive analysis of the data showed that the mean values of ventilation hours at and just after the revenue-relevant thresholds (96, 250, 500, and 1000 h) were higher than before the thresholds for most years. Accordingly, the rates of change at and shortly after the thresholds were also higher than otherwise. Furthermore, statistical analysis was performed to examine the differences in rates of change between the critical and non-critical thresholds. It was shown that the median and mean rates of change were significantly greater for the critical thresholds than for the non-critical thresholds. Thus, the null hypothesis that there is no difference in the rates of change between the critical and non-critical thresholds can be rejected. The application of bootstrap analysis confirmed the robustness of these results.

In summary, the results at the descriptive, exploratory, and inductive levels showed a clear trend toward increased ventilation hour frequency at the revenue-relevant thresholds. The results of this analysis may help inform strategies to reduce ventilation hour frequency, develop new ways of billing for ventilation therapy, and thereby reduce overall healthcare costs.

References

Bremer, P. (2021) 10 Jahre "Diagnosis Related Groups" (DRGs) in deutschen Krankenhäusern. Eine Zwischenbilanz aus ökonomischer Perspektive. https://www.statistik-bw.de/Service/Veroeff/Monatshefte/PDF/Beitrag15_11_08.pdf. Accessed 15 Jun 2022.

Busse, R., & Nimptsch, U. (2021). COVID-19-Pandemie: Historisch niedrige Bettenauslastung. *Dtsch Arztebl, 118*(10) A-504/B-426.

Geissler, A., Scheller-Kreinsen, D., Quintel, M., & Busse, R. (2012). DRG-Systeme in Europa. *Bundesgsundheitsbl, 55*, 633–642.

Handelsblatt. (2021). Bis zu 3000 Euro mehr im Jahr pro Versicherten: Studie warnt vor Kostenexplosion im Gesundheitssystem. https://www.handelsblatt.com/politik/deutschland/gesetzliche-krankenkassen-bis-zu-3000-euro-mehr-im-jahr-pro-versichertem-studie-warnt-vor-kostenexplosion-im-gesundheitssystem/27577274.html?ticket=ST-2241847-YCKmz5Nu3XW4wLsLKttx-ap3. Accessed 7 Dec 2021.

Hesterberg, T. (2015). What teachers should know about the bootstrap: Resampling in the undergraduate statistics curriculum. *The American Statistician, 69*(4), 371–386.

Kim, T. K. (2015). T test as a parametric statistic. *Korean Journal of Anesthesiology, 68*(6), 540–546.

Krzywinski, M., & Altman, N. (2014). Visualizing samples with box plots. *Nature Methods, 11*, 119–120.

Nelder, J. A., & Wedderburn, R. W. M. (1972). Generalized linear models. *Journal of the Royal. Series A (General), 135*(3), 370–384.

Rosner, B., Glynn, R. J., & Lee, M. L. (2003). Incorporation of clustering effects for the Wilcoxon rank sum test: A large-sample approach. *Biometrics, 59*(4), 1089–1098.

Sarikaya, A., & Gleicher, M. (2017). Scatterplots: Tasks, data, and designs. *IEEE Transactions on Visualization and Computer Graphics, 24*(1), 402–412.

Verhulst, B. (2016). In defense of P values. *AANA Journal, 84*(5), 305–308.

Xu Mengqiao, Zhang Ling, Li Wen, Xia Haoxiang. (2017). Mobility pattern of taxi passengers at intra-urban scale: Empirical study of three cities. 系科学与信息学(英文)5. 537–555.